Jimmy Swaggart
Bible
Commentary

Joshua
Judges
Ruth

JIMMY SWAGGART BIBLE COMMENTARY

- Genesis (639 pages) (11-201)
- Exodus (639 pages) (11-202)
- Leviticus (435 pages) (11-203)
- Numbers
  Deuteronomy (493 pages) (11-204)
- Joshua
  Judges
  Ruth (329 pages) (11-205)
- I Samuel
  II Samuel (528 pages) (11-206)
- I Kings
  II Kings (560 pages) (11-207)
- I Chronicles
  II Chronicles (528 pages) (11-226)
- Ezra
  Nehemiah
  Esther (288 pages) (11-208)
- Job (320 pages) (11-225)
- Psalms (688 pages) (11-216)
- Proverbs (320 pages) (11-227)
- Ecclesiastes
  Song Of Solomon (11-228)
- Isaiah (688 pages) (11-220)
- Jeremiah
  Lamentations (688 pages) (11-070)
- Ezekiel (508 pages) (11-223)
- Daniel (403 pages) (11-224)
- Hosea
  Joel
  Amos
  (will be ready Fall 2012) (11-229)
- Matthew (625 pages) (11-073)
- Mark (606 pages) (11-074)
- Luke (626 pages) (11-075)
- John (532 pages) (11-076)
- Acts (697 pages) (11-077)
- Romans (536 pages) (11-078)
- I Corinthians (632 pages) (11-079)
- II Corinthians (589 pages) (11-080)

- Galatians (478 pages) (11-081)
- Ephesians (550 pages) (11-082)
- Philippians (476 pages) (11-083)
- Colossians (374 pages) (11-084)
- I Thessalonians
  II Thessalonians (498 pages) (11-085)
- I Timothy
  II Timothy
  Titus
  Philemon (687 pages) (11-086)
- Hebrews (831 pages) (11-087)
- James
  I Peter
  II Peter (730 pages) (11-088)
- I John
  II John
  III John
  Jude (377 pages) (11-089)
- Revelation (602 pages) (11-090)

HOSEA
JOEL
AMOS

For prices and information please call: 1-800-288-8350
Baton Rouge residents please call: (225) 768-7000
Website: www.jsm.org • E-mail: info@jsm.org

JIMMY SWAGGART BIBLE COMMENTARY

Joshua
Judges
Ruth

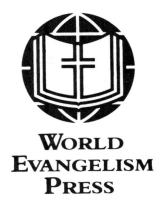

**WORLD
EVANGELISM
PRESS**

ISBN 978-1-934655-44-3
11-205 • COPYRIGHT © 2008 World Evangelism Press®
P.O. Box 262550 • Baton Rouge, Louisiana 70826-2550
Website: www.jsm.org • Email: info@jsm.org
(225) 768-8300
12 13 14 15 16 17 18 19 20 21 22 23 24 25 26 27 28 29 / CK / 19 18 17 16 15 14 13 12 11 10 9 8 7 6 5 4 3 2

TABLE OF CONTENTS

■

THE
BOOK OF JOSHUA

—■—

THE INTRODUCTION

The Hebrew name *"Joshua"* is *"Jesus"* in the Greek. So, the Joshua who led the Children of Israel into the Promised Land was a prefigurement of the Christ of Glory Who leads the Child of God into the Spiritual Promised Land.

Many have thought that the Land of Promise was a type of Heaven; it is not. It is a physical Type of the Spiritual Inheritance given to us in this great Christian walk. There were Jebusites, Hivites, Canaanites, and others in the Land of Promise. These were enemies of God's People. There is not such in Heaven.

THE DIVINE GREETING

"Moses My Servant is dead." Such is the Divine greeting to the already aged Joshua with which the Book that bears his name opens. It was a Message that must have tried even his fortitude; and it came from Him Who Alone could send it with assurance of perfect certitude. Moses was dead — just at the very moment, it would seem, when his people and those who had helped him to lead them needed his guidance most. But God's Ways aren't our ways. Moses was dead, but God was not dead!

Joshua had been *"anointed"* by Moses before the ascent of the Law-Giver to Pisgah, from which he would not return. In fact, they were never to see him again, or even to know where his remains were laid. They must now be content with the guidance of *"Moses' minister"* (Ex. 24:13; Num. 27:18; Deut. 1:38). It would seem that they loyally accepted Joshua. Certainly he accepted with

childlike trust and simplicity the high but heavy charge that was thus suddenly laid upon him. Neither elated nor depressed by it, he at once set to work to carry out the Divine command. In fact, the entirety of the remaining thirty years of his life are a calm, unwavering response to the exhortation of Jehovah.

VICTORIES

One might say that the victories of Joshua, of which we will study as it regards his great Book, were not only the subject of Prophecy, one might say, they were a Prophecy themselves — a Type and an Earnest of the Blessings which Jehovah had in store for His People, and on their darker side a Type and an Earnest of His Judgments upon those who refuse to know Him and find themselves, tragically so, fighting against Him.

So we see in this great Book of Joshua, the victories of this Spiritual and Military Leader, as a microcosm of ourselves. And that it is meant to be! As Joshua *"took the land"* we are as well to occupy that which the Lord has given us. There are many enemies there, and within the natural they cannot be conquered; however, if we follow the Lord as Joshua followed the Lord, we will find these victories in our experience, as he found them in his. God has the Way, and we must not veer from that Way.

JOSHUA AS A TYPE
OF CHRIST

I think as we go through this great Book of Joshua, it will be easy to see the conqueror as a Type of Christ. It is as follows:

1. Joshua began his life by sharing the

1

sufferings of his brethren in Egypt; so Jesus took upon Him the form of a Servant, and shared the lot of His Brethren.

2. The imperfect work of Moses was taken up and completed by Joshua: in a far higher sense it was taken up and completed by Christ; in other words, the Law was perfected in the Gospel.

3. In accordance with their common name, both, Joshua and Jesus, i.e., Joshua saved the people given to him from their enemies.

4. Both *"went forth conquering and to conquer";* and both conquered after being at first apparently defeated through the sins of others.

5. Joshua brought the Chosen People into the Promised Land, and gave them rest and a home in it. Jesus brings the Elect into the Kingdom prepared for us, and gives us rest and an Eternal Home in the *"many Mansions"* of the Father.

6. Both, Joshua and our Lord, entered into their Ministry on the banks of Jordan. Jesus as the *"Captain"* appeared to Joshua on those banks, while God spoke concerning Christ on the banks of that Jordan.

7. The Passover kept by Joshua and the Children of Israel on the banks of Jordan proclaims the Crucifixion of Christ, Who paid the supreme price in order to rescue the fallen sons of Adam's lost race.

8. Under Joshua the passage of Jordan as the road to the Land of Promise was freed from difficulty and danger. The river of death by which we must enter into our rest has been robbed of its terrors by Christ. Because He lives, we shall live also.

9. The twelve stones taken from the bed of Jordan and set up as witnesses to the people of their Deliverance may represent the Twelve Apostles who were living witnesses of His Resurrection, which Resurrection guaranteed our Resurrection as well.

10. Joshua, when he had completed his work, ascended the mountain of Ephraim and dwelt in security from his enemies. Jesus, having finished the work, which the Father gave Him to do (Jn. 17:4), ascended up on high and sat down on the Right Hand of God; *"From henceforth expecting till His enemies be made His footstool"* (Heb. 10:12-13).

NOTES

THE AUTHOR OF THE BOOK OF JOSHUA

The Talmud states that this Book was written by Joshua himself; that Eleazar wrote the account of Joshua's death, and that Phinehas added the Verses containing the narrative of the death of Eleazar.

While there is no proof of this, still, the evidence, I think, gives credence to the idea that Joshua wrote the Book himself.

The Book of Joshua is clearly a continuation of the Book of Deuteronomy. It commences with God's Charge to Joshua, embracing the extent of the dominion to be given to the Children of Israel, plus instructions are given to the great warrior as to the grounds of his confidence. He is to be successful, if he studies and keeps the Law of God, which he apparently did!

PERSONAL

It is May 23, 2006, Tuesday morning as I begin the Commentary on this Book. I have found in endeavoring to put on paper what I believe the Lord has given me, that each Book contains a tremendous lesson for the Believer, without which a spiritual gap will be left in the life of those who love the Lord. In other words, every Book in the Bible is of immense significance, and simply because every Book is inspired by the Holy Spirit.

We will find, I think, as we go along, that this Book of Joshua will not only ask many questions, but provide many answers. We will see ourselves in this great spiritual conflict, and in seeing ourselves, this will be what the Holy Spirit desires. As well, we will see the manner, the way, the direction that must be taken if victory is to be found and followed. It's all in this Book. If we do not glean from it, then the fault is ours. But by the Grace of God, glean we shall!

CHAPTER 1

(1) "NOW AFTER THE DEATH OF MOSES THE SERVANT OF THE LORD IT CAME TO PASS, THAT THE LORD SPOKE UNTO JOSHUA THE SON OF NUN,

MOSES' MINISTER, SAYING,

(2) "MOSES MY SERVANT IS DEAD; NOW THEREFORE ARISE, GO OVER THIS JORDAN, YOU, AND ALL THIS PEOPLE, UNTO THE LAND WHICH I DO GIVE TO THEM, EVEN TO THE CHILDREN OF ISRAEL.

(3) "EVERY PLACE THAT THE SOLE OF YOUR FOOT SHALL TREAD UPON, THAT HAVE I GIVEN UNTO YOU, AS I SAID UNTO MOSES.

(4) "FROM THE WILDERNESS AND THIS LEBANON EVEN UNTO THE GREAT RIVER, THE RIVER EUPHRATES, ALL THE LAND OF THE HITTITES, AND UNTO THE GREAT SEA TOWARD THE GOING DOWN OF THE SUN, SHALL BE YOUR COAST.

(5) "THERE SHALL NOT ANY MAN BE ABLE TO STAND BEFORE YOU ALL THE DAYS OF YOUR LIFE: AS I WAS WITH MOSES, SO I WILL BE WITH YOU: I WILL NOT FAIL YOU, NOR FORSAKE YOU.

(6) "BE STRONG AND OF A GOOD COURAGE: FOR UNTO THIS PEOPLE SHALL YOU DIVIDE FOR AN INHERITANCE THE LAND, WHICH I SWORE UNTO THEIR FATHERS TO GIVE THEM.

(7) "ONLY BE THOU STRONG AND VERY COURAGEOUS, THAT YOU MAY OBSERVE TO DO ACCORDING TO ALL THE LAW, WHICH MOSES MY SERVANT COMMANDED YOU: TURN NOT FROM IT TO THE RIGHT HAND OR TO THE LEFT, THAT YOU MAY PROSPER WHERESOEVER YOU GO.

(8) "THIS BOOK OF THE LAW SHALL NOT DEPART OUT OF YOUR MOUTH; BUT YOU SHALL MEDITATE THEREIN DAY AND NIGHT, THAT YOU MAY OBSERVE TO DO ACCORDING TO ALL THAT IS WRITTEN THEREIN: FOR THEN YOU SHALL MAKE YOUR WAY PROSPEROUS, AND THEN YOU SHALL HAVE GOOD SUCCESS.

(9) "HAVE NOT I COMMANDED YOU? BE STRONG AND OF A GOOD COURAGE; BE NOT AFRAID, NEITHER BE THOU DISMAYED: FOR THE LORD YOUR GOD IS WITH YOU WHERESOEVER YOU GO."

The pattern is:

1. As to how the Lord spoke to Joshua, we aren't told; however, the greater weight seems to point toward inward Revelation.

NOTES

2. Joshua begins his Ministry at the banks of Jordan, where Christ was baptized, and enters upon the public exercise of his Prophetic Office; I'm sure the Reader knows that the name Joshua is the Hebrew derivative of the Greek *"Jesus,"* the Name of our Blessed Lord Himself; Israel had dwelt in the wilderness for some forty years; it was now time for them to go into the Promised Land.

3. It was not God's Will that one foot breadth was to rest in the hands of its former owners; likewise, the Holy Spirit intends presently for everything in our lives to be removed which hinders our progress with the Lord; it is God's Will that we possess the entirety of the Promise, which pertains to total victory over the world, the flesh, and the Devil (James 4:5).

4. The area of Verse 4 includes modern Syria, Jordan, part of Iraq, and part of Arabia; all of this was never actually in the hands of the Israelites, save during the reigns of David and Solomon; however, during the coming Kingdom Age, Israel will possess all of that, and more.

5. Williams says, *"Moses, as representing the Law, could not bring Israel into the Promised Land; he must die, for he had made one failure under that Law, and possession of Canaan by Law could only be by a perfect obedience to it.*

"Man, being a sinner, cannot give this perfect obedience. Joshua, Type of the risen Saviour, brought Israel into the goodly Land. Grace, operating in the Power of the Holy Spirit, which it always does, can bring men into the enjoyment of that which the Law, because of man's moral weakness, on which it acts, can never do."[1]

6. Moses was a servant in the Wilderness, Joshua, a son in the Land. The subject of Deuteronomy is the Wilderness; that of Joshua is the Land. Most Christian people are satisfied to be servants in the Wilderness; few ambition to be sons in the Land.

Joshua's success depended upon his obedience to his two companions — the Eternal Word, manifested in Verse 6, and the Written Word, manifested in Verse 8; that is, Jesus and the Bible. Obedience to such companionship alone gives a victorious Christian experience.

7. Prosperity depended upon a strict adherence to the Law of God. Whereas Israel, at that time, only had a partial Revelation, the Law, now, we have the entirety of the Revelation of God, given in the entirety of His Word. It, and it alone, portrays the Way. To deviate from the Word of God is to deviate from prosperity. To adhere to the Word of God is to prosper, and to prosper in all things.

THE COMMISSION

The Lord had promised this great Land to the Children of Israel; however, promise is one thing, possession is another. God said, *"I, even I, do give you the Land."* Such was the Promise, but the one condition of possession was the placing of the foot upon it. This meant war, and to be certain, Satan will contest our every advance, and every foot of the way.

The Children of Israel were delivered out of Egypt without any fight or war. God did it all! Likewise, Redemption to the newfound Christian is all of God and not of him, with the exception of simply believing. All Israel had to do to be released from Egypt was to believe God. All the sinner has to do to be delivered from satanic bondage is to believe God; however, when it comes to Possession of all this that God has promised us, this is another matter entirely. We have to fight for every foot of spiritual ground that we take, and Satan does not give ground easily.

WARFARE

That it is warfare, of that there is no debate. Paul told Timothy, *"This charge I commit unto you, son Timothy* (refers to a command or injunction), *according to the Prophecies which went before on you* (probably refers to the time frame of Acts 16:1-3), *that you by them might war a good warfare* (we aren't told exactly what the Prophecies were, but that they spoke of an assignment to leadership in the army of King Jesus); *"Holding Faith . . .* (Maintaining Faith in Christ and the Cross)*"* (I Tim. 1:18-19).

That there will be war, of that there is no doubt; however, the great contention is as to how this war is to be conducted. On this rests defeat or victory. Regrettably, most of

the modern Church has no idea as to how this warfare is to be conducted, how it is to be addressed, how it is to be fought!

If it is to be noticed, Paul told Timothy, as it regards this warfare, that he must *"hold Faith."*

What did the Apostle mean by that?

He then said in the same Epistle, *"Fight the good fight of Faith* (in essence, the only fight we're called upon to engage; every attack by Satan against the Believer, irrespective of its form, is to destroy or seriously weaken our Faith; he wants to push our Faith from the Cross to other things), *lay hold on Eternal Life* (we do such by understanding that all Life comes from Christ, and the means is the Cross), *whereunto you are also Called* (Called to follow Christ), *and have professed a good profession before many witnesses.* (This does not refer to a particular occasion, but to the entirety of his life for Christ)*"* (I Tim. 6:12).

This is the only fight that we are called upon to engage, is the *"Good fight of Faith."* In a sense that is the same thing as *"holding Faith."*

Now again, what did Paul mean by that?

FIGHT THE GOOD FIGHT OF FAITH

This *"fight"* is in the realm of *"Faith."* So, what are we talking about when we mention *"Faith?"*

Just to use the term *"Faith,"* and let it drop there, really says nothing. As someone has well said, anything that says too much in the end actually says nothing.

When Paul speaks of Faith, without exception, he is always speaking of Faith in Christ and what Christ did at the Cross. That is the same thing as believing the Word of God, inasmuch as the Word is the Story of Christ and Him Crucified.

Satan will do everything within his power to stop the Believer from placing his Faith exclusively in Christ and the Cross. To be frank, he doesn't mind too much if your faith is merely in Christ. He knows that if Christ is divorced from the Cross, then the means by which God gives us all things, has just been removed. Let us say it this way:

Christ is the Source and the Cross is the Means.

This refers to the fact that everything we receive from our Saviour, and I mean everything, comes to us by the means of the Cross. In other words, we could not have anything from the Lord, be it Salvation, the Baptism with the Holy Spirit, Divine Healing, Blessings, Righteousness, Fruit of the Spirit, etc., without the Cross. In fact, if one attempts to believe God by placing his faith in something other than Christ and the Cross, the Jesus which remains, is *"another Jesus,"* which means that it is a fabrication (II Cor. 11:4).

To start this Commentary off right, and to give us the foundation on which Joshua won all his victories, which we will see a little later, let us give the following formula.

The Believer should consider the following very closely:

FOCUS: The Lord Jesus Christ (Col. 2:9-10);

OBJECT OF FAITH: The Cross of Christ (Rom. 6:3-5; Gal. 2:20-21);

POWER SOURCE: The Holy Spirit (Rom. 8:1-2, 11); and,

RESULTS: Victory (Rom. 6:14).

Now the Reader should study this little diagram very carefully, because what you're looking at is God's Prescribed Order of Victory.

Now let's turn it around, using the same formula, but look at it in the manner in which most are attempting to presently live for God.

FOCUS: Works;

OBJECT OF FAITH: Performance;

POWER SOURCE: Self; and,

RESULTS: Defeat.

Therefore, the way in which we engage this warfare is by placing our Faith exclusively in Christ and what He has done for us at the Cross. Then the Holy Spirit will grandly and gloriously help us, in fact, guaranteeing the victory.

A GUARANTEE AGAINST DEFEAT?

In a sense, yes! However, that needs qualification.

While one is most definitely on the right road to victory when one places one's Faith exclusively in Christ and the Cross, this doesn't mean that Satan is going to fold his tent and leave. In fact, he possibly will gather even greater forces in order to do what he

NOTES

can to stop you. In other words, he is going to test your Faith, and test it mightily, and the Lord will give him latitude to do so.

In this test of faith, you will fail. It's not *"if I fail,"* but *"when I fail."* There has never been a human being who didn't, in one way or the other; however, there is a difference in the type of failure that results when one is on the right road, than when one is on the wrong road. When one is on the right road, so to speak, even though the failure hurts, still, one knows that there is victory just around the bend. When the Holy Spirit through Paul said, *"Sin shall not have dominion over you,"* He meant exactly what He said. Every Believer who has his Faith anchored solidly in Christ and the Cross, which at the same time means that it's anchored solidly in the Word, can be assured of total and complete victory. It may be a time in coming, and there may be a few battles between now and then, but come it will!

POSSESSION

As God has designed Redemption perfectly, He has also designed possession of the Land perfectly. The allowing of great enemies to contest and hinder our progress builds Spiritual Character, Faith, and Maturity in the Child of God. As we study this great Book of Joshua, we are, in effect, studying our own Christian life. As the blueprint for victory was given by God to Joshua to *"take the land,"* likewise, this is the same blueprint for victory in our own lives.

The following has already been given in the overview; however, due to the fact that what has been said is so very, very important, please allow me the latitude of saying it again.

Moses, as representing the Law, could not bring Israel into the Promised Land. He must die, for he had made one failure under that Law and possession of Canaan by Law could only be by perfect obedience to it. Man, being a sinner, cannot give this perfect obedience.

Joshua was a Type of the risen Saviour and would bring Israel into that goodly Land. Grace, operating in the Power of the Holy Spirit, can bring men into the enjoyment of that which the Law, because of man's moral weakness, on which it acts, can never be.

THE RULE OF FAITH

When the question is asked, *"What is the rule of faith?"* For the Catholic Church, its answer would be, *"The Church and its teaching."* Regrettably, it would be the same for many Protestant Churches as well!

God's Answer in this Chapter and in all other Chapters is *"The Bible."*

He said, *"This Book of the Law shall not depart out of your mouth; but you shall meditate therein day and night, that you may observe to do according to all that is written therein: for then you shall make your way prosperous, and then you shall have good success"* (Vs. 8).

That's about as clear as it can get!

While it is certainly true that the Bible is the rule of Faith, perhaps the following will help us to understand it a little better.

The Bible in its entirety is the Story of Jesus Christ and Him Crucified (I Cor. 1:23). Actually, the strain of this great Truth began immediately after the Fall, with the Lord telling Satan through the serpent, *"And I will put enmity* (animosity) *between you and the woman* (presents the Lord now actually speaking to Satan, who had used the serpent; in effect, the Lord is saying to Satan, 'You used the woman to bring down the human race, and I will use the woman as an instrument to bring the Redeemer into the world, Who will save the human race'), *and between your seed* (mankind which follows Satan) *and her Seed* (the Lord Jesus Christ)*; it* (Christ) *shall bruise your head* (the victory that Jesus won at the Cross [Col. 2:14-15])*, and you shall bruise His Heel* (the sufferings of the Cross)*"* (Gen. 3:15).

It is spelled out plainly in the Fourth Chapter of Genesis, as it records the saga of Cain and Abel.

We see the Sacrificial System instituted on the first page of human history, which was a Type of the Innocent Victim Who would come, namely the Lord Jesus Christ, and Who would give His Life as a Sacrifice for dying humanity.

The Lord gave to Abraham the meaning of *"Justification by Faith,"* even telling him how this would be brought about, which

NOTES

would be through the death of an innocent victim. In other words, it was by death that man would be redeemed; however, the Lord did not tell the Patriarch as to what type of death this would be (Gen. 22:13-14).

It was to Moses that the Lord gave the means by which this death would occur. It would be by the Cross (Num. 21:8-9).

Jesus addressed this when He spoke to Nicodemus saying, *"And as Moses lifted up the serpent in the wilderness, even so must the Son of Man be lifted up"* (Jn. 3:14).

He then said, *"And I, if I be lifted up from the Earth* (refers to His Death at Calvary; He was 'lifted up' on the Cross; the 'Cross' is the Foundation of all victory)*, will draw all men unto Me* (refers to the Salvation of all who come to Him, believing what He did, and trusting in His atoning Work).

"This He said, signifying what death He should die (Reynolds says, 'In these Words, we learn that the attraction of the Cross of Christ will prove to be the mightiest, and most sovereign motive ever brought to bear on the human will, and, when wielded by the Holy Spirit as a Revelation of the matchless Love of God, will involve the most sweeping judicial sentence that can be pronounced upon the world and its prince.')*"* (Jn. 12:32-33).

THE WORD OF THE LORD TO JOSHUA

The following Verse is very dear to me personally. It says:

"Have not I commanded you? Be strong and of a good courage; be not afraid, neither be thou dismayed: for the LORD your God is with you wheresoever you go" (Vs. 9).

Frances and I began in Evangelistic Work in 1956. Donnie was two years old. If I remember correctly, the time of which I speak was January of 1958.

For the last two years, while preaching meetings here and there, I also held down a full-time job; however, feeling led of the Lord to go full time into Evangelistic Work, I quit the job I had, because I felt that's what the Lord wanted me to do. Our first meeting that January was in a little town in north Louisiana by the name of Sterlington.

I preached two or three nights, and then

came down so sick that I had to be taken to the hospital. The doctor told me that I had pneumonia.

I transferred to another hospital closer to home. If I remember correctly, I only stayed there one night. The nurse who was on duty, at least when I was there, had about the most profane mouth of any woman I've ever seen or heard. Almost every word out of her mouth was profanity.

After staying there the one night, sometime during the next morning, she came into the room, and saw me rummaging through the little closet, and asked me as to what I was doing. I related to her, *"I'm trying to find my trousers."*

She asked, *"What are you going to do with your trousers?"* Only she added a few expletives.

I retorted, *"If I can find my pants I'm going home."*

She let me know in no uncertain terms that I was not going to do that, but I persisted. Her parting words were, *"If you leave we are no longer responsible."*

To be frank, I had no confidence in their responsibility anyway.

Still with pneumonia, Frances drove us home, I was still so sick I could hardly hold my head up.

The next two or three days I was bedridden, and Satan took full advantage of that.

Almost every time I would turn on the radio (we did not then have a Television Set), I would hear one of the songs of one of my cousins. In fact, at that time, if I remember correctly, Jerry Lee was battling Elvis Presley for the number one spot in the nation. I would turn the dial and one of Mickey's songs would be playing. I would then turn it again, and one of Carl's songs would be airing. All of these were first cousins of mine (Jerry Lee Lewis, Mickey Gilley, and Carl McVoy).

At this time I was so sick I couldn't put my feet to the floor. At the same time, the thoughts went through my mind constantly as to how I was going to pay the bills.

THE TIME OF VICTORY

It was Wednesday night, and Frances and Donnie had gone to prayer meeting. As I lay there in the bed that night, Satan, as stated,

took full advantage of the situation.

I felt a darkened presence come into that room, and it was at the time, the most powerful I had ever experienced. Satan began to say to me, *"How are you going to pay the bills? How are you going to pay the note at the Bank on this little house?"* And then He said, *"You call yourself an Evangelist, and you are so sick you cannot even put your feet to the floor. You have no meetings to preach, and the truth is you'll probably starve to death."*

He went on to say, *"The man driving Jerry Lee's car makes as much money in a month as you make the entire year. You are a fool."*

There isn't a Believer who hasn't experienced something of this nature as Satan presses in for the kill.

I remember that night, as I began to pray, asking the Lord to help me. My Bible was lying by my side on the bed. I eagerly clutched at it, trying to open it, asking the Lord for His help.

I did not open the Bible to Joshua 1:9. Struggling with it, it opened to this very Verse of Scripture, and I know beyond the shadow of a doubt, that it was the Lord who did it. He knew exactly what I needed.

The words of this Ninth Verse seemed to be capitalized. They leaped up from the page, and I will never forget it:

"Have not I commanded you? Be strong and of a good courage; be not afraid, neither be thou dismayed: for the LORD your God is with you wheresoever you go."

This was the Word of the Lord to me. A Word that has stuck with me from that day until now. He was telling me, even as He had told Joshua so long, long ago, *"I am commanding you."* In other words, it doesn't matter what the situation looks like, it doesn't matter about circumstances, it doesn't matter about the present problems. Forget these things and *"Be strong and of a good courage; be not afraid, neither be thou dismayed."* The Lord was telling me to have Faith in Him. He was telling me that I didn't have anything to worry about. He was telling me that victory was mine, if I would only believe it.

And then it said, *"For the LORD your God is with you wheresoever you go."*

I have stood on that Word from then until

now. There have been some dark days in the meantime; however, the Lord has never failed me, and I know that He never will!

THE PRESENCE OF THE LORD

As the Lord gave me His Word that night, as well, His Presence filled my heart and life. In fact, it literally filled that room. I remember thinking; I don't have to stay in this bed any longer. With that, I gently placed my feet on the floor, arose, and started to walk, praising the Lord.

Now what I'm going to say may sound a little bit silly, but it was victory to me then. When Frances and Donnie came home that night about an hour or so later, Frances found me walking from room to room (the little house was small, only four rooms), and I was saying this over and over:

"Elvis can have 'Hound Dog' if he wants him, but I'll take the Holy Spirit." "Jerry Lee can have 'Great Balls Of Fire' if wants it, but I'll take Holy Ghost Fire."

"What a mighty God we serve,
"What a mighty God we serve,
"Angels bow before Him,
"Heaven and Earth adore Him,
"What a mighty God we serve."

So, this Ninth Verse of Joshua, Chapter 1 means very much to me personally. As it was the Lord's Word to Joshua, it was His Word to me.

Oh yes, I realize the circumstances were altogether different. Joshua was responsible for an entire nation, while my small effort only concerned myself, but yet that's not quite right.

Because what the Lord did for me that night, in future years helped me to touch this world for Christ, literally winning untold hundreds of thousands of souls to the Lord Jesus.

As well, I believe that I have the Authority of the Lord to say this to you who are reading these words. As it was the Word of the Lord to Joshua, as it was the Word of the Lord to me, I believe it is the Word of the Lord also to you:

"Have not I commanded you? Be strong and of a good courage; be not afraid, neither be thou dismayed: for the LORD your

God is with you wheresoever you go."

Even as I dictate these words, I sense the Presence of God, and I sense it mightily. And I believe the Lord is speaking right now to my heart saying, *"As I was real to Joshua so long, long ago, and as I was real to you when you began your Ministry those years ago, I will be just as real to you today, and to anyone and everyone who will dare to believe My Word."*

(10) "THEN JOSHUA COMMANDED THE OFFICERS OF THE PEOPLE, SAYING,

(11) "PASS THROUGH THE HOST, AND COMMAND THE PEOPLE, SAYING, PREPARE YOU VICTUALS; FOR WITHIN THREE DAYS YOU SHALL PASS OVER THIS JORDAN, TO GO IN TO POSSESS THE LAND, WHICH THE LORD YOUR GOD GIVES YOU TO POSSESS IT.

(12) "AND TO THE REUBENITES, AND TO THE GADITES, AND TO HALF THE TRIBE OF MANASSEH, SPOKE JOSHUA, SAYING,

(13) "REMEMBER THE WORD WHICH MOSES THE SERVANT OF THE LORD COMMANDED YOU, SAYING, THE LORD YOUR GOD HAS GIVEN YOU REST, AND HAS GIVEN YOU THIS LAND.

(14) "YOUR WIVES, YOUR LITTLE ONES, AND YOUR CATTLE, SHALL REMAIN IN THE LAND WHICH MOSES GAVE YOU ON THIS SIDE JORDAN; BUT YOU SHALL PASS BEFORE YOUR BRETHREN ARMED, ALL THE MIGHTY MEN OF VALOUR, AND HELP THEM;

(15) "UNTIL THE LORD HAVE GIVEN YOUR BRETHREN REST, AS HE HAS GIVEN YOU, AND THEY ALSO HAVE POSSESSED THE LAND WHICH THE LORD YOUR GOD GIVES THEM: THEN YOU SHALL RETURN UNTO THE LAND OF YOUR POSSESSION, AND ENJOY IT, WHICH MOSES THE LORD'S SERVANT GAVE YOU ON THIS SIDE JORDAN TOWARD THE SUNRISING."

The structure is:

1. Israel could have possessed the Land some 38 years earlier, had they only evidenced faith. But unbelief caused them to languish in the wilderness for some 38 extra years; likewise, far too many modern Christians languish in a Spiritual Wilderness because

of misplaced faith.

To inherit the Promised Land, we must, without fail, evidence Faith in Christ and the Cross, which will give the Holy Spirit latitude to work in our lives, Who Alone can help us to possess all that God has promised (I Cor. 1:17-18, 21, 23; 2:2).

2. Jesus Christ is the Source of all things, while the Cross is the Means by which these things are given to us.

3. Had the two Tribes and the half Tribe permitted God to chose for them, how much happier and safer they would have been! But they chose for themselves land on the wrong side of Jordan, and brought upon themselves many sorrows and early captivity (I Ki. 22:3).

Such is the sad experience of Christian people who plan for themselves and do not have fellowship with the thoughts of God. God's Plan was to conquer Canaan and then the land stretching from the Jordan to the Euphrates. The two Tribes and the half Tribe thought the reverse would be the better plan. It wasn't! Even as man's plans are never the better plan.

GOD'S WILL!

As we've already stated, the Lord had a Perfect Plan for Israel. It was conceived in Heaven, birthed in Heaven, and planned in Heaven. Everything was worked out by the Lord, even down to the smallest details. None of it was of man . . . all of it was of God.

However, the Tribes of Reuben and Gad, along with the half Tribe of Manasseh, were not satisfied with God's Plans, but rather inserted their own.

They wanted now to occupy land on the eastern side of Jordan. Was this what the Lord had chosen for them? No! But it's what they wanted.

Man is very capable of making his own plans and then asking God to bless those plans. To be truthful, God can never really bless such. He may tolerate it, but unless He conceives the plans, gives birth to the plans, and then carries out the plans, they cannot be what they ought to be.

THE PERFECT WILL OF GOD

Every Believer should want nothing but the Perfect Will of God. If there is such a

thing as a permissive will, we should not desire such, but only God's Perfect Will. Only then is such guaranteed for Blessings.

Paul said: *"Present your bodies a Living Sacrifice, holy, acceptable unto God, which is your reasonable service.*

"Be not conformed to this world, but be ye transformed by the renewing of your mind, that you may prove what is that good, and acceptable, and perfect, Will of God" (Rom. 12:1-2).

The idea is, the only *"will"* that is *"acceptable"* unto God, is a *"Perfect Will."* To be sure, He Alone has such!

As far as we know, the Tribes of Reuben, Gad, and the half Tribe of Manasseh were the first to go into captivity. The Scripture says of them, *"And they transgressed against the God of their Fathers, and went a whoring after the gods of the people of the land, whom God destroyed before them.*

"And the God of Israel stirred up the spirit of Pul king of Assyria, and the spirit of Tilgath-pilneser king of Assyria, and He carried them away, even the Reubenites, and the Gadites, and the half Tribe of Manasseh" (I Chron. 5:25-26).

The Holy Spirit is here quick to point out that it was these particular Tribes who first lost their way. Even though it was approximately 150 years after their fathers had settled that part of the land, still, I personally believe that their getting out of the Will of God those many long years before, is what ultimately brought on their downfall.

While the mills of God may grind slowly, they always grind exceedingly fine, meaning, they miss nothing.

(16) "AND THEY ANSWERED JOSHUA, SAYING, ALL THAT YOU COMMAND US WE WILL DO, AND WHERESOEVER YOU SEND US, WE WILL GO.

(17) "ACCORDING AS WE HEARKENED UNTO MOSES IN ALL THINGS, SO WILL WE HEARKEN UNTO YOU: ONLY THE LORD YOUR GOD BE WITH YOU, AS HE WAS WITH MOSES.

(18) "WHOSOEVER HE BE WHO DOES REBEL AGAINST YOUR COMMANDMENT, AND WILL NOT HEARKEN UNTO YOUR WORDS IN ALL THAT YOU COMMAND HIM, HE SHALL BE PUT TO DEATH; ONLY

BE STRONG AND OF A GOOD COURAGE."

The exegesis is:

1. Obedience is easy when all goes well with us, and when it makes little demand upon our faith.

2. The worthlessness of man's promises of fidelity at the close of this Chapter contrasts with the worthfulness of God's Promises of faithfulness at the opening of the Chapter.

3. Verse 18 illustrates the disobedience and folly of the natural heart. Man is always willing to obey a human rather than a Divine Law. These men who now condemn to death any who refuse to obey Joshua, themselves refuse to obey Jehovah.

OBEDIENCE?

These individuals in response to Joshua's leadership seemed to say the right thing. In fact, they did say the right thing; however, saying something and then doing it is quite different.

We must all know the period of struggle, when, *"after the inward man,"* we *"delight in the Law of God"* (Rom. 7:22-23), *but find another law in our members at conflict with it."* So must we learn to find the only deliverance from *"the body of this death,"* in Jesus Christ our Lord, is through Faith in Him and what He has done for us at the Cross (Rom. 6:1-14).

The truth is, despite our good intentions, we really cannot properly obey, even at this present time, even under the New Covenant, unless we seek to render obedience according to God's Prescribed Order.

GOD'S PRESCRIBED ORDER OF VICTORY

If we know this Divine Order, which is given to us in the Word of God, and faithfully attempt to obey, we will find the help of the Holy Spirit, without Whose help any progress is impossible, Who without reservation will come to our aid, and constantly. In fact, we cannot really be anything for the Lord, do anything for the Lord, have anything from the Lord, unless it is given to us by the Holy Spirit. He Alone is able to make us what we ought to be (I Cor. 3:16).

In brief, God's Prescribed Order of Victory is that we understand Christ is the Source of

NOTES

all things, while the Cross is the Means. This means that every single thing we receive from God, and I mean everything, comes to us strictly from Christ, but by and through the Cross. Without the Cross, we could not have had anything from the Lord. The Cross of Christ has made it all possible (I Cor. 1:17-18, 23; 2:2; Gal. 2:20-21; Chpt. 5; 6:14).

This means that our Faith must be anchored constantly and consistently in the Cross of Christ, and if we fully believe that everything comes to us by the means of the Cross, then it will be easy for us to anchor our Faith there; however, if we vacillate as it regards the Object of our Faith being the Cross, then we have problems.

But, the Cross of Christ being the Object of our Faith, the Holy Spirit will then begin to work mightily on our behalf, Who Alone, as previously stated, can make us what we ought to be (Rom. 8:1-2, 11).

Any true Christian wants to live right, wants to do right, wants to be right, wants to bring forth fruit for the Lord, wants to grow in Grace and the Knowledge of the Lord. In fact, that is an inbred spirit within the hearts and lives of all who are truly Born-Again. In fact, such a desire, such a hunger and thirst, are placed there by the Holy Spirit in the realm of the Divine Nature. But all of this can be obtained in only one way, and that is by and through Christ and what Christ has done for us at the Cross.

The following should be noted:

THE BIBLE IS THE STORY OF JESUS CHRIST AND HIM CRUCIFIED

The following will give us a brief summary of what the Bible is all about. If we understand it in this fashion, then we will understand it as we should. The First Chapter of the Gospel of John spells it out.

The First Verse tells us that the entirety of the Bible is about Jesus Christ.

John said, and I quote from the EXPOSITOR'S STUDY BIBLE, which I will use throughout the entirety of this Volume: *"In the beginning* (does not infer that Christ as God had a beginning, because as God He had no beginning, but rather refers to the time of Creation [Gen. 1:1]) *was the Word* (the Holy Spirit through John describes

Jesus as *'the Eternal Logos'*), *and the Word was with God* (*'was in relationship with God,'* and expresses the idea of the Trinity), *and the Word was God* (meaning that He did not cease to be God during the Incarnation; He *'was'* and *'is'* God from eternity past to eternity future)" (Jn. 1:1).

This one Verse plainly and clearly tells us that Jesus Christ is God, and that He is the Eternal Word. So, this tells us that the entirety of the Bible is about Jesus Christ.

And now the Fourteenth Verse tells us why God became Man. It says, *"And the Word was made flesh* (refers to the Incarnation, *'God becoming Man'*), *and dwelt among us* (refers to Jesus, although Perfect, not holding Himself aloft from all others, but rather lived as all men, even a peasant), (*and we beheld His Glory, the Glory as of the Only Begotten of the Father,*) (speaks of His Deity, although hidden from the eyes of the merely curious; while Christ laid aside the expression of His Deity, He never lost the possession of His Deity) *full of Grace and Truth* (as *'flesh,'* proclaimed His Humanity, *'Grace and Truth'* His Deity)" (Jn. 1:14).

And now the Twenty-ninth Verse of this same Chapter tells us why the Eternal Word became flesh and dwelt among us. It says:

"The next day (refers to the day after John had been questioned by the emissaries from the Sanhedrin) *John sees Jesus coming unto him* (is, no doubt, after the Baptism of Jesus, and the temptation in the wilderness), *and said, Behold the Lamb of God* (proclaims Jesus as the Sacrifice for sin, in fact, the Sin-Offering, Whom all the multiple millions of offered lambs had represented), *which takes away the sin of the world* (animal blood could only cover sin, it could not take it away; but Jesus offering Himself as the Perfect Sacrifice took away the sin of the world; He not only cleansed acts of sin but, as well, addressed the root cause [Col. 2:14-15])" (Jn. 1:29).

So, in Three Verses of Scripture found in the First Chapter of John, we find Who Jesus is, what Jesus is, and what He did!

THE FOUNDATION

The following Passage gives us the foundation of the great Redemption Plan. Peter said:

"Forasmuch as you know that you were not redeemed with corruptible things, as silver and gold (presents the fact that the most precious commodities [silver and gold] could not redeem fallen man), *from your vain conversation* (vain lifestyle) *received by tradition from your fathers* (speaks of original sin that is passed on from father to child at conception);

"But with the Precious Blood of Christ (presents the payment, which proclaims the poured out Life of Christ on behalf of sinners), *as of a Lamb without blemish and without spot* (speaks of the lambs offered as substitutes in the old Jewish economy; the Death of Christ was not an execution or assassination, but rather a Sacrifice; the Offering of Himself presented a Perfect Sacrifice, for He was Perfect in every respect [Ex. 12:5]):

"Who verily was foreordained before the foundation of the world (refers to the fact that God, in His Omniscience, knew He would create man, man would Fall, and man would be Redeemed by Christ going to the Cross; this was all done before the Universe was created; this means the Cross of Christ is the Foundation Doctrine of all Doctrine, referring to the fact that all Doctrine must be built upon that Foundation, or else it is specious), *but was manifest in these last times for you* (refers to the invisible God Who, in the Person of the Son, was made visible to human eyesight by assuming a human body and human limitations)" (I Pet. 1:18-20).

Pure and simple, this Passage of Scripture tells us that the Cross of Christ is the foundation of all that we have in the Lord. It was formulated by the Godhead, at least in the Mind of the Godhead, even before the foundation of the world. This means, and this is very important, that every single doctrine in the Bible must be built upon this foundation of the Cross, and if not, it will be error. In fact, that's the reason that the Church presently is loaded down with false doctrine. It doesn't understand the Cross, and in many cases, if not most, doesn't even really believe in the Cross; consequently, it is an open target for the powers of Satan.

If a doctrine is built squarely on the Cross of Christ, then in some way it will come out right, otherwise, wrong!

OLD TESTAMENT TYPOLOGY

All the typology in the Old Testament, which included the entirety of the Sacrificial System, which was originated on the very first page of human history (Gen., Chpt. 4), and, as well, the entirety of the Law of Moses, everything about all of this, and I mean all of it, points in some way to Christ in either His Atoning, Mediatorial, or Intercessory Work.

Paul referred to all of the Old Testament Economy as *"A shadow of things to come"* (Col. 2:17).

The great Apostle also said, *"But when the fullness of the time was come* (which completed the time designated by God that should elapse before the Son of God would come), *God sent forth His Son* (it was God Who acted; the Law required man to act; this requirement demonstrated man's impotency; the Son of God requires nothing from man other than his confidence), *made of a woman* (pertains to the Incarnation, God becoming Man), *made under the Law* (refers to the Mosaic Law; Jesus was subject to the Jewish legal economy, which He had to be, that is if He was to redeem fallen humanity; in other words, He had to keep the Law perfectly, which no human being had ever done, but He did),

To redeem them who were under the Law (in effect, all of humanity is under the Law of God which man, due to his fallen condition, could not keep; but Jesus came and redeemed us by keeping the Law perfectly, and above all satisfying its penalty on the Cross, which was death), *that we might receive the adoption of sons* (that we could become the sons of God by adoption, which is carried out by Faith in Christ and what He did at the Cross)*"* (Gal. 4:4-5).

As stated, everything under the Jewish Law pointed to Christ, in effect, the Cross, of which the entire Sacrificial System was a Type. When Israel began to leave the Cross, so to speak, that's when they lost their way, and went into captivity (Deut., Chpt. 28).

The Sacrificial System was the heart of the Old Jewish System, and the Sacrificial System in its entirety, pointed to the Cross, as should be overly obvious (Ex. 12:13).

THE NEW COVENANT

The Old Testament was a Pattern for the New Covenant, meaning, through typology, allegorical examples, illustrations, and examples, it pointed straight to Christ and the Cross.

As Israel looked forward to the coming Redeemer, we now look backward to the Redeemer Who has already come. In the Old Testament they looked forward to a Prophetic Jesus, while we look back to an historical Jesus. As the Cross was the centerpiece of the Old Economy, symbolized by the Sacrificial System, likewise, we now have the Finished Work, and it is all centered up in the Cross of Christ. Let us be blunt:

If the Church leaves the Cross, it will destroy itself exactly as did Israel of Old. In fact, the Apostle Paul laid it out in no uncertain terms. He said:

"For if God spared not the natural branches (Israel), *take heed lest He also spare not you* (again refers to the Church, as is obvious).

"Behold therefore the goodness and severity of God (don't mistake the Goodness of God for license)*: on them which fell, severity* (speaks of Judgment which came on Israel, God's chosen People)*; but toward you, goodness, if you continue in His Goodness* (proclaims the conditions; the continuing of that *'Goodness'* pertains to continued Faith in Christ and the Cross)*: otherwise you also shall be cut off* (is the modern Church on the edge of that even now? Rev. 3:15-22 tells us this is the case!)*"* (Rom. 11:21-22).

Therefore, it is the Cross of Christ, or it is spiritual destruction! There is no in-between.

CHAPTER 2

(1) "AND JOSHUA THE SON OF NUN SENT OUT OF SHITTIM TWO MEN TO SPY SECRETLY, SAYING, GO VIEW THE LAND, EVEN JERICHO. AND THEY WENT, AND CAME INTO AN HARLOT'S HOUSE, NAMED RAHAB, AND LODGED THERE."

The exegesis is:

1. The *"house"* spoken of in Verse 1 was an Inn of sorts. The two spies did not know

that Rahab was a harlot. As well, some have attempted to claim that Rahab had been forced into temple prostitution; however, the Greek Text of Hebrews 11:31 proves that she was a common harlot.

2. The *"two spies"* served no military purpose whatsoever. So why did Joshua send them?

The Lord told him to do so, because of Rahab, even though Joshua did not know or understand such at the time. The Lord knew that Faith lodged in the heart of this harlot, and God will go to any lengths to honor Faith (Heb., Chpt. 11).

3. In a sense, the two spies were Types of *"the Word of God"* and *"the Holy Spirit."* These two *"Spies"* are in the world presently, attempting to reconcile man to God.

4. Also in a sense Rahab, was a Type of the Church that will be raptured out before the Great Tribulation.

JERICHO AND THE TWO SPIES

Let's look at Jericho:

This city is one of the oldest in the world, already a city of antiquity by the time of Joshua. It probably derived its name from the moon-god *"Yarih."*

Located at the northern extremity of the Dead Sea, it was the entrance to Canaan from the East. In fact, at the time of Joshua, it was a mighty fortress. It was known for commerce as well as for agriculture. The proximity to the Dead Sea made the citizens dealers in salt, bitumen, and sulphur. But irrespective of the city itself in the natural, the spiritual implications involved present a tremendous lesson for us.

This was the entrance to the Promised Land, and it barred Israel's progress. Its conquest, at least in the natural, was impossible to Israel, for its walls were great and high. But yet, it had to be subdued.

It is a type of Satan's fortresses, which he places in our path, in order to keep us from the great things of God. In fact, we receive nothing from the Lord, without us defeating the satanic forces of darkness in some way. So, in order to take the Promised Land, to have what God had promised them, to enjoy this land of milk and honey, Jericho had to be first subdued. Is there a Jericho

hindering your progress? Is there a Jericho keeping you from having that which the Lord has promised you? Is there a Jericho, which stands in your way?

As we go forward with our study, we will see God's Way, and we will find out that this is the only way that victory can be brought about. Unfortunately, all too often, Christians attempt to gain victories in the flesh, which can never happen. It can only be done by the Power of the Holy Spirit.

THE TWO SPIES

There was absolutely no military reason for Joshua to send these two spies to Jericho in order to spy out the land. This battle would not be fought by natural means anyway, so whatever information they brought back, at least as it regards military information, would be useless. So it must be that the Lord impressed upon Joshua to send in these two men.

I think it can only be concluded that Rahab was the reason for their being sent. Even though this woman was a vile sinner, which we will deal with momentarily, still, evidence is that a cry of Faith was in her soul. That cry of Faith would be answered by the Lord, as every cry of Faith is always answered by the Lord.

I do not think it would be a stretch of the imagination, as well, to portray what happened at Jericho, to be a portend of that which is soon to happen in this world, and we speak of the coming Great Tribulation, and above all, the Rapture of the Church.

Considering the entirety of the population of the city, whatever it may have been, Rahab and her family were the only ones who were spared. As well, considering the entirety of the population of the world, which presently stands at approximately six and one half billion people (in 2006), the number of people who are truly Born-Again at this time, and who will make the Rapture, is truly small. So, Rahab definitely could be a Type of the Church, which will be delivered out of the coming Judgment.

These *"two spies,"* could well represent *"the Word of God,"* and *"the Holy Spirit,"* sent into this world.

The only way that Rahab and her family

could be spared, was by adhering totally to what they were told by the two spies. They were not to question it, not to add to it, or take from it. Their lives, their souls, everything they had depended totally and completely upon what the two spies related to them. It is the same presently with the Word of God, on which the Holy Spirit works exclusively.

If Rahab had changed the instructions in any way, she would never have been spared. I'm afraid presently that much of the modern Church is most definitely attempting to change the instructions. The Word of God is being replaced presently with religious books which refer to themselves as *"Bibles,"* and I speak of those such as the *"Message Bible,"* etc., but which in reality are not Bibles at all. How do I know?

These are *"thought for thought"* translations, even if that, which can never pass Spiritual and Scriptural muster. If you as a Believer do not have a *"word for word"* translation, such as the King James, then you really don't have a Bible. And to be frank, there are only two or three word for word translations available.

Some counter that by stating, *"I can't understand the King James,"* etc.

First of all, if you have something that you can understand, and it's not really the Word of God, you have not done yourself any good whatsoever. In fact you have done yourself irreparable harm. A road map that is wrong, will never lead one to the right destination. Blueprints that are faulty, will never build a house that will stand. Jesus said so!

The Holy Spirit functions entirely on, within, and by the Word of God. In fact, He is the Author of the Word. Peter said:

"For the Prophecy (the word *'Prophecy'* is used here in a general sense, covering the entirety of the Word of God, which means it's not limited merely to predictions regarding the future) *came not in old time by the will of man* (did not originate with man)*: but Holy men of God spoke as they were moved by the Holy Spirit.* (This proclaims the manner in which the Word of God was written and, thereby, given unto us)*"* (II Pet. 1:21).

Remember this, we aren't speaking here from a position of personal preference, but

NOTES

rather that which pertains to eternal consequences. If the Word of God is misinterpreted, the person will die eternally lost. So, considering the implications, considering the eternal consequences, I think it would certainly be wise for every Believer to *"make his calling and election sure"* (II Pet. 1:10).

The idea is, if it's not the pure Word of God, meaning that which has not been compromised, then the Holy Spirit, without Whom we receive nothing, will not, in fact, cannot function. He functions alone and entirely on the Word of God. So, if we want the Moving and Operation of the Holy Spirit within our hearts and lives, we had better make certain that we truly have the Word of God in our possession, and not some hybrid. In view of that, I would strongly recommend that the reader secure for themselves THE EXPOSITOR'S STUDY BIBLE. It is King James, but totally different than any type of Study Bible, to our knowledge, that has ever been produced. The explanation of each Scripture is given right with the Scripture. In other words, the explanation is not at the bottom of the page, or the side of the page, or at the back of the book. It is embedded with the actual Scripture itself, making it extremely user-friendly. So, the idea that the King James cannot be understood, has in a sense, been laid to rest.

RAHAB

The following is derived from the work of George Williams. He said:

"Rahab was a debauched member of a doomed race. Yet Grace saved her. She based her plea for Salvation upon the fact that she was justly ordained by God to destruction. Many people refuse to bestir themselves in the matter of personal Salvation because of the belief that if they are ordained to be saved, they will be saved, and if ordained to be lost, they will be lost, which constitutes an erroneous interpretation of predestination.

"All sinners are justly ordained to be lost (Rom. 5:12) and therefore, all sinners may be saved. Rahab prefaced her plea for Salvation by declaring that she knew all were doomed to destruction, and because of this Divine Judgment she asked for a true token that would assure her of her safety in the

Day of Wrath that was coming."[1]

THE WAY OF SALVATION

Rahab was immediately provided with a way of Salvation. It was a very simple way. She had but to bind a scarlet cord in a window. A child could do that. Salvation today from the Wrath to come is equally simple. Trusting in the Lord Jesus Christ, and in His Precious Blood, secures Eternal Salvation.

"Rahab lost not a moment in making her calling and election sure. She bound the scarlet cord in the window. And directly she did so she was saved — that is, she was in safety, and assured of safety. Prior to binding the scarlet line in the window, she was ordained to destruction, but from the moment she trusted that 'true token,' she was ordained to Salvation."

THE ASSURANCE OF SALVATION

Her assurance of Salvation was not founded upon an inward experience, but upon an outward evidence — that is, the scarlet line. And it was perfection; in herself imperfection. Looking upon that *"true token,"* and believing the testimony respecting it, she was assured of deliverance in the Day of Doom that was coming. Thus, the outward token gave an inward peace. The Believer in Jesus enjoys a similar peace. The preciousness of Christ's Blood, and the testimony of the Holy Scriptures concerning it, is the outward token, which brings assurance of Salvation to the heart that trusts Christ. It was vain for Rahab to seek for Salvation upon the ground of personal worthiness; for she was vile indeed. It is equally vain for the most moral to claim Salvation today, for all have sinned, none are righteous, and all are under sentence of death (Rom. 5:12).

RAHAB AND THE LORD JESUS CHRIST

"A faith that is born of God always evidences itself by seeking the Salvation of others. Rahab pleads for her father, her mother, her brothers, her sisters and all belonging to them; and they were all saved.

"The moral effect of a Divine Faith is further seen in Rahab. She became a good

woman, and joined the people of God, married one of its princes, and her name shines in the genealogy of Jesus Christ." (Mat. 1:5).

(2) "AND IT WAS TOLD THE KING OF JERICHO, SAYING, BEHOLD, THERE CAME MEN IN HITHER TO NIGHT OF THE CHILDREN OF ISRAEL TO SEARCH OUT THE COUNTRY.

(3) "AND THE KING OF JERICHO SENT UNTO RAHAB, SAYING, BRING FORTH THE MEN WHO ARE COME TO YOU, WHICH ARE ENTERED INTO YOUR HOUSE: FOR THEY BE COME TO SEARCH OUT ALL THE COUNTRY.

(4) "AND THE WOMAN TOOK THE TWO MEN, AND HID THEM, AND SAID THUS, THERE CAME MEN UNTO ME, BUT I DID NOT KNOW WHERE THEY CAME:

(5) "AND IT CAME TO PASS ABOUT THE TIME OF SHUTTING OF THE GATE, WHEN IT WAS DARK, THAT THE MEN WENT OUT: WHERE THE MEN WENT I DO NOT KNOW: PURSUE AFTER THEM QUICKLY; FOR YOU SHALL OVERTAKE THEM.

(6) "BUT SHE HAD BROUGHT THEM UP TO THE ROOF OF THE HOUSE, AND HID THEM WITH THE STALKS OF FLAX, WHICH SHE HAD LAID IN ORDER UPON THE ROOF.

(7) "AND THE MEN PURSUED AFTER THEM THE WAY TO JORDAN UNTO THE FORDS: AND AS SOON AS THEY WHICH PURSUED AFTER THEM WERE GONE OUT, THEY SHUT THE GATE."

The diagram is:

1. We know from the Scriptural narrative, that Rahab lied to the two men sent to her by the king as it regards the two spies. The sacred historian simply narrates the fact, and makes no comment whatever upon it.

2. The roofs of houses, then as now, were flat in those regions. She hid the men on the roof under stalks of flax. The germ of Faith was already stirring in her heart, and it was Faith that would be amply rewarded. We must not judge Rahab, for all of this was shortly before her conversion. To be sure, we must not judge Rahab at all.

3. Despite her past, this woman would go down in Biblical history as one of the greatest women of God ever. In fact, she would be in the genealogy of Christ, and nothing

could be greater than that (Mat. 1:5).

FAITH

Faith begins in the heart of the sinner, placed there by the Holy Spirit, even before conversion. In fact, it has to begin before conversion, or there could be no conversion.

What was it that stirred this woman's heart to begin with, especially considering the lifestyle that she was leading as a harlot?

At this time, and with over two million Israelites camped on the other side of Jordan, the entirety of the city was abuzz with these proceedings. It seems from what Rahab will say momentarily, that all the victories of the recent past regarding Israel were well known in Jericho. As well, Israel's deliverance from Egypt, and the opening of the waters of the Red Sea, were all well known.

It would seem that from this, in some way, Faith began to build in the hearts of these people. In those days, everything was attributed to the god of the particular people or country involved. Consequently, it was known that the God of Israel must be stronger than the many gods of Egypt, because Egypt had been left a wreck upon the deliverance of these people. As well, it would have been deduced that Jehovah was greater than the gods of the Amorites, etc. Therefore, whatever was said, whatever was deduced from all of this, Faith begins to build in the heart of Rahab, on which the Holy Spirit worked.

While the entirety of the city, as stated, was rife with all of this information, still, it was Rahab alone, and her family, which chose to believe in the God of Israel. Quite possibly this dear lady was sick of her supposed god, *"Chemosh,"* which she had been worshipping. It was quite common for little children to be offered up to this god as a burnt offering, which was carried on quite often. This, no doubt, sickened Rahab, with what little she knew about Jehovah striking a positive chord in her heart. At any rate, it would lead to her Salvation, and a place in Biblical history, all out of proportion to mere human thoughts.

The story of Rahab cannot be said to be anything but a story of Faith. It is Faith which believed God, and such Faith is always honored and recognized.

NOTES

(8) "AND BEFORE THEY WERE LAID DOWN, SHE CAME UP UNTO THEM UPON THE ROOF;

(9) "AND SHE SAID UNTO THE MEN, I KNOW THAT THE LORD HAS GIVEN YOU THE LAND, AND THAT YOUR TERROR IS FALLEN UPON US, THAT ALL THE INHABITANTS OF THE LAND FAINT BECAUSE OF YOU.

(10) "FOR WE HAVE HEARD HOW THE LORD DRIED UP THE WATER OF THE RED SEA FOR YOU, WHEN YOU CAME OUT OF EGYPT; AND WHAT YOU DID UNTO THE TWO KINGS OF THE AMORITES, WHO WERE ON THE OTHER SIDE JORDAN, SIHON AND OG, WHOM YOU UTTERLY DESTROYED.

(11) "AND AS SOON AS WE HAD HEARD THESE THINGS, OUR HEARTS DID MELT, NEITHER DID THERE REMAIN ANY MORE COURAGE IN ANY MAN, BECAUSE OF YOU: FOR THE LORD YOUR GOD, HE IS GOD IN HEAVEN ABOVE, AND IN EARTH BENEATH.

(12) "NOW THEREFORE, I PRAY YOU, SWEAR UNTO ME BY THE LORD, SINCE I HAVE SHOWED YOU KINDNESS, THAT YOU WILL ALSO SHOW KINDNESS UNTO MY FATHER'S HOUSE, AND GIVE ME A TRUE TOKEN:

(13) "AND THAT YOU WILL SAVE ALIVE MY FATHER, AND MY MOTHER, AND MY BRETHREN, AND MY SISTERS, AND ALL THAT THEY HAVE, AND DELIVER OUR LIVES FROM DEATH.

(14) "AND THE MEN ANSWERED HER, OUR LIFE FOR YOURS, IF YOU UTTER NOT THIS OUR BUSINESS. AND IT SHALL BE, WHEN THE LORD HAS GIVEN US THE LAND, THAT WE WILL DEAL KINDLY AND TRULY WITH YOU.

(15) "THEN SHE LET THEM DOWN BY A CORD THROUGH THE WINDOW: FOR HER HOUSE WAS UPON THE TOWN WALL, AND SHE DWELT UPON THE WALL.

(16) "AND SHE SAID UNTO THEM, GET YOU TO THE MOUNTAIN, LEST THE PURSUERS MEET YOU; AND HIDE YOURSELVES THERE THREE DAYS, UNTIL THE PURSUERS BE RETURNED: AND AFTERWARD MAY YOU GO YOUR WAY."

The synopsis is:

1. Rahab's Faith is shown by the expression, *"has given"*; what God wills, she regarded as already done.

2. The declaration of Verse 11, bearing in mind the circumstances of the person who uttered it, is as remarkable as Peter's *"You are the Christ, the Son of the Living God"* (Mat. 16:16-17). Upon the utterance of this statement of Faith, Rahab was Saved, which was evidenced in her obedience regarding the *"true token,"* i.e., *"the red cord."*

3. Williams says, *"Rahab was a debauched member of a doomed race. Yet Grace saved her. She based her plea for Salvation upon the fact that she was justly ordained by God to destruction.*

"Many people refuse to bestir themselves in the matter of personal Salvation because of the belief that if they are ordained to be saved, they will be saved, and if ordained to be lost, they will be lost; however, all sinners are justly ordained to be lost, and in this context, all are sinners (Rom. 5:12) and, therefore, all sinners may be saved."[2]

4. Rahab prefaced her plea for Salvation by declaring that she knew all were doomed to destruction, and because of this Divine Judgment, she asked for a true token that would assure of her safety in the Day of Wrath that was coming. That true token, the red cord, was given.

A Faith that is born of God always evidences itself by seeking the Salvation of others; her petition was answered favorably.

THE PLEA FOR SALVATION

From the conversation of Rahab, it is evident that all the surrounding nations knew of the tremendous Miracles performed by Jehovah in Egypt, and especially the waters of the Red Sea drying up for Passage by the Israelites. Also, she was very well acquainted with recent victories, pertaining to Sihon and Og. In hearing these accounts, and in them being discussed over and over, which they no doubt were, in some way the story of these great victories ignited a spark of Faith in the heart of this poor woman. She knew little of Jehovah; however, she knew enough to know that Jehovah was greater and stronger than all the gods of Egypt, etc. and upon

that fact, she was in the process of making some decisions within her heart.

The Holy Spirit, knowing and seeing the heart of this dear lady, irrespective of her debauched occupation, irrespective of the terrible vice which gripped her, irrespective of what had transpired in the past, the Holy Spirit would move favorably upon her Faith, which He had tendered her way in the first place.

WHY RAHAB AND NOT OTHERS IN JERICHO?

It has ever been in that fashion. Many hear the Gospel, but only a minute few accept the Gospel. As to exactly what causes most to say *"no,"* and some few to say *"yes,"* is known only to God. This we do know:

God does not tamper with the free moral agency of mankind. He will move upon people, deal with people, speak to people, bring events to pass to impress people, but He will never force the issue. The decision must be, whether *"yes"* or *"no,"* that of the individual.

But yet, as we see the Word of God, we know it is imperative that all be given an opportunity, whatever their decision. The Holy Spirit is insistent upon that. Jesus Himself said:

"Go ye into all the world (the Gospel of Christ is not merely a western Gospel, as some claim, but is for the entirety of the world), *and preach the Gospel to every creature* (*'preaching'* is God's method, as is here plainly obvious; as well, it is imperative that every single person have the opportunity to hear; this is the responsibility of every Believer).

"He who believes (believes in Christ and what He did for us at the Cross) *and is baptized* (baptized into Christ, which is done by Faith [Rom. 6:3-5] not water baptism) *shall be Saved; but he who believes not shall be damned* (Jn. 3:16)" (Mk. 16:15-16).

If Jesus had been speaking in this Verse of *"Water Baptism,"* He then would have also said, *"But he who believes not, and is not baptized in water, shall be damned."* But He didn't say that, but rather *"He who believes."*

The words of the Great Commission given in Matthew are a little different, because the emphasis is different. Jesus said:

"*Go ye therefore* (applies to any and all who follow Christ, and in all ages), *and teach all nations* (should have been translated, '*and preach to all nations,*' for the word '*teach*' here refers to a '*proclamation of truth*'), *baptizing them in the Name of the Father, and of the Son, and of the Holy Spirit* (presents the only formula for Water Baptism given in the Word of God):

"*Teaching them* (means to give instruction) *to observe all things* (the whole Gospel for the whole man) *whatsoever I have commanded you* (not a suggestion): *and, lo, I am with you always* (It is I, Myself, God, and Man, Who am — not '*will be*' — hence, forever present among you, and with you as Companion, Friend, Guide, Saviour, God), *even unto the end of the world* (should have been translated '*age*'). *Amen* (it is the guarantee of My Promise)" (Mat. 28:19-20).

(17) "AND THE MEN SAID UNTO HER, WE WILL BE BLAMELESS OF THIS YOUR OATH WHICH YOU HAVE MADE US SWEAR.

(18) "BEHOLD, WHEN WE COME INTO THE LAND, YOU SHALL BIND THIS LINE OF SCARLET THREAD IN THE WINDOW WHICH YOU DID LET US DOWN BY: AND YOU SHALL BRING YOUR FATHER, AND YOUR MOTHER, AND YOUR BRETHREN, AND ALL YOUR FATHER'S HOUSEHOLD, HOME UNTO YOU.

(19) "AND IT SHALL BE, THAT WHOSOEVER SHALL GO OUT OF THE DOORS OF YOUR HOUSE INTO THE STREET, HIS BLOOD SHALL BE UPON HIS HEAD, AND WE WILL BE GUILTLESS: AND WHOSOEVER SHALL BE WITH YOU IN THE HOUSE, HIS BLOOD SHALL BE ON OUR HEAD, IF ANY HAND BE UPON HIM.

(20) "AND IF YOU UTTER THIS OUR BUSINESS, THEN WE WILL NOT HONOR YOUR OATH WHICH YOU MADE US TO SWEAR."

The overview is:

1. Upon the request of Rahab, the Way of Salvation was immediately made clear and plain to her; it was a very simple way; all she had to do was to hang a piece of scarlet cloth in the window; a child could do that; as well, Salvation presently from the Wrath

NOTES

to come is equally simple; trusting in the Lord Jesus Christ, and in His Precious Blood, of which the scarlet cord was a Type, secures eternal Salvation.

2. The assurance of Salvation in Rahab was not built upon an inward experience, but rather upon an outward evidence — that is, the scarlet line. In it was perfection; in herself imperfection. Looking upon that "*true token*" and believing the Testimony respecting it, she was assured of deliverance in the Day of Doom that was coming. Thus, the outward token gave an inward peace.

The Believer in Jesus enjoys a similar peace. The preciousness of Christ's Blood, and the Testimony of the Holy Scriptures concerning it, is the outward token which brings assurance of Salvation to the heart that trusts Christ.

It was vain for Rahab to seek for Salvation upon the ground of personal worthiness; for she was vile indeed. It is equally vain for the most moral to claim Salvation today, for all have sinned, none are righteous, and all are under sentence of death (Rom. 5:12).

3. The condition was that the red cord would hang from the window, and that all must stay in the house where the window was. To leave the house would leave its protection. Safety was guaranteed for all who remained in the house, destruction for all who left the house. It is the same with the Blood of Christ, which the scarlet cord represented.

As long as we remain in the house of safety provided by the Blood, we are safe. To leave this house of safety, which is Faith in Christ and Him Crucified, guarantees destruction.

THE SCARLET CORD

Scarlet, or rather crimson, is the color of blood. Like the blood on the door-posts in Egypt, it was to be the sign which the destroying messengers of God's vengeance were to respect and pass by. That scarlet cord alone could insure safety. And it could insure the safety only of those who trusted in it alone. It must be taken, therefore, as the Type of Salvation through the Blood of Christ Alone.

Let the reader understand, the only means of Salvation, is Faith and Trust in Christ and what He did for us at the Cross, where He there shed His Life's Blood in order that we might be Saved. The Scripture says:

"But now in Christ Jesus (proclaims the basis of all Salvation) *you who sometimes* (times past) *were far off* (far from Salvation) *are made nigh* (near) *by the Blood of Christ.* (The Sacrificial Atoning Death of Jesus Christ transformed the relations of God with mankind. In Christ, God reconciled not a nation, but *'a world'* to Himself [II Cor. 5:19])" (Eph. 2:13).

WHY IS THE BLOOD, OF WHICH THE SCARLET CORD WAS A TYPE, SO IMPORTANT?

The Scripture tells us, *"For the life of the flesh is in the blood"* (Lev. 17:11).

As it regards payment for sin, God demanded life in payment, but it had to be a perfect life, which would necessitate perfect blood. No human being could do that, simply because the Fall had poisoned the entirety of the human race, and for all time.

So, in order to circumvent this terrible problem, the problem of the Fall, God would become Man, have a body, a special Body prepared for Him, and then He would be born of the Virgin Mary, which would bypass, so to speak, the results of the Fall. His Body was Perfect, and due to being Virgin born, His Blood was Perfect. In fact, Simon Peter referred to it as *"Precious Blood"* (I Pet. 1:19).

When Christ hung on the Cross, shedding His Life's Blood, which was Perfect Blood, which came from a Perfect Body, which came from a Perfect Life, God accepted this poured out Life as payment, total payment, for all sin, past, present, and future (Jn. 3:16).

In fact, every animal offered in sacrifice, at least according to the directions of the Lord, was to be a Substitute for the One Who was to come, namely, the Lord Jesus Christ (Gen., Chpt. 4).

So, the Blood is important, but only as it is the Blood of our Lord and Saviour Jesus Christ. And it is important, supremely important, only as it was shed, and shed for you and me.

When He poured out His Life, this atoned for all sin, as stated, past, present, and future, at least for all who will believe (Rom. 3:22).

Regrettably and sadly the modern Church

is dispensing with the Cross, which means they are dispensing with the Blood, which means they are dispensing with Salvation. As stated, the Cross of Christ is the only thing that stands between man and eternal Hell. As well, the Cross of Christ is the only thing that stands between the Church and total apostasy.

(21) "AND SHE SAID, ACCORDING UNTO YOUR WORDS, SO BE IT, AND SHE SENT THEM AWAY, AND THEY DEPARTED: AND SHE BOUND THE SCARLET LINE IN THE WINDOW.

(22) "AND THEY WENT, AND CAME UNTO THE MOUNTAIN, AND ABODE THERE THREE DAYS, UNTIL THE PURSUERS WERE RETURNED: AND THE PURSUERS SOUGHT THEM THROUGHOUT ALL THE WAY, BUT FOUND THEM NOT.

(23) "SO THE TWO MEN RETURNED, AND DESCENDED FROM THE MOUNTAIN, AND PASSED OVER, AND CAME TO JOSHUA THE SON OF NUN, AND TOLD HIM ALL THINGS THAT BEFELL THEM:

(24) "AND THEY SAID UNTO JOSHUA, TRULY THE LORD HAS DELIVERED INTO OUR HANDS ALL THE LAND; FOR EVEN ALL THE INHABITANTS OF THE COUNTRY DO FAINT BECAUSE OF US."

The construction is:

1. Rahab lost not a moment in making her calling and election sure. She bound the scarlet line in the window; and as directly she did so, she was Saved — that is, she was in safety, and assured of safety.

2. Prior to binding the scarlet line in the window, she was ordained to destruction, but, from the moment she trusted that *"true token,"* she was ordained to Salvation, as well as all her family, provided they stayed in the house, which means that they placed their trust in the scarlet line as well.

3. The report of the two spies as it was given to Joshua, was one of Faith, which was totally unlike the report that had been given some 38 years earlier, which doomed a generation to die in the wilderness (Num., Chpt. 13).

THE GOOD REPORT

The report of the two spies was that already their enemies are disheartened and dispirited at the thought of the Great Name Jehovah, under the protection of which the Israelites fight.

Concerning this, Pulpit says, *"So does the faithful soldier of Christ ever become a source of encouragement to his Brethren. He who trusts in the Lord, and goes steadfastly about His work, never fails to find the enemies of the Lord 'fainting because of' His soldiers. It is only the cowardly and distrustful who find the 'children of Anak,' and 'cities walled up to heaven' — that is, insuperable difficulties and tasks beyond their powers. They who set themselves in earnest to combat the enemies of God, and will neither make a compact with him, nor be 'afraid of their faces,' are sure of victory. Sometimes the walls of some fortress of sin will fall as if by a miracle. Sometimes the enemy will only be discomfited after the prolonged and exhausting efforts of a battle of Beth-horon. But the servants of God on the eve of a new conflict with the powers of evil may safely address their fellow-warriors in the words, 'Truly the Lord has delivered into our hands all the land.'"*[3]

VICTORY

The Child of God is to never think anything but *"victory."* In fact, with the Lord leading Joshua and the Children of Israel, irrespective of the forces against them, they simply could not lose. Who is able to stand up against Jehovah? Who is able to overcome Him? Who is able to discomfit Him? Of course, the entire world joined together could not overcome the Lord. We fight under His Banner! We face Satan and his cohorts, not in our own strength, but rather in His Strength.

The truth is, the victory was won at Calvary some 2,000 years ago. It is not a conflict that is in doubt, but a conflict that has already been fought and won.

Admittedly, Satan has been allowed to continue since that time, but only under the strict supervision of the Lord. In other words, the Evil One can do nothing except the Lord gives him permission to do so (Job, Chpts. 1-2).

WHY HAS THE LORD ALLOWED SATAN TO CONTINUE?

Considering that the Evil One was totally

defeated at Calvary, that is a good question (Col. 2:14-15).

However, Satan, believe it or not, is not the problem of the Believer. Satan has been allowed to continue in order for our Sanctification. We need an adversary, that we may grow in Grace and the Knowledge of the Lord; that we might grow in Faith and Trust; that we might learn to use our Faith, and to use it as required.

The great problem of the Believer is the problem of *"self."* In other words, self is our biggest enemy, and what do we mean by that.

First of all, we are a self, and we will always be a self. So, when a person comes to Christ, that individual does not cease to be a self.

THE PROBLEM OF SELF

First of all I will give the answer to the *"self problem."* Jesus Himself gave us the means and the way of victory.

He said, *"At that day* (after the Resurrection, and the coming of the Holy Spirit on the Day of Pentecost) *you shall know that I am in My Father* (speaks of Deity; Jesus is God!), *and you in Me* (has to do with our Salvation by Faith), *and I in you* (enables us to live a victorious life [Gal. 2:20])*"* (Jn. 14:20).

Self is safe, only when it is hidden totally and completely in Christ.

The great problem with self is that it seeks to depend on its own strength, its own power, its own intellectualism, its own ability, etc., instead of depending solely and totally upon Christ and what Christ has done at the Cross. This is the great battleground for the Christian. This is what Paul was talking about when he said, *"For the flesh* (in this case, evil desires) *lusts against the Spirit* (is the opposite of the Holy Spirit), *and the Spirit against the flesh* (it is the Holy Spirit Alone, Who can subdue the flesh; He does so, as we have repeatedly stated, by our Faith being placed exclusively in the Cross)*: and these are contrary the one to the other* (these two can never harmonize; as Paul has stated, the old nature must be cast out, which the Holy Spirit Alone can do)*: so that you cannot do the things that you would.* (Without the Holy Spirit, Who works by the Cross, the Believer cannot live a Holy life)*"* (Gal. 5:17).

Some attempt to claim that the name or

word *"spirit"* as given in this Verse is not the Holy Spirit, but rather the human spirit; however, when we look at the entirety of the Chapter, we know that Paul is speaking of the Holy Spirit, and not the spirit of man. For instance, he said in Verse 18, *"But if you be led of the Spirit, you are not under the Law."* He then went on to talk about the *"Fruit of the Spirit"* in Verses 22 and 23. So, the entire associating Text is speaking of the Holy Spirit and not the spirit of the individual.

As well, *"Young's Literal Translation of the Holy Bible,"* which does so from the Greek Text, proclaims the fact that Paul is speaking here of the Holy Spirit.

WHAT IS THE DIFFERENCE IN THE FLESH AND SELF?

The *"flesh"* is, one might say, the ability of *"self."* It is all the things that we can do of our own strength and intellectualism, whatever that might be. Within itself, there is really nothing wrong with that; however, the idea is, as given through Paul by the Holy Spirit, what needs to be done in the heart and life of the Believer, cannot be carried out by *"the flesh,"* i.e., *"our own strength and ability."* It just simply cannot be done that way; however, it's very difficult for Believers to admit this; or if they do admit it, they will turn around and continue to try to bring to pass in their lives that which can only be accomplished by the Spirit. Let me say it again:

Everything and anything that we must have done within our hearts and lives as Believers, and I'm speaking of being done by the Lord, to make us what we ought to be, there is no way that we within ourselves, no matter how hard we try, no matter the effort put forth, that we can bring these things to pass. It cannot be done. Paul also said:

"For to be carnally minded is death (this doesn't refer to watching too much Television, as some think, but rather to trying to live for God outside of His Prescribed Order; the results will be sin and separation from God)*; but to be Spiritually minded is life and peace* (God's Prescribed Order is the Cross; this demands our constant Faith in that Finished Work, which is the Way of the Holy Spirit).

NOTES

"Because the carnal mind is enmity against God (once again, this refers to attempting to live for God by means other than the Cross, which places one *'against God'*): *for it is not subject to the Law of God, neither indeed can be* (in its simplest form means that what is being done, whatever it may be, it's not in God's Prescribed Order, which is the Cross).

"So then they who are in the flesh cannot please God (refers to the Believer attempting to live his Christian life by means other than Faith in Christ and the Cross)*"* (Rom. 8:6-8).

This is the great problem of the Church, and in fact, the great problem of the Believer.

GOD'S PRESCRIBED ORDER OF VICTORY

The Lord has but one Way, and because it is the only Way that is needed.

Jesus Christ is the Source of all that we need and, as well, the Cross is the Means, by which everything is given to us. Whatever it is that we need, the Lord has always had it, as should be overly obvious; however, it was only through the Cross that it could be given to us, because it was at the Cross where all sin was atoned, making it possible for the Holy Spirit to come and abide permanently within the hearts and lives of Believers (Jn. 14:16-17).

As it regards *"God's Prescribed Order,"* all the Believer has to do is to subscribe to the following:

A. Every single thing that comes to us does so exclusively through the Cross of Christ. It is the Cross which has made it all possible. Do you believe that? Do you understand that?

The truth is, many, if not most, in the modern Church want to give the credit to something else other than the Cross of Christ. When this is done, such a Believer sets himself on a road to trouble, if not disaster.

B. Considering that it is the Cross of Christ which is the means by which everything is given to us, then our Faith must be exclusively in Christ and what He has done for us at the Cross (Jn. 3:3, 16; Rom. 5:1-2; 6:1-14; I Cor. 1:17-18, 21, 23; 2:2; Gal., Chpt. 5; 6:14).

C. When the Cross of Christ becomes the sole Object of our Faith, then the Holy Spirit, Who works exclusively within the perimeters of the Finished Work of Christ, will work mightily on our behalf, taking that which is of Christ, and revealing it to us (Jn. 16:14; Rom. 8:1-2, 11).

So there you have in a nutshell, so to speak, God's Prescribed Order of Victory. It is *"The Cross of Christ,"* and then *"our Faith,"* and then *"the Holy Spirit."*

CHAPTER 3

(1) "AND JOSHUA ROSE EARLY IN THE MORNING; AND THEY REMOVED FROM SHITTIM, AND CAME TO JORDAN, HE AND ALL THE CHILDREN OF ISRAEL, AND LODGED THERE BEFORE THEY PASSED OVER."

The construction is:

1. The evidence is, that at this particular time the Lord had not told Joshua as to exactly how they would pass over Jordan, just that it would be done.

2. The Jordan River is normally only about 50-100 feet wide; however, during the spring of every year during those times, it would flood, until it was approximately a mile and a half wide, and about 40 feet deep. It doesn't do that now because so much water is siphoned out of the River to irrigate crops.

3. The crossing of the Jordan is a Type of the Baptism with the Holy Spirit, with deliverance from Egypt being a Type of Salvation.

PREPARATIONS TO CROSS OVER

"Shittim" was approximately ten miles due east of the Jordan River. Evidently this was where the Children of Israel were camped.

The word *"Shittim"* means *"a place of the wood, and with scourging thorns.* In essence, it was a type of the wilderness experience, and would be their last camping place before crossing the Jordan. The wilderness experience is about over.

Some have concluded that the crossing of the Jordan is the same thing as dying and going to Heaven; however, the Promised Land, which is supposed to be a type of

Heaven, as we will find, is filled with enemies. There are no enemies in Heaven; therefore, the Promised Land is not a type of Heaven as some teach. It is rather a Type of the Baptism with the Holy Spirit.

To be sure, when one is baptized with the Holy Spirit, Satan knowing that that person can now be of extreme danger to him, and his kingdom of darkness, will do all within his power to oppose such a Child of God. To be sure, we now have the means to win the victory, and in every capacity; however, we come back to the age-old problem of the *"flesh"* and *"self."* As stated, the *"flesh"* is the means by which *"self"* attempts to carry forth its design. It is the greatest hindrance to the Holy Spirit.

If, in fact, the deliverance from Egypt is a Type of Salvation, which it is, and if the *"wilderness experience"* is a type of refusing the Baptism with the Holy Spirit, then those who walk this particular path, a path of disobedience, the situation becomes dire indeed! If the Believer doesn't go on and be Baptized with the Holy Spirit, precious few are going to make it. In fact, every single person who was delivered out of Egypt from 20 years old and upward, died in the wilderness, with the exception of Joshua and Caleb. They, in effect, evidenced Faith, and the Lord accredited to them entrance to the Promised Land, which they will now experience.

THE BAPTISM WITH THE HOLY SPIRIT

The great Prophet Joel prophesied and thereby predicted the *"former rain"* and the *"latter rain"* (Joel 2:23). This speaks of the outpouring of the Holy Spirit.

The *"former rain"* took place from the Day of Pentecost throughout the Early Church, a time frame of approximately 100 years. The Church then began to apostatize, finally degenerating into what is now known as the Catholic Church. In fact, the Catholic Church came into being over several hundreds of years. It was a gradual process.

In the early days of the Seventh Century, when it finally began to exert total control, the world was plunged into the Dark Ages. It did not come out of those Dark Ages until the Reformation, which came about in the 1400's.

At approximately the turn of the Twentieth Century, the *"latter rain"* outpouring commenced. Since that time, several hundreds of millions of people have been baptized with the Holy Spirit with the evidence of speaking with other tongues (Acts 2:4).

The Lord is very patient with His People. For instance, during the Dark Ages, when very little Gospel of any nature was preached, the Lord dealt with the people according to the light they then had. Don't misunderstand, there had to be a modicum of Faith, and that Faith had to register in Christ, in order for people to be Saved. But as is understood, precious few were actually Saved during the Dark Ages, and simply because there was precious little Gospel actually being preached.

But once the light of the Reformation began to spread around the world, and then the Spirit Baptism began to be poured out upon hungry hearts, inasmuch as light was given, in fact, more light than Believers had had since the former rain, the Lord then expected, and now expects much more of those who are Saved. If Believers presently reject the Baptism with the Holy Spirit, which is always accompanied by speaking with other tongues as the Spirit of God gives the utterance, it presents itself as a serious thing indeed! If light is given, and light is rejected, the Scripture I think plainly tells us, that what little light was formerly had is now taken away, and given to those who have accepted the light, whatever that light might be (Mat. 25:14-30).

(2) "AND IT CAME TO PASS AFTER THREE DAYS, THAT THE OFFICERS WENT THROUGH THE HOST;

(3) "AND THEY COMMANDED THE PEOPLE, SAYING, WHEN YOU SEE THE ARK OF THE COVENANT OF THE LORD YOUR GOD, AND THE PRIESTS THE LEVITES BEARING IT, THEN YOU SHALL REMOVE FROM YOUR PLACE, AND GO AFTER IT.

(4) "YET THERE SHALL BE A SPACE BETWEEN YOU AND IT, ABOUT TWO THOUSAND CUBITS BY MEASURE: COME NOT NEAR UNTO IT, THAT YOU MAY KNOW THE WAY BY WHICH YOU MUST

GO: FOR YOU HAVE NOT PASSED THIS WAY HERETOFORE.

(5) "AND JOSHUA SAID UNTO THE PEOPLE, SANCTIFY YOURSELVES: FOR TOMORROW THE LORD WILL DO WONDERS AMONG YOU.

(6) "AND JOSHUA SPOKE UNTO THE PRIESTS, SAYING, TAKE UP THE ARK OF THE COVENANT, AND PASS OVER BEFORE THE PEOPLE. AND THEY TOOK UP THE ARK OF THE COVENANT, AND WENT BEFORE THE PEOPLE."

The composition is:

1. The *"Priests"* who carried the Ark on their shoulders, and the staves on each side of the Ark were for that very purpose, were Types of Christ, Who Alone has the Glory of God, represented by the Ark. Jesus said to the prospective Disciples, *"Follow Me."* He is still saying the same thing to millions of people. Regrettably, far too many are following other things.

2. Before the Cross, men could not approach God, at least not directly, because the blood of bulls and goats could not take away sins (Heb. 10:4). Since the Cross, we are invited to come boldly to the Throne of Grace, and to do so as often as we like (Heb. 4:16).

3. The people were to make certain they were ceremonially clean, for that was the best they could do at that time.

4. As is here obvious, all the plans were God's Plans, and not at all of man; a perfect blueprint is laid out here for us; we should not fail to use it.

INSTRUCTIONS GIVEN BY THE HOLY SPIRIT TO JOSHUA

As we will see, every direction, every plan for crossing the Jordan, was given by God. Joshua, nor any of the great Officers of Israel, contributed anything toward this which was to be done. It all came from the Lord. This should be a lesson for us!

Whatever it is, the Lord knows the way. Whatever we may think, we don't know the way. So the only way that we're going to have victory in our lives, is to do the thing exactly as the Lord has instructed us to do.

We will see in this example laid out before us, that the Cross of Christ is the Means by which we receive everything. Of course, it is the Holy Spirit Who makes it real to our lives, and we also know, and beyond the shadow of a doubt, that the Lord Jesus is the Source; but still, the Cross is the Means by which everything is done, in other words, the manner and the way that we receive all things from God.

THE ARK OF THE COVENANT

The *"Ark of the Covenant"* was the Dwelling Place of God in His Journey with Israel. Actually, He dwelt between the Mercy Seat and the Cherubim (Ex. 25:22; I Sam. 4:4).

The Ark of the Covenant was in a sense, a Type of the Throne of God.

The Ark contained the two tables of the Decalogue (The Ten Commandments), which constituted the documentary basis of God's Redemptive Covenant with Israel (Ex. 34:28-29). This Redemption involved the Life Blood of the Redeemer (Ex. 24:8). The New Testament speaks appropriately of the death of the One Who makes the *"Will,"* or *"Testament"* (Heb. 9:16-18), and hence, of the *"Ark of His Testament"* (Rev. 11:19).

The *"Ark of the Covenant"* represented in typology the *"New Covenant,"* which was and is all in Christ and what He did for us at the Cross.

Along with the two tablets of stone on which the Ten Commandments were inscribed, there was a pot of Manna placed in the Ark. The *"Manna"* was a Type of the Word of God.

As well, Aaron's rod, which budded (Num. 17:10), was also placed in the Ark. The Budded Rod typified the Death and Resurrection of Christ.

Once every year the Ark achieved its ultimate Sacramental significance in the Day of Atonement service (Lev. 16:2). After insuring his personal safety through a protecting cloud of Incense above it, Aaron would sprinkle the Ark's Cover, or Mercy Seat, seven times with blood: first with the blood of a bull, slain as a Sin Offering for himself, and then with that of a goat for the people, so as to cleanse Israel *"from all its sins . . . before the Lord"* (Lev. 16:30).

In pictorial fashion, Grace (the Blood of the Testament) thus became an intervening cover between the Holiness of God (the Glory Cloud) and the verdict of Divine Justice upon the conduct of man.

The Ark of God was never to be used as some type of magic talisman, which would guarantee a victory for Israel. While the Lord commanded it to be used at times, it was only under His Guidance and Direction. In other words, we do not tell the Lord what to do, He tells us what to do.

THE PRIESTS, A TYPE OF CHRIST

The Ark was to be carried on the shoulders of Priests, who were Types of Christ. No one else could touch the Ark under penalty of death.

Jesus said, *"I am the Way, the Truth, and the Life. No one comes to the Father, but by Me"* (Jn. 14:6). Let me put it this way:

A. The only way to God is through Jesus Christ (Jn. 14:6).

B. The only way to Jesus Christ is through the Cross (Lk. 9:23; 14:27).

C. The only way to the Cross is an abnegation of self (Lk. 9:23).

FOLLOW THE ARK

The Scripture plainly says, *"And go after it."* It also stated that there should be a space *"Between you and it, about 2,000 cubits by measure."* This was a little over a half mile.

As stated, the people could not come near the Ark, with the penalty of death imposed upon anyone who did, other than the appointed Priests. The reason was the following:

The blood of bulls and goats could not take away sins (Heb. 10:4), so this means that the sin debt remained over the heads, so to speak, of every single person in Israel.

When Jesus went to the Cross, shedding His Life's Blood in order that we might be Saved, He there atoned for all sin, past, present, and future (Jn. 1:29). In atoning for all sin, He lifted the sin debt, meaning that the debt was totally and completely paid, meaning that it was no longer owed by those who would accept Christ as Saviour and Lord.

Now that the Cross of Christ is a fact, meaning that all sin has been atoned, this means the sin debt is completely lifted, once again for those who believe, meaning that now Believers can come unto the very Throne of God, and do so at any time. Concerning this, the Scripture says:

"Let us therefore come boldly unto the Throne of Grace (presents the Seat of Divine Power, and yet the Source of boundless Grace), *that we may obtain Mercy* (presents that which we want first), *and find Grace to help in time of need* (refers to the Goodness of God extended to all who come, and during any *'time of need'*; all made possible by the Cross)" (Heb. 4:16).

"But now (since the Cross) *has He* (the Lord Jesus) *obtained a more excellent Ministry* (the New Covenant in Jesus' Blood is superior, and takes the place of the Old Covenant in animal blood), *by how much also He is the Mediator of a Better Covenant* (proclaims the fact that Christ officiates between God and man according to the arrangements of the New Covenant), *which was established upon Better Promises.* (This presents the New Covenant, explicitly based on the cleansing and forgiveness of all sin, which the Old Covenant could not do)" (Heb. 8:6).

SANCTIFICATION

The people were told to *"sanctify yourselves: for tomorrow the Lord will do wonders among you."*

"Sanctification" in Old Testament time was somewhat different than now.

Due to the fact that the Holy Spirit could not reside in the hearts and lives of Believers, as He can now, their sanctification then consisted mostly of outward observances. They were to bathe themselves, wash their clothing, thereby presenting themselves before the Lord.

Since the Cross, making it possible for the Holy Spirit to come in and abide permanently within our hearts and lives, Sanctification takes on a brand-new process. The word *"sanctify"* or *"Sanctification"* actually means *"to be set apart exclusively unto the Lord."* Now, the Holy Spirit institutes and instigates the Sanctification process, with the requirement on our part being that our Faith rests supremely in Christ and the Cross. This gives the Holy Spirit latitude to work in our lives.

The problem with modern Christians is that we attempt to sanctify ourselves, which

NOTES

we cannot do. As stated, this is a Work of the Holy Spirit; Who Alone can carry out the process. As well, it is a process, which, in effect, never ends, all made possible by the Cross (Rom. 8:1-2, 11).

(7) "AND THE LORD SAID UNTO JOSHUA, THIS DAY WILL I BEGIN TO MAGNIFY YOU IN THE SIGHT OF ALL ISRAEL, THAT THEY MAY KNOW THAT, AS I WAS WITH MOSES, SO I WILL BE WITH YOU.

(8) "AND YOU SHALL COMMAND THE PRIESTS WHO BEAR THE ARK OF THE COVENANT, SAYING, WHEN YOU ARE COME TO THE BRINK OF THE WATER OF JORDAN, YOU SHALL STAND STILL IN JORDAN."

The exegesis is:

1. While deliverance from Egypt could definitely be described as a Type of the Salvation experience, it also could be Typed as Deliverance from the domination of the sin nature (Rom. 6:14).

In fact, while in Egypt, the Lord referred to the Israelites as *"My People"* (Ex. 3:7). They were Saved, not by being delivered out of Egypt, but by trusting in the Abrahamic Covenant, which, in effect, was *"Justification by Faith"* (Gen. 15:6). That Deliverance was effected, even as it is effected presently, by Faith in the slain lamb (Ex. 12:13).

2. In the wilderness, Israel ceased to have faith in the slain lamb, and thereby wandered aimlessly for some 38 years, and with an entire generation dying in that wasteland. Regrettably and sadly, millions of modern Christians follow suit. They take their faith away from the slain lamb and place it in something else. Such a direction always guarantees death.

3. Crossing the Jordan, as we have stated, is a Type of the Baptism with the Holy Spirit, for it is impossible to claim the Promises of God without the Leading, Guidance, and Power of the Spirit, Who, however, always works within the framework of Christ and the Cross (Rom. 8:2).

FACING PROBLEMS ACCORDING TO THE DIRECTION OF THE HOLY SPIRIT

The River Jordan presented a formidable

obstacle to Israel as it regarded their entering the Promised Land, especially considering that it was now at flood tide. As stated, normally the Jordan River is only about 50-100 feet wide; however, in those years, due to not drawing water out of the River for irrigation, every spring the River would flood. According to Scholars, it was probably about a mile and a half wide, and about 40 feet deep. The Holy Spirit, without a doubt, chose the most inopportune time of the year for the crossing to be made. In fact, without a Miracle, it was virtually impossible for some three million Israelites, along with all of their herds, to get across this obstacle.

Even if they had built a small fleet of boats, it would have taken upwards of a year to get everyone across this body of water. So, in effect, there was nothing physically that could be done to speed up the process. It was either God or nothing!

The directions were, that the Priests bearing the Ark of the Covenant, were to come *"to the brink of the water of Jordan,"* referring to the edge of the River. They were to *"stand still in Jordan."*

Every advancement made by the Child of God is always met by a formidable obstacle presented by Satan. To be sure, the Lord allows Satan certain latitude, in order to teach Believers Faith and Trust. We have to learn and understand, that there is nothing God cannot do. That whatever obstacles that Satan throws in our path, whatever they might be, the Lord can easily help us around them, over them, through them, etc. He is not limited, unless we limit Him by our unbelief.

As well, as here typified, we do not overcome problems by trying to ignore them, or by trying to confess that they do not exist. It would have been useless for Joshua and the Children of Israel to confess that the Jordan River wasn't there. How silly can we be?! Problems, obstacles, hindrances, difficulties, cannot be confessed away; they must be met head-on, but we must remember as to how they are met head-on.

The Lord didn't tell the Officers, the mighty men of Israel, to go stand on the edge of Jordan. Neither did the Lord tell any of the Children of Israel to perform this task. It was instructed that the Priests who were

bearing the Ark of the Covenant were to themselves, go to the brink of Jordan, and there stand in that body of water. We should learn a lesson from this.

All too often we attempt to do things which we cannot do. Inasmuch as the Priests who were bearing the Ark were Types of Christ, and the Ark itself was a Type of the Throne of God, it was Christ Alone Who could perform this task. Listen to Paul, as it regards living this Christian life:

"I am crucified with Christ (as the Foundation of all Victory; Paul, here, takes us back to Rom. 6:3-5): *nevertheless I live* (have New Life); *yet not I* (not by my own strength and ability), *but Christ lives in me* (by virtue of me dying with Him on the Cross, and being raised with Him in Newness of Life): *and the life which I now live in the flesh* (my daily walk before God) *I live by the Faith of the Son of God* (the Cross is ever the Object of my Faith), *Who loved me, and gave Himself for me* (which is the only way that I could be Saved).

He then said, *"I do not frustrate the Grace of God* (if we make anything other than the Cross of Christ the Object of our Faith, we frustrate the Grace of God, which means we stop its action, and the Holy Spirit will no longer help us): *for if Righteousness come by the Law* (any type of Law), *then Christ is dead in vain.* (If I can successfully live for the Lord by any means other than Faith in Christ and the Cross, then the Death of Christ was a waste)" (Gal. 2:20-21).

In a nutshell, so to speak, we face obstacles, and ever how large they might be, by making certain that our Faith is anchored squarely in Christ and the Cross, which is the same thing as one's Faith being anchored squarely in the Word, for they are all synonymous, which then allows the Holy Spirit the proper latitude within my life, Who can bring about whatever it is that I need (Rom. 6:1-14; 8:1-2, 11).

The idea is, go towards your problem instead of running from it, but at the same time make certain that it is Christ Who leads the charge. Our Faith in His Cross guarantees that (I Cor. 1:17-18, 23; 2:2; Gal., Chpt. 5).

(9) "AND JOSHUA SAID UNTO THE CHILDREN OF ISRAEL, COME HITHER

AND HEAR THE WORDS OF THE LORD YOUR GOD.

(10) "AND JOSHUA SAID, HEREBY YOU SHALL KNOW THAT THE LIVING GOD IS AMONG YOU, AND THAT HE WILL WITHOUT FAIL DRIVE OUT FROM BEFORE YOU THE CANAANITES, AND THE HITTITES, AND THE HIVITES, AND THE PERIZZITES, AND THE GIRGASHITES, AND THE AMORITES, AND THE JEBUSITES.

(11) "BEHOLD, THE ARK OF THE COVENANT OF THE LORD OF ALL THE EARTH PASSES OVER BEFORE YOU INTO JORDAN.

(12) "NOW THEREFORE TAKE YOU TWELVE MEN OUT OF THE TRIBES OF ISRAEL, OUT OF EVERY TRIBE A MAN.

(13) "AND IT SHALL COME TO PASS, AS SOON AS THE SOLES OF THE FEET OF THE PRIESTS WHO BEAR THE ARK OF THE LORD, THE LORD OF ALL THE EARTH, SHALL REST IN THE WATERS OF JORDAN, THAT THE WATERS OF JORDAN SHALL BE CUT OFF FROM THE WATERS THAT COME DOWN FROM ABOVE; AND THEY SHALL STAND UPON AN HEAP."

The pattern is:

1. These heathen tribes typify enemies of the flesh which seek to hinder our progress with the Lord; victory can come to the Believer only as the Believer maintains his Faith in Christ and the Cross, which gives the Holy Spirit latitude to work within our lives (Rom. 6:3-14; 8:1-2, 11).

2. Christ, of which the Ark of the Covenant was a Type, has gone before us and secured the victory; Faith and Trust in Him guarantees us His Victory; to be sure, it is a Victory, which He has won solely for us.

3. The number "twelve" is God's number of Government; however, it is His Government, and not that of man; this means that man must not dilute it in any way.

4. What is God's Government? Of course, it is His Word, but it can be summed up in the statement, "Jesus Christ and Him Crucified" (I Cor. 1:23; Gal. 6:14).

5. The Priests being a Type of Christ as well, the moment their feet touched the waters, the waters fled; such is the Power of

Christ over the enemies of our soul. But, understand, Jordan will flee only before Christ, and not at all before us.

THE WORD OF THE LORD

Joshua will now address Israel, and he tells them at the beginning, "Come hither and hear the Words of the LORD your God." In other words, what Israel would hear would not be the mere words of Joshua, as weighty as they may have been, but rather, "The Words of the LORD."

THE LIVING GOD AND THE ENEMIES OF ISRAEL

The Lord tells Joshua to tell the people that there, in fact, are enemies in the Promised Land. He even names the Tribes, seven in totality.

The Lord could have done any number of things to rid the land of these enemies of the People of God; however, He allowed them to remain, in order that Israel, as stated, might learn Faith and Trust.

He said that "without fail" He would drive out these enemies; however, that depended, as we shall later see, on obedience to the Word of God. It is always obedience! We are given the Word, and we are to obey that Word, whatever it might be.

THE LORD OF ALL THE EARTH

Israel was the only monotheistic Nation on the face of the Earth. This meant that they worshipped one God, Jehovah. The other nations of the world were polytheistic, which means they worshipped many gods. But the Scripture in this Eleventh Verse plainly tells us, that Jehovah is "the LORD of all the Earth," and not these heathenistic gods, which, in effect, were no gods at all!

At this present time (in 2006) there are about two billion people on the Earth who go under the guise of "Christian." There are about one billion Protestants, and about one billion Catholics. Of course, as to how many people in this number are truly Saved, only the Lord would know. But one thing is certain, that number is probably infinitesimally small.

There are about one billion Muslims, and about one half billion Buddhists, and Shintoists. The balance of the world is made up of atheists, and whatever! So, the situation now is not so very much different than it was 3,500 years ago at the time of Joshua. But irrespective of the religious beliefs of these false religions, Jesus Christ is still the *"LORD of all the Earth."* One day soon, He will reign Personally from Jerusalem. This reign will commence almost immediately after the Second Coming (Rev., Chpt. 19).

THE GOVERNMENT OF GOD

Now Joshua is told by the Lord to *"take you twelve men out of the Tribes of Israel, out of every Tribe a man."* We aren't given any information here as to what these men were to do; however, Joshua 4:1 sheds some light on the subject.

As we have stated, the number *"twelve"* in the Bible stands for the Government of God. There were Twelve Tribes of Israel, and Twelve Apostles. As we have also stated, the Government of God is the Word of God.

One of the greatest problems in the Church, and a problem which seems to have always existed, is that religious man attempts to replace the Government of God with his own government, whatever that might be. Many religious Denominations begin in the right way, looking solely to the Word of God. They are then blessed somewhat, and then begin to intrude upon the Government of the Lord, attempting to replace it with their own government. It always brings tragedy.

One particular time and speaking to a religious leader, he had stated something, which was obviously unscriptural. I kindly made mention of this to him, and his answer was very revealing.

He did not deny that what he said was unscriptural, but rather, he stated, *"but that is our tradition."* It didn't really matter about the situation being unscriptural, it's just what we want to do. Such a direction always spells disaster.

The Word of God must be the criteria for all things. We must not veer from the Word, deviate from the Word, add to the Word, or take from the Word. Jesus said, *"Man shall not live by bread alone, but by every Word that proceeds out of the Mouth of God"* (Mat. 4:4).

We have a tendency, tragically enough, to

not obey the admonition of our Lord, but rather to substitute something to take its place, which always leads to disaster. The Government of God must never be abrogated, weakened, or substituted in any way!

THE PROMISE OF THE LORD

Now the Children of Israel, according to the Thirteenth Verse, knows as to how they're going to cross this Jordan. The Lord is going to perform a Miracle, in fact, a Miracle of unprecedented proportions.

The actual terminology in the Hebrew is, *"and they shall stand, one heap,"* referring to the waters of Jordan.

Some claim that it was an earthquake that caused this. Whatever it is that the Lord used to bring about this tremendous Miracle, really doesn't matter. The idea is, it was not happenchance, or happenstance, but rather, a Miracle generated totally by the Lord. At least this is what the Lord said that He would do, and which, as we shall see, He most definitely did do!

(14) "AND IT CAME TO PASS, WHEN THE PEOPLE REMOVED FROM THEIR TENTS, TO PASS OVER JORDAN, AND THE PRIESTS BEARING THE ARK OF THE COVENANT BEFORE THE PEOPLE;

(15) "AND AS THEY WHO BORE THE ARK WERE COME INTO JORDAN, AND THE FEET OF THE PRIESTS WHO BORE THE ARK WERE DIPPED IN THE BRIM OF THE WATER, (FOR JORDAN OVERFLOWED ALL HIS BANKS ALL THE TIME OF HARVEST,)

(16) "THAT THE WATERS WHICH CAME DOWN FROM ABOVE STOOD AND ROSE UP UPON AN HEAP VERY FAR FROM THE CITY OF ADAM, THAT IS BESIDE ZARETAN: AND THOSE WHO CAME DOWN TOWARD THE SEA OF THE PLAIN, EVEN THE SALT SEA, FAILED, AND WERE CUT OFF: AND THE PEOPLE PASSED OVER RIGHT AGAINST JERICHO.

(17) "AND THE PRIESTS WHO BORE THE ARK OF THE COVENANT OF THE LORD STOOD FIRM ON DRY GROUND IN THE MIDST OF JORDAN, AND ALL THE ISRAELITES PASSED OVER ON DRY GROUND, UNTIL ALL THE PEOPLE WERE

PASSED CLEAN OVER JORDAN."

The exposition is:

1. No doubt, Jericho, due to the fact of Jordan being flooded now about a mile and a half wide, felt somewhat safe, thinking that Israel could not cross the swollen river. They reckoned without the Power of God.

2. The opening of the Jordan can be construed as none other than one of the greatest Miracles ever performed by the Lord; furthermore, the Lord had them to cross opposite Jericho, with the inhabitants of that city no doubt observing this spectacle.

3. Many people think of Jordan as described here, as a type of death, with Canaan as a Type of Heaven; however, while Jordan is a type of death, it is rather a type of the death of the flesh, with Canaan a Type of our possession of the Promises of God, and by the Power of the Holy Spirit. In other words, the Promised Land is a Type of the inheritance of the Child of God, but which can be obtained only by the Power of the Holy Spirit.

THE GREAT MIRACLE

The idea of the opening of the Jordan seems to have been, that the Lord effected the opening some 15 or 20 miles above where Israel was camped, with a dry river bed running all the way then to the Dead Sea, into which the Jordan normally emptied. Considering that nearly 3 million people had to cross, plus all of their herds, ever how many there were, the actual crossing had to be several miles wide, which it no doubt was. I wonder what the thoughts of the inhabitants of Jericho were, as they observed this miraculous happening, watching hundreds of thousands of the Children of Israel cross the dry river bed? I suspect that Rahab and her family, were watching intently as well, and remembering every moment the promise that the two spies had made to her that she and her family would be spared.

Let it be understood, that the God of Miracles of yesterday, is still the God of Miracles today. Far too many claim the days of Miracles are over; however, there is nothing in the Word of God that substantiates such a claim. In fact, the Lord changes not.

CHAPTER 4

(1) "AND IT CAME TO PASS, WHEN ALL THE PEOPLE WERE CLEAN PASSED OVER JORDAN, THAT THE LORD SPOKE UNTO JOSHUA, SAYING,

(2) "TAKE YOU TWELVE MEN OUT OF THE PEOPLE, OUT OF EVERY TRIBE A MAN,

(3) "AND COMMAND YOU THEM, SAYING, TAKE YOU HENCE OUT OF THE MIDST OF JORDAN, OUT OF THE PLACE WHERE THE PRIESTS' FEET STOOD FIRM, TWELVE STONES, AND YOU SHALL CARRY THEM OVER WITH YOU, AND LEAVE THEM IN THE LODGING PLACE, WHERE YOU SHALL LODGE THIS NIGHT.

(4) "THEN JOSHUA CALLED THE TWELVE MEN, WHOM HE HAD PREPARED OF THE CHILDREN OF ISRAEL, OUT OF EVERY TRIBE A MAN:

(5) "AND JOSHUA SAID UNTO THEM, PASS OVER BEFORE THE ARK OF THE LORD YOUR GOD INTO THE MIDST OF JORDAN, AND TAKE YOU UP EVERY MAN OF YOU A STONE UPON HIS SHOULDER, ACCORDING UNTO THE NUMBER OF THE TRIBES OF THE CHILDREN OF ISRAEL:

(6) "THAT THIS MAY BE A SIGN AMONG YOU, THAT WHEN YOUR CHILDREN ASK YOUR FATHERS IN TIME TO COME, SAYING, WHAT MEAN YOU BY THESE STONES?

(7) "THEN YOU SHALL ANSWER THEM, THAT THE WATERS OF JORDAN WERE CUT OFF BEFORE THE ARK OF THE COVENANT OF THE LORD; WHEN IT PASSED OVER JORDAN, THE WATERS OF JORDAN WERE CUT OFF: AND THESE STONES SHALL BE FOR A MEMORIAL UNTO THE CHILDREN OF ISRAEL FOREVER.

(8) "AND THE CHILDREN OF ISRAEL DID SO AS JOSHUA COMMANDED, AND TOOK UP TWELVE STONES OUT OF THE MIDST OF JORDAN, AS THE LORD SPOKE UNTO JOSHUA, ACCORDING TO THE NUMBER OF THE TRIBES OF THE CHILDREN OF ISRAEL, AND CARRIED THEM OVER WITH THEM UNTO THE PLACE

WHERE THEY LODGED, AND LAID THEM DOWN THERE.

(9) "AND JOSHUA SET UP TWELVE STONES IN THE MIDST OF JORDAN, IN THE PLACE WHERE THE FEET OF THE PRIESTS WHICH BORE THE ARK OF THE COVENANT STOOD: AND THEY ARE THERE UNTO THIS DAY.

(10) "FOR THE PRIESTS WHICH BORE THE ARK STOOD IN THE MIDST OF JORDAN, UNTIL EVERYTHING WAS FINISHED THAT THE LORD COMMANDED JOSHUA TO SPEAK UNTO THE PEOPLE, ACCORDING TO ALL THAT MOSES COMMANDED JOSHUA: AND THE PEOPLE HASTED AND PASSED OVER.

(11) "AND IT CAME TO PASS, WHEN ALL THE PEOPLE WERE CLEAN PASSED OVER, THAT THE ARK OF THE LORD PASSED OVER, AND THE PRIESTS, IN THE PRESENCE OF THE PEOPLE.

(12) "AND THE CHILDREN OF REUBEN, AND THE CHILDREN OF GAD, AND HALF THE TRIBE OF MANASSEH, PASSED OVER ARMED BEFORE THE CHILDREN OF ISRAEL, AS MOSES SPOKE UNTO THEM:

(13) "ABOUT FORTY THOUSAND PREPARED FOR WAR PASSED OVER BEFORE THE LORD UNTO BATTLE, TO THE PLAINS OF JERICHO.

(14) "ON THAT DAY THE LORD MAGNIFIED JOSHUA IN THE SIGHT OF ALL ISRAEL; AND THEY FEARED HIM, AS THEY FEARED MOSES, ALL THE DAYS OF HIS LIFE."

The construction is:

1. We will find in this Fourth Chapter that there are two distinct memorials set up, both consisting of twelve stones each.

2. Four facts are stated about these stones. They were *"taken,"* they were *"carried"* they were *"laid down,"* and they were *"set up."* The origin of the stones was the deep bed of Jordan; their purpose was to testify that Israel owed her entrance into the goodly land only and wholly to Divine Grace and Power.

In the Baptism of Christ, the Believer dies to his old life and rises into a New Life; and we are reminded that as to our moral origin, we were buried beneath the waters of the Wrath of God; that as to our present

NOTES

position, we are now set up upon Resurrection ground; and it is our duty to testify daily to the Glory of Christ, the one and only Saviour. The Lord Jesus Christ said to the Pharisees that if the children were silent, the very stones would cry out! These stones set up at Gilgal cried out day and night!

3. The first memorial could, no doubt, be referred to as Jordan stones, but these spoken of in the Ninth Verse must be referred to as Wilderness stones. These twelve stones buried on the bottom of the Jordan River, where the feet of the Priests had stood, signify the death and burial of Israel's forty years of unbelief and sinning in the Wilderness.

The Lord is saying to Israel that that time is over, buried, out of sight, and forgotten, typical of all our sins of the past, that is, if we have properly trusted Christ (I Jn. 1:9). Unfortunately, far too many modern Christians seem to take delight in diving down to the bottom of Jordan, spiritually speaking, and retrieving those stones and bringing them to the surface, thereby constantly reminding people of such-and-such sin. I would hope we could see the terrible insult to Christ that such a thing is, and, in fact, that such action is sinful and wicked. Sins forgiven are to never be held over someone's head.

4. What a scene this must have been! The majestic Ark of the Covenant held on the shoulders of the Priests, all in the midst of Jordan, with the waters held up by the mighty Power of God, that the people could walk across on dry ground, flood or not!

5. Joshua was a Type of Christ, Who actually carried the Hebrew name *"Joshua,"* which means *"Saviour."* The Greek derivative is *"Jesus."*

JORDAN STONES AND WILDERNESS STONES

Verse 2 says, *"Take you twelve men out of the people."* This was a man for each Tribe. The number 12, as previously stated, represents government. As well, it meant that every single person who passed across enjoyed the same type of Salvation. None were Saved more than others; likewise, the *"born-again"* experience for the most vile libertine is the same as the Salvation experience for the good moral man. Both are horribly lost; both must have a glorious Salvation; consequently, the Salvation is the same for both.

These twelve men, one from each Tribe, were to take a stone each to Gilgal and set them up as a memorial. Incidentally, the name *"Gilgal"* means *"rolled away."* Where Israel was encamped, and what Israel was instructed by the Lord to do, all, in effect, stated, *"the wilderness experience of doubt and death is all rolled away. It is no more held against us. It is gone, forever gone!"*

THE TESTIMONY

In the years to come, even the centuries to come, when the children would ask their fathers, *"What mean ye by these stones?"* the Testimony was to be the same. They were to tell the children how the Lord delivered them.

As well, ever the same testimony must be of the Salvation experience. As it was for the fathers, so for the children. The Message must not change.

The stones represent the great Power of God in delivering Israel from the wilderness as well as from Egypt. The great Rock, the Lord Jesus Christ, represents our Salvation and must be told the same to the children as to the fathers. God help us when the children ask, *"What means this?"* That we will have instantly the miraculous story, *"Saved by Grace."*

THE MEMORIAL

The Seventh Verse says, *"Shall be for a memorial."* What is our memorial today? Too often times it is the rank message of modernism, which denies the Mighty Power of God, or the false cults that substitute *"another Ark,"* or then, sadly, the Church that preaches *"another gospel,"* which is the opposite of the Message, *"Jesus Christ and Him Crucified"* (I Cor. 1:23).

THE MESSAGE OF
THE CROSS

I'm afraid that presently, when the children ask as it regards what the Church presently believes, that the answer given them is no longer what it was yesteryear. The Message in the Early Church was, *"Jesus Christ*

and Him Crucified" (Rom. 6:1-14; I Cor. 1:17-18, 21, 23; 2:2; Gal. 2:20-21; Chpt. 5; 6:14; Col. 2:14-15).

Regrettably, most modern Churches have a program, in fact, a well-oiled program, but they have no message. Let it ever be understood that the reason for the Church, the purpose for the Church, the cause for the Church, is *"the Message."* As stated, the modern Church has no Message, it has only a program!

THE WILDERNESS STONES

The Ninth Verse, *"And Joshua set up twelve stones in the midst of Jordan."* These twelve stones were totally different from the twelve that they had taken out of Jordan. These could be called *"wilderness stones."* They represent the terrible failure, sin, and defeat of the wilderness. In effect, Joshua was saying, *"in the sea of God's forgetfulness."*

The Lord was telling Israel, *"The wilderness is forgotten; the failures are buried. They will be covered by the Jordan not to be remembered anymore."*

They were to be placed *"where the feet of the Priests which bore the Ark of the Covenant stood."* Every sin of the past is washed by the Blood of Jesus Christ. They are buried forever, not to be remembered against us anymore.

And it says, *"And they are there unto this day."* Those stones representing the horrible wilderness failure were to be covered by the waters of God's Grace. They were not to be seen anymore, nor were they to be remembered anymore. In the Eyes of God they no longer existed.

Sadly, too many Christians seem to delight in diving into the murky waters of life's Jordan, groping around on the bed of the sea of God's forgetfulness, and then when finding some stone, whether the correct one or not, delighting in bringing it to the surface and calling it to the attention of all concerned. How the Anger of God would have burned red hot if the Israelites had attempted to retrieve these buried wilderness stones! How God's Anger must burn red hot today when Christians attempt to retrieve, to remember, or to rehash that which God has forgiven, cleansed, and forgotten!

Likewise, when Satan comes to us attempting to bring his condemnation of past failures, we must do as Paul said, *"Forgetting those things which are behind."* Hallelujah!

What a sight this must have been, nearly three million people flooding across the dry bed of Jordan, with the Priests dressed in their royal garments holding the Ark of the Covenant on their shoulders. What must the inhabitants of Jericho thought! No doubt, stark fear filled their hearts, as well it should!

(15) "AND THE LORD SPOKE UNTO JOSHUA, SAYING;

(16) "COMMAND THE PRIESTS WHO BEAR THE ARK OF THE TESTIMONY, THAT THEY COME UP OUT OF JORDAN.

(17) "JOSHUA THEREFORE COMMANDED THE PRIESTS, SAYING, COME YE UP OUT OF JORDAN.

(18) "AND IT CAME TO PASS, WHEN THE PRIESTS WHO BORE THE ARK OF THE COVENANT OF THE LORD WERE COME UP OUT OF THE MIDST OF JORDAN, AND THE SOLES OF THE PRIESTS' FEET WERE LIFTED UP UNTO THE DRY LAND, THAT THE WATERS OF JORDAN RETURNED UNTO THEIR PLACE, AND FLOWED OVER ALL HIS BANKS, AS THEY DID BEFORE."

The construction is:

1. This is the Way of the Lord; He calls men and women, and then He speaks to them, giving leading and guidance; unfortunately, most of the Church have long since ceased to hear from the Lord, that is, if they ever heard from Him, and are thereby led by men; the results are obvious.

2. Williams says, *"There was but one way into Canaan and that the Divine Way made by the Ark of the Covenant."*[1]

3. There is but one way into Heaven. Jesus says, *"I am the Way."* The Ark typified Him — its precious wood, His Humanity; its gold, His Deity; its blood-sprinkled cover, His Atonement. As the Ark descended into the depth of Jordan and rolled back its waters, so Christ descended into the deep waters of the Wrath of God and opened the one way into Everlasting Life.

THE ARK OF THE COVENANT

If it is to be noticed, the Sixteenth Verse

proclaims the Ark of the Covenant being referred to as the *"Ark of the Testimony."* The word *"Testimony"* in the Hebrew means *"witness."* So it could be called the *"Ark of the Witness."*

This means that the Ark of the Covenant was a Witness given by God, of His Promises as it regards the coming Redeemer. The Ark witnessed to that Promise, that coming event!

When Israel no longer cared, and I'm referring to caring about the coming Redeemer, and which took place about a thousand years into the future, the Ark of the Covenant was lost. Some say that Jeremiah hid it in a cave, and did so immediately before the Babylonian invasion. One thing is known, when the Babylonians broke into the Holy of Holies of the Temple, there was no Ark of the Covenant present. What actually happened to it, we aren't told!

THE MIRACLE

The Eighteenth Verse says that the moment the Priests walked out of the bed of Jordan to yonder bank, at that moment, *"The waters of Jordan returned unto their place, and flowed over all his banks, as they did before."*

Some claim that this was merely an earthquake which took place, and had nothing to do with the Miracle-working Power of God. In other words, they are claiming a natural phenomenon. Nothing could be further from the truth!

As to exactly how the Lord did this thing, we aren't told. But this we do know, that whatever was done was supernatural, proven by the fact that the moment the Priests left the riverbed, that the waters returned. It would be impossible to calculate an earthquake and its effects to that degree. No! This was the Miracle-working Power of God, which opened that river, even though it was at flood tide. And let all know and understand, God is still in the Miracle-working business!

(19) "AND THE PEOPLE CAME UP OUT OF JORDAN ON THE TENTH DAY OF THE FIRST MONTH, AND ENCAMPED IN GILGAL, IN THE EAST BORDER OF JERICHO.

(20) "AND THOSE TWELVE STONES, WHICH THEY TOOK OUT OF JORDAN, DID

JOSHUA PITCH IN GILGAL.

(21) "AND HE SPOKE UNTO THE CHILDREN OF ISRAEL, SAYING, WHEN YOUR CHILDREN SHALL ASK THEIR FATHERS IN TIME TO COME, SAYING, WHAT MEAN THESE STONES?

(22) "THEN YOU SHALL LET YOUR CHILDREN KNOW, SAYING, ISRAEL CAME OVER THIS JORDAN ON DRY LAND.

(23) "FOR THE LORD YOUR GOD DRIED UP THE WATERS OF JORDAN FROM BEFORE YOU, UNTIL YOU WERE PASSED OVER, AS THE LORD YOUR GOD DID TO THE RED SEA, WHICH HE DRIED UP FROM BEFORE US, UNTIL WE WERE GONE OVER:

(24) "THAT ALL THE PEOPLE OF THE EARTH MIGHT KNOW THE HAND OF THE LORD, THAT IT IS MIGHTY: THAT YOU MIGHT FEAR THE LORD YOUR GOD FOREVER."

The exegesis is:

1. The name *"Gilgal"* means *"rolled away"*; their encampment in this place typified that the sins, doubt, and unbelief of the Wilderness had rolled away.

2. Gilgal was an appropriate place for these twelve memorial stones to be set up; in a sense, it was a new beginning for Israel; with Faith in Christ, any individual can have a new beginning.

3. The Miracles of the past, which the Lord has given us are to be related again and again, in essence, lived again and again. While we cannot live off past Miracles, they do give us Faith for the present times and the future, which they are meant to do.

4. Of the nearly three million people who left Egypt, some forty years before, only two of them would actually go into the Promised Land, Joshua and Caleb, other than those under twenty years of age; doubt and unbelief killed the others, while Faith brought Joshua and Caleb through.

THE SINS ARE ROLLED AWAY

"The tenth day of the first month," corresponds somewhat with our modern April. This was the time of the Barley harvest, the time of the Passover.

Presently, Jericho is about five miles due west of the Jordan River. Considering that

the river was a flood tide, then approximately a mile and a half wide, from the banks of the river then to Jericho was about three and a half miles. So, the area referred to as *"Gilgal,"* was probably about two miles from Jericho, or possibly as little as a mile and a half.

It is believed that the army of Jericho was powerful, and yet, they made no attempt to come against Israel. The reason? The reason was the manner in the way that Israel crossed the Jordan. The river being at flood tide, approximately a mile and a half wide and some forty feet deep, quite possibly the inhabitants of Jericho felt somewhat secure. And yet, there was the nagging truth of what had transpired some forty years before, when the Red Sea miraculously opened.

I personally think that the inhabitants of Jericho hardly knew what to do. Could they come out and fight people who had just seen and witnessed such a Miracle, and for whom this Miracle had been tendered? Therefore, they did what Verse 1 of the Sixth Chapter proclaims, *"Jericho was straitly shut up because of the Children of Israel: none went out, and none came in."*

I think that one could say, and without fear of contradiction, that most everything that Israel now did, was a type of Redemption, and the Moving and Operation of the Holy Spirit.

"Gilgal," as stated, was an appropriate place for them to camp. It spoke of a new beginning, especially considering that very name *"Gilgal"* meant *"rolled away."*

Every person in the world, in some way, has a *"past."* Of course, with some that *"past"* is extremely negative, and with others less so; nevertheless, a *"past"* of some sort is present with all.

Suffice to say that most would like to have certain parts of their past erased, which of course in the natural is impossible. But yet it can be done, just as this illustration of *"Gilgal"* gives to us. It can be done in Christ. As someone has well said:

"The Child of God has no past, while Satan has no future."

What a statement!

The Lord was telling Israel when they encamped at Gilgal, that the *"past"* is done away with. The terrible wilderness experience which lasted for some forty years, and which saw such heartache, dying and death, is now gone, erased, in fact, typified by the twelve stones which were placed in the darkened depths of Jordan.

The song says:

"He took my sins away, He took my sins away,
"He keeps me singing every day.
"I'm so glad, He took my sins away,
"He took my sins away!"

Israel had a new beginning, and any Believer can have a new beginning, irrespective as to what the past has been, if they will only look to Christ! Look to Christ! Look to Christ! Calvary erased the past and did so totally and completely and, as well, promised and guaranteed a brand-new future. Nothing in the world can touch that, nothing in the world can equal that, nothing in the world can even remotely approach that.

There is one more thing that needs to be said about the Lord. Some may read these words and say, *"Brother Swaggart, you don't understand, I've tried my best in the Lord to start over again and again, and I keep failing."*

As bad as that is, let it ever be understood, that God has no limitation on the times that one can *"begin again."* As long as we meet His Conditions, which is to simply confess our failure to Him, He will always be *"faithful and just to forgive us our sins, and to cleanse us from all unrighteousness"* (I Jn. 1:9).

THE MEMORIAL

As is obvious here, the Lord wanted future generations to never forget the great Miracle that had been performed on this tenth day of April, which was the first month of Israel's year. The exciting, supernatural, miraculous story, must be told again and again! And so should every Miracle given in the Word of God, as well as those that happen to us personally.

They should be told, *"That all the people of the Earth might know the Hand of the LORD, that it is mighty: that you might fear the LORD your God forever."*

Regrettably and sadly, this has not been done, and is not being done now, at least to

the degree it should; however, there is coming a day that the entirety of the Earth will *"know the Hand of the LORD."* I speak of the coming Kingdom Age when Jesus will rule and reign Personally from Jerusalem. Then and only then, things will be as they ought to be. Now the world points to the very opposite, global warming, or freezing temperatures, in other words, coming catastrophe for this world. To be sure, were it left in the hands of man, catastrophe it would be; however, Jesus Christ, its Creator is coming back. And as the song says, *"What a day that will be!"*

CHAPTER 5

(1) "AND IT CAME TO PASS, WHEN ALL THE KINGS OF THE AMORITES, WHICH WERE ON THE SIDE OF JORDAN WESTWARD, AND ALL THE KINGS OF THE CANAANITES, WHICH WERE BY THE SEA, HEARD THAT THE LORD HAD DRIED UP THE WATERS OF JORDAN FROM BEFORE THE CHILDREN OF ISRAEL, UNTIL WE WERE PASSED OVER, THAT THEIR HEART MELTED, NEITHER WAS THEIR SPIRIT IN THEM ANY MORE, BECAUSE OF THE CHILDREN OF ISRAEL.

(2) "AT THAT TIME THE LORD SAID UNTO JOSHUA, MAKE YOU SHARP KNIVES, AND CIRCUMCISE AGAIN THE CHILDREN OF ISRAEL THE SECOND TIME.

(3) "AND JOSHUA MADE HIM SHARP KNIVES, AND CIRCUMCISED THE CHILDREN OF ISRAEL AT THE HILL OF THE FORESKINS.

(4) "AND THIS IS THE CAUSE WHY JOSHUA DID CIRCUMCISE: ALL THE PEOPLE WHO CAME OUT OF EGYPT WHO WERE MALES, EVEN ALL THE MEN OF WAR, DIED IN THE WILDERNESS BY THE WAY, AFTER THEY CAME OUT OF EGYPT.

(5) "NOW ALL THE PEOPLE WHO CAME OUT WERE CIRCUMCISED: BUT ALL THE PEOPLE WHO WERE BORN IN THE WILDERNESS BY THE WAY AS THEY CAME FORTH OUT OF EGYPT, THEM THEY HAD NOT CIRCUMCISED.

(6) "FOR THE CHILDREN OF ISRAEL

WALKED FORTY YEARS IN THE WILDER-
NESS, TILL ALL THE PEOPLE WHO WERE
MEN OF WAR, WHICH CAME OUT OF
EGYPT, WERE CONSUMED, BECAUSE
THEY OBEYED NOT THE VOICE OF THE
LORD: UNTO WHOM THE LORD SWORE
THAT HE WOULD NOT SHOW THEM THE
LAND, WHICH THE LORD SWORE UNTO
THEIR FATHERS THAT HE WOULD GIVE
US, A LAND THAT FLOWS WITH MILK
AND HONEY.

(7) "AND THEIR CHILDREN, WHOM
HE RAISED UP IN THEIR STEAD, THEM
JOSHUA CIRCUMCISED: FOR THEY
WERE UNCIRCUMCISED, BECAUSE
THEY HAD NOT CIRCUMCISED THEM BY
THE WAY.

(8) "AND IT CAME TO PASS, WHEN
THEY HAD DONE CIRCUMCISING ALL
THE PEOPLE, THAT THEY ABODE IN
THEIR PLACES IN THE CAMP, TILL THEY
WERE WHOLE.

(9) "AND THE LORD SAID UNTO
JOSHUA, THIS DAY HAVE I ROLLED
AWAY THE REPROACH OF EGYPT FROM
OFF YOU. WHEREFORE THE NAME OF
THE PLACE IS CALLED GILGAL UNTO
THIS DAY."

The composition is:

1. Even though the hearts of the kings of
the Amorites melted with fear before Israel,
still, as Chapter 10 proclaims, they would oppose Israel. No matter what, Satan will oppose the Child of God, but victory is assured
if God's Way is followed, even as did Joshua.

2. Israel was about to smite the Seven Nations of Canaan with the Sword of the Lord.
Williams says, *"But before they were fitted
to use the Sword on others, they must themselves feel its sharpness and 'die beneath its
stroke.' This was illustrated in Circumcision, which in essence is a Type of the Cross.*

*"Separation was made and blood was
shed. We as Believers are to be separated
from the world, and this can only be done
by looking to Christ and the Cross, which
latter the blood symbolizes."*[1]

3. Only those who are fitted to use the
Sword of the Spirit, which is the Word of
God, who have themselves experienced the
death-stroke which it gives to *"Nature"* —
that is, to the natural man, his wisdom and

NOTES

his goodness. It is most bitter to a man to
learn that all his goodness must be slain with
the Sword of the Lord just as much as all his
badness. But to the true Believer, this is
most sweet; for it brings him into a Resurrection Life, and the Power of that Life takes
all strength from Satan. Man, as man, let
him be ever so religious, has no strength
against Satan. Jericho's walls never fall before him!

So, Circumcision was a symbol of Christ
and the Cross, and the price that He would
there pay in order to deliver fallen humanity.

4. In the face of the enemy, Joshua by circumcising all the men of war, rendered the
entirety of the male population helpless;
but their weakness would be their strength
(II Cor. 12:9-10).

5. The reproach of Egypt was dual. So
long as Israel wandered in the Wilderness,
Egypt reproached them with the taunt that
Jehovah could not bring them into the Promised Land; and, further, all of Egypt that attaches to a Servant of God is a reproach to
him. That double reproach was *"rolled away"*
at Gilgal.

SATAN'S FORTRESSES

This Chapter is a powerful portrayal of
what God demands in order that we have victory. His Demands will be totally opposite of
that which the world demands.

Jericho was a fortress. It barred Israel's
entrance into the Promised Land; likewise,
Satan has placed many fortresses at the entrance of the Promised Land to keep the
Child of God from inheriting that which God
has promised him. As Jericho's conquest was
impossible to Israel, at least as far as the flesh
was concerned, likewise, our victory respecting the great fortresses that Satan has reared
is impossible for us in the flesh as well. Let
us see what the Lord required of Israel that
day and what He requires of us today.

SATAN TREMBLES IN THE FACE
OF THE NAME OF JESUS

Verse 1 says, *"That their heart melted, neither was there spirit in them anymore, because of the Children of Israel."*

The First Verse of the Fifth Chapter
speaks of all of the kings with their mighty

fortresses who would oppose Israel. Yet, their *"heart melted."*

Satan would attempt to make us believe that our opposition is so formidable that it is hopeless, especially considering the times, possibly so that we tried and failed; however, in spiritual reality the opposite is true.

The Spirit of God had so worked on these enemies of Israel that they literally trembled in fear of the People of God. In spiritual reality Satan trembles in fear at the Power of God manifest in us. He doesn't want us to know it. He tries to hide it from us. He tries to make us believe that our opposition is so strong that we cannot hope to overcome. That is, in fact, one of his chief tactics. But, in reality, he is already defeated, and his heart is trembling in fear. In fact, he was defeated at Calvary's Cross, and defeated in totality.

We should understand this; we should know this. We should shout the praises of God constantly. We should understand that instead of fear plaguing us, it is fear that plagues the enemy, *"their heart melted."* All of us want these great victories, and in this Chapter we are given God's Blueprint for victory. It is:

A. The death of self;

B. The testimony to the Blood and of the Lamb;

C. Feeding on the Word of God; and,

D. Subjection to Christ as Lord.

DEATH TO SELF

Let us first look at *"death to self."* Verse 2 says, *"Make thee sharp knives, and circumcise again the Children of Israel the second time."*

The battle with self is never ended once and for all, at least will not be ended until the trump sounds, or until the Lord calls us home. We would like for this battle to end, and, at times, we may foolishly think that it has; however, self keeps cropping up. It is a constant conflict between the flesh and the Spirit, hence, the words, *"the second time."* The death to self is illustrated in Circumcision.

This Rite was a sign of *"separation."* Of course, the question is asked, *"separation from what?"* It is separation from self.

Most of the time when we think of separation, we are thinking of separation from the world. It certainly does include that. The world is an enemy to the Child of God; however, our biggest enemy, of which circumcision is a type, is *"self."* What type of *"self"* are we speaking of?

Strangely enough, the self part of man that must be separated by the Spirit of God (circumcised) is that which we would call *"good."* It is man's natural wisdom and goodness. It is most bitter for a man to learn that all his goodness must be slain with the Sword of the Lord just as much as all his badness. But to the Christian, this is most sweet, for it brings him into a Resurrection Life, and the Power of that Life takes all strength from Satan.

THE CROSS OF CHRIST

It was all done at the Cross. There, as we have previously stated, Jesus died that we might be saved from sin, but as well, from *"self."* Therefore, we are to look to the Cross exclusively, understanding that it is there where all victory was won (Rom. 6:1-14; Col. 2:14-15). This means that the Believer must anchor his Faith exclusively in Christ and the Cross, never allowing it to be moved anywhere else. It is the Cross! The Cross! The Cross!

Man, irregardless of his religion or his goodness, has no strength, personally speaking, against Satan. Jericho's walls never fall before him! But if death to all that we think of as good, wise, and beautiful is suffered, it then becomes a shelter, for what can Satan do with a dead man? Paul wrote, *"We are the circumcision, and have no confidence in the flesh."*

Circumcision, in fact, is a Type of the Cross and what Jesus did there. It is as follows:

A. The sharp knife is applied to the male member, which is a picture of what the Cross does to us in totality; however, we must die, of which the knife is a Type, and which we do die with Christ at Calvary. We are *"baptized into His Death. We are buried with Him by baptism into death. And by the Glory of the Father, we are raised with Him in Newness of Life"* (Rom. 6:3-4).

B. Upon the knife performing the Circumcision, blood is spilled, which is a Type of the Blood shed at Calvary's Cross, and done so by our Lord and Saviour Jesus Christ. As we die only in Him, as well, our blood is shed only in Him.

C. Circumcision was the physical sign of the great Covenant of God between Himself and His People. As stated, it was a physical picture of the Cross, which is no longer mandatory upon the male population of Believers, simply because Christ has fulfilled all the demands at Calvary's Cross. In other words, we now have a Better Covenant based on Better Promises (Heb. 8:6-8).

(10) "AND THE CHILDREN OF ISRAEL ENCAMPED IN GILGAL, AND KEPT THE PASSOVER ON THE FOURTEENTH DAY OF THE MONTH AT EVENING IN THE PLAINS OF JERICHO."

The pattern is:

1. This is the first Passover in the Promised Land.

2. Israel eating the Passover proclaims that her Redemption out of Egypt, and her position in the Land of Promise, were alike due to the preciousness of the Blood of the Lamb.

3. True spiritual victories can only be won where there is this Testimony to the Person and Work of the Lord Jesus Christ. Circumcision in symbolizing the Cross, also symbolized *"the death of self."* The Passover symbolizing the Cross presents a *"testimony to the Blood of the Lamb."*

THE PASSOVER

Verse 10 says, *"And kept the Passover."* Israel proclaimed her Redemption out of Egypt and her position in the Land of Promise by keeping the Passover. We proclaim our Redemption and dwelling because of the preciousness of the Blood of the Pascal Lamb. That is the reason that Paul with all of his education and worldly knowledge said, *"I determined not to know any thing among you save Jesus Christ, and Him Crucified"* (I Cor. 2:2).

Why?

Because the terrible bondages of humanity cannot be broken by the intellect, earthly wisdom, money, prestige, or education. It can only be broken by the Power of the shed blood of Jesus Christ. That was Israel's victory then;

this is our victory now. It is ever the Cross!

A description of the Passover is given in Exodus, Chapter 12. It is a perfect Type of the Cross.

It seems that Israel kept the Passover only one time in the wilderness, which was about a year after deliverance from Egypt (Num. 9:1-14). And now that they are to enter the Promised Land, they must enter by the Power of the Blood of the Lamb, symbolized by the Passover. This proclaimed Israel's strength. It was not their standing army, or their military strategy, but rather their dependence on the shed Blood of the Lamb. We must never forget that, because our strength is the same presently!

I am saddened by the thought that the modern Church is leaving the Cross. To do so not only invites destruction, but, in fact, is destruction. As we have previously stated, the only thing standing between mankind and eternal Hell is the Cross of Christ. That is a sobering statement, and oh so true!

When we walk through that Gate of Pearl in that city built foursquare, we will be there solely and completely because of Jesus and what He did at the Cross. We must never forget that! It is the Cross! The Cross! The Cross!

(11) "AND THEY DID EAT OF THE OLD CORN OF THE LAND ON THE MORROW AFTER THE PASSOVER, UNLEAVENED CAKES, AND PARCHED CORN IN THE SELFSAME DAY.

(12) "AND THE MANNA CEASED ON THE MORROW AFTER THEY HAD EATEN OF THE OLD CORN OF THE LAND; NEITHER HAD THE CHILDREN OF ISRAEL MANNA ANY MORE; BUT THEY DID EAT OF THE FRUIT OF THE LAND OF CANAAN THAT YEAR."

The structure is:

1. Manna was Angel's food.

2. It was sufficient for the Wilderness and its defective spiritual life; however, the *"old corn of the land"* symbolized the Word of God, and is a necessity of the strength needed for spiritual conquests.

3. Everything must be by the Word.

THE WORD OF THE LORD

The phrase, *"And they did eat of the old*

corn of the land," presents the first time this is mentioned. In fact, and as stated, for some forty years Israel had existed on Manna, which was Angel's food. But now, since they are in the Land, the *"strong meat of the Word"* is now needed. It is a must regarding the strength needed for spiritual conquests in the land of our inheritance.

Sadly, the Bible is presently talked about, merchandised, spoken of, analyzed, and dissected, but it is little read and meditated thereon. In fact, the present Church is almost a Bibleless family. Most of the preaching today is psychology in one form or the other. In fact, the Church has become so psychologized, that I think most Preachers little know or realize that they really aren't preaching the Word, but rather mouthing psychological jargon. It appeals to the flesh, but let it ever be understood, if it's not the Word of God, and we mean the pure Word of God, which means it hasn't been polluted or perverted by the additives of the world, then it will do no good. And to pull it down to the bottom line so-called, if the Message is not *"Jesus Christ and Him Crucified,"* in other words, the Cross, then it's not really the Gospel. Paul said:

"For Christ sent me not to baptize (presents to us a Cardinal Truth), *but to preach the Gospel* (the manner in which one may be saved from sin)*: not with wisdom of words* (intellectualism is not the Gospel), *lest the Cross of Christ should be made of none effect.* (This tells us in no uncertain terms that the Cross of Christ must always be the emphasis of the Message)" (I Cor. 1:17).

In this one Verse we are plainly and clearly told what the Gospel of Jesus Christ actually is. It is *"the Cross of Christ."* This means that the Preacher must preach Christ as the Source of all things from God, and the Cross as the Means by which all of these things are given to us. If anything else is preached, no matter how clever it might be, no matter how glib it might be, no matter how intellectual it might seem to be, it will bring no good news to the poor, heal no brokenhearts, bring no deliverance to captives, recover no sight for the blind, and will not set at liberty them who are bruised (Lk. 4:18).

NOTES

(13) "AND IT CAME TO PASS, WHEN JOSHUA WAS BY JERICHO, THAT HE LIFTED UP HIS EYES AND LOOKED, AND, BEHOLD, THERE STOOD A MAN OVER AGAINST HIM WITH HIS SWORD DRAWN IN HIS HAND: AND JOSHUA WENT UNTO HIM, AND SAID UNTO HIM, ARE YOU FOR US, OR FOR OUR ADVERSARIES?

(14) "AND HE SAID, NO; BUT AS CAPTAIN OF THE HOST OF THE LORD AM I NOW COME. AND JOSHUA FELL ON HIS FACE TO THE EARTH, AND DID WORSHIP, AND SAID UNTO HIM, WHAT SAYS MY LORD UNTO HIS SERVANT?

(15) "AND THE CAPTAIN OF THE LORD'S HOST SAID UNTO JOSHUA, LOOSE YOUR SHOE FROM OFF YOUR FOOT; FOR THE PLACE WHEREON YOU STAND IS HOLY. AND JOSHUA DID SO."

The construction is:

1. The *"Man"* of Verse 13, was a preincarnate appearance of Christ, Whom Joshua at first didn't recognize.

2. When the Lord revealed Himself, Joshua then recognized Him as the Lord. Concerning this, Williams says, *"An absolute condition of victory is full surrender to Christ as Lord. He must be accepted as Captain, be permitted to plan, and be fully obeyed."*[2]

3. The demand that the shoes be removed from Joshua's feet, and the removal of those shoes, guaranteed that He Who now spoke to Joshua was a Divine Person, actually, as stated, a preincarnate appearance of Christ.

4. The removal of the shoes in essence indicated that Joshua was giving up all ownership and leadership, thereby giving Christ total control.

We have four steps to victory listed in this Chapter.

They are:

A. The death of self — circumcision.

B. Testimony to the Blood of the Lamb — Passover.

C. Feeding on the Word of God — old corn of the land.

D. Subjection to Christ as Lord — pulling off the shoes.

SUBMISSION TO CHRIST

There must be a full surrender to Christ in all things, which can only be done by the

Believer going to the Cross (Lk. 9:23).

While in the wilderness Egypt reproached Israel with a taunt that Jehovah could not bring them into the Promised Land, and furthermore, all of Egypt that attaches itself to a Servant of God is a reproach to Him. Joshua would yield total authority to the *"Captain"* as he *"fell on his face to the earth, and did worship."* He would then ask the question, *"What says my Lord unto His Servant?"* The answer would be startling.

The Lord at the beginning of His Command would not mention the conquest of Jericho, the great victories to be won, or all the great things He would do for Israel. He merely said, *"Loose your shoe from off your foot; for the place whereon you stand is Holy."*

Unfortunately, the modern Child of God is so busy seeking riches, etc., that he seldom seeks that which is the most important. The most important is that which is *"holy."* How many thousands of Preachers are trying to defeat the Evil One when they have never met the *"Captain"* or stood on that which is *"holy."* This is the secret of the Church; not the subjection of the Jericho's, nor the defeat of the Amorites and the Canaanites, but that first we see Jesus and that which is Holy. Then, and only then will the Jericho's fall and the Amorites and the Canaanites be defeated.

Verse 9 told us, *"This day have I rolled away the reproach of Egypt from off you,"* and this can only get done as we follow the *"Captain."* We cannot roll that reproach away from ourselves or of ourselves, only *"The Captain"* can. As well, He does such by and through the Cross and only by and through the Cross!

CHAPTER 6

(1) "NOW JERICHO WAS STRAITLY SHUT UP BECAUSE OF THE CHILDREN OF ISRAEL: NONE WENT OUT, AND NONE CAME IN.

(2) "AND THE LORD SAID UNTO JOSHUA, SEE, I HAVE GIVEN INTO YOUR HAND JERICHO, AND THE KING THEREOF, AND THE MIGHTY MEN OF VALOUR.

(3) "AND YOU SHALL COMPASS THE CITY, ALL YOU MEN OF WAR, AND GO ROUND ABOUT THE CITY ONCE. THUS SHALL YOU DO SIX DAYS.

(4) "AND SEVEN PRIESTS SHALL BEAR BEFORE THE ARK SEVEN TRUMPETS OF RAMS' HORNS: AND THE SEVENTH DAY YOU SHALL COMPASS THE CITY SEVEN TIMES, AND THE PRIESTS SHALL BLOW WITH THE TRUMPETS.

(5) "AND IT SHALL COME TO PASS, THAT WHEN THEY MAKE A LONG BLAST WITH THE RAM'S HORN, AND WHEN YOU HEAR THE SOUND OF THE TRUMPET, ALL THE PEOPLE SHALL SHOUT WITH A GREAT SHOUT; AND THE WALL OF THE CITY SHALL FALL DOWN FLAT, AND THE PEOPLE SHALL ASCEND UP EVERY MAN STRAIGHT BEFORE HIM.

(6) "AND JOSHUA THE SON OF NUN CALLED THE PRIESTS, AND SAID UNTO THEM, TAKE UP THE ARK OF THE COVENANT, AND LET SEVEN PRIESTS BEAR SEVEN TRUMPETS OF RAMS' HORNS BEFORE THE ARK OF THE LORD.

(7) "AND HE SAID UNTO THE PEOPLE, PASS ON, AND COMPASS THE CITY, AND LET HIM WHO IS ARMED PASS ON BEFORE THE ARK OF THE LORD.

(8) "AND IT CAME TO PASS, WHEN JOSHUA HAD SPOKEN UNTO THE PEOPLE, THAT THE SEVEN PRIESTS BEARING THE SEVEN TRUMPETS OF RAMS' HORNS PASSED ON BEFORE THE LORD, AND BLEW WITH THE TRUMPETS: AND THE ARK OF THE COVENANT OF THE LORD FOLLOWED THEM.

(9) "AND THE ARMED MEN WENT BEFORE THE PRIESTS WHO BLEW WITH THE TRUMPETS, AND THE REREWARD CAME AFTER THE ARK, THE PRIESTS GOING ON, AND BLOWING WITH THE TRUMPETS.

(10) "AND JOSHUA HAD COMMANDED THE PEOPLE, SAYING, YOU SHALL NOT SHOUT, NOR MAKE ANY NOISE WITH YOUR VOICE, NEITHER SHALL ANY WORD PROCEED OUT OF YOUR MOUTH, UNTIL THE DAY I BID YOU SHOUT; THEN SHALL YOU SHOUT.

(11) "SO THE ARK OF THE LORD COMPASSED THE CITY, GOING ABOUT IT

ONCE: AND THEY CAME INTO THE CAMP, AND LODGED IN THE CAMP.

(12) "AND JOSHUA ROSE EARLY IN THE MORNING, AND THE PRIESTS TOOK UP THE ARK OF THE LORD.

(13) "AND SEVEN PRIESTS BEARING SEVEN TRUMPETS OF RAMS' HORNS BEFORE THE ARK OF THE LORD WENT ON CONTINUALLY, AND BLEW WITH THE TRUMPETS: AND THE ARMED MEN WENT BEFORE THEM; BUT THE REREWARD CAME AFTER THE ARK OF THE LORD, THE PRIESTS GOING ON, AND BLOWING WITH THE TRUMPETS.

(14) "AND THE SECOND DAY THEY COMPASSED THE CITY ONCE, AND RETURNED INTO THE CAMP: SO THEY DID SIX DAYS.

(15) "AND IT CAME TO PASS ON THE SEVENTH DAY, THAT THEY ROSE EARLY ABOUT THE DAWNING OF THE DAY, AND COMPASSED THE CITY AFTER THE SAME MANNER SEVEN TIMES: ONLY ON THAT DAY THEY COMPASSED THE CITY SEVEN TIMES.

(16) "AND IT CAME TO PASS AT THE SEVENTH TIME, WHEN THE PRIESTS BLEW WITH THE TRUMPETS, JOSHUA SAID UNTO THE PEOPLE, SHOUT; FOR THE LORD HAS GIVEN YOU THE CITY.

(17) "AND THE CITY SHALL BE ACCURSED, EVEN IT, AND ALL WHO ARE THEREIN, TO THE LORD: ONLY RAHAB THE HARLOT SHALL LIVE, SHE AND ALL WHO ARE WITH HER IN THE HOUSE, BECAUSE SHE HID THE MESSENGERS THAT WE SENT.

(18) "AND YOU, IN ANY WISE KEEP YOURSELVES FROM THE ACCURSED THING, LEST YOU MAKE YOURSELVES ACCURSED, WHEN YOU TAKE OF THE ACCURSED THING, AND MAKE THE CAMP OF ISRAEL A CURSE, AND TROUBLE IT.

(19) "BUT ALL THE SILVER, AND GOLD, AND VESSELS OF BRASS AND IRON, ARE CONSECRATED UNTO THE LORD: THEY SHALL COME INTO THE TREASURY OF THE LORD."

The exegesis is:

1. The strong fortress of Jericho barred Israel's entrance to the Land; Satan will always have such a fortress to hinder our

NOTES

spiritual progress; it was, in fact, impregnable, therefore, its conquest was impossible to Israel, but not impossible to God!

2. This was probably the strangest plan of battle ever formed.

3. The number *"seven"* as used here is not without purpose and design; Biblically the number symbolizes perfection, totality, and universality; these are God's Plans, and they always succeed; we should cease to make plans for ourselves, and let God plan for us; as stated, His Plans always succeed.

4. This was a *"shout"* of obedience and a *"shout"* of victory. Spiritually, the *"shout"* had everything to do with the wall falling down flat, but, physically and materially, it had no effect at all, as would be obvious. The wall falling down flat was strictly a Miracle of God.

5. The Lord didn't need Israel to march around Jericho seven days, or even one day, for the walls to fall down. So why did He have them do this?

It was to teach them trust, dependence on Him and obedience, even though they did not at all understand the directions, as neither would anyone; however, understanding what the Lord is doing is not necessarily the criteria, obedience is!

6. There is a problem that arises out of this illustration. Many have marched around particular obstacles, when the Lord had not said to do so, and when the ingredient was presumption instead of Faith. Let the Reader understand that presumption is just as bad as disobedience. Presumption brings reproach on the Work of the Lord just as bad as disobedience.

7. As a military maneuver, all of this marching was worse than useless. But it was not a military maneuver, but rather that which was Spiritual.

8. As it regards the Eighteenth Verse, unfortunately, there was one man who didn't obey, which caused Israel great trouble. Everything about the city was cursed by God, because it was wholly given over to idol worship. The modern Christian, likewise, must be very careful about his entanglement with the world. While we are *"in"* the world, we are not to be *"of"* the world. In fact, if the world gets into the Believer,

it is the same as water getting into the ship. Ruin is the result!

GOD'S PLAN FOR THE FALL OF JERICHO

Now that the Lord has brought Joshua to the place of total surrender and obedience, He will give him instructions concerning Jericho. So oftentimes we get them backwards. We want the great victory pronouncement over Jericho without coming to the place of Holiness. It does not work, as it cannot work. Now the Lord will give Joshua instructions.

The Second Verse says, *"And the LORD said unto Joshua."* He tells him first that he will have victory over Jericho, *"I have given into your hand Jericho."*

So many Christians make their plans by attempting to get God to bless them. We have it backwards. God must make the plans and then they will be blessed. Here, the Lord made the plans.

He then gives Joshua instructions. To the natural mind they would be foolish, *"go round about the city once. Thus shall you do six days."*

If one will notice, in the Fourth Verse the number *"seven"* is used repeatedly. There are *"seven"* Priests, *"seven"* trumpets, *"the seventh day,"* and then, *"seven times."* Why all of these sevens?

Everything in the Word of God is for an express purpose. Nothing is done for show or selfish occupation. All have tremendous Spiritual meaning.

In the Word of God the number *"seven,"* one might say is God's Number. It denotes perfection, completion, totality, universality, and all in all. Joshua, it must be remembered, is operating strictly in the spiritual sense. Regrettably, all too often we modern Christians operate in the worldly sense. We borrow our ideas from the world, insert them into that which is called Christianity, and pass it off as the Word of God. God will have none of it.

These are Spiritual Instructions of Faith. The world, the natural mind, or Jericho will have absolutely no idea what they mean, as the natural mind cannot understand the things of the Spirit (I Cor. 2:14).

Regrettably, most in the modern Church have little or no knowledge at all of the things of the Spirit; they only understand the things of the world.

THE PRIESTS AND THE ARK OF THE COVENANT

The Eighth Verse says, *"And the Ark of the Covenant of the LORD followed them."* Why were the seven Priests with the seven rams' horns placed before the Ark? Why not the Ark first?

The Priests were Types of Christ. The *"Ark of the Covenant"* was a Type of the very Throne of God. The idea is, Christ is the One Who has defeated the enemy, and has done so by going to the Cross. He is the Way, and the only Way to the very Throne of God; therefore, the seven Priests with their rams' horns going before the Ark, was in essence a statement that said that Jesus would one day open up the way to the very Throne of God, which He most definitely did at Calvary's Cross. As stated, every single thing done here has a Scriptural and Spiritual meaning. If we understand that meaning, we will understand God's Prescribed Order of Victory. That Prescribed Order is always the Cross of Christ.

THE LORD HAS CHOSEN THAT HE WORK THROUGH MEN

That is His Plan. If there are no men or women to work through, the Work of God is not done. The Ark of God will only follow Godly, consecrated, Holy men — and here is where we make our mistake.

Men are not necessarily Holy because of what they do. They are Holy because of what Jesus has done, and we speak of the Cross. Some think because someone has failed they are, thereby, unholy. If they have repented, however, there is no unholiness left. To be frank with you, there are no human beings who ever existed who have not failed. *"All have come short of the Glory of God"* (Rom. 3:23).

Now this is not merely speaking of the past tense. The Greek Text bears it out that all of us, even the best of us, are continually coming short of the Glory of God.

In fact, if lack of failure is a criteria for

being used of God, although God certainly places no premium on failure, then the Bible *"greats"* could never have been used. So, if you are allowing Satan (or men) to tell you that because you have failed you can never be used of God again, please remember this:

The ones telling you this have failed over and over again and are now doing the service of Satan by mouthing their unbelief. The only failure that will prohibit an individual from marching around Jericho and ultimately blowing the victory note on the rams' horns and being followed by the Ark of the Lord is the failure of not believing. And, regrettably, most of the modern Church is saddled with that failure.

PERFECT BELIEVERS?

God is not looking for perfect men, because the truth is, there aren't any. He is looking for those who will be *"poor and of a contrite spirit, and will tremble at His Word"* (Isa. 66:2). This is God's Method. God will follow the men who will obey Him. To be frank, He is looking for individuals who will admit their failures and repent before God, and then hear from Heaven, pick up their rams' horn and march around the Jericho walls of their obstacles. The Ark of God will follow a person like that, and the walls will fall down flat.

Hallelujah!

SHOUT!

The Tenth Verse says two things:
1. *"You shall not shout."*
2. *"Then shall you shout."*

From the Word of God we are told here there is a time to shout and a time not to shout. Why could they not shout at the beginning? Millions today in Christendom are shouting when there is actually nothing to shout about. They have not heard from Heaven. They have not seen the *"Captain of the LORD of Hosts."* They have not pulled off their shoes or stood on Holy Ground. Faith doesn't have to scream to make itself heard. So many trumpet the loudness of their profession to cover up the barrenness of their possession. In fact, much of the shouting in modern Churches is superficial, hollow, and only on the surface. So, when

should we shout?

The Scripture says, *"then,"* which means after we have obeyed the Lord and done exactly what He has told us to do.

I think one can say without fear of Scriptural contradiction, that the criteria for the *"shout,"* is that one's Faith be placed exclusively in Christ and what Christ has done for us at the Cross (Rom. 6:1-14; 8:1-2, 11; I Cor. 1:17-18, 21, 23; 2:2).

THE CROSS OF CHRIST AND THE SHOUT OF VICTORY

The reason the *"shout of victory"* and that's what this is, is placed exclusively in the Cross of Christ is simply because it was there, at the Cross, where total and complete victory was won, and for all time. Everything about the description given in this Chapter points to the Cross of Christ.

1. The number *"seven"* of Verse 4, which is God's Number of perfection, points exclusively to a perfect Salvation all afforded by the Cross of Christ.

2. As stated, seven Priests went before the Ark blowing seven trumpets, all signifying Christ, and what He would do to redeem humanity, which was done by the means of the Cross.

3. The *"shout"* signified victory by Faith. If it is to be noticed, they shouted before the walls fell down, and not after. In fact, it's easy to shout after the victory, but it takes real Faith to shout before the victory is evident.

Considering what Jesus did at the Cross, there is a *"shout of victory"* in the Cross and, in fact, the *"shout of victory"* is found only in the Cross. Everything else is superficial, hollow, shallow, and without substance.

(20) "SO THE PEOPLE SHOUTED WHEN THE PRIESTS BLEW WITH THE TRUMPETS: AND IT CAME TO PASS, WHEN THE PEOPLE HEARD THE SOUND OF THE TRUMPET, AND THE PEOPLE SHOUTED WITH A GREAT SHOUT, THAT THE WALL FELL DOWN FLAT, SO THAT THE PEOPLE WENT UP INTO THE CITY, EVERY MAN STRAIGHT BEFORE HIM, AND THEY TOOK THE CITY.

(21) "AND THEY UTTERLY DESTROYED ALL THAT WAS IN THE CITY, BOTH MAN AND WOMAN, YOUNG AND OLD, AND OX,

AND SHEEP, AND ASS, WITH THE EDGE OF THE SWORD."

The exegesis is:

1. Had Israel attempted to take Jericho without the leading of the Lord, casualties would have been great.

2. Following the Lord, there is no record that there were any casualties whatsoever among the army of Israel.

3. The army of Israel was commanded to kill all the people in the city, even the children, because the city was wholly given over to idolatry, with all of its attendant immorality, which was gross to say the least — all with the exception of Rahab and her family.

THE FALL OF JERICHO

The Twentieth Verse says, *"They took the city."* As stated, there is no record that even one Israelite was lost. This is God's Way. Sometimes we win great victories albeit with great loss. This is a sure sign that much flesh has been associated with what little of the Holy Spirit we have allowed to function; consequently, that is why we suffer loss.

Here there is no loss at all, *"they took the city."* The reason that there was no loss is obvious. They followed the instructions of Faith to the letter.

THE LEADING OF THE SPIRIT

Believers reading the Old Testament, and the account of these tremendous Miracles, seemed to think that it was easier then, than now. In other words, that it was easier then for people to believe and to see God do great things than at the present time. Not so!

In fact, the Holy Spirit, since the Cross, now abiding in the hearts and lives of all Believers, and doing so permanently, and there for the express purpose of serving as our Helper, to be sure, His Leading and Guidance is far more pronounced presently than in former times. Jesus said:

"Howbeit when He, the Spirit of Truth, is come (which He did on the Day of Pentecost), *He will guide you into all Truth* (if our Faith is properly placed in Christ and the Cross, the Holy Spirit can then bring forth Truth to us; He doesn't guide into some Truth, but rather 'all Truth'): *for He shall not speak of Himself* (tells us not only what

He does, but Whom He represents)*; but whatsoever He shall hear, that shall He speak* (doesn't refer to lack of knowledge, for the Holy Spirit is God, but rather He will proclaim the Work of Christ only)*: and He will show you things to come* (pertains to the New Covenant, which would shortly be given)" (Jn. 16:13).

In fact, and concerning this very thing, Paul said, *"But now* (since the Cross) *has He* (the Lord Jesus) *obtained a more excellent Ministry* (the New Covenant in Jesus' Blood is superior, and takes the place of the Old Covenant in animal blood), *by how much also He is the Mediator of a Better Covenant* (proclaims the fact that Christ officiates between God and man according to the arrangements of the New Covenant), *which was established upon Better Promises.* (This presents the New Covenant, explicitly based on the cleansing and forgiveness of all sin, which the Old Covenant could not do.)

He then said, *"For if that First Covenant had been faultless* (proclaims the fact that the First Covenant was definitely not faultless; as stated, it was based on animal blood, which was vastly inferior to the Precious Blood of Christ), *then should no place have been sought for the Second* (proclaims the necessity of the New Covenant).

"For finding fault with them (the First Covenant was actually designed to glaringly portray the fault of the people, which it successfully did), *He said* (Jer. 31:31), *Behold, the days come, saith the Lord, when I will make a New Covenant with the House of Israel and with the House of Judah* (that New Covenant was in Christ and what He did at the Cross; regrettably, Israel rejected Him)" (Heb. 8:6-8).

There are some Miracles that God performed in Old Testament times, which He has not repeated, but only because the necessity of such isn't present. For example, God opened the Red Sea, but considering all the events which transpired, there hasn't been a need to do such again.

There is a great difference in the Holy Spirit being with a person, which He was before the Cross, which He only could be, then being in that Person, residing permanently, therefore, helping us constantly.

Jesus said so:

"*Even the Spirit of Truth* (the Greek says, '*the Spirit of the Truth,*' which refers to the Word of God; actually, He does far more than merely superintend the attribute of Truth, as Christ '*is Truth*' [I Jn. 5:6]); *Whom the world cannot receive* (the Holy Spirit cannot come in to the heart of the unbeliever until that person makes Christ his or her Saviour; then He comes in), *because it sees Him not neither knows Him* (refers to the fact that only Born-Again Believers can understand the Holy Spirit and know Him): *but you know Him* (would have been better translated, '*But you shall get to know Him*'); *for He dwells with you* (before the Cross), *and shall be in you* (which would take place on the Day of Pentecost and forward, because the sin debt has been forever paid by Christ on the Cross, changing the disposition of everything)" (Jn.14:17).

The truth is, if we as Believers will fully consecrate ourselves, make certain that our Faith is anchored properly in Christ and the Cross, and that we do not allow it to be moved elsewhere, to be sure, the Holy Spirit will then lead us and guide us to a far greater degree. He wants to help! He wants to lead! He wants to guide! He wants to empower! But so oftentimes we do things which are totally contrary to the Word of God, which greatly hinders the Holy Spirit and His Work within our hearts and lives, as should be obvious.

For instance, most Christians, sadly and regrettably, have their faith placed in anything and everything except Christ and the Cross. In fact, most Christians understand the Cross not at all as it regards their Sanctification, i.e., their everyday living for God. As a result, whether they realize it or not, they are actually living in a state of Spiritual Adultery, which as should be obvious, greatly hinders the Holy Spirit and what He can do (Rom. 7:1-4).

TOTAL DESTRUCTION OF THE ENEMY

The Twenty-first Verse says, "*And they utterly destroyed all.*"

To properly understand this Verse, we must bring it over into the New Covenant, into our everyday life and living for the Lord.

This means that every vestige of temper, jealousy, ambition, pride, deceit, and envy, etc., must be "*utterly destroyed*" in our lives. There must be nothing there of the flesh. But the problem is this:

We try to destroy the flesh with the flesh. We fail as ever we must. Flesh cannot destroy flesh. Sickness cannot heal sickness. Sin cannot save from sin. All the rules of legalism in our Churches cannot set one captive free. It can make evident more sin, which is the last thing we want, but legalism, i.e., the flesh, cannot set anyone free. But when the Spirit of God has His Perfect and complete Way, all is "*utterly destroyed.*"

THE FLESH

Paul used the term "*the flesh*" over and over (Rom. 8:1, 3-7), in fact, he said, "*So then they who are in the flesh cannot please God*" (Rom. 8:8).

The Holy Spirit through the Apostle used the term "*flesh,*" to describe human capabilities, intellectualism, knowledge, ability, power, etc. Within themselves, these things aren't necessarily wrong; however, the wrong comes in when we try to live for God by the means of the flesh, in other words, by our own capabilities. It simply cannot be done, and when we attempt to do so, to live for God after this fashion, this greatly insults Christ. Even as Paul said, such an effort greatly displeases the Lord.

WHY?

Despite what we think, and as we have already stated, it is impossible for the Believer to live for God, to work for God, to experience the Fruit of the Spirit in our lives, to grow in Grace and the Knowledge of the Lord, by the means of the "*flesh.*" It cannot be done. But yet, this is where the Church runs aground and, in fact, where all of us at one time or the other have run aground. The Church keeps coming up with one fad after the other, all proposing to develop something in our lives, all to no avail. A perfect example is "*The Purpose Driven Life,*" which is all of the flesh, and will bring about no positive results whatsoever. There is only one way that the Believer can successfully live for the Lord.

GOD'S PRESCRIBED ORDER
OF VICTORY

If it is to be noticed, I have used this heading, *"God's Prescribed Order of Victory,"* several times already in this Volume. I do it for purpose. It is so important, that I want you the reader to know perfectly well what the Bible teaches as it regards our living for the Lord. Nothing could be more important. Let's again say it this way. Even though it is repetitive, it is worth reading and studying several times.

FOCUS: The Lord Jesus Christ (Jn. 14:6);

OBJECT OF FAITH: The Cross of Christ (Rom. 6:3-14);

POWER SOURCE: The Holy Spirit (Rom. 8:1-2, 11); and,

RESULTS: Victory (Rom. 6:14).

Even though what we have given is extremely abbreviated, if you the Believer will meditate on this little short diagram, asking the Holy Spirit to give you leading and guidance, it will begin to become crystal clear.

Let's look at it again from the way this little formula is used by most modern Christians.

FOCUS: Works!

OBJECT OF FAITH: Performance!

POWER SOURCE: Self!

RESULTS: Defeat!

WHY IS THE CROSS OF CHRIST
SO IMPORTANT?

Because the Bible says so! (Gen. 3:15; Ex. 12:13; Isa. 53; Rom. 6:1-14; I Cor. 1:17-18, 21, 23; 2:2; Gal., Chpt. 5; 6:14; Eph. 2:13-18; Col. 2:14-15).

It was at the Cross that all sin was atoned. Because of all sin being atoned, Satan and all of his cohorts, i.e., fallen angels, demon spirits, etc., were defeated (Col. 2:15). Sin is the legal right that Satan has to hold mankind in bondage. With all sin atoned, which it was at Calvary's Cross, Satan has lost that legal right; consequently, he can place men presently in bondage only by the consent of the governed.

What do we mean by that?

The unredeemed person gives Satan consent to place him in bondage by refusing Jesus Christ. Regrettably, Believers do the

same identical thing, when they place their faith in something other than the Cross of Christ. Let us say it again even as we've already said it any number of times:

"Christ is the Source of everything we receive from God, and whatever it might be, while the Cross is the Means by which it is given to us."

Much of the modern Church preaches Jesus, but without the Cross. Some do so out of ignorance, and some do so out of unbelief. Either way, the damage is done!

It was to the Apostle Paul that the meaning of the New Covenant was given (Gal. 1:1-12). In fact, the meaning of the New Covenant is actually the meaning of the Cross, even as the meaning of the Cross is the meaning of the New Covenant. In graphic form, Paul also gave this to us in his description of the Lord's Supper, which characterizes and epitomizes the New Covenant. It is all in the Cross (I Cor. 11:24-34).

That's the reason we boldly declare that *"The Purpose Driven Life"* scheme is not of God. This tale doesn't hold up Christ and the Cross, but rather works of the Law, i.e., laws devised by men. I'm sure that the writer of this book would vehemently deny that his efforts constitute nothing but Law; however, the following must be recognized, that is if we are to be Scriptural.

If we aren't preaching *"Jesus Christ and Him Crucified,"* i.e., *"the Cross,"* then pure and simple, whatever it is we are preaching and teaching has to be law. There are only two places that the Believer can be. That is Grace and Law. If we are in Grace, that is functioning in Grace, we can only do so by our Faith placed squarely in Christ and the Cross. Everything else constitutes Law. So, for Believers to claim they are functioning in Grace, when they are omitting and ignoring the Cross, places such a person, despite their claims, in an unscriptural position. Paul said:

"For Christ sent me not to baptize, but to preach the Gospel: not with wisdom of words, lest the Cross of Christ should be made of none effect" (I Cor. 1:17).

He then said, *"For the preaching* (Word) *of the Cross is to them who perish foolishness; but unto us which are Saved it is the*

Power of God" (I Cor. 1:18).

And finally the Apostle said, *"For I determined not to know any thing among you, save Jesus Christ, and Him Crucified"* (I Cor. 2:2).

Paul's statement plainly tells us that with purpose and design he did not resort to the knowledge or philosophy of the world regarding the Preaching of the Gospel. He preached the Cross as the answer to man's dilemma, and the Cross alone as the answer to man's dilemma! That and that alone, the Cross, is the Message which will save the sinner, set the captive free, and give the Believer perpetual victory.

(22) "BUT JOSHUA HAD SAID UNTO THE TWO MEN WHO HAD SPIED OUT THE COUNTRY, GO INTO THE HARLOT'S HOUSE, AND BRING OUT THENCE THE WOMAN, AND ALL THAT SHE HAS, AS YOU SWORE UNTO HER.

(23) "AND THE YOUNG MEN WHO WERE SPIES WENT IN, AND BROUGHT OUT RAHAB, AND HER FATHER, AND HER MOTHER, AND HER BRETHREN, AND ALL THAT SHE HAD; AND THEY BROUGHT OUT ALL HER KINDRED, AND LEFT THEM WITHOUT THE CAMP OF ISRAEL.

(24) "AND THEY BURNT THE CITY WITH FIRE, AND ALL WHO WERE THEREIN: ONLY THE SILVER, AND THE GOLD, AND THE VESSELS OF BRASS AND OF IRON, THEY PUT INTO THE TREASURY OF THE HOUSE OF THE LORD.

(25) "AND JOSHUA SAVED RAHAB THE HARLOT ALIVE, AND HER FATHER'S HOUSEHOLD, AND ALL THAT SHE HAD; AND SHE DWELLS IN ISRAEL EVEN UNTO THIS DAY; BECAUSE SHE HID THE MESSENGERS, WHICH JOSHUA SENT TO SPY OUT JERICHO."

The construction is:

1. Salvation by the scarlet cord was not only simple, it was also sure. When the Day of Wrath came, it gave the safety it promised. Thus will it be in the Day of the Wrath to come. That Day will prove how sure is the Salvation which follows upon simply trusting Jesus (Williams).[1]

2. Although slated for destruction, the Faith of Rahab saved her. Rahab married Salmon, one of the princes of Israel. She is

included in our Lord's Genealogy (Mat. 1:5). To what heights of glory her Faith took her, and so may it be for all who will dare to believe God. The Lord took her harlotry and turned it into holiness. He took the curse that was upon her and turned it into a Blessing. What He did for her, He will, as well, do for me and you.

3. The entirety of the family of Rahab was saved and because the entirety of her family placed themselves under the protection of the shed Blood of the Lamb, typified by the Red Cord.

RAHAB

The story of this dear lady, is one of the grandest in all of Biblical history. A poor lost daughter of Adam's fallen race, even having given over her life to total licentiousness, she was made an example of Grace, and simply because of her Faith in Christ. She and her family were the only ones in the entirety of the city of Jericho that took advantage of the Grace of God.

If the leaders of Jericho had come to Joshua and stated that they wished to accept Israel's God, namely Jehovah, thereby rejecting their heathenistic idols, they would have been spared to a person, exactly as were Rahab and her family. They did not do that and were totally lost!

Rahab is a type of the entirety of the human race, lost, heathenistic, without God, without hope, but Faith brought her out of this morass of sin and shame, exactly as Faith has brought out untold millions.

THE WRATH OF GOD

The modern Church has almost totally set aside the great Biblical Truth of the Wrath of God, typified in the destruction of Jericho. But let the following be understood:

God is unalterably opposed to sin, and in every form! The Scripture plainly says:

"For the Wrath of God (God's Personal Emotion with regard to sin) *is revealed from Heaven* (this anger originates with God) *against all ungodliness and unrighteousness of men* (God must unalterably be opposed to sin), *who hold the truth in unrighteousness* (who refuse to recognize Who God is, and What God is)" (Rom. 1:18). As we have

previously stated, the only thing standing between mankind and the Wrath of God, is the Cross of Christ.

Men may argue that His Wrath is not now being evidenced. While that is true in many cases, still, the term *"Wrath of God"* actually speaks of man being condemned to eternal Hell, and placed there forever and forever. If men refuse Christ and the Cross, which is the answer for sin and the only answer for sin, eternal Hell will be the result, which is the Wrath of God.

Jericho was totally destroyed, typifying the Wrath of God against sin and, as well, typifying what is going to happen to all who reject the Lord Jesus Christ. It may be a while in coming, but come it shall (Rev. 20:11-15).

(26) "AND JOSHUA ADJURED THEM AT THAT TIME, SAYING, CURSED BE THE MAN BEFORE THE LORD, WHO RISES UP AND BUILDS THIS CITY JERICHO: HE SHALL LAY THE FOUNDATION THEREOF IN HIS FIRSTBORN, AND IN HIS YOUNGEST SON SHALL HE SET UP THE GATES OF IT.

(27) "SO THE LORD WAS WITH JOSHUA: AND HIS FAME WAS NOISED THROUGHOUT ALL THE COUNTRY."

The structure is:

1. The object of this solid pronouncement was to preserve Jericho as a spot devoted to God forever. And for this reason a curse was pronounced upon anyone who should attempt to build a city upon the devoted spot.

2. It does not seem that it was forbidden to build habitations on the spot, for Jericho is frequently mentioned in the New Testament. What seems to have been forbidden was the erection of a fortified city.

3. This curse pronounced by Joshua actually fell on the reckless Hiel (I Ki. 16:34); he saw the laying of its foundation marked by the death of his eldest son, while the death of his youngest followed its completion.

CHAPTER 7

(1) "BUT THE CHILDREN OF ISRAEL COMMITTED A TRESPASS IN THE ACCURSED THING: FOR ACHAN, THE SON

OF CARMI, THE SON OF ZABDI, THE SON OF ZERAH, OF THE TRIBE OF JUDAH, TOOK OF THE ACCURSED THING: AND THE ANGER OF THE LORD WAS KINDLED AGAINST THE CHILDREN OF ISRAEL.

(2) "AND JOSHUA SENT MEN FROM JERICHO TO AI, WHICH IS BESIDE BETH-AVEN, ON THE EAST SIDE OF BETHEL, AND SPOKE UNTO THEM, SAYING, GO UP AND VIEW THE COUNTRY. AND THE MEN WENT UP AND VIEWED AI.

(3) "AND THEY RETURNED TO JOSHUA, AND SAID UNTO HIM, LET NOT ALL THE PEOPLE GO UP; BUT LET ABOUT TWO OR THREE THOUSAND MEN GO UP AND SMITE AI; AND MAKE NOT ALL THE PEOPLE TO LABOUR THERE; FOR THEY ARE BUT FEW.

(4) "SO THERE WENT UP THERE OF THE PEOPLE ABOUT THREE THOUSAND MEN: AND THEY FLED BEFORE THE MEN OF AI.

(5) "AND THE MEN OF AI SMOTE OF THEM ABOUT THIRTY AND SIX MEN: FOR THEY CHASED THEM FROM BEFORE THE GATE EVEN UNTO SHEBARIM, AND SMOTE THEM IN THE GOING DOWN: WHEREFORE THE HEARTS OF THE PEOPLE MELTED, AND BECAME AS WATER.

(6) "AND JOSHUA RENT HIS CLOTHES, AND FELL TO THE EARTH UPON HIS FACE BEFORE THE ARK OF THE LORD UNTIL THE EVENTIDE, HE AND THE ELDERS OF ISRAEL, AND PUT DUST UPON THEIR HEADS.

(7) "AND JOSHUA SAID, ALAS, O LORD GOD, WHEREFORE HAVE YOU AT ALL BROUGHT THIS PEOPLE OVER JORDAN, TO DELIVER US INTO THE HAND OF THE AMORITES, TO DESTROY US? WOULD TO GOD WE HAD BEEN CONTENT, AND DWELT ON THE OTHER SIDE JORDAN!

(8) "O LORD, WHAT SHALL I SAY, WHEN ISRAEL TURNS THEIR BACKS BEFORE THEIR ENEMIES!

(9) "FOR THE CANAANITES AND ALL THE INHABITANTS OF THE LAND SHALL HEAR OF IT, AND SHALL ENVIRON US ROUND, AND CUT OFF OUR NAME FROM THE EARTH: AND WHAT WILL YOU DO UNTO YOUR GREAT NAME?"

The exegesis is:

1. Sin, as we shall see, was the cause of this debacle. If one single member of the community of Israel violated the specific Laws laid down by God imposed on them, the whole body was liable for his sin, until it had purged itself by a public act of restitution.

So, Paul regards the Corinthian Church as polluted by the presence of one single offender until he was publicly expelled, or he repented. There is some evidence that he repented (I Cor. 5:2, 6-7; II Cor. 2:4-11).

2. Had Joshua prayed about Ai, and it doesn't seem that he did, the sin would have been immediately discovered and defeat avoided. The danger after a victory is evident, because of over confidence. In such an atmosphere, it is easy to forget to pray.

3. Hidden sin was the cause of this failure. In the life of victory, God is the One and Only strength of the Believer; he has no other strength. But God cannot give that strength if sin be indulged. If He did, He would deny His Own Nature, which is Holiness. When He acts in Power, in the midst of His People, He must act in harmony with His Own Nature; and hence, He must judge sin in the camp of Israel with the same *"fierce anger"* with which He judged it in the city of Jericho. That Judgment in both cases was death.

4. Sin can be overcome in the life of the Believer only by the Believer looking exclusively to Christ and the Cross. It is at the Cross where sin was addressed, and only at the Cross. When the Believer places his Faith exclusively in Christ and the Cross, and it must be in both, the Holy Spirit will then work mightily in the heart and life of such a Believer, giving total and complete victory (Rom. 8:1-2, 11; I Cor. 1:17-18, 21, 23; 2:2; Gal. 6:14; Col. 2:14-15).

5. It doesn't take very much for the Faith of even the strongest Saint, such as Joshua, to be weakened. He had just seen one of the greatest Moves of God in the history of man, the opening of the Jordan River, and the destruction of the city of Jericho without the loss of a single Israelite. So why will he now question the Lord?

If there is a problem, then it's not the Lord's fault, but rather ours!

NOTES

DEFEAT AND HIDDEN SIN

Joshua, Chapter 7 shows us the reason for failure in the life of the Christian — sin. As sin stopped the advance of God's People in the Land of Promise, so sin will stop the advance of God's People today. God's Holiness cannot abide sin. Likewise, God's Grace cannot refuse forgiveness to those who will truly repent. Sadly, there is very little evidence that Achan repented.

The First Verse says, *"And the anger of the Lord was kindled."* Nothing angers God like sin; He cannot abide it, whether in the life of Moses or whether in the life of Achan. A hidden sin was the cause of Israel's defeat. In the life of victory, God is the one and only strength of the Christian who within Himself, has no strength. But God cannot give that strength if sin be present. If He did, He would deny His Own Nature, which is Holiness. When He acts in Power in the midst of His People, He must act in harmony with His Own Nature. Hence, He must judge sin in the camp of Israel with the same *"fierce anger"* with which He judged it in the city of Jericho. That Judgment, as previously stated, in both cases was death.

REPENTANCE

But if the discovery and Judgment of sin is painful, and if there is faithfulness in dealing with it, then Grace gives both Blessing and Victory, and the Valley of Achor, which had been a valley of death, now becomes a Door of Hope (Hos. 2:15). Sin must be feared, but neither its bitterness nor its punishment should be dreaded, for it is at this point that God resumes His Victory — having fellowship with His Child.

WHAT IS REPENTANCE?

Repentance means to turn about, to have a change of mind, to express regret. Repentance used as a verb means the act of turning about, while Repentance used as a noun means the result of such action.

True Repentance actually refers to a basic change in man's attitude toward God. That attitude cannot actually be changed unless in some way it becomes a part of the Cross of Christ. We have a picture of this at the very dawn of time, actually on the first page of human history. It is the story of Cain and Abel.

The Lord had shown the First Family that despite the Fall, they could have communion with Him and forgiveness of sins; however, it could only be by the means of the slain lamb, which was a representative of the Redeemer, Who would eventually come, the Lord Jesus Christ. Abel offered up the correct Sacrifice and received that which God promised, while Cain rejected it, thereby offering up his own sacrifice, which God could not accept. The end result was that Cain murdered his brother; therefore, at the very beginning the foundation is laid for all that God does, and the result of refusing that which He has given.

Cain did not refuse to build an altar, neither did he refuse to offer sacrifice, he just refused to offer the sacrifice that God demanded, which was an innocent victim, in essence, the lamb. The Church, if we would use that term, has continued to follow this pattern down through the ages. Only a small part in the Church has trusted in Christ and the Cross, while the far greater majority has gone the way of Cain, i.e., offering up its own sacrifice, which God can never accept.

At this particular time (2006) the problem is more acute than ever. I speak of *"The Purpose Driven Life"* scheme! I speak of the *"Confession Message"*! I speak of *"Denominationalism"*! Of course, there are 101 other false directions that one could name as well.

If it is looked at closely, it will be found that all of these schemes parrot that which was carried out by Cain so long, long ago! Man doesn't refuse to build an altar; neither does he refuse to offer up sacrifice, he just wants to offer up a sacrifice of his own making.

THE REVELATION OF THE CROSS

After some six years of concentrated prayer, and I speak of both morning and night, the Lord, in 1997 began to open up to me the great Revelation of the Cross. To be sure, it was not anything new, actually that which had been given to the Apostle Paul. In fact, I was taken by the Holy Spirit directly to the Sixth and Eighth Chapters of Romans. This Revelation has changed my life, my heart,

my Ministry and, in fact, every facet of my life and living. I will forever thank the Lord, and as the songwriter said, *"The Old Rugged Cross Made the Difference."*

As this great Revelation, and primarily I speak of the Cross as it refers to Sanctification, began to be opened up to me, which, in fact, it continues to open up even unto this very hour, to be sure, I could not wait to proclaim to the world what the Lord had given me.

I had labored in ignorance of this great Truth all of my Christian experience, and this particular ignorance caused me untold failure, shame, and humiliation, and before the entirety of the world at that; however, as someone has well said, *"desperation always precedes Revelation."* I cannot guarantee that this happens with every person, but I know it happened with Paul, and I know it happened with me. The desperation definitely did precede the Revelation.

At any rate, I couldn't wait to tell the story. I knew that the majority of the Church world, even as I, was ignorant of the Cross of Christ as it regards Sanctification. In other words, I knew that it did not know nor understand that the Believer must have his Faith anchored squarely in the Cross of Christ in order for the Holy Spirit to work in one's life, which is the only way that victory can be ascertained.

But I found to my dismay that most were not interested. And then I found to my utter dismay that the cause and the reason were unbelief. Most in the modern Church simply do not believe that what Jesus did at the Cross answers man's dilemma, and does so in totality. It would, regrettably and sadly, rather turn to its own schemes and fads, or most of all, to humanistic psychology. Thank God, some few have accepted, are accepting, and I know shall accept, but the majority, as always, has gone, sadder still, by the way of Cain (Gen., Chpt. 4).

REPENTANCE WITHOUT THE CROSS!

Actually, repentance without the Cross, and I refer to basically understanding the Cross as it refers to our every day living for God, cannot really be effected as it should be. Let me explain:

Most of the time the sin that one commits is not really the problem. It is only a symptom of the real problem. The tragedy is, most Believers do not know nor understand what the real problem is.

The real problem is man's rebellion against God's Prescribed Order of Victory, which is, *"Jesus Christ and Him Crucified"* (I Cor. 1:23). In other words, if the Believer has placed his faith in something other than Christ and the Cross, then failure is going to inevitably be the result. In fact, it cannot be otherwise. That's the real problem, faith placed in the wrong object.

But if the Believer doesn't know and understand that, his life, and I speak of those who truly know the Lord, will be one of *"sinning and repenting," "sinning and repenting!"* Such a life doesn't exactly fall out to the *"abundance"* of which Jesus spoke (Jn. 10:10).

So, the Believer addresses himself to the failure, whatever it might be, all to no avail. As stated, he is merely treating the symptom. He will find that this type of existence is little more than a merry-go-round, with the situation of *"sinning"* and *"repenting"* being repeated over and over again. As stated, it is because he is addressing the symptoms only, and not the real cause.

WHAT IS TRUE REPENTANCE?

True Repentance is the Believer not only repenting of the *"bad"* he has committed, but the *"good"* as well! Now what do we mean by repenting of the *"good"*?

By using the word *"good,"* we are referring to the *"flesh."* We are referring to man's own ability, his own intelligence, his own prowess, his own capabilities, all used, and in a good way at that, trying to overcome the world. Because these things are *"good"* it fools us. But the truth is as follows:

Man cannot effect, within himself, what needs to be effected. In other words, man cannot make himself righteous or holy, irrespective as to who he is and how hard he tries, or how consecrated or dedicated to the Lord he might be. That might come as a shock to most! Many will read that and look at it in disbelief, and simply because man is always very proud of the *"flesh,"* and especially

religious man. Let's look at Abraham.

Regarding this example, I quote George Williams: *"The effect of the birth of Isaac was to make manifest the character of Ishmael. Ishmael hated him, and so did Hagar, Ishmael's mother. Prompted by her, he sought to murder Isaac (Gal. 4:29), and with his mother was justly expelled. Both merited the severer sentence of death. Thus the birth of Isaac, which filled Sarah's heart with mirth, filled Hagar's with murder.*

"Isaac and Ishmael symbolized the new and the old nature in the Believer. Sarah and Hagar typified the two covenants of works and grace, of bondage and liberty (Gal. 4). The birth of the new nature demands the expulsion of the old. It is impossible to improve the old nature. The Holy Spirit says in Romans 8 that 'it is enmity against God, that it is not subject to the Law of God, neither indeed can be.' If therefore it cannot be subject to the Law of God, how can the old nature be improved?

"How foolish therefore appears the doctrine of moral evolution! The Divine way of Holiness is to 'put off the old man' just as Abraham 'put off Ishmael'. Man's way of holiness is to improve the 'old man,' that is, to improve Ishmael. The effort is both foolish and hopeless. Of course the casting out of Ishmael was 'very grievous in Abraham's sight,' because it always costs a struggle to cast out this element of bondage, that is, salvation by works. For legalism is dear to the heart. Ishmael was the fruit, and to Abraham the fair fruit of his own energy and planning."[1]

Therefore, he did not give up Ishmael easily, and we do not give up the works of our flesh easily as well, and especially the religious works.

But they must be given up, all of them, with our Faith placed totally and completely in Christ and the Cross, which then gives the Holy Spirit latitude to work in our hearts and lives. In that manner, and that manner only, can the Believer walk in victory. That is God's Way, and His only Way! That's how we repent of the *"good,"* which, in effect, is the good side of *"the Tree of the Knowledge of Good and Evil"* (Gen. 2:17). This is true Repentance, and is the only type of Repentance that will fall out to victory — Repentance with the Cross of Christ as the Foundation (I Cor. 1:17-18).

In the final analysis, the problem is not the Canaanites, or what they will say, but the problem is sin. The only way to address sin, and to address it properly, is to take it to the Cross. Unfortunately, the modern Church is trying to address it with humanistic psychology, or a bevy of schemes and fads, all psychologically laced. Let us say it again:

The only answer for sin is the Cross!

(10) "AND THE LORD SAID UNTO JOSHUA, GET THEE UP; WHEREFORE LIEST THOU THUS UPON YOUR FACE?

(11) "ISRAEL HAS SINNED, AND THEY HAVE ALSO TRANSGRESSED MY COVENANT WHICH I COMMANDED THEM: FOR THEY HAVE EVEN TAKEN OF THE ACCURSED THING, AND HAVE ALSO STOLEN, AND DISSEMBLED ALSO, AND THEY HAVE PUT IT EVEN AMONG THEIR OWN STUFF.

(12) "THEREFORE THE CHILDREN OF ISRAEL COULD NOT STAND BEFORE THEIR ENEMIES, BUT TURNED THEIR BACKS BEFORE THEIR ENEMIES, BECAUSE THEY WERE ACCURSED: NEITHER WILL I BE WITH YOU ANYMORE, EXCEPT YOU DESTROY THE ACCURSED FROM AMONG YOU.

(13) "UP, SANCTIFY THE PEOPLE, AND SAY, SANCTIFY YOURSELVES AGAINST TOMORROW: FOR THUS SAITH THE LORD GOD OF ISRAEL, THERE IS AN ACCURSED THING IN THE MIDST OF YOU, O ISRAEL: YOU CAN NOT STAND BEFORE YOUR ENEMIES, UNTIL YOU TAKE AWAY THE ACCURSED THING FROM AMONG YOU.

(14) "IN THE MORNING THEREFORE YOU SHALL BE BROUGHT ACCORDING TO YOUR TRIBES: AND IT SHALL BE, THAT THE TRIBE WHICH THE LORD TAKES SHALL COME ACCORDING TO THE FAMILIES THEREOF; AND THE FAMILY WHICH THE LORD SHALL TAKE SHALL COME BY HOUSEHOLDS; AND THE HOUSEHOLD WHICH THE LORD SHALL TAKE SHALL COME MAN BY MAN.

(15) "AND IT SHALL BE, THAT HE WHO IS TAKEN WITH THE ACCURSED THING

SHALL BE BURNT WITH FIRE, HE AND ALL WHO HE HAS: BECAUSE HE HAS TRANSGRESSED THE COVENANT OF THE LORD, AND BECAUSE HE HAS WROUGHT FOLLY IN ISRAEL."

The exegesis is:

1. Verse 12 proclaims the greatest example that God will not bless anyone if there is unconfessed sin in one's life. As He wouldn't bless Israel because of Achan, likewise He will not bless us presently if we attempt to harbor sin.

2. The *"accursed thing"* falls into many categories. The only way it can be defeated is for the Believer to express his Faith exclusively in Christ and what Christ has done at the Cross. Then, and only then, can and will the Holy Spirit work within one's life, Who Alone can remove the *"accursed thing"* (Rom. 6:3-14; I Cor. 1:17-18, 23; Gal. 6:14).

3. The enemies of the Lord would claim that the demand by the Lord that Achan and his family be killed is barbaric; however, the truth is, it is the sin that is barbaric, because it allows Satan to *"steal, kill, and destroy"* (Jn. 10:10). Instructions had been plainly and clearly given to the entirety of the army of Israel that no spoil was to be taken in Jericho by the soldiers, or anyone else of the Tribes of Israel. So, to disobey this was to do so in the Face of God, and with defiance and arrogance, which, if allowed to continue, would wreck Israel.

If someone has a contagious disease, it is not cruel to quarantine that person where they cannot infect others. In fact, it would be cruel not to do so.

No, the Lord was not cruel in what He demanded; He would have been cruel not to have done so.

SIN

The Lord said in the Eleventh Verse, *"Israel has sinned."* One sin brought all the nation to defeat and caused God to stop His Blessings. In fact, it was one sin which caused Adam and the whole race to be under the present curse (Gen. 2:19; Rom. 5:12-21). One sin brings the same result as committing all sins; at least as far as sin itself is concerned (James 2:9-10).

It is certainly true, that some sins are

worse than others. Jesus said so! (Jn. 19:11). But yet, and as stated, even one sin makes a person a sinner.

When Christians start bragging about the fact that they have not committed certain sins, thinking this makes them better than others, they need to think again.

There are thousands of individuals who are incarcerated in penal institutions who did not kill anyone. But still, they are in prison just the same, and because of committing other types of crime. As stated, some sins are definitely worse than others, but all sin is bad, grievously bad!

SIN AND THE CROSS

I do not personally believe that any Christian can properly understand sin until he first of all understands the Cross. It was at the Cross that all sin was addressed, and properly atoned. And to be sure, it was our sins which put Him there. Once one sees the Cross, and sees it properly, and I'm referring to the Cross as it applies to our everyday life and living, then one begins to see sin in its proper light. It's not a pretty picture.

The reason that one can then see and understand sin to a greater degree, is because now one properly sees oneself. Again, the picture is not pleasant to behold!

The Cross of Christ shows everything up for what it actually is. It tells us how black sin is, how ungodly we are, and none of us enjoy very much hearing such a Truth.

When one properly sees the Cross, one then properly sees his own unrighteousness. He begins to see and understand that his only hope is in Christ and what Christ did at the Cross. He ceases to look to his own righteousness, realizing how far short it falls. But once again, all of this comes about because of a proper understanding of the Cross. Regrettably, not many in the modern Church understand the Cross, at least as it refers to our Sanctification. Quite possibly they don't desire to understand it, and for all the obvious reasons.

The Cross of Christ exposes man for what he really is, totally unable to save himself, and in any capacity, and Christ for Who He really is, the Saviour of mankind. Man is not too happy about admitting to either.

WHY WAS ISRAEL'S SIN SO BAD AS IT REGARDED JERICHO?

All sin constitutes a breaking of the Commandments of the Lord. In other words, we do what He tells us not to do.

Why is that so bad?

God knows where sin leads. He knows that it is the cause of all heartache, destruction, pain, sickness, suffering, and sorrow. He knows what the end result will be. It's like the spread of a contagious disease. If it's not stopped, it will destroy everything in its path. We only see the immediate results of sin, and that only in part. God sees sin and the bitter results even unto the bitter end.

Very near our office in Baton Rouge, La., they are building an interchange on Interstate 10. They recently placed some huge concrete crossbeams across the entirety of the highway, where another crossway would be built. They found a crack in one of those giant crossbeams, and demanded immediately that all work stop, at least as it regarded the crossbeams.

They were concerned that salt water from Hurricane Katrina had gotten into the crack and onto the steel reinforcements, which could cause it to rust, thereby weakening the crossbeam, which in the future could cause a catastrophe. Thankfully the water had not reached the steel reinforcement and so there was no damage.

But that is similar to sin. No matter how strong we may think we are, and that goes for every part of our life and living, sin will tear down the very strongest, even entire nations, as it has wrecked empires in the past. In fact, America's greatest danger is sin!

THE PRICE

One begins to understand just how bad sin is, when we realize the price that God had to pay in order for this terrible problem to be properly addressed. That price was the giving of His Only Son, and giving Him as a Sacrifice, actually impaled on Calvary's Cross (Jn. 3:16). Only when one understands that, can one properly understand sin, at least as far as we poor human beings can understand such.

As one Preacher said, *"Look at the Cross*

and the dying Saviour. Look at the horror and the agony of it all. Watch Him as He did bear the penalty for our iniquity, and then say, 'my sin did that!'"

WHY THE CROSS IS SO IMPORTANT!

The Cross alone deals with sin. Nothing else will as nothing else can. This is the reason the Cross of Christ is so important, actually, the single most important thing that mankind faces. Without the Cross, there is no remission of sin. And when we use the term *"the Cross,"* we are actually speaking of what Jesus did there in the giving of Himself, in the shedding of His Own Precious Blood (Eph. 2:13-18). That's the reason the Church sins so greatly when it ignores the Cross and thereby substitutes its own so-called remedy. It is the story of Cain all over again.

We've said it repeatedly, and we'll say it again:

The only thing standing between mankind and eternal Hell is the Cross of Christ.

The only thing standing between the Church and total apostasy is the Cross of Christ.

There are many who think that we are harsh and criticize us greatly because we point out the terrible error of *"The Purpose Driven Life"* debacle. We do so, because, as stated, it's the sin of Cain all over again. It is the substitute of something other than the Cross of Christ. The same can be said for the *"Word of Faith"* doctrine, plus the *"Government of Twelve,"* plus *"Denominationalism,"* etc. This is the reason that *"humanistic psychology"* is so wrong. All of these efforts are an attempt to deal with sin by means other than the Cross. Let us say it again:

There is only one remedy for sin and that is the Cross of Christ. Paul said:

"But this Man (this Priest, Christ Jesus), *after He had offered One Sacrifice for sins forever* (speaks of the Cross), *sat down on the Right Hand of God* (refers to the great contrast with the Priests under the Levitical System, who never sat down because their work was never completed; the work of Christ was a 'Finished Work,' and needed no repetition);

"From henceforth expecting till His enemies be made His footstool. (These enemies

are Satan and all fallen Angels and demon spirits, plus all who follow Satan.)

"For by one Offering He has perfected forever them who are Sanctified. (Everything one needs is found in the Cross [Gal. 6:14])" (Heb. 10:12-14).

(16) "SO JOSHUA ROSE UP EARLY IN THE MORNING, AND BROUGHT ISRAEL BY THEIR TRIBES; AND THE TRIBE OF JUDAH WAS TAKEN:

(17) "AND HE BROUGHT THE FAMILY OF JUDAH; AND HE TOOK THE FAMILY OF THE ZARHITES: AND HE BROUGHT THE FAMILY OF THE ZARHITES MAN BY MAN; AND ZABDI WAS TAKEN:

(18) "AND HE BROUGHT HIS HOUSEHOLD MAN BY MAN; AND ACHAN, THE SON OF CARMI, THE SON OF ZABDI, THE SON OF ZERAH, OF THE TRIBE OF JUDAH, WAS TAKEN.

(19) "AND JOSHUA SAID UNTO ACHAN, MY SON, GIVE, I PRAY YOU, GLORY TO THE LORD GOD OF ISRAEL, AND MAKE CONFESSION UNTO HIM; AND TELL ME NOW WHAT YOU HAVE DONE; HIDE IT NOT FROM ME.

(20) "AND ACHAN ANSWERED JOSHUA, AND SAID, INDEED I HAVE SINNED AGAINST THE LORD GOD OF ISRAEL, AND THUS AND THUS HAVE I DONE:

(21) "WHEN I SAW AMONG THE SPOILS A GOODLY BABYLONISH GARMENT, AND TWO HUNDRED SHEKELS OF SILVER, AND A WEDGE OF GOLD OF FIFTY SHEKELS WEIGHT, THEN I COVETED THEM, AND TOOK THEM; AND, BEHOLD, THEY ARE HID IN THE EARTH IN THE MIDST OF MY TENT, AND THE SILVER UNDER IT."

The construction is:

1. We find in all of this, that sin is a terrible detriment to the forward motion of the Work of God, whether in our immediate lives, or whether in the Work of the Lord in general.

2. It is the Work of the Holy Spirit in our lives, exactly as He functioned in this scenario of our study, to rid us of all sin.

3. While the Bible doesn't teach sinless perfection, it most definitely does teach victory over sin, and in every capacity, in other words, as Believers, that sin not dominate

us in any fashion. This can be accomplished only by the Believer looking exclusively to Christ and the Cross, which then gives the Holy Spirit latitude to work within our lives; Who Alone can bring about the desired results (Rom. 6:14).

A LACK OF REPENTANCE

There is no hint in the Text that Achan sincerely repented. After the Holy Spirit had pointedly marked him as the guilty one, still, he only admitted as to what was done. There seemed to be no true contrition, no true Repentance before God. While he possibly was sorry, it was only that he was sorry that he was caught.

The Twenty-first Verse says that Achan's sin was *"a goodly Babylonish garment, and two hundred shekels of silver, and a wedge of gold of fifty shekels weight."* Achan had heard the command, *"And you, in any wise keep yourselves from the accursed thing"* (Josh. 6:18).

It seemed to be willful sin with no regard for the Word of God and was apparently accompanied by very little temptation. Babylon and money have a fateful attraction for the Christian. He finds these things among the unconverted around him, as they found them in Jericho, and his heart covets them. This explains, at least a part of the weakness of the modern Church.

These sins are enjoyed instead of being confessed and forsaken. God has, therefore, withdrawn His Power, and there is universal weakness and defeat. Fellowship with God can only be enjoyed if resolute separation from all evil be observed.

It seems that Achan's family joined with him in the stealing of these items and in their hiding of them. They would also join with him in the Judgment.

Furthermore, their sin, the Fifth Verse says, had caused the death of *"about thirty and six men"* the wages of sin is always death (Rom. 6:23).

WILLFUL SIN AND
UNWILLFUL SIN

No sin is excusable before God or man, irrespective if it's willful or unwillful. In some way, it will still bring about its catastrophic

NOTES

results. We must never forget that!

What is the difference in *"willful sin"* and *"unwillful sin?"*

Willful sin is that indulged and engaged by Achan and his family, inward, as stated, there seemed to be very little temptation. While temptation for the Christian is in some ways, always present, still, temptation was not Achan's problem, but rather self-will.

For instance, as we bring it up to modern times, and which has been the case untold millions of times down through the ages, when Believers purposefully set a course that is wrong, simply because that is what they want to do, that is willful sin. At the present time, there are hundreds if not thousands of religious leaders who know better, but simply because they desire to curry the favor of others, they embark upon a course that is not of God, meaning that it is not Scriptural. It might be popular and, in fact, almost everything that Satan has in the religious sense is popular, but, of course, it's not Scriptural; therefore, it is wrong, dead wrong!

One might say that every single Preacher in the country who follows *"The Purpose Driven Life"* scheme, is engaging in willful sin. They know better. And if they don't know better, if they call themselves Preachers, they certainly ought to know better.

All willful sin in some way starts with a rejection of the Cross of Christ. In other words, the individual makes a conscious decision that he, and for whatever reason or reasons, will not accept the Cross as the answer to man's dilemma, but rather chooses something else. That is willful sin. It is the sin of Judas.

Can one repent of such a sin?

Most definitely they can, and the Lord will most definitely forgive, cleanse, wash, and restore (I Jn. 1:9); however, the truth is, most will not repent, but plunge deeper into the morass of wrong direction. Listen to Paul:

"Beware of dogs (the Apostle is addressing the Judaizers, who were Jews from Jerusalem who claimed Christ, but insisted on Believers keeping the Law as well; all of this was diametrically opposed to Paul's Gospel of Grace, in which the Law of Moses had no part; as well, by the use of the word *'dogs,'* the Apostle was using the worst slur; in

fact, the word *'dogs'* was used by Jews for homosexuals; so, Paul is, in essence, saying that these Judaizers were to the Gospel of Jesus Christ as homosexuality is to the human race — a perversion of the worst order), *beware of evil workers* (they denigrated the Cross), *beware of the concision.* (This presents a Greek word Paul uses as a play upon the Greek word *'Circumcision,'* which was at the heart of the Law Gospel of the Judaizers)" (Phil. 3:2).

The Apostle then said, *"Brethren, be followers together of me* (be *'fellow-imitators'*), *and mark them which walk so as you have us for an example* (observe intently).

"(For many walk [speaks of those attempting to live for God outside of the victory and rudiments of the Cross of Christ], *of whom I have told you often, and now tell you even weeping* [this is a most serious matter], *that they are the enemies of the Cross of Christ* [those who do not look exclusively to the Cross of Christ must be labeled *'enemies'*]:

"Whose end is destruction [if the Cross is ignored, and continues to be ignored, the loss of the soul is the only ultimate conclusion], *whose god is their belly* [refers to those who attempt to pervert the Gospel for their own personal gain], *and whose glory is in their shame* [the material things they seek, God labels as *'shame'*], *who mind earthly things.)* (This means they have no interest in Heavenly things, which signifies they are using the Lord for their own personal gain)" (Phil. 3:17-19).

That is willful sin!

Unwillful sin, concerns sin in which the Believer engages, but doesn't want to do so and, in fact, is trying with all of his might and strength not to do so, but fails anyway. The Seventh Chapter of Romans is replete with this information.

When Paul wrote the Seventh Chapter, he was writing it about himself; however, the information given pertained to the time immediately after his conversion and Baptism with the Holy Spirit, but yet with a lack of knowledge as it regards how to live for God. For a period of time, possibly even several years, he tried to live for God by the keeping of Commandments, regrettably and

sadly, almost identically to the manner in which most of the modern Church functions.

When he wrote the Seventh Chapter, he understood perfectly the Ways of the Lord, as it regards victory, because the Lord had already given him the Revelation as it regards the meaning of the New Covenant, which, in effect, was and is the meaning of the Cross. But the Apostle is inspired by the Holy Spirit to tell us, that unless we follow the Prescribed Order laid down by the Lord, which is found in the Sixth Chapter of Romans, that we will repeat the Seventh Chapter of Romans all over again, and no matter how hard we may try to function otherwise. In other words, the *"sin nature"* which results in the *"Law of Sin and Death,"* is ruling in such a Believer's life. Let me say it again:

Regrettably, due to modern Believers having such little knowledge of the Cross, at least as it refers to Sanctification, the sin nature is ruling most Christians. Perhaps the great Seventh Chapter of Romans can be summed up in the Fifteenth Verse. The Apostle said:

"For that which I do (the failure) *I allow not* (should have been translated, *'I understand not'*; these are not the words of an unsaved man, as some claim, but rather a Believer who is trying and failing)*: for what I would, that do I not* (refers to the obedience he wants to render to Christ, but rather fails; why? As Paul explained, the Believer is married to Christ, but is being unfaithful to Christ by spiritually cohabiting with the Law, which frustrates the Grace of God; that means the Holy Spirit will not help such a person, which guarantees failure [Gal. 2:21])*; but what I hate, that do I* (refers to sin in his life which he doesn't want to do, and, in fact, hates, but finds himself unable to stop; unfortunately, due to the fact of not understanding the Cross as it refers to Sanctification, this is, as stated, the plight of most modern Christians)" (Rom. 7:15).

Now don't misunderstand, even though such a Believer, even as Paul is trying not to fail the Lord and, in fact, hates the failure, still, sin will always bring forth very negative results. But yet, God as should be obvious, looks at such a person in a different light then he does those who are engaging in *"willful sin."* Both Paul and Achan are perfect examples.

I hardly think that any Believer would think that the Lord looked upon Paul at this particular time of his life, even though he was sinning and sinning greatly, whatever it may have been, in the same manner that he looked at Achan during the time of Joshua. To be sure, we have this scenario played out before us presently even on a daily basis. Let us say it again:

Achan engaged in *"willful sin,"* while Paul engaged in *"unwillful sin."* But yet let not the Believer think that simply because it is unwillful, that God overlooks the situation. The party is still guilty, and the end result is going to be extremely hurtful. In fact, even though it is unwillful sin, in such a life, the situation will get worse and worse, with the sin becoming more and more pronounced.

THE ONLY ANSWER FOR SIN IS THE CROSS OF CHRIST

Whether it's *"willful sin,"* or *"unwillful sin,"* there is no other solution for this problem, but the Cross of Christ. To walk in victory, the Believer must place his Faith exclusively in Christ and the Cross, which at the same time means that such a Believer must denounce everything else. While I love the Church to which I belong, still, it within itself as an institution cannot give me one iota of victory over sin. While Christian disciplines are necessary for the Believer, no matter how faithfully engaged, they will present no victory whatsoever. While manifestations of the Holy Spirit are desirable, still, as wonderful as they are, they will bring about no victory.

It is only Faith in Christ and what He has done for us at the Cross, and Faith I might quickly add on a continuing, even daily basis, which will bring about the desired results. The Holy Spirit Alone can make our lives what they ought to be, and He works exclusively within the framework of the Finished Work of Christ. He doesn't demand much of us, but He does demand that our Faith be totally and completely in Christ and the Cross, and nothing else (Rom. 6:1-14; 8:1-2, 11; I Cor. 1:17-18, 23; 2:2; Gal. 6:14).

WHY WOULD ANYONE BE AN ENEMY OF THE CROSS?

The reasons are, I suppose, as many and varied, as there are rejecters of the Cross.

It's not an easy thing to reject the Cross of Christ, because the story of the Cross is actually the story of the Bible, as the story of the Bible is the story of the Cross.

While we receive many letters and e-mails in opposition to our position as it regards the Cross of Christ, and it being the only avenue of victory for the Child of God, still, most of these individuals, whomever they might be, attack us personally instead of the Doctrine which we espouse. While some make a feeble attempt to denigrate the Doctrine of the Cross, most don't even try, simply because, and as stated, the story of the Cross is the story of the Bible.

This automatically states that such individuals are not really attempting to live according to the Word of God, but rather according to some other word, whether developed by someone else or of themselves.

For starters, the Cross of Christ eliminates every other spiritual crutch. It cuts the legs out from under good works, denominationalism, and a myriad of other things that one might be able to name. It lays all of that waste. In respect to this, Paul said:

"Yea doubtless, and I count all things but loss for the excellency of the knowledge of Christ Jesus my Lord (the knowledge of the Lord Jesus which Paul gained through the experience of intimate companionship and communion with Him)*: for Whom I have suffered the loss of all things* ('For Whose sake I have been caused to forfeit')*, and do count them but dung, that I may win Christ* (next to Christ, everything else is nothing),

"And be found in Him (to be united with Christ by a living Faith, which has as its Object the Cross of Christ)*, not having my own Righteousness* ('not having any Righteousness which can be called my own')*, which is of the Law* (pertains to Law-keeping; he was done with that)*, but that which is through the Faith of Christ* (what He did at the Cross)*, the Righteousness which is of God by Faith* (a spotless Righteousness made possible by the Cross, and imputed by God

to all who exhibit Faith in Christ and the Cross)" (Phil. 3:8-9).

The Apostle then said, *"That I may know Him* (referring to what Christ did at the Cross), *and the power of His Resurrection* (refers to being raised with Him in *'Newness of Life'* [Rom. 6:3-5]), *and the fellowship of His sufferings* (regarding our Trust and Faith placed in what He did for us at the Cross), *being made conformable unto His death* (to conform to what He did for us at the Cross, understanding that this is the only means of Salvation and Sanctification)" (Phil. 3:10).

When Paul spoke of the *"loss of all things,"* he was referring to many things, his family, the place and position he had once had and held as a Pharisee, actually, once held in high esteem by the ruling hierarchy of Israel, etc. All of that had to go, and go completely. Most religious leaders are not willing to do that.

It is sad, but many Preachers if not most, seek to gain the plaudits of fellow Preachers, whom they desire to impress. As a result, they compromise the Word of God!

Paul set the example for us. We can please God, or we can please men, we can't please both. Concerning this, Jesus said:

"But in vain they do worship Me (worship that was not accepted by God indicative of much of the modern Church as well!), *teaching for doctrines the commandments of men* (anything that adds to or takes away from the Word of God)" (Mat. 15:9).

(22) "SO JOSHUA SENT MESSENGERS, AND THEY RAN UNTO THE TENT; AND, BEHOLD, IT WAS HID IN HIS TENT, AND THE SILVER UNDER IT.

(23) "AND THEY TOOK THEM OUT OF THE MIDST OF THE TENT, AND BROUGHT THEM UNTO JOSHUA, AND UNTO ALL THE CHILDREN OF ISRAEL, AND LAID THEM OUT BEFORE THE LORD.

(24) "AND JOSHUA, AND ALL ISRAEL WITH HIM, TOOK ACHAN THE SON OF ZERAH, AND THE SILVER, AND THE GARMENT, AND THE WEDGE OF GOLD, AND HIS SONS, AND HIS DAUGHTERS, AND HIS OXEN, AND HIS ASSES, AND HIS SHEEP, AND HIS TENT, AND ALL THAT HE HAD: AND THEY BROUGHT THEM UNTO THE VALLEY OF ACHOR.

NOTES

(25) "AND JOSHUA SAID, WHY HAVE YOU TROUBLED US? THE LORD SHALL TROUBLE YOU THIS DAY. AND ALL ISRAEL STONED HIM WITH STONES, AND BURNED THEM WITH FIRE, AFTER THEY HAD STONED THEM WITH STONES.

(26) "AND THEY RAISED OVER HIM A GREAT HEAP OF STONES UNTO THIS DAY. SO THE LORD TURNED FROM THE FIERCENESS OF HIS ANGER. WHEREFORE THE NAME OF THAT PLACE WAS CALLED, THE VALLEY OF ACHOR, UNTO THIS DAY."

The diagram is:

1. Achan involved his family in the like ruin with himself. The use of the plural in the Hebrew Text suggests that they, like Sapphira, were privy to the theft (Acts 5:1-2).

2. If the discovery and Judgment of sin be painful, and if there be faithfulness in dealing with it, then Grace gives both Blessing and Victory, and the Valley of Achor becomes a Door of Hope (Hos. 2:15). In other words, if true Repentance is engaged, the Lord will always forgive (I Jn. 1:9).

3. Let the Reader understand that Israel was under Law, whereas presently we are under Grace. Observing what Law is, and how it must be enforced, should cause every Believer to shrink back from engaging in Law.

If the Christian tries to live by Law, which, regrettably, the far greater majority of the modern Church is attempting to do, Law, incidentally, devised by man, but still Law nevertheless, they are then brought under its curse (Gal. 3:10). And to be sure, that's not the way that any Believer wants to live.

4. This is the Age of Grace, all made possible by the Cross, and comes to the Child of God in an uninterrupted flow, which is the only way we can successfully live for God, providing the Believer places his Faith exclusively in Christ and the Cross. This is imperative (Gal., Chpt. 5).

THE JUDGMENT OF GOD

As we've already stated, there is no evidence that Achan or any member of his family truly repented. As also stated, they were sorry they were caught, but as far as any true contrition before the Lord, none seems to be present, therefore, they had to suffer the just penalty of the Law.

Why did the Lord forgive David of his terrible sin, which on the surface seemed to be much worse, and not forgive Achan and his family?

As the Fifty-first Psalm bears out, David truly repented, while, as stated, there is no evidence that Achan or his family repented at all. This is evident from the statement by Joshua when he said, *"Why have you troubled us? The LORD shall trouble you this day"* (Vs. 25).

And yet, in the last Verse of this Chapter, with the words *"the Valley of Achor,"* we are given a note of hope.

The Prophet Hosea said, *"And I will give her her vineyards from thence, and the Valley of Achor for a Door of Hope: and she shall sing there, as in the days of her youth, and as in the day when she came up out of the land of Egypt"* (Hos. 2:15). In effect, this says:

"The Valley of Achor for a Door of Hope," (signals back to a vale of horror as described in Joshua 7:24, but which is to become for Israel *"a Door of Hope"* and, as well, for all individuals, at least those who will subscribe to the Grace of God.

The truth is presented here by the Holy Spirit that where the Wrath of God justly fell, the Grace of God is to brightly shine. The valley of horror becomes the vale of hope. Such was Calvary — a place of horror to the Suffering Saviour under the Wrath of God, but a door of hope to the redeemed sinner under the Grace of God.

Thus, this *"Valley of Achor"* proclaims to the Believer who has suffered defeat that the very area of such defeat can become their area of victory.

CHAPTER 8

(1) "AND THE LORD SAID UNTO JOSHUA, FEAR NOT, NEITHER BE THOU DISMAYED: TAKE ALL THE PEOPLE OF WAR WITH YOU, AND ARISE, GO UP TO AI: SEE, I HAVE GIVEN INTO YOUR HAND THE KING OF AI, AND HIS PEOPLE, AND HIS CITY, AND HIS LAND:

(2) "AND YOU SHALL DO TO AI AND HER KING AS YOU DID UNTO JERICHO AND HER KING: ONLY THE SPOIL THEREOF, AND THE CATTLE THEREOF, SHALL YOU TAKE FOR A PREY UNTO YOURSELVES: YOU MUST LAY AN AMBUSH FOR THE CITY BEHIND IT.

(3) "SO JOSHUA AROSE, AND ALL THE PEOPLE OF WAR, TO GO UP AGAINST AI: AND JOSHUA CHOSE OUT THIRTY THOUSAND MIGHTY MEN OF VALOUR, AND SENT THEM AWAY BY NIGHT.

(4) "AND HE COMMANDED THEM, SAYING, BEHOLD, YOU SHALL LIE IN WAIT AGAINST THE CITY, EVEN BEHIND THE CITY: GO NOT VERY FAR FROM THE CITY, BUT ALL OF YOU BE READY:

(5) "AND I, AND ALL THE PEOPLE WHO ARE WITH ME, WILL APPROACH UNTO THE CITY: AND IT SHALL COME TO PASS, WHEN THEY COME OUT AGAINST US, AS AT THE FIRST, THAT WE WILL FLEE BEFORE THEM,

(6) "(FOR THEY WILL COME OUT AFTER US) TILL WE HAVE DRAWN THEM FROM THE CITY; FOR THEY WILL SAY, THEY FLEE BEFORE US, AS AT THE FIRST: THEREFORE WE WILL FLEE BEFORE THEM.

(7) "THEN YOU SHALL RISE UP FROM THE AMBUSH, AND SEIZE UPON THE CITY: FOR THE LORD YOUR GOD WILL DELIVER IT INTO YOUR HAND.

(8) "AND IT SHALL BE, WHEN YOU HAVE TAKEN THE CITY, THAT YOU SHALL SET THE CITY ON FIRE: ACCORDING TO THE COMMANDMENT OF THE LORD SHALL YOU DO. SEE, I HAVE COMMANDED YOU."

The overview is:

1. If God gives something, then the obtaining of such treasure must be done in God's Way; the problem with the modern Church is that it has abrogated God's Government, instituted government of its own devisings, papered it with a Scripture or two and then labeled it as *"God's Government"*; that which man conceives is never of God, irrespective as to how religious it may be.

2. When God gives directions, victory is the guaranteed result; a proper relationship with Him through prayer, the study of the

Word, and above all, constant Faith in Christ and the Cross, such will then guarantee proper leading.

3. The taking of these cities, and the destruction of them, along with the need of the particular time, as well were symbolic of the victory that is to be won within our present-day lives and living; the Promised Land was God's Land; consequently, all enemies must be put to the sword; likewise, we as Believers now belong to the Lord; everything in our lives that is not proper must be subjected to the Sword of the Spirit, with the Fire of the Spirit burning out the dross (Mat. 3:11; Eph. 6:17).

DIRECTIONS GIVEN BY THE LORD

Verse 1 says, *"I have given into your hand the king of Ai, and his people, and his city, and his land."* Victories are easily won in the path of simplicity and Faith, but if sin has been indulged, it causes considerable pain to win even small victories. Even though sin had by now been put away, still, much difficulty was engaged in order to win the victory at Ai. All the people had to be mustered, and an ambushment had to be set, Israel had to pretend to flee! Nothing of this was seen in the capture of Jericho. So, the glaring example is set before us!

A PERSONAL EXPERIENCE

On one of our trips to Israel, I asked the guide if he could take us to where the city of Ai had been located. As well, I wanted to follow the route that Joshua would have taken from Jericho to this particular place.

From Jericho to Ai, one has to cross a mountain range, and even though it's not far, still, the mountains have to be traversed. So, about the only way he could have gone was the way that we went because of the lay of the land. The guide related to us that there was no way that anyone presently could know where Ai did actually exist, because no ruins remain. And yet we were taken to the place, which seemed to be the only logical site for the city, and where no doubt it had been situated.

Going up the mountain about half way to the supposed site of Ai, one could look out

over the entirety of the Jordan valley, at least at that particular location. It is easy to see where Gilgal would have been located, and where the Jordan was crossed, which was the opposite of Jericho.

Why was all of this important to me?

I wanted to go to the site of Ai and go the way that Joshua, no doubt, went because it's in the Bible, and there is nothing more important than the Word of God. In fact, that's what makes the entirety of the Holy Land so very, very interesting. Were we speaking of mere historical narratives, that would be something else; however, inasmuch as we're speaking of the very site where these Biblical events took place, in other words, where God was tremendously involved, then they become very important, at least they do to me.

When Joshua first went against Ai, there is no Biblical record that he sought the Lord as to what he should do; consequently, defeat was his, with some thirty-six men dying. Now, he most definitely seeks the Lord, and the Lord gives him implicit directions, as it regards how the city is to be approached. Had he prayed the first time, quite possibly the defeat could have been avoided.

We make a grave mistake when we take the Way of the Lord for granted. To be overconfident is just as bad as to be faithless. Either way, self is in the way.

This means that the Believer should seek the Lord about everything, even the things which seem to be small, which Ai at the beginning definitely seemed to be. However, small situations can turn into big situations, and fast, especially if we do not have the mind of the Lord.

(9) "JOSHUA THEREFORE SENT THEM FORTH: AND THEY WENT TO LIE IN AMBUSH, AND ABODE BETWEEN BETH-EL AND AI, ON THE WEST SIDE OF AI: BUT JOSHUA LODGED THAT NIGHT AMONG THE PEOPLE.

(10) "AND JOSHUA ROSE UP EARLY IN THE MORNING, AND NUMBERED THE PEOPLE, AND WENT UP, HE AND THE ELDERS OF ISRAEL, BEFORE THE PEOPLE TO AI.

(11) "AND ALL THE PEOPLE, EVEN THE PEOPLE OF WAR WHO WERE WITH

HIM, WENT UP, AND DREW NEAR, AND CAME BEFORE THE CITY, AND PITCHED ON THE NORTH SIDE OF AI: NOW THERE WAS A VALLEY BETWEEN THEM AND AI.

(12) "AND HE TOOK ABOUT FIVE THOUSAND MEN, AND SET THEM TO LIE IN AMBUSH BETWEEN BETH-EL AND AI, ON THE WEST SIDE OF THE CITY.

(13) "AND WHEN THEY HAD SET THE PEOPLE, EVEN ALL THE HOST THAT WAS ON THE NORTH OF THE CITY, AND THEIR LIERS IN WAIT ON THE WEST OF THE CITY, JOSHUA WENT THAT NIGHT INTO THE MIDST OF THE VALLEY.

(14) "AND IT CAME TO PASS, WHEN THE KING OF AI SAW IT, THAT THEY HASTED AND ROSE UP EARLY, AND THE MEN OF THE CITY WENT OUT AGAINST ISRAEL TO BATTLE, HE AND ALL HIS PEOPLE, AT A TIME APPOINTED, BEFORE THE PLAIN; BUT HE DID NOT KNOW THAT THERE WERE LIERS IN AMBUSH AGAINST HIM BEHIND THE CITY.

(15) "AND JOSHUA AND ALL ISRaAEL MADE AS IF THEY WERE BEATEN BEFORE THEM, AND FLED BY THE WAY OF THE WILDERNESS.

(16) "AND ALL THE PEOPLE WHO WERE IN AI WERE CALLED TOGETHER TO PURSUE AFTER THEM: AND THEY PURSUED AFTER JOSHUA, AND WERE DRAWN AWAY FROM THE CITY.

(17) "AND THERE WAS NOT A MAN LEFT IN AI OR BETH-EL, WHO WENT NOT OUT AFTER ISRAEL: AND THEY LEFT THE CITY OPEN, AND PURSUED AFTER ISRAEL.

(18) "AND THE LORD SAID UNTO JOSHUA, STRETCH OUT THE SPEAR THAT IS IN YOUR HAND TOWARD AI; FOR I WILL GIVE IT INTO YOUR HAND. AND JOSHUA STRETCHED OUT THE SPEAR THAT HE HAD IN HIS HAND TOWARD THE CITY.

(19) "AND THE AMBUSH AROSE QUICKLY OUT OF THEIR PLACE, AND THEY RAN AS SOON AS HE HAD STRETCHED OUT HIS HAND: AND THEY ENTERED INTO THE CITY, AND TOOK IT, AND HASTED AND SET THE CITY ON FIRE.

(20) "AND WHEN THE MEN OF AI LOOKED BEHIND THEM, THEY SAW, AND, BEHOLD, THE SMOKE OF THE CITY ASCENDED UP TO HEAVEN, AND THEY HAD NO POWER TO FLEE THIS WAY OR THAT WAY: AND THE PEOPLE WHO FLED TO THE WILDERNESS TURNED BACK UPON THE PURSUERS.

(21) "AND WHEN JOSHUA AND ALL ISRAEL SAW THAT THE AMBUSH HAD TAKEN THE CITY, AND THAT THE SMOKE OF THE CITY ASCENDED, THEN THEY TURNED AGAIN, AND SLEW THE MEN OF AI.

(22) "AND THE OTHER ISSUED OUT OF THE CITY AGAINST THEM; SO THEY WERE IN THE MIDST OF ISRAEL, SOME ON THIS SIDE, AND SOME ON THAT SIDE: AND THEY SMOTE THEM, SO THAT THEY LET NONE OF THEM REMAIN OR ESCAPE.

(23) "AND THE KING OF AI THEY TOOK ALIVE, AND BROUGHT HIM TO JOSHUA."

The pattern is:

1. God numbers exactly those who would do battle in His Service. It was then physical as well as Spiritual; it is now altogether Spiritual.

The fight at present is *"the good fight of Faith"* (I Tim. 6:12-13). This *"fight"* in which we are called upon to engage pertains to our Faith. This refers to one exclusively placing one's Faith in Christ and the Cross. The Cross must never be separated from Christ, and we speak of its benefits (Eph. 2:13-18; Gal. 6:14).

2. The Lord told Joshua to stretch out the spear toward the city, which was a symbol of Faith.

3. Everything in our lives not proper with the Lord must be slain, and can be slain, but only by the Believer placing his Faith exclusively in Christ and the Cross (Rom. 6:3-14).

4. Israel had the army of Ai between two forces, soldiers of Israel on one side, and soldiers of Israel on the other side. Such is indicative of our Spiritual Warfare presently, with Faith in the Word on one side, and the Victory of the Cross on the other. If we stay between these two mighty forces, we will win the victory exactly as did Joshua.

NOTES

VICTORY OVER THE ENEMY

The Lord gave Joshua minute instructions as to how he was to proceed regarding the taking of the city of Ai. Joshua was not to deviate one iota from those instructions. As is obvious, it was the Word of the Lord, and the account is given to us in the Bible.

It is the same presently! We must not deviate from the Word of the Lord in any respect. If we stay true to the Word, victory, and in every capacity will be ours. If we forsake the Word for our own meanderings, there will be no victory. And regrettably and sadly, that's exactly what the modern Church is doing. It is functioning in the strength of its own mental stratagems, with the Word of God given little consideration, if any at all. As a result, while there is much machinery, much activity, the truth is, virtually no one is getting Saved, virtually no one is being delivered; virtually no one is being baptized with the Holy Spirit, etc.

THE CROSS OF CHRIST
IS THE FOUNDATION
OF ALL VICTORY

Many Christians have it in their minds that if they are not bound by alcohol, or drugs, or nicotine, or immorality, etc., that everything is well and good. The truth is, there are millions of people who do not know the Lord, and make no claim on the Lord whatsoever, who are not bound by those things either. In fact, those things are but symptoms of the real problem, with the real problem being *"self."* Now we're getting down, proverbially speaking, where the rubber meets the road.

Most Christians have had so little instruction as it regards *"self,"* that they have very little idea as to what one is talking about when this subject is broached; however, Paul had more to say about *"self,"* which he referred to as the *"flesh,"* than anything else. The Holy Spirit did this, because this is the real problem with the Child of God. There is no way that self can be put in its proper place, without the Believer understanding the Cross, which alone is the answer for self and sin. So, if the Believer ignores the Cross, disbelieves the Message of the Cross, or is

ignorant as it regards the Cross, there will be precious little victory regarding self, as it pertains to such Believers. The truth is, the Holy Spirit Alone can perfect our lives as they should be. Even then, it is definitely not easy, and neither is it done quickly. In fact, Job is the great example of such in the Word of God.

JOB

A quote from George Williams. He said:

"The Book of Job proclaims the discovery of the 'worthlessness' of self, and that such is the first step in the Christian experience, with the 'worthfulness,' of Christ being the last step.

"Job does not symbolize an unconverted but rather, a converted man. It was necessary that one of God's children should be chosen for this trial; for the subject of the Book is not the conversion of the sinner, but the consecration of the Saint. It is evident that an unconverted man needs to be brought to the end of himself; but that a man who feared God, who was perfect, and who hated evil, should also need this, is not so clear. Here comes the mystery of the Book.

"God uses Satan, calamity, and sickness, to be His instruments in creating character and making men partakers of His Holiness."

Actually, these things did not perfect holiness in Job's life, as such things cannot do so; however, they did get his attention, which they were designed to do, and we might quickly say, then and now. So, the Hand that used these instruments belonged to God. Therefore, the facts of this Book explain to Christian people, who, like Job, are conscious of personal integrity, why calamities, sorrows, and diseases are permitted to afflict them.

Williams went on to say, *"The effect of the Divine action was that Job 'abhorred himself.' This language shows that he had thought well of himself. His creed was orthodox, for he approached God through Sacrifice, and his conduct was faultless, for he was a just man and hated evil. But these sharp trials, and especially the anger, which the unjust accusations of his friends stirred up in his heart, revealed to himself unknown depths of moral ugliness; and, finally, his being challenged to measure himself with God, made him conscious that in him, that is, in his 'flesh,' there dwelt no good thing. This is a deep and painful experience, which all Christian people have not reached.*"[1]

It boils down to the following: we do it God's Way and gain the Victory, or we do it our way or the way of someone else, and gain no victory at all, but rather abject defeat.

(24) "AND IT CAME TO PASS, WHEN ISRAEL HAD MADE AN END OF SLAYING ALL THE INHABITANTS OF AI IN THE FIELD, IN THE WILDERNESS WHEREIN THEY CHASED THEM, AND WHEN THEY WERE ALL FALLEN ON THE EDGE OF THE SWORD, UNTIL THEY WERE CONSUMED, THAT ALL THE ISRAELITES RETURNED UNTO AI, AND SMOTE IT WITH THE EDGE OF THE SWORD.

(25) "AND SO IT WAS, THAT ALL WHO FELL THAT DAY, BOTH OF MEN AND WOMEN, WERE TWELVE THOUSAND, EVEN ALL THE MEN OF AI.

(26) "FOR JOSHUA DREW NOT HIS HAND BACK, WHEREWITH HE STRETCHED OUT THE SPEAR, UNTIL HE HAD UTTERLY DESTROYED ALL THE INHABITANTS OF AI.

(27) "ONLY THE CATTLE AND THE SPOIL OF THAT CITY ISRAEL TOOK FOR A PREY UNTO THEMSELVES, ACCORDING UNTO THE WORD OF THE LORD WHICH HE COMMANDED JOSHUA.

(28) "AND JOSHUA BURNT AI, AND MADE IT AN HEAP FOR EVER, EVEN A DESOLATION UNTO THIS DAY.

(29) "AND THE KING OF AI HE HANGED ON A TREE UNTIL EVENTIDE: AND AS SOON AS THE SUN WAS DOWN, JOSHUA COMMANDED THAT THEY SHOULD TAKE HIS CARCASE DOWN FROM THE TREE, AND CAST IT AT THE ENTERING OF THE GATE OF THE CITY, AND RAISE THEREON A GREAT HEAP OF STONES, THAT REMAINS UNTO THIS DAY."

The overview is:

1. The individuals of Ai were so steeped in sin and idolatry that one Archeologist stated, *"The God of Israel, Who gave instructions that all of these heathen tribes in the land of Canaan be exterminated, did future*

NOTES

generations an untold service."

2. Had these heathen been allowed to remain, knowing the human heart, Israel would have been corrupted. Regrettably, after the death of Joshua, some were allowed to remain, and the corruption of Israel is exactly what took place.

If weights and sins in our lives aren't exterminated, which can only be exterminated by the Cross, they will ultimately wreck us (Heb. 12:1-2).

3. Extermination of these idolaters was demanded by the Lord, and because to do otherwise would have put Israel in great danger. It is the same with sin in our present-day lives. It must be exterminated, which means to be rooted out completely, or else it will ultimately exterminate us. One or the other must go!

THE EXTERMINATION OF ALL THE PEOPLE OF AI

Certain archeologists in excavating these particular areas in Canaan have said, *"The evil in which these people engaged themselves such as incest, bestiality, homosexuality, as well as wholesale human sacrifice to idols, so corrupted them that their destruction to protect other nations and future generations was demanded."*

Therefore, God gave instructions that they were to all be destroyed, men, women, and children. At times and in certain places even the animals were destroyed; however, at Ai the Twenty-seventh Verse says, *"Only the cattle and the spoil of that city Israel took for a prey unto themselves, according unto the Word of the LORD."*

The spiritual moral of this illustration pertains to the demand that all sin be eliminated from the heart and life of the Believer. While the Bible doesn't teach sinless perfection, it definitely does teach that sin is not to have dominion over us, in other words, we as Believers are no longer ruled by the sin nature (Rom. 6:14).

As we have already said in any number of ways in this Volume, and will continue to say so, the only way that such a position of victory can be reached in the heart and life of the Believer, which most definitely is the intention of the Holy Spirit, is that the Faith of the Believer ever have the Cross of Christ as its eternal Object. Then and only then will the Holy Spirit work within our lives as He desires to do so, bringing about His Fruit (Gal. 5:22-23).

THE FRUIT OF THE SPIRIT

As far as results are concerned, it probably could be said that there is nothing greater than the development of the Fruit of the Spirit in one's life. That Fruit is:

"Love, Joy, Peace, Longsuffering, Gentleness, Goodness, Faith, Meekness, and Temperance."

We must remember, that this *"Fruit"* is *"of the Spirit,"* which means that the development of such is in His Domain entirely. In other words, it is not possible for human endeavor, no matter how consecrated or dedicated to the Lord, to develop this *"Fruit."* In fact, when we try to do this in our own power and strength, the end result is always the very opposite. It can be done, but only by and through the Holy Spirit.

The manner in which this is done by the Holy Spirit, even as the entirety of the Fifth Chapter of Galatians brings out, is by and through the Cross of Christ. Even though the word *"Cross"* is little mentioned in this Chapter, still, it is actually the subject matter.

Paul did say in the Sixth Chapter, *"But God forbid that I should glory* (boast), *save in the Cross of our Lord Jesus Christ* (what the opponents of Paul sought to escape at the price of insincerity is the Apostle's only basis of exultation), *by Whom the world is crucified unto me, and I unto the world"* (The only way we can overcome the world, and I mean the only way, is by placing our Faith exclusively in the Cross of Christ and keeping it there)" (Gal. 6:14).

To be sure, the *"Fruit of the Spirit"* cannot be developed until the world first of all is overcome.

Also, *"Fruit"* is not developed overnight. It's a time-consuming process, referring to the fact, that what we ought to be in Christ, is not reached quickly or easily, which should be overly obvious.

Also, *"Fruit"* has to be cultivated. If left to its own, it will be overgrown with weeds, and we speak in the natural, which will

NOTES

greatly stunt its progress. It is the same way with the Christian experience.

Unless we as Believers properly cultivate this *"Fruit of the Spirit,"* which is our responsibility, and designed intentionally in this manner by the Holy Spirit, we will never see a true development. Once again, such cultivation comes about not by *"works,"* but rather by *"Faith,"* but by Faith being in the proper object, which is always the Cross of Christ. Then and then only can this *"Fruit"* be developed.

THE HOLY SPIRIT AND THE CROSS OF CHRIST

Before the Cross, where the sin debt was forever settled, animal blood served as a stop-gap measure, so to speak, but was woefully inadequate. In fact, animal blood in the realm of clean animals such as lambs, etc., could not remove the terrible sin debt; therefore, it remained unpaid.

Because of such, the Holy Spirit could not come in to hearts and lives to abide permanently. In fact, He could only come in to the hearts of a certain few, actually those who had been called for a certain task. He helped them to perform that task (I Sam. 16:13), and then departed. That's why Jesus said to His Disciples the week of His Passion, *"Even the Spirit of Truth; Whom the world cannot receive, because it sees Him not, neither knows Him: but you know Him; for He dwells with you, and shall be in you"* (Jn. 14:17). Plainly and simply our Lord told His Disciples, and all other Believers as well that while the Holy Spirit most definitely dwelt with them, He did not at that time (before the Cross) dwell in them. This would come about after the Cross.

At the Cross, Jesus atoned for all sin, past, present, and future, at least for all who will believe (Jn. 3:16; Col. 2:14-15). This paid the sin debt, and paid it totally and completely, with nothing left owing. As a result, the Holy Spirit, and all due to the Cross, can come in to the heart and life of the Believer, and dwell there permanently, which He most definitely does at conversion (I Cor. 3:16). In other words, it's the Cross that made it possible for the Holy Spirit to make the Believer His permanent Home.

As a result, the Holy Spirit works entirely within the framework of the Finished Work of Christ. In fact, He will work no other way. Paul said:

"For the Law of the Spirit of Life in Christ Jesus has made me free from the Law of Sin and Death" (Rom. 8:2).

We are told in this Verse, that this is a *"Law,"* meaning that it is a Law that was devised by the Godhead sometime in eternity past. The phrase, *"In Christ Jesus,"* always and without exception, refers to what Christ did at the Cross. So this *"Law"* of the way the Spirit works, is ensconced totally and completely *"In Christ Jesus,"* referring to what He did for us at the Cross. That's the reason that we proclaim, and boldly, that the Holy Spirit will not work outside of the framework of the Cross of Christ. The Cross is what gives Him the legal right to do what He does in our lives, hence, the word *"Law"* being used in this respect.

The Lord doesn't require much of us in this great Plan, but He does require one thing, and that is Faith; however, it must be Faith in Christ and the Cross, and Christ and the Cross exclusively, or the Holy Spirit is greatly hindered, thereby unable to develop His Fruit within our lives.

THE CROSS AND PERFECTION

As we've already stated several times, the Bible does not teach sinless perfection as it regards the Child of God, in fact, that will not come about until the First Resurrection of Life, when we shall be changed (I Cor., Chpt. 15). However, it does teach perfection, but it is perfection that is in Christ, and Christ Alone.

When the Believer places his Faith exclusively in Christ and what Christ has done for us at the Cross, our Lord then gives us His Perfection, which is all done by Grace, i.e., *"The Goodness of God."*

The Whole Burnt Offering of the Old Testament proclaims Christ giving the Believer His Perfection, i.e., *"His all!"* The *"Sin-Offering,"* presents Christ taking on Himself all of our sin. So we have the former Offering giving us His Perfection, while the latter Offering takes all of our sin.

In fact, those particular Offerings of the

Old Testament were Types and Shadows, while the Cross of Christ is the fulfillment of such.

Righteousness is imputed to the Believer, only as the Believer exercises Faith in Christ and the Cross. If the Believer tries to bring about Righteousness by his own machinations, the only thing that he will develop is self-righteousness. Even though Saved and baptized with the Holy Spirit, still, within ourselves we cannot perfect anything in our hearts and lives which need to be perfected. That can be done only by the Holy Spirit, and let us say it again.

Our Faith must be anchored squarely in Christ and the Cross, and remain squarely in Christ and the Cross, even renewing it on a daily basis (Lk. 9:23). This being done, and continuing to be done, in fact, never ceasing to be done, the Holy Spirit can then work mightily, thereby developing His Fruit, which translates into Righteousness and Holiness (Rom., Chpts. 6, 8; Gal., Chpt. 5).

(30) "THEN JOSHUA BUILT AN ALTAR UNTO THE LORD GOD OF ISRAEL IN MOUNT EBAL,

(31) "AS MOSES THE SERVANT OF THE LORD COMMANDED THE CHILDREN OF ISRAEL, AS IT IS WRITTEN IN THE BOOK OF THE LAW OF MOSES, AN ALTAR OF WHOLE STONES, OVER WHICH NO MAN HAS LIFT UP ANY IRON: AND THEY OFFERED THEREON BURNT OFFERINGS UNTO THE LORD, AND SACRIFICED PEACE OFFERINGS.

(32) "AND HE WROTE THERE UPON THE STONES A COPY OF THE LAW OF MOSES, WHICH HE WROTE IN THE PRESENCE OF THE CHILDREN OF ISRAEL.

(33) "AND ALL ISRAEL, AND THEIR ELDERS, AND OFFICERS, AND THEIR JUDGES, STOOD ON THIS SIDE THE ARK AND ON THAT SIDE BEFORE THE PRIESTS THE LEVITES, WHICH BORE THE ARK OF THE COVENANT OF THE LORD, AS WELL THE STRANGER, AS HE WHO WAS BORN AMONG THEM; HALF OF THEM OVER AGAINST MOUNT GERIZIM, AND HALF OF THEM OVER AGAINST MOUNT EBAL; AS MOSES THE SERVANT OF THE LORD HAD COMMANDED BEFORE, THAT THEY SHOULD BLESS THE PEOPLE OF ISRAEL.

(34) "AND AFTERWARD HE READ ALL THE WORDS OF THE LAW, THE BLESSINGS AND CURSINGS, ACCORDING TO ALL THAT IS WRITTEN IN THE BOOK OF THE LAW.

(35) "THERE WAS NOT A WORD OF ALL THAT MOSES COMMANDED, WHICH JOSHUA READ NOT BEFORE ALL THE CONGREGATION OF ISRAEL, WITH THE WOMEN, AND THE LITTLE ONES, AND THE STRANGERS WHO WERE CONVERSANT AMONG THEM."

The synopsis is:

1. According to the Word of the Lord, the Altar was built on Mount Ebal, the Mount of Cursing, which relates to the curse of sin, and not Mount Gerizim, the Mount of Blessing.

2. Christ, Who Alone perfectly obeyed the Law, had, therefore, enjoyed, as a Man, its Blessing, yet, voluntarily, in love for those who, by sinning, had incurred its curse, ascended the hill of malediction, and, in His Own Person, suffered the Judgment, and thus, brought out from under the curse those who were sentenced to death (Gal. 3:13-14).

3. Regrettably, the modern Church is attempting to build the Altar, i.e., *"The Cross,"* that is, if the Cross is considered at all, on Mount Gerizim, the Mount of Blessing, which is a denial of the real problem of man, which is sin.

4. The Altar, a Type of the Cross, built of stones, unshaped, symbolizes the fact that we must not add to the Cross nor take from the Cross.

5. All of Israel stood at the foot of Mount Gerizim, the Mount of Blessing, where the Ark of the Covenant was then located, and pronounced Blessings upon Israel; but let it be understood, all of these Blessings were predicated on a proper understanding of the *"Altar"* and its use.

6. It is incumbent upon us presently, as Preachers of the Gospel, to announce to the entirety of the Church the Word of the Lord, taking nothing from it nor adding anything to it.

THE MOUNT OF CURSING AND THE MOUNT OF BLESSING

These two mountains, situated in the very heart of Israel, were to serve as mute reminders of the Blessings of God, and of the Curse that would follow if the Word of God was ignored.

Strangely enough, Joshua was instructed by the Lord to build the Altar, which was a Type of the Cross on *"Mount Ebal,"* which was the Mount of Cursing.

Why did the Lord instruct Joshua to build the *"Altar,"* which, as stated, was a Type of the Cross, on the Mount of Cursing, instead of the Mount of Blessing?

The answer is simple!

The *"Curse"* is man's problem, not the Blessing! Man doesn't need deliverance from the Blessing, he needs Deliverance from the curse — the curse brought on by the Fall.

Unfortunately, we presently have Churches that are all blessing Churches, which are in the greater number, or all cursing Churches. Either one is wrong.

For the Church to be what it ought to be, it must recognize that man's problem is sin, and the only solution to that problem is the Cross of Christ. That properly addressed, the Blessing will automatically come. But unfortunately, there are very few modern Churches that fall into the category of treating the problem as it should be treated. In fact, most do not even admit that the problem of the Believer is sin. And as previously stated, and many times, the only solution for sin is the Cross of Christ. There is no other, as there need be no other.

THE ALTAR

As well, the Thirty-first Verse declares that this Altar was to be built out of *"whole stones,"* meaning that no stones had been trimmed by an instrument of iron, etc.

This tells us that man must not tamper with the Altar, i.e., *"The Cross."* It must not be taken from or added to.

Men do not mind so much Crosses or Altars of their own making. In fact, the Church world is full of them. *"The Purpose Driven Life"* is a case in point. So is Denominationalism, and scores of other schemes and fads that one might address. No, the Lord will have none of that.

Man must understand, and believing man most of all, that the Source of all that we receive from Heaven is the Lord Jesus Christ; however, the Means by which we receive it is the Cross, and none other. Everything else must go. There must never be an altar constructed that is devised and designed by man. The only Altar, which our Lord will accept is the Altar on which the Saviour died.

THE WORD OF GOD

As well, linked with the *"Altar,"* was the Word of God. The Thirty-second Verse says: *"And he wrote there upon the stones a copy of the Law of Moses, which he wrote in the presence of the Children of Israel."* This Word of God was then read to all of Israel, including the little children, and even the strangers which were among them.

This tells us that the Word of God is applicable to all. In fact, there is no such thing as a Western Gospel, or an Eastern Gospel, etc. There is only one Gospel for the entirety of the world (Jn. 3:16).

CHAPTER 9

(1) "AND IT CAME TO PASS, WHEN ALL THE KINGS WHICH WERE ON THIS SIDE JORDAN, IN THE HILLS, AND IN THE VALLEYS, AND IN ALL THE COASTS OF THE GREAT SEA OVER AGAINST LEBANON, THE HITTITE, AND THE AMORITE, THE CANAANITE, THE PERIZZITE, THE HIVITE, AND THE JEBUSITE, HEARD THEREOF;

(2) "THAT THEY GATHERED THEMSELVES TOGETHER, TO FIGHT WITH JOSHUA AND WITH ISRAEL, WITH ONE ACCORD."

The pattern is:

1. These two Verses proclaim an example of the enemy coming against the Child of God, and with reinforcements.

2. As Joshua and Israel of old, if directions from the Lord are sought and received, victory will be sure.

3. To be certain, that which Satan brings against us as a Child of God, is always more, far more than we can hope to overcome within our own strength and power; therefore, if we attempt to come against the evil

one in the wrong way, we will be defeated. If we do it God's Way, which is the Way of the Cross, victory will be certain (Rom. 6:14).

THE ATTACK OF SATAN

Joshua and Israel would now face the concentrated forces of Satan, in fact, in a far greater manner than their previous conflicts. In fact, without the help of God, there was no way they could succeed; however, that help, thankfully, would definitely be forthcoming.

The phrase of Verse Two, *"with one accord,"* means that all of these heathen tribes were in perfect agreement as it regards the destruction of Israel. That's the reason they joined together. Likewise, the Pharisees and the Sadducees joined together, even though they normally hated each other, in order to crucify Christ.

The Believer must understand that the forces arrayed against him, are far greater than that with which, as it regards his own capabilities, he can contend.

DAVID AND GOLIATH

Other than the example before us here regarding Joshua, one of the greatest illustrations in the Bible is that of David and Goliath. This giant, as would be overly obvious, could not be subdued by natural means. Due to his size, and the way they had to fight in those days, such was impossible.

The Holy Spirit means for us to understand that, in effect, this is what we as Believers are facing. Unfortunately, the greater majority of the modern Church seems to little realize that. And how do I know that?

I know it simply because of the foolish schemes and fads they keep proposing in order to deal with this monster — the monster called sin, propelled by the powers of darkness. Paul clearly and plainly told us, *"For we wrestle not against flesh and blood* (our foes are not human; however, Satan constantly uses human beings to carry out his dirty work), *but against principalities* (rulers or beings of the highest rank and order in Satan's kingdom), *against powers* (the rank immediately below the *'Principalities'*), *against the rulers of the darkness of this world* (those who carry out the instructions of the *'Powers'), against spiritual wickedness in high places.* (This refers to demon spirits)" (Eph. 6:12).

The very fact that we are not wrestling against flesh and blood tells us that human means are woefully incapable of coming out victorious against such odds. It simply cannot be done. But yet it must be done!

Jesus defeated every power of darkness at the Cross (Col. 2:14-15). This is where Satan and all of his minions were totally and completely defeated. In fact, none were left undefeated. So, it's at the Cross where we win the victory, and because it is there that the victory has already been won. That's the reason Paul said, *"We preach Christ Crucified"* (I Cor. 1:23).

That's the reason the Apostle also said, *"I determined not to know any thing among you save Jesus Christ, and Him Crucified"* (I Cor. 2:2).

That's the reason he also said, *"God forbid that I should glory, save in the Cross of our Lord Jesus Christ . . ."* (Gal. 6:14).

And finally, *"The preaching of the Cross is to them who perish foolishness; but unto us who are Saved it is the Power of God"* (I Cor. 1:18).

Let me say it again. That's why we preach the Cross so strongly, so constantly, and with such force and vigor. We know, and beyond the shadow of a doubt, that what is opposing us is so much more powerful than we are; therefore, we must have the resources of God on our side, or else we will fail.

THE RESOURCES OF GOD

Of course, virtually every Christian who opposes the Cross, will claim that they have the resources of God on their side. They are fond of exclaiming, *"I can do all things through Christ Who strengthens me."*

The truth is, we can have the resources of God on our side, but only in one way, and that is through the Cross.

The Power of God is registered in the Holy Spirit (Acts 1:8). Considering, as we have repeatedly stated, that the Holy Spirit works entirely within the framework of the Finished Work of Christ, then we should understand that the Cross is the Means by which all of these resources are made available to

us (Rom. 8:2). But regrettably, the far greater percentage of the modern Church either ignores the Cross, or opposes the Cross. Either way, disaster is imminent!

So, we come down to the problem of Faith. Do we really believe that what Jesus did at the Cross answers every question, solves every problem, and is the answer, the solution to our difficulties? We either believe it or we don't.

In 1997 the Lord began to open up to me the great Revelation of the Cross. To be sure, it was not something new, actually that which had been given to the Apostle Paul. He first of all showed me the problem, which is the sin nature, i.e., *"sin."* A few days later He showed me that the solution to that problem of sin, and the only solution, is the Cross of Christ. He took me to the great Sixth Chapter of Romans. And then several weeks later, He showed me how the Holy Spirit works in all of this (Rom. 8:1-2, 11).

We teach that the Cross of Christ is the only thing standing between mankind and eternal Hell!

We teach that the Cross of Christ is the only thing standing between the Church and total apostasy!

So, the question is, do we believe that or do we believe something else? Let me say it again.

As the forces were arrayed against Joshua, far greater than he could even hope to handle, he had to have a Miracle from God, that is if Israel was to gain the victory. As we shall see, that Miracle was forthcoming.

We as Believers have already had the greatest Miracle of all given to us, which guarantees victory, and for all time. It is the great Victory won by Christ at Calvary's Cross, which was ratified in totality by His Resurrection. All victory is centered up in Him and what He has done for us at the Cross. Believe that, rest in that, claim that, and total Victory is yours! (Gal., Chpt. 5).

(3) "AND WHEN THE INHABITANTS OF GIBEON HEARD WHAT JOSHUA HAD DONE UNTO JERICHO AND TO AI,

(4) "THEY DID WORK WILILY, AND WENT AND MADE AS IF THEY HAD BEEN AMBASSADORS, AND TOOK OLD SACKS

UPON THEIR ASSES, AND WINE BOT-TLES, OLD, AND RENT, AND BOUND UP;

(5) "AND OLD SHOES AND CLOUTED UPON THEIR FEET, AND OLD GAR-MENTS UPON THEM; AND ALL THE BREAD OF THEIR PROVISION WAS DRY AND MOULDY.

(6) "AND THEY WENT TO JOSHUA UNTO THE CAMP AT GILGAL, AND SAID UNTO HIM, AND TO THE MEN OF ISRAEL, WE BE COME FROM A FAR COUNTRY: NOW THEREFORE MAKE YOU A LEAGUE WITH US.

(7) "AND THE MEN OF ISRAEL SAID UNTO THE HIVITES, PERADVENTURE YOU DWELL AMONG US; AND HOW SHALL WE MAKE A LEAGUE WITH YOU?

(8) "AND THEY SAID UNTO JOSHUA, WE ARE YOUR SERVANTS, AND JOSHUA SAID UNTO THEM, WHO ARE YOU? AND FROM WHERE DO YOU COME YOU?

(9) "AND THEY SAID UNTO HIM, FROM A VERY FAR COUNTRY YOUR SERVANTS ARE COME BECAUSE OF THE NAME OF THE LORD YOUR GOD: FOR WE HAVE HEARD THE FAME OF HIM, AND ALL THAT HE DID IN EGYPT,

(10) "AND ALL THAT HE DID TO THE TWO KINGS OF THE AMORITES, WHO WERE BEYOND JORDAN, TO SIHON KING OF HESHBON, AND TO OG KING OF BASHAN, WHICH WAS AT ASHTAROTH.

(11) "WHEREFORE OUR ELDERS AND ALL THE INHABITANTS OF OUR COUN-TRY SPOKE TO US, SAYING, TAKE VICT-UALS WITH YOU FOR THE JOURNEY, AND GO TO MEET THEM, AND SAY UNTO THEM, WE ARE YOUR SERVANTS: THEREFORE NOW MAKE YOU A LEAGUE WITH US.

(12) "THIS OUR BREAD WE TOOK HOT FOR OUR PROVISION OUT OF OUR HOUSES ON THE DAY WE CAME FORTH TO GO UNTO YOU; BUT NOW, BEHOLD, IT IS DRY, AND IT IS MOULDY:

(13) "AND THESE BOTTLES OF WINE, WHICH WE FILLED, WERE NEW; AND, BEHOLD, THEY BE RENT: AND THESE OUR GARMENTS AND OUR SHOES ARE BECOME OLD BY REASON OF THE VERY LONG JOURNEY.

(14) "AND THE MEN TOOK OF THEIR VICTUALS, AND ASKED NOT COUNSEL

NOTES

AT THE MOUTH OF THE LORD.

(15) "AND JOSHUA MADE PEACE WITH THEM, AND MADE A LEAGUE WITH THEM, TO LET THEM LIVE: AND THE PRINCES OF THE CONGREGATION SWORE UNTO THEM."

The exposition is:

1. Gibeon, from where these men had come, was actually only about fifteen miles west of Jericho. They were claiming it was many, many miles!

2. While these men were Hivites, evi-dently, their city Gibeon had not thrown in their lot with the balance of the Hivites who were bitterly opposed to Joshua and Israel.

3. In listing the victories won by Israel, and recorded in Verse 10, to buttress their deceit, they carefully neglected to mention Jericho and Ai, which were recent victories.

4. In the Fourteenth Verse, the Holy Spirit is careful to delineate this failure on the part of Israel. At Ai, Israel trusted her own strength, and did not seek the Face of the Lord, and was defeated. At Gibeon, she trusted her own wisdom, and did not seek the Face of the Lord, and was defeated! The sharp lesson taught at Ai was quickly forgot-ten. Such is the natural heart!

5. Williams says, "*Satan is more to be dreaded as a humble supplicant than as a roaring lion. To make him flee, he only needs to be resisted; but to stand against his wiles, the whole armor of God must be employed.*

"*Had Joshua asked counsel at the Mouth of the Lord instead of putting the moldy bread of the Gibeonites into his own mouth, so to speak, he would not have fallen into this snare. Satan, through the mouth of the Gibeonite abundantly quoted the Bible to Joshua (Vss. 6, 9-10, 24), just as afterwards he did to the greater than Joshua, but the Lord defeated him with three Verses out of the Law.*"[1]

Had Joshua so acted, he would have got-ten the victory as well.

6. Satan can only deceive the Christian when we take the management into our own hands, instead of consulting the Lord.

THE SUBTERFUGE OF THE GIBEONITES

Questions loom large here!

First of all, had these men come to Joshua, immediately telling him as to who they were, seeking peace, what would the answer of the Lord have been?

Staring death in the face, can the Gibeonites be blamed for the position they took?

Had the Gibeonites accepted Jehovah as their God, and there is some evidence they did, can we fault these people?

COUNSEL AT THE MOUTH OF THE LORD

The Holy Spirit is quick to point out the fact that Joshua did not *"Ask counsel at the Mouth of the LORD,"* which proclaims the fact that the Lord was displeased with the action of the great warrior; however, there is no record that the Lord reprimanded the Gibeonites at all for what they had done.

To answer one of the previous questions, even though the Hivites were scheduled for destruction, still, had they been totally open with Joshua, telling him immediately as to who they were and where they resided, in fact, that they were only about fifteen miles distance, and offered to convert to Jehovah from their heathen gods, I cannot help but believe that the Lord would have readily accepted them. In fact, I know that He would have.

There is no record of anyone ever coming to the Lord, and if they are sincere, being turned away. The Scripture plainly tells us:

"All who the Father gives Me shall come to Me (refers to all, whomever they may be, whether Israelites, Gentiles, Pharisees, Scoffers, Harlots, or even the very Castaways of the Devil)*; and him who comes to Me I will in no wise cast out* (proclaims to all a promise of unparalleled proportion; no one has ever been turned away, and no one will ever be turned away)*"* (Jn. 6:37).

Once again we are brought face-to-face with a great truth that we must seek the Face of the Lord about everything, be it little or large. Nothing is unimportant to His all-seeing Eye. Nothing is insignificant as it regards His Child; therefore, we as Believers must seek His Leading and Guidance as it regards every facet of all life and living of our existence.

So, upon the subterfuge of the Gibeonites, *"Joshua made peace with them, and made a*

league with them, to let them live: and the princes of the congregation swore unto them."

(16) "AND IT CAME TO PASS AT THE END OF THREE DAYS AFTER THEY HAD MADE A LEAGUE WITH THEM, THAT THEY HEARD THAT THEY WERE THEIR NEIGHBORS, AND THAT THEY DWELT AMONG THEM.

(17) "AND THE CHILDREN OF ISRAEL JOURNEYED, AND CAME UNTO THEIR CITIES ON THE THIRD DAY. NOW THEIR CITIES WERE GIBEON, AND CHEPHIRAH, AND BEEROTH, AND KIRJATH-JEARIM.

(18) "AND THE CHILDREN OF ISRAEL SMOTE THEM NOT, BECAUSE THE PRINCES OF THE CONGREGATION HAD SWORN UNTO THEM BY THE LORD GOD OF ISRAEL. AND ALL THE CONGREGATION MURMURED AGAINST THE PRINCES.

(19) "BUT ALL THE PRINCES SAID UNTO ALL THE CONGREGATION, WE HAVE SWORN UNTO THEM BY THE LORD GOD OF ISRAEL: NOW THEREFORE WE MAY NOT TOUCH THEM."

The composition is:

1. The word of the Child of God is to be as the Word of the Lord.

2. That word being given, Joshua was honor-bound to uphold it.

3. Now that these Gibeonites had been accepted, although by subterfuge, still, they were to be defended, which they were. This proclaims the fact that the Lord defends all who belong to Him.

THE WAYS OF THE LORD

Satan can only deceive Christians when they take management into their own hands instead of consulting the Lord. Communion with God gives a Spiritual instinct, which discerns an enemy and refuses to make him an ally.

Even though the Covenant by Joshua with the Gibeonites was made and was unlawful, still, the Lord did not punish them for making this Covenant; however, when Israel long afterward broke the Covenant, the Lord punished them for doing so (II Sam. 21:1-9). The Lord let Israel make this mistake without intervening, as He will oftentimes do with us as well.

(20) "THIS WE WILL DO TO THEM; WE WILL EVEN LET THEM LIVE, LEST WRATH BE UPON US, BECAUSE OF THE OATH WHICH WE SWORE UNTO THEM.

(21) "AND THE PRINCES SAID UNTO THEM, LET THEM LIVE; BUT LET THEM BE HEWERS OF WOOD AND DRAWERS OF WATER UNTO ALL THE CONGREGATION; AS THE PRINCES HAD PROMISED THEM.

(22) "AND JOSHUA CALLED FOR THEM, AND HE SPOKE UNTO THEM, SAYING, WHEREFORE HAVE YOU BEGUILED US, SAYING, WE ARE VERY FAR FROM YOU; WHEN YOU DWELL AMONG US?

(23) "NOW THEREFORE YOU ARE CURSED, AND THERE SHALL NONE OF YOU BE FREED FROM BEING BONDMEN, AND HEWERS OF WOOD AND DRAWERS OF WATER FOR THE HOUSE OF MY GOD.

(24) "AND THEY ANSWERED JOSHUA, AND SAID, BECAUSE IT WAS CERTAINLY TOLD YOUR SERVANTS, HOW THAT THE LORD YOUR GOD COMMANDED HIS SERVANT MOSES TO GIVE YOU ALL THE LAND, AND TO DESTROY ALL THE INHABITANTS OF THE LAND FROM BEFORE YOU, THEREFORE WE WERE SORE AFRAID OF OUR LIVES BECAUSE OF YOU, AND HAVE DONE THIS THING.

(25) "AND NOW, BEHOLD, WE ARE IN YOUR HAND: AS IT SEEMS GOOD AND RIGHT UNTO YOU TO DO UNTO US, DO.

(26) "AND SO DID HE UNTO THEM, AND DELIVERED THEM OUT OF THE HAND OF THE CHILDREN OF ISRAEL, THAT THEY SLEW THEM NOT.

(27) "AND JOSHUA MADE THEM THAT DAY HEWERS OF WOOD AND DRAWERS OF WATER FOR THE CONGREGATION, AND FOR THE ALTAR OF THE LORD, EVEN UNTO THIS DAY, IN THE PLACE WHICH HE SHOULD CHOOSE."

The construction is:

1. The Gibeonites became the Nethinim. The word means *"given,"* i.e., devoted to the sanctuary of Jehovah.

2. Their lives were spared because the princes of Israel had taken an oath to them in the Name of Johovah; but, because of their deceit, they were condemned to be drawers of water to the House of the Lord. They were not condemned to domestic slavery to the Israelites, but rather to *"the congregation,"* which refers to the Tabernacle, and later the Temple.

3. Grace, therefore, brought them into the glory and joy of Psalms 84:10, and instructed David to appoint them to high position in the Temple (Ezra 8:20). In fact, they were the first to return with Ezra and Nehemiah from Babylonian captivity, pledging themselves to keep the statutes given by God to Moses (Ezra 2:43-58; Neh. 7:60).

4. The Gibeonites, i.e., *"Nethinim"* are last read of in Nehemiah 3:26; 10:28; and 11:21, as making their homes outside the watergate of Jerusalem. Why the water-gate? Because being near the water supply, they could more readily discharge the honorable bondage to which Joshua had condemned them, of being drawers of water to the Temple of Jehovah. Thus, a curse justly pronounced by Law becomes, by Grace, a Blessing.

One must shout *"Hallelujah!"*

HEWERS OF WOOD AND DRAWERS OF WATER

The meaning of the phrase, *"Hewers of wood and drawers of water,"* was that they were to hew wood for the Sacrificial Offerings for the Brazen Altar and to carry water for the Brazen Laver in which the Priests would wash, plus other things pertaining to the sacrifices that needed water. These were to be their duties.

The Law condemned them as the Law must, for it says in the Twenty-third Verse, *"Now therefore you are cursed."* However, Grace, because of Calvary, brought them into glory and joy. The curse was turned into a Blessing, in fact, because of Calvary (Gal. 3:13-14).

The final results were, they were ever so close to the Spirit and Presence of God. As they hewed the wood and would bring it close to the Brazen Altar, they, no doubt, sensed the glorious Presence of God constantly. As they drew the water and brought it close to the Brazen Laver, they were close to the Glory of God. There is no greater place where anyone could be.

THE CURSE AND CALVARY

The picture of these Gibeonites is a perfect

picture of humanity under the curse, and, thereby condemned; however, it is also a perfect picture of Calvary and the Word of God that sets the captive free. It seems these Gibeonites understood perfectly how the Lord had blessed them. They would become in Bible terminology, and as stated, the *"Nethinims."*

Even though as heathen they lied to Joshua about their domicile, etc. But still, one, I think must applaud them. They did all they knew to do, and the results were, that God blessed them for many centuries into the future.

As we've already stated, this, in fact, is a perfect picture of the individual who comes to the Lord. Most, sad to say, don't come to Christ with all the right motives. Some come because of a fear of Hell. Others come because of a fear of dying. But whatever the reason for their coming, the Lord never turns anyone away, and gives equally alike life everlasting to all who will believe.

He then takes us and brings us into His Glory, just as He gave the Gibeonites a place of prominence as it regards the Tabernacle and then the Temple.

What a wonderful, mighty, glorious, and loving God that we serve!

CHAPTER 10

(1) "NOW IT CAME TO PASS, WHEN ADONI-ZEDEC KING OF JERUSALEM HAD HEARD HOW JOSHUA HAD TAKEN AI, AND HAD UTTERLY DESTROYED IT; AS HE HAD DONE TO JERICHO AND HER KING, SO HE HAD DONE TO AI AND HER KING; AND HOW THE INHABITANTS OF GIBEON HAD MADE PEACE WITH ISRAEL, AND WERE AMONG THEM;

(2) "THAT THEY FEARED GREATLY, BECAUSE GIBEON WAS A GREAT CITY, AS ONE OF THE ROYAL CITIES, AND BECAUSE IT WAS GREATER THAN AI, AND ALL THE MEN THEREOF WERE MIGHTY.

(3) "WHEREFORE ADONI-ZEDEC KING OF JERUSALEM, SENT UNTO HOHAM KING OF HEBRON, AND UNTO PIRAM KING OF JARMUTH, AND UNTO JAPHIA

KING OF LACHISH, AND UNTO DEBIR KING OF EGLON, SAYING,

(4) "COME UP UNTO ME, AND HELP ME, THAT WE MAY SMITE GIBEON: FOR IT HAS MADE PEACE WITH JOSHUA AND WITH THE CHILDREN OF ISRAEL.

(5) "THEREFORE THE FIVE KINGS OF THE AMORITES, THE KING OF JERUSALEM, THE KING OF HEBRON, THE KING OF JARMUTH, THE KING OF LACHISH, THE KING OF EGLON, GATHERED THEMSELVES TOGETHER, AND WENT UP, THEY AND ALL THEIR HOSTS, AND ENCAMPED BEFORE GIBEON, AND MADE WAR AGAINST IT."

The pattern is:

1. This is the first mention of Jerusalem in the Bible, as a proper name; it was mentioned first, about five hundred years earlier, as *"Salem."*

2. When anyone makes peace with the Divine Joshua, he brings upon himself the anger of his companions. Thus it was with Gibeon; however, Joshua was able to protect and deliver the Gibeonites. Our Lord is able to deliver from our enemies those who know Him as their Peace.

3. If it is to be noticed, Satan always comes against us with overwhelming odds; consequently, we cannot hope to gain the victory against him unless we function in the manner of the Lord. What is that manner?

That manner is the Cross of Christ, and our Faith in that Finished Work, which then gives the Holy Spirit latitude to work within our lives (Rom. 6:1-14; 8:1-2, 11; I Cor. 1:17-18, 23; 2:2; Gal. 6:14).

THE CONFEDERATION OF EVIL

Now we come to one of the greatest Miracles ever recorded in the annals of human history. Satan will attempt to destroy the People of God. If Joshua had once depended upon the flesh in this episode, as he did at Ai, or with the Gibeonites, all would have been lost. But as he depended totally upon the Spirit, all was won.

The Gibeonites had now been brought over to Israel's God; consequently, the former friends of the Gibeonites became very angry and sought to destroy all. The Fourth Verse says, *"Come up with me, and help me, that we may smite Gibeon: for it has made peace with Joshua."* The moment the person comes to Jesus Christ, though many who were formerly friends, now become enemies. The Fifth Verse says, *"And made war against Gibeon."*

This is the first mention of Jerusalem as such in Scripture. It was referred to formerly as *"Salem,"* during the time of Abraham (Gen. 14:18). The name *"Jerusalem"* means *"peace or peaceful."* The name *"Salem"* means the same thing. Unfortunately, it has known anything but peace, almost from its very beginning.

Why?

It is the city of Jerusalem where on Earth God chose to place His Name. Solomon said:

"If Your people go out to battle against their enemy, whithersoever You shall send them, and shall pray unto the LORD toward the city which you have chosen, and toward the house that I have built for Your Name" (I Ki. 8:44).

Due to the fact that God has placed His Name there, Satan has contested it from then until now. This is the reason for the great conflict in Israel at present.

Israel has done everything within her power to appease the Palestinians, basically offering them, as it regards land area, about everything they demanded; however, the Palestinians also demand east Jerusalem as their Capital, which Israel will not do and, in fact, cannot do. So, the conflict continues and, in fact, will continue until the Second Coming.

So, what is viewed presently in Israel is but a continuing of what has transpired, as stated, for the last 3,500 years.

At the time of our Text, Jerusalem was inhabited by Adoni-zedec. His name means *"sovereign, controller, lord, master, owner."* Thus, from the name of this king, we find the efforts of Satan to control that which belongs to God. This is typical of our own persons, life and living. I speak of Believers. Satan seeks to totally and completely control, to literally *"own"* the Believer. He tries to do so through the sin nature, having it control the Believer, which it most certainly shall, if the Believer attempts to live for God by any means other than Faith being placed entirely

in the Cross of Christ and remaining in the Cross of Christ, which then gives the Holy Spirit latitude to help in our hearts and lives, making us what we ought to be (Acts 1:8; Rom. 8:1-2, 11).

However, as we shall see in this particular Chapter, no matter the power of the forces arrayed against us, no matter the overwhelming odds, no matter as it regards our own personal liabilities, *"He Who is within us, is greater than he who is in the world"* (I Jn. 4:4).

(6) "AND THE MEN OF GIBEON SENT UNTO JOSHUA TO THE CAMP TO GILGAL, SAYING, SLACK NOT YOUR HAND FROM YOUR SERVANTS; COME UP TO US QUICKLY, AND SAVE US, AND HELP US: FOR ALL THE KINGS OF THE AMORITES WHO DWELL IN THE MOUNTAINS ARE GATHERED TOGETHER AGAINST US.

(7) "SO JOSHUA ASCENDED FROM GILGAL, HE, AND ALL THE PEOPLE OF WAR WITH HIM, AND ALL THE MIGHTY MEN OF VALOUR.

(8) "AND THE LORD SAID UNTO JOSHUA, FEAR THEM NOT: FOR I HAVE DELIVERED THEM INTO YOUR HAND; THERE SHALL NOT A MAN OF THEM STAND BEFORE YOU.

(9) "JOSHUA THEREFORE CAME UNTO THEM SUDDENLY, AND WENT UP FROM GILGAL ALL NIGHT."

The composition is:

1. Let the Believer understand that it is our Heavenly Joshua Alone Who can help us. No one else can.

2. He does so by us evidencing Faith in Him and what He has done for us at the Cross. Then, and then only, the Holy Spirit can work mightily on behalf of us against the powers of darkness. To be sure, He has never lost a battle (Rom. 6:1-14; 8:1-2, 11; Gal. 6:14).

3. As Joshua was told by the Lord that he need not fear the enemy, likewise, that same Promise is for us presently.

THE HELP PROVIDED BY THE LORD

The appeal by the Gibeonites to Joshua was quick and to the point, *"Come up to us quickly, and save us, and help us."*

What a plea!

What a petition!

First of all, they appealed to Joshua for help. Some may quickly retort that they had no other recourse. That is true, but neither do we.

The tragedy is, far too many Christians think they do have other recourses. I speak of humanistic psychology! I speak of our own personal strength and ability! In fact, the list is long; however, the truth is, as it comes to the powers of darkness, which every Christian faces, there is no help but the Lord Jesus Christ. We appeal to others in vain. So, as Joshua was the only help for the Gibeonites of that time, as stated, it is the same presently, the Lord Jesus is our only help now. Satan, however, works overtime, proposing every type of scheme and fad, all devised by men, proposing to be of service and help. Despite the fact, that almost the entirety of the modern Church has opted for these foolish directions, as stated, they provide no help whatsoever.

As it regards the human dilemma, the Cross of Christ is the only answer, the only solution, the only cure. There is no other, as there need be no other.

(10) "AND THE LORD DISCOMFITED THEM BEFORE ISRAEL, AND KILLED THEM WITH A GREAT SLAUGHTER AT GIBEON, AND CHASED THEM ALONG THE WAY THAT GOES UP TO BETH-HORON, AND SMOTE THEM TO AZEKAH, AND UNTO MAKKEDAH.

(11) "AND IT CAME TO PASS, AS THEY FLED FROM BEFORE ISRAEL, AND WERE IN THE GOING DOWN TO BETH-HORON, THAT THE LORD CAST DOWN GREAT STONES FROM HEAVEN UPON THEM UNTO AZEKAH, AND THEY DIED: THEY WERE MORE WHICH DIED WITH HAILSTONES THAN THEY WHOM THE CHILDREN OF ISRAEL KILLED WITH THE SWORD."

The pattern is:

1. The distance from Azekah to Makkedah was about 25 miles.

2. The Power of the Lord is not limited respecting those who have Faith in Him; however, such Power is available only if we go according to His Direction, and not from the position of presumption.

3. All victory is found in the Cross of

NOTES

our Lord Jesus Christ, and only in the Cross (I Cor. 1:18).

4. The Lord has the elements at His disposal, as is here obvious.

VICTORY

The Scripture plainly says, *"And the LORD discomfited them before Israel . . ."* while Israel definitely did fight the enemy, still, the artillery of the Lord in the capacity of hailstones, probably weighing 20 to 30 pounds each or more, did incalculable damage, as would be obvious. As stated, the Lord has the elements at His disposal, which He can use anytime He so desires.

There is no need to try to explain this as a freak of nature, etc. This was a Miracle from God, for God is a God of Miracles.

While Israel may have suffered some few casualties, the evidence is, that they didn't. In other words, it seems they did not lose a man, nor even suffered one man to be wounded, which, of course, is a Miracle within itself.

In fact, Israel could have had this type of help from the Lord on a constant basis, even unending, all the way to the time of Christ. They then could have accepted Him as Saviour, Lord, and Messiah, which would have saved the world now, some 2,000 years of bloodshed and sorrow. But regrettably, Israel did not follow that course.

IS SUCH VICTORY, AS ISRAEL
EXPERIENCED THEN,
AVAILABLE TO US PRESENTLY?

Yes, and even more!

We now have a much Better Covenant based on much Better Promises (Heb. 8:6).

Israel was raised up by the Lord as a nation to give the world the Word of God, which they did and, as well, to serve as the womb of the Messiah, which they also did. So, His dealings with them were somewhat different than His dealings presently with the Church, inasmuch as the Church is worldwide. But let it be understood, that whatever is needed, the Lord is available, and desires to help us greatly.

While Christians do not presently have nations arrayed against us, as Israel of old, our opposition comes directly from Satan in the form of demon spirits, etc. As a Child of God, by using the Name of Jesus, we have authority over these spirits, all made possible by what Jesus did at the Cross (I Jn. 4:4).

A PERSONAL EXPERIENCE

If I remember correctly, the year was 1953. Frances and I had been married only about a year. I was just starting to preach. As well, my knowledge of the Word of God was very deficient also. I have thought many times, if I had then had THE EXPOSITOR'S STUDY BIBLE how much grief and sorrow could have been avoided. I could include the COMMENTARIES in that as well.

At any rate, as it regards the time in question, Frances had gone to bed. I was sitting on the couch at the other end of the little mobile home, which was our home at the time, attempting to read the Bible. There was a little country road that ran immediately beside our little mobile home, which afforded some privacy, and I had been walking up and down that road attempting to pray, but without much success.

In those days I didn't know too very much about demonic oppression, but that's what I was experiencing that evening.

I finally went to bed, and the Lord gave me a dream. The dream pertained, as I look back, not only to that particular period of time, but, as well, what I would face in the distant future.

THE DREAM

In the dream I found myself in a house, a place with which I was not familiar. I remember looking around the room where I found myself, wondering what I was doing there. I did not know where it was, or to whom it belonged.

There was no furniture in the room, not even a window in the walls, only a door, which led outside.

My first thought was, *"I've got to get out of this place!"*

But before I could make any move toward the door, all of a sudden, there appeared in the door the most hideous looking creature that I had ever seen. It must have stood at least 8 feet tall, and had the face of a man and the body of a bear. It was lumbering

NOTES

toward me, as if to say, *"I have you now."*

As I looked at its face, and especially its eyes, it seemed like all the evil of the ages was registered on that countenance and in those eyes. In fact, the very strength of the power of that thing seemed to emanate from him, so much so, that I fell to the floor unable to even stand. In other words my legs wouldn't hold me.

I remember feeling around over the floor trying to find something with which to defend myself, but there was nothing. Of course, if I had found something, I was so weak that there was nothing I could do.

This thing was almost over me, and I knew that it was intending to kill me.

THE NAME OF JESUS

Without premeditation, without thinking, and even though fear gripped me to such an extent that I had no strength left, I shouted it as loud as I could, *"In the Name of Jesus."* Even though I shouted, using all the strength I had, still, my voice was so weak that it was barely above a whisper.

But yet, even though I had no personal strength, the Power of that Name literally exploded over that demon spirit. It screamed, clutching its head and, in fact, kept screaming, like someone had hit it in the head with a ball bat. That's how much of an affect the Name of Jesus had.

Something else I feel I must state, my personal physical weakness, had no bearing whatsoever on the strength, the Power, the validity of that Name. I think we should remember that.

As this thing continued screaming and began to stagger backwards, I slowly began to gather strength and started to arise. I stood to my feet and said it again, this time with more strength, *"In the Name of Jesus."*

When I said it the second time, this man/beast fell to the floor, still screaming, still clutching its head, and writhing like a snake that had just received a deathblow. Now, instead of it towering over me, I was towering over it.

For the third time I opened my mouth, but without exerting any strength at all, and again said, *"In the Name of Jesus!"*

This time, my voice literally boomed off

the walls, as if it was connected to a public address system, and that without me putting forth any effort whatsoever.

THE HOLY SPIRIT

And then I heard it. I didn't see anything, but I heard it, and heard it distinctly.

I heard the *"sound of the mighty rushing wind"* of the Holy Spirit.

I cannot describe it any better than that; it was like a rushing mighty wind. It swept through that room, and hit that demon spirit still writhing on the floor, and despite its huge bulk, swept it out the front door like it was no more than a piece of tissue paper. In my dream I walked to the door, and I could see it in the distance like a leaf in the wind being swept away, until it was no longer visible.

I woke myself up worshipping and speaking in other Tongues, with the Power of God all over me.

I knew the Lord had given me the dream; however, at that particular time, beyond the present need I really did not understand what it all meant.

Down through the many years, I believe I have come to understand now what the Lord was telling me that night of so long ago.

He was telling me, that I would face the concentrated powers of darkness, and would almost be overcome. But in the dream He showed me the Power of the Name of Jesus and, as well, the Power of the Holy Spirit. In fact, the two, the Name of Jesus, and the Holy Spirit, one might say, are indivisible. Without the mighty Baptism with the Holy Spirit, without His Power, I do not personally think that any Believer can know the Power, the Strength, the Glory, and the Wonder of *"The Name of Jesus"* (Mk. 16:17).

(12) "THEN SPOKE JOSHUA TO THE LORD IN THE DAY WHEN THE LORD DELIVERED UP THE AMORITES BEFORE THE CHILDREN OF ISRAEL, AND HE SAID IN THE SIGHT OF ISRAEL, SUN, STAND THOU STILL UPON STILL UPON GIBEON; AND YOU, MOON, IN THE VALLEY OF AJALON.

(13) "AND THE SUN STOOD STILL, AND THE MOON STAYED, UNTIL THE PEOPLE HAD AVENGED THEMSELVES UPON THEIR ENEMIES. IS NOT THIS WRITTEN

IN THE BOOK OF JASHER? SO THE SUN STOOD STILL IN THE MIDST OF HEAVEN, AND HASTED NOT TO GO DOWN ABOUT A WHOLE DAY.

(14) "AND THERE WAS NO DAY LIKE THAT BEFORE IT OR AFTER IT, THAT THE LORD HEARKENED UNTO THE VOICE OF A MAN: FOR THE LORD FOUGHT FOR ISRAEL."

The exposition is:

1. The book of Jasher is no longer in existence, nor any of its copies, that is if there were copies.

2. The sun standing still, so to speak, is said to be confirmed by State documents of Egypt, China, and even Mexico, which record this double-day.

It is said that Herodotus, and Lord Kingsborough, in his history of the Mexicans, and the Chinese philosopher Huai-nan-Tzu quoted these records.

The hill of Gibeon, at the moment when Joshua spoke, was behind him to the east, and the sun was setting in front of him to the west. It was evening, and a continuance of daylight was needed in order to complete the victory.

3. God is a Miracle-working God. The Bible opens with Miracles, continues with Miracles, and concludes with Miracles, i.e., *"proclaims them into the eternal future."*

THE GREAT MIRACLE

Several things are said in these amazing Passages.

A. First of all, Joshua asked of the Lord a Miracle, in fact, a Miracle of unprecedented proportions.

B. Considering that this Miracle involved the rotation of the Earth, inasmuch as it evidently stopped on its axis, this Miracle could very well have been even greater than the opening of the Red Sea, in other words, the greatest Miracle performed by the Lord for Israel.

C. The Scripture says, *"There was no day like that before it or after it."*

D. As well, it is said that the Lord hearkened that day to a man, to Joshua, as He had never hearkened to a man previously.

E. *"The LORD fought for Israel."* Most definitely He did.

(15) "AND JOSHUA RETURNED, AND ALL ISRAEL WITH HIM, UNTO THE CAMP TO GILGAL.

(16) "BUT THESE FIVE KINGS FLED, AND HID THEMSELVES IN A CAVE AT MAKKEDAH.

(17) "AND IT WAS TOLD JOSHUA, SAYING, THE FIVE KINGS ARE FOUND HID IN A CAVE AT MAKKEDAH.

(18) "AND JOSHUA SAID, ROLL GREAT STONES UPON THE MOUTH OF THE CAVE, AND SET MEN BY IT FOR TO KEEP THEM:

(19) "AND STAY YE NOT, BUT PURSUE AFTER YOUR ENEMIES, AND SMITE THE HINDMOST OF THEM; SUFFER THEM NOT TO ENTER INTO THEIR CITIES: FOR THE LORD YOUR GOD HAS DELIVERED THEM INTO YOUR HAND.

(20) "AND IT CAME TO PASS, WHEN JOSHUA AND THE CHILDREN OF ISRAEL HAD MADE AN END OF SLAYING THEM WITH A VERY GREAT SLAUGHTER, TILL THEY WERE CONSUMED, THAT THE REST WHICH REMAINED OF THEM ENTERED INTO FENCED CITIES.

(21) "AND ALL THE PEOPLE RETURNED TO THE CAMP TO JOSHUA AT MAKKEDAH IN PEACE: NONE MOVED HIS TONGUE AGAINST ANY OF THE CHILDREN OF ISRAEL.

(22) "THEN SAID JOSHUA, OPEN THE MOUTH OF THE CAVE, AND BRING OUT THOSE FIVE KINGS UNTO ME OUT OF THE CAVE.

(23) "AND THEY DID SO, AND BROUGHT FORTH THOSE FIVE KINGS UNTO HIM OUT OF THE CAVE, THE KING OF JERUSALEM, THE KING OF HEBRON, THE KING OF JARMUTH, THE KING OF LACHISH, AND THE KING OF EGLON.

(24) "AND IT CAME TO PASS, WHEN THEY BROUGHT OUT THOSE KINGS UNTO JOSHUA, THAT JOSHUA CALLED FOR ALL THE MEN OF ISRAEL, AND SAID UNTO THE CAPTAINS OF THE MEN OF WAR WHICH WENT WITH HIM, COME NEAR, PUT YOUR FEET UPON THE NECKS OF THESE KINGS. AND THEY CAME NEAR, AND PUT THEIR FEET UPON THE NECKS OF THEM.

(25) "AND JOSHUA SAID UNTO THEM, FEAR NOT, NOR BE DISMAYED, BE STRONG AND OF A GOOD COURAGE: FOR THUS SHALL THE LORD DO TO ALL YOUR ENEMIES AGAINST WHOM YOU FIGHT.

(26) "AND AFTERWARD JOSHUA SMOTE THEM, AND SLEW THEM, AND HANGED THEM ON FIVE TREES: AND THEY WERE HANGING UPON THE TREES UNTIL THE EVENING.

(27) "AND IT CAME TO PASS AT THE TIME OF THE GOING DOWN OF THE SUN, THAT JOSHUA COMMANDED, AND THEY TOOK THEM DOWN OFF THE TREES, AND CAST THEM INTO THE CAVE WHEREIN THEY HAD BEEN HID, AND LAID GREAT STONES IN THE CAVE'S MOUTH, WHICH REMAIN UNTIL THIS VERY DAY."

The composition is:

1. Verse 19 proclaims the fact that they were not to be diverted from the purpose of annihilating the enemy by the important news that the heads of the confederacy were in their hands.

2. The Twenty-fourth Verse tells us that there is but one way to deal with sin, and that is to place the triumphant foot of Faith upon its neck, and put it to death. It is impossible to improve sin, just as, in the Judgment of God, it was impossible for Israel to improve these five kings. Man, in his folly, tries to improve what is opposed to God; but the failure of his efforts ever reveals its foolishness. There is no such thing as moral evolution. The Cross of Christ is the only answer for sin, and to be sure, sin is the problem.

3. The great promise of Verse 25, and even greater, is available to us as well. Paul said, *"Sin* (the sin nature) *shall not have dominion over you"* (Rom. 6:14); however, there is only one way that such victory can be assured.

The Believer must understand that all things come to us from God by the Person of Christ with the Means being the Cross (Rom. 6:13-14). The Holy Spirit, Who Alone can bring about these victories, and Who works exclusively within the perimeters of the Finished Work of Christ, will then do great and mighty things for us (Rom. 8:1-2, 11).

4. As stated, victory over sin, of which all of this is a type, can only come about by it being utterly destroyed within our lives. This was all made possible at the Cross, and only

at the Cross. There sin was dealt with, as it regards its cause and its effect (Jn. 1:29).

TOTAL VICTORY OVER THE ENEMY

While, of course, all of this portrayed the great victory given to Israel by the Lord, still, the example holds a great lesson for us in our present life and living for the Lord.

Joshua did not allow any of the enemy to remain alive, at least as it regarded the bulk of their armies. This included the kings as well.

As it regards these kings, when they were brought before Joshua, he made them prostrate themselves on the ground, that is, if they didn't do it willingly, and then told his Captains to *"put your feet upon the necks of these kings."* This speaks of total and complete victory on the part of Israel.

As well, this proclaims how we are presently to conquer sin within our lives. In other words, it is not to conquer us, we are to conquer it. We can do such, however, only by functioning in the manner laid out by the Lord, which is Faith in Christ and the Cross, and that consistently (Rom. 6:1-14; 8:1-2, 11; I Cor. 1:17-18, 21, 23; 2:2; Gal., Chpt. 5; 6:14; Col. 2:14-15).

After these enemies were killed, they then *"hanged them on five trees."* When evening came, however, according to the Law of Moses, they were taken down with their bodies entombed in a nearby cave (Deut. 21:22-23).

(28) "AND THAT DAY JOSHUA TOOK MAKKEDAH, AND SMOTE IT WITH THE EDGE OF THE SWORD, AND THE KING THEREOF HE UTTERLY DESTROYED, THEM, AND ALL THE SOULS WHO WERE THEREIN; HE LET NONE REMAIN: AND HE DID TO THE KING OF MAKKEDAH AS HE DID UNTO THE KING OF JERICHO.

(29) "THEN JOSHUA PASSED FROM MAKKEDAH, AND ALL ISRAEL WITH HIM, AND TO LIBNAH, AND FOUGHT AGAINST LIBNAH:

(30) "AND THE LORD DELIVERED IT ALSO, AND THE KING THEREOF, INTO THE HAND OF ISRAEL; AND HE SMOTE IT WITH THE EDGE OF THE SWORD, AND ALL THE SOULS WHO WERE THEREIN; HE LET NONE REMAIN IN IT; BUT DID UNTO THE KING THEREOF AS HE DID

UNTO THE KING OF JERICHO.

(31) "AND JOSHUA PASSED FROM LIBNAH, AND ALL ISRAEL WITH HIM, UNTO LACHISH, AND ENCAMPED AGAINST IT, AND FOUGHT AGAINST IT:

(32) "AND THE LORD DELIVERED LACHISH INTO THE HAND OF ISRAEL, WHICH TOOK IT ON THE SECOND DAY, AND SMOTE IT WITH THE EDGE OF THE SWORD, AND ALL THE SOULS WHO WERE THEREIN, ACCORDING TO ALL THAT HE HAD DONE TO LIBNAH.

(33) "THEN HORAM KING OF GEZER CAME UP TO HELP LACHISH; AND JOSHUA SMOTE HIM AND HIS PEOPLE, UNTIL HE HAD LEFT HIM NONE REMAINING.

(34) "AND FROM LACHISH JOSHUA PASSED UNTO EGLON, AND ALL ISRAEL WITH HIM; AND THEY ENCAMPED AGAINST IT, AND FOUGHT AGAINST IT:

(35) "AND THEY TOOK IT ON THAT DAY, AND SMOTE IT WITH THE EDGE OF THE SWORD, AND ALL THE SOULS WHO WERE THEREIN HE UTTERLY DESTROYED THAT DAY, ACCORDING TO ALL THAT HE HAD DONE TO LACHISH.

(36) "AND JOSHUA WENT UP FROM EGLON, AND ALL ISRAEL WITH HIM, UNTO HEBRON; AND THEY FOUGHT AGAINST IT:

(37) "AND THEY TOOK IT, AND SMOTE IT WITH THE EDGE OF THE SWORD, AND THE KING THEREOF, AND ALL THE CITIES THEREOF, AND ALL THE SOULS WHO WERE THEREIN; HE LEFT NONE REMAINING, ACCORDING TO ALL THAT HE HAD DONE TO EGLON; BUT DESTROYED IT UTTERLY, AND ALL THE SOULS WHO WERE THEREIN.

(38) "AND JOSHUA RETURNED, AND ALL ISRAEL WITH HIM, TO DEBIR; AND FOUGHT AGAINST IT:

(39) "AND HE TOOK IT, AND THE KING THEREOF, AND ALL THE CITIES THEREOF; AND THEY SMOTE THEM WITH THE EDGE OF THE SWORD, AND UTTERLY DESTROYED ALL THE SOULS WHO WERE THEREIN; HE LEFT NONE REMAINING: AS HE HAD DONE TO HEBRON, SO HE DID TO DEBIR, AND TO THE KING THEREOF; AS HE HAD DONE ALSO TO LIBNAH, AND TO HER KING.

(40) "SO JOSHUA SMOTE ALL THE COUNTRY OF THE HILLS, AND OF THE SOUTH, AND OF THE VALE, AND OF THE SPRINGS, AND ALL THEIR KINGS: HE LEFT NONE REMAINING, BUT UTTERLY DESTROYED ALL WHO BREATHED, AS THE LORD GOD OF ISRAEL COMMANDED.

(41) "AND JOSHUA SMOTE THEM FROM KADESH-BARNEA EVEN UNTO GAZA, AND ALL THE COUNTRY OF GOSHEN, EVEN UNTO GIBEON.

(42) "AND ALL THESE KINGS AND THEIR LAND DID JOSHUA TAKE AT ONE TIME, BECAUSE THE LORD GOD OF ISRAEL FOUGHT FOR ISRAEL.

(43) "AND JOSHUA RETURNED, AND ALL ISRAEL WITH HIM, UNTO THE CAMP TO GILGAL."

The synopsis is:

1. If it is to be noticed, it was not the stratagem of Israel that won these victories, but rather the Lord, Who told Joshua what to do. If we seek the Face of the Lord, as we should, as well, He will give us guidance and direction. Jesus said so (Jn. 16:13-15).

2. No sin of any nature is to be left remaining in our lives. But let us say it again, because it is so very, very important:

Victory for the Child of God can be obtained only by looking exclusively to Christ, understanding that everything He gives us is by the Means of the Cross; consequently, the Cross must ever be the Object of our Faith. Then the Holy Spirit will gloriously work on our behalf (Rom. 8:1-2, 11).

Before the conflict ever began, a preincarnate appearance of Christ to Joshua was afforded the warrior, with the Scripture referring to Him as *"The Captain of the LORD's Host"* (Josh. 5:13-15). This means that Christ was the secret of all Victory, as Christ is always the secret of all Victory.

WE ARE ABLE TO GO UP AND TAKE THE COUNTRY

Over and over again in the balance of the Tenth Chapter, concerning victory at particular cities, the words are used, *"He utterly destroyed them"* (Vs. 28).

The Thirtieth Verse says, *"He let none remain in it."*

Verse Thirty-three says, *"Until he had left

him none remaining."*

Verse Thirty-five, *"He utterly destroyed that day, according to all."*

And finally, Verse Thirty-seven says, *"He left none remaining."*

Over and over again throughout the Chapter these words are used. To be sure, the Holy Spirit was not merely being repetitive to fill up space. The lesson should be very obvious.

Every vestige of envy, jealousy, pride, lust, immorality, uncontrollable temper, and above all, all self-will must be rooted out of the life of the Child of God. There must be *"None remaining."* The Holy Spirit is insistent in this, *"None remaining."* That which remains is forever a snare to us. Ultimately, it will rise up and destroy us. Let us say it again, *"There must be none remaining."*

There are those faint of heart who believe that it is impossible to overcome all the efforts of darkness. It is not impossible because the Forty-second Verse says, *"The LORD God of Israel fought for Israel."*

We cannot hope to root out these enemies ourselves. Flesh cannot defeat flesh; sickness cannot heal sickness; man cannot cure man. The secret is found in the Forty-third Verse, *"And Joshua returned, and all Israel with him, unto the camp to Gilgal."* What is the secret?

GILGAL

Gilgal was the place of circumcision, which stood for separation. It meant victory over the flesh and over self-will. It must be completely understood that when all was destroyed in these cities, not only was all the bad destroyed, but all the good was destroyed as well.

Likewise, the Christian knows that the evil must be destroyed, but at the same time, finds it very difficult to destroy the good. Our good works, man-made consecration, and extreme religiosity all may seem good, but they must be destroyed along with that which is evil, or else the evil will come back to haunt us, because man's self-will, which stems from the flesh, always leads to the works of the flesh as is recorded in the Epistle of Paul to the Galatians (Gal. 5:19-21).

As we keep saying over and over, the Cross

is the answer to all sin, the flesh, the good, the bad, and the ugly, so to speak! As well, it is the only answer.

CHAPTER 11

(1) "AND IT CAME TO PASS, WHEN JABIN KING OF HAZOR HAD HEARD THOSE THINGS, THAT HE SENT TO JOBAB KING OF MADON, AND TO THE KING OF SHIMRON, AND TO THE KING OF ACHSHAPH,

(2) "AND TO THE KINGS WHO WERE ON THE NORTH OF THE MOUNTAINS, AND OF THE PLAINS SOUTH OF CHINNEROTH, AND IN THE VALLEY, AND IN THE BORDERS OF DOR ON THE WEST,

(3) "AND TO THE CANAANITE ON THE EAST AND ON THE WEST, AND TO THE AMORITE, AND THE HITTITE, AND THE PERIZZITE, AND THE JEBUSITE IN THE MOUNTAINS, AND TO THE HIVITE UNDER HERMON IN THE LAND OF MIZPEH.

(4) "AND THEY WENT OUT, THEY AND ALL THEIR HOST WITH THEM, MUCH PEOPLE, EVEN AS THE SAND THAT IS UPON THE SEA SHORE IN MULTITUDE, WITH HORSES AND CHARIOTS VERY MANY.

(5) "AND WHEN ALL THESE KINGS WERE MET TOGETHER, THEY CAME AND PITCHED TOGETHER AT THE WATERS OF MEROM, TO FIGHT AGAINST ISRAEL.

(6) "AND THE LORD SAID UNTO JOSHUA, BE NOT AFRAID BECAUSE OF THEM: FOR TOMORROW ABOUT THIS TIME WILL I DELIVER THEM UP ALL SLAIN BEFORE ISRAEL: YOU SHALL HOUGH THEIR HORSES, AND BURN THEIR CHARIOTS WITH FIRE.

(7) "SO JOSHUA CAME, AND ALL THE PEOPLE OF WAR WITH HIM, AGAINST THEM BY THE WATERS OF MEROM SUDDENLY; AND THEY FELL UPON THEM.

(8) "AND THE LORD DELIVERED THEM INTO THE HAND OF ISRAEL, WHO SMOTE THEM, AND CHASED THEM UNTO GREAT ZIDON, AND UNTO MISREPHOTHMAIM, AND UNTO THE VALLEY OF MIZPEH EASTWARD; AND THEY SMOTE THEM, UNTIL THEY LEFT THEM NONE REMAINING.

(9) "AND JOSHUA DID UNTO THEM AS THE LORD BADE HIM: HE HOUGHED THEIR HORSES, AND BURNT THEIR CHARIOTS WITH FIRE.

(10) "AND JOSHUA AT THAT TIME TURNED BACK, AND TOOK HAZOR, AND SMOTE THE KING THEREOF WITH THE SWORD: FOR HAZOR BEFORETIME WAS THE HEAD OF ALL THOSE KINGDOMS.

(11) "AND THEY SMOTE ALL THE SOULS WHO WERE THEREIN WITH THE EDGE OF THE SWORD, UTTERLY DESTROYING THEM: THERE WAS NOT ANY LEFT TO BREATHE: AND HE BURNT HAZOR WITH FIRE."

The overview is:

1. Hazor was about 90 miles due north of Gilgal, meaning it was about 10 miles north of the Sea of Galilee.

2. The hamstringing of the horses made them unfit for war, but not for agriculture.

3. Israel had no horses or chariots, but yet they defeated these enemies, who were far, far superior to them regarding military warfare; Israel defeated them, because the Lord was with Israel.

4. Williams says, *"The frequent mention of Hazor (Vss. 1, 10-11, 13) introduces a great principle. Hazor was the center of power of that part of the world. Natural wisdom would propose to make it the seat of government, so that it should be that for God, which before it had been for the world. But God will in no wise allow the world's seat of power to become that of His People. His People were to depend exclusively on Him, and to dwell with Him at Gilgal. Accordingly, Hazor is totally destroyed. Not a vestige of its former power must remain to compete with Gilgal. The center and source of power must be all Divine."*[1]

5. The Fire of the Spirit as recorded in Verse 11, will destroy every vestige of the world within our lives, if we will only look to Christ and the Cross (Mat. 3:11).

VICTORY OVER NORTHERN CANAAN

Chapter 11 is the continued saga of conquest. All the land must be eradicated of the enemy. All must be subdued, for this land is God's Land; likewise, since Jesus has come into the heart of the Child of God, all of the enemy must be eradicated. Every semblance of the world, the flesh, and the Devil must be put away. Now the house is to become a Temple of the Holy Spirit (I Cor. 3:16).

The conflict in the northern part of the Holy Land once again sees a confederation of the enemy against Joshua. The Fourth Verse says, *"Even as the sand that is upon the sea shore in multitude, with horses and chariots very many."* Satan's efforts against us are always accompanied by a multitude. He comes *"As a roaring lion."* If one does not depend totally upon the Lord Jesus Christ, our Heavenly Joshua, and what He did for us at the Cross of Calvary, then fear will overcome the individual.

FEAR NOT

The Sixth Verse says, *"And the LORD said unto Joshua, Be not afraid because of them."*

Over and over again the Lord keeps saying throughout the entirety of the Bible, *"Fear not,"* or statements such as *"Be not afraid of them."*

Fear is, no doubt, one of the greatest weapons that Satan has and one of the Christian's greatest problems. We look at circumstances, and then we begin to fear. To be frank, fear is a spirit. Paul said, *"For God has not given us the spirit of fear . . ."* (II Tim. 1:7). Please allow me to speak more clearly:

Every single Christian has been attacked numerous times by *"A spirit of fear."* Please believe me, this is far more than just a negative thought. It is actually a spirit of darkness sent by one of the *"principalities"* or *"powers,"* or one of the *"rulers of the darkness of this world,"* or maybe even by *"spiritual wickedness in high places"* (Eph. 6:12).

We have been taught that a negative confession would occasion such. It certainly can play a part in it; however, most of the time the negative confession comes about because of the *"spirit of fear,"* and not the cause of such. To be sure, this is a spirit that can definitely be felt by the Child of God. During such times, everything looks hopeless. The odds against us look absolutely overwhelming. Every problem seems to be bigger than life all because of a *"spirit of fear."*

Our defense against such is as follows:

A. The Word of God (Jn. 1:1-3);

B. The Whole Armour of God (Eph., Chpt. 6);

C. The Name of Jesus (Mk., Chpt. 16);

D. The Cross of Christ (Rom. 6:1-14); and,

E. The Holy Spirit (Rom. 8:1-2, 11).

These are our weapons. So the Lord would say to Joshua, *"Be not afraid."*

When we study this Book of Joshua, we make a mistake if we relegate it totally and solely to Israel and her ridding all enemies out of the Holy Land. All of this is meant to portray to us as well, even at this present time, the manner in which victory can be ours. In fact, the only manner in which victory can be ours.

THE SPIRITUAL

While everything as it pertains to the Child of God is Spiritual, and flows over into other aspects of our life and living, such as the physical, the financial, etc., still, Israel's conflict was more so in the physical than anything else. Ours now, even though flowing over into every aspect of our life and living, is mostly Spiritual. At any rate, the answer is the same. It does not change.

In all things, we must follow the Word of the Lord. Then and only then will victory be ours, whether Israel of old, or whether of Believers at the present time.

(12) "AND ALL THE CITIES OF THOSE KINGS, AND ALL THE KINGS OF THEM, DID JOSHUA TAKE, AND SMOTE THEM WITH THE EDGE OF THE SWORD, AND HE UTTERLY DESTROYED THEM, AS MOSES THE SERVANT OF THE LORD COMMANDED.

(13) "BUT AS FOR THE CITIES THAT STOOD STILL IN THEIR STRENGTH, ISRAEL BURNED NONE OF THEM, SAVE HAZOR ONLY; THAT DID JOSHUA BURN.

(14) "AND ALL THE SPOIL OF THESE CITIES, AND THE CATTLE, THE CHILDREN OF ISRAEL TOOK FOR A PREY TO THEMSELVES; BUT EVERY MAN THEY SMOTE WITH THE EDGE OF THE SWORD, UNTIL THEY HAD DESTROYED THEM, NEITHER LEFT THEY ANY TO BREATHE.

(15) "AS THE LORD COMMANDED MOSES HIS SERVANT, SO DID MOSES

COMMAND JOSHUA, AND SO DID JOSHUA; HE LEFT NOTHING UNDONE OF ALL THAT THE LORD COMMANDED MOSES.

(16) "SO JOSHUA TOOK ALL THAT LAND, THE HILLS, AND ALL THE SOUTH COUNTRY, AND ALL THE LAND OF GOSHEN, AND THE VALLEY, AND THE PLAIN, AND THE MOUNTAIN OF ISRAEL, AND THE VALLEY OF THE SAME;

(17) "EVEN FROM THE MOUNT HALAK, THAT GOES UP TO SEIR, EVEN UNTO BAAL-GAD IN THE VALLEY OF LEBANON UNDER MOUNT HERMON: AND ALL THEIR KINGS HE TOOK, AND SMOTE THEM, AND SLEW THEM.

(18) "JOSHUA MADE WAR A LONG TIME WITH ALL THOSE KINGS.

(19) "THERE WAS NOT A CITY THAT MADE PEACE WITH THE CHILDREN OF ISRAEL, SAVE THE HIVITES THE INHABITANTS OF GIBEON: ALL OTHER THEY TOOK IN BATTLE.

(20) "FOR IT WAS OF THE LORD TO HARDEN THEIR HEARTS, THAT THEY SHOULD COME AGAINST ISRAEL IN BATTLE, THAT HE MIGHT DESTROY THEM UTTERLY, AND THAT THEY MIGHT HAVE NO FAVOUR, BUT THAT HE MIGHT DESTROY THEM, AS THE LORD COMMANDED MOSES.

(21) "AND AT THAT TIME CAME JOSHUA, AND CUT OFF THE ANAKIMS FROM THE MOUNTAINS, FROM HEBRON, FROM DEBIR, FROM ANAB, AND FROM ALL THE MOUNTAINS OF JUDAH, AND FROM ALL THE MOUNTAINS OF ISRAEL: JOSHUA DESTROYED THEM UTTERLY WITH THEIR CITIES.

(22) "THERE WAS NONE OF THE ANAKIMS LEFT IN THE LAND OF THE CHILDREN OF ISRAEL: ONLY IN GAZA, IN GATH, AND IN ASHDOD, THERE REMAINED.

(23) "SO JOSHUA TOOK THE WHOLE LAND, ACCORDING TO ALL THAT THE LORD SAID UNTO MOSES; AND JOSHUA GAVE IT FOR AN INHERITANCE UNTO ISRAEL ACCORDING TO THEIR DIVISIONS BY THEIR TRIBES. AND THE LAND RESTED FROM WAR."

The diagram is:

1. Regarding Verse 13, it should have been translated, *"But as for the cities that stood*

NOTES

still in their strength, Israel burned none of them, save Hazor only."

2. The Fifteenth Verse proclaims the fact that *"obedience to the Lord"* was the secret of Joshua's strength.

3. All of this is symbolic of the victories we must win in our Christian experience. But let the Reader understand, God does not give victory to sinful men, but only to His Son, the Lord Jesus Christ, which was paid for at the Cross. The Believer, properly in Christ, can have this victory, but only as we are properly in Christ, which can only be by virtue of the Cross and our Faith in that Finished Work (Jn. 14:20).

4. Those spoken of in Verse 22 were the giants, a product of the union of fallen angels and women (Gen. 6:4). The offspring of those who remained in Gaza, etc., which would later be the country of the Philistines would be destroyed many years later by David. Goliath was one of them (I Sam., Chpt. 17). Why the Lord didn't have Joshua to defeat these as well, we aren't told; however, we do know that everything the Lord does is for purpose and reason. In other words, everything that pertains to His Children is a test. How will we act? How will we react?

5. It is believed that the conquest of Canaan took possibly from five to seven years.

WARFARE FOR THE LORD

Once again we look at the command of the Lord that Joshua should kill all, both young and old, both men and women, and even little children in these particular cities. Many blanch at this, not understanding God's reasons.

These people had become so unspeakably vile, so unspeakably evil, that even the children were grossly infected, which means that the Lord had to perform a surgical procedure, so to speak, to remove these individuals, in order that the body politic may be spared. It is the same as a cancer in a physical body. The cancer must be removed, even though it causes the loss of blood and much pain and suffering. Still, if the physical body is to be saved, the surgical procedure must be carried out. So it was with those heathen tribes in the land of Canaan.

If at any time, any of these Tribes had repented, and thereby turned to Jehovah, even as did, it seems, the Gibeonites, they would have been spared. The Lord will never turn anyone away, who earnestly and sincerely comes to Him. But they did not do that, insisting rather upon destroying God's People; therefore, they had to be taken out. In fact, the Lord would have been cruel not to have done so.

SIN IS CONTAGIOUS

Sin is far worse than most Believers know or understand. In fact, it seeks to drag the person or the nation down, and it actually knows no end to the depths of its destruction. To try to explain that, one could only proclaim the fact of Hell, where all Christ rejecters will go.

That's the reason that sin cannot be allowed to continue in the life of the Believer. The Lord has given Believers the means by which victory; even total victory can be ours. The problem is, far too many Believers simply don't believe. And what do I mean by that?

I mean that the majority of those who refer to themselves as *"Christians,"* simply do not believe that what Jesus did at Calvary's Cross answered and answers every single sin, transgression, iniquity, bondage, and evil passion. It excluded none, including all.

How do I know that the majority of Christendom rejects the Cross?

I know it from personal experience.

When we go into a community with Son-Life Radio, beaming and broadcasting the Gospel of *"Jesus Christ and Him Crucified"* some twenty-four hours a day, seven days a week, the opportunity is laid before every Believer as it regards the veracity of the Cross of Christ. A few receive and accept, while most don't.

Why?

UNBELIEF!

The major problem is unbelief. Most simply do not believe that what Jesus did at the Cross answers and meets every need.

The truth is, the answer to the sin problem and in every capacity is the Cross, and the only answer is the Cross!

Why is that so hard to believe? To accept?

To understand?

The truth is, it's not hard to understand. In fact, the Holy Spirit refers to the Message of the Cross as the *"simplicity that is in Christ"* (II Cor. 11:3).

IS THE REASON THEOLOGICAL OR MORAL?

The reason is moral!

If the reason for rejecting the Cross was theological, that would mean that it's too difficult to understand; however, as I have just quoted the Word of God, the Message of the Cross is not difficult to understand, in fact, even a child can understand it. So, the problem is not theological but rather moral.

What do we mean by the problem being moral?

We mean that the reason that the Cross is rejected, is on moral grounds. In other words, it is a matter of pride, self-will, self-righteousness, etc.

People are like sheep the Bible tells us. They follow shepherds. If those shepherds are corrupt, thereby going in the wrong direction of false doctrine, most sheep regrettably, will continue to follow. The trouble is, most of those who are referred to as *"religious leaders,"* are, in fact, *"wolves in sheep's clothing."* Listen to what our Lord said!

WOLVES IN SHEEP'S CLOTHING

I quote from THE EXPOSITOR'S STUDY BIBLE.

"Beware of false prophets, which come to you in sheep's clothing, but inwardly they are ravening wolves ('beware of false prophets' is said in the sternest of measures! there will be and are false prophets, and are some of Satan's greatest weapons).

"You shall know them by their fruits (this is the test as given by Christ as it regards identification of false prophets and false apostles). *Do men gather grapes of thorns, or figs of thistles?* (It is impossible for false doctrine, generated by false prophets, to bring forth good fruit.)

"Even so every good tree brings forth good fruit; but a corrupt tree brings forth evil fruit (the good fruit is Christlikeness, while the evil fruit is self-likeness).

"A good tree cannot bring forth evil fruit,

neither can a corrupt tree bring forth good fruit (the *'good tree'* is the Cross, while the *'corrupt tree'* pertains to all of that which is other than the Cross).

"Every tree that brings not forth good fruit is hewn down, and cast into the fire (Judgment will ultimately come on all so-called gospel, other than the Cross [Rom. 1:18]).

"Wherefore by their fruits you shall know them (the acid test).

Our Lord then went on to say: *"Not everyone who says unto Me, Lord, Lord, shall enter into the Kingdom of Heaven* (the repetition of the word *'Lord'* expresses astonishment, as if to say: *'Are we to be disowned?'*); *but he who does the Will of My Father which is in Heaven* (what is the Will of the Father? Verse 24 tells us).

"Many will say to Me in that day, Lord, Lord, have we not prophesied in Your Name? And in Your Name have cast out devils? and in Your Name done many wonderful works? (These things are not the criteria, but rather Faith in Christ and what Christ has done for us at the Cross [Eph. 2:8-9, 13-18]. The Word of God Alone is to be the judge of doctrine.)

"And then will I profess unto them, I never knew you (again we say, the criteria alone is Christ and Him Crucified [I Cor. 1:23]): *depart from Me, you who work iniquity* (we have access to God only through Christ, and access to Christ only through the Cross, and access to the Cross only through a denial of self [Lk. 9:23]; any other message is judged by God as *'iniquity,'* and cannot be a part of Christ [I Cor. 1:17])*" (Mat. 7:15-23).

The last Verse of the Eleventh Chapter says, *"So Joshua took the whole land."* This is exactly what the Lord intends as it regards all that we are supposed to have in Christ and, in fact, all for which Christ paid such a price.

CHAPTER 12

(1) "NOW THESE ARE THE KINGS OF THE LAND, WHICH THE CHILDREN OF ISRAEL SMOTE, AND POSSESSED THEIR LAND ON THE OTHER SIDE JORDAN TOWARD THE RISING OF THE SUN, FROM

THE RIVER ARNON UNTO MOUNT HERMON, AND ALL THE PLAIN ON THE EAST:

(2) "SIHON KING OF THE AMORITES, WHO DWELT IN HESHBON, AND RULED FROM AROER, WHICH IS UPON THE BANK OF THE RIVER ARNON, AND FROM THE MIDDLE OF THE RIVER, AND FROM HALF GILEAD, EVEN UNTO THE RIVER JABBOK, WHICH IS THE BORDER OF THE CHILDREN OF AMMON;

(3) "AND FROM THE PLAIN TO THE SEA OF CHINEROTH ON THE EAST, AND UNTO THE SEA OF THE PLAIN, EVEN THE SALT SEA ON THE EAST, THE WAY TO BETH-JESHIMOTH; AND FROM THE SOUTH, UNDER ASHDOTH-PISGAH:

(4) "AND THE COAST OF OG KING OF BASHAN, WHICH WAS OF THE REMNANT OF THE GIANTS, WHO DWELT AT ASHTAROTH AND AT EDREI,

(5) "AND REIGNED IN MOUNT HERMON, AND IN SALCAH, AND IN ALL BASHAN, UNTO THE BORDER OF THE GESHURITES AND THE MAACHATHITES, AND HALF GILEAD, THE BORDER OF SIHON KING OF HESHBON.

(6) "THEM DID MOSES THE SERVANT OF THE LORD AND THE CHILDREN OF ISRAEL SMITE: AND MOSES THE SERVANT OF THE LORD GAVE IT FOR A POSSESSION UNTO THE REUBENITES, AND THE GADITES, AND THE HALF TRIBE OF MANASSEH."

The exegesis is:

1. Williams says, *"As we study this Chapter, we will find where there was faithfulness, there was rest; but where Israel was disobedient, thereby not destroying all which they were commanded to destroy, there was compromise and defeat; this is an ever-present principle in the experience of the Believer."*[1]

2. To a mind which is governed by the spirit of this world, Chapters in the Bible which contain lists of names are uninteresting, but not so to those who sit where Mary sat, when she hungrily listened to Christ (Lk. 10:38-42); we hang with appetite over every word that the Holy Spirit has written; consequently, to such Believers the list of victories in this Chapter is full of interest, because they mirror our own victories.

3. The *"Sea of Chinneroth"* was the *"Sea of Galilee."*

CONQUESTS

At first glance, this Chapter seems to be uninteresting; however, to the Holy Spirit and to those who know and understand this great Christian life, this Chapter is freighted with victory. The list of these kings and their cities defeated by the people of God represents a tremendous victory in the halls of Heaven. They are typical of our victories in the Spirit.

Verse 1 says, *"Now these are the kings of the land, which the Children of Israel smote."* And then it says, *"and possessed their land."*

The inheritance that God has given us as Christians still must be taken. The only way we can possess it is to drive out the enemies (jealousy, envy, malice, pride, lust, etc.). It is a Promised Land; it is given to us by God. It is our inheritance, but at the same time, we have to take it by force in Faith.

Whatever area of Spiritual Land that pride, jealousy, greed, or self-will, is occupying cannot be ours. The question must be asked, *"How many of us have actually possessed all the land?"*

HOW DO WE POSSESS OUR INHERITANCE?

As we have said repeatedly in this Volume, and will continue to say, there is only one way that we can have all that for which Jesus paid such a price.

Considering the price that He paid, which was Calvary's Cross, doesn't it stand to reason that He wants us to have all for which He paid this great price? I think so!

So how do we obtain this great Blessing?

We obtain it in one way, and only in one way. It is all done by Faith. Paul said:

"Therefore being Justified by Faith (this is the only way one can be justified; refers to Faith in Christ and what He did at the Cross), *we have peace with God* (justifying peace) *through our Lord Jesus Christ* (what He did at the Cross):

"By Whom also we have access by Faith into this Grace (we have access to the Goodness of God by Faith in Christ) *wherein we stand* (wherein alone we can stand), *and*

rejoice in hope (a hope that is guaranteed) *of the Glory of God* (our Faith in Christ always brings Glory to God; anything else brings glory to self, which God can never accept)" (Rom. 5:1-2).

Paul then said, *"For by Grace* (the Goodness of God) *are you Saved through Faith* (Faith in Christ, with the Cross ever as it's Object)*; and that not of yourselves* (none of this is of us, but all is of Him)*: it is the Gift of God* (anytime the word *'Gift'* is used, God is speaking of His Son and His Substitutionary Work on the Cross, which makes all of this possible)*:*

"Not of works (man cannot merit Salvation, irrespective what he does), *lest any man should boast* (boast in his own ability and strength; we are allowed to boast only in the Cross [Gal. 6:14])" (Eph. 2:8-9).

However, and as stated, the Faith registered here must, and without exception, be in Christ and what He did at the Cross. That must ever be the Object of our Faith. This means that Christ must never be separated from the Cross, nor the Cross separated from Christ.

WHAT DO WE MEAN BY THE WORD *"CROSS"*?

Paul uses the word *"Cross"* somewhat as a synonym or even a metaphor.

The word *"synonym"* means, *"one of two or more words or expressions of the same language that have the same or nearly the same meaning and some or all senses."* It also means, *"a symbolic or figurative name."*

The word *"metaphor"* means, *"a figure of speech in which a word or phrase literally denoting one kind of object or idea is used in place of another to suggest a likeness or analogy between them."*

In other words, Paul used the word *"Cross"* to denote the entirety of the great Salvation/ Redemption Plan (I Cor. 1:17-18; 2:2; Gal. 6:14; Eph. 3:18). He wasn't speaking of a wooden beam, and neither was he trying to put Christ back on the Cross. Such an idea is ludicrous to say the least!

In actuality, he was and is speaking of the benefits of what Jesus did as it regards His Death, and what it accomplished. These are benefits which accrue from that great

Sacrifice, and which come to us in an unending stream, and can come to us only by that means. The truth is, the Story of the Bible, the entirety of the Bible, is the story of man's Fall (Gen., Chpt. 3), and the manner in which man was redeemed from that Fall, which is through Christ and the Cross, and which takes up the entirety of the balance of the Word of God. To promote something else as the answer, and we speak of anything other than the Cross of Christ, is to promote something which is not in the Bible.

If we are to possess all for which such a price was paid, we must do it God's Way, which is *"Jesus Christ and Him Crucified"* (I Cor. 1:23).

(7) "AND THESE ARE THE KINGS OF THE COUNTRY WHICH JOSHUA AND THE CHILDREN OF ISRAEL SMOTE ON THIS SIDE JORDAN ON THE WEST, FROM BAAL-GAD IN THE VALLEY OF LEBANON EVEN UNTO THE MOUNT HALAK, THAT GOES UP TO SEIR; WHICH JOSHUA GAVE UNTO THE TRIBES OF ISRAEL FOR A POSSESSION ACCORDING TO THEIR DIVISIONS;

(8) "IN THE MOUNTAINS, AND IN THE VALLEYS, AND IN THE PLAINS, AND IN THE SPRINGS, AND IN THE WILDERNESS, AND IN THE SOUTH COUNTRY; THE HITTITES, THE AMORITES, AND THE CANAANITES, THE PERIZZITES, THE HIVITES, AND THE JEBUSITES:

(9) "THE KING OF JERICHO, ONE; THE KING OF AI, WHICH IS BESIDE BETH-EL, ONE;

(10) "THE KING OF JERUSALEM, ONE; THE KING OF HEBRON, ONE;

(11) "THE KING OF JARMUTH, ONE; THE KING OF LACHISH, ONE;

(12) "THE KING OF EGLON, ONE; THE KING OF GEZER, ONE;

(13) " THE KING OF DEBIR, ONE; THE KING OF GEDER, ONE;

(14) "THE KING OF HORMAH, ONE; THE KING OF ARAD, ONE;

(15) "THE KING OF LIBNAH, ONE; THE KING OF ADULLAM, ONE;

(16) "THE KING OF MAKKEDAH, ONE; THE KING OF BETH-EL, ONE;

(17) "THE KING OF TAPPUAH, ONE; THE KING OF HEPHER, ONE;

NOTES

(18) "THE KING OF APHEK, ONE; THE KING OF LASHARON, ONE;

(19) "THE KING OF MADON, ONE; THE KING OF HAZOR, ONE;

(20) "THE KING OF SHIMRON-MERON, ONE; THE KING OF ACHSHAPH, ONE;

(21) "THE KING OF TAANACH, ONE; THE KING OF MEGIDDO, ONE;

(22) "THE KING OF KEDESH, ONE; THE KING OF JOKNEAM OF CARMEL, ONE;

(23) "THE KING OF DOR IN THE COAST OF DOR, ONE; THE KING OF THE NATIONS OF GILGAL, ONE;

(24) "THE KING OF TIZRAH; ONE: ALL THE KINGS THIRTY AND ONE."

The construction is:

1. On the Wilderness side of Jordan, Israel conquered only two kings, on the Canaan side thirty-one. The reason?

The Children of Israel departed from the Word of the Lord as it regards the initial settling of the eastern side. Had they followed the Lord's Directions minutely they, no doubt, could have conquered many more.

2. Those who are satisfied to stop short of claiming and enjoying all the exceeding great and precious Promises of the New Covenant win but few victories over sin and self and the world, but those who go on unto perfection (Heb. 6:1) win many victories.

3. It is encouraging and touching to read of these thirty-one victories so definitely and individually recorded. There were not just thirty victories, but thirty-one. Each victory was important in the Eye of God and precious to the Heart of God, however uninteresting and small they might appear to man. In fact, no victory over the enemy is small to God's Mind.

CHAPTER 13

(1) "NOW JOSHUA WAS OLD AND STRICKEN IN YEARS; AND THE LORD SAID UNTO HIM, YOU ARE OLD AND STRICKEN IN YEARS, AND THERE REMAINS YET VERY MUCH LAND TO BE POSSESSED.

(2) "THIS IS THE LAND THAT YET REMAINS: ALL THE BORDERS OF THE

PHILISTINES, AND ALL GESHURI,

(3) "FROM SIHOR, WHICH IS BEFORE EGYPT, EVEN UNTO THE BORDERS OF EKRON NORTHWARD, WHICH IS COUNTED TO THE CANAANITE: FIVE LORDS OF THE PHILISTINES; THE GAZA-THITES, AND THE ASHDOTHITES, THE ESHKALONITES, THE GITTITES, AND THE EKRONITES; ALSO THE AVITES:

(4) "FROM THE SOUTH, ALL THE LAND OF THE CANAANITES, AND THE MEARAH THAT IS BESIDE THE SIDONIANS, UNTO APHEK, TO THE BOR-DERS OF THE AMORITES:

(5) "AND THE LAND OF THE GIBLITES, AND ALL LEBANON, TOWARD THE SUNRISING, FROM BAAL-GAD UNDER MOUNT HERMON UNTO THE ENTERING INTO HAMATH.

(6) "ALL THE INHABITANTS OF THE HILL COUNTRY FROM LEBANON UNTO MISREPHOTH-MAIM, AND ALL THE SIDONIANS, THEM WILL I DRIVE OUT FROM BEFORE THE CHILDREN OF IS-RAEL: ONLY DIVIDE YOU IT BY LOT UNTO THE ISRAELITES FOR AN INHER-ITANCE, AS I HAVE COMMANDED YOU."

The structure is:

1. Joshua, at this time, was 101 years of age.

2. The account in this Chapter given to us concerning the possession of the land, or the lack thereof, points to every Believer that which the Lord has prepared for us; however, there are enemies between the Promise and the Possession. God has a Per-fect Plan for us, but, regrettably, so few of us press through to that Perfect Plan. We all too often stop short!

3. The words, *"There remains yet very much land to be possessed,"* should strike long, hard, and true to the heart of every Believer.

4. We must remember, it is the Holy Spirit Who is delineating these things.

MUCH LAND YET TO BE POSSESSED

We must remember that these words are the Words of the Holy Spirit. Verse 1 says, *"And the LORD said unto him;"* consequently, the words are extremely precious. As well, that which we glean should be powerful.

We learn from this that God had a Perfect Plan for Israel as He has for us today. There was absolutely nothing uncertain in His Ar-rangements, but, on the contrary, everything was orderly and well defined. As in the Twelfth Chapter, great victories were re-corded and itemized. Still, the Lord would gently remind them, *"There remains yet very much land to be possessed."*

So often the flesh becomes weary and stops short of God's best for our lives. That is the bane of Christendom. We never quite take all the land.

THE BORDERS

Verse 2 says, *"This is the land that yet remains."* This means that the Holy Spirit has perfectly drawn out *"the borders."* That is what He intends for us to take. If we come short of total victory, we fail the Lord, which means that we leave land unpossessed. How many enemies remain unsubdued in the hearts of Christians?

As previously stated, while all of this most definitely pertained to Israel and her posses-sion of the Promised Land, still, it is a blue-print for our own life and living. We must never forget that! As we've stated regarding notes on the last Chapter, there were *"thirty-one"* victories, not thirty, or twenty-eight, etc. This means that the Holy Spirit writes down all the victories as well as the defeats, and all are precious to Him, as all should be pre-cious to us.

The borders which the Lord has drawn off for you, present that which God intends for you to have, and for which our Lord has paid a frightful price.

As it regards taking the land, several things should be noted.

First of all, if at first we don't succeed, and most don't, we must not quit nor give up. We must keep trying, and I'm speaking of trying for victory in every respect. Re-member this:

If we fail it's not the Cross which has failed, but rather us. In some way, it's always our Faith. So if we stumble on this road of pos-sessing the land, we must get up, spiritu-ally speaking, dust ourselves off, and con-tinue on toward total and complete victory. If we won't quit, this victory will be ours and in totality.

Thank the Lord that our Heavenly Father does not lose patience with us. He bears long and hard with us, for He has purchased us at great price. This means that all of Heaven is pulling for our victory, and total Victory at that. In fact, and I think I can say without fear of contradiction, that there is a great host in Heaven who is watching our progress, or the lack thereof. So much is at stake, far more than we could ever even begin to comprehend.

Keep your eye on Christ and what He has done for you at the Cross. Never allow your Faith to be moved from that great Sacrifice, and you will find the Holy Spirit, Who Alone can give us what we need and make of us what we ought to be, working mightily on our behalf (Rom. 6:1-14; 8:1-2, 11).

OLD AND STRICKEN IN YEARS

This First Verse, *"Now Joshua was old and stricken in years; and the Lord said unto him, You are old and stricken in years, and there remains yet very much land to be possessed,"* is very dear to me personally.

As I dictate these notes I was seventy-one years old March 15, 2006. As the sands of time have taken their toll, I hear the voice of my Master saying, even as He said to Joshua so long ago, *"You are old and stricken in years . . ."* this means that despite Joshua's age, the Lord still expected of him that the balance of the land would be possessed. At the same time, this means that the Lord would enable him, despite his age, to carry out this task.

As Joshua of old, despite my age, I do not feel that what God has called me to do has yet been accomplished. Likewise, as He helped the great warrior of old, I believe that He will help me. The land that remains, whatever it might be, must be possessed. This speaks of us personally, but above all, it speaks of that which God has called us to do.

(7) "NOW THEREFORE DIVIDE THIS LAND FOR AN INHERITANCE UNTO THE NINE TRIBES, AND THE HALF TRIBE OF MANASSEH,

(8) "WITH WHOM THE REUBENITES AND THE GADITES HAVE RECEIVED THEIR INHERITANCE, WHICH MOSES GAVE THEM, BEYOND JORDAN EASTWARD, EVEN AS MOSES THE SERVANT OF THE LORD GAVE THEM;

(9) "FROM AROER, THAT IS UPON THE BANK OF THE RIVER ARNON, AND THE CITY THAT IS IN THE MIDST OF THE RIVER, AND ALL THE PLAIN OF MEDEBA UNTO DIBON;

(10) "AND ALL THE CITIES OF SIHON KING OF THE AMORITES, WHICH REIGNED IN HESHBON, UNTO THE BORDER OF THE CHILDREN OF AMMON;

(11) "AND GILEAD, AND THE BORDER OF THE GESHURITES AND MAACHATHITES, AND ALL MOUNT HERMON, AND ALL BASHAN UNTO SALCAH;

(12) "ALL THE KINGDOM OF OG IN BASHAN, WHICH REIGNED IN ASHTAROTH AND IN EDREI, WHO REMAINED OF THE REMNANT OF THE GIANTS: FOR THESE DID MOSES SMITE, AND CAST THEM OUT.

(13) "NEVERTHELESS THE CHILDREN OF ISRAEL EXPELLED NOT THE GESHURITES, NOR THE MAACHATHITES: BUT THE GESHURITES AND THE MAACHATHITES DWELL AMONG THE ISRAELITES UNTIL THIS DAY.

(14) "ONLY UNTO THE TRIBES OF LEVI HE GAVE NONE INHERITANCE; THE SACRIFICES OF THE LORD GOD OF ISRAEL MADE BY FIRE ARE THEIR INHERITANCE, AS HE SAID UNTO THEM."

The structure is:

1. The Holy Spirit in this Chapter delineates the areas which have not yet been taken, but which must be taken. He is doing the same thing in our lives presently.

2. The word *"nevertheless"* of Verse 13 proclaims failure among the people of God to possess all that was promised. Such is the sad condition of far too many Believers. While some victories are won, *"nevertheless"* some things remain — things which steal, kill, and destroy. How many enemies remain unsubdued in the hearts of Believers?

3. There's only one way that victory can be attained in the life of the Christian. Not ten ways, not five ways, not even two ways, only one way.

All victory over sin, and in every capacity, and, to be sure, sin is the problem, was

NOTES

purchased and thereby attained at the Cross of Calvary (Eph. 2:13-18; Col. 2:14-15; Gal., Chpt. 5; 6:14).

As a result, the Believer's Faith and this is so very, very important, must ever have the Cross of Christ as its Object (Rom. 6:3-14). If the Believer is faithful in anchoring his Faith in the Cross of Christ, and maintaining his Faith in the Cross of Christ, the Holy Spirit, Who works exclusively within the perimeters of the Finished Work of Christ, will, without fail, subdue every enemy within our hearts and lives (Rom. 8:1-2, 11). That, and that alone, is God's Prescribed Order of Victory; otherwise, instead of the Believer subduing the enemies of his soul, the enemies of his soul will subdue him.

LANDS YET UNCONQUERED

As the Holy Spirit was very faithful and prompt in delineating the cities and kings which had now been defeated and taken, He is likewise diligent to enumerate the areas which had not yet been taken by Israel.

As well, these areas and people are specified by the Holy Spirit, such as the *"Geshurites and the Maachathites,"* which Verse 13 says, *"dwell among the Israelites until this day."*

How is the Holy Spirit evaluating us presently? Does He speak of pride, of envy, of immorality of some nature, of self-will, and then say, *"they dwell in the heart of such and such Believer until this day?"*

Some enemies of our soul are easily defeated, while some enemies are extremely difficult. And as we have repeatedly stated, and will continue to state, the only way to victory is through the Cross of Christ.

I'VE TRIED THE CROSS
AND IT FAILED!

In one way or the other, I've heard that statement a number of times, *"I've tried the Cross and it failed!"*

No, the Cross didn't fail, it's you or me who failed, not the Cross. To say that the Cross failed is at the same time to say that what Jesus did at the Cross was insufficient, Jesus failed to defeat every enemy, to gain the total victory, therefore, what He did is not trustworthy.

While any sane Christian would strongly

denounce such a statement, and rightly so, still, whether it is realized or not, when anyone claims that the Cross has failed, that's what they are actually saying.

The Cross of Christ is not a magic talisman. It's not some little magic charm that wards off every problem and difficulty. It is rather a belief system, in other words, the Object of our Faith.

When the Believer places his Faith exclusively in Christ and the Cross, first of all he must realize, that even though he may think his faith is exclusively placed, it actually isn't. The clinging vines of the flesh are still there, and to a much greater degree than we realize. It is so much in man, even the best of Christians to look to the flesh, to depend on self, to devise religious means and schemes of proposed victory. We load it down with Scriptures, and we think because of doing such that it is Scripturally correct. Most of the time it isn't!

So we must be patient with ourselves, understanding that this is a growth process. Some of us grow faster than others, some of us grow slower than others. But this one thing that can be guaranteed, the growth will take place if the Believer maintains his Faith in Christ and the Cross (Rom. 6:1-14; 8:1-2, 11; Gal. 6:14).

Next, it's not a question of *"if I fail,"* but rather, *"when I fail."* That may sound like something negative, but it happens to be the truth.

This is not an easy sojourn. Satan will muster all the forces at his disposal, to trip you up, to hinder you. This trip is definitely not uneventful. But the following is certain:

When your Faith is in Christ and the Cross exclusively, no matter the failures, as hurtful as they might be, no matter the times you slip, you are now on the right path, and you definitely will begin to know victory in your life, and know victory more and more. If you don't quit, you most definitely will come to the place that *"the sin nature will no longer have dominion over you"* (Rom. 6:14).

THE SIN NATURE

The entirety of the Sixth Chapter of Romans deals with the sin nature, which tries to dominate the Child of God and, in fact, will dominate the Child of God, if such a Believer doesn't adhere to God's Prescribed Order of Victory. What is the sin nature?

It is the inclination of the individual toward sin, toward transgression, toward iniquity. Before you came to Christ, you were ruled totally and completely, twenty-four hours a day, by the sin nature. When you came to Christ, the sin nature became dormant, that is inactive; however, if we do not follow God's Prescribed Order as stated, we will find the sin nature very quickly having a resurrection.

The sin nature is a result of the Fall. At that time, man fell from a position of total God consciousness, down to a far lower level of total self-consciousness. In other words, God ceased to be a part in any capacity of life and living. That's the reason that Jesus told Nicodemus, *"You must be born again"* (Jn. 3:3).

Unfortunately, many preachers claim that once a person comes to Christ that such a person no longer has a sin nature. That's strange when we consider that the Holy Spirit devoted an awful lot of time and attention telling us how to overcome something, when in reality it doesn't even exist. The truth is, the sin nature most definitely does exist in the heart and life of the Believer; however, the Believer need have no problem with it, that is if the Believer functions entirely according to the Word of God.

Some seventeen times in the Sixth Chapter of Romans, the Holy Spirit through Paul refers to the sin nature.

In the original Greek Text, in which this Epistle was written, in front of the word *"sin"* (some fifteen times in that one Chapter) is what is referred to as the definite article. Therefore, when Paul asked, *"Shall we continue in sin, that Grace may abound?"*, he actually said, *"Shall we continue in 'the sin'. . . ."* The word *"the"* is what is referred to as the definite article.

Whenever the definite article is used, or else the word *"sin"* is used as a noun, as it is in Verse 14, Paul is not speaking of acts of sin, but rather the sin nature or it could be referred to as the evil nature. In Verse 15 of this Sixth Chapter of Romans Paul uses the word *"sin"* without the definite article, which

means that he is referring to acts of sin in that particular Verse; however, in all the other Verses of that Chapter, he is referring to the *"sin nature"* when he uses the word *"sin."*

Now we might ask the question as to why the King James translators did not apply the definite article (the) in front of the word sin where it is used?

Probably they translated it as they did simply because in English it is often times clumsy to place the word *"the"* in front of the word *"sin."* At any rate, because of the way they did translate it, which was not the best way, most people do not understand that Paul is dealing with the sin nature, but think that he is dealing with acts of sin.

The *"sin nature"* is the biggest problem for the Child of God, and that despite the fact that most modern Believers don't even understand or know what the sin nature actually is.

VICTORY OVER THE SIN NATURE

God has only one Order of Victory as it regards the sin nature, and that is the Cross of Christ, and Faith in that Finished Work. Listen again to Paul:

In the first two Verses of the Sixth Chapter of Romans the Holy Spirit through the Apostle tells us that the problem is sin. Never mind that you are now a Believer, even Spirit-filled, still, the problem is sin. While many Preachers, Churches, and even entire denominations deny this fact, I'll leave it up to you. You can accept what they say or you can accept what the Holy Spirit through Paul said. He tells us plainly in those first two Verses that the problem is sin.

Immediately then he tells us the answer, the solution, to the dilemma. It is the Cross of Christ. He said, and I quote from THE EXPOSITOR'S STUDY BIBLE:

"Know you not, that so many of us as were baptized into Jesus Christ (plainly says that this Baptism is into Christ and not water [I Cor. 1:17; 12:13; Gal. 3:27; Eph. 4:5; Col. 2:11-13]) *were baptized into His Death?* (When Christ died on the Cross, in the Mind of God, we died with Him; in other words, He became our Substitute, and our identification with Him in His Death gives us all the benefits for which He died; the idea is

that He did it all for us!)

"Therefore we are buried with Him by baptism into death (not only did we die with Him, but we were buried with Him as well, which means that all the sin and transgression of the past were buried; when they put Him in the Tomb, they put all of our sins into that Tomb as well)*: that like as Christ was raised up from the dead by the Glory of the Father, even so we also should walk in Newness of Life* (we died with Him, we were buried with Him, and His Resurrection was our Resurrection to a *'Newness of Life'*).

"For if we have been planted together (with Christ) *in the likeness of His Death* (Paul proclaims the Cross as the instrument through which all Blessings come; consequently, the Cross must ever be the Object of our Faith, which gives the Holy Spirit latitude to work within our lives), *we shall be also in the likeness of His Resurrection* (we can have the *'likeness of His Resurrection,'* i.e., *'live this Resurrection Life,'* only as long as we understand the *'likeness of His Death,'* which refers to the Cross as the means by which all of this is done)" (Rom. 6:3-5).

The answer is the Cross of Christ, and the only answer is the Cross of Christ! For a more complete treatment of the sin nature, please see our Study Guide, *"The Sin Nature, The Cross of Christ Series."*

(15) "AND MOSES GAVE UNTO THE TRIBE OF THE CHILDREN OF REUBEN INHERITANCE ACCORDING TO THEIR FAMILIES.

(16) "AND THEIR COAST WAS FROM AROER, THAT IS ON THE BANK OF THE RIVER ARNON, AND THE CITY THAT IS IN THE MIDST OF THE RIVER, AND ALL THE PLAIN BY MEDEBA;

(17) "HESHBON, AND ALL HER CITIES THAT ARE IN THE PLAIN; DIBON, AND BAMOTH-BAAL, AND BETH-BAAL-MEON,

(18) "AND JAHAZA, AND KEDEMOTH, AND MEPHAATH,

(19) "AND KIRJATHAIM, AND SIBMAH, AND ZARETH-SHAHAR IN THE MOUNT OF THE VALLEY,

(20) "AND BETH-PEOR, AND ASHDOTH-PISGAH, AND BETH-JESHIMOTH,

(21) "AND ALL THE CITIES OF THE

PLAIN, AND ALL THE KINGDOM OF SIHON KING OF THE AMORITES, WHICH REIGNED IN HESHBON, WHOM MOSES SMOTE WITH THE PRINCES OF MIDIAN, EVI, AND REKEM, AND ZUR, AND HUR, AND REBA, WHICH WERE DUKES OF SIHON, DWELLING IN THE COUNTRY."

The structure is:

1. All of these places and names represent victories by God's People over their enemies. Considering that the Holy Spirit inspired all of this, even down to naming the places, portrays to us a tremendous truth.

2. In Heaven, the Lord enumerates our victories, which are all precious in His Sight, and, as well, mentions the failures, and does so by using the word *"nevertheless"* in Verse 13 . . . until that enemy is overcome, and then the record is expunged from the books.

3. To be sure, Satan will do his best to hinder in every capacity. As should be obvious, he doesn't want us to win any victories; however, we definitely can have all that the Lord has promised us, and we must not stop short of total Victory in Christ and the Cross, coupled with our Faith, which gives the Holy Spirit latitude to work. We can, spiritually speaking, possess the entirety of the land (Rom. 8:2, 11).

(22) "BALAAM ALSO THE SON OF BEOR, THE SOOTHSAYER, DID THE CHILDREN OF ISRAEL SLAY WITH THE SWORD AMONG THEM WHO WERE SLAIN BY THEM."

The construction is:

1. If Balaam originally was a true Prophet of God, the tragedy is that he sold his gift to the highest bidder, and was reduced in the Mind of God to nothing more than a *"soothsayer."* How many modern Prophets fall into the same category?

2. It seems, instead of returning to his own land, he went to visit the Midianites, whose elders had joined in the invitation given by Moab (Num. 22:7), and persuaded them to entice the Israelites into idolatry and licentiousness (Num., Chpt. 25). For this crime, he met with the punishment he had deserved, and was involved in the destruction which fell on the Midianites by God's express command, in consequence of

their treachery (Num. 25:16-18).

3. When the Gifts of God are prostituted, even as they were with Balaam, and sadly and regrettably with so many presently, in one way or the other, destruction will come, again, exactly as it did with Balaam.

(23) "AND THE BORDER OF THE CHILDREN OF REUBEN WAS JORDAN, AND THE BORDER THEREOF. THIS WAS THE INHERITANCE OF THE CHILDREN OF REUBEN AFTER THEIR FAMILIES, THE CITIES AND THE VILLAGES THEREOF."

The exegesis is:

1. The borders of Reuben's inheritance seem to go from the River Arnon, which was about half way the length of the Dead Sea, and went a little ways north past the Dead Sea, with the Jordan River as its western boundary.

2. If it is to be noticed, everything is neatly cataloged so to speak, whether victories or defeats. As well, the exact location of the inheritance is described, all typical of what we are in Christ, and what we are to have in Christ.

3. Whatever the inheritance, the Lord drew the boundaries, and in totality. This means that the Tribes were not to infringe upon the territory of others. This should be a great lesson for us as well!

Far too many modern Believers attempt to function in a calling which the Lord has not given them. Every time such an effort spells trouble.

Every Believer should avidly seek the Face of the Lord as it regards the boundaries of his own personal inheritance, so to speak. He should then ask the Lord to help him function in that capacity and, in fact, be exactly what God wants us to be.

(24) "AND MOSES GAVE INHERITANCE UNTO THE TRIBE OF GAD, EVEN UNTO THE CHILDREN OF GAD ACCORDING TO THEIR FAMILIES.

(25) "AND THEIR COAST WAS JAZER, AND ALL THE CITIES OF GILEAD, AND HALF THE LAND OF THE CHILDREN OF AMMON, UNTO AROER THAT IS BEFORE RABBAH;

(26) "AND FROM HESHBON UNTO RAMATH-MIZPEH, AND BETONIM; AND FROM MAHANAIM UNTO THE BORDER

NOTES

OF DEBIR;

(27) "AND IN THE VALLEY, BETH-ARAM, AND BETHNIMRAH, AND SUCCOTH, AND ZAPHON, THE REST OF THE KINGDOM OF SIHON KING OF HESHBON, JORDAN AND HIS BORDER, EVEN UNTO THE EDGE OF THE SEA OF CHINNERETH ON THE OTHER SIDE JORDAN EASTWARD.

(28) "THIS IS THE INHERITANCE OF THE CHILDREN OF GAD AFTER THEIR FAMILIES, THE CITIES, AND THEIR VILLAGES."

The diagram is:

1. As is obvious here, God had a Perfect Plan for each Tribe in Israel and, in fact, a Perfect Plan for each person. He no less has a Perfect Plan for us presently as well.

2. There was nothing uncertain in His Arrangements, but, on the contrary, everything was orderly and well defined.

3. There is a difference between the Gifts of God and the enjoyment of those gifts; and, accordingly, how many enemies remain unsubdued in the hearts of Christian People.

4. Several times it is stated in this Chapter that Moses gave the land east of the Jordan to the two Tribes and a half. When dealing with the possessions west of the Jordan it is repeated with emphasis that *"God gave them."*

(29) "AND MOSES GAVE INHERITANCE UNTO THE HALF TRIBE OF MANASSEH: AND THIS WAS THE POSSESSION OF THE HALF TRIBE OF THE CHILDREN OF MANASSEH BY THEIR FAMILIES.

(30) "AND THEIR COAST WAS FROM MAHANAIM, ALL BASHAN, ALL THE KINGDOM OF OG KING OF BASHAN, AND ALL THE TOWNS OF JAIR, WHICH ARE IN BASHAN, THREESCORE CITIES:

(31) "AND HALF GILEAD, AND ASHTAROTH, AND EDREI, CITIES OF THE KINGDOM OF OG IN BASHAN, WERE PERTAINING UNTO THE CHILDREN OF MACHIR THE SON OF MANASSEH, EVEN TO THE ONE HALF OF THE CHILDREN OF MACHIR BY THEIR FAMILIES.

(32) "THESE ARE THE COUNTRIES WHICH MOSES DID DISTRIBUTE FOR INHERITANCE IN THE PLAINS OF MOAB, ON THE OTHER SIDE JORDAN,

BY JERICHO, EASTWARD.

(33) "BUT UNTO THE TRIBE OF LEVI MOSES GAVE NOT ANY INHERITANCE: THE LORD GOD OF ISRAEL WAS THEIR INHERITANCE, AS HE SAID UNTO THEM."

The overview is:

1. No victory over the enemy is small to God's Mind.

2. Christ is the Source of all Blessings, while the Cross is the Means of those Blessings.

3. Twice in this Chapter (Vss. 14 and 33) the special glory which was Levi's is recorded; that is, that he had no inheritance other than Jehovah the God of Israel; that was his Inheritance, and what an Inheritance it was.

It was Grace that brought Levi this great Blessing, as Grace alone could bring the Blessing.

A curse was leveled on both Simeon and Levi nearly 300 years before, and because of their murder of the Shechemites (Gen., Chpt. 34). Now almost with Jacob's dying breath, he prophesied over all of his sons who were the progenitor of the great Tribes of Israel. In these prophesies both Simeon and Levi were cursed (Gen. 49:5-7).

But Grace brought both of them from this place of the curse, to a place of victory, which is exactly what happens to any person who comes to Christ. They're brought from sin unto Salvation, from darkness to light, from Hell to Heaven!

CHAPTER 14

(1) "AND THESE ARE THE COUNTRIES WHICH THE CHILDREN OF ISRAEL INHERITED IN THE LAND OF CANAAN, WHICH ELEAZER THE PRIEST, AND JOSHUA THE SON OF NUN, AND THE HEADS OF THE FATHERS OF THE TRIBES OF THE CHILDREN OF ISRAEL DISTRIBUTED FOR INHERITANCE TO THEM.

(2) "BY LOT WAS THEIR INHERITANCE, AS THE LORD COMMANDED BY THE HAND OF MOSES, FOR THE NINE TRIBES, AND FOR THE HALF TRIBE.

(3) "FOR MOSES HAD GIVEN THE

INHERITANCE OF TWO TRIBES AND AN HALF TRIBE ON THE OTHER SIDE JORDAN: BUT UNTO THE LEVITES HE GAVE NONE INHERITANCE AMONG THEM.

(4) "FOR THE CHILDREN OF JOSHEPH WERE TWO TRIBES, MANASSEH AND EPHRAIM: THEREFORE THEY GAVE NO PART UNTO THE LEVITES IN THE LAND, SAVE CITIES TO DWELL IN, WITH THEIR SUBURBS FOR THEIR CATTLE AND FOR THEIR SUBSTANCE.

(5) "AS THE LORD COMMANDED MOSES, SO THE CHILDREN OF ISRAEL DID, AND THEY DIVIDED THE LAND."

The diagram is:

1. The words *"by lot"* in Verse 2 had to do with the Urim and the Thummim; whatever these things were, they were kept in a pouch on the back of the breastplate of the High Priest; some think they were two stones with the word *"yes"* on one, and the word *"no"* on the other; however, that description is only speculative.

2. Whatever were the *"Urim and the Thummim"* it was the Holy Spirit Who parceled off the land and its boundaries, and did so through the means of these items.

3. The indication is, the Holy Spirit Alone parceled out the land on the western side of the Jordan, but that seemed not to be the case on the eastern side. And let it be known, anything in which the Holy Spirit doesn't have full sway, will present itself with problems later on.

VICTORY

This is a Victory Chapter, and we should rejoice in it.

The Second Verse says, *"By lot was their inheritance."* Eleazar, the High Priest, now acted with Joshua to divide the land by lot as instructed by Moses. The High Priest alone had the Urim and Thummim, by which the lots would be cast. In other words, the dividing of the land was not according to political stance, position, power, or prestige. The borders were designed by the Holy Spirit. Whatever the Tribe of Ephraim received, it was designed by the Holy Spirit. That which Judah received was by the Holy Spirit, and so forth as it regarded the entirety of the nine and a half Tribes on the western side of the Jordan.

There were really thirteen Tribes counting the Tribe of Levi; however, they were not considered a Tribe as far as inheritance of the land was concerned. The two sons of Joseph (Manasseh and Ephraim) took the part of their father; therefore, regarding the sons of Jacob, Joseph, his true son was not included, and instead, his two grandsons, sons of Joseph, took the place of Joseph and of Levi. As far as the Levites were concerned, the Lord was their Inheritance so that they could be ministers of the whole Nation.

Sadly, little by little, the present-day Church structure of denominations and denominationalism has gradually usurped authority over the Holy Spirit. God's Biblical order of calling men and women to preach the Gospel and then designating where they should go to preach has been replaced by man, who, according to denominational politics, divides the land himself; however, it must be noted that whatever the Holy Spirit does, He will bless, but whatever man does, the Holy Spirit will not bless. So, by and large, we have an unblessed Church, at least as it regards spiritual things.

(6) "THEN THE CHILDREN OF JUDAH CAME UNTO JOSHUA IN GILGAL: AND CALEB THE SON OF JEPHUNNEH THE KENEZITE SAID UNTO HIM, YOU KNOW THE THING THAT THE LORD SAID UNTO MOSES THE MAN OF GOD CONCERNING ME AND YOU IN KADESH-BARNEA.

(7) "FORTY YEARS OLD WAS I WHEN MOSES THE SERVANT OF THE LORD SENT ME FROM KADESH-BARNEA TO SPY OUT THE LAND; AND I BROUGHT HIM WORD AGAIN AS IT WAS IN MY HEART.

(8) "NEVERTHELESS MY BRETHREN WHO WENT UP WITH ME MADE THE HEART OF THE PEOPLE MELT: BUT I WHOLLY FOLLOWED THE LORD MY GOD.

(9) "AND MOSES SWORE ON THAT DAY, SAYING, SURELY THE LAND WHEREON YOUR FEET HAVE TRODDEN SHALL BE YOUR INHERITANCE, AND YOUR CHILDREN'S FOR EVER, BECAUSE YOU HAVE WHOLLY FOLLOWED THE LORD MY GOD.

(10) "AND NOW, BEHOLD, THE LORD HAS KEPT ME ALIVE, AS HE SAID, THESE

NOTES

FORTY AND FIVE YEARS, EVEN SINCE THE LORD SPOKE THIS WORD UNTO MOSES, WHILE THE CHILDREN OF ISRAEL WANDERED IN THE WILDERNESS: AND NOW, LO, I AM THIS DAY FOURSCORE AND FIVE YEARS OLD.

(11) "AS YET I AM AS STRONG THIS DAY AS I WAS IN THE DAY THAT MOSES SENT ME: AS MY STRENGTH WAS THEN, EVEN SO IS MY STRENGTH NOW, FOR WAR, BOTH TO GO OUT, AND TO COME IN.

(12) "NOW THEREFORE GIVE ME THIS MOUNTAIN, WHEREOF THE LORD SPOKE IN THAT DAY; FOR YOU HEARD IN THAT DAY HOW THE ANAKIMS WERE THERE, AND THAT THE CITIES WERE GREAT AND FENCED: IF SO BE THE LORD WILL BE WITH ME, THEN I SHALL BE ABLE TO DRIVE THEM OUT, AS THE LORD SAID.

(13) "AND JOSHUA BLESSED HIM, AND GAVE UNTO CALEB THE SON OF JEPHUNNEH HEBRON FOR AN INHERITANCE.

(14) "HEBRON THEREFORE BECAME THE INHERITANCE OF CALEB THE SON OF JEPHUNNEH THE KENEZITE UNTO THIS DAY, BECAUSE THAT HE WHOLLY FOLLOWED THE LORD GOD OF ISRAEL.

(15) "AND THE NAME OF HEBRON BEFORE WAS KIRJATH-ARBA; WHICH ARBA WAS A GREAT MAN AMONG THE ANAKIMS. AND THE LAND HAD REST FROM WAR."

The overview is:

1. Out of all this, Caleb's Faith shines like the sun. His was a Divine Faith. Such Faith overcomes the world.

2. Williams says, *"Giant sins entrenched on strong mountains are helpless before a Faith that is born of God. This fact may be experienced by any and all Believers, if they will but wholly follow the Lord as did Caleb."*[1]

3. The record proclaims that Caleb, because of his Faith in God, took possession of this mountain, and expelled the greatest of the giants whose name was Arba. The result was that Kirjath-Arba — that is, the city of Arba — became Hebron — that is, *"fellowship,"* for that's what Hebron means! As well, where there is true Faith, there is *"rest from war."*

CALEB

Beginning with the Sixth Verse to the conclusion of the Chapter, we have the shining light of Faith. It pertains to Caleb. This man was born in Egypt, but his Faith would defeat the enemy and gain a place of such victory that the Holy Spirit would graphically record it.

His Faith in the Eleventh Verse says, *"As yet I am as strong this day as I was in the day that Moses sent me."* This is the boast of Faith, and it must be noted that Faith alone can boast (Gal. 6:14).

This was not the idle boast of an old man who hates to see his strength fading away; it was Truth, for afterward, he expelled three great giants from his inheritance (Judg. 1:20). No doubt, Caleb lived to enjoy his possession many years. If he remained alive as long as Joshua, who was near the same age, he enjoyed it no less than 25 or 30 years.

Caleb's Faith will claim the great mountains for a possession and not only expel the giants but even Arba, the greatest of the giants!

GIVE ME THIS MOUNTAIN

Caleb's words in the Twelfth Verse speak out to us even today, *"Now therefore give me this mountain."* One can sense the Presence and the Spirit of God even in pronouncing the words, *"Now therefore give me this mountain."* This should be the cry of every Child of God as it regards spiritual victories.

Others may be satisfied but not Caleb. Faith is never satisfied. It must take all the land. It must expel all the giants. Its testimony forever will be, *"If the LORD will be with me, then I shall be able to drive them out, as the LORD said."*

The Thirteenth Verse says, *"And Joshua blessed him, and gave unto Caleb the son of Jephunneh Hebron for an inheritance."* There were five reasons that Joshua could grant this request.

A. Because of the Prophecy of Verse 9, *"Surely the land whereon your feet have trod shall be your inheritance, and your children's for ever."*

B. Caleb's faithfulness (Num. 14:24).

C. Because of it being the request of a mighty man of Faith in Israel, one of only two of the old generation who came out of Egypt (Num. 14:23-24).

D. The land requested was in the Judah portion of which Caleb was a member (I Chron. 4:1-15).

E. Because of the Will of God by the Urim and Thummim (Ex. 28:30).

In other words, it was promised to him by the Word of the Lord; therefore, every single Child of God can have that which is promised to him in the Word of God. He has promised every one of us Victory if we will have Faith and believe Him.

The key is the Fourteenth Verse. It says, *"Because that he wholly followed the LORD God of Israel."* That was the key to Victory in that day, it is the key to Victory in our day.

CHAPTER 15

(1) "THIS THEN WAS THE LOT OF THE TRIBE OF THE CHILDREN OF JUDAH BY THEIR FAMILIES: EVEN TO THE BORDER OF EDOM THE WILDERNESS OF ZIN SOUTHWARD WAS THE UTTERMOST PART OF THE SOUTH COAST.

(2) "AND THEIR SOUTH BORDER WAS FROM THE SHORE OF THE SALT SEA, FROM THE BAY THAT LOOKS SOUTHWARD:

(3) "AND IT WENT OUT TO THE SOUTH SIDE TO MAALEH-ACRABBIM, AND PASSED ALONG TO ZIN, AND ASCENDED UP ON THE SOUTH SIDE UNTO KADESH-BARNEA, AND PASSED ALONG TO HEZRON, AND WENT UP TO ADAR, AND FETCHED A COMPASS TO KARKAA:

(4) "FROM THENCE IT PASSED TOWARD AZMON, AND WENT OUT UNTO THE RIVER OF EGYPT; AND THE GOINGS OUT OF THAT COAST WERE AT THE SEA: THIS SHALL BE YOUR SOUTH COAST.

(5) "AND THE EAST BORDER WAS THE SALT SEA, EVEN UNTO THE END OF JORDAN. AND THEIR BORDER IN THE NORTH QUARTER WAS FROM THE BAY OF THE SEA AT THE UTTERMOST PART OF JORDAN:

(6) "AND THE BORDER WENT UP TO

NOTES

BETH-HOGLA, AND PASSED ALONG BY THE NORTH OF BETH-ARABAH; AND THE BORDER WENT UP TO THE STONE OF BOHAN THE SON OF REUBEN:

(7) "AND THE BORDER WENT UP TOWARD DEBIR FROM THE VALLEY OF ACHOR, AND SO NORTHWARD, LOOKING TOWARD GILGAL, THAT IS BEFORE THE GOING UP TO ADUMMIM, WHICH IS ON THE SOUTH SIDE OF THE RIVER: AND THE BORDER PASSED TOWARD THE WATERS OF EN-SHEMESH, AND THE GOINGS OUT THEREOF WERE AT EN-ROGEL:

(8) "AND THE BORDER WENT UP BY THE VALLEY OF THE SON OF HINNOM UNTO THE SOUTH SIDE OF THE JEBUSITE; THE SAME IS JERUSALEM: AND THE BORDER WENT UP TO THE TOP OF THE MOUNTAIN THAT LIES BEFORE THE VALLEY OF HINNOM WESTWARD, WHICH IS AT THE END OF THE VALLEY OF THE GIANTS NORTHWARD:

(9) "AND THE BORDER WAS DRAWN FROM THE TOP OF THE HILL UNTO THE FOUNTAIN OF THE WATER OF NEPHTOAH, AND WENT OUT TO THE CITIES OF MOUNT EPHRON; AND THE BORDER WAS DRAWN TO BAALAH, WHICH IS KIRJATH-JEARIM:

(10) "AND THE BORDER COMPASSED FROM BAALAH WESTWARD UNTO MOUNT SEIR, AND PASSED ALONG UNTO THE SIDE OF MOUNT JEARIM, WHICH IS CHESALON, ON THE NORTH SIDE, AND WENT DOWN TO BETH-SHEMESH, AND PASSED ON TO TIMNAH:

(11) "AND THE BORDER WENT OUT UNTO THE SIDE OF EKRON NORTHWARD: AND THE BORDER WAS DRAWN TO SHICRON, AND PASSED ALONG TO MOUNT BAALAH, AND WENT OUT UNTO JABNEEL; AND THE GOINGS OUT OF THE BORDER WERE AT THE SEA.

(12) "AND THE WEST BORDER WAS TO THE GREAT SEA, AND THE COAST THEREOF. THIS IS THE COAST OF THE CHILDREN OF JUDAH ROUND ABOUT ACCORDING TO THEIR FAMILIES."

The diagram is:

1. Judah was the Tribe from which Jesus would come.

2. By far, Judah had the largest portion.

NOTES

In fact, her portion was so large that the Tribe of Simeon had her portion within the portion of Judah, but which only took up a small part of that vast area.

The portion of Simeon included the city of Beersheba. Judah's portion extended all the way from Jerusalem in the north to the brook of Egypt due south, a distance of well over a hundred miles.

3. Judah, being the Royal Tribe, and Joseph having the birthright, which was forfeited by Reuben, were the first to receive their portions in the goodly Land.

JUDAH

Verse 1 says, *"This then was the lot of the Tribe of the Children of Judah."* Judah was given the first inheritance.

Why?

From this great Tribe of Judah would come the Messiah. It had been prophesied by Jacob (Gen. 49:10).

As well, Judah would be the Tribe that would hold the torch of Faith higher for a longer period of time than any of the other Tribes. Amazingly enough, in Verse after Verse we are given the exact instructions by the Holy Spirit. Nothing was left to chance.

Also, for each and every Child of God the Lord has a distinct plan. Its borders in the spiritual sense are carefully defined. God help us to occupy and to carry out exactly what He has called us to do, which in effect, although spiritually speaking, constitutes our borders as well.

It is delightful to read of this apportionment. When God enriches His People everything is real, substantial, and definite. He gives largely; and His Blessings may, without fear of disappointment, be counted just as this Chapter records the 116 cities given to Judah.

But a life of Blessing with God has definite borders, just as the lot of Judah had its divinely marked boundaries. It is important that God should choose a lot in life for each one of His People, and that we should be satisfied with that lot and its limitations.

(13) "AND UNTO CALEB THE SON OF JEPHUNNEH HE GAVE A PART AMONG THE CHILDREN OF JUDAH, ACCORDING TO THE COMMANDMENT OF THE LORD

TO JOSHUA, EVEN THE CITY OF ARBA THE FATHER OF ANAK, WHICH CITY IS HEBRON.

(14) "AND CALEB DROVE THENCE THE THREE SONS OF ANAK, SHESHAI, AND AHIMAN, AND TALMAI, THE CHILDREN OF ANAK.

(15) "AND HE WENT UP THENCE TO THE INHABITANTS OF DEBIR: AND THE NAME OF DEBIR BEFORE WAS KIRJATH-SEPHER.

(16) "AND CALEB SAID, HE WHO SMITES KIRJATH-SEPHER, AND TAKES IT, TO HIM WILL I GIVE ACHSAH MY DAUGHTER TO WIFE.

(17) "AND OTHNIEL THE SON OF KENAZ, THE BROTHER OF CALEB, TOOK IT: AND HE GAVE HIM ACHSAH HIS DAUGHTER TO WIFE.

(18) "AND IT CAME TO PASS, AS SHE CAME UNTO HIM, THAT SHE MOVED HIM TO ASK OF HER FATHER A FIELD: AND SHE LIGHTED OFF HER ASS; AND CALEB SAID UNTO HER, WHAT WOULD YOU?

(19) "WHO ANSWERED, GIVE ME A BLESSING; FOR YOU HAVE GIVEN ME A SOUTH LAND; GIVE ME ALSO SPRINGS OF WATER. AND HE GAVE HER THE UPPER SPRINGS, AND THE NETHER SPRINGS."

The overview is:

1. The Holy Spirit is quick to record the victory of Othniel, as He is quick to record our victories also. These victories we must win and, in fact, can only win by the virtue of our Faith in Christ and what He has done for us at the Cross.

2. Achsah's Faith is to be commended. She asked for a "Blessing," and, to be sure, the Lord will always honor such a request. Her father gave her the Springs of Water, which would water the land, making it very fertile. This is a Type of the Holy Spirit, given to those who ask (Lk. 11:13). Without the Springs of Water, the land was basically worthless. With the springs, it was extremely valuable.

3. Likewise, without the Holy Spirit, of which these springs, in a sense, were a Type, the life of the Believer is by and large unproductive. With Christ and the Cross as the Object of the Believer's Faith, such a life will be extremely fertile and productive.

NOTES

GIVE ME A BLESSING

Caleb proved equal to the Faith which he boasted.

The area that he was given, and which he requested, was that of the giants. In other words, what he was to have, he would have to take. It is the same as it regards the Blessings of the Lord presently. They are there, but we have to take them, and we have to take them from the enemy. As well, the enemy is not weak or inexperienced, but rather strong and powerful, exactly as were the giants; however, they were all expelled *"Anak, Sheshai, Ahiman, and Talmai."* As stated, his Faith was equal to the task!

Another part of that awarded to Caleb was taken by his brother, Othniel. This man was Israel's first deliverer and ruler; his Faith grew exceedingly, even as he showed boldness in battle.

For this great feat of arms, Caleb gave to Othniel his daughter Achsah to be his wife.

This young lady proved to be a woman of Faith. Pulpit says, *"She coveted a prize that is as yet beyond her reach. She said to her father, 'Give me a blessing.' And then she said, 'you have given me a south* (dry, barren) *land; give me also springs of water.'"*

How expressive is this of that yearning of the heart by virtue of which it cannot rest content with present possessions, but is ever reaching forth towards something more, a richer inheritance, a more complete Blessing, the perfect filling up of its capacity, the sense of absolute Blessing. Pulpit goes on to say, *"There is an appetite in the soul of man, which is not only insatiable, but often becomes more intense the more it is fed with finite gratifications."*[1]

Achsah's request is immediately granted. She receives from her father a *"completed Blessing,"* the richer land added to the poorer to supplement its deficiency.

This tells us that God is ever ready to respond to every pure aspiration of our nature. He who *"opens His Hand and satisfies the wants of true spiritual desire of which we are conscious contains in itself the pledge of its own fulfillment."*

Christ is God's Answer to the soul's deepest craving. In Him is the fullness of all satisfying good. *"Whosoever drinks of the water that I shall give him shall never thirst; but the water that I shall give him shall be in him a well of water springing up into Everlasting Life"* (Jn. 4:14). In Him we find the rest of absolute contentment.

The cry of every Believer to the Lord, and from pure motives should be, *"Give me a Blessing!"* As the request of Achsah was answered and met, likewise, the honest and sincere heart will find the same from our Heavenly Father. The Blessing will be given.

A PERSONAL EXPERIENCE

The request, *"Give me a blessing,"* is very real and dear to me personally.

I honestly don't remember the month, or even the year. It is now 2006 (the time of this writing), it must have been somewhere near 2002.

At any rate, I was in our Television Studio televising a special which would be aired very shortly. Frances and Donnie were with me.

The day before, our Television Director called me, and asked what song I wanted played on the program. At the moment I couldn't think of a particular song, so I told him, *"Play the song that aired on the Telecast Sunday."* To be frank I didn't even remember what the song was. But I know now that the Lord was guiding events.

As we began the special that day, and the song began to play, I found out that it was one of our choir songs entitled, *"Your Blessing is Coming Through."*

As the song played, and the closer it came to the end, I could sense the Presence of the Lord. The words are:

"Your Blessing, your Blessing, is coming through
"Your Blessing, your Blessing, is coming through
"He'll pour you out a Blessing
"You won't have room to receive,
"Your Blessing, your Blessing is coming through."

Waiting for the song to finish, those words kept going deep into my heart, *"Your Blessing, your Blessing is coming through."*

When the song finished, and I began to

speak, the Lord in the meantime changed the entire direction of my Message. It zeroed in on the words, *"Your Blessing, your Blessing is coming through."*

That particular day the Lord spoke to my heart and, in essence, told me, *"The Blessing of this Ministry is now beginning."* And so it has, and in every way possible.

However, I'm definitely not satisfied. I feel like we still have much work to do. In fact, and as stated, I believe the Lord has spoken to my heart, exactly as he did to Joshua, *"You are old and stricken in years, and there remains yet very much land to be possessed"* (Josh. 13:1).

I am believing for more people to be Saved than ever before, more Believers to be baptized with the Holy Spirit, more Believers through the great Message of the Cross, to begin to walk the Walk of Victory. The words of Achsah keep ringing in my ears and settling in my heart, *"Give me a Blessing!"* I cannot believe that the Lord will not fulfill that request to its utmost heights and its utmost depths. *"Give me a Blessing!"*

(20) "THIS IS THE INHERITANCE OF THE TRIBE OF THE CHILDREN OF JUDAH ACCORDING TO THEIR FAMILIES.

(21) "AND THE UTTERMOST CITIES OF THE TRIBE OF THE CHILDREN OF JUDAH TOWARD THE COAST OF EDOM SOUTHWARD WERE KABZEEL, AND EDER, AND JAGUR,

(22) "AND KINAH, AND DIMONAH, AND ADADAH,

(23) "AND KEDESH, AND HAZOR, AND ITHNAN,

(24) "ZIPH, AND TELEM, AND BEALOTH,

(25) "AND HAZOR, HADATTAH, AND KERIOTH, AND HEZRON, WHICH IS HAZOR,

(26) "AMAM, AND SHEMA, AND MOLADAH,

(27) "AND HAZAR-GADDAH, AND HESHMON, AND BETH-PALET,

(28) "AND HAZAR-SHUAL, AND BEER-SHEBA, AND BIZJOTHJAH,

(29) "BAALAH, AND IIM, AND AZEM,

(30) "AND ELTOLAD, AND CHESIL, AND HORMAH,

(31) "AND ZIKLAG, AND MADMANNAH,

AND SANSANNAH,

(32) "AND LEBAOTH, AND SHILHIM, AND AIN, AND RIMMON: ALL THE CITIES ARE TWENTY AND NINE, WITH THEIR VILLAGES:

(33) "AND IN THE VALLEY, ESHTAOL, AND ZOREAH, AND ASHNAH,

(34) "AND ZANOAH, AND EN-GANNIM, TAPPUAH, AND ENAM,

(35) "JARMUTH, AND ADULLAM, SOCOH, AND AZEKAH,

(36) "AND SHARAIM, AND ADITHAIM, AND GEDERAH, AND GEDEROTHAIM; FOURTEEN CITIES WITH THEIR VILLAGES:

(37) "ZENAN, AND HADASHAH, AND MIGDAL-GAD,

(38) "AND DILEAN, AND MIZPEH, AND JOKTHEEL,

(39) "LACHISH, AND BOZKATH, AND EGLON,

(40) "AND CABBON, AND LAHMAM, AND KITHLISH,

(41) "AND GEDEROTH, BETH-DAGON, AND NAAMAH, AND MAKKEDAH; SIXTEEN CITIES WITH THEIR VILLAGES:

(42) "LIBNAH, AND ETHER, AND ASHAN,

(43) "AND JIPHTAH, AND ASHNAH, AND NEZIB,

(44) "AND KEILAH, AND ACHZIB, AND MARESHAH; NINE CITIES WITH THEIR VILLAGES:

(45) "EKRON, WITH HER TOWNS AND HER VILLAGES:

(46) "FROM EKRON EVEN UNTO THE SEA, ALL THAT LAY NEAR ASHDOD, WITH THEIR VILLAGES:

(47) "ASHDOD WITH HER TOWNS AND HER VILLAGES, GAZA WITH HER TOWNS AND HER VILLAGES, UNTO THE RIVER OF EGYPT, AND THE GREAT SEA, AND THE BORDER THEREOF:

(48) "AND IN THE MOUNTAINS, SHAMIR, AND JATTIR, AND SOCOH,

(49) "AND DANNAH, AND KIRJATH-SANNAH, WHICH IS DEBIR,

(50) "AND ANAB, AND ESHTEMOH, AND ANIM,

(51) "AND GOSHEN, AND HOLON, AND GILOH; ELEVEN CITIES WITH THEIR VILLAGES:

(52) "ARAB, AND DUMAH, AND ESHEAN,

(53) "AND JANUM, AND BETH-TAPPUAH, AND APHEKAH,

(54) "AND HUMTAH, AND KIRJATH-ARBA, WHICH IS HEBRON, AND ZIOR; NINE CITIES WITH THEIR VILLAGES:

(55) "MAON, CARMEL, AND ZIPH, AND JUTTAH,

(56) "AND JEZREEL, AND JOKDEAM, AND ZANOAH,

(57) "CAIN, GIBEAH, AND TIMNAH; TEN CITIES WITH THEIR VILLAGES:

(58) "HALHUL, BETH-ZUR, AND GEDOR,

(59) "AND MAARATH, AND BETH-ANOTH, AND ELTEKON; SIX CITIES WITH THEIR VILLAGES:

(60) "KIRJATH-BAAL, WHICH IS KIRJATH-JEARIM, AND RABBAH; TWO CITIES WITH THEIR VILLAGES:

(61) "IN THE WILDERNESS, BETH-ARABAH, MIDDIN, AND SECACAH,

(62) "AND NIBSHAN, AND THE CITY OF SALT, AND ENGEDI; SIX CITIES WITH THEIR VILLAGES."

The diagram is:

1. If it is to be noted, the Holy Spirit identifies each city given to Judah and specifically so. Likewise the Lord enumerates all that He gives unto us. What are we doing with it?

2. While these places were given to Judah, still, they had to take them, and do so by force, which meant they had to have the help of the Lord. Likewise, we have to have the help of the Lord in taking the Promise within our lives.

3. What is given to us was done so at great price — I speak of the price paid by Christ at Calvary's Cross. We should treasure it highly!

(63) "AS FOR THE JEBUSITES THE INHABITANTS OF JERUSALEM, THE CHILDREN OF JUDAH COULD NOT DRIVE THEM OUT: BUT THE JEBUSITES DWELL WITH THE CHILDREN OF JUDAH AT JERUSALEM UNTO THIS DAY."

The exegesis is:

1. Jerusalem remained in the power of the Jebusite until David, a Type of Israel's mighty King, captured it. In how many lives is found a fortress opposed to the Government of the Lord, which ought to have been conquered at the beginning.

2. Satan knew that Jerusalem would ultimately become the Capital of Israel; therefore, he would seek to make it his stronghold, which he did for many, many years.

3. This tells us that the very area in the Believer's life which is ungodly, and which the Believer has the greatest difficulty in conquering, is the very area which the Holy Spirit desires to make our strong suit, in essence, His Capital. This is why the battle is so intense in such a capacity. Spiritually speaking, the Jebusite must be driven out of the land, with nothing left of that former enemy.

THE JEBUSITES

Failure to drive out the Jebusites by Judah was a glaring failure of faith on their part. With the help of the Lord, as with all their other victories, they could have easily carried out this task. For some reason, they didn't.

Consequently, the Jebusites would be a thorn in Israel's flesh all the days of the Judges on up until the time of David. David would be the first one to expel the Jebusites from the city where the Lord would place His Name, Jerusalem.

As a Child of God, the area in your life that Satan fights and hinders the most is the area where God wants to place His greatest Glory. The Jebusite must go. He must not be allowed to stay. The reason for Satan's obstinacy is because of the plans that the Lord has for this area of your Spiritual life. Satan desires to erect a stronghold in the heart and life of every Believer, a stronghold which he occupies, and which greatly hinders and weakens the Child of God. To be sure, he is not easy to dislodge, as is proven here from the Scriptures. The Jebusites would remain in this stronghold, right in the midst of Israel for some four hundred years. In fact, the very first thing that David did upon becoming King of Israel was to take the stronghold of the Jebusites, with Jerusalem then becoming the capital city of Israel.

Concerning the spiritual aspect of such, Paul said:

PULLING DOWN STRONGHOLDS

"For though we walk in the flesh (refers to the fact that we do not yet have Glorified Bodies), *we do not war after the flesh* (after

NOTES

our own ability, but rather by the Power of the Spirit)*:

"(For the weapons of our warfare are not carnal (carnal weapons consist of those which are man devised), *but mighty through God* (the Cross of Christ [I Cor. 1:18]) *to the pulling down of strong holds;)*

"Casting down imaginations (philosophic strongholds; every effort man makes outside of the Cross of Christ), *and every high thing that exalts itself against the Knowledge of God* (all the pride of the human heart), *and bringing into captivity every thought to the obedience of Christ* (can be done only by the Believer looking exclusively to the Cross, where all Victory is found; the Holy Spirit will then perform the task)" (II Cor. 10:3-5).

As we've already stated in the notes following the Passages of Scripture, these strongholds erected by Satan in our lives, can only be pulled down by Faith in Christ and what Christ has done for us at the Cross. The Holy Spirit will then work mightily on our behalf; however, the great problem with the modern Church, and perhaps it's always been a problem, is that we attempt to pull down these strongholds by means other than Christ and the Cross, and our Faith in that Finished Work. No matter how good it may seem to be on the surface, such efforts simply will not work.

We must remember, that even though we are Saved and baptized with the Holy Spirit, still, we within ourselves, which refers to our own capabilities, simply cannot do what needs to be done, whatever that might be. Of course, the immediate retort to that is, *"The Lord is helping me."*

Of course, the Lord will help us all that He can; however, if our faith is in anything other than Christ and the Cross, this greatly limits the Lord as to what He can do. In fact, with faith being improperly placed, such a direction constitutes spiritual adultery on the part of the Believer.

WHAT IS SPRITUAL ADULTERY?

Spiritual adultery is the Believer who is married to Christ (Rom. 7:1-4), and who must be faithful to Christ, but instead seeks about regarding other things concerning living this life. In other words, the Believer resorts to man-devised schemes, such as *"The Purpose Driven Life,"* etc. That constitutes spiritual adultery (Rom. 7:1-4). In such a state, the Holy Spirit, even though He definitely will remain in our lives, and will do all He can, still, He will not help us commit spiritual adultery, as should be overly obvious. In that situation, and sadly the situation in which the majority of the modern Church finds itself, most modern Christians are receiving precious little help from the Lord; consequently, Satan is able to erect his strongholds, which he is doing presently, I think, at an unprecedented rate.

When we get to the commentary on II Samuel, we will see how David took the stronghold of the Jebusites, which path of victory is opened up to us presently, and even in a greater way, because we now have a better Covenant based on better Promises (Heb. 8:6).

CHAPTER 16

(1) "AND THE LOT OF THE CHILDREN OF JOSEHPH FELL FROM JORDAN BY JERICHO, UNTO THE WATER OF JERICHO ON THE EAST, TO THE WILDERNESS THAT GOES UP FROM JERICHO THROUGHOUT MOUNT BETH-EL,

(2) "AND GOES OUT FROM BETH-EL TO LUZ, AND PASSES ALONG UNTO THE BORDERS OF ARCHI TO ATAROTH,

(3) "AND GOES DOWN WESTWARD TO THE COAST OF JAPHLETI, UNTO THE COAST OF BETH-HORON THE NETHER, AND TO GEZER: AND THE GOINGS OUT THEREOF ARE AT THE SEA.

(4) "SO THE CHILDREN OF JOSHEPH, MANASSEH AND EPHRAIM, TOOK THEIR INHERITANCE."

The pattern is:

1. As stated, Judah's allotment was given first because it was from the Tribe of Judah that the Messiah would come; likewise, Joseph was a Type of Christ; therefore, his sons would be next in line to receive their portion of the Promised Land.

2. The words *"the lot"* proclaim the fact that their portion was decided by the Urim and Thummim. In other words, the Holy

Spirit drew the boundaries.

3. It seems from Joshua 17:14 that Joseph was dissatisfied with his lot; but the True Joseph in Psalms 16:6, declared that the lines had fallen to Him in pleasant places, and that He had a goodly heritage. He then added in Psalms 125:3, that the rod of the wicked should not rest upon the lot of the righteous.

4. The two Tribes and a half (Reuben, Gad, and Manasseh) chose for themselves. They did not wait for God to give them their portion; and, therefore, the rod of the wicked very soon rested upon their self-chosen lot.

5. The whole land was, in effect, first given to Judah and Joseph, the other Tribes receiving their portions according as they stood in relationship to the Royal and First-born sons of Jacob. These sons, united, typify Christ, to Whom the whole land is promised (Ps. 2, 110).

6. All was according to the Word of the Lord. The casting of lots, the men who were to cast them, the divisions by Families, by Tribes, and by Names — all were Divine — nothing was left either to the will or wisdom of man.

(5) "AND THE BORDER OF THE CHILDREN OF EPHRAIM ACCORDING TO THEIR FAMILIES WAS THUS: EVEN THE BORDER OF THEIR INHERITANCE ON THE EAST SIDE WAS ATAROTH-ADDAR, UNTO BETH-HORON THE UPPER;

(6) "AND THE BORDER WENT OUT TOWARD THE SEA TO MICHMETHAH ON THE NORTH SIDE; AND THE BORDER WENT ABOUT EASTWARD UNTO TAANATH-SHILOH, AND PASSED BY IT ON THE EAST TO JANOHAH;

(7) "AND IT WENT DOWN FROM JANOHAH TO ATAROTH, AND TO NAARATH, AND CAME TO JERICHO, AND WENT OUT AT JORDAN.

(8) "THE BORDER WENT OUT FROM TAPPUAH WESTWARD UNTO THE RIVER KANAH; AND THE GOINGS OUT THEREOF WERE AT THE SEA. THIS IS THE INHERITANCE OF THE TRIBE OF THE CHILDREN OF EPHRAIM BY THEIR FAMILIES.

(9) "AND THE SEPARATE CITIES FOR THE CHILDREN OF EPHRAIM WERE AMONG THE INHERITANCE OF THE

CHILDREN OF MANASSEH, ALL THE CITIES WITH THEIR VILLAGES.

(10) "AND THEY DROVE NOT OUT THE CANAANITES WHO DWELT IN GEZER: BUT THE CANAANITES DWELL AMONG THE EPHRAIMITES UNTO THIS DAY, AND SERVE UNDER TRIBUTE."

The overview is:

1. The portions were allotted *"according to their families."* This expressed the measure of their need; and it was richly supplied.

2. In Ephesians, the Believer's *"lot"* is given not in proportion to either faith or need *"but according to His Riches."*

3. Concerning all of this, Williams says, *"The meanings of the Hebrew names of the towns and mountains, etc., which on the one side separated a Tribe from the world, and on the other side, from a brother-Tribe, are full of valuable teaching for the Christian. They plainly show how fellowship with evil on the one hand, or a lack of fellowship with truth on the other hand sap faith and rob the servant of God of power to drive out the inhabitants of the Land."*[1]

4. The Children of Ephraim could not drive out the inhabitants of those cities, so the Canaanite would dwell in the Land; but the day will come when Israel's mighty King will take possession of the Land, and then there will be *"no more the Canaanite in the House of the LORD"* (Zech. 14:21).

THE FAILURE OF EPHRAIM

As the Children of Judah did not drive out the Jebusites, likewise, the Children of Ephraim did not drive the Canaanites out of Gezer. All of this was in direct disobedience to the Word of the Lord. The Canaanites still in the land were a witness to the failure of Israel to accomplish God's Will. Why they did not obey the Lord we aren't told; however, we will always suffer when we neglect God's Will for worldly convenience, or for whatever reason.

Bringing this thing up to us presently, the Canaanites remaining in the land were a type of sins remaining in the heart of the modern Believer. Most of the land of that time was conquered. But there were these glaring omissions. The heart of the Believer is conquered by Christ. Christ sits enthroned

there. With the Canaanite there as well, and in a sense enthroned in some capacity, one can easily now see the dichotomy.

Sin always retains its old character of destruction, and must be ever regarded as dangerous (Rom. 7:23).

The Canaanites although not driven out, were, in fact, forced to serve under tribute; however, that is actually not God's Way. There must be no vestige of sin left! It all must be rooted out, and rooted out in its entirety!

The idea is, *"tribute"* seems to suggest a compromise. One cannot compromise with sin, and even as the future portrayed, the Canaanite left in the land, would ultimately cause Israel tremendous problems; likewise, sin remaining in the life of the Christian, although subdued, will ultimately cause great problems. It must be, as stated, rooted out in its entirety.

CHAPTER 17

(1) "THERE WAS ALSO A LOT FOR THE TRIBE OF MANASSEH; FOR HE WAS THE FIRSTBORN OF JOSEPH; TO WIT, FOR MACHIR THE FIRSTBORN OF MANASSEH, THE FATHER OF GILEAD: BECAUSE HE WAS A MAN OF WAR, THEREFORE HE HAD GILEAD AND BASHAN.

(2) "THERE WAS ALSO A LOT FOR THE REST OF THE CHILDREN OF MANASSEH BY THEIR FAMILIES; FOR THE CHILDREN OF ABIEZER, AND FOR THE CHILDREN OF HELEK, AND FOR THE CHILDREN OF ASRIEL, AND FOR THE CHILDREN OF SHECHEM, AND FOR THE CHILDREN OF HEPHER, AND FOR THE CHILDREN OF SHEMIDA: THESE WERE THE MALE CHILDREN OF MANASSEH THE SON OF JOSEPH BY THEIR FAMILIES.

(3) "BUT ZELOPHEHAD, THE SON OF HEPHER, THE SON OF GILEAD, THE SON OF MACHIR, THE SON OF MANASSEH, HAD NO SONS, BUT DAUGHTERS: AND THESE ARE THE NAMES OF HIS DAUGHTERS, MAHLAH, AND NOAH, HOGLAH, MILCAH, AND TIRZAH.

(4) "AND THEY CAME NEAR BEFORE

ELEAZAR THE PRIEST, AND BEFORE JOSHUA THE SON OF NUN, AND BEFORE THE PRINCES, SAYING, THE LORD COMMANDED MOSES TO GIVE US AN INHERITANCE AMONG OUR BRETHREN. THEREFORE ACCORDING TO THE COMMANDMENT OF THE LORD HE GAVE THEM AN INHERITANCE AMONG THE BRETHREN OF THEIR FATHER.

(5) "AND THERE FELL TEN PORTIONS TO MANASSEH, BESIDE THE LAND OF GILEAD AND BASHAN, WHICH WERE ON THE OTHER SIDE JORDAN;

(6) "BECAUSE THE DAUGHTERS OF MANASSEH HAD AN INHERITANCE AMONG HIS SONS: AND THE REST OF MANASSEH'S SONS HAD THE LAND OF GILEAD.

(7) "AND THE COAST OF MANASSEH WAS FROM ASHER TO MICHMETHAH, THAT LIES BEFORE SHECHEM; AND THE BORDER WENT ALONG ON THE RIGHT HAND UNTO THE INHABITANTS OF EN-TAPPUAH.

(8) "NOW MANASSEH HAD THE LAND OF TAPPUAH: BUT TAPPUAH ON THE BORDER OF MANASSEH BELONGED TO THE CHILDREN OF EPHRAIM;

(9) "AND THE COAST DESCENDED UNTO THE RIVER KANAH, SOUTHWARD OF THE RIVER: THESE CITIES OF EPHRAIM ARE AMONG THE CITIES OF MANASSEH: THE COAST OF MANASSEH ALSO WAS ON THE NORTH SIDE OF THE RIVER, AND THE OUTGOINGS OF IT WERE AT THE SEA:

(10) "SOUTHWARD IT WAS EPHRAIM'S, AND NORTHWARD IT WAS MANASSEH'S, AND THE SEA IS HIS BORDER; AND THEY MET TOGETHER IN ASHER ON THE NORTH, AND IN ISSACHAR ON THE EAST.

(11) "AND MANASSEH HAD IN ISSACHAR AND IN ASHER BETH-SHEAN AND HER TOWNS, AND IBLEAM AND HER TOWNS, AND THE INHABITANTS OF DOR AND HER TOWNS, AND THE INHABITANTS OF EN-DOR AND HER TOWNS, AND THE INHABITANTS OF TAANACH AND HER TOWNS, AND THE INHABITANTS OF MEGIDDO AND HER TOWNS, EVEN THREE COUNTRIES.

NOTES

(12) "YET THE CHILDREN OF MANASSEH COULD NOT DRIVE OUT THE INHABITANTS OF THOSE CITIES; BUT THE CANAANITES WOULD DWELL IN THAT LAND.

(13) "YET IT CAME TO PASS, WHEN THE CHILDREN OF ISRAEL WERE WAXED STRONG, THAT THEY PUT THE CANAANITES TO TRIBUTE; BUT DID NOT UTTERLY DRIVE THEM OUT."

The exposition is:

1. Some four times the Holy Spirit records the Faith of the five daughters of Zelophehad (Num. 26:33; 27:1; 36:11; Josh. 17:4).

Even though they were women, and no provision had been made for them in the Law, as it regards inheritance, their Faith claimed such just the same as their male counterparts. As well, through Faith, they forged a path, not only for themselves, but for all other families in Israel where all the offspring were females.

2. We are told in the Sixth Verse where these daughters of Zelophehad had their inheritance. It was on the west side of the Jordan River. (Manasseh had a portion on both sides of the Jordan River.)

3. The Thirteenth Verse proclaims the fact that once again, we have the Word of God being compromised, which would fall out to tremendous problems and trouble later on for Israel.

COMPROMISE

The Israelites, as is obvious in Scripture, were promised the possession of the land of Canaan on condition that they should exterminate its inhabitants. They did not do this.

Why?

It was either because they thought it would be too difficult, or else they found the process of exacting tribute to be, they thought, the better choice. As we have addressed in the past, the command to exterminate the inhabitants of the land was not just an arbitrary choice on the part of God. It was given because of the terrible depravity of these people. As well, the attractiveness of their sins was ever in view. In fact, this *"attractiveness"* would later become a tremendous problem for Israel.

THE ATTRACTIVENESS AND POWER OF SIN

Some time ago over the SonLife Radio Network, actually on Gabriel's program, a dear lady called in as it regards the attraction of the world.

She went on to mention that while her daughter might go to some places that may not be desirable for a Christian, she always took another Christian with her, the lady said, which somehow was supposed to lessen the danger.

The truth is, it lessened the danger not at all. Sin has a power that is far beyond our comprehension.

In the first place, and as stated, sin is attractive. Satan would not propose something that has no lure. To be sure, that lure has attracted untold millions of young people, with destruction every time in view.

But along with the attraction, the power of sin is such as to defy all description. That's the reason the child cannot be allowed to decide for himself as it regards vices. The parents must relate to the child, and in no uncertain terms, the right and the wrong of certain situations. The facts are, if that child tries sin in any form, bondage is just around the corner. It must be remembered, that every alcoholic in this nation or the world for that matter, began with their first drink. It is the same with the first cigarette, the first act of immorality, the first hit of drugs, etc.

Sin is not such that it can be experimented with, and then laid down if so desired. Untold millions find they can't lay it down.

So, the Canaanites would prove to be a terrible adversary in the future. While now they pay tribute to Israel, the time would come when Israel would pay tribute to them, and that's always the case! We get it out or it gets us out!

(14) "AND THE CHILDREN OF JOSEPH SPOKE UNTO JOSHUA, SAYING, WHY HAVE YOU GIVEN ME BUT ONE LOT AND ONE PORTION TO INHERIT, SEEING I AM A GREAT PEOPLE, FORASMUCH AS THE LORD HAS BLESSED ME HITHERTO?

(15) "AND JOSHUA ANSWERED THEM, IF YOU BE A GREAT PEOPLE, THEN GET YOU UP TO THE WOOD COUNTRY, AND CUT DOWN FOR YOURSELF THERE IN THE LAND OF THE PERIZZITES AND OF THE GIANTS, IF MOUNT EPHRAIM BE TOO NARROW FOR YOU.

(16) "AND THE CHILDREN OF JOSEPH SAID, THE HILL IS NOT ENOUGH FOR US: AND ALL THE CANAANITES WHO DWELL IN THE LAND OF THE VALLEY HAVE CHARIOTS OF IRON, BOTH THEY WHO ARE OF BETH-SHEAN AND HER TOWNS, AND THEY WHO ARE OF THE VALLEY OF JEZREEL.

(17) "AND JOSHUA SPOKE UNTO THE HOUSE OF JOSEPH, EVEN TO EPHRAIM AND TO MANASSEH, SAYING, YOU ARE A GREAT PEOPLE, AND HAVE GREAT POWER: YOU SHALL NOT HAVE ONE LOT ONLY:

(18) "BUT THE MOUNTAIN SHALL BE YOURS: FOR IT IS A WOOD, AND YOU SHALL CUT IT DOWN: AND THE OUTGOINGS OF IT SHALL BE YOURS; FOR YOU SHALL DRIVE OUT THE CANAANITES, THOUGH THEY HAVE IRON CHARIOTS, AND THOUGH THEY BE STRONG."

The pattern is:

1. The boasting, discontent, unbelief, selfishness, and cowardice of the Children of Joseph was, with fine scorn, rebuked by Joshua, who was himself of the Tribe of Joseph.

2. Despite the encouragement given by Joshua, the Children of Joseph did not drive the Canaanites out, as Verses 11 through 13 show.

3. The reason for this was that they did not trust in God, but preferred an unworthy compromise with neighbors, who, however rich in warlike material, were sunk in sensuality and sloth.

COMPLAINTS

Ephraim and Manasseh, sons of Joseph want a larger lot. They boast as to how great they are and, therefore, feel that they should have a greater allotment. In other words, they were dissatisfied with what the Holy Spirit had allotted for them, so they demand more.

How so much like many Christians who are not satisfied with that which the Lord has given them, but demand more. The truth is, when such is the case, they are not even realizing the full potential, not nearly so, for what they presently have. Even if such people are given more, it will conclude by very little that is positive being carried out.

Joshua's challenge to them was: *"If you are such a great people, then prove it by conquering more of the land."* He then told them, *"Destroy the giants."* In essence, the great warrior says to them, *"If you and Ephraim are so great and worthy, use your greatness and power for the good of yourselves and others, and none will grudge you what in this way you win."*

The truth is, it is foolish to complain of our lot until, as we have stated, we have made the best use of it. The Ephraimites had not cleared their forests, yet they complained of the narrowness of their possession. Too many Christians bury their one talent simply because it is not five. We have no excuse for complaints before we have made the full use of what we presently possess.

The truth is, God wants us to ask for more. So, the sons of Joseph were not wrong in asking; however, before they asked they should have first developed what they presently had. And so should we!

CHAPTER 18

(1) "AND THE WHOLE CONGREGATION OF THE CHILDREN OF ISRAEL ASSEMBLED TOGETHER AT SHILOH, AND SET UP THE TABERNACLE OF THE CONGREGATION THERE. AND THE LAND WAS SUBDUED BEFORE THEM."

The exposition is:

1. Shiloh was about twenty-five miles north of Jerusalem. It was pretty much in the center of the land.

2. The Tabernacle remained at Shiloh and Gibeon for some 300 years, and ceased to be used when replaced by Solomon's Temple.

3. The Tabernacle symbolized Grace while the Temple foreshadowed Glory. Both are found in Jesus, the God of Grace and Glory.

THE TABERNACLE

The strength of Israel was the Tabernacle, because it foreshadowed Christ. In fact, every single thing about the Tabernacle, its

sacred furniture, its rituals and ceremonies, its construction, in fact all that pertained to it, symbolized Christ in either His Atoning, Mediatorial, or Intercessory Work. As stated, the *"Tabernacle"* was the nerve center of Israel, and simply because it represented Christ and, therefore, the Power of God.

The Spirit and Power of God is the strength of the Church; however, the Church seems to be aware of that not at all. It depends mostly on man's whims, schemes and fads, along with humanistic psychology. Oh yes, the machinery of the Church is large and runs well, but there is none of the Moving and Operation of the Holy Spirit, or precious little, and He seems not to be missed at all.

The name *"Shiloh,"* came to be another name for the coming Christ. So, when *"the Children of Israel assembled together at Shiloh,"* in a sense, they were assembled together in order to meet with Christ.

(2) "AND THERE REMAINED AMONG THE CHILDREN OF ISRAEL SEVEN TRIBES, WHICH HAD NOT YET RECEIVED THEIR INHERITANCE.

(3) "AND JOSHUA SAID UNTO THE CHILDREN OF ISRAEL, HOW LONG ARE YOU SLACK TO GO TO POSSESS THE LAND, WHICH THE LORD GOD OF YOUR FATHERS HAS GIVEN YOU?

(4) "GIVE OUT FROM AMONG YOU THREE MEN FOR EACH TRIBE: AND I WILL SEND THEM, AND THEY SHALL RISE, AND GO THROUGH THE LAND, AND DESCRIBE IT ACCORDING TO THE INHERITANCE OF THEM; AND THEY SHALL COME AGAIN TO ME.

(5) "AND THEY SHALL DIVIDE IT INTO SEVEN PARTS: JUDAH SHALL ABIDE IN THEIR COAST ON THE SOUTH, AND THE HOUSE OF JOSEPH SHALL ABIDE IN THEIR COASTS ON THE NORTH.

(6) "YOU SHALL THEREFORE DESCRIBE THE LAND INTO SEVEN PARTS, AND BRING THE DESCRIPTION HITHER TO ME, THAT I MAY CAST LOTS FOR YOU HERE BEFORE THE LORD OUR GOD.

(7) "BUT THE LEVITES HAVE NO PART AMONG YOU; FOR THE PRIESTHOOD OF THE LORD IS THEIR INHERITANCE: AND GAD, AND REUBEN, AND HALF THE TRIBE OF MANASSEH, HAVE RECEIVED

THEIR INHERITANCE BEYOND JORDAN ON THE EAST, WHICH MOSES THE SERVANT OF THE LORD GAVE THEM.

(8) "AND THE MEN AROSE, AND WENT AWAY: AND JOSHUA CHARGED THEM WHO WENT TO DESCRIBE THE LAND, SAYING, GO AND WALK THROUGH THE LAND, AND DESCRIBE IT, AND COME AGAIN TO ME, THAT I MAY HERE CAST LOTS FOR YOU BEFORE THE LORD IN SHILOH.

(9) "AND THE MEN WENT AND PASSED THROUGH THE LAND, AND DESCRIBED IT BY CITIES INTO SEVEN PARTS IN A BOOK, AND CAME AGAIN TO JOSHUA TO THE HOST AT SHILOH.

(10) "AND JOSHUA CAST LOTS FOR THEM IN SHILOH BEFORE THE LORD: AND THERE JOSHUA DIVIDED THE LAND UNTO THE CHILDREN OF ISRAEL ACCORDING TO THEIR DIVISIONS."

The overview is:

1. Seven of the Tribes, as we see here, had been very slow to proceed forward. That is symbolic of far too many Christians. Is it possible that our Heavenly Joshua is asking the same question of modern Christians, as Joshua asked of Israel of old? How long are you slack . . . ?

2. Evidently, these individuals who were to spy out the land were to describe what they desired regarding the petitioning of the land, with the Lord, of course, having the final say.

3. This tells us that it is perfectly proper for Believers to describe to the Lord what we want, but always with the idea that our primary objective is the Will of God, which means that it's what He wants.

HOW LONG ARE YOU SLACK
TO POSSESS THE LAND?

Why must the Holy Spirit have to ask us the same question over and over again?

Israel is now in the land, the Promised Land, but yet, they are slow to carry out the Will of God. Why?

So many times, self-will or slothfulness, or both hinder us from having God's best in our hearts and lives.

Under the New Covenant, I think that it can be said that there is no limit to what the modern Believer can possess in the Lord, if such a Believer will exercise Faith, thereby putting God first in all things. That goes for the Preacher and the Laity. God is no respecter of persons.

But the truth is, all too many modern Believers are satisfied to just be Saved. In other words, while all Believers, and I speak of true Believers, definitely have *"more abundant life,"* only a few Believers are truly enjoying their *"more abundant life"* (Jn. 10:10).

THE CROSS OF CHRIST AND
POSSESSING THE LAND

For my sixty odd years of studying the Word of God, I am fully convinced that it is impossible for Believers to properly grow in Grace and the Knowledge of the Lord, without first understanding the Cross. Listen to Paul:

"But God be thanked, that you were the servants of sin (slaves to the sin nature, what we were before we were Saved), *but you have obeyed from the heart that form of Doctrine* (Jesus Christ and Him Crucified; understanding that all things come to the Believer from God by the means of the Cross) *which was delivered you* (the Lord gave this 'form of Doctrine' to Paul, and he gave it to us in his Epistles)" (Rom. 6:17).

What *"form of Doctrine"* is Paul speaking of?

He is taking Believers back to Verses 3 through 5 of the Sixth Chapter of Romans. He is reminding us that we were *"baptized into His Death, buried with Him by baptism into death, and raised with Him in Newness of Life."* In other words, that *"form of Doctrine"* is the Cross of Christ.

ALL CHRISTIAN MATURITY IS
PREDICATED ON ONE'S
UNDERSTANDING OF
THE CROSS

This is one of the reasons that so many of these schemes and fads of modern day religion are so eagerly accepted. There is no, or at least precious little, spiritual maturity. Let me say it again:

The maturity of the Believer, which speaks of our growing in Grace and the Knowledge of the Lord, depends totally upon our understanding of the Cross.

No understanding, no maturity!

Little understanding, little maturity!

Much understanding, much maturity!

Once the Cross begins to be understood, then the parts and pieces of the Word of God, so to speak, begin to come together. Now Spiritual Growth begins. Peter said:

"But grow in Grace (presents the only way the Saint can grow), *and in the Knowledge of our Lord and Saviour Jesus Christ.* (This *'knowledge'* refers not only to Who Christ is [the Lord of Glory], but, as well, What He did in order that we might be Redeemed, which points to the Cross)" (II Pet. 3:18).

WHAT DOES IT MEAN TO GROW IN GRACE?

If it is to be noticed, the Lord did not say *"Grow in Law,"* etc., but rather *"Grow in Grace."*

One can only grow in Grace as one properly understands the Cross as it refers to Sanctification. That knowledge is simple:

We must understand that every single thing we receive from God comes to us from our Lord and Saviour as the Source. We must also understand, that the Cross is the Means by which all of this is done.

The Grace of God is simply the Goodness of God extended to undeserving Saints. That Goodness is extended to us on an unending basis, whenever our Faith is properly placed in the Cross, and remains in the Cross; consequently, now we can *"Grow in Grace."* Without a proper knowledge of the Cross, growth in Grace presents itself literally as an impossibility. Failing, regarding growth in Grace, then the *"Knowledge of our Lord and Saviour Jesus Christ,"* comes to a grinding halt also. One cannot truly know the *"Person"* of Christ without a proper understanding of the Cross, as one cannot properly know the *"purpose"* of Christ without understanding the Cross.

So, to possess the land, there has to be a proper understanding of the Finished Work of Christ.

(11) "AND THE LOT OF THE TRIBE OF THE CHILDREN OF BENJAMIN CAME UP ACCORDING TO THEIR FAMILIES: AND THE COAST OF THEIR LOT CAME

FORTH BETWEEN THE CHILDREN OF JUDAH AND THE CHILDREN OF JOSEPH.

(12) "AND THEIR BORDER ON THE NORTH SIDE WAS FROM JORDAN; AND THE BORDER WENT UP TO THE SIDE OF JERICHO ON THE NORTH SIDE, AND WENT UP THROUGH THE MOUNTAINS WESTWARD; AND THE GOINGS OUT THEREOF WERE AT THE WILDERNESS OF BETH-AVEN.

(13) "AND THE BORDER WENT OVER FROM THENCE TOWARD LUZ, TO THE SIDE OF LUZ, WHICH IS BETHEL, SOUTHWARD; AND THE BORDER DESCENDED TO ATAROTH-ADAR, NEAR THE HILL THAT LIES ON THE SOUTH SIDE OF THE NETHER BETH-HORON.

(14) "AND THE BORDER WAS DRAWN THENCE, AND COMPASSED THE CORNER OF THE SEA SOUTHWARD, FROM THE HILL THAT LIES BEFORE BETH-HORON SOUTHWARD; AND THE GOINGS OUT THEREOF WERE AT KIRJATH-BAAL, WHICH IS KIRJATH-JEARIM, A CITY OF THE CHILDREN OF JUDAH: THIS WAS THE WEST QUARTER.

(15) "AND THE SOUTH QUARTER WAS FROM THE END OF KIRJATH-JEARIM, AND THE BORDER WENT OUT ON THE WEST, AND WENT OUT TO THE WELL OF WATERS OF NEPHTOAH:

(16) "AND THE BORDER CAME DOWN TO THE END OF THE MOUNTAIN THAT LIES BEFORE THE VALLEY OF THE SON OF HINNOM, AND WHICH IS IN THE VALLEY OF THE GIANTS ON THE NORTH, AND DESCENDED TO THE VALLEY OF HINNOM, TO THE SIDE OF JEBUSI ON THE SOUTH, AND DESCENDED TO EN-ROGEL,

(17) "AND WAS DRAWN FROM THE NORTH, AND WENT FORTH TO EN-SHEMESH, AND WENT FORTH TOWARD GELILOTH, WHICH IS OVER AGAINST THE GOING UP OF ADUMMIM, AND DESCENDED TO THE STONE OF BOHAN THE SON OF REUBEN,

(18) "AND PASSED ALONG TOWARD THE SIDE OVER AGAINST ARABAH NORTHWARD, AND WENT DOWN UNTO ARABAH:

(19) "AND THE BORDER PASSED ALONG TO THE SIDE OF BETH-HOGLAH NORTHWARD: AND THE OUTGOINGS OF THE

BORDER WERE AT THE NORTH BAY OF THE SALT SEA AT THE SOUTH END OF JORDAN: THIS WAS THE SOUTH COAST.

(20) "AND JORDAN WAS THE BORDER OF IT ON THE EAST SIDE. THIS WAS THE INHERITANCE OF THE CHILDREN OF BENJAMIN, BY THE COASTS THEREOF ROUND ABOUT, ACCORDING TO THEIR FAMILIES.

(21) "NOW THE CITIES OF THE TRIBE OF THE CHILDREN OF BENJAMIN ACCORDING TO THEIR FAMILIES WERE JERICHO, AND BETH-HOGLAH, AND THE VALLEY OF KEZIZ.

(22) "AND BETH-ARABAH, AND ZEMARAIM, AND BETH-EL,

(23) "AND AVIM, AND PARAH, AND OPHRAH,

(24) "AND CHEPHAR-HAAMMONAI, AND OPHNI, AND GABA; TWELVE CITIES WITH THEIR VILLAGES:

(25) "GIBEON, AND RAMAH, AND BEEROTH,

(26) "AND MIZPEH, AND CHEPHIRAH, AND MOZAH,

(27) "AND REKEM, AND IRPEEL, AND TARALAH,

(28) "AND ZELAH, ELEPH, AND JEBUSI, WHICH IS JERUSALEM, GIBEAH, AND KIRJATH; FOURTEEN CITIES WITH THEIR VILLAGES. THIS IS THE INHERITANCE OF THE CHILDREN OF BENJAMIN ACCORDING TO THEIR FAMILIES."

The exegesis is:

1. The Lord provided for Benjamin a plot sufficiently large to amply take care of each family.

2. No one family, therefore, needed to be apprehensive as to the supply of its necessities.

3. Actually, Jerusalem was situated in the Tribe of Benjamin, in a sense straddling the border of both Benjamin and Judah.

THE TRIBE OF BENJAMIN

The Sixteenth Verse says, *"The valley of the giants."* These giants were called by various names and were placed there by Satan to hinder the coming of the Messiah. They would attempt to corrupt the population by evil and subdue it by force. They were the results of the union of fallen angels and evil women (Gen. 6:2-4). Without further

NOTES

explanation, their origin was totally of evil. They were a formidable power but were defeated by the People of God.

Likewise, there are *"giants"* in our own inheritance. Who are the giants in your life? If so, they cannot be defeated by natural means. All the efforts of man fall down when attempting to assuage the terrible problems caused by envy, jealousy, pride, and greed. The changed heart is the only answer. Jesus Christ and Him Crucified is that answer. He is not only the answer for the sinner, but He is the answer for the Believer as well. He and He Alone can subdue these giants. Please remember, this is a battle to the death. No quarter is asked or given; you defeat the giants in Christ, or the giants will defeat you.

THE VALLEY OF THE GIANTS

This *"valley of the giants"* was in the inheritance of Benjamin. Saul, the first king of Israel would be a product of Benjamin, and so would the beloved Paul of the Book of Acts. Sadly, Saul would not defeat his giants, but Paul most definitely would (Rom. 8:1-2, 11).

Yes, all have giants; all have to fight them. All either win or lose according to their dependence on Christ. No wonder Paul, of the Tribe of Benjamin of the valley of the giants would say, *"I am crucified with Christ* (as the Foundation of all Victory; Paul, here, takes us back to Rom. 6:3-5)*: nevertheless I live* (have New Life)*; yet not I* (not by my own strength and ability)*, but Christ lives in me* (by virtue of me dying with Him on the Cross, and being raised with Him in Newness of Life)*: and the life which I now live in the flesh* (my daily walk before God) *I live by the Faith of the Son of God* (the Cross is ever the Object of my Faith)*, Who loved me, and gave Himself for me* (which is the only way that I could be Saved)" (Gal. 2:20).

CHAPTER 19

(1) "AND THE SECOND LOT CAME FORTH TO SIMEON, EVEN FOR THE TRIBE OF THE CHILDREN OF SIMEON ACCORDING TO THEIR FAMILIES: AND THEIR INHERITANCE WAS WITHIN

THE INHERITANCE OF THE CHILDREN OF JUDAH.

(2) "AND THEY HAD IN THEIR IN- HERITANCE BEERSHEBA, AND SHEBA, AND MOLADAH,

(3) "AND HAZAR-SHUAL, AND BALAH, AND AZEM,

(4) "AND ELTOLAD, AND BETHUL, AND HORMAH,

(5) "AND ZIKLAG, AND BETH- MARCABOTH, AND HAZAR-SUSAH,

(6) "AND BETH-LEBAOTH, AND SHARUHEN; THIRTEEN CITIES AND THEIR VILLAGES:

(7) "AIN, REMMON, AND ETHER, AND ASHAN; FOUR CITIES AND THEIR VILLAGES:

(8) "AND ALL THE VILLAGES THAT WERE ROUND ABOUT THESE CITIES TO BAALATH-BEER, RAMATH OF THE SOUTH. THIS IS THE INHERITANCE OF THE TRIBE OF THE CHILDREN OF SIMEON ACCORDING TO THEIR FAMILIES.

(9) "OUT OF THE PORTION OF THE CHILDREN OF JUDAH WAS THE INHER- ITANCE OF THE CHILDREN OF SIMEON: FOR THE PART OF THE CHILDREN OF JUDAH WAS TOO MUCH FOR THEM: THEREFORE THE CHILDREN OF SIMEON HAD THEIR INHERITANCE WITHIN THE INHERITANCE OF THEM."

The composition is:

1. Simeon, because of his misconduct (Gen. 49:7) was under a curse. As a result, he was really to have no inheritance in the Promised Land. And so he didn't, and again, so he did!

2. Judah shared her inheritance with the outcast brother and thus, doubled her joy. Dividing Divine Blessing with others doubles it. This is a great principle, and should moti- vate our actions at all times.

3. Thus it was that Simeon, justly doomed to wrath, was taken up in Grace — the curse being turned into a Blessing — and given a seat among the sons at the King's table; for the Lord sprang out of Judah (Heb. 7:14).

4. Simeon was saved by Grace, not by works; the name means "hearing." The Holy Spirit in Galatians 3:2 contrasts salvation by doing and Salvation by hearing, and teaches that only upon the latter principle

NOTES

can sinners be given a portion in the Heav- enly Canaan (Williams).[1]

5. In truth, Simeon and Judah proclaim a type of the human race, as well as our Lord in His Grace. The whole of the human race is cursed. But our Heavenly Judah, by His Grace, and certainly not through any good thing that we have done, has made room for us in His most glorious Inheritance. And, to be sure, a place in Judah's Inheritance is the greatest position of all. As stated, Grace shines in the First and Ninth Verses of this Nineteenth Chapter of Joshua.

THE INHERITANCE OF SIMEON

The very phrase, "The inheritance of Simeon," speaks of the Grace of God. It was not to be, because a curse was pronounced upon them. What had they done? In fact, this curse was pronounced on both Simeon and Levi.

As recorded in Genesis, Chapter 34, both Simeon and Levi slaughtered all the men of the village of Shechem, because one of the young men of the city, a prince, had violated their sister Dinah.

Of the incident, Jacob said to Simeon and Levi, "You have troubled me to make me to stink among the inhabitants of the land . . ." (Gen. 34:30).

Because of this deed that was done, when Jacob, on his dying bed was prophesying over all of his sons as it regarded the Tribes which would spring from them, he said of Simeon and Levi, "Instruments of cruelty are in their habitations . . . Cursed be their anger, for it was fierce; and their wrath, for it was cruel: I will divide them in Jacob, and scatter them in Israel" (Gen. 49:5, 7). And now nearly 300 years later, they must face this curse; however, and as stated, it would be turned into a Blessing.

How?

Simeon, as we see in this Nineteenth Chapter, is given a part of Judah, while the Tribe of Levi became the Priestly Tribe. While they were truly scattered over Israel, still, in a sense, they had the greatest Inheritance of all — the Lord of Glory.

As we've already stated, this is a beautiful story of Grace. It is the story in a sense of the entirety of the human family, at least for all who will believe.

Due to the Fall, every human being is under a curse — the curse of the broken Law. But when Jesus, our Heavenly Judah went to the Cross, He removed the curse, by paying the price for our Redemption, which satisfied the demands of a thrice-Holy God. Paul said:

"*Christ has redeemed us from the curse of the Law* (He did so on the Cross), *being made a curse for us* (He took the penalty of the Law, which was death): *for it is written, Cursed is every one who hangs on a tree* (Deut. 21:22-23):

"*That the Blessing of Abraham* (Justification by Faith) *might come on the Gentiles through Jesus Christ* (what He did at the Cross); *that we might receive the Promise of the Spirit through Faith.* (All sin was atoned at the Cross which lifted the sin debt from believing man, making it possible for the Holy Spirit to come into the life of the Believer and abide there forever [Jn. 14:16-17])" (Gal. 3:13-14).

(10) "AND THE THIRD LOT CAME UP FOR THE CHILDREN OF ZEBULUN ACCORDING TO THEIR FAMILIES: AND THE BORDER OF THEIR INHERITANCE WAS UNTO SARID:

(11) "AND THEIR BORDER WENT UP TOWARD THE SEA, AND MARALAH, AND REACHED TO DABBASHETH, AND REACHED TO THE RIVER THAT IS BEFORE JOKNEAM;

(12) "AND TURNED FROM SARID EASTWARD TOWARD THE SUNRISING UNTO THE BORDER OF CHISLOTH-TABOR, AND THEN GOES OUT TO DABERATH, AND GOES UP TO JAPHIA,

(13) "AND FROM THENCE PASSES ON ALONG ON THE EAST TO GITTAH-HEPHER, TO ITTAH-KAZIN, AND GOES OUT OF REMMON-METHOAR TO NEAH;

(14) "AND THE BORDER COMPASSES IT ON THE NORTH SIDE TO HANNATHON: AND THE OUTGOINGS THEREOF ARE IN THE VALLEY OF JIPHTHAH-EL:

(15) "AND KATTATH, AND NAHALLAL, AND SHIMRON, AND IDALAH, AND BETH-LEHEM: TWELVE CITIES WITH THEIR VILLAGES.

(16) "THIS IS THE INHERITANCE OF THE CHILDREN OF ZEBULUN ACCORDING

NOTES

TO THEIR FAMILIES, THESE CITIES WITH THEIR VILLAGES."

The diagram is:

1. The listing of all of these villages and cities may seem to be useless trivia, especially considering that it all took place about 3,500 years ago; however, the Holy Spirit had a purpose in all of this, with, among other things, every one of these places being a symbol of what the Lord has given unto us.

2. However unfaithful man may prove himself to be, God ever remains faithful, for He cannot deny Himself. Therefore, He did not fail to point out in detail to His People all that belonged to them.

3. It is very beautiful to learn from these Chapters how minutely, patiently, and repeatedly, our Lord describes to His People the goodly Land which He had given them; and to notice how He divided it to them by families so that all should share alike, and no one family be preferred before another.

THE INHERITANCE OF ZEBULUN

If one studies carefully the Prophecies Jacob gave in Genesis, Chapter 49 concerning the various Tribes and then the location and the borders given in these Chapters, one would see what seems to be a slight discrepancy, but, actually, on further investigation the true meaning becomes clear.

For instance, in Genesis 49:13 and Deuteronomy 33:19, the prediction is that the portion of Zebulun is to be on the Sea and a haven for ships; however, the inheritance given to Zebulun by Joshua at this particular time was not on the Sea and was, thereby no haven for ships. So, what we must understand is this:

The Prophecies that were given by Jacob pertain not only to the possession of the land in the days of Joshua, but also to the coming great Millennial Reign, which has not yet come. In the Millennium the allotment of land will be on a different principle. Each of the twelve great portions will run west from the Euphrates and the Persian Gulf to the Mediterranean, giving each Tribe an outlet by water (Ezek., Chpt. 48).

(17) "AND THE FOURTH LOT CAME

OUT TO ISSACHAR, FOR THE CHILDREN OF ISSACHAR ACCORDING TO THEIR FAMILIES.

(18) "AND THEIR BORDER WAS TOWARD JEZREEL, AND CHESULLOTH, AND SHUNEM,

(19) "AND HAPHRAIM, AND SHIHON, AND ANAHARATH,

(20) "AND RABBITH, AND KISHION, AND ABEZ,

(21) "AND REMETH, AND EN-GANNIM, AND EN-HADDAH, AND BETH-PAZZEZ;

(22) "AND THE COAST REACHES TO TABOR, AND SHAHAZIMAH, AND BETH-SHEMESH; AND THE OUTGOINGS OF THEIR BORDER WERE AT JORDAN: SIXTEEN CITIES WITH THEIR VILLAGES.

(23) "THIS IS THE INHERITANCE OF THE TRIBE OF THE CHILDREN OF ISSACHAR ACCORDING TO THEIR FAMILIES, THE CITIES AND THEIR VILLAGES."

The exegesis is:

1. The portion given to Issachar was very small, with Judah being approximately thirty times larger or more. In fact, the Tribe of Manasseh, which bordered Issachar, was at least six or seven times larger.

2. Jezreel was in Issachar, which was the beginning of the Valley of Megiddo, where many of the great battles of Israel were fought.

3. The extreme northeastern tip of Issachar is about five miles south of the Sea of Galilee.

(24) "AND THE FIFTH LOT CAME OUT OF THE TRIBE OF THE CHILDREN OF ASHER ACCORDING TO THEIR FAMILIES.

(25) "AND THEIR BORDER WAS HELKATH, AND HALI, AND BETEN, AND ACHSHAPH,

(26) "AND ALAMMELECH, AND AMAD, AND MISHEAL; AND REACHES TO CARMEL WESTWARD, AND TO SHIHOR-LIBNATH;

(27) "AND TURNS TOWARD THE SUNRISING TO BETH-DAGON, AND REAHCES TO ZEBULUN, AND TO THE VALLEY OF JIPHTHAH-EL TOWARD THE NORTH SIDE OF BETH-EMEK, AND NEIEL, AND GOES OUT TO CABUL ON THE LEFT HAND,

(28) "AND HEBRON, AND REHOB, AND HAMMON, AND KANAH, EVEN UNTO GREAT ZIDON;

(29) "AND THEN THE COAST TURNS

NOTES

TO RAMAH, AND TO THE STRONG CITY TYRE; AND THE COAST TURNS TO HOSAH; AND THE OUTGOINGS THEREOF ARE AT THE SEA FROM THE COAST TO ACHZIB:

(30) "UMMAH ALSO, AND APHEK, AND REHOB: TWENTY AND TWO CITIES WITH THEIR VILLAGES.

(31) "THIS IS THE INHERITANCE OF THE TRIBE OF THE CHILDREN OF ASHER ACCORDING TO THEIR FAMILIES, THESE CITIES WITH THEIR VILLAGES."

The diagram is:

1. The Tribe of Asher occupied at least a third of the country we now know as Lebanon, actually all the way to Zidon, which included the city of Tyre also.

2. The Tribe bordered the Mediterranean.

3. Four of the Tribes bordered the Mediterranean, Asher, Manasseh (the half Tribe of Manasseh), Dan (its southern portion), and Judah.

(32) "THE SIXTH LOT CAME OUT TO THE CHILDREN OF NAPHTALI, EVEN FOR THE CHILDREN OF NAPHTALI ACCORDING TO THEIR FAMILIES.

(33) "AND THEIR COAST WAS FROM HELEPH, FROM ALLON TO ZAANANNIM, AND ADAMI, NEKEB, AND JABNEEL, UNTO LAKUM; AND THE OUTGOINGS THEREOF WERE AT JORDAN:

(34) "AND THEN THE COAST TURNS WESTWARD TO AZNOTH-TABOR, AND GOES OUT FROM THENCE TO HUKKOK, AND REACHES TO ZEBULUN ON THE SOUTH SIDE, AND REACHES TO ASHER ON THE WEST SIDE, AND TO JUDAH UPON JORDAN TOWARD THE SUNRISING.

(35) "AND THE FENCED CITIES ARE ZIDDIM, ZER, AND HAMMATH, RAKKATH, AND CHINNERETH,

(36) "AND ADAMAH, AND RAMAH, AND HAZOR,

(37) "AND KEDESH, AND EDREI, AND EN-HAZOR,

(38) "AND IRON, AND MIGDAL-EL, HOREM, AND BETH-ANATH, AND BETH-SHEMESH; NINETEEN CITIES WITH THEIR VILLAGES.

(39) "THIS IS THE INHERITANCE OF THE TRIBE OF THE CHILDREN OF NAPHTALI ACCORDING TO THEIR FAMILIES, THE CITIES AND THEIR VILLAGES."

The construction is:

1. Concerning the Tribe of Naphtali the Prophet Isaiah said:

"Nevertheless the dimness shall not be such as was in her vexation, when at the first He lightly afflicted the land of Zebulun and the land of Naphtali, and afterward did more grievously afflict her by the way of the sea, beyond Jordan, in Galilee of the nations" (Isa. 9:1).

The translation from the Hebrew to the English is thought by some Scholars referring to this Verse, as to not have been as sufficient as it could have been.

The major weakness in the translation seems to be the latter part where it says, *"and afterward did more grievously afflict her."* This should have been translated, *"So, in the latter time, He has brought honor on the way of the Sea."*

Actually, the *"Way of the Sea"* has reference to the *"Sea of Galilee,"* where Christ carried out most of His Ministry.

The *"Galilee of the nations"* refers to the district where the far greater number of His Miracles were performed.

2. The Tribe of Naphtali, therefore, would be honored to see the greatest Ministry and the greatest array of Miracles that man has ever known, that and those of the Lord Jesus Christ.

3. While Jesus came from the Tribe of Judah, most of His Ministry was carried out in the area of the Tribe of Naphtali.

(40) "AND THE SEVENTH LOT CAME OUT FOR THE TRIBE OF THE CHILDREN OF DAN ACCORDING TO THEIR FAMILIES.

(41) "AND THE COAST OF THEIR INHERITANCE WAS ZORAH, AND ESHTAOL, AND IR-SHEMESH,

(42) "AND SHAALABBIN, AND AJALON, AND JETHLAH,

(43) "AND ELON, AND THIMNATHAH, AND EKRON,

(44) "AND ELTEKEH, AND GIBBETHON, AND BAALATH,

(45) "AND JEHUD, AND BENE-BERAK, AND GATH-RIMMON,

(46) "AND ME-JARKON, AND RAKKON, WITH THE BORDER BEFORE JAPHO.

(47) "AND THE COAST OF THE CHILDREN OF DAN WENT OUT TOO LITTLE

NOTES

FOR THEM: THEREFORE THE CHILDREN OF DAN WENT UP TO FIGHT AGAINST LESHEM, AND TOOK IT, AND SMOTE IT WITH THE EDGE OF THE SWORD, AND POSSESSED IT, AND DWELT THEREIN, AND CALLED LESHEM, DAN, AFTER THE NAME OF DAN THEIR FATHER.

(48) "THIS IS THE INHERITANCE OF THE TRIBE OF THE CHILDREN OF DAN ACCORDING TO THEIR FAMILIES, THESE CITIES WITH THEIR VILLAGES."

The structure is:

1. The Forty-seventh Verse proclaims the fact of Dan taking a portion up north, which was about 100 miles from their southern portion.

2. The southern portion of Dan bordered the Mediterranean. The inheritance assigned to them, the southern portion, was extremely small, but it was also extremely fertile.

3. Sampson is the only hero this Tribe produced, and his exploits were limited to a very narrow area, and his influence apparently to his own Tribe.

(49) "WHEN THEY HAD MADE AN END OF DIVIDING THE LAND FOR INHERITANCE BY THEIR COASTS, THE CHILDREN OF ISRAEL GAVE AN INHERITANCE TO JOSHUA THE SON OF NUN AMONG THEM:

(50) "ACCORDING TO THE WORD OF THE LORD THEY GAVE HIM THE CITY WHICH HE ASKED, EVEN TIMNATH-SERAH IN MOUNT EPHRAIM: AND HE BUILT THE CITY, AND DWELT THEREIN.

(51) "THESE ARE THE INHERITANCES, WHICH ELEAZAR THE PRIEST, AND JOSHUA THE SON OF NUN, AND THE HEADS OF THE FATHERS OF THE TRIBES OF THE CHILDREN OF ISRAEL, DIVIDED FOR AN INHERITANCE BY LOT IN SHILOH BEFORE THE LORD, AT THE DOOR OF THE TABERNACLE OF THE CONGREGATION. SO THEY MADE AN END OF DIVIDING THE COUNTRY."

The overview is:

1. We learn here that the Lord distributed the land to Israel; He employed Eleazar, Joshua, and the Chiefs as His Agents; the distribution was by lot, i.e., the Urim and Thummim. The lots were drawn at the door of the Tabernacle; and it all took place

at Shiloh.

2. From all of this we learn the lesson that they are happy, and well provided for, who allow God to choose for them.

3. Joshua, in not choosing for himself until all the others had received their portions, furnishes another pleasing proof of the beauty of His Character. His Character may be said to be almost perfect. There is nothing recorded to his disparagement except that he objected to a particular situation, for which Moses reprimanded him (Num. 11:27-29).

4. We know that he chose his area according to the Commandment of the Lord. This means that it was, as well, by the means of the Urim and the Thummim.

TIMNATH-SERAH

Verses 49 through 51 give us a beautiful example of Faith and of a great hunger for God. When all had been divided to the Tribes, the Forty-ninth Verse says, *"The Children of Israel gave an inheritance to Joshua the son of Nun among them."* It says that this inheritance was given to him *"according to the Word of the LORD."*

Evidently, it seems that some did not believe that Joshua should receive this inheritance; however, when the Word of the Lord was sought, it was found that the Promise was there.

Likewise, Satan by using Christians (he almost always uses Christians) will try to tell the hungry heart that *"it is not possible,"* or *"the days of Miracles are over,"* or *"it is not for today,"* etc. To whom will you listen, unbelieving men or the Word of God? Joshua paid no attention to what men said. His desires were according to what was said by the Word of God.

If the Word of God says that you can have Salvation (and it does), then regardless of what man says, you can have it (Rom. 10:9-10). If the Word of God says you can have healing (and it does), then regardless of what man says, you can have it (James 5:14). If the Word of God says you can be an overcomer (and it does), regardless of what man says you can have it (Rom. 6:14).

If the Word of God says you can have the Baptism with the Holy Spirit with the evidence of speaking with other Tongues (and

it does), then regardless of what man says, you can have it (Acts 2:4). The Word of God must be the criteria. It must be the Standard.

ASK AND YOU SHALL RECEIVE

The Fiftieth Verse says, *"Which he asked."* Jesus said to *"ask"* and we would receive (Lk., Chpt. 11). Over and over again we are told to ask. James said, *"We have not because we ask not."* And then he went on to say that so often when we do ask, it is to *"consume it upon our lusts"* (James 4:2-3).

Joshua asked for this added inheritance. If you want healing from the Lord, ask for it. If you want victory in certain areas of your life, ask for it. If you want the Baptism with the Holy Spirit, ask for it. If you don't get it the first time, keep asking. This is what Jesus said in the Eleventh Chapter of Luke.

For what did Joshua ask? He asked for *"Timnath-serah."*

THE MEANING OF TIMNATH-SERAH

Even though this occasion took place some 3,500 years before the Day of Pentecost, still, it has a semblance of the Baptism with the Holy Spirit. Let's look at it in that light.

A. The Scripture says, *"The Children of Israel gave an inheritance to Joshua the son of Nun among them."*

The Baptism with the Holy Spirit is a part of the Inheritance that we have in Christ. Jesus said to His Disciples and His followers immediately before His ascension, *"that they should not depart from Jerusalem, but wait for the Promise of the Father"* (Acts 1:4). That Promise was *"the Baptism with the Holy Spirit"* (Acts 1:5).

Unfortunately, there are many presently who will tell the Believer *"that's not for today."* But let every Believer understand, that the Baptism with the Holy Spirit is made possible to us because of what Jesus did at the Cross, and we can have it today, even as untold millions have been filled. It's a part of the Inheritance (Rom. 8:17).

B. It was given to him, *"according to the Word of the Lord."* This means that it doesn't matter what other people say, how much they claim it's no longer for today, or that it passed away with the Apostles, etc. The truth is, *"The Word of the Lord"* says that we can have it, and that's enough (Acts 2:4; 19:1-7).

C. He asked for this inheritance. We are to ask for the Holy Spirit. Jesus said, *"If you then, being evil, know how to give good gifts unto your children: how much more shall your Heavenly Father give the Holy Spirit to them who ask Him?"* (Lk. 11:13).

D. He asked for the city of *"Timnath-serah."*

"Timnath" means *"the portion that remains."* This is typical of the Holy Spirit.

After the believing sinner comes to Christ, is Born-Again, there is a portion that remains. That portion doesn't make one more Saved, but, in fact, is made possible by being Saved. It is the Baptism with the Holy Spirit.

"Serah" means *"city of the Sun."* Even though it was speaking of the orb that shines in the heavens, still, it most definitely could refer to *"the Son,"* i.e., *"The City of the Son."*

This speaks of victory, and total victory at that.

"Here the Sun is always shining,
"Here the skies are always bright;
"'Tis no place for gloomy Christians
  to abide,
"For my soul is filled with music,
"And my heart with pure delight,
"And I'm living on the Hallelujah side."

The Holy Spirit, i.e., *"The portion that remains,"* will help you to *"build the city and dwell therein."*

CHAPTER 20

(1) "THE LORD ALSO SPOKE UNTO JOSHUA, SAYING,

(2) "SPEAK TO THE CHILDREN OF IS-RAEL, SAYING, APPOINT OUT FOR YOU CITIES OF REFUGE, WHEREOF I SPOKE UNTO YOU BY THE HAND OF MOSES:

(3) "THAT THE SLAYER WHO KILLS ANY PERSON UNAWARES AND UNWIT-TINGLY MAY FLEE THERE: AND THEY SHALL BE YOUR REFUGE FROM THE AVENGER OF BLOOD.

(4) "AND WHEN HE WHO DOES FLEE UNTO ONE OF THOSE CITIES SHALL STAND AT THE ENTERING OF THE GATE

OF THE CITY, AND SHALL DECLARE HIS CAUSE IN THE EARS OF THE ELDERS OF THAT CITY, THEY SHALL TAKE HIM INTO THE CITY UNTO THEM, AND GIVE HIM A PLACE, THAT HE MAY DWELL AMONG THEM.

(5) "AND IF THE AVENGER OF BLOOD PURSUE AFTER HIM, THEN THEY SHALL NOT DELIVER THE SLAYER UP INTO HIS HAND; BECAUSE HE SMOTE HIS NEIGHBOUR UNWITTINGLY, AND HATED HIM NOT BEFORETIME.

(6) "AND HE SHALL DWELL IN THAT CITY, UNTIL HE STAND BEFORE THE CONGREGATION FOR JUDGMENT, AND UNTIL THE DEATH OF THE HIGH PRIEST WHO SHALL BE IN THOSE DAYS: THEN SHALL THE SLAYER RETURN, AND COME UNTO HIS OWN CITY, AND UNTO HIS OWN HOUSE, UNTO THE CITY FROM WHERE HE FLED.

(7) "AND THEY APPOINTED KEDESH IN GALILEE IN MOUNT NAPHTALI, AND SHECHEM IN MOUNT EPHRAIM, AND KIRJATH-ARBA, WHICH IS HEBRON, IN THE MOUNTAIN OF JUDAH.

(8) "AND ON THE OTHER SIDE JOR-DAN BY JERICHO EASTWARD, THEY AS-SIGNED BEZER IN THE WILDERNESS UPON THE PLAIN OUT OF THE TRIBE OF REUBEN, AND RAMOTH IN GILEAD OUT OF THE TRIBE OF GAD, AND GOLAN IN BASHAN OUT OF THE TRIBE OF MANASSEH.

(9) "THESE WERE THE CITIES AP-POINTED FOR ALL THE CHILDREN OF ISRAEL, AND FOR THE STRANGER WHO SOJOURNS AMONG THEM, THAT WHO-SOEVER KILLS ANY PERSON AT UN-AWARES MIGHT FLEE THERE, AND NOT DIE BY THE HAND OF THE AVENGER OF BLOOD, UNTIL HE STOOD BEFORE THE CONGREGATION."

The exegesis is:

1. There were to be six cities of refuge, for *"six"* is the number of man, signifying man's weaknesses, imperfection, hence, the need for such cities.

2. The cities of refuge were not for mur-derers, but rather to protect those who had killed someone accidentally; protect them from members of the family of the victim who

sought revenge, and for whatever reason.

3. The High Priest, as referred to in Verse 6, is a Type of Christ. When the High Priest died, the man was free to return to his home, and would be protected by Law. When Jesus died on the Cross, this made it possible for men to be free, at least those who would accept Him, of which all of this was a Type (Rom. 8:2).

4. Concerning this, Williams said, *"Hebrews 6:18 sets forth Christ as the City of Refuge for sinners guilty of His Blood; and the six cities appointed by Joshua display, by the meaning of their names, something of the sufficiency of that Saviour; for in Him is found: Holiness"* (Kedesh); *"Strength"* (Shechem); *"Fellowship"* (Hebron); *"Happiness"* (Golan). *"God puts Holiness first and Happiness last, man reverses this."*[1]

CITIES OF REFUGE

The government of Israel was then a Theocracy. This means that it was ruled by God through a man, at that time Joshua. The Lord would just a little later rule through the Judges, and then through the kings of Israel, always with Prophets making their great contribution.

The Lord, as obvious here, proclaimed that six cities must be established throughout Israel, which would be referred to as *"Cities of Refuge."* Individuals who accidentally kill someone, could flee to those cities, that is if friends or relatives of the deceased were trying to exact vengeance. Safely ensconced in one of these cities, these individuals could not touch the man involved.

However, the man had to stay there until the High Priest died, and then he could return by Law to his natural home, and not fear the vengeance of the friends or relatives of the deceased. This had a tremendous spiritual meaning.

The High Priest was a Type of Christ. The demand that the individual must stay in the city of refuge until the High Priest died, referred to Christ Who would come, and would die on the Cross of Calvary. All who believe in Him and what He did at the Cross, could go free, i.e., *"Be Saved."* This is the spiritual meaning of these demands.

Concerning this very thing, the Apostle

Paul said:

"That by two immutable things (they are the Promise to Abraham of the coming Redeemer, and the Oath given as it regards Christ being a Priest forever after the Order of Melchisedec), *in which it was impossible for God to lie* (refers to the moral impossibility of such), *we might have a strong consolation* (refers to assurance), *who have fled for refuge to lay hold upon the hope set before us* (carries the idea of the sinner fleeing to one of the Cities of Refuge in Israel; in effect, he was fleeing to the High Priest who has offered Atonement for him and his sin [Deut. 4:42]; using that as a Type, we are to flee as well to our High Priest, the Lord Jesus Christ):

"Which hope we have as an anchor of the soul, both sure and steadfast (presents the Apostle changing the illusion from safety in the Cities of Refuge to a ship reaching harbor after a tempestuous voyage, knowing that her anchor is sure and steadfast), *and which enters into that within the Veil* (refers to the Holy of Holies, which Jesus has entered on our behalf)*"* (Heb. 6:18-19).

GOD'S DIRECTION FOR OUR LIVES

Verse 2 says, *"Appoint out for you cities of refuge."* This provision by God portrayed God's Mercy, Compassion, and Grace. It proclaims in beautiful material form how He goes to extremes to bring the sinner home. The need for the cities of refuge, shows man's cruelty; cruelty that was even attached to God's People. The fact of the cities of refuge, shows that God is not man and is ever striving to bring the wayward home.

To the unspiritual eye, God's command in previous Chapters to slay all (concerning the heathen) would seem somewhat contradictory considering the extra length that God would go regarding the Salvation of His Own; however, it must be remembered that the Canaanites, the Jebusites, and others had *"filled up"* their cup of iniquity. In their evil they had gone beyond redemption (Gen. 15:16).

Verse 7 says, *"And they appointed,"* this was done by the Urim and the Thummim. The six cities are listed in Verses 7 and 8. They display by the meaning of their names the intention of God's direction for our lives. They are as follows:

A. KEDESH: The word means *"Holiness."* By this we know that God's first demand is Holiness.

B. SHECHEM: This word means *"Strength."* From this we see that our real Strength lies in Holiness.

C. HEBRON: This means *"Fellowship."* Now that we are in Holiness and, thereby, receiving Strength, there can be Fellowship with God.

D. BEZER: The word means *"Safety."* When there is Fellowship with God, there is always Safety.

E. RAMOTH: This word means *"Uplifting."* Now, in God's progression we can see the Blessing as it begins to come.

F. GOLAN: The word means *"Happiness."* If you will notice, God puts Holiness first, and Happiness last. Man, sadly, reverses this, and there is little happiness.

THE DEATH OF THE HIGH PRIEST

The Sixth Verse says, *"Until the death of the High Priest,"* meaning that once the High Priest died, as stated, the individual could then leave the city of refuge and go back to his home and his possessions.

This is a picture of Israel in the last days restored to the Promised Land from which she, the slayer of the Messiah, has been exiled. This will not be totally fulfilled until the Coming of the Lord.

He will appear as the dead yet living High Priest (*"I am He Who lives and was dead."*) At the occasion of that Restoration, then, all the great promises that God made to the Prophets of old will be fulfilled and realized. Sadly, God's Will is very slow to be carried out, and yet, ultimately His Plan, although oftentimes delayed, will always be carried out. And so it will be with Israel in that coming glad day.

CHAPTER 21

(1) "THEN CAME NEAR THE HEADS OF THE FATHERS OF THE LEVITES UNTO ELEAZAR THE PRIEST, AND UNTO

JOSHUA THE SON OF NUN, AND UNTO THE HEADS OF THE FATHERS OF THE TRIBES OF THE CHILDREN OF ISRAEL;

(2) "AND THEY SPOKE UNTO THEM AT SHILOH IN THE LAND OF CANAAN, SAYING, THE LORD COMMANDED BY THE HAND OF MOSES TO GIVE US CITIES TO DWELL IN, WITH THE SUBURBS THEREOF FOR OUR CATTLE.

(3) "AND THE CHILDREN OF ISRAEL GAVE UNTO THE LEVITES OUT OF THEIR INHERITANCE, AT THE COMMANDMENT OF THE LORD, THESE CITIES AND THEIR SUBURBS.

(4) "AND THE LOT CAME OUT FOR THE FAMILIES OF THE KOHATHITES: AND THE CHILDREN OF AARON THE PRIEST, WHICH WERE OF THE LEVITES, HAD BY LOT OUT OF THE TRIBE OF JUDAH, AND OUT OF THE TRIBE OF SIMEON, AND OUT OF THE TRIBE OF BENJAMIN, THIRTEEN CITIES.

(5) "AND THE REST OF THE CHILDREN OF KOHATH HAD BY LOT OUT OF THE FAMILIES OF THE TRIBE OF EPHRAIM, AND OUT OF THE TRIBE OF DAN, AND OUT OF THE HALF TRIBE OF MANASSEH, TEN CITIES.

(6) "AND THE CHILDREN OF GERSHON HAD BY LOT OUT OF THE FAMILIES OF THE TRIBE OF ISSACHAR, AND OUT OF THE TRIBE OF ASHER, AND OUT OF THE TRIBE OF NAPHTALI, AND OUT OF THE HALF TRIBE OF MANASSEH IN BASHAN, THIRTEEN CITIES.

(7) "THE CHILDREN OF MERARI BY THEIR FAMILIES HAD OUT OF THE TRIBE OF REUBEN, AND OUT OF THE TRIBE OF GAD, AND OUT OF THE TRIBE OF ZEBULUN, TWELVE CITIES.

(8) "AND THE CHILDREN OF ISRAEL GAVE BY LOT UNTO THE LEVITES THESE CITIES WITH THEIR SUBURBS, AS THE LORD COMMANDED BY THE HAND OF MOSES.

(9) "AND THEY GAVE OUT OF THE TRIBE OF THE CHILDREN OF JUDAH, AND OUT OF THE TRIBE OF THE CHILDREN OF SIMEON, THESE CITIES WHICH ARE HERE MENTIONED BY NAME,

(10) "WHICH THE CHILDREN OF AARON, BEING OF THE FAMILIES OF

THE KOHATHITES, WHO WERE OF THE CHILDREN OF LEVI, HAD: FOR THEIRS WAS THE FIRST LOT.

(11) "AND THEY GAVE THEM THE CITY OF ARBA THE FATHER OF ANAK, WHICH CITY IS HEBRON, IN THE HILL COUNTRY OF JUDAH, WITH THE SUBURBS THEREOF ROUND ABOUT IT.

(12) "BUT THE FIELDS OF THE CITY, AND THE VILLAGES THEREOF, GAVE THEY TO CALEB THE SON OF JEPHUNNEH FOR HIS POSSESSION.

(13) "THUS THEY GAVE TO THE CHILDREN OF AARON THE PRIEST HEBRON WITH HER SUBURBS, TO BE A CITY OF REFUGE FOR THE SLAYER; AND LIBNAH WITH HER SUBURBS,

(14) "AND JATTIR WITH HER SUBURBS, AND ESHTEMOA WITH HER SUBURBS,

(15) "AND HOLON WITH HER SUBURBS, AND DEBIR WITH HER SUBURBS,

(16) "AND AIN WITH HER SUBURBS, AND JUTTAH WITH HER SUBURBS, AND BETH-SHEMESH WITH HER SUBURBS; NINE CITIES OUT OF THOSE TWO TRIBES.

(17) "AND OUT OF THE TRIBE OF BENJAMIN, GIBEON WITH HER SUBURBS, GEBA WITH HER SUBURBS,

(18) "ANATHOTH WITH HER SUBURBS, AND ALMON WITH HER SUBURBS; FOUR CITIES.

(19) "ALL THE CITIES OF THE CHILDREN OF AARON, THE PRIESTS, WERE THIRTEEN CITIES WITH THEIR SUBURBS.

(20) "AND THE FAMILIES OF THE CHILDREN OF KOHATH, THE LEVITES WHICH REMAINED OF THE CHILDREN OF KOHATH, EVEN THEY HAD THE CITIES OF THEIR LOT OUT OF THE TRIBE OF EPRHAIM.

(21) "FOR THEY GAVE THEM SHECHEM WITH HER SUBURBS IN MOUNT EPHRAIM, TO BE A CITY OF REFUGE FOR THE SLAYER; AND GEZER WITH HER SUBURBS,

(22) "AND KIBZAIM WITH HER SUBURBS, AND BETH-HORON WITH HER SUBURBS; FOUR CITIES.

(23) "AND OUT OF THE TRIBE OF DAN, ELTEKEH WITH HER SUBURBS, GIBBETHON WITH HER SUBURBS,

(24) "AIJALON WITH HER SUBURBS, GATH-RIMMON WITH HER SUBURBS, FOUR CITIES.

(25) "AND OUT OF THE HALF TRIBE OF MANASSEH, TANACH WITH HER SUBURBS, AND GATH-RIMMON WITH HER SUBURBS; TWO CITIES.

(26) "ALL THE CITIES WERE TEN WITH THEIR SUBURBS FOR THE FAMILIES OF THE CHILDREN OF KOHATH WHO REMAINED.

(27) "AND UNTO THE CHILDREN OF GERSHON, OF THE FAMILIES OF THE LEVITES, OUT OF THE OTHER HALF TRIBE OF MANASSEH THEY GAVE GOLAN IN BASHAN WITH HER SUBURBS, TO BE A CITY OF REFUGE FOR THE SLAYER; AND BEESH-TERAH WITH HER SUBURBS; TWO CITIES.

(28) "AND OUT OF THE TRIBE OF ISSACHAR, KISHON WITH HER SUBURBS, DABAREH WITH HER SUBURBS,

(29) "JARMUTH WITH HER SUBURBS, EN-GANNIM WITH HER SUBURBS; FOUR CITIES.

(30) "AND OUT OF THE TRIBE OF ASHER, MISHAL WITH HER SUBURBS, ABDON WITH HER SUBURBS,

(31) "HELKATH WITH HER SUBURBS, AND REHOB WITH HER SUBURBS; FOUR CITIES.

(32) "AND OUT OF THE TRIBE OF NAPHTALI, KEDESH IN GALILEE WITH HER SUBURBS, TO BE A CITY OF REFUGE FOR THE SLAYER; AND HAMMOTH-DOR WITH HER SUBURBS, AND KARTAN WITH HER SUBURBS; THREE CITIES.

(33) "ALL THE CITIES OF THE GERSHONITES ACCORDING TO THEIR FAMILIES WERE THIRTEEN CITIES WITH THEIR SUBURBS.

(34) "AND UNTO THE FAMILIES OF THE CHILDREN OF MERARI, THE REST OF THE LEVITES, OUT OF THE TRIBE OF ZEBULUN, JOKNEAM WITH HER SUBURBS, AND KARTAH WITH HER SUBURBS,

(35) "DIMNAH WITH HER SUBURBS, NAHALAL WITH HER SUBURBS; FOUR CITIES.

(36) "AND OUT OF THE TRIBE OF REUBEN, BEZER WITH HER SUBURBS, AND JAHAZAH WITH HER SUBURBS,

(37) "KEDEMOTH WITH HER SUB-URBS, AND MEPHAATH WITH HER SUB-URBS; FOUR CITIES.

(38) "AND OUT OF THE TRIBE OF GAD, RAMOTH IN GILEAD WITH HER SUB-URBS, TO BE A CITY OF REFUGE FOR THE SLAYER; AND MAHANAIM WITH HER SUBURBS,

(39) "HESHBON WITH HER SUBURBS, JAZER WITH HER SUBURBS; FOUR CIT-IES IN ALL.

(40) "SO ALL THE CITIES FOR THE CHILDREN OF MERARI BY THEIR FAMI-LIES, WHICH WERE REMAINING OF THE FAMILIES OF THE LEVITES, WERE BY THEIR LOT TWELVE CITIES."

The construction is:

1. The *"Kohathites"* of Verse 4 were of the Tribe of Levi, and were in charge of the Vessels of the Sanctuary (Num. 3:31).

2. The *"Gershonites"* of Verse 6, also of the Tribe of Levi, were in charge of the Tabernacle proper (Num. 3:25).

3. The *"Merarites"* of Verse 7, also of the Tribe of Levi, were in charge of the structure of the Tabernacle (Num. 3:36).

4. The Lord did not at all fail to provide for the Tribe of Levi, even though they had brought upon themselves a curse due to their slaughter of the Shechemites (Gen., Chpt. 34). As a result, Judgment scattered them in Israel, but Grace made them a Kingdom of Priests and gave them forty-eight cities with their pasture-lands. Some three times this was declared to have been the Commandment of the Lord (Vss. 2-3, 8).

5. Six cities were appointed as cities of refuge (20:7-8); however, Chapter 21 only mentions five of these cities: Verse 13, Hebron; Verse 21, Shechem; Verse 27, Bashan; Verse 32, Kedesh; and Verse 38, Ramoth. *"Bezer"* is not mentioned. Why? Joshua 22:10-34 may provide the answer.

An Altar, which was the product of man's imagination, rebellious imagination we might quickly add, was set up close to Bezer. This neutralized it as a city of refuge.

Why?

God has but one center of Atonement and Blessing in Type, and that is Calvary. Any other center, even an exact pattern, denies that Divine Center. Bezer's sufficiency as a

refuge was based upon the atoning Sacrifices at Shiloh, as was everything else in Israel. The erection of the Reubenite altar destroyed that sufficiency, because it destroyed that base.

In this present modern Age, man is putting forth all types of solutions as imitations of Christ's atoning Work; consequently, the Cross has been set aside. But let it ever be known, there is no other refuge for sinners, only the Cross! Only the Cross! Only the Cross! (Rom. 6:1-14; I Cor. 1:17-18, 21, 23; 2:2; Gal., Chpt. 5; 6:14; Col. 2:14-15).

THE INHERITANCE OF THE LEVITES

As we dealt with the Tribe of Simeon in the Nineteenth Chapter, we now deal with the Tribe of the Levites. Both, as previously stated, had been cursed some 300 years before, when the founders of the Tribes, Simeon and Levi, committed terrible acts of atrocity. The curse came from Jacob on his dying bed, as he addressed all the Tribes of Israel, which were then only families (Gen. 49:5-7).

The Prophecy which threatened to *"scatter them in Israel"* was to be fulfilled for the benefit of the whole people. Instead of a portion for himself, Levi, as we have been repeatedly informed, was to have *"the LORD God of Israel for his Inheritance"* (Josh. 13:33; 14:3; 18:7). Now that the portions had been assigned to all the other Tribes, this portion could be assigned to the Levites, from which Tribe all the Priests came, and all those who worked with the Tabernacle, etc.

The cities assigned to them, didn't mean that the entire city was theirs for a possession, but that they could purchase land in these cities and build houses, and it would belong to them, etc. These cities were scattered all over the entirety of Israel.

(41) "ALL THE CITIES OF THE LEVITES WITHIN THE POSSESSION OF THE CHIL-DREN OF ISRAEL WERE FORTY AND EIGHT CITIES WITH THEIR SUBURBS.

(42) "THESE CITIES WERE EVERY ONE WITH THEIR SUBURBS ROUND ABOUT THEM: THUS WERE ALL THESE CITIES."

The pattern is:

1. Inasmuch as these cities were scattered all over Israel, this meant that Priests were

also scattered all over Israel, which had a tendency to direct Israel to things spiritual, as it was intended by the Lord.

2. The Priests, all from the Tribe of Levi, although all Levites were not Priests, were meant to serve as a mediator between God and Israel. This had to be at that time, simply because the Cross was yet future, and the Cross alone would pay the terrible sin debt owed by man to God, but which man was unable to pay.

3. Since the Cross, there is no more need for human intermediaries, Christ having taken that place. The Scripture says of Him, and I quote from THE EXPOSITOR'S STUDY BIBLE:

PRIESTS

"For there is one God (manifested in three Persons — God the Father, God the Son, and God the Holy Spirit), and one Mediator between God and men, the Man Christ Jesus (He can only be an adequate Mediator Who has sympathy with and an understanding of both parties, and is understandable by and clear to both; in other words, Jesus is both God and Man, i.e., 'Very God and Very Man');

"Who gave Himself a ransom for all (refers to the fact that our Lord's Death was a spontaneous and voluntary Sacrifice on His Part; the word 'ransom' refers to the price He paid, owed by man to God, which was His Precious Blood [I Pet. 1:18-20]), to be testified in due time. (This refers to the planning of this great Work, which took place 'before the foundation of the World' [I Pet. 1:18-20], unto the 'due time' of its manifestation, which refers to when Christ was Crucified)" (I Tim. 2:5-6).

This means that no man since the Cross should refer to himself as a Priest, nor should any individual refer to anyone as a Priest. With the death of Christ on the Cross, this totally and completely did away with the office of the Priesthood. Jesus is now our Great High Priest. Paul said:

"If therefore perfection were by the Levitical Priesthood (in effect, says this was not the case), (for under it the people received the Law,) (This proclaims the fact that if the Levitical Priesthood [which was a part of the

Law] was changed, which it was, then the Law had to be changed also.) what further need was there that another Priest should rise after the Order of Melchisedec (since the Levitical Priesthood brought nothing to completion, not merely another Priest was needed, but another Priest of a different kind altogether), and not be called after the Order of Aaron? (This presents the fact that the Order of Aaron must give way to the Order of Melchisedec, a better Priesthood, which it was always meant to do.)

"For the Priesthood being changed (refers to the Priestly Order of Aaron now being abrogated to make way for the original Priesthood that preceded it, which, in effect, had predicted this very thing), there is made of necessity a change also of the Law. (The connection between the Priesthood and the Law means a change in one involves a change in the other)" (Heb. 7:11-12).

Paul then said, "Now of the things which we have spoken this is the sum (refers to what Paul will now give as it regards the meaning of all this): We have such an High Priest, Who sat on the Right Hand of the Throne of the Majesty in the Heavens (the very fact that Christ is now seated in the Heavens at the Right Hand of God proves His Work is a Finished Work);

"A Minister of the Sanctuary (as Paul uses the word 'Minister,' it speaks both of Priestly service to God and of service to man), and of the True Tabernacle (the true Dwelling Place of God, which is in the Heavens), which the Lord pitched, and not man. (This refers to the fact that Moses pitched the earthly Tabernacle, but God formed the True Tabernacle.)

"For every High Priest is ordained to offer Gifts and Sacrifices (portrays the High Priests of old serving as mediators between God and men): wherefore it is of necessity that this Man (Christ Jesus) have somewhat also to offer. (A Priest must have a Sacrifice to offer. Christ offered Himself. This was His one great and all embracing Sacrifice, satisfying all the Types of the Old Covenant and abolishing all its Offerings for sin.)

"For if He (the Lord Jesus) were on Earth, He should not be a Priest (refers to the fact that Christ was not of the Levitical Order,

NOTES

and due to His Sacrifice of Himself, no more earthly Priests are now needed, which, as should be obvious, completely abrogates the Catholic Priesthood)" (Heb. 8:1-4), or any other type of Priesthood. Christ is our Great High Priest, and Christ Alone is our Great High Priest, and will be so forever. As well, He is the only one who is needed.

(43) "AND THE LORD GAVE UNTO IS-RAEL ALL THE LAND WHICH HE SWORE TO GIVE UNTO THEIR FA-THERS; AND THEY POSSESSED IT, AND DWELT THEREIN.

(44) "AND THE LORD GAVE THEM REST ROUND ABOUT, ACCORDING TO ALL THAT HE SWORE UNTO THEIR FA-THERS: AND THERE STOOD NOT A MAN OF ALL THEIR ENEMIES BEFORE THEM; THE LORD DELIVERED ALL THEIR EN-EMIES INTO THEIR HAND.

(45) "THERE FAILED NOT OUGHT OF ANY GOOD THING WHICH THE LORD HAD SPOKEN UNTO THE HOUSE OF ISRAEL; ALL CAME TO PASS."

The overview is:

1. The Book of Joshua is the story of the Promised Land and its Possession. Even though the Lord gave it to Israel, they had to take it, which must be a lesson for us presently.

2. The Promise and the Possession are two different things. The Lord has designed it that we have to use our Faith and Trust in Him in order to possess the land. If we follow His Word exactly, we will see nothing but Victory. If we veer from the de-signed course, a course incidentally laid out by the Lord, we will suffer defeat. So, as a Believer, we should study this Book of Joshua intently, for it is, in Type, God's Blueprint for Victory.

3. While the Lord definitely did deliver these enemies into their hand, at times, Is-rael failed to do her part regarding Faith (16:10; 17:12-13).

4. All Promises of God given to us, will most definitely come to pass, exactly as they did here, if we will only dare to believe Him. As well, such Faith, must always have as its Object, the Cross of Christ (Rom. 6:1-14; I Cor. 1:17-18, 23; 2:2; Eph. 2:13-18; Gal. 6:14; Col. 2:14-15).

CHAPTER 22

(1) "THEN JOSHUA CALLED THE REUBENITES, AND THE GADITES, AND THE HALF TRIBE OF MANASSEH,

(2) "AND SAID UNTO THEM, YOU HAVE KEPT ALL THAT MOSES THE SERVANT OF THE LORD COMMANDED YOU, AND HAVE OBEYED MY VOICE AND ALL THAT I COMMANDED YOU:

(3) "YOU HAVE NOT LEFT YOUR BRETHREN THESE MANY DAYS UNTO THIS DAY, BUT HAVE KEPT THE CHARGE OF THE COMMANDMENT OF THE LORD YOUR GOD.

(4) "AND NOW THE LORD YOUR GOD HAS GIVEN REST UNTO YOUR BRETH-REN, AS HE PROMISED THEM: THERE-FORE NOW RETURN YE, AND GET YOU UNTO YOUR TENTS, AND UNTO THE LAND OF YOUR POSSESSION, WHICH MOSES THE SERVANT OF THE LORD GAVE YOU ON THE OTHER SIDE JORDAN.

(5) "BUT TAKE DILIGENT HEED TO DO THE COMMANDMENT AND THE LAW, WHICH MOSES THE SERVANT OF THE LORD CHARGED YOU, TO LOVE THE LORD YOUR GOD, AND TO WALK IN ALL HIS WAYS, AND TO KEEP HIS COMMAND-MENTS, AND TO CLEAVE UNTO HIM, AND TO SERVE HIM WITH ALL YOUR HEART AND WITH ALL YOUR SOUL.

(6) "SO JOSHUA BLESSED THEM, AND SENT THEM AWAY: AND THEY WENT UNTO THEIR TENTS.

(7) "NOW TO THE ONE HALF OF THE TRIBE OF MANASSEH MOSES HAD GIVEN POSSESSION IN BASHAN: BUT UNTO THE OTHER HALF THEREOF GAVE JOSHUA AMONG THEIR BRETHREN ON THIS SIDE JORDAN WESTWARD. AND WHEN JOSHUA SENT THEM AWAY ALSO UNTO THEIR TENTS, THEN HE BLESSED THEM,

(8) "AND HE SPOKE UNTO THEM, SAYING, RETURN WITH MUCH RICHES UNTO YOUR TENTS, AND WITH VERY MUCH CATTLE, WITH SILVER, AND WITH GOLD, AND WITH BRASS, AND WITH IRON, AND WITH VERY MUCH RAIMENT:

DIVIDE THE SPOIL OF YOUR ENEMIES WITH YOUR BRETHREN.

(9) "AND THE CHILDREN OF REUBEN AND THE CHILDREN OF GAD AND THE HALF TRIBE OF MANASSEH RETURNED, AND DEPARTED FROM THE CHILDREN OF ISRAEL OUT OF SHILOH, WHICH IS IN THE LAND OF CANAAN, TO GO UNTO THE COUNTRY OF GILEAD, TO THE LAND OF THEIR POSSESSION, WHEREOF THEY WERE POSSESSED, ACCORDING TO THE WORD OF THE LORD BY THE HAND OF MOSES."

The structure is:

1. The Lord had kept His Promise to Israel, as it regards taking the land, and even against overwhelming odds.

2. Now Joshua charges them that they should keep their promise to the Lord, that is, to serve Him *"With all your heart and with all your soul."*

3. It seems that the spoil, as it regards cattle, silver, and gold, etc., was to be divided among all the families of Israel, which means that as far as these things were concerned, they were rich.

REUBEN, GAD, AND MANASSEH

It is remarkable that during the entirety of this time of taking the land of Canaan, which probably took approximately seven or more years, there seemed not to be one single time of complaint or murmuring, unless we would conclude the mild complaint of the Tribe of Joseph as being worthy of note. This is a Miracle within itself, when we consider that the thirty-eight plus years of sojourn in the wilderness was one complaint after the other. Perhaps they learned their lesson!

For seven or more years, the men of the three Tribes listed above, had been away from their families helping Joshua and the other Tribes defeat the Canaanites and others. It was now time for them to go home. They would go home with riches, and of every description. They had promised Joshua they would be faithful to their task, even though it certainly would work a hardship on their families, and it seems they were true to their Promise (Num. 32:16-38).

(10) "AND WHEN THEY CAME UNTO THE BORDERS OF JORDAN, THAT ARE

IN THE LAND OF CANAAN, THE CHILDREN OF REUBEN AND THE CHILDREN OF GAD AND THE HALF TRIBE OF MANASSEH BUILT THERE AN ALTAR BY JORDAN, A GREAT ALTAR TO SEE TO."

The exposition is:

1. Such an altar was sternly forbidden by God; for it opened the door to idolatry.

2. There was to be only one place for the Altar, the place which God appointed, which now was Shiloh (Deut. 12:5-8).

3. Jesus Christ and Him Crucified is the answer (I Cor. 1:23). Anything else proposed, even that which looks right, but is not actually the Cross, must be rejected out of hand, because God has rejected all such things. He accepts the Cross of Christ and nothing else!

THE FALSE ALTAR

This altar was built close to Bezer, one of the cities of refuge. Yet, it seems that this *"City of Refuge"* was seldom, if ever, used because of this false altar that was built nearby.

God had but one center of Blessing, in Type, and that would be Calvary. Any other altar, even an exact pattern, denied the Divine Altar.

Man is forever attempting to imitate Christ's atoning Work; therefore, he adds other altars of supposed spiritual blessing, which, in reality, attack God's only refuge for sinners.

The latter portion of this Tenth Verse says, *"A great altar to see to."* How many *"great altars"* has man built or is building? They may look good and very similar to Calvary. Actually, the unspiritual eye probably couldn't tell the difference, but the difference is great. God's Altar, which is Calvary, will set men free. Man's *"great altar"* will set no one free.

THE LORD'S SUPPER

While the Lord's Supper, or that which we refer to as such, presents itself as a beautiful Type, example, or portrayal of the Cross of Christ, still, if we think the taking of such, instead of what it represents, brings some type of Blessing, then we miss the point altogether. In fact, we sin!

The taking of the Lord's Supper, which every Believer certainly should do, is to be a reminder of what Jesus did at the Cross in the giving of Himself. The Holy Spirit through Paul clearly and plainly brought to our attention the words of our Lord when He said, *"This do in remembrance of Me"* (I Cor. 11:24). Let us say it again, the ceremony or ritual within itself, no matter how much one might take it will bring about no Blessing, no Spiritual help, etc.

The other day I watched a Preacher over Television, with whom I was not acquainted, extol the virtues of taking the Lord's Supper, insinuating, actually even stating, that if one takes the Lord's Supper, and does so often, that this ritual will bring about untold blessings, etc. Pure and simple this is *"another altar,"* or in the words of the Apostle Paul, *"another Jesus"* (II Cor. 11:4).

That's why the great Apostle also stated, *"For Christ sent me not to baptize, but to Preach the Gospel: not with wisdom of words, lest the Cross of Christ should be made of none effect"* (I Cor. 1:17).

The great Apostle was not speaking disparagingly of Water Baptism. No! He was merely stating that the emphasis must always be on the Cross of Christ, and nothing, even the great Ordinances of the Church such as Water Baptism, the Lord's Supper, etc., must take the place of the Cross. If it does, we make *"the Cross of Christ of none effect."*

Satan will do anything and everything he can to move one's Faith from the Cross of Christ to other things, and he doesn't too very much care what the other things are. In fact, he will most definitely use very Scriptural things such as the Lord's Supper, Water Baptism, etc., to accomplish this task. Simply because what he is substituting is very Scriptural in its own right and, in fact, very sacred, it fools and deceives many Believers. The truth is, it's *"another altar."*

(11) "AND THE CHILDREN OF ISRAEL HEARD SAY, BEHOLD, THE CHILDREN OF REUBEN AND THE CHILDREN OF GAD AND THE HALF TRIBE OF MANASSEH HAVE BUILT AN ALTAR OVER AGAINST THE LAND OF CANAAN, IN THE BORDERS OF JORDAN, AT THE PASSAGE OF THE CHILDREN OF ISRAEL.

(12) "AND WHEN THE CHILDREN OF ISRAEL HEARD OF IT, THE WHOLE CONGREGATION OF THE CHILDREN OF

NOTES

ISRAEL GATHERED THEMSELVES TOGETHER AT SHILOH, TO GO UP TO WAR AGAINST THEM.

(13) "AND THE CHILDREN OF ISRAEL SENT UNTO THE CHILDREN OF REUBEN, AND TO THE CHILDREN OF GAD, AND TO THE HALF TRIBE OF MANASSEH, INTO THE LAND OF GILEAD, PHINEHAS THE SON OF ELEAZAR THE PRIEST,

(14) "AND WITH HIM TEN PRINCES, OF EACH CHIEF HOUSE A PRINCE THROUGHOUT ALL THE TRIBES OF ISRAEL; AND EACH ONE WAS AN HEAD OF THE HOUSE OF THEIR FATHERS AMONG THE THOUSANDS OF ISRAEL.

(15) "AND THEY CAME UNTO THE CHILDREN OF REUBEN, AND TO THE CHILDREN OF GAD, AND TO THE HALF TRIBE OF MANASSEH, UNTO THE LAND OF GILEAD, AND THEY SPOKE WITH THEM, SAYING,

(16) "THUS SAITH THE WHOLE CONGREGATION OF THE LORD, WHAT TRESPASS IS THIS THAT YOU HAVE COMMITTED AGAINST THE GOD OF ISRAEL, TO TURN AWAY THIS DAY FROM FOLLOWING THE LORD, IN THAT YOU HAVE BUILT YOU AN ALTAR, THAT YOU MIGHT REBEL THIS DAY AGAINST THE LORD?

(17) "IS THE INIQUITY OF PEOR TOO LITTLE FOR US, FROM WHICH WE ARE NOT CLEANSED UNTIL THIS DAY, ALTHOUGH THERE WAS A PLAGUE IN THE CONGREGATION OF THE LORD.

(18) "BUT THAT YOU MUST TURN AWAY THIS DAY FROM FOLLOWING THE LORD? AND IT WILL BE, SEEING YOU REBEL TODAY AGAINST THE LORD, THAT TOMORROW HE WILL BE WROTH WITH THE WHOLE CONGREGATION OF ISRAEL.

(19) "NOTWITHSTANDING, IF THE LAND OF YOUR POSSESSION BE UNCLEAN, THEN PASS YE OVER UNTO THE LAND OF THE POSSESSION OF THE LORD, WHEREIN THE LORD'S TABERNACLE DWELLS, AND TAKE POSSESSION AMONG US: BUT REBEL NOT AGAINST THE LORD, NOR REBEL AGAINST US, IN BUILDING YOU AN ALTAR BESIDE THE ALTAR OF THE LORD OUR GOD.

(20) "DID NOT ACHAN THE SON OF ZERAH COMMIT A TRESPASS IN THE

ACCURSED THING, AND WRATH FELL ON ALL THE CONGREGATION OF ISRAEL? AND THAT MAN PERISHED NOT ALONE IN HIS INIQUITY.

(21) "THEN THE CHILDREN OF REUBEN AND THE CHILDREN OF GAD AND THE HALF TRIBE OF MANASSEH ANSWERED, AND SAID UNTO THE HEADS OF THE THOUSANDS OF ISRAEL,

(22) "THE LORD GOD OF GODS, THE LORD GOD OF GODS, HE KNOWS, AND ISRAEL HE SHALL KNOW; IF IT BE IN REBELLION, OR IF IN TRANSGRESSION AGAINST THE LORD, (SAVE US NOT THIS DAY,)

(23) "THAT WE HAVE BUILT US AN ALTAR TO TURN FROM FOLLOWING THE LORD, OR IF TO OFFER THEREON BURNT OFFERING OR MEAT OFFERING, OR IF TO OFFER PEACE OFFERINGS THEREON, LET THE LORD HIMSELF REQUIRE IT;

(24) "AND IF WE HAVE NOT RATHER DONE IT FOR FEAR OF THIS THING, SAYING, IN TIME TO COME YOUR CHILDREN MIGHT SPEAK UNTO OUR CHILDREN, SAYING, WHAT HAVE YOU TO DO WITH THE LORD GOD OF ISRAEL?

(25) "FOR THE LORD HAS MADE JORDAN A BORDER BETWEEN US AND YOU, YOU CHILDREN OF REUBEN AND CHILDREN OF GAD; YOU HAVE NO PART IN THE LORD: SO SHALL YOUR CHILDREN MAKE OUR CHILDREN CEASE FROM FEARING THE LORD.

(26) "THEREFORE WE SAID, LET US NOW PREPARE TO BUILD US AN ALTAR, NOT FOR BURNT OFFERING, NOR FOR SACRIFICE:

(27) "BUT THAT IT MAY BE A WITNESS BETWEEN US, AND YOU, AND OUR GENERATIONS AFTER US, THAT WE MIGHT DO THE SERVICE OF THE LORD BEFORE HIM WITH OUR BURNT OFFERINGS, AND WITH OUR SACRIFICES, AND WITH OUR PEACE OFFERINGS; THAT YOUR CHILDREN MAY NOT SAY TO OUR CHILDREN IN TIME TO COME, YOU HAVE NO PART IN THE LORD.

(28) "THEREFORE SAID WE, THAT IT SHALL BE, WHEN THEY SHOULD SO SAY TO US OR TO OUR GENERATIONS IN TIME TO COME, THAT WE MAY SAY

AGAIN, BEHOLD THE PATTERN OF THE ALTAR OF THE LORD, WHICH OUR FATHERS MADE, NOT FOR BURNT OFFERINGS, NOR FOR SACRIFICES; BUT IT IS A WITNESS BETWEEN US AND YOU.

(29) "GOD FORBID THAT WE SHOULD REBEL AGAINST THE LORD, AND TURN THIS DAY FROM FOLLOWING THE LORD, TO BUILD AN ALTAR FOR BURNT OFFERINGS, FOR MEAT OFFERINGS, OR FOR SACRIFICES, BESIDE THE ALTAR OF THE LORD OUR GOD THAT IS BEFORE HIS TABERNACLE.

(30) "AND WHEN PHINEHAS THE PRIEST, AND THE PRINCES OF THE CONGREGATION AND HEADS OF THE THOUSANDS OF ISRAEL WHICH WERE WITH HIM, HEARD THE WORDS THAT THE CHILDREN OF REUBEN AND THE CHILDREN OF GAD AND THE CHILDREN OF MANASSEH SPOKE, IT PLEASED THEM.

(31) "AND PHINEHAS THE SON OF ELEAZAR THE PRIEST SAID UNTO THE CHILDREN OF REUBEN, AND TO THE CHILDREN OF GAD, AND TO THE CHILDREN OF MANASSEH, THIS DAY WE PERCEIVE THAT THE LORD IS AMONG US, BECAUSE YOU HAVE NOT COMMITTED THIS TRESPASS AGAINST THE LORD: NOW YOU HAVE DELIVERED THE CHILDREN OF ISRAEL OUT OF THE HAND OF THE LORD.

(32) "AND PHINEHAS THE SON OF ELEAZAR THE PRIEST, AND THE PRINCES, RETURNED FROM THE CHILDREN OF REUBEN, AND FROM THE CHILDREN OF GAD, OUT OF THE LAND OF GILEAD, UNTO THE LAND OF CANAAN, TO THE CHILDREN OF ISRAEL, AND BROUGHT THEM WORD AGAIN.

(33) "AND THE THING PLEASED THE CHILDREN OF ISRAEL; AND THE CHILDREN OF ISRAEL BLESSED GOD, AND DID NOT INTEND TO GO UP AGAINST THEM IN BATTLE, TO DESTROY THE LAND WHEREIN THE CHILDREN OF REUBEN AND GAD DWELT.

(34) "AND THE CHILDREN OF REUBEN AND THE CHILDREN OF GAD CALLED THE ALTAR ED: FOR IT SHALL BE A WITNESS BETWEEN US THAT THE LORD IS GOD."

The pattern is:

1. Verse 34 should have been translated, *"And the sons of Reuben and the sons of Gad gave a name to the altar, 'For it is a witness between us.'"*

2. The account does not say that God was well-pleased; nor does it say that Joshua asked counsel of God in the matter.

3. The truth is, it was not well-pleasing to the Lord, and Eleazar the High Priest should have demanded that it be torn down. As stated, there is only one Altar, and that is Calvary. No matter what other type of Altar may be built, and we speak in the spiritual sense, it cannot be allowed to stand.

MAN'S ALTARS

Man is continually building altars which contain no bloody sacrifice. Man loves these types of altars. The altar outlined in this Chapter contained no sacrifice. Calvary's Altar is effective only because it contained the Sacrifice, Who was Jesus Christ. The Twenty-third Verse says, *"Or if to offer thereon Burnt Offering or Meat Offering,"* which they did not, neither could not.

The Twenty-seventh Verse says, *"But that it may be a witness between us."* God does not require that type of witness. Religious man's actions are always crowded with religious effort. It, thereby, seems like a good *"witness"* to the world; unfortunately, the world, by and large, accepts this false witness, and so does most of the Church.

The Thirty-third Verse says, *"And the thing pleased the Children of Israel,"* but it does not say, as stated, that it pleased God. There is no evidence that Joshua or the leaders of Israel sought counsel of the Lord regarding this matter. Israel formed her own positive conclusion because it *"looked so right."* Most of what today passes for Gospel pleases the Church, but it does not please God.

The Thirty-fourth Verse says, *"Call the altar Ed."* The word *"Ed"* means witness or testimony. Regrettably, most of the witness and testimony of the present-day Church is a barren, sacrificeless, sterile altar. It is an altar that receives very little criticism from the world. So much of the Church is *"well-pleased"* with it. But it must be remembered that it is an altar of man's making and,

consequently, will not set one single, solitary soul free from the bondage of sin.

Satan pays little mind to our building of altars; and actually, he is the author of most altar building. It can look like Calvary; it can be pointed to with great delight. He finds no fault with that because he knows that it will set no captive free.

Admittedly, the Altar of Calvary is ugly. It is bloody and rejected by all of the world and almost all of the Church. But the Altar called Calvary, of which there is no other, because no other is needed, still sets men free and, in fact, it is the only Altar that will set men free!

CHAPTER 23

(1) "AND IT CAME TO PASS A LONG TIME AFTER THAT THE LORD HAD GIVEN REST UNTO ISRAEL FROM ALL THEIR ENEMIES ROUND ABOUT, THAT JOSHUA WAXED OLD AND STRICKEN IN AGE.

(2) "AND JOSHUA CALLED FOR ALL ISRAEL, AND FOR THEIR ELDERS, AND FOR THEIR HEADS, AND FOR THEIR JUDGES, AND FOR THEIR OFFICERS, AND SAID UNTO THEM, I AM OLD AND STRICKEN IN AGE:

(3) "AND YOU HAVE SEEN ALL THAT THE LORD YOUR GOD HAS DONE UNTO ALL THESE NATIONS BECAUSE OF YOU; FOR THE LORD YOUR GOD IS HE WHO HAS FOUGHT FOR YOU.

(4) "BEHOLD, I HAVE DIVIDED UNTO YOU BY LOT THESE NATIONS THAT REMAIN, TO BE AN INHERITANCE FOR YOUR TRIBES, FROM JORDAN, WITH ALL THE NATIONS THAT I HAVE CUT OFF, EVEN UNTO THE GREAT SEA WESTWARD.

(5) "AND THE LORD YOUR GOD, HE SHALL EXPEL THEM FROM BEFORE YOU, AND DRIVE THEM FROM OUT OF YOUR SIGHT; AND YOU SHALL POSSESS THEIR LAND, AS THE LORD YOUR GOD HAS PROMISED UNTO YOU.

(6) "BE YE THEREFORE VERY COURAGEOUS TO KEEP AND TO DO ALL THAT IS WRITTEN IN THE BOOK OF THE

LAW OF MOSES, THAT YOU TURN NOT ASIDE THEREFROM TO THE RIGHT HAND OR TO THE LEFT;

(7) "THAT YOU COME NOT AMONG THESE NATIONS, THESE WHO REMAIN AMONG YOU; NEITHER MAKE MENTION OF THE NAME OF THEIR GODS, NOR CAUSE TO SWEAR BY THEM, NEITHER SERVE THEM, NOR BOW YOURSELVES UNTO THEM:

(8) "BUT CLEAVE UNTO THE LORD YOUR GOD, AS YOU HAVE DONE UNTO THIS DAY.

(9) "FOR THE LORD HAS DRIVEN OUT FROM BEFORE YOU GREAT NATIONS AND STRONG: BUT AS FOR YOU, NO MAN HAS BEEN ABLE TO STAND BEFORE YOU UNTO THIS DAY.

(10) "ONE MAN OF YOU SHALL CHASE A THOUSAND: FOR THE LORD YOUR GOD, HE IT IS WHO FIGHTS FOR YOU, AS HE HAS PROMISED YOU.

(11) "TAKE GOOD HEED THEREFORE UNTO YOURSELVES, THAT YOU LOVE THE LORD YOUR GOD.

(12) "ELSE IF YOU DO IN ANY WISE GO BACK, AND CLEAVE UNTO THE REMNANT OF THESE NATIONS, EVEN THESE WHO REMAIN AMONG YOU, AND SHALL MAKE MARRIAGES WITH THEM, AND GO IN UNTO THEM, AND THEY TO YOU:

(13) "KNOW FOR A CERTAINTY THAT THE LORD YOUR GOD WILL NO MORE DRIVE OUT ANY OF THESE NATIONS FROM BEFORE YOU; BUT THEY SHALL BE SNARES AND TRAPS UNTO YOU, AND SCOURGES IN YOUR SIDES, AND THORNS IN YOUR EYES, UNTIL YOU PERISH FROM OFF THIS GOOD LAND WHICH THE LORD YOUR GOD HAS GIVEN YOU.

(14) "AND, BEHOLD, THIS DAY I AM GOING THE WAY OF ALL THE EARTH: AND YOU KNOW IN ALL YOUR HEARTS AND IN ALL YOUR SOULS, THAT NOT ONE THING HAS FAILED OF ALL THE GOOD THINGS WHICH THE LORD YOUR GOD SPOKE CONCERNING YOU; ALL ARE COME TO PASS UNTO YOU, AND NOT ONE THING HAS FAILED THEREOF.

(15) "THEREFORE IT SHALL COME TO PASS, THAT AS ALL GOOD THINGS ARE COME UPON YOU, WHICH THE LORD

YOUR GOD PROMISED YOU; SO SHALL THE LORD BRING UPON YOU ALL EVIL THINGS, UNTIL HE HAS DESTROYED YOU FROM OFF THIS GOOD LAND WHICH THE LORD YOUR GOD HAS GIVEN YOU.

(16) "WHEN YOU HAVE TRANSGRESSED THE COVENANT OF THE LORD YOUR GOD, WHICH HE COMMANDED YOU, AND HAVE GONE AND SERVED OTHER GODS, AND BOWED YOURSELVES TO THEM; THEN SHALL THE ANGER OF THE LORD BE KINDLED AGAINST YOU, AND YOU SHALL PERISH QUICKLY FROM OFF THE GOOD LAND WHICH HE HAS GIVEN UNTO YOU."

The exegesis is:

1. The *"long time"* of Verse 1 was approximately 8 years.

2. All the enemies were not yet driven out, but the Promise is given here that if the people will obey the Lord, to be sure, total victory will be the result, with no enemies left. Thus far, no enemies stood before them, at least for those who truly followed the Lord. Continued victory is promised here!

3. Israel is told here that prosperity depends upon their fidelity to the Bible; it is the same presently! We must not add to the Word of God, nor take from the Word of God.

4. Presently, any form of worship that is not anchored squarely in *"Jesus Christ and Him Crucified"* can only be construed as idolatry (I Cor. 1:17-18, 21, 23; 2:2).

5. Regarding Verse 14, from that time until now, about 3,500 years, the same thing can still be said; not one Word of the Lord has ever failed, and, in fact, cannot fail.

6. Verse 15 proclaims the fact, as the Lord blesses for obedience, at the same time, He will send Judgment for disobedience; this must not be forgotten!

THE EXHORTATION

Verse 1 says, *"After that the LORD had given rest unto Israel from all their enemies."* As we have stated several times, the Book of Joshua is a Blueprint outline for Victory. In this Book we have seen much war, as every Christian sees constant warfare with Satan; however, if we follow the Lord, there will come a time of *"rest"* from all of our enemies.

The *"rest"* that is being spoken of here can only come in Christ, with our Faith in Him and what He did for us at the Cross. It must ever be the Cross, for as Christ is the Source, the Cross is the Means, by which all great things are given unto us.

As long as we're trying to defeat the enemy in our own strength, there will be no victory and there will be no *"rest."* But once Christ becomes predominant within our Spiritual experience, and He is doing the living in us, then we will have *"rest."* Joshua will give the criteria for continued victory and, thereby, continued *"rest."* It is as follows:

A. *"And to do all that is written in the Book of the Law of Moses,"* in other words, fidelity to the Bible. The Word of God must be the criteria for every Child of God. We must be very careful that we *"turn not aside therefrom to the right hand or to the left."* The bane of the modern Church is, in fact, turning either to the right or to the left.

B. *"That you come not among these nations"* refers to separation. Remember, it is not isolation but separation. *"Come out from among them, and be ye separate, says the Lord"* (II Cor. 6:17).

C. *"But cleave unto the LORD your God."* This, of course, speaks of our love for God. We are to love Him as Jesus said, with all *"our heart, our mind, our soul, and our strength."* There you have the criteria:

- The Word of God;
- Separation from the world; and,
- Love for God.

If this is done, then, as the Tenth Verse says, *"One man of you shall chase a thousand."* There is no power like the Child of God who is abiding by the Book, separating himself from the world, and loving the Lord with all of his heart.

Then we can expect *"not one thing will fail of all the good things which the LORD your God spoke concerning you."*

THE WARNING

The warning is, *"When you have transgressed the Covenant of the LORD your God . . . you shall perish quickly from off the good land which He has given unto you."* Sadly, that is exactly what happened;

likewise, it will happen with any Child of God who turns away from the Lord. In other words, we cannot have the Bible, separation from the world, the Love of God and continued unrepentant transgressions at the same time; one or the other must go. God help us to choose that the transgressions go.

CHAPTER 24

(1) "AND JOSHUA GATHERED ALL THE TRIBES OF ISRAEL TO SHECHEM, AND CALLED FOR THE ELDERS OF ISRAEL, AND FOR THEIR HEADS, AND FOR THEIR JUDGES, AND FOR THEIR OFFICERS; AND THEY PRESENTED THEMSELVES BEFORE GOD.

(2) "AND JOSHUA SAID UNTO ALL THE PEOPLE, THUS SAITH THE LORD GOD OF ISRAEL, YOUR FATHERS DWELT ON THE OTHER SIDE OF THE FLOOD IN OLD TIME, EVEN TERAH, THE FATHER OF ABRAHAM, AND THE FATHER OF NACHOR: AND THEY SERVED OTHER GODS.

(3) "AND I TOOK YOUR FATHER ABRAHAM FROM THE OTHER SIDE OF THE FLOOD, AND LED HIM THROUGHOUT ALL THE LAND OF CANAAN, AND MULTIPLIED HIS SEED, AND GAVE HIM ISAAC.

(4) "AND I GAVE UNTO ISAAC JACOB AND ESAU: AND I GAVE UNTO ESAU MOUNT SEIR, TO POSSESS IT; BUT JACOB AND HIS CHILDREN WENT DOWN INTO EGYPT.

(5) "AND I SENT MOSES ALSO AND AARON, AND I PLAGUED EGYPT, ACCORDING TO THAT WHICH I DID AMONG THEM: AND AFTERWARD I BROUGHT YOU OUT.

(6) "AND I BROUGHT YOUR FATHERS OUT OF EGYPT: AND YOU CAME UNTO THE SEA; AND THE EGYPTIANS PURSUED AFTER YOUR FATHERS WITH CHARIOTS AND HORSEMEN UNTO THE RED SEA.

(7) "AND WHEN THEY CRIED UNTO THE LORD, HE PUT DARKNESS BETWEEN YOU AND THE EGYPTIANS, AND

BROUGHT THE SEA UPON THEM, AND COVERED THEM; AND YOUR EYES HAVE SEEN WHAT I HAVE DONE IN EGYPT: AND YOU DWELT IN THE WILDERNESS A LONG SEASON.

(8) "AND I BROUGHT YOU INTO THE LAND OF THE AMORITES, WHICH DWELT ON THE OTHER SIDE JORDAN; AND THEY FOUGHT WITH YOU: AND I GAVE THEM INTO YOUR HAND, THAT YOU MIGHT POSSESS THEIR LAND; AND I DESTROYED THEM FROM BEFORE YOU.

(9) "THEN BALAK THE SON OF ZIPPOR, KING OF MOAB AROSE AND WARRED AGAINST ISRAEL, AND SENT AND CALLED BALAAM THE SON OF BEOR TO CURSE YOU:

(10) "BUT I WOULD NOT HEARKEN UNTO BALAAM; THEREFORE HE BLESSED YOU STILL: SO I DELIVERED YOU OUT OF HIS HAND.

(11) "AND YOU WENT OVER JORDAN, AND CAME UNTO JERICHO: AND THE MEN OF JERICHO FOUGHT AGAINST YOU, THE AMORITES, AND THE PERIZZITES, AND THE CANAANITES, AND THE HITTITES, AND THE GIRGASHITES, THE HIVITES, AND THE JEBUSITES; AND I DELIVERED THEM INTO YOUR HAND.

(12) "AND I SENT THE HORNET BEFORE YOU, WHICH DROVE THEM OUT FROM BEFORE YOU, EVEN THE TWO KINGS OF THE AMORITES; BUT NOT WITH YOUR SWORD, NOR WITH YOUR BOW.

(13) "AND I HAVE GIVEN YOU A LAND FOR WHICH YOU DID NOT LABOUR, AND CITIES WHICH YOU BUILT NOT, AND YOU DWELL IN THEM; OF THE VINEYARDS AND OLIVEYARDS WHICH YOU PLANTED NOT DO YOU EAT.

(14) "NOW THEREFORE FEAR THE LORD, AND SERVE HIM IN SINCERITY AND IN TRUTH: AND PUT AWAY THE GODS WHICH YOUR FATHERS SERVED ON THE OTHER SIDE OF THE FLOOD, AND IN EGYPT; AND SERVE YE THE LORD.

(15) "AND IF IT SEEM EVIL UNTO YOU TO SERVE THE LORD, CHOOSE YOU THIS DAY WHOM YOU WILL SERVE; WHETHER THE GODS WHICH YOUR FATHERS SERVED WHO WERE ON THE OTHER SIDE OF THE FLOOD, OR THE GODS OF THE AMORITES, IN WHOSE LAND YOU DWELL: BUT AS FOR ME AND MY HOUSE, WE WILL SERVE THE LORD.

(16) "AND THE PEOPLE ANSWERED AND SAID, GOD FORBID THAT WE SHOULD FORSAKE THE LORD, TO SERVE OTHER GODS;

(17) "FOR THE LORD OUR GOD, HE IT IS WHO BROUGHT US UP AND OUR FATHERS OUT OF THE LAND OF EGYPT, FROM THE HOUSE OF BONDAGE, AND WHICH DID THOSE GREAT SIGNS IN OUR SIGHT, AND PRESERVED US IN ALL THE WAY WHEREIN WE WENT, AND AMONG ALL THE PEOPLE THROUGH WHOM WE PASSED:

(18) "AND THE LORD DROVE OUT FROM BEFORE US ALL THE PEOPLE, EVEN THE AMORITES WHICH DWELT IN THE LAND: THEREFORE WILL WE ALSO SERVE THE LORD; FOR HE IS OUR GOD.

(19) "AND JOSHUA SAID UNTO THE PEOPLE, YOU CANNOT SERVE THE LORD: FOR HE IS AN HOLY GOD; HE IS A JEALOUS GOD; HE WILL NOT FORGIVE YOUR TRANSGRESSIONS NOR YOUR SINS.

(20) "IF YOU FORSAKE THE LORD, AND SERVE STRANGE GODS, THEN HE WILL TURN AND DO YOU HURT, AND CONSUME YOU, AFTER THAT HE HAS DONE YOU GOOD."

The exegesis is:

1. The Children of Israel, according to Verse 1, were gathered at the Tabernacle, where the Altar and the Ark of the Covenant were.

2. When Grace found Abraham, he was an idolater. In fact, in one way or the other, all who do not know the Lord are guilty of the sin of idolatry. With many it is the worship of *"self."* Even in Christendom, idols are plentiful, although in a different form than during the time of Joshua. Many worship their Churches, their denominations, etc.

3. As Verse 3 and following proclaim, the Lord was the author of all these things, as it pertained to Abraham, and those who followed him.

4. From this Chapter, we learn that

NOTES

Joshua stood in the office of the Prophet. We find the proof of this in Verses 2 and 27. In fact, everything between these two Verses, and including those Verses, is prophetic.

5. It was the Will of the Lord that Israel would spend a short period of time in the wilderness, in order that they might learn Faith and trust in Him. That time frame would have been approximately 2 years; however, they instead would spend approximately 40 years in the wilderness because of unbelief. It was truly *"a long season."*

6. As long as Israel served the Lord, the Lord fought for them, even using the hornet to do so, as Verse 12 proclaims.

7. There were 7 nations in Canaan, which opposed Israel, and which were defeated by the Lord. The number *"seven"* is God's number of totality, perfection, and completeness. It means that evil in every form opposed Israel.

8. Verse 15 proclaims the fact that even though the Godly warrior cannot answer for others, he does answer for himself; and his answer should be the answer for every human being on Earth.

9. While Verse 18 proclaims the fact that the people answered correctly, still, the near future would prove that their hearts were not exactly according to their words.

10. The idea of the Nineteenth Verse is, the word *"forgive,"* as used here, *"signifies to remove or to bear the burden of guilt."* In other words, God could not do such if proper Atonement is not made, which is the proper Sacrifice, which is a Type of the Cross, and Faith in that Sacrifice.

"Transgressions" signify *"a breach of covenant."* One can have Forgiveness, Mercy, and Grace only on the basis of the Crucified Christ, and Faith in that atoning Work (Jn. 3:16; Eph. 2:8-9).

11. In all of this, God doesn't change; He rewards obedience, and brings Judgment on disobedience.

A REMINDER AND A WARNING

This will be Joshua's final address to Israel. The First Verse says, *"They presented themselves before God."* What a statement! What an awesome thought to *"present ourselves before God."* And yet, Christians in

whom the Spirit of God constantly abides (I Cor. 3:16) are constantly *"presenting themselves before God."*

Beginning with the Second Verse, the address begins. It says, *"They served other gods."* This tells us that God did not choose Abraham because he was godly, good, or righteous. In fact, he was an idolater. It was Grace that looked at this idolater and saw something in his heart that would respond to God and, thereby, chose him. The sentence, *"They served other gods,"* could well apply to each and every one of us; likewise, we have not been brought to Jesus because of our goodness but because of His Grace.

The word in the Third Verse, *"and gave him Isaac,"* was the first tangible promise of the Coming Seed, the Lord Jesus Christ. It must be continually remembered that every single Blessing that comes to the Child of God is because of our Heavenly Isaac, the Lord Jesus Christ. God does not and, in fact, cannot bless poor, fallen, sinful man. He can only bless Christ Who is in converted man.

The Sixth Verse will forever record God's Great Salvation Plan, *"And I brought your fathers out of Egypt."* And then we are given the catalog of the great victories that came to Israel.

Over and over again Satan will tell us there are no victories; however, we should ever point to the Eleventh Verse, where it names all the enemies of our soul, and then says, *"I delivered them into your hand."* Hallelujah! The song says:

"We've come this far by Faith, leaning on the Lord."
"Trusting in His Holy Word, He's never failed me yet."

The Fifteenth Verse pictures man's free-moral agency, *"choose you this day whom you will serve."* This means that the doctrine of unconditional eternal security as taught by some, is a fallacious doctrine. In other words, unscriptural. Our serving God is always by choice. We choose to get in, and if we so desire, we can choose to get out; however, I will say, as Joshua stated eternally, *"but as for me and my house, we will serve the LORD."*

THE CHOICE THE BELIEVER MUST MAKE

While this experience is a choice on our part (Jn. 3:16; Rev. 22:17), still, we must understand what that choice actually is. First of all let's see what it isn't!

Most Christians are taught that once they come to the Lord, then they have the power (willpower) to say *"yes"* to the Lord and *"no"* to sin. That is totally wrong! If one follows that direction, one is going to fail.

Why?

That particular direction puts the emphasis on self, which God cannot bless. The Believer must understand, that we are just as dependent on the Lord for Sanctification after we get Saved, as we were as a sinner to get Saved. Regrettably, most modern Christians are trying to live for God by the means of willpower. Such cannot be done. Listen to Paul, and I will quote from THE EXPOSITOR'S STUDY BIBLE:

"For I know that in me, (that is, in my flesh,) dwells no good thing (speaks of man's own ability, or rather the lack thereof in comparison to the Holy Spirit, at least when it comes to spiritual things)*: for to will is present with me* (Paul is speaking here of his willpower; regrettably, most modern Christians are trying to live for God by means of willpower, thinking falsely that since they have come to Christ, they are now free to say *'no'* to sin; that is the wrong way to look at the situation; the Believer cannot live for God by the strength of willpower; while the will is definitely important, it alone is not enough; the Believer must exercise Faith in Christ and the Cross, and do so constantly; then he will have the ability and strength to say *'yes'* to Christ, which automatically says, *'no'* to the things of the world)*; but how to perform that which is good I find not* (outside of the Cross, it is impossible to find a way to do good)*"* (Rom. 7:18).

SO WHAT IS THE CHOICE THE BELIEVER MUST MAKE?

The choice is, do I place my Faith exclusively in Christ as the Source and the Cross as the Means, which is the same thing as placing it in the Word of God, or do I place

my faith elsewhere? That is the choice! If you as a Believer place your faith in anything other than the Cross of Christ, this greatly hinders the Holy Spirit, Who works exclusively within the perimeters of the Finished Work of Christ (Rom. 8:2). Then the Believer is pretty much left on his own. Listen again to Paul:

"I do not frustrate the Grace of God (if we make anything other than the Cross of Christ the Object of our Faith, we frustrate the Grace of God, which means we stop its action, and the Holy Spirit will no longer help us)*: for if Righteousness come by the Law* (any type of Law), *then Christ is dead in vain.* (If I can successfully live for the Lord by any means other than Faith in Christ and the Cross, then the Death of Christ was a waste)*"* (Gal. 2:21).

WHAT DOES IT REALLY MEAN TO FRUSTRATE THE GRACE OF GOD?

While we've already given the answer in brief, and because it's so very, very important, let us elaborate.

First of all, the Grace of God is simply the Goodness of God extended to undeserving Believers. There is nothing that any of us can do to deserve Grace, i.e., *"the Goodness of God."* We receive His Grace, i.e., *"Goodness"* by simply exerting Faith in Christ and what He did for us at the Cross (Rom. 6:1-14; I Cor. 1:17-18, 23; 2:2). This means that His Grace is received solely and totally by Faith, and never by works.

In other words, for this Grace to come to us in an uninterrupted flow, which the Lord intends for it to do, and which we must have if we are to live an overcoming, victorious life, then our Faith must be properly placed. That proper place is always the Cross of Christ (Gal., Chpt. 5; Eph. 2:13-18; Col. 2:14-15).

When we place our faith in something else, anything else, it doesn't really matter what it is, and no matter how good it may seem to be on the surface, in effect, we are insulting Christ. We are saying what His Word does not say.

We are claiming that we have the ability within ourselves to do what needs to be done. We are claiming, whether we realize it or not, that what Jesus did at the Cross was insufficient, and we have to add something to what He has done.

I would hope it would be obvious by now, as to the arrogance of such thinking; however, that's where most Christians are! When we place our faith in something else other than Christ and the Cross, we immediately frustrate the Grace of God, which means that we stop His Flow, or at least seriously hinder that Flow, which spells disaster for the Believer. The word *"frustrate"* in the Greek is *"atheteo,"* and means, *"to set aside, to disesteem, to neutralize or violate, to reject."* I would hope we would see as to how serious the situation is, as it regards frustrating the Grace of God.

Any Believer can survive only by the means of the Grace of God. But the truth is, most Believers think they can do the job pretty well on their own.

This is proved by the millions who have embraced the *"Purpose Driven Life"* scheme, or the *"Government of Twelve"* scheme, or *"Humanistic Psychology,"* or *"Denominationalism,"* or a myriad of other types of *"works religion."* Let's say it this way:

Anything, and I mean anything, that is not strictly *"Christ and Him Crucified,"* will fall out to frustrating the Grace of God. The only way that the Grace of God will continue to come to the Believer, and do so, as stated, on an uninterrupted basis, is for the Believer to always understand that Christ is the Source of all things, while the Cross is the Means.

So, the *"choice"* the Believer has is, *"Do I place my Faith exclusively in Christ and the Cross, or in something else?"*

DECEPTION

Sadly, millions of Believers are deceived. They think their faith is in Christ and the Cross, when in reality, it's in something else.

A short time ago, actually on the Fourth of July, having the day off, I had the opportunity to observe several Christian programs over Television, which I do not ordinarily do.

Most, in one way or the other, were teaching two things:

A. Self-improvement and
B. Morality.

To the ear of the Believer that is not very spiritual, meaning, they really don't know the Word as they should, these two subjects, seem to be exactly what the Church needs. In fact, self-improvement is the great pastime of this nation. In fact, it is the same with most Believers.

The preacher who is teaching and preaching self-improvement has a large audience, and simply because every Believer wants to improve themselves.

The truth is, it is impossible for self to improve self. We may think we can, we may be told we can, but it cannot be done. It most definitely needs to be done, and it most definitely must be done, but it can't be done by self.

In other words, the manner and the way in which self-improvement is being taught and preached, even though a few Scriptures are used, and even though the Name of the Lord is banded about constantly, still, what's being taught is the ways of the world.

I heard one program for a few minutes, and the dear lady was exclaiming that Believers must change their attitude. While that is certainly a desirable goal, still, man is not going to change his situation by changing his attitude. The truth is, within himself, he can't change his attitude, no matter how hard he tries.

Intertwined in all of this is the teaching of morality. Now everybody knows that we need a higher standard of morality. Even the world agrees with that. In fact, the world has their own brand of morality, which the Church seems to have adopted.

There is only one way that self can be improved, only one way that God's Standard of Morality can be reached. Let's look at that way.

SELF-IMPROVEMENT AND MORALITY

Once again, we go back to the Cross. In other words, the only way that self can be improved, or that God's Standard of Morality can be reached, is by the Believer placing his or her Faith exclusively in Christ and the Cross. This emphatically states that the Believer understands that whatever is needed he cannot do himself. In fact, and as stated, the Holy Spirit Alone can bring about these desired results. Even then, meaning that the Believer's Faith is properly placed, which insures the help of the Holy Spirit, it's not easy.

The clinging vines of the Fall hold to us so tightly, that it is hard for the Believer even though Faith is rightly placed, to come to the place he ought to be, and flat-out impossible otherwise! But this is where the great problem begins:

The modern Church doesn't want to agree that it cannot attain or achieve this place and position of improvement or God's Standard of Morality, by its own machinations. It refuses to admit that the Cross of Christ is the only way, and I mean the only way. It refuses to admit that it is making, by its efforts otherwise, *"The Cross of Christ of none effect"* (I Cor. 1:17). But that's exactly what is happening.

Admittedly, the thousands will not flock to the Message of the Cross. It will only be one here and one there. In fact, the thousands will most definitely flock to the self-improvement message and the morality message, because it appeals to the flesh. But Paul stated:

"So then they who are in the flesh cannot please God (refers to the Believer attempting to live his Christian Life by means other than Faith in Christ and the Cross)" (Rom. 8:8).

DESTRUCTION!

Now let the reader understand, that all of this of which we speak, does not fall out to a mere preference on our part, but rather to life or death. It is that serious!

Paul also said:

"Brethren, be followers together of me (be 'fellow-imitators'), *and mark them which walk so as you have us for an example* (observe intently).

"(For many walk [speaks of those attempting to live for God outside of the victory and rudiments of the Cross of Christ], *of whom I have told you often, and now tell you even weeping* [this is a most serious matter], *that they are the enemies of the Cross of Christ* [those who do not look exclusively to the Cross of Christ must be labeled 'enemies']:

"Whose end is destruction [if the Cross is ignored, and continues to be ignored, the loss of the soul is the only ultimate conclusion], *whose god is their belly* [refers to those who attempt to pervert the Gospel for their own personal gain], *and whose glory is in their shame* [the material things they seek, God labels as 'shame'], *who mind earthly things.)* (This means they have no interest in Heavenly things, which signifies they are using the Lord for their own personal gain)" (Phil. 3:17-19).

If the Believer misses it here, then the Believer stands to miss it altogether, which means the loss of the soul (Gal. 1:8-9).

AS FOR ME AND MY HOUSE WE WILL SERVE THE LORD!

Verse 15 of the final Chapter of Joshua, which gives the final address of Joshua to Israel, in a sense, closes by saying, *"But as for me and my house, we will serve the LORD."*

The world pulls and tugs at the Christian in order that the Christian may depart from God's Way; unfortunately, most of the modern Church has gone the way of the world and does the same thing. So, when the Believer stakes his claim on the good ground of Faith in Christ and what Christ has done at the Cross, the ire and the anger of the Church is going to be directed his way. Paul referred to that as the *"offence of the Cross"* (Gal. 5:11).

(21) "AND THE PEOPLE SAID UNTO JOSHUA, NO; BUT WE WILL SERVE THE LORD.

(22) "AND JOSHUA SAID UNTO THE PEOPLE, YOU ARE WITNESSES AGAINST YOURSELVES THAT YOU HAVE CHOSEN YOU THE LORD, TO SERVE HIM. AND THEY SAID, WE ARE WITNESSES.

(23) "NOW THEREFORE PUT AWAY, SAID HE, THE STRANGE GODS WHICH ARE AMONG YOU, AND INCLINE YOUR HEART UNTO THE LORD GOD OF ISRAEL.

(24) "AND THE PEOPLE SAID UNTO JOSHUA, THE LORD OUR GOD WILL WE SERVE, AND HIS VOICE WILL WE OBEY.

(25) "SO JOSHUA MADE A COVENANT WITH THE PEOPLE THAT DAY, AND SET THEM A STATUTE AND AN ORDINANCE IN SHECHEM."

The structure is:

1. The people were called upon to witness their own proclamation, which they did.

2. Verse 23 proves that there was still idolatry among the Israelites, despite the great things done for them by the Lord. This is why John the Beloved said, *"Little children, keep yourselves from idols"* (I Jn. 5:21).

3. A Covenant was made that day as Joshua finished his address, but regrettably, a Covenant that Israel didn't keep.

IDOLATRY

Sadly, Joshua knew that, even as he spoke to them, that the people were idolaters. The Twenty-third Verse says, *"Now therefore put away, said he, the strange gods which are among you."* How strange it was for Israel to have these idols (albeit hidden) after they had seen God do such great and mighty things! How strange is it for us today to continue to have idols, when we have seen God do such great things. An idol is anything that takes the place of God. But let's be a little more definitive:

Anything in which the Believer places his faith other than Christ and the Cross, constitutes an idol. Of course, Believers do not think of such in that capacity, but that's exactly what it is. In the Eyes of God, Whose Eyes Alone matter, anything and everything which is not strictly according to the Word of God, which is *"Jesus Christ and Him Crucified,"* is constituted as an idol. It doesn't matter that Believers would not dare think of such in that capacity, the truth is, that's the way that God looks at the situation. In the Eyes of the Lord, they are *"strange gods."*

(26) "AND JOSHUA WROTE THESE WORDS IN THE BOOK OF THE LAW OF GOD, AND TOOK A GREAT STONE, AND SET IT UP THERE UNDER AN OAK, THAT WAS BY THE SANCTUARY OF THE LORD.

(27) "AND JOSHUA SAID UNTO ALL THE PEOPLE, BEHOLD, THIS STONE SHALL BE A WITNESS UNTO US; FOR IT HAS HEARD ALL THE WORDS OF THE LORD WHICH HE SPOKE UNTO US: IT SHALL BE THEREFORE A WITNESS UNTO YOU, LEST YOU DENY YOUR GOD.

(28) "SO JOSHUA LET THE PEOPLE DEPART, EVERY MAN UNTO HIS INHERITANCE."

NOTES

The pattern is:

1. Joshua used a stone as a witness. The Lord told the Pharisees that the very stones were prepared to give their testimony to His Person and Mission (Lk. 19:40).

2. This would be the last time that many of those in Israel, actually most, would see Joshua, one of the greatest men of God who ever lived.

3. Under Joshua, the people had tremendous leadership. Without proper leadership, the Church languishes and falls by the wayside.

THE MONUMENT OF WITNESS

Joshua was a Prophet and knew that God was speaking these words through him. The Twenty-seventh Verse says, *"For it has heard all the words of the LORD which He spoke unto us."* Joshua was speaking not only of Israel but *"this stone."* Jesus, likewise, as stated, told the Pharisees that if the people stop praising Him, the very stones would cry out. He could have had this moment in mind when He uttered those words.

The truth is, every single thing becomes a witness either for us or against us, and simply because God's Creation bears witness to the Creator. The idea is, there is no excuse!

The people had promised to obey the Word of the Lord. While God always keeps His Promises, it is very difficult for man in turn to keep his promises, whether to God or man.

(29) "AND IT CAME TO PASS AFTER THESE THINGS, THAT JOSHUA THE SON OF NUN, THE SERVANT OF THE LORD, DIED, BEING AN HUNDRED AND TEN YEARS OLD.

(30) "AND THEY BURIED HIM IN THE BORDER OF HIS INHERITANCE IN TIMNATH-SERAH, WHICH IS IN MOUNT EPHRAIM, ON THE NORTH SIDE OF THE HILL OF GAASH.

(31) "AND ISRAEL SERVED THE LORD ALL THE DAYS OF JOSHUA, AND ALL THE DAYS OF THE ELDERS WHO OVERLIVED JOSHUA, AND WHICH HAD KNOWN ALL THE WORKS OF THE LORD, THAT HE HAD DONE FOR ISRAEL.

(32) "AND THE BONES OF JOSEPH,

WHICH THE CHILDREN OF ISRAEL BROUGHT UP OUT OF EGYPT, BURIED THEY IN SHECHEM, IN A PARCEL OF GROUND WHICH JACOB BOUGHT OF THE SONS OF HAMOR THE FATHER OF SHECHEM FOR AN HUNDRED PIECES OF SILVER: AND IT BECAME THE INHERITANCE OF THE CHILDREN OF JOSEPH.

(33) "AND ELEAZAR THE SON OF AARON DIED; AND THEY BURIED HIM IN A HILL THAT PERTAINED TO PHINEHAS HIS SON, WHICH WAS GIVEN HIM IN MOUNT EPHRAIM."

The overview is:

1. No higher accolade could be given to any man or woman than to refer to them as *"the Servant of the LORD."* Joshua closed his life with the full consciousness that he had discharged the duties God had imposed upon him, and had done so without failure of Faith.

2. Tradition says that they carved the rising sun on the stone placed over the entrance to the tomb. This commemorated the tremendous Miracle wrought by the Lord, when Joshua asked for the day to be lengthened that the victory may be complete. God honored his request.

3. We see here the value of personal influence. All the days of Joshua's government were only fourteen years, and all the days of the Elders who outlived only three years; and then came Israel's swift lapse into the abominations of idolatry.

4. Incidentally, both Joseph and Joshua each lived to be 110 years of age (Gen. 50:23-26).

5. A glorious Chapter here closes, with now a darker Chapter concerning Israel about to begin.

JOSHUA, THE SERVANT OF THE LORD

The Thirtieth Verse says, *"And they buried him in the border of his inheritance in Timnath-serah."* As we have stated, the words *"Timnath-serah"* mean *"the portion that remains."* They buried him in it because he had obtained it.

God help us in this great and glorious day of Grace to at least do as well. Tradition says, as stated, that at the entrance of Joshua's tomb, the figure of the shining Sun was

carved into the solid rock, signifying the man who made the Sun to stand still, and did so by his Faith.

The Thirty-first Verse proclaims the tremendous value of proper leadership. When that Leadership died, and we speak of Joshua and Eleazar the High Priest, Israel sadly and regrettably, quickly went into apostasy.

Every generation must have a move of God. No generation can live off the past experiences of the generation prior to them. Each must have their own Calvary, their own Resurrection, and their own Pentecost, so to speak.

JOSEPH

In the last Chapter of Genesis (50:26), we have a record of the death of Joseph and him being in a coffin in Egypt. Here, in the last Chapter of Joshua we have the final reference to Joseph being brought out of Egypt and buried in Shechem in the burying place of Abraham, Isaac, and Jacob. It was as well, Joseph's inheritance, which he obtained by Faith;

Even though Egypt beckoned so strongly to Joseph, it never claimed him, neither did it claim Jacob, their heart and their Faith were ever in Canaan.

CONCLUSION

It is July 5, 2006, as I conclude the commentary notes on this great Book of Joshua.

Its study has sharpened my Faith, and has given me a strong determination, that the entirety of the inheritance must be possessed. My prayer is that the Lord will help us mightily. Within ourselves, we cannot do it; however, with Him, we can do all that He has promised us.

"In Heavenly love abiding,
"No change my heart shall fear;
"And safe is such confiding,
"For nothing changes here.
"The storm may roar without me,
"My heart may low be laid,
"But God is round about me,
"And cannot be dismayed."

"Wherever He may guide me,
"No fear shall turn me back;
"My Shepherd is beside me,

"And nothing shall I lack.
"His Wisdom ever waketh,
"His sight is never dim;
"He knows the way He takes,
"And I will walk with Him."

"Green pastures are before me,
"Which yet I have not seen;
"Bright skies will soon be o'er me,
"Where darkest clouds have been.
"My hope I cannot measure,
"My path to life is free;
"My Saviour is my treasure,
"And He will walk with me."

BIBLIOGRAPY

CHAPTER 1

[1] George Williams, *The Student's Commentary On The Holy Scriptures*, Grand Rapids, Kregel Publications, 1949, pg. 108.

CHAPTER 2

[1] George Williams, *The Student's Commentary on the Holy Scriptures*, Grand Rapids, Kregel Publications, 1949, pg. 109.
[2] Ibid., pg. 109.
[3] H.D.M Spence, *The Pulpit Commentary: Vol. 3*, Grand Rapids, Eerdmans Publishing Company, 1978, pg. 42.

CHAPTER 4

[1] George Williams, *The Student's Commentary On The Holy Scriptures*, Grand Rapids, Kregel Publications, 1949, pg. 110.

CHAPTER 5

[1] George Williams, *The Student's Commentary On The Holy Scriptures*, Grand Rapids, Kregel Publications, 1949, pg. 111.
[2] Ibid., pg. 111.

CHAPTER 6

[1] George Williams, *The Student's Commentary On The Holy Scriptures*, Grand Rapids, Kregel Publications, 1949, pg. 112.

CHAPTER 7

[1] George Williams, *The Student's Commentary On The Holy Scriptures*, Grand Rapids, Kregel Publications, 1949, pg. 25.

CHAPTER 8

[1] George Williams, *The Student's Commentary On The Holy Scriptures*, Grand Rapids, Kregel Publications, 1949, pg. 274.

CHAPTER 9

[1] George Williams, *The Student's Commentary On The Holy Scriptures*, Grand Rapids, Kregel Publications, 1949, pg. 114.

CHAPTER 11

[1] George Williams, *The Student's Commentary On The Holy Scriptures*, Grand Rapids, Kregel Publications, 1949, pg. 115.

CHAPTER 12

[1] George Williams, *The Student's Commentary On The Holy Scriptures*, Grand Rapids, Kregel Publications, 1949, pg. 115.

CHAPTER 14

[1] George Williams, *The Student's Commentary On The Holy Scriptures*, Grand Rapids, Kregel Publications, 1949, pg. 116.

CHAPTER 15

[1] H.D.M Spence, *The Pulpit Commentary: Vol. 3*, Grand Rapids, Eerdmans Publishing Company, 1978, pg. 253.

CHAPTER 16

[1] George Williams, *The Student's Commentary On The Holy Scriptures*, Grand Rapids, Kregel Publications, 1949, pg. 117.

CHAPTER 19

[1] George Williams, *The Student's Commentary On The Holy Scriptures*, Grand Rapids, Kregel Publications, 1949, pg. 118.

CHAPTER 20

[1] George Williams, *The Student's Commentary On The Holy Scriptures*, Grand Rapids, Kregel Publications, 1949, pg. 119.

NOTES

REFERENCE BOOKS

Atlas Of The Bible — Rogerson
Hymns For The Family Of God
Strong's Exhaustive Concordance Of The Bible
The Interlinear Greek — English New Testament — George Ricker Berry
The New Bible Dictionary — Tyndale
The Pulpit Commentary — H.D.M. Spence
The Student's Commentary On The Holy Scriptures — George Williams
The Zondervan Pictorial Encyclopedia Of The Bible
Vine's Expository Dictionary Of New Testament Words
Webster's New Collegiate Dictionary
Young's Literal Translation Of The Holy Bible

NOTES

THE
BOOK OF JUDGES

THE INTRODUCTION

The glory of the great victories of the Book of Joshua stand as a beacon of light in the midst of a darkened world; however, sadly and regrettably, Judges is a Book of defeat — defeat that resulted from unbelief and disobedience. Joshua is now dead, but God is not; hence, there is no reason for defeat, even as there is no reason for defeat regarding our present-day lives and living. As Believers, especially considering that we now have a much better Covenant based on much better Promises, defeat should not be a part of our experience; however, sadly and regrettably, it is, and for all of us!

It is July 5, 2006 as I begin commentary on this great Book. I find with every Book of the Bible, that great Truths, on which are placed great emphasis are found in each Book that's not found in other Books of the Bible. Probably one could say, and without fear of contradiction, that it's the emphasis, and placed such by the Holy Spirit, we might quickly add, which brings out the great Truth, and makes the difference. Judges will be no exception to this rule. Tremendous Truths will be given to us; therefore, we pray that the Lord will help us to dig out these Spiritual nuggets of gold.

AUTHORSHIP OF JUDGES

It is stated by the Jewish Talmud that Samuel the Prophet wrote both the Books of Judges and Ruth.

This much is guaranteed, the entirety of the Book of Judges, as well as the other sixty-five Books of the Bible are definitely the Word of God. This means that the account is given

accurately and is the truth. It means there is no contradiction and, thereby, no error.

Modern theologians tend to discount the Miracles, etc., and simply because they do not believe that God performs Miracles. No, there is no mythology as it regards the Book of Judges, or any other parts of the Bible. What the Text says, is the truth of the matter.

THE TIME FRAME OF THE BOOK OF JUDGES

Once again, all type of dates and time frames have been given as it regards the time of the Judges. Some claim it was only about 200 years in duration, with others going slightly higher.

The Apostle Paul emphatically stated that the space of time was *"430 years"* (Acts 13:20). I think we will be safe in assuming that the great Apostle was correct.

THE BASIC TEACHING OF THE BOOK OF JUDGES

Concerning this, the following is derived from the New Bible Dictionary:

GOD'S WRATH REGARDING SIN

Israel's hope for survival was dependent upon their intertribal unity, yet such co-operative effort rose only from a common dedication to their God. Loss of Faith meant extinction (Judg. 2:11, 14; 5:8-9, 16-18).

GOD'S MERCY UPON REPENTANCE

Even oppression served as a medium of Divine Grace, and for Israel's edification. In other words, the Lord over and over used such oppression as a whip so to speak, to bring Israel in line (Judg. 2:16; 3:1-4).

MAN'S TOTAL DEPRAVITY

For after each deliverance, *"whenever the Judge died, they turned back and behaved worse than their fathers"* (Judg. 2:19).

Individualistic society had demonstrated its inherent inadequacy, for man on his own inevitably goes wrong (Judg. 17:6). Israel needed a king, though indeed only such a king as should accomplish the ultimate Will of God (Judg. 8:23; 9:6, 56).

Thus, the author of Judges was one of civilization's first true historians, not simply recording events, but then interpreting the facts on the basis of an explicit philosophy of history. As to the permanent validity of his Deuteronomy philosophy of retribution, one must grant that in those early days, when revelation was more limited, providence operated more obviously than at present. But his basic principles remain eternally sound: the sinning nation shall be punished, the repentant shall be Saved, and all man-created systems must ultimately fail.

All of this tells us, that the only valid hope of history lies in the Coming of Christ, the King.

CHAPTER 1

(1) "NOW AFTER THE DEATH OF JOSHUA IT CAME TO PASS, THAT THE CHILDREN OF ISRAEL ASKED THE LORD, SAYING, WHO SHALL GO UP FOR US AGAINST THE CANAANITES FIRST, TO FIGHT AGAINST THEM?

(2) "AND THE LORD SAID, JUDAH SHALL GO UP: BEHOLD, I HAVE DELIVERED THE LAND INTO HIS HAND.

(3) "AND JUDAH SAID UNTO SIMEON HIS BROTHER, COME UP WITH ME INTO MY LOT, THAT WE MAY FIGHT AGAINST THE CANAANITES; AND I LIKEWISE WILL GO WITH YOU INTO YOUR LOT. SO SIMEON WENT WITH HIM.

(4) "AND JUDAH WENT UP; AND THE LORD DELIVERED THE CANAANITES AND THE PERIZZITES INTO THEIR HAND: AND THEY KILLED OF THEM IN BEZEK TEN THOUSAND MEN.

(5) "AND THEY FOUND ADONI-BEZEK IN BEZEK: AND THEY FOUGHT AGAINST HIM, AND THEY KILLED THE CANAANITES AND THE PERIZZITES.

(6) "BUT ADONI-BEZEK FLED; AND THEY PURSUED AFTER HIM, AND CAUGHT HIM, AND CUT OFF HIS THUMBS AND HIS GREAT TOES.

(7) "AND ADONI-BEZEK SAID, THREESCORE AND TEN KINGS, HAVING THEIR THUMBS AND THEIR GREAT TOES CUT OFF, GATHERED THEIR MEAT UNDER MY TABLE: AS I HAVE DONE, SO GOD HAS REQUITED ME. AND THEY BROUGHT HIM TO JERUSALEM, AND THERE HE DIED."

The structure is:

1. Joshua died, but God didn't die! They *"asked the LORD"* as to what they should do, which is what they should have done. In fact, we as Believers should ask the Lord about everything.

2. Christ came from the Tribe of Judah; so, in essence, the Lord is saying that if we follow our Heavenly Judah, victory will be ours.

3. Simeon had been cursed because of the slaughter of the Shechemites, which, of course, had taken place many years before. The curse meant that they would have no inheritance in Israel, when, in fact, Israel possessed the land; however, the Tribe of Judah, which had the largest inheritance of all, gave Simeon an inheritance within their inheritance (Josh. 19:1; Gen. 49:5-7).

Likewise, the whole of humanity was cursed because of the Fall; consequently, we had no inheritance. But our Heavenly Judah made a way for us, by giving us a part in His Inheritance. If we go with Judah, i.e., *"our Heavenly Judah,"* we are guaranteed the Victory.

4. Evidently, Adoni-Bezek had committed the same atrocity on some 70 lesser kings, which rendered them helpless to hold a sword, or to properly run. Apparently, the leaders of the Tribe of Judah had heard about his atrocities, and treated him accordingly.

THE VICTORY GIVEN TO JUDAH

In the first eighteen Verses there is a beautiful proclamation of Judah's victories as given by God.

Verse 1 says, *"The Children of Israel asked the LORD, saying, Who shall go up for us against the Canaanites first, to fight against them?"*

This means they inquired by the Urim and Thummim. It was done so through the High Priest. Judges will start out with such victory and will conclude with such ugly defeat. The reason for victory was obvious, they *"asked the LORD."*

Every Believer should ask the Lord concerning every move that is made. We should earnestly want, desire, and seek His Counsel and Guidance. The beloved John said that the Holy Spirit will *"lead us into all truth"* — if we would but ask.

Verse 2 proclaims, *"And the LORD said, Judah shall go up."* The Lord will always answer if we will always ask and believe.

Verse 3 records a beautiful Type of the Grace of God. It says, *"And Judah said unto Simeon his brother, Come up with me into my lot, that we may fight against the Canaanites."*

Simeon was Jacob's son; he would be the head of a great Tribe, and, yet, Simeon had been cursed by God because of the slaughter of the Shechemites (Gen., Chpt. 34). The curse had been given in the form of a Prophecy; it had been severe, Simeon, as well as Levi, who also had been a part of the slaughter, would be scattered in Israel (Gen. 49:5-7). In other words, there would be no inheritance for them; however, whenever the land was parceled out to the various Tribes, as is recorded in the Book of Joshua, Judah was given so much that the they invited the Tribe of Simeon to come partake of their inheritance. This is a beautiful Type of Christ's relationship with the sinner Saved by Grace.

Simeon, a type of every poor, fallen, demented specimen of humanity, is invited by the Lord Jesus Christ, Who sprang from the Tribe of Judah, to come up into His Inheritance. The old song says:

"Hallelujah what a thought, Jesus, full
Salvation brought,
"Victory, yes victory."
"Let the powers of sin assail, Heaven's
Grace shall never fail,
"Victory, yes victory."

The Third Verse says, *"And I likewise will go with you into your lot."* If we go with our Heavenly Judah into His lot, then He will go

with us into our lot. He will, so to speak, help us fight the Canaanites. He will guarantee us the Victory. What a beautiful Type. Simeon, who had nothing, now has everything. And so the Scripture says, *"So Simeon went with him."* God help us to go with *"Him,"* for *"He"* is our only Hope.

"Adoni-bezek" seemed to head up the heathen forces. He was apprehended by the army of Judah, and taken captive. The Scripture says, *"And caught him, and cut off his thumbs and his great toes."*

God had given the command that this man was to be killed, not tortured. When the Church leaves the Ways of God, it always resorts to cruelty.

THE STATE OF THE TIME OF THE JUDGES

Following the death of Joshua, there was not a central government established for the Hebrew nation. Instead, the country consisted of Twelve independent Tribes existing like a confederacy, with no unifying force except God. This type of Government is referred to as a *"Theocracy,"* which means that God was to be the direct Ruler of the nation; however, the people did not always serve God, but often fell away into idolatry. There were periods of anarchy, civil war, and the ever-present threat of extermination by their enemies.

This period is known as the Dark Ages of Hebrew history, as the Israelites went through several cycles of bondage and Deliverance. They would forget God; then an oppressor would come in and subdue the people, placing them under bondage. They would then cry out to God for help; and He would send a deliverer in the form of a Judge to help them, and they would be delivered from the enemy. Before long, they would again fail to walk close to the Lord, fall back into sin, and the whole process was repeated.

The exact duration of the time of the Judges is uncertain; however, it is believed to be exactly as Paul said, 450 years (Acts 13:20). The period of the Judges is between Joshua's death and the rise of Samuel. It was a time of transition, with the scattered Tribes being held together only by a common faith.

The name for the Book *"Judges"* comes

from the Twelve military leaders known as Judges whom the Lord raised up to deliver the Nation. As the young Nation, consisting of a loose confederacy with no stable government, forsook the Lord and became easy prey for enemy invasion, the Judges were raised up to deliver the people and to help rule them. The Book of Judges, sadly, reveals Israel's deep, internal corruption.

(8) "NOW THE CHILDREN OF JUDAH HAD FOUGHT AGAINST JERUSALEM, AND HAD TAKEN IT, AND SMITTEN IT WITH THE EDGE OF THE SWORD, AND SET THE CITY ON FIRE.

(9) "AND AFTERWARD THE CHILDREN OF JUDAH WENT DOWN TO FIGHT AGAINST THE CANAANITES, WHO DWELT IN THE MOUNTAIN, AND IN THE SOUTH, AND IN THE VALLEY.

(10) "AND JUDAH WENT AGAINST THE CANAANITES WHO DWELT IN HEBRON: (NOW THE NAME OF HEBRON BEFORE WAS KIRJATH-ARBA:) AND THEY KILLED SHESHAI, AND AHIMAN, AND TALMAI.

(11) "AND FROM THENCE HE WENT AGAINST THE INHABITANTS OF DEBIR: AND THE NAME OF DEBIR BEFORE WAS KIRJATH-SEPHER:

(12) "AND CALEB SAID, HE WHO SMITES KIRJATH-SEPHER, AND TAKES IT, TO HIM WILL I GIVE ACHSAH MY DAUGHTER TO WIFE.

(13) "AND OTHNIEL THE SON OF KENAZ, CALEB'S YOUNGER BROTHER, TOOK IT: AND HE GAVE HIM ACHSAH HIS DAUGHTER TO WIFE.

(14) "AND IT CAME TO PASS, WHEN SHE CAME TO HIM, THAT SHE MOVED HIM TO ASK OF HER FATHER A FIELD: AND SHE LIGHTED FROM OFF HER ASS; AND CALEB SAID UNTO HER, WHAT WILL YOU?

(15) "AND SHE SAID UNTO HIM, GIVE ME A BLESSING: FOR YOU HAVE GIVEN ME A SOUTH LAND; GIVE ME ALSO SPRINGS OF WATER. AND CALEB GAVE HER THE UPPER SPRINGS AND THE NETHER SPRINGS."

The overview is:

1. Even though the Children of Judah took Jerusalem, it seems they didn't hold it.

2. The Tenth Verse speaks of the giants.

NOTES

They evidently were defeated by Caleb (Josh. 15:14).

3. If the field was to be given to the daughter of Caleb, then she felt she also had the right to ask for the Springs of Water to make the field fertile, which she did, and which she received. In a sense, the Springs are a Type of the Holy Spirit, without which there would be no Spiritual Fertility in our lives.

FAITH

Verses 12 through15 once again, record the great feat of Faith concerning Caleb's daughter and her husband, Othniel, who incidentally would become the first Judge of Israel.

It must be ever remembered that our Faith is the only thing that can go down to our children. Many Christians wonder why their children do not live for God. Quite possibly, it is because we passed to them everything but Faith.

Faith in Jesus Christ will insure their Salvation and, therefore, their Victory. The *"Springs of Water"* of the Fifteenth Verse proclaim the eternal, continued Blessing of Faith. God will always honor it.

Several times the Holy Spirit in the Bible will proclaim this great story of Faith concerning Caleb and his family. It was done for a reason.

The Lord wants to give us *"Springs of Living Water,"* but it must come by Faith. This is the type of *"Water"* that Jesus was speaking of to the Samaritan woman at Jacob's well. *"If you drink of this water you will thirst again, but if you drink of the water that I shall give, it shall be in you a well of water springing up unto Everlasting Life"* (Jn. 4:13-14).

(16) "AND THE CHILDREN OF THE KENITE, MOSES' FATHER IN LAW, WENT UP OUT OF THE CITY OF THE PALM TREES WITH THE CHILDREN OF JUDAH INTO THE WILDERNESS OF JUDAH, WHICH LIES IN THE SOUTH OF ARAD; AND THEY WENT AND DWELT AMONG THE PEOPLE.

(17) "AND JUDAH WENT WITH SIMEON HIS BROTHER, AND THEY KILLED THE CANAANITES WHO INHABITED ZEPHATH, AND UTTERLY DESTROYED IT. AND THE NAME OF THE

CITY WAS CALLED HORMAH.

(18) "ALSO JUDAH TOOK GAZA WITH THE COAST THEREOF, AND ASKELON WITH THE COAST THEREOF, AND EKRON WITH THE COAST THEREOF.

(19) "AND THE LORD WAS WITH JUDAH; AND HE DROVE OUT THE INHABITANTS OF THE MOUNTAIN; BUT COULD NOT DRIVE OUT THE INHABITANTS OF THE VALLEY, BECAUSE THEY HAD CHARIOTS OF IRON.

(20) "AND THEY GAVE HEBRON UNTO CALEB, AS MOSES SAID: AND HE EXPELLED THENCE THE THREE SONS OF ANAK.

(21) "AND THE CHILDREN OF BENJAMIN DID NOT DRIVE OUT THE JEBUSITES WHO INHABITED JERUSALEM; BUT THE JEBUSITES DWELL WITH THE CHILDREN OF BENJAMIN IN JERUSALEM UNTO THIS DAY."

The composition is:

1. The Sixteenth Verse declares that Moses' father-in-law (probably should have been translated brother-in-law) whose name was Hobab, who declined to go with Moses when invited some time earlier, evidently, ultimately excepted Moses' offer (Num. 10:29-30).

2. In Verse 3, it says, *"Simeon went with Judah,"* because the places which follow were all in Judah's portion; but now we read, *"Judah went with Simeon,"* because the place named was in Simeon's portion (Josh. 19:4).

3. The first phrase of the Nineteenth Verse, *"The LORD was with Judah,"* means that they could definitely have driven out those with the chariots of iron had they only exercised proper Faith; evidently, they didn't! The truth is, without God, it was all impossible for Israel, but, with the Lord, all things are possible.

4. The same held true for Benjamin as it regards Verse 21, even as it did for Judah; they evidently did not exercise proper Faith. The *"Jebusites,"* one of the most fierce and warlike tribes, continued to inhabit Jerusalem until the time of David, when he expelled them, nearly 500 years later. That's a long time to have an enemy in one's very midst; however, it is typical of Satan endeavoring to build strongholds in our lives. Only proper Faith in Christ and the Cross,

which gives the Holy Spirit latitude to work in our lives, can bring about victory over the world, the flesh, and the Devil. Far too many Believers have *"Jebusites"* in their life and living!

THE LORD WAS WITH JUDAH

The Nineteenth Verse gives the secret of *"Victory"* and of *"defeat."* It says, *"And the LORD was with Judah: and he drove out the inhabitants of the mountain."*

There was nothing Judah could not do whenever the Tribe depended on the Lord. However, the latter portion of the Verse says, *"But could not drive out the inhabitants of the valley, because they had chariots of iron."*

Here is a glaring disposition of eyes that had been on the Lord but now are on *"chariots of iron."* How easy it is for us to take our eyes from the Lord and to begin to look at Satan's weapons. The God Who tore down the Jericho walls could easily destroy the chariots of iron, but Judah, evidently, ceased to believe Him.

Along the same line, Verse 21 says, *"And the Children of Benjamin did not drive out the Jebusites who inhabited Jerusalem."* Therefore, it says, *"but the Jebusites dwell with the Children of Benjamin in Jerusalem unto this day."*

Jerusalem was to be the city where God would place His Name, and Satan would contest it mightily.

The Jebusites were some of the most fearsome and warlike people who faced Israel. Benjamin's faith failed; therefore, this thorn in Israel's side would remain there until David would dispossess them. If we allow any *"Jebusite"* to remain in our Spiritual Inheritance, he will forever be a thorn in our flesh and a blight on our Christian experience. He must be rooted out.

Beautifully enough, between Verses 19 and 21, which record terrible defeats, once again, the great Faith of Caleb stands out. It says, *"He expelled thence the three sons of Anak."* These were giants, but Caleb's Faith prevailed. The Holy Spirit intended to put this account in juxtaposition against the failure of Judah and Benjamin.

The Holy Spirit also proclaims the fact that *"the LORD was with Judah."* That is telling us that whatever needed to be done, could have been done, if Judah, and the same goes for Benjamin, had only exercised proper Faith, and pressed the issue, which God most definitely would have honored. He honored it for Caleb, and He definitely would have honored it for them.

OPPOSITION BY THE POWERS OF DARKNESS

Many Christians have the erroneous idea, that if God is in something, there will never be a problem. The truth is, the very opposite is the fact. If the Lord is in something, Satan, as should be obvious, is going to contest it every foot of the way, and every hour of the day. He will do everything within his power to stop the progress of the Lord.

Of course, the Lord can do anything as ought to be obvious; however, He works through people, and if people fail Him, He has so designed His Work, that He will allow the failure to happen. All of this, is for our benefit. He wants us to learn trust and obedience.

Praying Hyde was once asked the question, *"Does Satan contest every Believer?"* His answer was revealing.

He said, *"Satan doesn't know most Christians exist. They are causing him no trouble; therefore, he little opposes them, if at all."*

Whether that is totally correct or not I cannot answer; however, one thing I do know, that if a person is truly doing something for the Lord, and the results are obvious, one can be doubly certain that Satan is going to do everything within Hell's power to try to stop that which is being done. And most of the time, he will use other Christians to carry out his perfidious designs. Simon Peter said:

"Beloved, think it not strange concerning the fiery trial which is to try you (trials do not merely happen; they are designed by Wisdom and Operated by Love; Job proved this), *as though some strange thing happened unto you* (your trial, whatever it is, is not unique; many others are experiencing the same thing!)*:*

But rejoice (despite the trial), *inasmuch as you are partakers of Christ's sufferings* (refers to suffering for Righteousness' sake); *that, when His Glory shall be revealed* (refers

to His Second Coming), *you may be glad also with exceeding joy.* (There will be great joy in the heart of every Saint when we come back with the Lord at the Second Coming)" (I Pet. 4:12-13).

Concerning the Work of God, I like what Dr. John R. Rice once said: *"If it was easy, anybody could do it!"*

The truth is, it isn't easy; however, victory is sure, as stated, if the Lord is in the project.

THE JEBUSITES

The *"Jebusites,"* the inhabitants of Jerusalem, will prove to be a thorn in Israel's side, and for nearly 500 years. They would be expelled by David when he became king. Satan had a grand design in all of this.

He knew that Jerusalem (Jebus) would be ultimately chosen by God for His Capital in this world. He knew this is where the Temple would be built, with the Altar of Sacrifice, which made it possible for individuals to be redeemed. So, the Evil One would use all of his powers to hold the city, and for all the obvious reasons. In other words, he would not make it easy for the People of God.

The tragedy is, the Jebusites could have been driven out at any time, had the People of God exercised the proper Faith. Regrettably, for the entirety of this some 500 years, and as it pertained to all of the Judges, not one was able to expel the Jebusites. Caleb expelled his giants, but Benjamin did not succeed in expelling his. Unfortunately, when Caleb died, there seemed to be no one of like Faith to take his place.

That's the reason that most religious denominations lose their way. At a given point they exercise all of their energy in protecting the Denomination, i.e., the institution. They forget that it's not the institution, but rather mighty men and women of God who exercise Faith, which brings about the victory. So, after a while, the institution, despite how large it might be, or how materially rich it might be, becomes little more than an empty shell.

All of this, in a sense, is a type of our own personal lives. Satan seeks to erect a stronghold in our lives, a stronghold of weakness, of sloth, of vice, or whatever it might be, all designed to hinder our way with God, and above all to keep the Holy Spirit from having His Way within our lives. Unfortunately, the Evil One is all too successful. But we must remember, if the Jebusite is not driven out of our lives, the Jebusite will take over our lives. There is no in-between with the Lord, it is either victory or defeat!

(22) "AND THE HOUSE OF JOSEPH, THEY ALSO WENT UP AGAINST BETH-EL: AND THE LORD WAS WITH THEM.

(23) "AND THE HOUSE OF JOSEPH SENT TO DESCRY BETH-EL. (NOW THE NAME OF THE CITY BEFORE WAS LUZ.)

(24) "AND THE SPIES SAW A MAN COME FORTH OUT OF THE CITY, AND THEY SAID UNTO HIM, SHOW US, WE PRAY YOU, THE ENTRANCE INTO THE CITY, AND WE WILL SHOW YOU MERCY.

(25) "AND WHEN HE SHOWED THEM THE ENTRANCE INTO THE CITY, THEY SMOTE THE CITY WITH THE EDGE OF THE SWORD; BUT THEY LET GO THE MAN AND ALL HIS FAMILY.

(26) "AND THE MAN WENT INTO THE LAND OF THE HITTITES, AND BUILT A CITY, AND CALLED THE NAME THEREOF LUZ: WHICH IS THE NAME THEREOF UNTO THIS DAY.

(27) "NEITHER DID MANASSEH DRIVE OUT THE INHABITANTS OF BETH-SHEAN AND HER TOWNS, NOR TAANACH AND HER TOWNS, NOR THE INHABITANTS OF DOR AND HER TOWNS, NOR THE INHABITANTS OF IBLEAM AND HER TOWNS, NOR THE INHABITANTS OF MEGIDDO AND HER TOWNS: BUT THE CANAANITES WOULD DWELL IN THAT LAND.

(28) "AND IT CAME TO PASS, WHEN ISRAEL WAS STRONG, THAT THEY PUT THE CANAANITES TO TRIBUTE, AND DID NOT UTTERLY DRIVE THEM OUT.

(29) "NEITHER DID EPHRAIM DRIVE OUT THE CANAANITES THAT DWELT IN GEZER; BUT THE CANAANITES DWELT IN GEZER AMONG THEM.

(30) "NEITHER DID ZEBULUN DRIVE OUT THE INHABITANTS OF KITRON, NOR THE INHABITANTS OF NAHALOL; BUT THE CANAANITES DWELT AMONG THEM, AND BECAME TRIBUTARIES.

(31) "NEITHER DID ASHER DRIVE OUT THE INHABITANTS OF ACCHO, NOR THE

INHABITANTS OF ZIDON, NOR OF AHLAB, NOR OF ACHZIB, NOR OF HELBAH, NOR OF APHIK, NOR OF REHOB:

(32) "BUT THE ASHERITES DWELT AMONG THE CANAANITES, THE INHABITANTS OF THE LAND: FOR THEY DID NOT DRIVE THEM OUT.

(33) "NEITHER DID NAPHTALI DRIVE OUT THE INHABITANTS OF BETH-SHEMESH, NOR THE INHABITANTS OF BETH-ANATH; BUT HE DWELT AMONG THE CANAANITES, THE INHABITANTS OF THE LAND: NEVERTHELESS THE INHABITANTS OF BETH-SHEMESH AND OF BETH-ANATH BECAME TRIBUTARIES UNTO THEM.

(34) "AND THE AMORITES FORCED THE CHILDREN OF DAN INTO THE MOUNTAIN: FOR THEY WOULD NOT SUFFER THEM TO COME DOWN TO THE VALLEY:

(35) "BUT THE AMORITES WOULD DWELL IN MOUNT HERES IN AIJALON, AND IN SHAALBIM: YET THE HAND OF THE HOUSE OF JOSEPH PREVAILED, SO THAT THEY BECAME TRIBUTARIES.

(36) "AND THE COAST OF THE AMORITES WAS FROM THE GOING UP TO AKRABBIM, FROM THE ROCK, AND UPWARD."

The composition is:

1. By the phrase, *"And the LORD was with them,"* we are shown what God can do, regarding the heart which trusts Him. But the ground won by Faith can only be held by Faith; and very soon, therefore, the Canaanite and the Philistine recovered possession of what they had lost.

2. The man of Verse 26 was determined to build what God had determined to destroy. He had an opportunity to know the God of Israel, but rebelled against that opportunity.

Rahab's action was the reverse. She and her family were the only ones saved out of the doom of Jericho. But Grace changed her heart, and she joined the People of God.

3. As failure after failure is recorded, it doesn't mean that Israel didn't have the power to drive out the heathen, but rather that they just simply disobeyed God, and let them remain, which proved to be exactly what the Lord said would happen. Instead of Israel winning the heathen to Jehovah, the heathen

won the People of God to their heathen idols. It is the same with the modern Church.

While the Bible does not teach isolation from the world, it definitely does teach separation. We are *"in"* the world, but never to be *"of"* the world. The ship is in the water, but trouble comes, and greatly so, when the water gets in the ship (II Cor. 6:14-18; 7:1).

4. As stated, if the enemy is allowed to remain, he will ultimately make a slave out of the Believer. The situation had become so bad in Israel that the Tribe of Dan could not even live in the valley, or plant crops therein; they were virtual prisoners in their own land; and so it is.

THE FAILURE OF ISRAEL

Williams says, *"The Book of Joshua records the inheritance possessed: the Book of Judges the inheritance despised. The Book contrasts the faithfulness of God and the faithlessness of Israel."*[1]

There is but one way to deal with anything in the heart, or life, which is opposed to Christ and that one way is to put it to death, and not to try and just keep it in subjection.

The Scripture says that many of the Tribes failed to obey the Lord in driving out the heathen which occupied the land, but rather *"put them to tribute."* This was not the command of God. His command was extermination. There is no way that we can make sin work for us. Jealousy, envy, and pride, of which these things were types, cannot become friends and cannot serve us. We will destroy them, or they will ultimately destroy us, as these enemies ultimately destroyed Israel.

Man's problem is and, in fact, always has been, he thinks that he knows more than God. He thinks he has a better way; however, whatever it is that man thinks, if he doesn't obey the Lord, and obey Him in totality, the end result will not be pleasant, to say the least!

WHY DID THE TRIBES NOT OBEY THE LORD?

The reasons are probably many and varied. At the moment, it was easier to let the heathen stay than it was to drive them out. As well, they reasoned in their minds evidently, that they could make these heathen tribes

work for them, *"put them to tribute."* They couldn't see any problem with that, even though it was a direct disobedience to the Word of God. The Lord had said *"drive them out,"* and the Holy Spirit is careful to record the fact that they didn't. It is meant to be a warning to us presently.

Modern Churches forsake the Gospel, thereby inserting their own brand, which they seem to think is a better way. In other words, they try to make the passions of the people, which are always sinful to work for them. So the Preacher trims the Message, and no longer talks about sin or sinners. Nothing is said to make people feel uncomfortable, not even in the slightest. Everything is *"uplifting,"* etc. But the truth is, this Spiritual Pablum will not lift man out of the morass of evil in which he finds himself, but will only seek to drive him deeper. Such preachers, and the world is full of them, will have to answer to God one day and, as well, answer to the souls that they're causing to be lost.

"There is a way that seems right unto a man, but the end thereof are the ways of death" (Prov. 14:12).

CHAPTER 2

(1) "AND AN ANGEL OF THE LORD CAME UP FROM GILGAL TO BOCHIM, AND SAID, I MADE YOU TO GO UP OUT OF EGYPT, AND HAVE BROUGHT YOU UNTO THE LAND WHICH I SWORE UNTO YOUR FATHERS; AND I SAID, I WILL NEVER BREAK MY COVENANT WITH YOU.

(2) "AND YOU SHALL MAKE NO LEAGUE WITH THE INHABITANTS OF THIS LAND; YOU SHALL THROW DOWN THEIR ALTARS: BUT YOU HAVE NOT OBEYED MY VOICE: WHY HAVE YOU DONE THIS?

(3) "WHEREFORE I ALSO SAID, I WILL NOT DRIVE THEM OUT FROM BEFORE YOU; BUT THEY SHALL BE AS THORNS IN YOUR SIDES, AND THEIR GODS SHALL BE A SNARE UNTO YOU.

(4) "AND IT CAME TO PASS, WHEN THE ANGEL OF THE LORD SPOKE THESE

WORDS UNTO ALL THE CHILDREN OF ISRAEL, THAT THE PEOPLE LIFTED UP THEIR VOICE, AND WEPT.

(5) "AND THEY CALLED THE NAME OF THAT PLACE BOCHIM: AND THEY SACRIFICED THERE UNTO THE LORD."

The structure is:

1. The *"Angel of the LORD"* of Verse 1 was actually a preincarnate appearance of Christ.

2. The Lord has never broken a Covenant, but, most definitely, man breaks it repeatedly.

3. The question, *"Why have you done this?"* The Lord continues to ask of many Believers! As stated, if we make a league with the world, the world doesn't become more Christian, but rather we become more worldly.

4. If Israel disobeyed the Lord, He would withhold His help; in that case, Israel could but fail! It is the same with us presently!

5. Exactly where *"Bochim"* was, we aren't told, but many think that it was near Shiloh. In fact, the sacrifices were probably carried out at Shiloh. It seems that the people repented; however, it is also obvious that their repentance was shallow. Bochim means, *"weeping."*

WHY HAVE YOU DONE THIS?

The picture this Chapter portrays is of a people who have left their God. They have gone in their own directions with little thought as to the Will of the Lord.

The First Verse says, *"And an Angel of the LORD came up from Gilgal to Bochim."* This is really, as stated; the Lord Himself Who has come up to Bochim. Gilgal was Israel's first headquarters after crossing Jordan. It was also where Israel had experienced her first circumcision in the land and her first Passover.

The Tabernacle was now at Shiloh (Josh. 18:1). It would seem that the Lord would have been there residing between the Mercy Seat and the Cherubim; however, it is quite possible that God never intended for the Tabernacle to be moved to Shiloh, desiring that it remain at Gilgal. This one thing is certain:

The Lord wasn't in the Tabernacle at Shiloh, but rather was at Gilgal.

It seems that one of the few good things that happened there involved Hannah. She was praying that she might conceive, and

that the Lord would give her a baby boy. The Lord answered her prayer. She and her husband did conceive and the result was one of the greatest Prophets who ever lived, Samuel.

The Holy Spirit did not see fit to explain why the Lord was at Gilgal and not at Shiloh. This we do know; it was at Gilgal that the Lord was last seen (Josh. 5:13-15). It was at Gilgal that Israel received the Power by which she overcame the Canaanite.

The inward exercises of the heart, the putting to death of the members, which are upon the Earth, referring to true circumcision, has no outward glory. It is unimportant in the eyes of man, and it makes man little in his own eyes but fills the soul with Power, making the Presence of God real. Even then strength would not be shown at Gilgal — it would be shown at Jericho; however, the strength was obtained at Gilgal. This principle is the secret of overcoming.

THE MODERN CHURCH

But when Gilgal was forsaken, it was discovered that the Lord with His Almighty Power had been there and, seemingly, was still there. He comes up from Gilgal. The result of leaving Gilgal was to weep in the valley of Bochim. The tears were shed for lost blessings. Still, the people did not return to Gilgal. Praise and Power at Gilgal were exchanged for weeping and weakness at Bochim.

How much is this the picture of the modern Church. The Second Verse will echo through the ages as spoken by the Lord, *"but you have not obeyed My Voice: why have you done this?"*

THE CONVICTING POWER OF THE HOLY SPIRIT

The Fourth Verse records the response of the people to the convicting Power of the Holy Spirit, *"the people lifted up their voice, and wept."*

Israel was under such conviction that she would weep; however, she was not sorry enough for her backsliding to repent before God. Weeping that does not precede true Biblical Repentance only represents powerful Holy Spirit conviction. It does not necessarily represent the people acceding to that conviction.

At times Israel was penitent when God dealt with them, but at other times their hearts were hardened beyond any breaking. A general process of hardening continued in Israel from here to the time that there was no turning back, so God permitted them to go into captivity. This broke the people temporarily (Ezra 3:12; Neh. 8:9). Then Israel lapsed into hardness of heart again until, by the time the Messiah came, there was not the slightest indication of brokenness or willingness on the part of the people to do the Will of God, apart from a few Godly ones who wept much because of the impending destruction (Mat. 24:34-39; Lk. 19:41). The leaders of Israel promoted a mob spirit against Christ and through hardness of heart the Nation was destroyed (Acts 7:51-52; 28:25-31).

C. Morse Ward, Revival time speaker, made the following statement. He said, *"True Holy Spirit conviction is as scarce as the proverbial hen's teeth."*

Our dear brother was absolutely correct!

Services for the most part are geared presently to where the Holy Spirit has no opportunity to place anyone under conviction. For true Holy Spirit conviction to be present and prevalent, the Word of God must be truly preached, and preached under the Anointing of the Spirit (Lk. 4:18-19). This means that *"sin"* must be labeled as the problem, and that the only solution for this problem is *"Jesus Christ and Him Crucified"* (I Cor. 1:23). Unfortunately, there is not much preaching anymore against sin. In fact, sin is hardly even mentioned in most modern Church circles.

The seeker sensitive Churches, so-called, claim that if sin is mentioned, that will offend people and keep them from coming to Church. The Word of Faith Preachers claim that if the preacher preaches about sin, then this will create a sin consciousness in people, which will cause them to sin. In other words, the way to keep people from sinning, they say, is to simply not mention sin.

That is strange when one considers in the Sixth Chapter of Romans alone, the Apostle Paul mentions sin some seventeen times. And that's just one of his Chapters. Evidently, Paul had not heard of this new light that has been given to our Word of Faith friends. Too bad that he wasn't properly enlightened.

NOTES

Concerning Holy Spirit conviction, Jesus said, *"And when He* (the Holy Spirit) *is come, He will reprove* (the word means *'convict'*) *the world of sin* (the supreme sin of rejecting Christ), *and of Righteousness* (Jesus is Righteousness, and declared so by the Resurrection), *and of Judgment* (Satan was judged at Calvary, and all who follow him are likewise judged)*:*

"Of sin, because they believe not on Me (to reject Christ and the Cross is to reject Salvation)*;*

"Of Righteousness, because I go to My Father (Jesus presented a spotless Righteousness to the Father, namely Himself, which pertained to His Sacrifice at Calvary, that was accepted by God; consequently, that Righteousness is imputed to all who will believe in Him and His Work on the Cross), *and you see Me no more* (meaning that His Work was Finished)*;*

"Of judgment, because the prince of this world is judged (Satan was completely defeated at Calvary and, thereby, judged as eternally condemned; all who follow him will suffer his fate, the Lake of Fire, and that fate will be forever and forever [Rev. 20:12-15])*"* (Jn. 16:8-11).

Without Holy Spirit conviction, sinners cannot be saved. Without Holy Spirit conviction Christians who stray cannot be brought back to the right path. Without Holy Spirit conviction, the Work of God is stopped dead in its tracks.

When true Holy Spirit conviction settles in upon the hearts of men and women, many times, exactly as did Israel, they weep, and rightly so. At the same time, they feel like they're hanging over Hell on a rotten stick and it's going to break at any moment. That's the way they should feel. And that's what the modern Ministry doesn't want or desire.

So the upshot is, considering that there is almost no Holy Spirit conviction at this particular time, this means that the Church is being filled with unsaved people, but yet made to believe that they are saved. Nothing could be worse than that!

Without Holy Spirit conviction, the Believer doesn't know what is right and doesn't know what is wrong. He doesn't understand the Word of God, and is not led by the Spirit, which should be overly obvious. It is tragic, when virtually the entirety of the modern Church falls into this category.

THE WORKING OF THE HOLY SPIRIT AND THE CROSS

The Holy Spirit, of which we will have much to say in this Volume, works entirely within the framework of the Finished Work of Christ. In fact, He will not work outside of the atoning Work of our Saviour at Calvary's Cross. In other words, it is the Cross which gives the Holy Spirit the latitude to legally work. Paul said:

"For the Law (that which we are about to give is a Law of God, devised by the Godhead in eternity past [I Pet. 1:18-20]; this Law, in fact, is *'God's Prescribed Order of Victory'*) *of the Spirit* (Holy Spirit, i.e., *'the way the Spirit works'*) *of Life* (all life comes from Christ, but through the Holy Spirit [Jn. 16:13-14]) *in Christ Jesus* (any time Paul uses this term or one of its derivatives, he is, without fail, referring to what Christ did at the Cross, which makes this *'life'* possible) *has made me free* (given me total Victory) *from the Law of Sin and Death* (these are the two most powerful Laws in the Universe; the *'Law of the Spirit of Life in Christ Jesus'* alone is stronger than the *'Law of Sin and Death'*; this means that if the Believer attempts to live for God by any manner other than Faith in Christ and the Cross, he is doomed to failure)" (Rom. 8:2).

If we obey the Lord, we can expect His Blessings. Disobedience brings the reverse.

Without the Lord Israel could not hope to drive out these heathen tribes. In actuality, the Lord said to them, *"I will not drive them out from before you."* As a result He went on to say, *"They shall be as thorns in your sides, and their gods shall be a snare unto you"* (Vs. 3).

It is the same presently! If we obey the Lord the Holy Spirit is with us to help us; however, if we disobey Him, the Holy Spirit simply will not help and that which we have erroneously accepted, will turn out to be *"thorns in our sides."*

(6) "AND WHEN JOSHUA HAD LET THE PEOPLE GO, THE CHILDREN OF ISRAEL WENT EVERY MAN UNTO HIS

INHERITANCE TO POSSESS THE LAND.

(7) "AND THE PEOPLE SERVED THE LORD ALL THE DAYS OF JOSHUA, AND ALL THE DAYS OF THE ELDERS WHO OUTLIVED JOSHUA, WHO HAD SEEN ALL THE GREAT WORKS OF THE LORD, THAT HE DID FOR ISRAEL.

(8) "AND JOSHUA THE SON OF NUN, THE SERVANT OF THE LORD, DIED, BEING AN HUNDRED AND TEN YEARS OLD.

(9) "AND THEY BURIED HIM IN THE BORDER OF HIS INHERITANCE IN TIMNATH-HERES, IN THE MOUNT OF EPHRAIM, ON THE NORTH SIDE OF THE HILL GAASH.

(10) "AND ALSO ALL THAT GENERATION WERE GATHERED UNTO THEIR FATHERS: AND THERE AROSE ANOTHER GENERATION AFTER THEM, WHICH KNEW NOT THE LORD, NOR YET THE WORKS WHICH HE HAD DONE FOR ISRAEL."

The construction is:

1. The events of Verses 1 through 5 happened after Joshua died.

2. The statement about Joshua and the Elders is repeated here designedly by the Holy Spirit in order to justify the righteous indignation and words of the Angel of Jehovah.

3. Qualified leadership is a must, and by the word *"qualified"* we're speaking of those who are truly called of the Lord, and are truly trying to follow the Lord, even as Joshua.

JOSHUA

The Scripture is emphatic. As long as Joshua lived, and those who served under him, Israel prospered, because they were properly led. But when Joshua died, and *"all that generation were gathered unto their fathers,"* the Scripture then plainly says, *"there arose another generation after them, which knew not the LORD, nor yet the works which He had done for Israel."* Why didn't they know?

They didn't know because they didn't have proper leadership. They had Preachers so to speak, who were not preaching the truth, were not close to God and, in fact, really didn't even know the Lord. How so similar to modern times!

Improper leadership was the problem with

Israel then, and improper leadership is the problem with the modern Church now! In fact, I think one could say, and not be fearful of Scriptural contradiction, that this has always been the problem. Paul's first Letter, was to the Thessalonians, a Church. His last Letter was written to a Preacher, Timothy. This tells us that the Church, without proper leadership, is of no consequence. And when we speak of Leadership, we're not speaking of degrees from a university, but rather the Call of God, closeness to God, and being led by the Lord. Such were Joshua and those with him, and such must be the same presently.

(11) "AND THE CHILDREN OF ISRAEL DID EVIL IN THE SIGHT OF THE LORD, AND SERVED BAALIM:

(12) "AND THEY FORSOOK THE LORD GOD OF THEIR FATHERS, WHICH BROUGHT THEM OUT OF THE LAND OF EGYPT, AND FOLLOWED OTHER GODS, OF THE GODS OF THE PEOPLE WHO WERE ROUND ABOUT THEM, AND BOWED THEMSELVES UNTO THEM, AND PROVOKED THE LORD TO ANGER.

(13) "AND THEY FORSOOK THE LORD, AND SERVED BAAL AND ASHTAROTH.

(14) "AND THE ANGER OF THE LORD WAS HOT AGAINST ISRAEL, AND HE DELIVERED THEM INTO THE HANDS OF SPOILERS WHO SPOILED THEM, AND HE SOLD THEM INTO THE HANDS OF THEIR ENEMIES ROUND ABOUT, SO THAT THEY COULD NOT ANY LONGER STAND BEFORE THEIR ENEMIES.

(15) "WHITHERSOEVER THEY WENT OUT, THE HAND OF THE LORD WAS AGAINST THEM FOR EVIL, AS THE LORD HAD SAID, AND AS THE LORD HAD SWORN UNTO THEM: AND THEY WERE GREATLY DISTRESSED."

The exegesis is:

1. Some six times the phrase, *"The Children of Israel did evil in the sight of the LORD,"* is used in the Book of Judges; in all of these six Passages, the definite article, *"the evil,"* should be used; it means *"idolatry"* (Judg. 2:11; 3:7, 12; 4:1; 6:1; 10:6; 13:1).

2. The Doctrine of this Chapter is that the Lord cannot give victories to the flesh (Rom. 8:8). These people had seen God move mightily at the crossing of the Jordan, the fall of Jericho and many other similar victories; however, Miracles, as wonderful as they are, seldom, if ever, hold people to the tried-and-true. It is Faith alone which can accomplish that and, above all, Faith in the correct Object, which is Christ and the Cross, i.e., the Word of God (I Cor. 1:17-18, 21, 23; 2:2).

3. *"Baal"* and *"Ashtaroth"* are frequently coupled together; this was the god of the Zidonians; their worship was accompanied by the most vile immoralities.

4. Gods invented by men are served faithfully; however, the fact that Israel was at perpetual war with Jehovah proclaims the fact that the Lord was not an invention of man; as the Lord had worked for Israel, He now works against Israel; God hasn't changed; what He did then, He does now!

APOSTASY

These Verses portray to us a subject, which presently is little heard. It gives us an awful view of the Wrath of God, which is excited by willful sin.

The phrase *"He sold them,"* carries the idea of Him taking His Hand of protection away from them, and actually helping their enemies to do them harm. It is a frightful place for anyone to be in.

This is exactly what happened to Israel when they crucified Christ.

Sometime ago in a Message aired over Television, I made the statement that Israel doomed themselves when they said to Pilate concerning Christ, *"We have no king but Caesar"* (Jn. 19:15). They then said, *"His Blood be on us, and on our children"* (Mat. 27:25).

The idea is, when they did this, they took themselves out from under the Hand of God and did so purposely, which then made them targets for all of their enemies, but with no help from the Lord.

I had one Jewish leader in America to write me. He was very hostile.

He was angry because I had stated that the terrible problems of the Jewish people from then until now have been caused by their rejection of Christ. He wanted to say that Christ had nothing to do with it.

I answered him by saying, that God is not vengeful and certainly not against those He refers to as *"His people"* but when people purposely take themselves out from under the Hand of God, they have then opened themselves up to the powers of darkness. And to be sure, Satan will have no mercy. It was not God who created the situation, it was the Jews themselves.

I had another Jewish friend to say to me, *"What you are talking about happened nearly 2,000 years ago. We had no part in that, etc."* My answer to him was somewhat brief. I said, *"No, you had no part in the Crucifixion of Christ, but you hate Him now just as much as they did then."*

He just stood there looking at me, in fact, having no answer, because he knew what I was saying was right.

Because of improper leadership, Israel now goes into apostasy. They worship and serve the gods of the heathen tribes among them, exactly as the Lord said would happen.

THE DISPENSATION OF GRACE

Many read these Passages, and then proclaim that God doesn't do such now, because we are living in the Dispensation of Grace.

It might come as a shock to most; however, God demands more now out of Believers, even in this Dispensation of Grace, than He did then with Israel. Listen again to Paul:

"And the times of this ignorance (before the Cross) *God winked at; but now* (since the Cross) *commands all men every where to repent"* (Acts 17:30).

This tells us that God demands more at the present time out of Believers, even then He did at that time.

Let it be understood, no man gets by with sin. It has always wreaked its frightful toll, and it continues to wreak a frightful toll.

SIN AND THE CROSS

Our Lord dealt with sin at the Cross. It is dealt with in no other way, as it can be dealt with in no other way. This means that all of the ridiculous means by which preachers attempt to deal with sin outside of the Cross, are meaningless, fruitless, and not only don't help people, but rather hurt them.

It was at the Cross where the need was met! It was at the Cross where all sin was atoned! It was at the Cross that our Lord

was *"bruised for our iniquities."* And if we try to deal with sin by any means other than the Cross, there will be no positive solution. In fact, sin will take its deadly toll despite all the efforts of man otherwise.

One might say that sin is like acid. It eats until it's stopped, and it cannot be stopped other than by Faith in Christ and what Christ did at the Cross.

That's the reason that Paul said, *"We preach Christ Crucified"* (I Cor. 1:23; 2:2). If the Preacher preaches anything else, no matter how intellectual it might be, no matter how slick it may be produced, no matter how educated it might be, no matter how cleverly delivered, it will help no one, not even a little bit. As stated, it will rather do harm, because it will lead people away from the true help they can find in Christ and the Cross.

Is your Pastor preaching the Cross?

WHAT DOES IT MEAN TO PREACH THE CROSS?

It means that the Preacher must first of all understand, that everything we receive from God comes to us from Christ as the Source and the Cross as the Means. In other words, we receive nothing except the Cross is the means of what we are given. That means that the Believer's Faith must be in Christ and the Cross exclusively.

When the preacher believes this, then he will preach it. And to be sure, this will expose all false doctrine, for everything other than Christ and the Cross is false. As well, the Cross proclaims what man actually is, and Who Christ actually is. Nothing else does, as nothing else can.

When I speak of *"preaching the Cross,"* I'm not meaning that the Cross is mentioned once in a while, but rather that it is the foundation of our Faith, and the foundation of our Faith exclusively.

(16) "NEVERTHELESS THE LORD RAISED UP JUDGES, WHICH DELIVERED THEM OUT OF THE HAND OF THOSE WHO SPOILED THEM.

(17) "AND YET THEY WOULD NOT HEARKEN UNTO THEIR JUDGES, BUT THEY WENT A WHORING AFTER OTHER GODS, AND BOWED THEMSELVES UNTO

THEM: THEY TURNED QUICKLY OUT OF THE WAY WHICH THEIR FATHERS WALKED IN, OBEYING THE COMMANDMENTS OF THE LORD; BUT THEY DID NOT SO.

(18) "AND WHEN THE LORD RAISED THEM UP JUDGES, THEN THE LORD WAS WITH THE JUDGE, AND DELIVERED THEM OUT OF THE HAND OF THEIR ENEMIES ALL THE DAYS OF THE JUDGE: FOR IT REPENTED THE LORD BECAUSE OF THEIR GROANINGS BY REASON OF THEM WHO OPPRESSED THEM AND VEXED THEM.

(19) "AND IT CAME TO PASS, WHEN THE JUDGE WAS DEAD, THAT THEY RETURNED, AND CORRUPTED THEMSELVES MORE THAN THEIR FATHERS, IN FOLLOWING OTHER GODS TO SERVE THEM, AND TO BOW DOWN UNTO THEM; THEY CEASED NOT FROM THEIR OWN DOINGS, NOR FROM THEIR STUBBORN WAY.

(20) "AND THE ANGER OF THE LORD WAS HOT AGAINST ISRAEL; AND HE SAID, BECAUSE THAT THIS PEOPLE HAS TRANSGRESSED MY COVENANT WHICH I COMMANDED THEIR FATHERS, AND HAVE NOT HEARKENED UNTO MY VOICE;

(21) "I ALSO WILL NOT HENCEFORTH DRIVE OUT ANY FROM BEFORE THEM OF THE NATIONS WHICH JOSHUA LEFT WHEN HE DIED:

(22) "THAT THROUGH THEM I MAY PROVE ISRAEL, WHETHER THEY WILL KEEP THE WAY OF THE LORD TO WALK THEREIN, AS THEIR FATHERS DID KEEP IT, OR NOT.

(23) "THEREFORE THE LORD LEFT THOSE NATIONS, WITHOUT DRIVING THEM OUT HASTILY; NEITHER DELIVERED HE THEM INTO THE HAND OF JOSHUA."

The diagram is:

1. The Hebrew word for *"Judge"* means *"one who sets right what has been put wrong."* We will find that all of these Judges were all distinguished by some disability, as will appear when each one's history is studied, and they will be found to illustrate the principle that God uses weak things to confound the mighty (I Cor. 1:27).

2. With these Judges, God gave gracious

NOTES

Revivals; but, after each Revival, the nation fell into deeper sin and bondage.

3. Without proper spiritual leadership, as stated, basically every time the Church will go into apostasy. That is the problem with the modern Church. Its leadership, for all practical purposes, is man-appointed, which God can never recognize.

4. Everything, as it regards the Child of God, is a test. How will we act? How will we react?

JUDGES

Thirteen Judges appear in this Book: Twelve were chosen by God, and one was a usurper. Concerning this, Williams said, *"God raised up these Judges because 'His heart was grieved for the misery of Israel,' and 'yet they would not hearken unto their Judges' but corrupted themselves more and more with their idols. This fact contradicts the belief of those who say that Jehovah was invented by the Israelites, and was their tribal God, just as Chemosh was invented by the Moabites. But people always remain faithful to the god whom they invent, whereas there was perpetual contention between Jehovah and Israel. This fact is one of the many demonstrations that God is the one, true and only God, and that man's heart is incurably diseased by sin."*[1]

We have the history of the Early Church in the Book of Acts and the Epistles. Tragically, Church History proclaims the fact that the Church went into apostasy almost immediately after the death of the Apostles, and finally so deep into apostasy that the Catholic Church was the result. It took approximately 500 years for the Spiritual Declension to take its toll, which was a gradual process, as would be obvious. The ultimate result was the Pope, Priests, both which are totally unscriptural. Sadly, the religion of fallen man is not a gradual ascent to what is higher and better, but a declension to what is lower.

SELF-IMPROVEMENT AND MORALITY

Self-improvement is the message of the hour. The preachers who proclaim such, have vast audiences and, as well, are greatly popular with the world.

They claim that self can be improved by

the changing of one's habits, by putting on a smiley face, by changing one's association, by creating a new environment, etc. But let the reader understand, that there is no such thing as *"moral evolution."* In other words, and as already stated, man does not ascend to what is spiritually higher, but rather, declines to what is lower, that is unless certain steps are taken.

The facts are, and the truth is, there is no way that man by his own efforts, ability, strength, power, prowess, intellectualism, etc., can better himself. It cannot be done. It can be done, but not by those means. But man, and especially religious man, is loath to admit that.

So, the Preachers continue to give their little schemes and manufactured ways, claiming that whatever it is they are promoting, will accomplish the task. People like to hear such, because they like to think that it can be done; therefore, despite what the Bible says, they bite into this apple, but soon find to their dismay, that all of Satan's apples have worms.

THE TREE OF THE KNOWLEDGE OF GOOD AND OF EVIL

The self-improvement message, is a part of the good side of *"the Tree of the Knowledge of Good and Evil"* (Gen. 2:17). Because it is *"good,"* or at least thought to be so, it is eagerly accepted.

As it regards the bad side of this Tree, it is overly obvious as to what that is, and thereby opposed. It's the *"good side"* that deceives people, and intended so by Satan.

This *"good side"* consists of all the efforts made by man to bring Salvation to himself, i.e., self-improvement, etc. Let us state it again. There is no such thing as moral evolution. In other words, man cannot better himself by his efforts. Such a task can only be accomplished by the Holy Spirit. As we have repeatedly stated, the Holy Spirit works entirely within the framework of the Finished Work of Christ. He will not deviate from those perimeters. In fact, the Scripture refers to this as a *"Law"* (Rom. 8:2). It is all made possible by the Cross; therefore, the Believer must anchor his Faith exclusively in Christ and the Cross, which, in effect, is anchoring

NOTES

his Faith entirely in the Word. This is what Jesus was talking about when He spoke of Believers denying themselves, and taking up the Cross daily in order to follow Him (Lk. 9:23).

THE ANGER OF THE LORD AGAINST ISRAEL

When Israel was obedient, no man could stand before them, but now when disobedient, they could not stand before any man. When Israel was obedient, the Lord prospered them and made them victorious wherever they went, but now the Lord cursed them wherever they went. The question must be asked, *"Does God do the same today?"* The answer is obvious, most definitely yes.

The greatest sign of God's Love for His People, especially when they are rebellious, is His chastisement of them.

CHASTISEMENT

A most negative situation pertains to those who claim to be Christians and who have forsaken the Ways of God, and, yet, there is no chastisement. It is a sign they are no longer children but rather bastards (Heb. 12:8). Even though the Judgment registered against Israel was terrible, still, the Judgment itself was a sign that God loved them, was dealing with them, and was doing everything possible, even resorting to drastic means to bring them back to Himself.

In the midst of all of this God raised up Judges to champion His Cause and to lead Israel. It says, *"His heart was grieved for the misery of Israel,"* and *"yet they would not hearken unto their Judges,"* but corrupted themselves more and more with their idols. Therefore, it says, *"The anger of the LORD was hot against them."* Here, then, we see God's hatred of sin. Pulpit says, *"And if God is infinitely good and holy, and if He knows the full misery that sin has brought into His creation, with what other sentiment can He regard sin but with that of hatred and indignation? Sin excites a holy anger in His mind, and His hand must be stretched out to punish and to check. If we look at it closely, we must see that both of these are inevitable. God must look upon sin with displeasure, and He must act upon that displeasure. Evil must excite displeasure in One Who is perfectly good; and in the moral Governor of the universe such displeasure cannot be quiet and impotent, it must be active and effective."[2]*

PROVING ISRAEL

We see in the last few Verses of the Second Chapter, that the Lord purposely arranged the situation to where that some of the heathen tribes would be left in Israel until Joshua died. He did it, as the Scripture says, *"that through them I may prove Israel, whether they will keep the way of the LORD to walk therein, as their fathers did keep it, or not"* (Vs. 22).

Of course, the Lord, and because He has Perfect Knowledge, knew what Israel would do. He knew that they would not follow in the footsteps of Joshua, and would violate the Word of God. So, knowing that, why did the Lord put them to the test?

He did so in order that it might be a lesson to them. In fact, the Lord does all Believers this way, and constantly.

He sets up scenarios of His Own Devisings, of course, knowing what the outcome will be, but that it might be a test for us, a test in order that we might learn trust. Unfortunately, even though we read these accounts of Israel, with the thought in our mind, that had we been there we would not have done such a thing as they did, still, I wonder if we would have done any better?

In fact, the Lord presently has to work with us over and over again, dealing with us in all manner of ways, putting us to the test, all in order that we might ultimately see what He wants us to see. As stated, it is not easy, and it is not done quickly. So, even though we grieve over Israel's failures, even as we peruse the Text, the truth is, some of the grieving should be reserved for ourselves.

CHAPTER 3

(1) "NOW THESE ARE THE NATIONS WHICH THE LORD LEFT, TO PROVE ISRAEL BY THEM, EVEN AS MANY OF ISRAEL AS HAD NOT KNOWN ALL THE WARS OF CANAAN;

(2) "ONLY THAT THE GENERATIONS OF THE CHILDREN OF ISRAEL MIGHT KNOW, TO TEACH THEM WAR, AT THE LEAST SUCH AS BEFORE KNEW NOTHING THEREOF;

(3) "NAMELY, FIVE LORDS OF THE PHILISTINES, AND ALL THE CANAANITES, AND THE SIDONIANS, AND THE HIVITES WHO DWELT IN MOUNT LEBANON, FROM MOUNT BAAL-HERMON UNTO THE ENTERING IN OF HAMATH.

(4) "AND THEY WERE TO PROVE ISRAEL BY THEM, TO KNOW WHETHER THEY WOULD HEARKEN UNTO THE COMMANDMENTS OF THE LORD, WHICH HE COMMANDED THEIR FATHERS BY THE HAND OF MOSES.

(5) "AND THE CHILDREN OF ISRAEL DWELT AMONG THE CANAANITES, HITTITES, AND AMORITES, AND PERIZZITES, AND HIVITES, AND JEBUSITES:

(6) "AND THEY TOOK THEIR DAUGHTERS TO BE THEIR WIVES, AND GAVE THEIR DAUGHTERS TO THEIR SONS, AND SERVED THEIR GODS.

(7) "AND THE CHILDREN OF ISRAEL DID EVIL IN THE SIGHT OF THE LORD, AND FORGOT THE LORD THEIR GOD, AND SERVED BAALIM AND THE GROVES."

The diagram is:

1. The younger generation had not witnessed the Miracles of the recent past; they would now need to be proven, as to whether they would follow the Lord or heathen idols; every Believer, in one way or the other, is *"proven"*; this is not that the Lord might know, for He already knows, but rather, that we might know.

2. A considerable period of *"rest"* had followed Joshua's conquest, during which the younger Israelites had no experience of war; but, if they were to keep their hold of Canaan, it was needful that they understand war and victory; every generation of Believers must be *"proven"*; will they lean on the arm of flesh, or will they look to Christ and the Cross? Unfortunately, the sword held by most in the modern Church is not *"of the Spirit,"* which is actually the Word of God, but rather something else altogether (Eph. 6:17).

3. Friendship with the world doesn't make

the world more Godly, but rather the Christian more worldly.

THE GREAT TEST

By and large, the modern day Church has been taught that any difficulty, hindrance, obstacle, or disturbance is a sign of a lack of Faith. Perhaps this is the reason we have such puny Christians. The truth is, the lack of those things is a sign that the person is not in the Will of God, is not, therefore, hindering Satan, so, Satan lets him alone. For one who is truly in the Will of God, and is truly doing the Work of God, Satan, as should be obvious, is going to do everything within his power to hurt and hinder. The Apostle Paul is an excellent example of this.

This is Israel's third generation after coming out of Egypt. The generation under Moses was lost in the wilderness because of unbelief. The generation under Joshua who went into the Promised Land was mainly a victorious generation. This third generation will fail miserably. Can any move of God survive the second generation?

The first generation of the Early Church was victorious. The second generation was victorious as well; however, the third generation of what is referred to as the Early Church started the long decline into apostasy.

As we look at religious denominations presently, most, spiritually speaking, are but a shell of what they once were. They began in the fire, but by the third generation they were already starting down the long road to apostasy. It seems that the brighter the flame at the beginning, the faster the decline when it does begin. For instance, the present-day Pentecostal denominations, hold little resemblance to their beginnings.

When Peter in Acts, Chapter 3 said to the lame man at the gate, *"Silver and gold have I none; but such as I have give I thee,"* he had the Power of God to set this captive free. Someone once said that the Church no longer has to say, *"Silver and gold have we none,"* but at the same time, neither can it say to the lame man at the gate, *"In the Name of Jesus Christ of Nazareth rise up and walk."*

OPPOSITION

The Church is tempered by opposition.

NOTES

One might say that by the same amount of God that it has in it, by that same degree it will be opposed. Much God, much opposition. A little of God, a little opposition. No God, no opposition.

The Lord allows *"the Philistines, the Canaanites, and others"* to put us to the proof that we may learn our own feebleness and God's ability to keep and bless us. It must always be remembered that prosperity without trial deadens the soul. There must be trial to hone Faith, Trust, and Dependence on God.

The Lord can instantly and easily take away and remove every Philistine or Canaanite, so to speak; however, He allows the things to remain in order *"to prove the Child of God by them."*

How so different the teaching of the Bible from the modern-day Church. In the Bible, trials and tests were the keys to one's Faith, which again, is exampled by Paul (II Cor. 4:7-18). Today, unfortunately, money and prosperity are the keys, they say, to one's faith.

A FAILED TEST

Regrettably, the *"proving of Israel,"* did not turn out very well. The Sixth Verse says, *"And they took their daughters* (the daughters of the heathen) *to be their wives, and gave their daughters to their sons* (the sons of the heathen), *and served their gods."*

In Joshua, Chapter 23, three requirements are listed, which God expects of His People. They are:

1. The Word of God, the Bible must be the criteria for all things.

2. Separation from the world is an absolute must; however, that doesn't mean isolation.

3. One is to love the Lord with all of one's heart.

Unfortunately, all three of these requirements were forsaken by Israel. They turned their back on the Word of God, and they mingled with the world, for the Seventh Verse says, *"And forgot the LORD their God, and served Baalim and the groves."* What a sad indictment!

TO TRAIN ISRAEL FOR WAR

One of the reasons that the Lord left the

enemies in the land until the death of Joshua, was in order that this new generation *"might know, to teach them war"* (Vs. 2).

This tells us that the opposition will always be fierce against the Child of God. While presently it is not physical enemies that we as Believers face, most assuredly, we definitely do face Spiritual Enemies, even as outlined by the Apostle Paul. He said:

"Finally, my Brethren, be strong in the Lord (be continually strengthened, which one does by constant Faith in the Cross), *and in the power of His Might.* (This power is at our disposal. The Source is the Holy Spirit, but the means is the Cross [I Cor. 1:18].)

"Put on the whole Armour of God (not just some, but all), *that you may be able to stand against the wiles of the Devil.* (This refers to the 'stratagems' of Satan.)

"For we wrestle not against flesh and blood (our foes are not human; however, Satan constantly uses human beings to carry out his dirty work), *but against principalities* (rulers or beings of the highest rank and order in Satan's kingdom), *against powers* (the rank immediately below the 'Principalities'), *against the rulers of the darkness of this world* (those who carry out the instructions of the 'Powers'), *against spiritual wickedness in high places.* (This refers to demon spirits)" (Eph. 6:10-12).

Peter said, *"Beloved, think it not strange concerning the fiery trial which is to try you* (trials do not merely happen; they are designed by wisdom and operated by love; Job proved this), *as though some strange thing happened unto you* (your trial, whatever it is, is not unique; many others are experiencing the same thing!)" (I Pet. 4:12).

HOW DO MODERN BELIEVERS FIGHT THIS WAR?

Actually, whether it was Israel of old, or Believers presently, it is all done by Faith. Let us explain!

Two things are in operation as it regards the Saint of God. They are:

A. The Holy Spirit within our hearts and lives is desiring to bring about His Fruit, which pertains to our Sanctification, thereby, the development of Righteousness and Holiness. The Holy Spirit Alone can

accomplish this.

B. Satan comes against us with every power at his disposal in order to hinder us, and preferably, even to stop us, in order that the Holy Spirit not be able to carry out this task.

Now the war sets in, and please believe me, it is war.

Paul said, and concerning this very thing, *"This charge I commit unto you, son Timothy* (refers to a command or injunction), *according to the Prophecies which went before on you* (probably refers to the time frame of Acts 16:1-3), *that you by them might war a good warfare* (we aren't told exactly what the Prophecies were, but that they spoke of an assignment to leadership in the army of King Jesus);

"Holding faith . . ." (maintaining Faith in Christ and the Cross)" (I Tim. 1:18-19).

The Apostle also said, *"For though we walk in the flesh* (refers to the fact that we do not yet have Glorified Bodies), *we do not war after the flesh* (after our own ability, but rather by the Power of the Spirit):

"(For the weapons of our warfare are not carnal [carnal weapons consist of those which are man-devised], *but mighty through God* [the Cross of Christ (I Cor. 1:18)] *to the pulling down of strongholds;)*

"Casting down imaginations (philosophic strongholds; every effort man makes outside of the Cross of Christ), *and every high thing that exalts itself against the Knowledge of God* (all the pride of the human heart), *and bringing into captivity every thought to the obedience of Christ* (can be done only by the Believer looking exclusively to the Cross, where all Victory is found; the Holy Spirit will then perform the task)" (II Cor. 10:3-5).

THIS WAR OR STRUGGLE IS ACTUALLY WITH THE SIN NATURE

In the Sixth Chapter of Romans Paul tells us how to overcome the sin nature. (Please see our Study Guide: THE SIN NATURE, THE CROSS OF CHRIST SERIES.)

Some seventeen times in this one Chapter, Paul uses the word *"sin."* Fifteen of the times in the original Text, he used the definite article making it read *"the sin."* When this is done, it means that Paul is not speaking of acts of sin, but rather the sin principal, or the sin nature. So, and as stated, this Chapter is given over to telling us how to overcome the sin nature.

WHAT IS THE SIN NATURE?

The sin nature simply refers to the nature of the human being to sin or do wrong. It is a result of the Fall in the Garden of Eden.

When Adam fell, he fell from total God consciousness, down to the far, far lower level of total self-consciousness. Of course, Eve fell with him.

Due to the fact that Adam, in a sense, is the father of us all, in essence, we fell with him. This means that every baby born from then until now has been born in sin. It is called *"original sin."* In this original sin the very nature of the human being is to do wrong, to transgress, to commit iniquity, to disobey the Word of God. As stated, that is one's nature, hence, called *"the sin nature"* or *"the evil nature."*

All unredeemed people are ruled totally and completely, twenty-four hours a day, by the sin nature; however, when the person comes to Christ, the sin nature, although not removed, is at that time made ineffective. Paul said:

"Knowing this, that our old man is crucified with Him (all that we were before conversion), *that the body of sin might be destroyed* (the power of sin broken), *that henceforth we should not serve sin* (the guilt of sin is removed at conversion, because the sin nature no longer rules within our hearts and lives. The word *'destroyed'* should have been translated *'ineffective,'* thereby reading, *'that the body of sin might be made ineffective')"* (Rom. 6:6).

So, at the moment of conversion, the sin nature is made ineffective, which means it's dormant, which means that it holds no power over the Child of God. It is made this way strictly and totally by the Cross (Rom. 6:3-5). That's what Paul is talking about when he uses the two words *"knowing this."*

Knowing what?

Knowing that we were *"baptized into His Death, buried with Him by baptism into death, and raised with Him in Newness of Life."*

That's the way we got saved, and that's the way we stay saved.

If we keep our Faith exclusively in Christ and the Cross, the sin nature will forever remain dormant and cause us no problem; however, this is where the *"war"* comes in. Satan will do his best to move us from Faith in Christ and the Cross to other things, and he doesn't too much care what the other things are. Paul referred to this as *"the good fight of Faith"* (I Tim. 6:12). In fact, this will be a fight that will never end, even being carried forth on a daily basis. That's why Jesus said:

"If any man will come after Me (the criteria for Discipleship), *let him deny himself* (not asceticism as many think, but rather that one denies one's own willpower, self-will, strength, and ability, depending totally on Christ), *and take up his cross* (the benefits of the Cross, looking exclusively to what Jesus did there to meet our every need) *daily* (this is so important, our looking to the Cross; that we must renew our Faith in what Christ has done for us, even on a daily basis, for Satan will ever try to move us away from the Cross as the Object of our Faith, which always spells disaster), *and follow Me* (Christ can be followed only by the Believer looking to the Cross, understanding what it accomplished, and by that means alone [Rom. 6:3-5, 11, 14; 8:1-2, 11; I Cor. 1:17-18, 21, 23; 2:2; Gal. 6:14; Eph. 2:13-18; Col. 2:14-15])" (Lk. 9:23).

The only way the Believer can walk in Victory, in other words, to fight this war successfully, and, as stated, a war it is, is for the Believer to keep his Faith exclusively in Christ and the Cross, ever knowing that Christ is the Source while the Cross is the Means.

(8) "THEREFORE THE ANGER OF THE LORD WAS HOT AGAINST ISRAEL, AND HE SOLD THEM INTO THE HAND OF CHUSHAN-RISHATHAIM KING OF MESOPOTAMIA: AND THE CHILDREN OF ISRAEL SERVED CHUSHAN-RISHATHAIM EIGHT YEARS.

(9) "AND WHEN THE CHILDREN OF ISRAEL CRIED UNTO THE LORD, THE LORD RAISED UP A DELIVERER TO THE CHILDREN OF ISRAEL, WHO DELIVERED THEM, EVEN OTHNIEL THE SON OF KENAZ, CALEB'S YOUNGER BROTHER.

(10) "AND THE SPIRIT OF THE LORD

NOTES

CAME UPON HIM, AND HE JUDGED ISRAEL, AND WENT OUT TO WAR: AND THE LORD DELIVERED CHUSHAN-RISHATHAIM KING OF MESOPOTAMIA INTO HIS HAND; AND HIS HAND PREVAILED AGAINST CHUSHAN-RISHATHAIM.

(11) "AND THE LAND HAD REST FORTY YEARS. AND OTHNIEL THE SON OF KENAZ DIED."

The overview is:

1. Idolatry always leads to slavery in some way. For Israel, it was to a heathen power; presently, it is to Satan himself. And we must remember, any worship that's not anchored in Christ and the Cross is unscriptural and, in fact, in one way or the other, is idolatry!

2. Any time that Israel cried to the Lord, irrespective as to how wrong they had previously been, He always heard their cry, and answered with Deliverance. It is the same presently! No matter the problem, if you will sincerely cry to the Lord, He will hear and answer, irrespective as to what you may have done in the past that is wrong.

3. Othniel was the first Judge of Israel. He was able to perform this mighty feat of valor, because the *"Spirit of the LORD"* was upon him. The secret then was the Spirit of the Lord, and the secret now is the Spirit of the Lord. There are all type of things greater than we are, but there is nothing greater than the Spirit of the Lord, for He is God (Jn. 14:17-20).

4. After the death of Othniel, Israel will, once again, be without proper leadership and apostasy was the result, as apostasy is always the result in such case.

OTHNIEL, THE FIRST JUDGE

Verse Eight gives us an interesting statement. It says, *"He sold them."* The statement has reference to a transaction being completed. Even though the people to whom they were sold (Mesopotamians) had no idea of what God was doing, still, the Lord knew.

In effect, He would sell them as slaves to these people. What would the Lord receive in return?

Hopefully, He would receive a repentant people and that's exactly what happened, for the Ninth Verse says, *"And when the Children of Israel cried unto the LORD, the LORD*

raised up a deliverer."

This deliverer was the first Judge of Israel. His name was *"Othniel."* He was Caleb's nephew.

The people under great bondage *"cried unto the LORD,"* which is exactly what the Lord desired. Sometimes we Christians have to be placed under very trying circumstances before we will *"cry unto the Lord."*

It seems that Othniel had some of Caleb's Faith. It doesn't happen all the time, but many times, those around a great leader such as Caleb, will receive of his anointing. Othniel did!

THE SPIRIT OF THE LORD

The Tenth Verse says, *"And the Spirit of the LORD came upon him."* I want the reader to notice how the Lord was in charge of everything.

The Lord used the Philistines and the Canaanites, to *"prove"* His People (Vss. 3-4). He used the Mesopotamians as His Instrument of chastisement (Vs. 8). He used *"Othniel"* to deliver Israel unto their Repentance (Vss. 9-10). The *"Spirit of the LORD"* was the answer. In fact, it is the only answer. It is sad, but the majority of the modern Church knows little, or absolutely nothing about *"the Spirit of the Lord."*

The involvement of the Holy Spirit with Believers before the Cross was totally different than after the Cross.

Why?

The answer was the sin debt.

Paul said, *"For it is not possible that the blood of bulls and of goats should take away sins. (The word 'impossible' is a strong one. It means there is no way forward through the blood of animals. As well, it applies to all other efforts made by man to address the problem of sin, other than the Cross)"* (Heb. 10:4).

This means that animal sacrifices were not sufficient to remove the sin debt which hung over every human being, and actually goes back to original sin. While animal sacrifices served as a stopgap measure, so to speak, that was about as much as could be done. That's why Jesus said to His Disciples, *"And I will pray the Father, and He shall give you another Comforter ('Parakletos,' which means 'One called to the side of another to help'), that He may abide with you forever* (before the Cross, the Holy Spirit could only help a few individuals, and then only for a period of time; since the Cross, He lives in the hearts and lives of Believers, and does so forever)*;*

"Even the Spirit of Truth (the Greek says, *'The Spirit of the Truth,'* which refers to the Word of God; actually, He does far more than merely superintend the attribute of Truth, as Christ *'is Truth'* [I Jn. 5:6]; *Whom the world cannot receive* (the Holy Spirit cannot come into the heart of the unbeliever until that person makes Christ his or her Saviour; then He comes in), *because it sees Him not, neither knows Him* (refers to the fact that only Born-Again Believers can understand the Holy Spirit and know Him): *but you know Him* (would have been better translated, *'But you shall get to know Him'*); *for He dwells with you* (before the Cross), *and shall be in you* (which would take place on the Day of Pentecost and forward, because the sin debt has been forever paid by Christ on the Cross, changing the disposition of everything)*"* (Jn. 14:16-17).

The notes following the Text derived from THE EXPOSITOR'S STUDY BIBLE have already explained what I'm about to say, but due to the tremendous significance, please allow me this repetition.

BEFORE THE CROSS

Before the Cross, and, as stated, due to the fact that the blood of bulls and goats couldn't remove the sin debt, the Holy Spirit was limited as to what He could do with Believers. For instance, He could not come into any heart and life and abide forever. He could only come in to certain ones (and I emphasize certain ones), in order to help them carry out the tasks required of them, such as Othniel. When that task was completed, He left.

Since the Cross, and due to the fact that all sin was removed at the Cross, and because all sin was atoned, the Holy Spirit can now come into hearts and lives and abide forever, which He most definitely does at conversion (Jn. 14:18).

In fact, before the Cross, when Believers died, they could not go to Heaven. Instead, they were taken down into Paradise, which is in the heart of the Earth, actually, separated

from the burning side of Hell only by a great gulf (Lk., Chpt. 16). In fact, they were actually captives of Satan in this place, even though they were comforted. In other words, Satan could not do anything to them, but still, they were in the wrong place.

Actually, they awaited the Cross. When the Cross was a fact, immediately, the Scripture says that Jesus went down into Paradise and *"led captivity captive"* (Eph. 4:8).

The phrase *"He led captivity captive,"* is strange. It actually means, that all of the Saints who lived before the Cross, and who were in Paradise, and all were, He made all of them His captives, thereby removing them from Satan's domain. They had been captives of Satan in a sense, and now they are captives of the Lord Jesus Christ, all made possible by the Cross.

Now when Believers die, they instantly go to Heaven and to be with the Lord Jesus Christ (Phil. 1:23).

Before the Cross only certain Believers had the Holy Spirit, and then only for periods of time. Now, since the Cross, every single Believer has the Holy Spirit, and has Him constantly, meaning that He will abide in our hearts and lives forever (Jn. 14:16).

(12) "AND THE CHILDREN OF ISRAEL DID EVIL AGAIN IN THE SIGHT OF THE LORD: AND THE LORD STRENGTHENED EGLON THE KING OF MOAB AGAINST ISRAEL, BECAUSE THEY HAD DONE EVIL IN THE SIGHT OF THE LORD.

(13) "AND HE GATHERED UNTO HIM THE CHILDREN OF AMMON AND AMALEK, AND WENT AND SMOTE ISRAEL, AND POSSESSED THE CITY OF PALM TREES.

(14) "SO THE CHILDREN OF ISRAEL SERVED EGLON THE KING OF MOAB EIGHTEEN YEARS."

The synopsis is:

1. If it is to be noticed, it was the Lord Who strengthened Eglon, the king of Moab, even though this heathen had no personal knowledge of the reason for his military strength. As well, the Lord directed the mind of this man toward Israel.

Why?

Unless, it seems, Israel was in dire straits, she simply would not function properly. So the Lord brought upon them great misery through this heathen king.

2. All of this tells us that the Lord presently does the same thing with Believers who are going in the wrong direction. Paul called it, *"chastisement"* (Heb. 12:5-14). Sometimes the Lord uses sickness, sometimes he uses the unredeemed, etc.; however, everything He does, irrespective as to what it might be, is all done for our good. So, even though the person who wrongs us, that is, if the Lord uses such, is wrong himself or herself in what is being done, to be sure, such an individual will answer to the Lord. Still, we must understand that the Lord has allowed such, and not allow bitterness to get into our heart toward such a person. Even though the Lord may use such, it doesn't mean that He condones their action. To be sure, as Eglon, they will ultimately answer.

3. Eighteen years of bondage weren't necessary at all; it was because they had done evil in the sight of the Lord.

APOSTASY

It seems that this will continue to be Israel's disposition, *"doing evil"* and being sold into the hands of the enemy; *"crying to God,"* and the Lord raising up a deliverer for them. And then, sadly, the situation will be repeated over and over again.

All evil is forever *"in the sight of the Lord."* It is the Lord Who judges what is evil and what is not evil. Regrettably, today America and Canada as well as the rest of the world go about setting their own standards for what is right and wrong, completely ignoring the Word of God; however, we must ever understand that the Bible is the only criteria for what is right and wrong, because the Bible is the Word of God. When it is abandoned, a nation is then left to drift aimlessly, as America, sadly and regrettably, drifts today.

Still, the sad disposition of Israel with their spiritual ups and downs is the plight of most of modern Christendom.

THE LORD EITHER CAUSES OR ALLOWS ALL THAT HAPPENS TO A BELIEVER

We should read the heading very carefully, because it is ever so true.

Every Believer is *"bought with a price"*

(I Cor. 6:20). That price was and is the shed Blood of the Lord Jesus Christ, which was shed at Calvary's Cross. It is ever the case that one learns the worth of something by the price that is paid.

Inasmuch as we are bought with a price, and, thereby, belong to the Lord, and belong to Him in totality, this means that every single thing that happens to us as a Believer, is either caused or allowed by the Lord. While He definitely does not cause us to sin, that being our own perfidiousness, still, He does allow such, but with the understanding that we will have to reap the consequences; and those consequences are never pretty.

And then again, the Lord definitely does cause some things to happen, such as here with Israel. Even though this wicked king, Eglon, didn't know what was happening, it was the Lord Who strengthened Him, and set his mind toward Israel, in order that Israel might be chastised. Of course, and as previously stated, there was a method to what the Lord was doing.

He knew that Israel would not repent, would not live right, would not do right, would not act right, unless they were forced to do so; therefore, the Lord forces the issue by causing this evil king to come against His People. They stayed under his oppression for *"eighteen years,"* and we might quickly add, eighteen years, which were totally unnecessary.

UNNECESSARY YEARS OF TROUBLE

How many of us fall into the same category! We suffer when we don't need to suffer, we hurt when we don't need to hurt, we do without when we don't need to do without, and simply because the Bible clearly says, *"the way of the transgressors is hard"* (Prov. 13:15).

God's Way is His Holy Word. It's our road map, our blueprint, so to speak, the Way to Life, and Eternal Life at that. We can abide by God's Word and reap the benefits, of which there are many, or we can disobey that Word, and thereby spurn the many pleadings to come back to the right way, and ultimately suffer disastrous consequences.

But the tragedy is, most modern Believers, despite the plethora of Bibles, simply do not know the Word of God. And then on top of that, Satan has brought against the Word of God a full-fledged attack that is different, maybe than any attack he has ever fomented. He is bringing out these *"thought for thought"* so-called translations, which in reality are no translations at all. At best they can be concluded to be religious books, because they certainly aren't the Word of God. Concerning the Bible, Jesus said, *"Man shall not live by bread alone, but by every Word that proceeds out of the Mouth of God"* (Mat. 4:4).

This means that every *"Word"* in the Bible is important in the Eyes of God. That's the reason we state that for the individual to have a true Bible, one must have a word for word translation, of which the King James is one. There are, in fact, two or three, but not many. In fact, I would strongly encourage the Reader to get for yourself THE EXPOSITOR'S STUDY BIBLE, which we believe is one of the most helpful study Bibles in the world. If you already have one, I think you know what I'm talking about, and you should thereby endeavor to get a copy for each of your loved ones. It would be one of the best investments you ever made.

All of this tells us that at this very moment, the Lord, Who loves you dearly, is either working to bless you, or to bring chastisement on you, depending upon your obedience or disobedience of the Word. You should consider that very carefully.

(15) "BUT WHEN THE CHILDREN OF ISRAEL CRIED UNTO THE LORD, THE LORD RAISED THEM UP A DELIVERER, EHUD THE SON OF GERA, A BENJAMITE, A MAN LEFTHANDED: AND BY HIM THE CHILDREN OF ISRAEL SENT A PRESENT UNTO EGLON THE KING OF MOAB.

(16) "BUT EHUD MADE HIM A DAGGER WHICH HAD TWO EDGES, OF A CUBIT LENGTH; AND HE DID GIRD IT UNDER HIS RAIMENT UPON HIS RIGHT THIGH.

(17) "AND HE BROUGHT THE PRESENT UNTO EGLON KING OF MOAB: AND EGLON WAS A VERY FAT MAN.

(18) "AND WHEN HE HAD MADE AN END TO OFFER THE PRESENT, HE SENT AWAY THE PEOPLE WHO BORE THE PRESENT.

(19) "BUT HE HIMSELF TURNED AGAIN FROM THE QUARRIES THAT WERE BY GILGAL, AND SAID, I HAVE A SECRET ERRAND UNTO YOU, O KING: WHO SAID, KEEP SILENCE. AND ALL WHO STOOD BY HIM WENT OUT FROM HIM.

(20) "AND EHUD CAME UNTO HIM; AND HE WAS SITTING IN A SUMMER PARLOUR, WHICH HE HAD FOR HIMSELF ALONE. AND EHUD SAID, I HAVE A MESSAGE FROM GOD UNTO YOU. AND HE AROSE OUT OF HIS SEAT.

(21) "AND EHUD PUT FORTH HIS LEFT HAND, AND TOOK THE DAGGER FROM HIS RIGHT THIGH, AND THRUST IT INTO HIS BELLY:

(22) "AND THE HAFT ALSO WENT IN AFTER THE BLADE; AND THE FAT CLOSED UPON THE BLADE, SO THAT HE COULD NOT DRAW THE DAGGER OUT OF HIS BELLY; AND THE DIRT CAME OUT.

(23) "THEN EHUD WENT FORTH THROUGH THE PORCH, AND SHUT THE DOORS OF THE PARLOUR UPON HIM, AND LOCKED THEM.

(24) "WHEN HE WAS GONE OUT, HIS SERVANTS CAME; AND WHEN THEY SAW THAT, BEHOLD, THE DOORS OF THE PARLOUR WERE LOCKED, THEY SAID, SURELY HE COVERS HIS FEET IN HIS SUMMER CHAMBER.

(25) "AND THEY TARRIED TILL THEY WERE ASHAMED: AND, BEHOLD, HE OPENED NOT THE DOORS OF THE PARLOUR; THEREFORE THEY TOOK A KEY, AND OPENED THEM: AND, BEHOLD, THEIR LORD WAS FALLEN DOWN DEAD ON THE EARTH."

The synopsis is:

1. In some way, each one of these Judges expressed some form of weakness; Othniel was the son of a younger brother; Ehud was left-handed; Shamgar had but an ox goad; Deborah was a woman; Gideon was the least in the poorest family in Manasseh; Jephthah was the son of a harlot; and Samson was a Nazarite.

2. We learn from the Nineteenth Verse, that idols had been set up at Gilgal — an outrage upon the hallowed associations of that sacred spot; it was the Dwelling-place of the Angel of Jehovah, or had been (2:1).

Gilgal pictures the broken and contrite heart in which God dwells. If He be grieved away from such an heart, very quickly it becomes the home of graven images.

3. The *"Message from God"* is always that every enemy in our life be put to the Sword, i.e., *"the Sword of the Spirit,"* which is the Word of God, which means that the enemy not merely be defeated, but slain (Eph. 6:17).

EHUD, THE SECOND JUDGE

Ehud was of the Tribe of Benjamin. Not much is known of him with the exception of what he did to deliver Israel.

Some would claim that he did wrong by killing Eglon; however, there is no hint in Scripture that what he did was displeasing to the Lord. Quite the contrary, I think the only reasonable conclusion that one can arrive at is that what he did was not only sanctioned by the Lord, but directed by the Lord.

If it was wrong for Ehud to kill Eglon, then it was wrong for Israel to kill some 10,000 men of Moab in the battle of victory that followed the death of their king.

It was God who allowed the heathen king Eglon to gain supremacy over Israel and to rule them with an iron fist for eighteen years; therefore, it was God Who determined not only how long the subjugation would be, but, as well, when it would end, which it did.

THE FLESH MUST DIE

Ehud killing Eglon should be a lesson to us presently. Sin cannot be dealt with by any other fashion. It must be exterminated, i.e., *"killed."* To try to come to terms with sin, to try to compromise with sin, will not only leave one in bondage, but will deepen the bondage.

Ehud had the dagger in his belt. That dagger is a Type of the Word of God. He used it even as we are told to use the Word. His use of that dagger, made several statements.

First of all, he was saying that he was tired of this heathen king holding Israel as a captive. Second, even though he was only one man, he felt that he could do something about the situation, which he did. That means that you can do something about your situation also.

God doesn't demand a lot of things of us, but He does demand that we take the first step. Ehud took that first step, and that which followed set Israel free.

We have to look at the situation as though the victorious outcome depended totally upon us. While, of course, it may not, and probably doesn't, still, we must look at it in that fashion. Such portrays Faith, and instead of doing wrong Ehud evidenced Faith and great Faith at that!

Are you tired of Satan running over you? Take the dagger of the Word of God, plunge it into the belly of the beast, and plunge it so deep and hard that it will have the desired effect, and you will have the same results as did Ehud, and Israel as a whole.

GRAVEN IMAGES

The word *"quarries"* in Verses 19 and 26 should have been translated *"graven images."* How sad, as stated, that we learn here that idols had been set up at Gilgal, which had been the Dwelling-place of the Lord. How so much that Satan must have gloated in regard to this. Let us say it again and let us say it straight forward:

If the Lord is taken out of the heart, it very quickly becomes the home of graven images. And whatever we place ahead of the Lord becomes an image, i.e., *"an idol."* Regrettably, the modern Church is full of idols! In fact, the greatest idol of all, the most base idolatry of all, is the idol of religion!

(26) "AND EHUD ESCAPED WHILE THEY TARRIED, AND PASSED BEYOND THE QUARRIES, AND ESCAPED UNTO SEIRATH.

(27) "AND IT CAME TO PASS, WHEN HE WAS COME, THAT HE BLEW A TRUMPET IN THE MOUNTAIN OF EPHRAIM, AND THE CHILDREN OF ISRAEL WENT DOWN WITH HIM FROM THE MOUNT, AND HE BEFORE THEM.

(28) "AND HE SAID UNTO THEM, FOLLOW AFTER ME: FOR THE LORD HAS DELIVERED YOUR ENEMIES, THE MOABITES INTO YOUR HAND. AND THEY WENT DOWN AFTER HIM, AND TOOK THE FORDS OF JORDAN TOWARD MOAB, AND SUFFERED NOT A MAN TO PASS OVER.

(29) "AND THEY KILLED OF MOAB AT

THAT TIME ABOUT TEN THOUSAND MEN, ALL LUSTY, AND ALL MEN OF VALOUR; AND THERE ESCAPED NOT A MAN.

(30) "SO MOAB WAS SUBDUED THAT DAY UNDER THE HAND OF ISRAEL. AND THE LAND HAD REST FOURSCORE YEARS."

The composition is:

1. Ehud, the second Judge of Israel, blew the trumpet of war, because the Lord through him would deliver Israel; if there was ever a time in the modern Church to *"blow the trumpet,"* it is now!

2. Moab was on the eastern side of the Dead Sea; it was the area occupied, as well, by the Tribe of Reuben.

3. No casualties of Israel are listed; therefore, the indication is that there were none; when Israel had the Lord with them, nothing could defeat them, and when they didn't have the Lord, they were already defeated.

BLOW THE TRUMPET

Ehud was not satisfied by merely killing the king of Moab. He had something far greater in mind than that. He believed that through him the entirety of the Nation of Israel would be delivered, and would be delivered now. He had a grand plan in mind, no doubt nurtured by the Lord. He wanted total and complete victory. He wasn't satisfied with another Moab king taking the throne, which might have been a little more lenient with Israel. He wanted to be rid of this scurrilous bunch once and for all.

So, he blew a trumpet.

That trumpet would call all of Israel to war. How long it took for the news to get around, we aren't told, but get around it did. How many Israelites gathered we aren't told, as well, but we do know that the Lord helped them mightily. It was like they fed off the Faith of Ehud. In doing so they killed *"ten thousand mighty men"* of Moab. And every evidence is, that not one single Israelite was killed or wounded.

How in the world would such a thing be possible?

As previously stated, when the Lord was with Israel, they were capable of being the instrument of mighty Miracles. This is but one example! They had rest for eighty years.

NOTES

TOTAL VICTORY

What do you as a Believer want and desire in your life? Do you want partial victory, or do you want total Victory? To be sure, the Lord will accept nothing but total Victory. The Plans He has for us are Plans of total Victory, nothing partial!

One of the biggest problems of Believers is that we believe too little. We set our sights too low. My Grandmother said to me when I was a child, over and over, and I'll never forget it:

"Jimmy, God is a big God, so ask big."

I've never forgotten that. It has helped me to touch this world for Christ. *"God is a big God, so ask big!"*

We ask too little, and get that for which we ask, meaning we leave an awful lot on the table.

The Work of Calvary is a total and complete Work. As such, the Lord means for us to have a total and complete work within our lives. Nothing partial! Nothing half way! Nothing partway! He means for us to go all the way, not only killing this idol within our life, but all of its residue as well. Then and only then can we have *"rest."*

(31) "AND AFTER HIM WAS SHAMGAR THE SON OF ANATH, WHICH KILLED OF THE PHILISTINES SIX HUNDRED MEN WITH AN OX GOAD: AND HE ALSO DELIVERED ISRAEL."

The exposition is:

1. Other than the information given in this one Verse, nothing more is known of Shamgar, except the mention of him in Deborah's song (5:6).

2. The Text indicates that this one man, armed with nothing but an ox goad, which was something like a spear, killed six hundred Philistines, and did so single-handedly. Obviously, the Spirit of God helped him mightily.

3. Shamgar was the third Judge of Israel.

SHAMGAR, THE THIRD JUDGE OF ISRAEL

How in the world could one man armed with nothing but an ox goad, kill six hundred Philistines, and do it at one time?

How so much the enemies of the Lord enjoy ridiculing such statements in the Bible;

however, to do so, places one in the position of denying the Power of God, and in effect, calling the Holy Spirit, Who inspired this account, a liar — a position in which no sane person desires to be.

To be sure, it happened exactly as the Word of God gave the account.

An ox goad was not really even a spear. It amounted to little more than a sharp stick. But yet with this one item, this one insignificant weapon, this one man killed six hundred Philistines, and did it all at one time. Of course, he could only do such by the Power of God.

But all of this tells us what can be done with God! Without God, nothing! With God, anything and everything!

MIRACLES

I believe in a God of Miracles! I believe that God can do anything and, to be sure, He will do that for which the occasion calls.

As a Believer, we must not listen to the naysayers who claim the days of Miracles are over. Had those people been living during the time of Shamgar, they would have denied what he did, claiming that such Miracles passed away at the crossing of the Red Sea. When men don't want to believe God, they manufacture any and every excuse. But the truth is, God is a Miracle Working God! God desires and delights in doing mighty things for His People.

While He definitely is not an errand boy, and while He definitely is not a glorified bell-hop, meaning that He is at our beck and call, still, at times, He will do great and mighty things.

But at the same time, I believe that all of His great Action awaits a man or a woman of Faith. God is a Faith God, meaning that He operates totally upon the basis of Faith. While the Lord can do anything, still, He chooses to use men and women in order to function.

He used Shamgar. Who this man was, we aren't told! What his background was we aren't told! So that means that the Holy Spirit is telling us that whatever Shamgar was in the past is not worthy now of mention. It's only what he has done at the present, and he did something mighty at this time. He delivered Israel!

NOTES

CHAPTER 4

(1) "AND THE CHILDREN OF ISRAEL AGAIN DID EVIL IN THE SIGHT OF THE LORD, WHEN EHUD WAS DEAD.

(2) "AND THE LORD SOLD THEM INTO THE HAND OF JABIN KING OF CANAAN, WHO REIGNED IN HAZOR; THE CAPTAIN OF WHOSE HOST WAS SISERA, WHICH DWELT IN HAROSHETH OF THE GENTILES.

(3) "AND THE CHILDREN OF ISRAEL CRIED UNTO THE LORD: FOR HE HAD NINE HUNDRED CHARIOTS OF IRON; AND TWENTY YEARS HE MIGHTILY OPPRESSED THE CHILDREN OF ISRAEL."

The exposition is:

1. Again, we state, without proper spiritual leadership, the Church is like a ship without a rudder; regrettably, there isn't much leadership in the modern Church. And what little there is, has been rejected by institutionalized religion.

2. Having 900 chariots of iron tells us that Sisera was a mighty warlord. Satan always comes against the Child of God with his most powerful.

3. The words, *"mightily oppressed,"* proclaim the fact that Israel had virtually become slaves in their own land — slaves to Sisera; sin will take a person further than they want to go, at a price higher than they can afford to pay.

OPPRESSION

The Holy Spirit is very quick to relate that Ehud, who had been the spiritual leader of Israel at this time, was now dead. Regrettably, there was no one to take his place, and Israel once again drifted into spiritual declension, actually, gross idolatry! Let us state it again:

Without proper spiritual leadership, the Church cannot advance, cannot grow, at least in a spiritual sense, and thereby goes into apostasy.

One Chinese Believer on his first visit to the United States was asked the question, *"How do you see the Church in America?"*

His answer was most revealing: *"It's*

amazing," he said, *"as to the advancement the Church in America can make without God."*

Quite a statement, but oh so true!

Due to the gross sinfulness of Israel, the Scripture again, emphatically states that *"The LORD sold them* (sold Israel) *into the hand of Jabin king of Canaan."*

The word *"sold"* in the Hebrew is *"makar,"* and means, *"to sell as a slave."*

Why would the Lord do this, especially considering that it was being done to His chosen People?

As we have previously stated, the Lord by no means desires to do such a thing, as should be obvious. The Lord desires to bless His Children, and desires to do so greatly; however, the Lord loves His People enough, that He will take drastic measures, if He has to, in order to bring them back into line. The chastisement will be according to the degree of spiritual drift.

The people to whom He delivered then, were mighty and powerful, even with their chief captain, Sisera, heading up a powerful chariot army, actually consisting of *"900 chariots of iron."* In the natural, they were invincible; consequently, they terrorized Israel for twenty years.

All of these particular periods of time given in these accounts throughout the Book of Judges as it regards oppression, were all unnecessary. How much unnecessary trouble do we go through, simply because we get out of the Will of God, and do so because of self-will?

Israel was a Nation, so the Lord dealt with them accordingly. Today He deals with Believers on a different basis, because His Church is not a nation, at least as we think of such, but is made up of individual members all over the world. So, whatever the Lord does with us individually, is still in some way, a microcosm of what He did with Israel.

This doesn't mean that every bad thing that happens to a Believer is caused by the Believer's sinfulness, etc. While that certainly is the case at times, it's not the case all the time.

Irrespective, whatever it is that happens to a Believer, the Lord either caused it or allowed it; therefore, we must look at whatever it is that's taking place, and try to learn the lesson which the Holy Spirit desires to

NOTES

teach us, and by using the situation at hand, whatever it might be.

SPIRITUAL OPPRESSION

Every Believer, I think I can say without fear of contradiction, has at one time or the other experienced oppression from the Powers of Darkness. It affects a Believer as it regards their emotional stability or lack thereof, in the realm of fear, and even in some types of physical sickness. To be sure, such oppression makes life miserable. It doesn't have to be!

I know what it is to experience oppression, even to the point of it becoming so difficult, that I wondered if a human being could stand it. Actually, many times I related to the Lord that very complaint.

In ministering a few weeks ago at Family Worship Center, I was relating the very thing that I have just dictated, whenever the Lord began to bring to my mind the fact that since the Revelation of the Cross, I haven't experienced one moment of spiritual oppression. Not one single moment!

I didn't realize that until the Lord portrayed it to me even in the midst of that Message, which I then related to the people.

The reason that Believers suffer oppression, which causes all type of problems, is because their faith is in something other than Christ and the Cross. While they may claim it's in Christ, still, if it's not also in the Cross, then it is *"another Jesus"* they are serving, whether they realize such or not (II Cor. 11:4).

As we have said any number of times, it was at the Cross where all Victory was won, where all sin was addressed and atoned for, and where Satan was totally and completely defeated, which includes all of his minions of darkness. So, it is imperative that the Believer anchor his Faith exclusively in Christ and the Cross, understanding that Christ is always the Source while the Cross is the Means.

DEMON OPPRESSION AND DEMON POSSESSION

There is a vast difference in demon oppression and demon possession. The former operates from without, while the latter from within.

Despite what some Preachers say, it's impossible for a Christian to be demon possessed.

The Scripture emphatically tells us that all true Believers are temples of the Holy Spirit (I Cor. 3:16). To be sure, the Holy Spirit is not going to share His Quarters, so to speak, with demon spirits.

Moses wrote a long time ago, *"And the Blood shall be to you for a token upon the houses where you are: and when I see the Blood, I will pass over you, and the plague shall not be upon you to destroy you"* (Ex. 12:13).

This Passage emphatically tells us that the *"Blood"* protects the Believer from the powers of darkness, in the sense of destruction, etc. And to be sure, the *"Blood"* will protect the Believer against demon oppression, that is if the Believer understands that his Victory is totally and completely in the Cross, instead of his own personal works and ability, etc. Regrettably, most Christians simply don't understand that.

Many Preachers confuse *"demon oppression"* with *"demon possession."* The Scripture says:

"How God anointed Jesus of Nazareth with the Holy Spirit and with Power: Who went about doing good, and healing all who were oppressed of the Devil; for God was with Him" (Acts 10:38).

The word *"oppressed"* in the Greek is *"katadunasteno,"* and means *"to exercise dominion against."* In other words, demon oppression can force a Believer into a position, which they do not desire; however, this is not to be mistaken for demon possession. The answer as it regards demon oppression, as stated, is the Cross, always the Cross!

(4) "AND DEBORAH, A PROPHETESS, THE WIFE OF LAPIDOTH, SHE JUDGED ISRAEL AT THAT TIME.

(5) "AND SHE DWELT UNDER THE PALM TREE OF DEBORAH BETWEEN RAMAH AND BETH-EL IN MOUNT EPHRAIM: AND THE CHILDREN OF ISRAEL CAME UP TO HER FOR JUDGMENT.

(6) "AND SHE SENT AND CALLED BARAK THE SON OF ABINOAM OUT OF KEDESH-NAPHTALI, AND SAID UNTO HIM, HAS NOT THE LORD GOD OF ISRAEL COMMANDED, SAYING, GO AND DRAW TOWARD MOUNT TABOR, AND TAKE WITH YOU TEN THOUSAND MEN OF THE CHILDREN OF NAPHTALI AND OF THE

CHILDREN OF ZEBULUN?

(7) "AND I WILL DRAW UNTO YOU TO THE RIVER KISHON SISERA, THE CAPTAIN OF JABIN'S ARMY, WITH HIS CHARIOTS AND HIS MULTITUDE; AND I WILL DELIVER HIM INTO YOUR HAND.

(8) "AND BARAK SAID UNTO HER, IF YOU WILL GO WITH ME, THEN I WILL GO: BUT IF YOU WILL NOT GO WITH ME, THEN I WILL NOT GO.

(9) "AND SHE SAID, I WILL SURELY GO WITH YOU: NOTWITHSTANDING THE JOURNEY THAT YOU TAKE SHALL NOT BE FOR YOUR HONOUR; FOR THE LORD SHALL SELL SISERA INTO THE HAND OF A WOMAN. AND DEBORAH AROSE, AND WENT WITH BARAK TO KEDESH."

The pattern is:

1. This Chapter and the following could be cited as the women's Chapters. We find that Deborah's Faith brought about a great Victory, and Jael's fidelity destroyed a great tyrant. Both of these women were raised up by God for their respective Ministries. So, this puts to rest the idea that God does not call women to preach, etc. Paul said that in Christ *"there is neither male nor female: for you are all one in Christ Jesus"* (Gal. 3:28).

2. Williams says of Deborah, *"There was one heart that did not tremble before Sisera and his 900 chariots of iron. She 'sat as judge' under a palm tree near Beth-el. Her namesake, Rebecca's nurse was buried there, about 400 years back."*[1]

3. Deborah speaks here as a Prophetess, announcing God's Commands, not her own opinion; declaring God's Promises, not merely her own hopes or wishes.

4. We have little history on Barak; we do know that his faith seemed to be weak; he wanted someone near and visible upon whom he could lean; to such a feeble faith, the arm, even of a woman, gives more confidence than the Arm of God; consequently, God did not honor him, because he did not honor God; God is best honored by being trusted.

DEBORAH, THE FOURTH JUDGE

All of Israel trembled before Sisera, because he had 900 chariots of iron, but Deborah did not tremble. This woman's Faith would bring about a tremendous Victory, and another woman's fidelity (Jael) would destroy a great tyrant.

First of all, it is foolishness to think that God does not call women to preach. There are *"Prophets"* and there are *"Prophetesses."* Actually, the very first one to herald the great Gospel Message of the Resurrection of Jesus Christ was a woman, namely, *"Mary Magdalene."* We find here that God would use a woman, Deborah, to deliver the entire Nation of Israel. In fact, one of the greatest victories in the Bible is recorded as having been brought about by this woman. The Bible said that she was a *"Prophetess"* (Vs 4).

Evidently the Lord told her what to do as it regards the coming battle with Jabin the king of Canaan, whose military commander was Sisera.

She called on Barak to enlist the men, with the intention that he would lead the fight. It seems that he believed her, at least somewhat, but not enough to lead the attack. He wanted her to go with him, and then flatly stated, that if she did not go with him, that he would not lead the attack. She did go with him.

And yet, before we criticize Barak too harshly, we must remember, that it was to Deborah that the revelation was given, and not Barak. He was taking her word for all the things that were to happen; therefore, in the back of his mind he must have reasoned, that if Deborah was wrong, he was a dead man. Of that he was correct, but Deborah wasn't wrong.

I personally think that Deborah had such a reputation, that Barak should have believed her without question. He didn't, and to his eternal dismay! While the Lord used him, and did so greatly, still, he would find exactly as Deborah said, that the honor of the victory would go to a woman. That woman would be Jael.

(10) "AND BARAK CALLED ZEBULUN AND NAPHTALI TO KEDESH; AND HE WENT UP WITH TEN THOUSAND MEN AT HIS FEET: AND DEBORAH WENT UP WITH HIM.

(11) "NOW HEBER THE KENITE, WHICH WAS OF THE CHILDREN OF HOBAB THE FATHER IN LAW OF MOSES, HAD SEVERED HIMSELF FROM THE

NOTES

KENITES, AND PITCHED HIS TENT UNTO THE PLAIN OF ZAANAIM, WHICH IS BY KEDESH.

(12) "AND THEY SHOWED SISERA THAT BARAK THE SON OF ABINOAM WAS GONE UP TO MOUNT TABOR.

(13) "AND SISERA GATHERED TOGETHER ALL HIS CHARIOTS, EVEN NINE HUNDRED CHARIOTS OF IRON, AND ALL THE PEOPLE WHO WERE WITH HIM, FROM HAROSHETH OF THE GENTILES UNTO THE RIVER OF KISHON.

(14) "AND DEBORAH SAID UNTO BARAK, UP; FOR THIS IS THE DAY IN WHICH THE LORD HAS DELIVERED SISERA INTO YOUR HAND: IS NOT THE LORD GONE OUT BEFORE YOU? SO BARAK WENT DOWN FROM MOUNT TABOR, AND TEN THOUSAND MEN AFTER HIM.

(15) "AND THE LORD DISCOMFITED SISERA, AND ALL HIS CHARIOTS, AND ALL HIS HOST, WITH THE EDGE OF THE SWORD BEFORE BARAK; SO THAT SISERA LIGHTED DOWN OFF HIS CHARIOT, AND FLED AWAY ON HIS FEET.

(16) "BUT BARAK PURSUED AFTER THE CHARIOTS, AND AFTER THE HOST, UNTO HAROSHETH OF THE GENTILES: AND ALL THE HOST OF SISERA FELL UPON THE EDGE OF THE SWORD; AND THERE WAS NOT A MAN LEFT."

The structure is:

1. In the natural, what could Israel do against all of these iron chariots? However, they were not functioning in the natural, but rather by the Power of God.

2. The Hebrew word for *"discomfited"* implies supernatural discomfiture.

3. It was a defeat that was total, and there is no indication that the army of Israel lost even a single man. Without the Lord, some minor victories may be won, but at a fearful price. With Him, it is total Victory, at no loss whatsoever.

VICTORY

Sometime back on one of our trips to Israel, we happened to be in this particular valley through which the River Kishon ran; however, it is now no more than a trickling stream, if that.

And yet, the valley is a perfect setting for

chariots, which, no doubt, Sisera reasoned as it regards this conflict. In fact, considering that this valley spread out for quite a ways, and that he had 900 chariots of iron, he couldn't see how that he could lose.

I remember walking beside this little stream, knowing the Biblical history of the place, realizing that a tremendous victory had been here won for the Glory of God, it made me realize several things.

First of all, if we are in the Will of God, great and mighty things take place. Also, the Lord strongly desires, insists, that every single foe within our lives be rooted out and destroyed. Among other things, this is what this great example teaches us.

As the Lord that day fought for Israel, as the Fifth Chapter proclaims, He used the elements, because He is the Creator of those elements. In whatever manner they were used, Sisera didn't have a chance! There is no record that Israel lost even a single man.

THE MIRACLE-WORKING POWER OF GOD

The modern Church finds itself in the age where miracles are talked about constantly, but which, in fact, there are in reality, precious few Miracles, at least that can be seen. I personally believe that God is performing Miracles constantly on behalf of His Children. But I also believe that He is sorely displeased at things being labeled as miracles, which obviously aren't! Lies and liars are still looked at with disfavor by the Lord, to say the least!

And yet we realize that Satan uses all of this to keep godly people from believing the Lord. They get turned off by the chicanery, the subterfuge, the wild claims, etc. and rightly so!

But none of that stops God from truly performing Miracles, at least for those who will dare to believe Him, and who will not use such as a gimmick, etc.

As a present example, I personally feel that SonLife Radio is a Miracle. In the year 2000 the Lord told us to take the two Stations, which the Ministry then owned, and told me to change the programming entirely, with, in fact, all of the programming coming from Family Worship Center. When I broached

NOTES

our staff, almost to a person they did not believe that it would work. But I knew the Lord had spoken to my heart.

A week before the Lord spoke to me, despite the fact that the Ministry owned two Radio Stations, of which we had been trying to sell one for the last couple of years, I simply had no interest in Radio. My interest was in Television, etc. and then all of a sudden it happened.

The Lord told me what to do, how to program the Stations, and then told me to fill the land with Stations. In other words, that the Ministry was to purchase Stations all over this nation, in order that the Message of the Cross could go out to a hurting Church and a hurting world.

Now that may sound big; however, the truth was that the Ministry had no money. When I say we had no money, I mean we had no money. How in the world can one buy Stations, which are actually very expensive, when one has no money, and no way to get any money? But yet at this time (July 2006), the Ministry owns 82 Stations all over this nation, broadcasting the Message of the Cross 24 hours a day. That's a Miracle! And we give the Lord all the praise and all the glory.

I believe in a God of Miracles! I believe that He can do anything, and will do anything if it suits His Purpose. At the same time, I do not believe in lying about the situation claiming that which isn't there. As stated, a lie is a lie is a lie, irrespective as to how it is packaged.

(17) "HOWBEIT SISERA FLED AWAY ON HIS FEET TO THE TENT OF JAEL THE WIFE OF HEBER THE KENITE: FOR THERE WAS PEACE BETWEEN JABIN THE KING OF HAZOR AND THE HOUSE OF HEBER THE KENITE.

(18) "AND JAEL WENT OUT TO MEET SISERA, AND SAID UNTO HIM, TURN IN, MY LORD, TURN IN TO ME; FEAR NOT. AND WHEN HE HAD TURNED IN UNTO HER INTO THE TENT, SHE COVERED HIM WITH A MANTLE.

(19) "AND HE SAID UNTO HER, GIVE ME, I PRAY YOU, A LITTLE WATER TO DRINK; FOR I AM THIRSTY. AND SHE OPENED A BOTTLE OF MILK, AND GAVE HIM DRINK, AND COVERED HIM.

(20) "AGAIN HE SAID UNTO HER, STAND IN THE DOOR OF THE TENT, AND IT SHALL BE, WHEN ANY MAN DOES COME AND ENQUIRE OF YOU, AND SAY, IS THERE ANY MAN HERE? THAT YOU SHALL SAY, NO.

(21) "THEN JAEL HEBER'S WIFE TOOK A NAIL OF THE TENT, AND TOOK AN HAMMER IN HER HAND, AND WENT SOFTLY UNTO HIM, AND SMOTE THE NAIL INTO HIS TEMPLES, AND FASTENED IT INTO THE GROUND: FOR HE WAS FAST ASLEEP AND WEARY. SO HE DIED.

(22) "AND, BEHOLD, AS BARAK PURSUED SISERA, JAEL CAME OUT TO MEET HIM, AND SAID UNTO HIM, COME, AND I WILL SHOW YOU THE MAN WHOM YOU SEEK. AND WHEN HE CAME INTO HER TENT, BEHOLD, SISERA LAY DEAD, AND THE NAIL WAS IN HIS TEMPLES."

The construction is:

1. The mighty military commander of the Canaanites is reduced here to depending on a woman. Such are the Ways of the Lord, concerning those who oppose Him.

2. Williams says, *"God, Who energized Shamgar to destroy the Philistine with an ox goad, strengthened Jael to kill the Syrian with a tent-peg."*[2]

3. The Holy Spirit labels only two women as preeminently *"blessed among women"*; the one was Jael (Judg. 5:24), and the other, the Virgin Mary (Lk. 1:28). Mary, of course, is associated with the advent of Israel's, and the world's, Redeemer; Jael, with the Judgment of the Israel's oppressor.

GOD USES ANOTHER WOMAN

If it is to be noticed, the Scripture will most of the time point out that it is the Lord Who performs the task, yet, individuals of Faith will also be brought into it. They may perform the task, but at the same time, it is the Lord Who gives them the supernatural Power to do so. As well, at other times the Lord, distinctly and apart from men and women of Faith, will add to what is already being done. In this case it would say, *"They fought from heaven; the stars in their courses fought against Sisera"* (5:20). God is looking for Faith. Talent, ability, expertise, knowledge, and wisdom may play some tiny part in

NOTES

the things which are done, but, by and large, it is the Faith on which God focuses. We never honor God more than when we trust Him.

IS FAITH ALWAYS THE PRIMARY PRINCIPLE?

No!

The Will of God is always and without question, the primary principle, even though Faith is, as should be obvious, extremely important. Without Faith it's impossible to please God (Heb. 11:6).

The idea that everything that God does for us is predicated on the degree of our faith, is a wrong idea. Were that the case, that faith is the primary ingredient, then God could be forced to anything and everything, despite His Will in the matter. Please understand the following:

God will not allow His Word to be used against Himself. In other words, if it's not the Will of God for something to take place, no matter how much faith a person has, usually the Lord simply will not perform the task, whatever the task might be. Unfortunately, the modern Church has been left with the impression that if they had enough faith they could do thus and so. No way! Let me say it again:

God will not allow His Word to be used against Himself. What exactly do we mean by that?

For instance, Jesus said, *"Therefore I say unto you, What things soever you desire, when you pray, believe that you receive them, and you shall have them"* (Mk. 11:24).

Now on the surface, this Scripture presents, what seems to be, an open ended statement; however, the idea is, one seeking to do the Will of God, will want only what God desires.

The Lord will not allow any of His Children to demand and receive things, which He knows are going to be bad for them in the future, just as an earthly parent will not allow a child to have things that the parent knows will not be good for that child, at least at the particular time.

SPIRITUAL MATURITY IS PREDICATED ON THE KNOWLEDGE OF THE CROSS

The reader should read that heading

several times, and then meditate thereon.

The Believer cannot really grow in Grace, cannot really grow in the Knowledge of the Lord, cannot really develop properly, unless there is a proper knowledge of the Cross. That's the reason that we say, *"All spiritual maturity, or the lack thereof, is predicated solely on one's understanding of the Cross, or the lack thereof."*

At a particular time, the Disciples said to the Lord, *"Increase our Faith"* (Lk. 17:5).

The Lord answered them in a very strange way. He said:

"If you had Faith as a grain of mustard seed, you might say unto this sycamine tree, Be thou plucked up by the root, and be thou planted in the sea; and it should obey you" (Lk. 17:6).

He was telling them that it's not really the amount of faith, but rather the correct Object of Faith that makes the difference. That correct Object is the Cross (I Cor. 1:18).

As well, the removal of trees and mountains were proverbial figures of speech among the Jews at that time, expressing the overcoming of great difficulties.

Let us say it again:

It's not so very much the amount of Faith, which is the criteria, as important as Faith is, but more so, it is the correct Object of Faith, which makes the great difference.

The Disciples were as many today, thinking that if they could just increase their faith, they could do anything. Once again, were that the case, the person would then be God and, of course, such will never be the case!

The Lord used Jael to kill the mightiest military commander in that part of the world. She took him out with one blow. The Scripture said, *"Sisera lay dead, and the nail was in his temples"* (Judg. 4:22).

(23) "SO GOD SUBDUED ON THAT DAY JABIN THE KING OF CANAAN BEFORE THE CHILDREN OF ISRAEL.

(24) "AND THE HAND OF THE CHILDREN OF ISRAEL PROSPERED, AND PREVAILED AGAINST JABIN THE KING OF CANAAN, UNTIL THEY HAD DESTROYED JABIN KING OF CANAAN."

The exegesis is:

1. As I think should be obvious, this great victory over *"Jabin the king of Canaan"* was

one of the greatest recorded in Biblical history.

2. The beautiful thing about this victory was that which the Lord used in order to bring it about. He used two women.

This tells us that God is able to use anyone and anything.

3. Even though these women and others were used, still it was God Who performed the task.

CHAPTER 5

(1) "THEN SANG DEBORAH AND BARAK THE SON OF ABINOAM ON THAT DAY, SAYING,

(2) "PRAISE YE THE LORD FOR THE AVENGING OF ISRAEL, WHEN THE PEOPLE WILLINGLY OFFERED THEMSELVES.

(3) "HEAR, O YOU KINGS; GIVE EAR, O YOU PRINCES; I, EVEN I, WILL SING UNTO THE LORD; I WILL SING PRAISE TO THE LORD GOD OF ISRAEL.

(4) "LORD, WHEN YOU WENT OUT OF SEIR, WHEN YOU MARCHED OUT OF THE FIELD OF EDOM, THE EARTH TREMBLED, AND THE HEAVENS DROPPED, THE CLOUDS ALSO DROPPED WATER.

(5) "THE MOUNTAINS MELTED FROM BEFORE THE LORD, EVEN THAT SINAI FROM BEFORE THE LORD GOD OF ISRAEL.

(6) "IN THE DAYS OF SHAMGAR THE SON OF ANATH, IN THE DAYS OF JAEL, THE HIGHWAYS WERE UNOCCUPIED, AND THE TRAVELLERS WALKED THROUGH BYWAYS.

(7) "THE INHABITANTS OF THE VILLAGES CEASED, THEY CEASED IN ISRAEL, UNTIL THAT I DEBORAH AROSE, THAT I AROSE A MOTHER IN ISRAEL.

(8) "THEY CHOSE NEW GODS; THEN WAS WAR IN THE GATES: WAS THERE A SHIELD OR SPEAR SEEN AMONG FORTY THOUSAND IN ISRAEL?

(9) "MY HEART IS TOWARD THE GOVERNORS OF ISRAEL, WHO OFFERED THEMSELVES WILLINGLY AMONG THE PEOPLE. BLESS YE THE LORD.

(10) "SPEAK, YOU WHO RIDE ON WHITE ASSES, YOU WHO SIT IN JUDGMENT, AND WALK BY THE WAY.

(11) "THEY WHO ARE DELIVERED FROM THE NOISE OF ARCHERS IN THE PLACES OF DRAWING WATER, THERE SHALL THEY REHEARSE THE RIGHTEOUS ACTS OF THE LORD, EVEN THE RIGHTEOUS ACTS TOWARD THE INHABITANTS OF HIS VILLAGES IN ISRAEL: THEN SHALL THE PEOPLE OF THE LORD GO DOWN TO THE GATES."

The diagram is:

1. Victory precedes singing, while defeat precedes weeping.

2. The people willingly offered themselves to be used of the Lord, and the Lord willingly avenged Israel.

3. The *"kings"* and *"princes"* of Verse 3, were those of the enemy; they found out as to Who exactly was the God of Israel.

4. Verse 6 records the fact that Israel was so beaten down by the enemy that they were afraid to even walk on the road; because of sin, the People of God had been reduced to this low state.

5. Israel was guilty of idolatry as Verse 8 proclaims, which had reduced the people to being defenseless; the only defense against Satan is the Cross of Christ; anything else leaves the Believer defenseless (I Cor. 1:17-18).

6. Verse 9 proclaims the fact that the leaders in Israel were to *"Bless the LORD,"* because of the great victory that had been won.

7. Verse 10 proclaims the fact that Israel was not only to bless the Lord, they were also to speak the Blessings; and what they were to speak is set out in Verse 11.

8. The idea of Verse 11 is this: The water wells were where gossip was exchanged and news proclaimed; instead of the Syrians talking at these wells about their great victory over Israel, which would have been the case had they won, instead, Israel would boast; however, they were to boast about the *"righteous Acts of the LORD,"* and not the achievements of individuals.

THE SONG OF VICTORY

Judges, Chapter 5 is the proclamation of Revival. Verse 1 says, *"Then sang Deborah and Barak."*

This is a praise to God for Victory. Actually, there are some eight songs of praise recorded in Scripture other than the Psalms.

They are as follows:

A. Song of Moses (Ex. 15:1-19);

B. Song of Israel (Num. 21:17-18);

C. Song of Moses (Deut. 32:1-43);

D. Song of Deborah-Barak (Judg. 5:1-31);

E. Song of Hannah (I Sam. 2:1-10);

F. Song of David (II Sam. 22:1-51);

G. Song of the Redeemed (Rev. 5:8-10); and,

H. Song of Tribulation Saints (Rev. 15:3-4).

Verse 6 shows the terrible condition to which Israel had sunk because of her spiritual declension. The land was full of anarchy and confusion, everywhere being infested with bandits. No public road was safe, and the people of the villages were forced to live in fortified places or in great numbers together to protect themselves from roving bands of wicked men.

As all of this relates to us personally, the enemy of our soul so desires to destroy our inheritance that we can take little advantage of the great Blessings that God has afforded us. Of how many Christians can it be said that the highways of blessing are unoccupied, and the roads of victory untraveled?

IDOLATRY

The Eighth Verse tells us why:
"They chose new gods."

Regrettably, Israel chose gods that could not save them. They were overcome by their enemies, *"then was war in the gates."*

The Eighth Verse says, *"Was there a shield or spear seen among forty thousand in Israel?"* So, to face Sisera's 900 chariots of iron and his mighty army, God sent a ragtag army of ten thousand without weapons. We might add as well, that a woman was leading them. Israel had been reduced to this state once again because, *"they chose new gods."*

NEW GODS

Could it be said today that the Church as well, has chosen *"new gods"*?

The god of modern day Christianity is for the most part the god of humanistic psychoanalysis — psychology. Psychology is the religion of secularism and humanism. It is atheistic at its core. It's apostles are Freud, Skinner, Maslow, Rogers, and a host of other similar ilk. The Church, sadly, has bought it hook, line, and sinker.

The individuals mentioned, who are mostly atheistic or at least humanistic, have replaced Matthew, Mark, Luke, and John. As Israel desperately needed a *"Deborah"* and a Miracle from God, likewise, the Church needs the same.

(12) "AWAKE, AWAKE, DEBORAH: AWAKE, AWAKE, UTTER A SONG: ARISE, BARAK, AND LEAD YOUR CAPTIVITY CAPTIVE, YOU SON OF ABINOAM.

(13) "THEN HE MADE HIM WHO REMAINS HAVE DOMINION OVER THE NOBLES AMONG THE PEOPLE: THE LORD MADE ME HAVE DOMINION OVER THE MIGHTY.

(14) "OUT OF EPHRAIM WAS THERE A ROOT OF THEM AGAINST AMALEK; AFTER YOU, BENJAMIN, AMONG YOUR PEOPLE; OUT OF MACHIR CAME DOWN GOVERNORS, AND OUT OF ZEBULUN THEY WHO HANDLE THE PEN OF THE WRITER.

(15) "AND THE PRINCES OF ISSACHAR WERE WITH DEBORAH; EVEN ISSACHAR, AND ALSO BARAK: HE WAS SENT ON FOOT INTO THE VALLEY. FOR THE DIVISIONS OF REUBEN THERE WERE GREAT THOUGHTS OF HEART.

(16) "WHY ABODE YOU AMONG THE SHEEPFOLDS, TO HEAR THE BLEATINGS OF THE FLOCKS? FOR THE DIVISION OF REUBEN THERE WERE GREAT SEARCHINGS OF HEART.

(17) "GILEAD ABODE BEYOND JORDAN: AND WHY DID DAN REMAIN IN SHIPS? ASHER CONTINUED ON THE SEA SHORE, AND ABODE IN HIS BREACHES.

(18) "ZEBULUN AND NAPHTALI WERE A PEOPLE WHO JEOPARDED THEIR LIVES UNTO THE DEATH IN THE HIGH PLACES OF THE FIELD."

The structure is:

1. Verse 12 proclaims Deborah's going back to the time the Lord moved upon her with the Divine Call.

2. The Holy Spirit through Deborah delineates those who helped in the battle, and those who didn't. The Tribes of Ephraim, Benjamin, Zebulun, and Issachar helped bring about the victory.

3. Verse 16 proclaims the fact that God gives the *"Vision,"* and brings about *"provision"*;

NOTES

however, Satan then comes in, attempting to bring about *"division"*; this is what happened to Reuben, and the Holy Spirit is quick to say so.

4. The Seventeenth Verse probably pertains to the Tribe of Gad, which portion was on the east side of Jordan; they seemed to think that the conflict did not include them, simply because of their location.

5. The celebrated harbor of Joppa was in the Tribe of Dan. They did not want to interrupt their business, so the Tribe of Dan neglected to help.

6. The Holy Spirit speaks very highly of the two Tribes of Zebulun and Naphtali, as it regards this conflict.

AWAKE

It was time for Israel to be delivered from the terrible bondage of the Canaanites headed up by Jabin and Sisera. As the Holy Spirit looked at the situation in Israel, he found only a woman who would evidence the Faith required in order for this task to be carried out.

God uses people. While, of course, the Lord can use anything, even as we shall see in this Chapter, still, the greater thrust of His Work is always through individuals; however, these must be individuals, whether man or woman, who evidence Faith in the Lord, and due to that Faith, will believe God, and carry out the Will of God.

How many grand and glorious things does the Lord have ready, but they cannot be brought to fruition because He cannot find a man or a woman who will believe Him. As we say over and over again, the ingredient is Faith; however, the Faith registered must be in Christ and the Cross. God will honor no other kind (Rom. 6:1-14; Eph. 2:13-18; Col. 2:14-15).

While, of course, Christ and the Cross were only in Shadow in Old Testament times, still, the Sacrificial System was designed by the Lord to portray Christ and what He would do at the Cross. While it is true that Israel most of the time did not understand the meaning of the Sacrificial System, that in no way took away from its veracity. Regrettably, most modern Christians still do not understand, and despite all the Revelation, the meaning of Christ and the Cross.

The word *"awake"* repeated four times by the Holy Spirit is done so for emphasis. The number of times the word is used proclaims the tremendous significance of the mission at hand. As previously stated, this mission would result in one of the greatest Miracles performed by God in the entirety of Israel's history. In some way it might even rank close to the Miracle of the tumbling of the walls of Jericho, as well as other tremendous victories won by Joshua, etc.

This can be said for Deborah, she immediately set out to carry out that which the Lord told her to do.

The manner in which the Lord gave this Revelation to Deborah, and by using the words *"awake,"* proclaims the fact, as well, that Israel, at that time, it seems, was mired down in a spirit of lethargy. In other words, they saw no way out of this dilemma. How in the world could Israel who, in essence, had few weapons, come up against Sisera with his 900 chariots of iron.

For twenty years the Lord had allowed this bondage. During this time, even as the bondage deepened, with all of its attendant misery, the people seemingly forgot that God was a God of Miracles. If He was, they may have reasoned, why would He allow them to be in this condition?

Of course, Israel discounted the fact, and we do so as well, that their negative situation was not the fault of the Lord, but rather their own fault. They had gone into deep sin, even idol worship, hence, the reason for their present predicament. At any rate, they could see no way out of their dilemma.

At the same time, who would have thought that God would use a woman to bring about one of the greatest deliverances of all? One thing is certain, had the wisest men in Israel of that time been given the choice of choosing the one that would lead them in battle, it certainly would not have been Deborah; however, while men look on the outward, God looks on the heart. He found in Deborah a woman of Faith whom He could trust, and who would do what He told her to do.

DOMINION

The Thirteenth Verse proclaims the fact that the Lord told Deborah that He would

give her dominion over the king of the Canaanites, and their mighty military leader, Sisera. I wonder what Deborah thought when the Lord related this to her. How in the world could she as a woman have dominion over these individuals, especially considering that Sisera had 900 chariots of iron?

The truth is, God intended for Israel to have dominion over every single nation on the face of the Earth, and had they obeyed the Lord, that dominion would have been theirs. There will come a day, in the coming Kingdom Age, when Israel will finally realize this dominion, and because she finally realizes that it is all in Christ — the very One she crucified!

It is the Will of God presently, for every Believer to have dominion over the powers of darkness, over every sin that would so easily beset us, that we walk in perpetual victory. Paul said:

"For sin shall not have dominion over you (the sin nature will not have dominion over us if we as Believers continue to exercise Faith in the Cross of Christ; otherwise, the sin nature most definitely will have dominion over the Believer): *for you are not under the Law* (means that if we try to live this life by any type of law, no matter how good that law might be in its own right, we will conclude by the sin nature having dominion over us), *but under Grace* (the Grace of God flows to the Believer on an unending basis only as long as the Believer exercises Faith in Christ and what He did at the Cross; Grace is merely the Goodness of God exercised by and through the Holy Spirit, and given to undeserving Saints)" (Rom. 6:14).

Our method of victory presently is basically the same as it was with Deborah. Salvation and its means are the same, and for all time. It is, *"Jesus Christ and Him Crucified"* (I Cor. 1:23).

The Sacrificial System was instituted by the Lord at the very dawn of time, immediately after the Fall of Adam and Eve in the Garden of Eden. Through this System, God proclaimed to the First Family how, despite the Fall, they could have communion with Him, fellowship with Him, and forgiveness of sins. It would be through the slain lamb, which would be a Type of Christ, Who would ultimately come to this world and die on a Cross, in order that man might be Saved. A perfect description is given to us in the Fourth Chapter of Genesis. So, Salvation and its method have never changed and, in fact, will never change, because there is only one Saviour, as there has ever been only one Saviour, the Lord Jesus Christ.

THE HOLY SPIRIT AND THE TRIBES OF ISRAEL

Several of the Tribes joined in the great battle, but some did not. Of the ten thousand men who fought against Sisera, most came from the Tribes of Ephraim, Manasseh, Benjamin, Zebulun, Issachar, and Naphtali. Admittedly, some of these Tribes sent only a few men, but the rest of the Tribes did not help at all. The Holy Spirit, even as we shall see, records some of the excuses. We would do well to fasten our attention on what the Holy Spirit here says.

It is interesting that the Holy Spirit in this Fourteenth Verse refers to *"Amalek."*

Amalek pictures the old carnal nature. He was the grandson of Esau, who before and after birth tried to murder Jacob, and who preferred the mess of pottage to the birthright. This carnal nature wars against the Spirit; *"it is not subject to the Law of God, neither indeed can be"* (Rom. 8:7).

Actually, the first mention of the Bible in the Word of God is in connection with the hostility of the natural man to the Spiritual Man, with Amalek as the example (Ex. 17:14). *"The LORD swore that He would have war with Amalek from generation to generation"* (Ex. 17:16). Amalek is a type of the flesh, hence, the very first battle enjoined after Israel was delivered from Egypt (Ex. 17:8-16).

The Holy Spirit had Deborah to mention *"Amalek"* in this Fourteenth Verse, in order that we may understand the root of this struggle. As stated, Amalek is a type of the flesh, referring to man's personal power, prowess, intellectualism, ability, talent, etc. While these things within themselves aren't necessarily wrong, the wrong comes in, when we depend on them to help us live for God. The Holy Spirit through Paul referred to such as the *"flesh."* Amalek is a type of the flesh (Rom. 8:1-2, 8).

DIVISIONS

The Holy Spirit records that the Tribe of Issachar *"was with Deborah."* But when it came to the Tribe of Reuben, even though they had *"great thoughts of heart,"* as it regards the coming conflict, because of *"divisions"* the record is clear that they sent no men.

"Division" without a doubt is one of the greatest problems in the Work of God, and even in the modern Church. Satan, as should be obvious, is the author of division. As we have stated, God gives the *"Vision,"* and then makes *"Provision,"* for the *"Vision"* to be carried out; however, in order to stop this Vision from being carried out, the Devil often time succeeds in bringing about *"division."* The very word *"division"* dissected says *"di-vision,"* meaning that the vision dies.

What caused these divisions in the Tribe of Reuben?

Of course we know that the root cause is always the Devil, but when it comes to the individuals themselves, more than likely some wanted to send soldiers and some didn't.

And quite possibly the question posed by the Holy Spirit, *"Why abode thou among the sheepfolds, to hear the bleatings of the flocks?"* Proclaimed the fact that their herds meant more than freedom. In other words they were making money, and they didn't want that disturbed. How often is money put before the Work of God?

If Believers only understood, that if we seek first the Kingdom of God and His Righteousness, that we'll come out on top to a much greater degree than otherwise. So, if we tend first of all to God's business, He will attend to ours. Reuben would here be sanctioned by the Holy Spirit for time and eternity, and all because they did not obey the Lord. How many of us fall into the same category?

Gilead, which probably applies to the Tribe of Gad, the Scripture says, *"abode beyond Jordan."* They simply reasoned, *"this is not my fight,"* when in reality it was their fight as much as the fight of anyone else.

How many Believers do as did Gad, thinking that *"this does not apply to me."*

Many times we will attempt to raise funds over SonLife Radio in order to put in a new Station. We are always faced with a number of Christians at that time, when asked to give for this cause, who will contemplate in their minds, that this particular Station is not in their city, so it doesn't pertain to them. They conveniently forget, that someone paid for the Station that is, in fact, in their city, someone who did not know them, but helped to put that Station on the air simply because of a love for souls. But tragically, far too many consider that simply because they are *"beyond Jordan,"* whatever that would mean to them personally, that whatever the need is, it does not apply to them. The Holy Spirit is quick here to say otherwise!

The Scripture says that *"Dan remained in ships."* In other words, it was business as usual for the Tribe of Dan. They didn't want to interrupt what they were doing, in their making of money, to send soldiers to help against Jabin and Sisera, so they *"remained in their ships."*

The Tribe of Asher fell into the same category. They were busy unloading the goods brought on by the ships from the Tribe of Dan, so they as well did not send any soldiers, even though the call came to them. Again, the Holy Spirit is quick to point all of this out.

FAITHFULNESS

The Holy Spirit, as well, is quick to point out also that the Tribes of *"Zebulun and Naphtali"* did everything they could do as it regards the winning of this battle. The Scripture says, *"They jeoparded their lives unto the death in the high places of the field."* As the Spirit of God had pointed out the deficiencies of the other Tribes, He points out the efficiency of these two Tribes.

They heard the clarion call of Deborah, exactly as did the other Tribes, but they did something these other Tribes did not do. They responded to that call!

Actually, these two Tribes furnished the majority of the ten thousand men who fought the Canaanites. The other Tribes provided token numbers with Reuben, Gad, Dan, and Asher providing no one. How so like the Church regarding the great Work of God in taking the Gospel of Jesus to a lost world. Many do absolutely nothing toward the most important part of all, which is telling the

greatest story the world has ever known, the Story of the Lord Jesus Christ and His Power to save. Many, as the Tribes mentioned, give only a token amount to help further this cause, with a few doing most of the giving, and working.

It shouldn't be that way!

For every single individual who is Saved as a result of the precious shed Blood of the Lord Jesus Christ, to say the least, we are a debtor. It is incumbent upon all of us, to do the very best we can, whatever that might be, to help take this Gospel to others. We must make doubly certain that what we are supporting is truly of God. Unfortunately, most of the giving as it regards the Work of God, in fact, does not go to the Work of God, but something else altogether. That is tragic but true! In this Work for the Lord, it doesn't matter how poor the person may be, or how rich the person may be. The Lord expects us to be faithful with what we have, as little as that might be, or as much as that might be. Remember this:

The Lord has not called us to be successful, but He has called us to be faithful (Mat. 25:21).

(19) "THE KINGS CAME AND FOUGHT, THEN FOUGHT THE KINGS OF CANAAN IN TAANACH BY THE WATERS OF MEGIDDO; THEY TOOK NO GAIN OF MONEY.

(20) "THEY FOUGHT FROM HEAVEN; THE STARS IN THEIR COURSES FOUGHT AGAINST SISERA.

(21) "THE RIVER OF KISHON SWEPT THEM AWAY, THAT ANCIENT RIVER, THE RIVER KISHON. O MY SOUL, YOU HAVE TRODDEN DOWN STRENGTH.

(22) "THEN WERE THE HORSEHOOFS BROKEN BY THE MEANS OF THE PRANSINGS, THE PRANSINGS OF THEIR MIGHTY ONES.

(23) "CURSE YOU MEROZ, SAID THE ANGEL OF THE LORD, CURSE YOU BITTERLY THE INHABITANTS THEREOF; BECAUSE THEY CAME NOT TO THE HELP OF THE LORD, TO THE HELP OF THE LORD AGAINST THE MIGHTY."

The exegesis is:

1. The heathen kings of Verse 19 thought to plunder Israel. Instead, they would be plundered themselves.

2. According to Josephus, a great storm arose in the face of the Canaanites, which led to their utter defeat in this battle.

Regarding Verse 21, the *"River of Kishon"* is normally a very narrow stream; however, the storm evidently caused the river to flood, which played havoc with the chariots, etc.

3. The inhabitants of the city of Meroz could easily have been of great help and great service in this battle, but evidently refused to do so. The Holy Spirit tells us here that a curse was placed on them by the *"Angel of the LORD,"* in other words, the Lord Almighty!

4. When the Holy Spirit begins to do a certain thing, and Believers take a neutral position, they lose the manifestation and the experience of the Power of God. But if, like these people of Meroz they are so placed that they can help, but refuse to do so, then they bring death upon their souls.

THE WAYS OF THE LORD

In this valley where the River of Kishon ran, which is normally little more than a stream, Israel's ten thousand men without any weapons of war we might quickly add, would be meat, or so it seemed, for Sisera's chariots.

Incidentally, for these ten thousand men to face Sisera's 900 chariots of iron along with what was, no doubt, tens of thousands of his army, required tremendous Faith, especially when we consider that the People of God were almost defenseless, at least as it regards natural weaponry.

In fact, this valley is perfect for the operation of chariots. Sisera could not lose, or so he thought. However, the Twentieth Verse says, *"The stars in their courses fought against Sisera."*

The Fourth Verse says, *"And the heavens dropped, the clouds also dropped water,"* which means, that this small River, normally only a few feet across, became a raging torrent. With a great rain, this can happen in a few minutes time. It must have thrown his chariots around like fallen leaves.

The Twenty-second Verse uses the phrase, *"The pransings of their mighty ones."* This signified the arrogancy of Sisera and his military chieftains; however, their pransings were *"broken"* by the mighty Power of Almighty God.

NOTES

THE CURSE

The Twenty-third Verse records an indictment that should make the Church tremble. It says, *"Curse ye Meroz."*

It must be remembered that these words were given to Deborah by the Holy Spirit, *"said the Angel of the LORD."* This would have been the One we now know as the Lord Jesus Christ. He then says:

"Curse ye bitterly."

And then, *"because they came not to the help of the LORD, to the help of the LORD against the mighty."*

The Holy Spirit was careful to speak of the two Tribes who provided most of the soldiers. He was also careful to specify those who provided none. And then, *"Curse ye Meroz."*

Who these individuals were we do not know. But this we do know; they had the opportunity to come *"to the help of the LORD,"* and they did not do so.

How many in the modern Church fall into the position of the Tribes who did not help because of difficulties in their own ranks, and are actually *"cursed by the Angel of the Lord?"*

Whatever happened to these people of the town of Meroz, we aren't told; however, one can be certain that if a curse is leveled against a place by none other than the Lord Himself, that the situation did not turn out too positive.

Whenever the Lord carries out a mission, He expects all of His People to get behind that mission. None are excluded!

We can only go here by the Scriptural Text. It says that the Lord cursed this village Meroz, meaning that He stopped the flow of Blessing to them, which means that they did not enjoy the freedom that Israel now had, but something else all together. As stated, what happened to them we aren't told. How many modern Believers fall into the same category? How many could help but won't? Is it true that a curse is upon such who fall into that category presently? Only the Lord can answer that question; however, I think every Believer should take heed as to exactly how we respond to the Work of the Lord. A curse, especially that leveled by the Lord Himself, is not something to be trifled with.

(24) "BLESSED ABOVE WOMEN SHALL JAEL THE WIFE OF HEBER THE KENITE BE, BLESSED SHALL SHE BE ABOVE WOMEN IN THE TENT.

(25) "HE ASKED WATER, AND SHE GAVE HIM MILK; SHE BROUGHT FORTH BUTTER IN A LORDLY DISH.

(26) "SHE PUT HER HAND TO THE NAIL, AND HER RIGHT HAND TO THE WORKMEN'S HAMMER; AND WITH THE HAMMER SHE SMOTE SISERA, SHE SMOTE OFF HIS HEAD, WHEN SHE HAD PEIRCED AND STRICKEN THROUGH HIS TEMPLES.

(27) "AT HER FEET HE BOWED, HE FELL, HE LAY DOWN: AT HER FEET HE BOWED, HE FELL: WHERE HE BOWED, THERE HE FELL DOWN DEAD.

(28) "THE MOTHER OF SISERA LOOKED OUT AT A WINDOW, AND CRIED THROUGH THE LATTICE, WHY IS HIS CHARIOT SO LONG IN COMING? WHY TARRY THE WHEELS OF HIS CHARIOTS?

(29) "HER WISE LADIES ANSWERED HER, YES, SHE RETURNED ANSWER TO HERSELF,

(30) "HAVE THEY NOT SPED? HAVE THEY NOT DIVIDED THE PREY; TO EVERY MAN A DAMSEL OR TWO; TO SISERA A PREY OF DIVERS COLOURS, A PREY OF DIVERS COLOURS OF NEEDLEWORK, OF DIVERS COLOURS OF NEEDLEWORK ON BOTH SIDES, MEET FOR THE NECKS OF THEM WHO TAKE THE SPOIL?

(31) "SO LET ALL YOUR ENEMIES PERISH, O LORD: BUT LET THEM WHO LOVE HIM BE AS THE SUN WHEN HE GOES FORTH IN HIS MIGHT. AND THE LAND HAD REST FORTY YEARS."

The diagram is:

1. As stated, the only other woman spoken of in this fashion by the Holy Spirit, as described in Verse 24, was Mary, the Mother of our Lord.

2. To be killed in battle by a woman presented, at that time, the height of disgrace.

3. Verse 31 proclaims a victory, which was a foretaste of the final Victory over sin and death, which took place at the Cross, and is the glory of the Redeemed Church.

BLESSED!

When we consider that the Holy Spirit

NOTES

sanctioned the Blessing of Jael, in the same sense as the Virgin Mary, we tend to see how signally important this great victory actually was.

Incidentally, the name *"Jael"* means *"profitable for the Lord."* This dear lady most assuredly lived up to her name. She was most profitable for the Work of God.

As is obvious here, the Holy Spirit goes into detail as it regards how Jael put an end to the military career of Sisera.

CALVARY'S CROSS

Inasmuch as she drove a nail through his head, with the Scripture intimating that she then also cut off his head, this becomes a Type of the defeat of Satan at Calvary's Cross. This is the reason that the Holy Spirit gave her such a lordly Blessing, thereby placing her in a sense, in the same category as Mary the Mother of our Lord.

As stricken as Sisera was, as stricken was Satan at the Cross.

When Jesus died on the Cross, He atoned for all sin, past, present, and future, at least for all who will believe (Jn. 3:16).

"Sin" is the means, and we might quickly add the legal means, by which Satan holds man in bondage. Sin gives him that right; however, with all sin removed, which it was at the Cross, actually taken away and taken away forever, Satan lost that legal right.

So that being the case, how is it that he can hold anyone presently as a captive?

We realize that most of the world is in sinful captivity, and is actually a captive of Satan. How can this be if he was defeated at Calvary's Cross?

One might say that Satan places individuals into captivity simply because they give him consent.

How is this done?

For that which Christ did to be effective, one must believe and accept Him as Lord and Saviour. Regrettably, most of the world doesn't want to do that, so they remain in captivity.

But how does that explain the millions of Christians who are also in some way, a captive of Satan?

It is because they do not place their Faith in Christ and the Cross, but rather something else.

The Believer must understand that it was at the Cross, where all Victory was won (Col. 2:14-15; Eph. 2:13-18; Rom. 6:1-14). Consequently, for that Victory to be ours, and in totality, our faith must be placed where the Victory was won, and that is the Cross. Unfortunately, most Christians, as stated, have their faith in something else. But once the Believer has his faith anchored solidly in Christ and the Cross, the Holy Spirit, Who Alone can make us what we ought to be, will then work mightily on our behalf. He always works entirely within the framework of the Finished Work of Christ. In doing so, He demands that our Faith be according to that great Truth (Rom. 8:1-2, 11).

Deborah closes out her song by saying, *"So let all Your enemies perish, O LORD."* And then she said, *"but let them who love Him be as the Sun when he goes forth in his might."*

All *"enemies"* were defeated at Calvary's Cross. We will realize the full and complete glory of that, in the coming Kingdom Age, which is soon to begin.

CHAPTER 6

(1) "AND THE CHILDREN OF ISRAEL DID EVIL IN THE SIGHT OF THE LORD: AND THE LORD DELIVERED THEM INTO THE HAND OF MIDIAN SEVEN YEARS.

(2) "AND THE HAND OF MIDIAN PREVAILED AGAINST ISRAEL: AND BECAUSE OF THE MIDIANITES THE CHILDREN OF ISRAEL MADE THEM THE DENS WHICH ARE IN THE MOUNTAINS, AND CAVES, AND STRONG HOLDS.

(3) "AND SO IT WAS, WHEN ISRAEL HAD SOWN, THAT THE MIDIANITES CAME UP, AND THE AMALEKITES, AND THE CHILDREN OF THE EAST, EVEN THEY CAME UP AGAINST THEM;

(4) "AND THEY ENCAMPED AGAINST THEM, AND DESTROYED THE INCREASE OF THE EARTH, TILL YOU COME UNTO GAZA, AND LEFT NO SUSTENANCE FOR ISRAEL, NEITHER SHEEP, NOR OX, NOR ASS.

(5) "FOR THEY CAME UP WITH THEIR CATTLE AND THEIR TENTS, AND THEY CAME AS GRASSHOPPERS FOR MULTITUDE; FOR BOTH THEY AND THEIR CAMELS WERE WITHOUT NUMBER: AND THEY ENTERED INTO THE LAND TO DESTROY IT.

(6) "AND ISRAEL WAS GREATLY IMPOVERISHED BECAUSE OF THE MIDIANITES; AND THE CHILDREN OF ISRAEL CRIED UNTO THE LORD."

The overview is:

1. Despite what Israel had seen regarding the great victory over Sisera, they once again lapsed into apostasy.

2. The People of God, according to Verse 2, who were to be the strongest on the face of the Earth, are now reduced to living in dens and caves, because of fear.

3. The Fourth Verse declares that Israel was reduced to starvation; such are the wages of iniquity!

4. The Lord allowed all of this, because of Israel's idolatry; let not the Believer think that because this is the day of Grace God operates any differently; He doesn't!

5. As stated, irrespective as to what they had done, when Israel cried unto the Lord, without fail, He always heard and answered them; He will do the same presently (I Jn. 1:9).

ENSLAVEMENT

The closing prayer of Deborah was, *"So let all Your enemies perish, O LORD."* This prayer would have been answered had Israel during their forty years of rest after their great victory over Sisera, allowed the Lord to reign supreme within their lives, and thereby their Nation; but, regrettably, the First Verse of this Chapter says, *"And the Children of Israel did evil in the sight of the LORD."*

If one looks at God's People in the Book of Judges, then the Book becomes laborious to read; however, if one will look instead at the Lord and His Mercy and Grace in this great Book, then it takes on a totally different complexion.

The First Verse also says, *"And the LORD delivered them into the hand of Midian seven years."* The Lord chastises those He loves. He only resorts to these measures when all measures of Mercy and Grace have failed, but all is done in love with the express purpose of bringing His People back to Him.

CHASTISEMENT

If one observes Christians, at least those who refer to themselves as such, who constantly live in a state of rebellion with no Repentance, and seemingly no chastisement, one must come to the conclusion that one is looking at bastards and not children. The Children of Israel were the Lord's Children; therefore, He would chastise them to bring them back.

The Scripture emphatically states, and concerning this: *"My son, despise not you the chastening of the Lord, nor faint when you are rebuked of Him* (everything that happens to a Believer is either caused or allowed by the Lord; consequently, we should learn the lesson desired to be taught)*:

"For whom the Lord loves He chastens (God disciplines those He loves, not those to whom He is indifferent), *and scourges every son whom He receives.* (This refers to all who truly belong to Him.)

"If you endure chastening, God deals with you as with sons (chastening from the Lord guarantees the fact that one is a Child of God); *for what son is he whom the father chastens not?* (If an earthly father truly cares for his son, he will use whatever measures necessary to bring the boy into line. If an earthly father will do this, how much more will our Heavenly Father do the same?)

"But if you be without chastisement, whereof all (all true Believers) *are partakers, then are you bastards, and not sons.* (Many claim to be Believers while continuing in sin, but the Lord never chastises them. Such shows they are illegitimate sons, meaning they are claiming faith on a basis other than the Cross. The true son, without doubt, will be chastised at times.)

"Furthermore we have had fathers of our flesh which corrected us, and we gave them reverence (earthly parents): *shall we not much rather be in subjection unto the Father of spirits, and live?* ('Father of spirits' is contrasted to 'Fathers of the flesh.' The latter concerns our earthly parents. Their relation to us is limited. His is universal and Eternal.)

"For they verily for a few days chastened us after their own pleasure (the use of the word 'pleasure' indicates that the chastening may

or may not have been proper, as it regards our earthly parents); *but He for our profit* (presents the difference between human liability of error and the Perfect Knowledge of our Heavenly Father; He seeks our profit, and cannot err in the means He employs), *that we might be partakers of His Holiness.* (This presents the objective of the chastening and correction of God.)

"Now no chastening for the present seems to be joyous, but grievous (presents the fact that the trials we are at times exposed to do not give joy at that moment, and are often hard indeed to bear): *nevertheless afterward it yields the peaceable fruit of Righteousness unto them which are exercised thereby.* (All of this is carried out by the Holy Spirit for a specific purpose [Jn. 15:1-9])" (Heb. 12:5-11).

THE KINDRED OF ISRAEL

Midian was the son of Abraham by Keturah (Gen. 25:2-4). His descendants became bitter enemies of Israel in the days of Moses, who himself married a Midianite woman. The reason for such enmity is not stated. It appears from Numbers, Chapter 31 that the Midianites were destroyed as a nation, but they multiplied again and became the leaders of this great multitude who came against Israel at this time, in fact, during the time of Gideon. One might say, and considering that Midian was the half brother of Israel so to speak, that the greatest foe to the Child of God is his own household.

IMPOVERISHMENT

Verse 2 records how that Spiritual Declension had brought Israel to a terrible low, as all sin always does. The Scripture says, *"Because of the Midianites the Children of Israel made them the dens which are in the mountains, and caves, and strong holds."* Once again, Israel is a slave in her own inheritance. When one reads Verse 2, one realizes that this is the exact position to which Satan desires to bring every Believer.

The Children of Israel, God's chosen People, those to whom He had given the great Law, which made them the most blessed people on the face of the Earth, are now reduced to living in dens and caves, in other words, hiding out for fear of the Midianites.

How many Christians, spiritually speaking, suffer the same fate?

The Third Verse says, *"When Israel had sown."* This had to do with their crops. Then it says in the Fourth Verse, *"and destroyed the increase of the Earth . . . and left no sustenance for Israel, neither sheep. . . ."* This is exactly Satan's method. He wants to destroy your increase until there is no sustenance left. He does it by many and varied means, but he can do so only if the Believer strays from the path of obedience.

The Fifth Verse gives us Satan's method, *"as grasshoppers for multitude."* And then it says, *"without number."* Satan's methods vary little. He overwhelms us with the magnitude of the opposition brought against us. It is for but one purpose, *"and they entered into the land to destroy it."* Jesus used this term concerning Satan, *"to steal, to kill, and to destroy"* (Jn. 10:10).

The Holy Spirit in Verse 6 says, *"And Israel was greatly impoverished."* Impoverishment in one way or the other, always follows sinful failure. Repentance is the only answer. The Scripture says, *"The Children of Israel cried unto the LORD."*

This was the purpose of the Lord delivering Israel into the hand of Midian. He wanted them to be brought to a place where they would *"cry unto the LORD."* So many of the things that we chafe at are actually meant for our Blessing. The Lord squeezes us just enough so that we will cry out to Him, but even then our repentance too often is insincere and incomplete; nevertheless, *"crying unto the LORD"* is most definitely a positive beginning.

THE CROSS AND BLESSING

While an individual can definitely be Saved without understanding the implications of the Cross of Christ, and can remain Saved, still, a Believer cannot know the full Blessings of the Lord without properly understanding the Cross.

What do we mean by properly understanding the Cross?

Many Believers have a modicum of understanding regarding the Cross as it refers to Salvation, but virtually none at all as it refers to Sanctification. And yet, almost all

the teaching given by the Apostle Paul as it regards this great subject has to do with the Cross, as it pertains to our Sanctification.

What do we mean by Sanctification?

Unfortunately, the great Bible word *"Sanctification,"* is almost presently a nonword. This means that most of the Body of Christ have little understanding as to what Sanctification actually is.

Sanctification means that we are set apart from something unto something. In the case of the Believer, we are *"delivered from this present evil world,"* unto the Lord Jesus Christ (Gal. 1:4). It is the business of the Holy Spirit, in which He must have our co-operation, to get all the world out of us, and all of Christ in us. This doesn't make us more Saved, as one cannot be more Saved than when one trusts Christ at Salvation; however, one can definitely grow in Grace and the Knowledge of the Lord, thereby being developed in Righteousness and Holiness, with the Fruit of the Spirit becoming dominant within our lives. This is the purpose of the Holy Spirit, i.e., *"the Sanctification process."* It is not an easy task, or a quick task. And one simply cannot come to this place to where the Holy Spirit can carry out this tremendous work within our hearts and lives, without understanding the Cross as it refers to Sanctification.

This simply means that everything we receive from the Lord, and I mean everything, comes to us from Christ as the Source, and the Cross as the Means. It is the Cross of Christ, which makes everything possible. Then Blessings, even manifold Blessings, can and will come to the Child of God; however, these Blessings may be acutely different than we have at first been led to believe. They may mostly be in the realm of Righteousness and Holiness; however, there are no Blessings greater than that. That's what makes us *"Christlike!"*

IS IT WHO HE IS OR WHAT HE DID?

A young man asked me that question once, actually, he was ridiculing the Cross. He was insinuating, that the Cross was of little significance, and that everything we receive from the Lord comes to us because of Who the Lord actually is — God manifest in the flesh.

While *"Who"* He is, is of the utmost significance, as should be overly obvious, still, that's not what brings us Salvation. Let me explain.

Jesus Christ has always been God. Even when He became flesh, while He laid aside purposely the expression of His Deity, He never for a moment lost possession of His Deity. In other words, He never ceased to be God, even though He did not use His Powers of Deity while on Earth. He functioned as a man full of the Holy Spirit, and was thereby anointed by the Holy Spirit to carry forth the Miracles, etc. (Lk. 4:18-19).

As God, our Lord needed no anointing whatsoever, as should be obvious; however, as a man, the Man Christ Jesus, He most definitely did need the anointing.

And as an aside, if He needed the Holy Spirit, needed the anointing, where does that leave us? I think the answer is obvious.

And yet, even though Jesus was and is God, and ever shall be God, no one was Saved as a result of that. He was God when Adam and Eve fell. But they were not Saved merely because of that fact. Actually, there is no record that Adam and Eve ever came back to God.

For the some four thousand years from Adam to the Cross, Jesus was God, but no one during that time was Saved merely because of that, as important as that was. In fact, Jesus Christ, the Son of God, was the only One Who could have carried out this great Plan of Redemption. So it was absolutely imperative for Him to be Who He was — God manifested in the flesh.

But it was not until the Cross, not until His shed Blood, not until He said, *"Father, it is finished, into Your Hands I commend My Spirit,"* meaning that the price was now fully paid, that the Righteousness of a thrice-Holy God had been fully satisfied, that man could be Saved.

Of course, there were many who were Saved before the Cross, but they were Saved in the same identical way that we are now. The Sacrificial System, which God ordained immediately after the Fall, was a Type, a Shadow if you please, a Symbol, of the Lord Jesus Christ in the sacrificial offering of Himself.

In fact, there were literally millions of lambs, etc., offered up to God during that nearly four thousand years from Adam to the Cross. These sacrifices, all being Types of Christ and what He would do at Calvary's Cross, were but a stopgap measure, so to speak until Christ would come. People were Saved by believing not in the ritual or the ceremony of the Sacrificial System, but rather having Faith in what it represented, namely the coming Redeemer, the Lord Jesus. When Christ came, and went to Calvary's Cross, this satisfied all of the Old Covenant, and the Price that He paid, which was all done at the Cross. This made it possible that, *"whosoever will, may come and drink of the Water of Life freely"* (Rev. 22:17).

So, while it was absolutely imperative that He be Who He was, the Son of God, still, if He had remained that, and had not gone to the Cross, no one could have been Saved. It is *"what"* He did, and I continue to speak of the Cross, that makes it possible for our Redemption, and that alone!

That is the Gospel. Unfortunately, the modern Church doesn't too much see it that way. That's why Paul said: *"I marvel that you are so soon removed from Him* (the Holy Spirit) *Who called you into the Grace of Christ* (made possible by the Cross) *unto another gospel* (anything which doesn't have the Cross as its Object of Faith)*:*

"Which is not another (presents the fact that Satan's aim is not so much to deny the Gospel, which he can little do, as to corrupt it)*; but there be some who trouble you, and would pervert the Gospel of Christ* (once again, to make the Object of Faith something other than the Cross)*"* (Gal. 1:6-7).

And then Paul said, *"But though we* (Paul and his associates), *or an Angel from Heaven, preach any other gospel unto you than that which we have preached unto you* (Jesus Christ and Him Crucified), *let him be accursed* (eternally condemned; the Holy Spirit speaks this through Paul, making this very serious)*"* (Gal. 1:8).

Again we state, while Who He is, is of utmost significance, it is rather what He did, and we speak of the Cross, that makes every whit of Salvation possible (Jn. 3:16; Rev. 22:17).

(7) "AND IT CAME TO PASS, WHEN

THE CHILDREN OF ISRAEL CRIED UNTO THE LORD BECAUSE OF THE MIDIANITES,

(8) "THAT THE LORD SENT A PROPHET UNTO THE CHILDREN OF IS-RAEL, WHICH SAID UNTO THEM, THUS SAITH THE LORD GOD OF ISRAEL, I BROUGHT YOU UP FROM EGYPT, AND BROUGHT YOU FORTH OUT OF THE HOUSE OF BONDAGE;

(9) "AND I DELIVERED YOU OUT OF THE HAND OF THE EGYPTIANS, AND OUT OF THE HAND OF ALL WHO OPPRESSED YOU, AND DROVE THEM OUT FROM BE-FORE YOU, AND GAVE YOU THEIR LAND;

(10) "AND I SAID UNTO YOU, I AM THE LORD YOUR GOD; FEAR NOT THE GODS OF THE AMORITES, IN WHOSE LAND YOU DWELL: BUT YOU HAVE NOT OBEYED MY VOICE."

The synopsis is:

1. Why is it that so many Believers have to come to a place of utter defeat and hu-miliation, before they will properly cry to the Lord? If we would cry to the Lord at all times there would be no impoverishment, as ad-dressed in the previous Verses.

2. To their cry of distress, a Prophet is sent by the Lord; however, his call to Repen-tance is unheeded. This appears, as we shall see, from the fact that the men of Gideon's village wish to kill him, because he destroyed their idols.

3. The Ministry of the Prophet is to whip Believers into line with the Word of God. Regrettably, most of the time, their Messages are little appreciated.

THE PROPHET

As is obvious, there were Prophets at this particular time, as well as Prophetesses (4:4); however, the Office of the Prophet had not yet been established. In fact, Samuel would be the first man to stand in the Office of the Prophet, and because Israel then had a king.

It was by and through the Ministry of the Prophet that God guided Israel during Old Testament times. While the Prophet at times will foretell, which means to give a Word of Wisdom concerning the future, with some used greatly in that respect, such as Isaiah, etc., mostly, the Ministry of the True Prophet

was to serve as a Minister of Righteousness. It was their duty to point out the right and the wrong and to do so in no uncertain terms. As previously stated, often times their Mes-sages were strong, biting, critical, and at times even scathing. That's the reason they were not too much appreciated. In fact, Jesus said of Israel:

"O Jerusalem, Jerusalem (presents Jesus standing in the Temple when He gave this sorrowing account), you who kill the Proph-ets, and stone them which are sent unto you (presents the terrible animosity tendered to-ward these Messengers of God), how often would I have gathered your children together, even as a hen gathers her chickens under her wings, and you would not! (Proclaims ev-ery effort made by the Lord, and made 'of-ten,' to bring Israel back to her senses.)

"Behold, your house (the Temple or Jerusalem, are no longer God's habitation) is left unto you desolate (without God, which means they were at the mercy of Satan)" (Mat. 23:37-38).

Prophets under the New Covenant con-tinue to be a part of the fivefold Ministry (Eph. 4:11). And yet, there is a difference in the Office of the Prophet after the Cross then it was before the Cross.

Before the Cross, the Prophet in a sense, and I refer to godly Prophets, constituted the spiritual leaders of Israel. That is no longer the case under the New Covenant, although the Ministry of the true Prophet is still greatly needed, as should be obvious. Presently, it is the Apostle, which the Lord has set up as the titular leader of the Church.

The Office of the Apostle (Eph. 4:11), is that which is ordained by God and of God. In other words, just as men or women cannot be made a Prophet or a Prophetess by other men, likewise, Apostles fall into the same category. All constitute a Calling from God.

The Office of the Apostle is judged as such simply because of the Message that such a person has. Meaning, it is a Message, what-ever it might be, and which coincides per-fectly with the Word of God, and is that which the Church presently needs and desperately so. The Lord gives the Apostle such a Mes-sage, and through that Message, the Church receives guidance. Unfortunately, and as always, religious men attempt to usurp authority over the Call of God, and try to place leadership in the hands of elected officials of particular denominations, which God can never honor. While those particular denominational offices are not wrong within themselves, and can be used of God, still, that's not God's actual form of Government.

We learn from the Book of Acts and the Epistles, that the Lord leads the Church by the Ministry of the Apostle, and He continues to do such presently. While the enemy may do everything in his power to hinder the Message of the True Apostle (there are false ones) still, the Holy Spirit has a way of getting the Message out, whatever that Message might be.

The Lord now sends a Prophet to Israel in response to their cry.

This Prophet had, no doubt, been crying to Israel before now, but regrettably Israel wouldn't listen. Now the oppression by the Midianites has become so severe that they will now listen.

THE PROMISE

If it is to be noticed, the Lord through this unnamed Prophet takes Israel back to their deliverance out of Egypt and then reminds them of the Promise that He made to them, stipulating that if they would obey Him, He would drive all the enemies out of the land. In other words, He is telling them, that if they will believe Him now, He will still do exactly what He has promised. They need not fear these enemies, only that they should believe God.

As well, and in no uncertain terms, He is telling them that the reason for their present distress is because *"You have not obeyed My Voice."*

We should read those words very carefully, because they apply now, as then.

(11) "AND THERE CAME AN ANGEL OF THE LORD, AND SAT UNDER AN OAK WHICH WAS IN OPHRAH, THAT PERTAINED UNTO JOASH THE ABIEZRITE: AND HIS SON GIDEON THRESHED WHEAT BY THE WINEPRESS, TO HIDE IT FROM THE MIDIANITES.

(12) "AND THE ANGEL OF THE LORD APPEARED UNTO HIM, AND SAID UNTO

HIM, THE LORD IS WITH YOU, YOU MIGHTY MAN OF VALOUR.

(13) "AND GIDEON SAID UNTO HIM, OH MY LORD, IF THE LORD BE WITH US, WHY THEN IS ALL THIS BEFALLEN US? AND WHERE BE ALL HIS MIRACLES WHICH OUR FATHERS TOLD US OF, SAYING, DID NOT THE LORD BRING US UP FROM EGYPT? BUT NOW THE LORD HAS FORSAKEN US, AND DELIVERED US INTO THE HANDS OF THE MIDIANITES.

(14) "AND THE LORD LOOKED UPON HIM, AND SAID, GO IN THIS YOUR MIGHT, AND YOU SHALL SAVE ISRAEL FROM THE HAND OF THE MIDIANITES: HAVE NOT I SENT YOU?

(15) "AND HE SAID UNTO HIM, OH MY LORD, WHEREWITH SHALL I SAVE ISRAEL? BEHOLD, MY FAMILY IS POOR IN MANASSEH, AND I AM THE LEAST IN MY FATHER'S HOUSE.

(16) "AND THE LORD SAID UNTO HIM, SURELY I WILL BE WITH YOU, AND YOU SHALL SMITE THE MIDIANITES AS ONE MAN.

(17) "AND HE SAID UNTO HIM, IF NOW I HAVE FOUND GRACE IN YOUR SIGHT, THEN SHOW ME A SIGN THAT YOU TALK WITH ME.

(18) "DEPART NOT HENCE, I PRAY YOU, UNTIL I COME UNTO YOU, AND BRING FORTH MY PRESENT, AND SET IT BEFORE YOU. AND HE SAID, I WILL TARRY UNTIL YOU COME AGAIN.

(19) "AND GIDEON WENT IN, AND MADE READY A KID, AND UNLEAVENED CAKES OF AN EPHAH OF FLOUR; THE FLESH HE PUT IN A BASKET, AND HE PUT THE BROTH IN A POT. AND BROUGHT IT OUT UNTO HIM UNDER THE OAK, AND PRESENTED IT.

(20) "AND THE ANGEL OF GOD SAID UNTO HIM, TAKE THE FLESH AND THE UNLEAVENED CAKES, AND LAY THEM UPON THIS ROCK, AND POUR OUT THE BROTH. AND HE DID SO.

(21) "THEN THE ANGEL OF THE LORD PUT FORTH THE END OF THE STAFF THAT WAS IN HIS HAND, AND TOUCHED THE FLESH AND THE UNLEAVENED CAKES; AND THERE ROSE UP FIRE OUT OF THE ROCK, AND CONSUMED THE

FLESH AND THE ULEAVENED CAKES. THEN THE ANGEL OF THE LORD DEPARTED OUT OF HIS SIGHT.

(22) "AND WHEN GIDEON PERCEIVED THAT HE WAS AN ANGEL OF THE LORD, GIDEON SAID, ALAS, O LORD GOD! FOR BECAUSE I HAVE SEEN AN ANGEL OF THE LORD FACE TO FACE.

(23) "AND THE LORD SAID UNTO HIM, PEACE BE UNTO YOU; FEAR NOT: YOU SHALL NOT DIE.

(24) "THEN GIDEON BUILT AN ALTAR THERE UNTO THE LORD, AND CALLED IT JEHOVAH-SHALOM: UNTO THIS DAY IT IS YET IN OPHRAH OF THE ABIEZRITES."

The synopsis is:

1. The Israelites, God's chosen People, because of their sin, were hard-put to even feed themselves, much less enjoy prosperity, because the enemy took everything they had. Let's say it again: sin will take you further than you want to go, and cost you more than you can afford to pay.

2. The title *"Angel of the LORD,"* as given in the Twelfth Verse, is, in fact, a preincarnate appearance of the Lord Jesus Christ.

3. The Lord appeared to Gideon and said certain things to him. If He appeared to you at this moment, what would He say about you?

4. Oppression breathed in every word spoken by Gideon. The truth was, the Lord had not forsaken Israel, but, instead, Israel had forsaken the Lord. This was the reason for all of their problems.

5. The Lord, according to Verse 14, commissioned Gideon at this moment, and it is a commission of astounding proportions. Why Gideon?

6. The Fifteenth Verse proclaims at least one of the reasons that the Lord chose this man. He had an exalted opinion of the Lord, but none at all of himself. *"Meekness and lowliness"* are absolute necessities if one is to be truly used of God (Mat. 11:28-30).

7. Considering what the Lord has told him that he must do, Gideon wants to make certain that it is the Lord to Whom he is speaking, and not something else. So he asks for a sign.

8. The word *"presented"* as used in Verse 19, is a Hebrew word especially used of

NOTES

Sacrifices and Offerings (Amos 5:25).

9. The consuming of the Sacrifice by Fire from Heaven was the token of its being accepted. It was a Type of the Judgment of God, which would fall on the Lord Jesus Christ, necessitating His Death, in the giving of Himself as a Perfect Sacrifice, which would atone for the sins of man.

10. Gideon's action proclaims the fact that he based everything on the atoning Sacrifice. Faith in that Sacrifice, and what it represented, is the primary reason that the Lord chose Gideon. Faith in the atoning Work of Christ is the only Faith that God will recognize. Regrettably, as it regards the Church as a whole, this Type of Faith seems to be in short supply.

GIDEON THE FIFTH JUDGE

The *"Angel of the LORD"* referred to in Verse 11 is none other than the Lord Jesus Christ. He appeared unto Gideon.

In the Twelfth Verse Gideon is called by the Lord, *"You mighty man of valor,"* He previously said, *"The LORD is with you."* What a wonderful thing for the Lord to say about a man.

The spiritual declension of Israel must have grieved Gideon's heart greatly for the Lord to have addressed him in this manner. I wonder what God would say of each of us?

In the Thirteenth Verse Gideon would ask the question, *"where be all His Miracles which our fathers told us of?"* Gideon expressed the heart of so many Christians today who, having heard about the great things that God has done in the past, long for Him to do so today. There was a reason for no Miracles in Gideon's day, as there is a reason for precious few miracles in our day. The reason is sin.

MIGHTY

In Verses 12 and 14, the Lord refers to Gideon as *"mighty."*

He said this in the face of Gideon's statement, as recorded in Verse 15, *"I am the least in my father's house."* So how do we correlate the two?

What men refer to as *"mighty,"* and what God refers to as *"mighty"* are two different things all together. Paul said, regarding what the Lord said to him, and his response, *"My*

Grace is sufficient for you (speaks of enabling Grace, which is really the Goodness of God carried out by the Holy Spirit)*: for My Strength is made perfect in weakness.* (All Believers are weak, but the Lord tends to make us weaker, with the intention being that we then depend solely upon Him, thereby obtaining His Strength.) *Most gladly therefore will I rather glory in my infirmities* (because of the end result), *that the Power of Christ may rest upon me.* (If Paul needed so humbling and painful an experience of what the carnal nature is, it is evident that all Christians need it. Whatever weakens, belittles, and humiliates that proud and willful nature should be regarded by the Believer as most worthwhile)*"* (II Cor. 12:9).

Gideon looked at himself as weak, which he most definitely was, while the Lord called him *"mighty."*

The truth is, every single Believer, no matter how strong that Believer may think he personally is, when it comes to the powers of darkness, is weak.

THE CROSS

When the Lord appeared to Gideon, and told him, *"Surely I will be with you, and you shall smite the Midianites as one man,"* Gideon then offered up a sacrifice unto the Lord, which typified Calvary. The word *"presented"* in the Nineteenth Verse, as used here, and, as stated, is a Hebrew word especially used of Sacrifices and Offerings (Amos 5:25). In fact, all of this represented the Cross, and it was the secret of his strength.

Gideon was then told by the Lord, *"Take the flesh and the unleavened cakes, and lay them upon this rock, and pour out the broth."* That *"Rock,"* in essence, became an Altar.

This being done, the Lord *"put forth the end of the staff that was in His Hand, and touched the flesh and the unleavened cakes; and there rose up fire out of the rock, and consumed the flesh and the unleavened cakes."*

This fire was a Type of the Judgment of God that would fall upon Christ upon Calvary's Cross, instead of us, and at the same time, a symbol of the Holy Spirit, which would all be made possible by the Cross.

As is plain to see here in the Scriptures, Gideon's strength, along with his humility,

and the entirety of the Blessings of God, in fact, the very reason that the Lord chose this man, was all because of Gideon's Faith in the Sacrifice, i.e., *"The Cross of Christ."*

THE MODERN CHURCH AND THE CROSS OF CHRIST

The Cross of Christ is the Intersection, the Foundation, the Principal, actually, the Totality of the Christian experience. Take away the Cross, and there is nothing left. Unfortunately, the modern Church has removed the Cross, whether through it being ignored, or outright repudiated; nevertheless, the Cross is hardly anymore being preached in the modern Church. As a result, even though many of the mega-Churches are swollen with people, sadly and regrettably, for the most part they are unsaved. The truth is, there can be no true Salvation without the Cross. That's why Jesus Said, *"And I, if I be lifted up from the Earth* (refers to His Death at Calvary; He was *'lifted up'* on the Cross; the *'Cross'* is the Foundation of all Victory), *will draw all men unto Me* (refers to the Salvation of all who come to Him, believing what He did, and trusting in its atoning Work).

"This He said, signifying what death He should die (Reynolds says, *'In these Words, we learn that the attraction of the Cross of Christ will prove to be the mightiest, and most sovereign motive ever brought to bear on the human will, and, when wielded by the Holy Spirit as a Revelation of the matchless Love of God, will involve the most sweeping judicial sentence that can be pronounced upon the world and its prince.'*)*"* (Jn. 12:32-33).

WHY DOESN'T THE MODERN CHURCH PREACH THE CROSS?

There are many and varied reasons.

First of all, the Cross of Christ proclaims how bad that man actually is, and how good that God is, so good in fact, that He would send His Only Begotten Son to this cold, cruel world, in order to die on a Cross that man might be Saved. Man doesn't too much chafe at what the Lord does as it regards the Cross, but he most definitely does chafe at the idea that he is so wicked, so ungodly, that it would take the Cross for him to be Saved. Man doesn't like to think of himself in that capacity, and it is an affront to his pride to be told that; consequently, that's the reason that many Churches anymore do not preach the Cross. They openly state, that it is offensive, so it is not mentioned.

However, and as stated, and we will continue to state, by refusing to preach the Cross, they have taken the heart out of the Gospel, which means they are filling their Churches with people who have never really been Born-Again.

As well, the Cross is the constant reminder that sin is the problem. And again, man doesn't like to be reminded that he is a sinner, infected by this ungodly, loathsome leprosy of destruction. He likes to think of Himself as good, as benevolent, as a credit to the universe. But the truth is, and exactly as Paul said, the human race is so ungodly, so wicked, so perfidious, so demonic, that it is *"worthy of death"* (Rom. 1:32).

As an emblem, or a symbol, the Cross is accepted; however, that it is the ugly place of the blood-sodden spectacle of death and dying, which it most definitely was, it is rejected totally. Again we state, man doesn't like to admit that he is so evil and so vile that it took that in order for him to be Saved. But I like what one great Baptist Preacher said:

"Look at the awfulness of the Cross, the pain, the suffering, the shame, the humiliation, the awfulness of the poured out Blood, the dying and death of the Lamb of God, and then say, 'my sin did this!'"

As the first presentation was a Type of the Cross, now the Scripture plainly says that *"Gideon built an Altar there unto the LORD, and called it Jehovah-shalom."*

Once again we emphasize the fact, that Gideon most definitely knew the Lord, and knew Him by means of the Cross, which is the only way the Lord can be known. To use a New Testament vernacular, if it's not the Cross, then it's *"another Jesus"* (II Cor. 11:4).

(25) "AND IT CAME TO PASS THE SAME NIGHT, THAT THE LORD SAID UNTO HIM, TAKE YOUR FATHER'S YOUNG BULLOCK, EVEN THE SECOND BULLOCK OF SEVEN YEARS OLD, AND THROW DOWN THE ALTAR OF BAAL THAT YOUR FATHER HAS, AND CUT DOWN THE GROVE THAT IS BY IT:

(26) "AND BUILD AN ALTAR UNTO THE LORD YOUR GOD UPON THE TOP OF THIS ROCK, IN THE ORDERED PLACE, AND TAKE THE SECOND BULLOCK, AND OFFER A BURNT SACRIFICE WITH THE WOOD OF THE GROVE WHICH YOU SHALL CUT DOWN.

(27) "THEN GIDEON TOOK TEN MEN OF HIS SERVANTS, AND DID AS THE LORD HAD SAID UNTO HIM: AND SO IT WAS, BECAUSE HE FEARED HIS FATHER'S HOUSEHOLD, AND THE MEN OF THE CITY, THAT HE COULD NOT DO IT BY DAY, THAT HE DID IT BY NIGHT.

(28) "AND WHEN THE MEN OF THE CITY AROSE EARLY IN THE MORNING, BEHOLD, THE ALTAR OF BAAL WAS CAST DOWN, AND THE GROVE WAS CUT DOWN THAT WAS BY IT, AND THE SECOND BULLOCK WAS OFFERED UPON THE ALTAR THAT WAS BUILT.

(29) "AND THEY SAID ONE TO ANOTHER, WHO HAS DONE THIS THING? AND WHEN THEY INQUIRED AND ASKED, THEY SAID, GIDEON THE SON OF JOASH HAS DONE THIS THING.

(30) "THEN THE MEN OF THE CITY SAID UNTO JOASH, BRING OUT YOUR SON, THAT HE MAY DIE: BECAUSE HE HAS CAST DOWN THE ALTAR OF BAAL, AND BECAUSE HE HAS CUT DOWN THE GROVE THAT WAS BY IT.

(31) "AND JOASH SAID UNTO ALL WHO STOOD AGAINST HIM, WILL YOU PLEAD FOR BAAL? WILL YOU SAVE HIM? HE WHO WILL PLEAD FOR HIM, LET HIM BE PUT TO DEATH WHILE IT IS YET MORNING: IF HE BE A GOD, LET HIM PLEAD FOR HIMSELF, BECAUSE ONE HAS CAST DOWN HIS ALTAR.

(32) "THEREFORE ON THAT DAY HE CALLED HIM JERUB-BAAL, SAYING, LET BAAL PLEAD AGAINST HIM, BECAUSE HE HAS THROWN DOWN HIS ALTAR.

(33) "THEN ALL THE MIDIANITES AND THE AMALEKITES AND THE CHILDREN OF THE EAST WERE GATHERED TOGETHER, AND WENT OVER, AND PITCHED IN THE VALLEY OF JEZREEL.

(34) "BUT THE SPIRIT OF THE LORD

NOTES

CAME UPON GIDEON, AND HE BLEW A TRUMPET; AND ABIEZER WAS GATHERED AFTER HIM.

(35) "AND HE SENT MESSENGERS THROUGHOUT ALL MANASSEH; WHO ALSO WAS GATHERED AFTER HIM: AND HE SENT MESSENGERS UNTO ASHER, AND UNTO ZEBULUN, AND UNTO NAPHTALI; AND THEY CAME UP TO MEET THEM."

The exegesis is:

1. It seems that Gideon was basically the only one in his family who truly lived for God; his father worshipped *"Baal,"* one of the most vulgar, and hideous idol gods.

2. Gideon was instructed by the Lord to build an Altar where the altar of Baal had been; this is the crying need of the modern Church; it needs to turn from altars of its own making, and place its Faith exclusively in Christ and His Cross.

3. The *"grove"* was really idols of the *"Asherah,"* several of which evidently had been made out of wood; this was one of the most despicable of idols, actually a portrayal of the male member; this is how far that Gideon's family had sunk down spiritually.

4. Men grow angry when their idols are touched, and religious men most of all.

5. Those who follow idolatry, even in modern day religion, and to be sure, and sadly, the modern Church is full of it, respond to the Cross exactly as these men did to Gideon, wanting to kill him.

6. It seems as if the courage of Joash, Gideon's father was rising under the influence of his son's brave deed. In essence, he says that instead of Gideon being killed, that he, Joash would kill anyone who would plead for Baal. His answer was, *"Let Baal plead for himself"*; however, these heathen gods were nothing, only figments of man's imagination.

7. Gideon was given the nickname of *"Jerub-baal"* which means *"is an idol anything?"* This showed his contempt for these heathen gods.

8. The Thirty-third Verse proclaims the periodic foray of the Midianites into Israel, at which time they would plunder the land; they would find that their reception now would not be as before.

9. The whole family of Abiezer, so says

Verse 34, numbering probably thousands, sprang to Gideon's side; the Spirit of the Lord was upon him, and the blowing of the trumpet, in essence, said it was time to strike.

THROW DOWN THE ALTAR OF BAAL

In the Twenty-sixth Verse Gideon was instructed to *"offer a Burnt Sacrifice with wood of the grove."* This took Israel to Calvary. Even though Israel would not have understood the word *"Calvary,"* still, in symbolism, this is what it meant. The Lord is forever taking the Church back to Calvary.

The Thirtieth Verse says, *"Because he has cast down the altar of Baal,"* portrays to us that despite Israel's crying unto the Lord (Vs. 6), there was still no Repentance.

The men of the city would try to kill Gideon because of this. Despite the Prophet of God being sent and proclaiming God's Message to them, they were still worshipping Baal. Men do not repent easily, and without proper leadership they will not repent at all. It must be understood that the altar of Baal had been erected at Gideon's father's house (Vs. 25). The Scripture says, and emphatically so, *"Judgment must first begin at the house of God."* Gideon cannot hope to lead Israel into the destruction of their own idols until his is first destroyed. So, destroyed it is.

THE SPIRIT OF THE LORD

The Thirty-fourth Verse says, *"But the Spirit of the LORD came upon Gideon, and he blew a trumpet."*

If it is to be noticed here, the *"Spirit of the LORD"* is always connected in some way with the Cross of Christ, of which the Sacrificial System of the Old Testament was a Type. In fact, the Holy Spirit is unalterably intertwined so to speak, with the Cross of Christ, so much, in fact, that it is referred to in the Word of God as a *"Law."* Paul said:

"For the Law of the Spirit of Life in Christ Jesus has made me free from the Law of Sin and Death" (Rom. 8:2).

So we see here how that Holy Spirit works so closely with the Crucified Christ. It is the Crucifixion, i.e., *"the Cross,"* which gives the Holy Spirit the legal right to function as He does.

When we go to the Book of Revelation we see another perfect example of this. The Scripture says, and I quote from THE EXPOSITOR'S STUDY BIBLE:

"And I beheld, and, lo, in the midst of the Throne and of the four Beasts, and in the midst of the Elders, stood a Lamb as it had been slain (the Crucifixion of Christ is represented here by the word *'Lamb,'* which refers to the fact that it was the Cross which redeemed mankind; the slain Lamb Alone has redeemed all things), *having seven horns* (horns denote dominion, and *'seven'* denotes total dominion; all of this was done for you and me, meaning that we can have total dominion over the powers of darkness, and in every capacity; so there is no excuse for a lack of victory) *and seven eyes* (denotes total, perfect, pure, and complete illumination of all things Spiritual, which is again made possible for you and me by the Cross; if the Believer makes the Cross the Object of his Faith, he will never be drawn away by false doctrine), *which are the Seven Spirits of God sent forth into all the Earth* (signifying that the Holy Spirit, in all His Perfection and universality, functions entirely within the perimeters of the Finished Work of Christ; in other words, it is required that we ever make the Cross the Object of our Faith, which gives the Holy Spirit latitude, and guarantees the *'dominion,'* and the *'illumination'* [Isa. 11:2; Rom. 8:2])" (Rev. 5:6).

We see in this Passage in Revelation that the Holy Spirit is so intertwined with the slain Lamb, so to speak, that They are actually indivisible. This shows us how closely the Holy Spirit works with Christ, and that it is the Cross, which has made everything possible.

Therefore, when it said, *"But the Spirit of the LORD came upon Gideon,"* it had its links totally and completely to the Cross.

(36) "AND GIDEON SAID UNTO GOD, IF YOU WILL SAVE ISRAEL BY MY HAND, AS YOU HAVE SAID,

(37) "BEHOLD, I WILL PUT A FLEECE OF WOOL IN THE FLOOR; AND IF THE DEW BE ON THE FLEECE ONLY, AND IT BE DRY UPON ALL THE EARTH BESIDE, THEN SHALL I KNOW THAT YOU WILL SAVE ISRAEL BY MY HAND, AS YOU HAVE SAID.

(38) "AND IT WAS SO: FOR HE ROSE UP EARLY ON THE MORROW, AND THRUST THE FLEECE TOGETHER, AND WRINGED THE DEW OUT OF THE FLEECE, A BOWL FULL OF WATER.

(39) "AND GIDEON SAID UNTO GOD, LET NOT YOUR ANGER BE HOT AGAINST ME, AND I WILL SPEAK BUT THIS ONCE; LET ME PROVE, I PRAY YOU, BUT THIS ONCE WITH THE FLEECE; LET IT NOW BE DRY ONLY UPON THE FLEECE, AND UPON ALL THE GROUND LET THERE BE DEW.

(40) "AND GOD DID SO THAT NIGHT: FOR IT WAS DRY UPON THE FLEECE ONLY, AND THERE WAS DEW ON ALL THE GROUND."

The composition is:

1. Concerning this, Williams says, *"The double test with the fleece made plain to Gideon that God could withhold or grant blessing.*

2. *"He could bless Gideon, and no one else; and, on the other hand, He could bless everybody else, and not Gideon.*

3. *"Rahab and Jericho illustrate the one action and Ninevah and Jonah the other."*[1]

THE FLEECE

From this episode with Gideon concerning the fleece, millions of Believers through the centuries, for one reason or the other, have *"put out a fleece."*

The double test with the fleece made plain to Gideon that God could withhold Blessing or grant Blessing. It was all with the Lord. Even though man plays his part, it is God Who does the doing.

Was it wrong for Gideon to demand the sign of the fleece?

There is no record in the Word of God that the Lord reprimanded Gideon in any fashion, or was displeased in any fashion. In fact, he did exactly what Gideon requested.

But we must understand that Gideon little at that time had the Word of God, as it refers to past history. He did have the Word of the Lord by word of mouth, but having it as we have it today in the form of the Bible, even though the Pentateuch had already been written, still, considering the poverty of Gideon's house, he probably did not have a copy of that. But he definitely did have the visitation from the Lord, which occasioned the fleece.

Presently, considering the proliferation of the Word of God, there should not be any reason for a fleece, so to speak. But yet, I suppose that all of us at one time or the other, have *"put out a fleece"* before the Lord. Sometimes the Lord honors it, and sometimes He doesn't!

A PERSONAL EXAMPLE

SonLife Radio can truly be said to be a Miracle from God. But it did not begin easily.

The way this Network operates is by Satellite. The Mother Station in Baton Rouge provides all the programming, which means that whatever we program here is at the same time programmed on all of our other Stations all across the nation, and at the same time. As stated, it is done by Satellite.

But yet, it is absolutely imperative that one have the Mother Station, for without that, you can't feed the other Stations, as should be obvious.

We had made application for the Mother Station, which came to be WJFM-FM in about 1985. We were awarded the Station about three years later; however, there was a competing application, which means that someone was contesting our ownership. It went before the FCC (Federal Communications Commission) and we were awarded the Station again. In fact, this went on several times.

In the meantime, I found that they could keep contesting our ownership of the Station indefinitely. And that's exactly what they were doing.

We went ahead and took over the Station in 1996, that is if I remember the year correctly. (We had owned an A.M. Station in Baton Rouge for approximately 20 years, but now converted to the F.M., and sold the A.M.). But yet when we took over the Station, our legal counsel in Washington informed us that it was possible for us to lose the Station. In other words, the competing application could conceivably win out.

In 1999 the Lord gave me a great burden for Radio, told me how to program the Stations, and told me to put Stations all over

the nation. That we set out to do. But we still had hanging over our head, this legal problem, which did not seem to have a solution.

Then the F.C.C. changed the rules, which made it easier for the competing application to win their argument. This meant, we could lose the Station. This meant that the Stations we had, which were then only three or four if I remember correctly, could not be fed from the Mother Station, simply because we wouldn't have a Mother Station, that is if the Station was lost.

About this time, the competing individuals made several very bold threats that they were going to take the Station, all due to the changes in the rules, etc. To be frank, I did not know what to do, except take it to the Lord. In fact, we had done everything legally we could do, and were continuing to do so, but seemingly to no avail.

On the day in question, I went before the Lord, very heavy of heart.

The questions came thick and fast, *"Lord, You told me what to do with Radio. You told me to put Stations all over this nation, and that being the case, how could we now lose this Station?"*

Of course, we couldn't lose it, but at the same time, at a time like that it's very easy to see the problems, and not see the Promise of the Lord.

As I went to prayer that afternoon, as stated, my heart heavy regarding the situation, which we had struggled with for over fifteen years. But it actually looked, at least at this time, like we could lose the Station.

As I went before the Lord, I began to pour out my heart to Him, even in desperation. To be sure, I had prayed about the thing many, many times before, as would be obvious, but it now was different.

For the first time in memory, I put out a *"fleece"* before Him. I remember apologizing to the Lord, telling Him that I shouldn't need such, but if He would see fit to give me a sign, I would very much appreciate it.

I went on praying about other things, and actually forgot about the situation. And as I was praying, I quoted the words of a little chorus, which we sing at Family Worship Center continuously.

*"We are able to go up and take the
    country,
"And possess the land from Jordan unto
    the Sea.
"Though the giants may be there our
    way to hinder,
"Our Lord has given us the Victory."*

When I said that last line, the Presence of
the Lord came all over me, *"Our Lord has
given us the Victory."*

I knew that the Lord was answering my
petition. He had given me a sign.

Not long after, the problems miraculously
disappeared, and the Station was ours.

OUR LORD HAS GIVEN US THE VICTORY!

CHAPTER 7

(1) "THEN JERUB-BAAL, WHO IS
GIDEON, AND ALL THE PEOPLE WHO
WERE WITH HIM, ROSE UP EARLY, AND
PITCHED BESIDE THE WELL OF HAROD:
SO THAT THE HOST OF THE MIDIANITES
WERE ON THE NORTH SIDE OF THEM,
BY THE HILL OF MOREH, IN THE VALLEY.

(2) "AND THE LORD SAID UNTO
GIDEON, THE PEOPLE WHO ARE WITH
YOU ARE TOO MANY FOR ME TO GIVE
THE MIDIANITES INTO THEIR HANDS,
LEST ISRAEL VAUNT THEMSELVES
AGAINST ME, SAYING, MY OWN HAND
HAS SAVED ME.

(3) "NOW THEREFORE GO TO, PRO-
CLAIM IN THE EARS OF THE PEOPLE,
SAYING, WHOSOEVER IS FEARFUL AND
AFRAID, LET HIM RETURN AND DEPART
EARLY FROM MOUNT GILEAD. AND
THERE RETURNED OF THE PEOPLE
TWENTY AND TWO THOUSAND; AND
THERE REMAINED TEN THOUSAND.

(4) "AND THE LORD SAID UNTO
GIDEON, THE PEOPLE ARE YET TOO
MANY; BRING THEM DOWN UNTO THE
WATER, AND I WILL TRY THEM FOR YOU
THERE: AND IT SHALL BE, THAT OF
WHOM I SAY UNTO YOU, THIS SHALL GO
WITH YOU, THE SAME SHALL GO WITH
YOU; AND OF WHOMSOEVER I SAY UNTO
YOU, THIS SHALL NOT GO WITH YOU,

NOTES

THE SAME SHALL NOT GO.

(5) "SO HE BROUGHT DOWN THE
PEOPLE UNTO THE WATER: AND THE
LORD SAID UNTO GIDEON, EVERY ONE
WHO LAPS OF THE WATER WITH HIS
TONGUE, AS A DOG LAPS, HIM SHALL
YOU SET BY HIMSELF; LIKEWISE EVERY
ONE WHO BOWS DOWN UPON HIS
KNEES TO DRINK.

(6) "AND THE NUMBER OF THEM WHO
LAPPED, PUTTING THEIR HAND TO
THEIR MOUTH, WERE THREE HUNDRED
MEN: BUT ALL THE REST OF THE
PEOPLE BOWED DOWN UPON THEIR
KNEES TO DRINK WATER.

(7) "AND THE LORD SAID UNTO
GIDEON, BY THE THREE HUNDRED MEN
WHO LAPPED WILL I SAVE YOU, AND DE-
LIVER THE MIDIANITES INTO YOUR
HAND: AND LET ALL THE OTHER PEOPLE
GO EVERY MAN UNTO HIS PLACE.

(8) "SO THE PEOPLE TOOK VICTUALS
IN THEIR HAND, AND THEIR TRUMPETS:
AND HE SENT ALL THE REST OF ISRAEL
EVERY MAN UNTO HIS TENT, AND RE-
TAINED THOSE THREE HUNDRED MEN:
AND THE HOST OF MIDIAN WAS BE-
NEATH HIM IN THE VALLEY."

The construction is:

1. The nickname *"Jerub-baal"* is used
here by the Holy Spirit in order to proclaim
the fact that Gideon is opposed to all idols,
and of every description.

2. The cowardly were given the option of
returning home, and 22,000 did so; there is
no place for *"fear"* in the Work of God; the
Lord cannot use such, as is so very much
evidenced here.

3. Jonathan, Saul's son, would later say,
*"there is no restraint to the LORD to save by
many or by few"* (I Sam. 14:6).

Those who lapped water had their hands
free in order to fight, if necessary, and,
thereby, showed their diligence. There were
three hundred of these, and the Lord used
those particular people. In fact, He did not
really need anyone, as ought to be obvious,
but He allows us to participate in His Work,
in order to build us up in the Faith.

THREE HUNDRED MEN OF FAITH

This Chapter is the story of great Faith

and great Victory.

The ever continuing thrust of the Church is for more and more numbers. While it is certainly true that numbers are important, still, large numbers portray no great spirituality with God; actually, in this case, they would portray the very opposite. God is not looking for mere numbers; He is looking for men and women who have Faith. And irrespective of their small number, tremendous victories will be won.

A PERSONAL EXPERIENCE

Many years ago, while preaching a Campmeeting with A.N. Trotter, he said in one of his messages something I've never forgotten:

"The Church is running aground on three things: money, education, and people."

That needs to be looked at very closely. First of all, it takes money for all of us to operate. Second, God places no premium on ignorance, and last of all, we are here trying to reach people. But what the man meant was this:

If we trim our Spiritual sails, pervert the Word of God, depend on anything and everything other than the Holy Spirit, while we may get more money and more people, our getting them in the long run will be a wasted effort. It is the Gospel of Jesus Christ alone, and we mean the unperverted Gospel, which will set the captive free. Paul said to the Galatians, and should be said now as well, *"I marvel that you are so soon removed from Him* (the Holy Spirit) *Who called you into the Grace of Christ* (made possible by the Cross) *unto another gospel* (anything which doesn't have the Cross as it's Object of Faith):

"Which is not another (presents the fact that Satan's aim is not so much to deny the Gospel, which he can little do, as to corrupt it); *but there be some who trouble you, and would pervert the Gospel of Christ* (once again, to make the object of Faith something other than the Cross).

The Apostle then said, *"But though we* (Paul and his associates), *or an Angel from Heaven, preach any other gospel unto you than that which we have preached unto you* (Jesus Christ and Him Crucified), *let him be accursed* (eternally condemned; the Holy Spirit speaks this through Paul, making this

NOTES

very serious)" (Gal. 1:6-8).

PERVERTING THE GOSPEL

How does one pervert the Gospel?

To cut straight through to the bottom line, the Gospel of Jesus Christ is perverted, when anything is made the object of faith other than the Cross of Christ. We must remember that. It is the Cross or it is nothing!

"Pervert" in the Greek is *"metastrepho,"* and means, *"to twist, to turn around, to reverse, to turn back again."*

There is only one Gospel. Actually, Paul said:

"One Lord (Jesus Christ), *one Faith* (what He did at the Cross), *one Baptism* (our Salvation, referring to Believers baptized into Christ, which was done at the Cross; it has nothing to do with Water Baptism [Rom. 6:3-5])" (Eph. 4:5).

Simply said, there is *"one Faith."* If that Faith is followed, and followed minutely, which is the Message of the Cross, emphasized in the Word *"one Baptism,"* then the victory that comes from following that Faith will be realized.

Why is it that the Message of the Cross is possibly the most difficult for Believers to accept? That's a strange question!

One can understand the world, which knows nothing of the Cross, rejecting this which the Lord has done, but when one realizes that the Church is the greatest rejecter of all, then the situation becomes far more complex.

This struggle has always existed. It began almost immediately after the Garden of Eden episode. While it was a few years, still, the Fourth Chapter of Genesis records the saga of Cain and Abel. Cain did not desire to, and, in fact, would not accept what the Lord had demanded, which was the slain lamb, which represented Christ. He did not deny the need for sacrifice, nor the need for an Altar, but he denied what was to be offered up on that Altar, namely the slain lamb, which typified the coming Saviour.

During Paul's time, the greatest problem in the Church of that day was the Law/Grace issue. Or one might say, the works/Grace issue. One can understand, as stated, evil men rejecting this, but good men have a struggle with it as well. In fact, some good men reject it.

JAMES, THE LORD'S BROTHER

While James made the right decision as it regards the Gentiles accepting Christ, he made the wrong decision as it regards the Jews. He left them in Law bondage (Acts 15:7-21). While we dare not take away from the Godliness of James, I do believe that we are absolutely correct as it regards the decision that he made in Jerusalem concerning this issue. It was partially right, but again, partially wrong. How do I know it was wrong?

THE REVELATION

Paul stated, *"Then fourteen years after I went up again to Jerusalem with Barnabas* (was probably the Jerusalem Council [Acts 15:1-35]), *and took Titus with me also.*

"And I went up by Revelation (the Lord told him to go), *and communicated unto them that Gospel which I preach among the Gentiles* (the Message of the Cross), *but privately to them which were of reputation* (to at least some of the original Twelve), *lest by any means I should run, or had run, in vain.* (If the Twelve, or even James the Lord's Brother, repudiated His Gospel of Grace, at least as far as the Gentiles were concerned, this would create an insurmountable barrier)" (Gal. 2:1-2).

This Passage is very important. It concerned the matter of the Law/Grace issue.

The Lord by Revelation told Paul to go to Jerusalem and to explain the Message of the Cross, i.e., *"The New Covenant,"* to all who were there, and especially those who were in positions of leadership.

Now please understand, when Paul used the phrase, *"went up by Revelation"* he was speaking of the fact that what he now did was solely and totally of the Lord. This meant, that if His Gospel was rejected that, in essence, Jesus Christ was rejected. As stated, James did accept what Paul proclaimed, but only for the Gentiles. He did not accept it as it regards the Jews, which caused untold problems.

When we say that he didn't accept it as it regards the Jews, we are meaning that James along with the other Jews in Jerusalem,

continued to try to keep the Law, while at the same time proclaim the Lord Jesus Christ. Let me tell you some things about James.

IT IS THE MESSAGE OF THE CROSS ALONE

It is said that James prayed so much until he was reputed to have *"camel knees."* That means he knelt on his knees so much, that they flattened out like the knees of a camel. This tells us something.

It tells us how valuable, how important that a proper prayer life is, but at the same time, it also tells us, that a proper prayer life, even the type that James had, which was totally out of the ordinary as should be obvious, still, will not give one victory over the world, the flesh, and the Devil.

Now if the reader thinks that we are demeaning prayer, then the reader is completely missing the point all together. It is absolutely essential that every Believer have a prayer life. If not, there will be precious little or no relationship with the Lord. But what I am stating is, that if one thinks that one can overcome the world by a concentrated prayer life, as important as that prayer life is, and as much as that person will be blessed by that prayer life, they will find to their chagrin, that there is no victory in that capacity. While one can definitely find the answer to the questions while in prayer, and while prayer will grandly help and grandly add to what one is doing, still, the act of just praying so much, as valuable as it might be, will not bring about victory. When this happens, then prayer, which is the greatest Christian discipline, is turned into works, which the Lord can never honor.

It is also stated that James died a martyr's death, actually being thrown from the pinnacle of the Temple. So, no one can question this man's consecration or dedication to the Lord or his love for the Lord. But James, a good man, a Godly man, still, made the wrong choice as it regards the Jews, and Judgment was the result.

THE JUDGMENT OF GOD

When Paul presented his Message to the Jewish segment of the Church, some few accepted it, many, if not most, didn't. Did they die lost?

Some did, and some didn't. The Book of Hebrews is a testimony to what I've just stated.

It's not hard at all for men to accept religion, because religion is devised by men. The Cross is all of God and, therefore, it is difficult for many, if not most, to accept.

MY OWN HAND HAS SAVED ME

The latter portion of the Second Verse says, *"My own hand has saved me."* Man has ever wanted to have a hand in his own Salvation. Our *"own hand"* is probably the greatest hindrance to our spiritual victory. The old hymn says this:

"Nothing, either great or small,
"Nothing, sinner, no,
"Jesus did it, did it all,
"Long, long ago!"

The defeat by the Lord of the Midianites, was a type of the way and manner in which victory is won in our lives. The Lord positioned this battle so that none could say, *"my own hand has saved me,"* which man, and especially religious man, is so prone to do.

In fact, this very idea, this very claim is the seat of the problem. To accept the Cross is to disavow our own efforts and ability. To reject the Cross, means that one has opted for his own strength and ability, which God can never honor. Once again, that is the problem, and has always been the problem. That's one of the reasons the Cross is rejected.

Man loves to think that his own efforts, his own ability, his own strength, his own works, have contributed something to his Salvation, or his walk with God. In fact, Christians are very quick to tell the unsaved that their works cannot earn God's approval, then turn around and try to earn His approval as it regards living for Him. It can't be done! But we are loath to admit that.

In order to be Saved, the only thing the believing sinner can do is to place his Faith and trust in Christ. While he knows almost nothing about it, still, God requires him to believe in the Lord (Jn. 3:16).

When it comes to living for God, which concerns our every day walk, the situation is identical. It is the same!

The Christian is to simply place his Faith

in Christ and the Cross, and not allow it to be moved to anything else, constantly believing twenty-four hours a day. This means that he knows that Christ is the Source of all things, while the Cross is the Means!

Now how hard is that?

What is it about that that you don't understand?

The truth is, it's not hard at all. In fact, it's about the most simple thing that one could ever think or do. But yet, it is rejected in most Christian circles.

Why?

Men love to boast of who they are in the Lord, and what they do for the Lord. But Paul said:

"But God forbid that I should glory (boast), *save in the Cross of our Lord Jesus Christ* (what the opponents of Paul sought to escape at the price of insincerity is the Apostle's only basis of exultation), *by Whom the world is crucified unto me, and I unto the world* (The only way we can overcome the world, and I mean the only way, is by placing our Faith exclusively in the Cross of Christ and keeping it there)*" (Gal. 6:14).

FEAR

The Third Verse says, *"Whosoever is fearful and afraid, let him return and depart."* As we look at the story of Gideon, we are probably seeing close to the true percentage in the Church who really have Faith. Out of 32,000, only some 301 (counting Gideon) had Faith. That's about one percent of the total. It probably characterizes the modern-day Church. Out of this multitude fear was the greatest hindrance then, and fear is, no doubt, the greatest hindrance now. Fear always follows faithlessness.

The first word that fallen man (Adam) uttered was, *"I was afraid."* Most everything that is done in the world is done from a basis of fear. That is sad but true.

Wars begin because of fear. Most laws are made by Congress because of fear. Most Church splits occur because of fear. Most preachers do the faithless things they do simply because of fear — mostly man fear.

Fear always says that man is in control and places God in a secondary position. Faith says that God is in control, and makes little difference as to what man does.

LACK OF DILIGENCE

After those who were fearful went home, the Scripture says, *"and there remained ten thousand."* These people could certainly be construed as godly, and yet the Lord will send 9,700 home.

Why?

They were not vigilant. In other words, they bent down over the water in order to drink, which means they were then blind to the enemy. Three hundred did the opposite. They cupped the water in their hands and drank from their hands, thereby continuing their diligence.

God had truly called the 9,700, but not to be soldiers. That's probably one of the biggest problems in the modern Church.

God has a special work for *every single* Believer to do. But many times, said Believer doesn't want to do what God has called him to do. He wants to do something someone else is doing, because he thinks it looks exciting or romantic, or makes him look good, etc.

While it's hard enough trying to do what God has really called us to do, trying to do what He hasn't called us to do is flat out impossible. And yet, that is the position of far too many Believers.

God give us Believers who know what God has called them to do, and are setting about, trying with all of their ability and faith, to carry out that task. They are the ones who uphold the Church. They are Gideon's three hundred, so to speak!

(9) "AND IT CAME TO PASS THE SAME NIGHT, THAT THE LORD SAID UNTO HIM, ARISE, GET YOU DOWN UNTO THE HOST; FOR I HAVE DELIVERED IT INTO YOUR HAND.

(10) "BUT IF YOU FEAR TO GO DOWN, GO YOU WITH PHURAH YOUR SERVANT DOWN TO THE HOST:

(11) "AND YOU SHALL HEAR WHAT THEY SAY; AND AFTERWARD SHALL YOUR HANDS BE STRENGTHENED TO GO DOWN UNTO THE HOST. THEN WENT HE DOWN WITH PHURAH HIS SERVANT UNTO THE OUTSIDE OF THE ARMED MEN WHO WERE IN THE HOST.

NOTES

(12) "AND THE MIDIANITES AND THE AMALEKITES AND ALL THE CHILDREN OF THE EAST LAY ALONG IN THE VALLEY LIKE GRASSHOPPERS FOR MULTITUDE; AND THEIR CAMELS WERE WITHOUT NUMBER, AS THE SAND BY THE SEA SIDE FOR MULTITUDE.

(13) "AND WHEN GIDEON WAS COME, BEHOLD THERE WAS A MAN WHO TOLD A DREAM UNTO HIS FELLOW, AND SAID, BEHOLD, I DREAMED A DREAM, AND, LO, A CAKE OF BARLEY BREAD TUMBLED INTO THE HOST OF MIDIAN, AND CAME UNTO A TENT, AND SMOTE IT THAT IT FELL, AND OVERTURNED IT, THAT THE TENT LAY ALONG.

(14) "AND HIS FELLOW ANSWERED AND SAID, THIS IS NOTHING ELSE SAVE THE SWORD OF GIDEON THE SON OF JOASH, A MAN OF ISRAEL: FOR INTO HIS HAND HAS GOD DELIVERED MIDIAN, AND ALL THE HOST."

The overview is:

1. The *"host"* of Verse Ten consisted of approximately 135,000 men [8:10]; Gideon was to face this *"host"* with just 300 men; despite what the Lord had told him, one can well understand his consternation. He, no doubt, wondered how in the world the Lord would deliver that mighty host into His Hand!

2. Satan, it seems, always brings formidable odds against the Believer.

3. Gideon and his servant, standing outside the tent in the dark, overheard this conversation. Bread made from barley was the poorest of all bread; so the Lord is showing Gideon that one cake of barley bread, with God behind it, could overturn the greatest tent in the camp of Midian, symbolizing the leadership of the army of the enemy.

4. The dream and the interpretation are striking evidences of the terror which Gideon's name had already inspired among the Midianites; the Lord had placed the fear of Gideon into the hearts of the enemy.

THE ENCOURAGING WORD
TO GIDEON

The Ninth Verse says, *"That the LORD said unto him, Arise."* Fear always finds an excuse for not doing what God has said. Faith always says, *"Arise."*

How is it that the Lord did not reprimand Gideon for his fear, when 22,000 other Israelites were sent home because of fear?

I think it can be said without fear of contradiction, that every single Believer, even the very Godliest, as was Gideon, at times, entertains fear. But the difference is, Gideon and those like him, while possibly pausing for a moment, do not stop their advance. When he had clear direction from the Lord, he would follow that direction. Others, because of fear, will do nothing! That, God cannot abide.

Why did the Lord desire that Phurah the servant go with Gideon?

For all the obvious reasons, he desired that there be at least two who would hear (overhear) the dream that God had given to a Midianite. The Scripture says, *"In the mouths of two or three witnesses"* (Deut. 17:6; Mat. 18:16).

OPPOSITION

The Twelfth Verse says, *"Without number."* In other words, Satan's opposition was so overwhelming that it beggared description. If we are looking at the problem with fear, then, seemingly, the number continues to grow. If we are looking at it with Faith, we cease to see the number, but we see God.

The test designed by the Lord for Gideon was clear and simple. He was to defeat an army of 135,000 men (8:10). He had 300 men with which to do such!

Great numbers regarding opposition means absolutely nothing to the Lord. Please look carefully at the following:

"He tells the number of the stars; He calls them all by their names. (If we take this literally, and we certainly should, this means that God calls all the stars by name (Ps.147:4).

In the 1950's, astronomers claimed that there were about forty sextillion stars in the vast universe, which are suns to other planets. They have presently increased that number, but have left it open-ended. [Forty sextillion is the number forty followed by twenty-one zeroes.] At any rate, God knows the exact number, for He made them [Isa. 45:18].

It is said that there are approximately 500,000 words in Webster's Unabridged Dictionary. If all the names of all the stars were

put in books of this size, it would take Eighty Quadrillion books to list the name of every star. [Eighty Quadrillion is the number eighty followed by fifteen zeroes.])

Understanding this, I think we should come to the conclusion that God can do anything. In fact, He said to us:

"Now unto Him Who is able (presents God as the Source of all power) *to do exceeding abundantly above all that we ask or think* (so far beyond our comprehension that the Holy Spirit could give us this explanation only in these terms), *according to the power that works in us* (the word 'according' refers to the fact that this Power can work in us only as we follow God's Prescribed Order of Victory, which is the Cross and our Faith in that Finished Work; this then gives the Holy Spirit the latitude to use His Great Power on our behalf)*"* (Eph. 3:20).

THE DREAM

According to the Word of the Lord, Gideon and his servant went down to the encampment of the Midianites. The Scripture implies that it was night. According to instructions from the Lord, they must have silently placed themselves outside a tent, and thereby overheard the men conversing in that tent.

One of them told a dream. He said, *"I dreamed a dream, and, lo, a cake of barley bread tumbled into the host of Midian, and came unto a tent, and smote it that it fell, and overturned it, and the tent lay along."*

The dream seemed simple enough, but yet, it held a tremendous meaning.

The *"cake of barley bread"* was the poorest type of bread, that which basically was consumed by the poorest of the poor. In other words, the Lord was telling Gideon through this barley bread, that even though he (Gideon) was the poorest of the poor, still, a great victory would here be won.

When the *"cake of barley bread"* hit the tent, and did so with such force, that the tent fell, this symbolized the might and power of the Midianites falling and thereby defeated.

Certainly all dreams aren't from the Lord, and certainly some dreams are from the Lord.

A PERSONAL EXPERIENCE

If I remember correctly, the year was 1987.

I dreamed I was in a particular house, but which seemed to have no significance in the dream.

The dreamed opened with me fighting a gigantic serpent. The thing, if stretched out, would have probably been eight or ten feet long. At any rate, it was lightening fast as it attempted to strike me with its sharp fangs.

I had a sword with which to defend myself.

As I fought, I wasn't at all certain as to what the outcome would be. I was pouring out perspiration.

In the dream there was also a man standing by me and observing the situation. Somehow I knew it was the Lord.

As I was fighting furiously, I would look at Him occasionally, and He was watching me intently. He was dressed in a snow white garment, and there was a Radiance of Light about Him.

Looking at this Magnificence, this Glory, I wondered why He would not help me. In fact He never did, at least that which was observable. He just watched me and did so with a look of serenity and peace on His Countenance. In other words, He did not at all seem to be perturbed, even though I was fighting for my life.

At long last I struck the serpent a telling blow with the sword and it toppled over. I was soaked with perspiration, and physically exhausted. I turned around and looked at Him and He continued to look at me.

He then turned around to walk outside of the house, and motioned for me to follow.

I walked outside, following Him, and all of the sudden in the dream the very ground began to shake. At first, I thought it was an earthquake. But then I realized it was something else altogether.

There was a huge pole standing near me, but yet it wasn't a pole. It must have been fifty feet around its base, and it must have stood at least a hundred feet high. When I looked up I saw a gigantic head, and realized that this was a serpent. Every time it moved, it was so powerful, so large, that the very ground shook.

I remember standing there with the sword in my hand. I looked over at the figure dressed in flowing white standing beside me, and asked, *"Do I have to fight this as well?"*

This was the only time He spoke. He said, *"Yes, you've got to fight that as well."*

The dream then ended.

What did it all mean?

It meant several things, I think! It meant the powers that were coming against me, were so overwhelmingly large, so overwhelmingly big, that within myself I could do nothing. While I might win some small victories as exampled by the serpent that I did actually defeat, I could not hope to defeat this monster, at least within myself. And neither can any other Believer.

That's what the Church does not seem to realize. It doesn't seem to understand that the powers of darkness facing us are so much larger, so much greater, that we within ourselves could ever begin to hope to defeat. Consequently, there must be a greater way. And to be sure, there is a greater way.

But yet the modern Church seems to think that these things can be defeated by means other than Christ and the Cross. They cannot!

We are called upon to fight only one fight, and that's the *"good fight of Faith"* (I Tim. 6:12).

This means that we are to place our Faith exclusively in Christ and the Cross, not allowing Satan or anything else to move it elsewhere. To be sure, he most definitely will try. That's why it is called a *"fight,"* but it is a *"good fight,"* because it is a fight that we are guaranteed to win.

With this fight successfully fought, meaning that we keep our Faith exclusively in Christ and the Cross, the Holy Spirit, Who is God, will most definitely fight for us, and do so with all of His Almighty Power. While we can do little or nothing, He can do everything. In other words, the serpent of my dream is mincemeat for Him. We are guaranteed His Help, but only if we place our Faith exclusively in Christ and the Cross, and keep our Faith exclusively in Christ and the Cross (Rom. 6:1-14; 8:1-2, 11; Gal., Chpt. 5; 6:14).

(15) "AND IT WAS SO, WHEN GIDEON HEARD THE TELLING OF THE DREAM, AND THE INTERPRETATION THEREOF, THAT HE WORSHIPPED, AND RETURNED INTO THE HOST OF ISRAEL, AND SAID, ARISE; FOR THE LORD HAS DELIVERED

INTO YOUR HAND THE HOST OF MIDIAN.

(16) "AND HE DIVIDED THE THREE HUNDRED MEN INTO THREE COMPANIES, AND HE PUT A TRUMPET IN EVERY MAN'S HAND, WITH EMPTY PITCHERS, AND LAMPS WITHIN THE PITCHERS.

(17) "AND HE SAID UNTO THEM, LOOK ON ME, AND DO LIKEWISE: AND, BEHOLD, WHEN I COME TO THE OUTSIDE OF THE CAMP, IT SHALL BE THAT, AS I DO, SO SHALL YOU DO.

(18) "WHEN I BLOW WITH A TRUMPET, I AND ALL WHO ARE WITH ME, THEN BLOW YOU THE TRUMPETS ALSO ON EVERY SIDE OF ALL THE CAMP, AND SAY, THE SWORD OF THE LORD, AND OF GIDEON.

(19) "SO GIDEON, AND THE HUNDRED MEN WHO WERE WITH HIM, CAME UNTO THE OUTSIDE OF THE CAMP IN THE BEGINNING OF THE MIDDLE WATCH; AND THEY HAD BUT NEWLY SET THE WATCH: AND THEY BLEW THE TRUMPETS, AND BROKE THE PITCHERS THAT WERE IN THEIR HANDS.

(20) "AND THE THREE COMPANIES BLEW THE TRUMPETS, AND BROKE THE PITCHERS, AND HELD THE LAMPS IN THEIR LEFT HANDS, AND THE TRUMPETS IN THEIR RIGHT HANDS TO BLOW WITHAL: AND THEY CRIED, THE SWORD OF THE LORD, AND OF GIDEON.

(21) "AND THEY STOOD EVERY MAN IN HIS PLACE ROUND ABOUT THE CAMP; AND ALL THE HOST RAN, AND CRIED, AND FLED.

(22) "AND THE THREE HUNDRED BLEW THE TRUMPETS, AND THE LORD SET EVERY MAN'S SWORD AGAINST HIS FELLOW, EVEN THROUGHOUT ALL THE HOST: AND THE HOST FLED TO BETH-SHITTAH IN ZERERATH, AND TO THE BORDER OF ABEL-MEHOLAH, UNTO TABBATH."

The diagram is:

1. The three hundred were to watch Gideon, and do exactly what he was doing; the Lord, no doubt, had given him instructions as to exactly what he should do.

2. All were to blow the trumpets at a given signal, and all were to shout, *"The Sword of the LORD, and of Gideon."*

NOTES

3. Fear already gripped the enemy, and with the shouting, the glowing lights from the broken pitchers, along with the blowing of the trumpets, they imagined all sorts of things, which is exactly what the Lord intended, actually pushing the Midianites in that direction.

4. The Midianites, thinking the enemy was upon them, not being able, in the dark, to distinguish friend from foe, mistook their own people who were running from pursuing Israelites, and fell upon and slew one another. In fact, the Lord often used such tactics, and I refer to the enemy turning on each other.

THREE COMPANIES

The *"three companies"* of the Sixteenth Verse speak of the Divine Trinity. With this Power behind them and with Faith in God, they could not fail.

The *"trumpet"* was symbolic of the Word of God. That must be the proclamation of every Preacher of the Gospel, the blowing of the certain and sure sound.

The *"empty pitchers"* speak of our lack of trust in the flesh. God cannot fill that which is already full of self-will, and what does God fill it with?

The Scripture says, *"And lamps within the pitchers,"* which portrays the Word of God within the Believer, and active within the Believer. Jesus said, *"You are the light of the world,"* and we can be that light only as long as we are full of the Word of God.

BROKEN PITCHERS

The Nineteenth Verse says, *"And broke the pitchers."* The story is always that the Child of God must be broken before there can be any light given. Over and over again it says of Christ that He took the bread, blessed the bread, broke the bread, and then gave the bread (Mat. 26:26). Let's look at that a little closer:

A. He took the bread: Whenever we were Saved, Jesus took us out of the world, a world of sin and shame.

B. He blessed the bread: Immediately after the individual comes to Christ, Blessings commence. There is a reason for that. The Lord wants to show us how wonderful, how good that He actually is. He blesses us, and does so in a tremendous way.

C. He broke the bread: However, we cannot stay in the place of nothing but Blessing. If that would be the case, such would generate pride, which God can never tolerate. In other words, even though we may be blessed, we couldn't be a blessing to anyone else; consequently, the Lord must *"break"* us. This is not a pleasant process, and is actually very hurtful to the flesh. But we must forever realize, that what is hurtful to the flesh, is invigorating to the spirit. We must be broken!

D. He gave the bread: Only after we have been broken, can we then be given to a hurting and dying world. Unfortunately, we all too often attempt to give ourselves to the world, which can help the world not at all. We must give them Christ, and we can only do so after we have been properly broken. For the light to shine, the pitcher must be broken.

THE WEAPONS OF OUR WARFARE ARE NOT CARNAL

Paul said, *"(For the weapons of our warfare are not carnal* [carnal weapons consist of those which are man-devised], *but mighty through God* [the Cross of Christ (I Cor. 1:18)] *to the pulling down of strong holds;)*

"Casting down imaginations (philosophic strongholds; every effort man makes outside of the Cross of Christ), *and every high thing that exalts itself against the Knowledge of God* (all the pride of the human heart), *and bringing into captivity every thought to the obedience of Christ* (can be done only by the Believer looking exclusively to the Cross, where all Victory is found; the Holy Spirit, Who works entirely within the framework of the Finished Work of Christ, will then perform the task)" (II Cor. 10:4-5).

Believers must understand that we are facing powerful enemies. I speak of demon spirits, fallen angels, and even Satan himself. These foes are so powerful that they cannot be defeated by normal or natural means, in other words, by anything that man devises. They can be defeated, and defeated totally, but only if we function according to God's Prescribed Order. What is that Prescribed Order?

GOD'S PRESCRIBED ORDER OF VICTORY

The Sixth Chapter of Romans proclaims God's Prescribed Order of Victory.

The first two Verses proclaim to us that sin is the problem. Unfortunately, the far greater majority of the modern Church has totally disavowed sin. They claim that if sin is mentioned it might offend people, so they simply don't mention it. The Word of Faith camp claims that if sin is mentioned, it will create a sin consciousness in Believers, causing them to sin. So, they say the way to keep from sinning is that the preacher never mention sin. All of that is strange when we consider that the Apostle Paul mentioned sin seventeen times in the Sixth Chapter of Romans alone.

No, sin is the problem. And then the Holy Spirit through the Apostle tells us in Verses 3 through 5 what the remedy is. That remedy is the Cross of Christ. In these three Verses we are told that we are baptized into His Death, buried with Him by baptism into death, and raised with Him in Newness of Life. As would be obvious, this speaks of the Crucifixion.

This actually means, that when you accepted Christ, in the Mind of God, you were actually placed in Christ in His great atoning Work. In other words, He was our Substitute, and our identification with Him, gives us all for which He has paid such a price. It was all done at the Cross!

As a Believer we are to place our Faith exclusively in Christ and the Cross, maintain our Faith exclusively in Christ and the Cross, understanding that every single thing we receive from the Lord, comes to us from Christ as the Source, and the Cross as the Means. This being done, the Holy Spirit, Who works exclusively within the framework of the Atonement, will work mightily on our behalf. He doesn't request or require much of us, but He does require that our Faith be exclusively in Christ and the Cross. This means that the object of one's Faith, is one of the single most important aspects of the Believer's life and living. That Object of Faith must ever be the Cross of Christ (I Cor. 1:17-18, 23; 2:2; Gal. 6:14).

Actually, that to which Paul is addressing

himself in the Sixth Chapter of Romans is the sin nature, and how the Believer is to have dominion over this power of darkness. The trouble is, most Christians don't have the foggiest idea as to what the sin nature is, much less, how to walk in victory over this problem.

WHAT IS THE SIN NATURE?

The sin nature is simply the nature of the individual to do wrong. It is a result of the Fall in the Garden of Eden. Adam fell from total God-consciousness, down to the far, far lower level of total self-consciousness. Considering that Adam was the federal head of the human race, what happened to him, has happened to us all. That's the reason that Jesus is referred to by Paul as the *"Last Adam,"* and the *"Second Man"* (I Cor. 15:45-50). The Lord Jesus Christ as the *"Last Adam"* did for us what we could not do. He brought us out of the terrible problem caused by the first Adam. He did it all at the Cross.

However, whenever the believing sinner comes to Christ, even though the sin nature is at that time made completely dormant, in other words, causing no problem, unfortunately, it can be quickly resurrected.

The Sixth Chapter of Romans, in essence, tells us how to have victory over the sin nature, that it never again be resurrected within our hearts and lives. Unfortunately, due to the clinging vines of the Fall, it is virtually impossible for the Believer to go from Romans, Chapter Six, to Romans, Chapter Eight, without passing through Romans, Chapter Seven.

Why?

There is something even in the best of Believers that tends to think that we can accomplish this task of successfully living for God by our own means. Oh, we cover our efforts with all types of spiritual phraseology, and load it with Scriptures, but the truth is, it is so easy to depart from God's Prescribed Order, which is the Cross of Christ, and start depending on something else. There is an offense to the Cross (Gal. 5:11).

And what is that offense?

THE OFFENSE OF THE CROSS

The offense of the Cross is the wounding

NOTES

of human pride. While the Believer readily admits that the unredeemed cannot be Saved unless they quit depending on their good works, and thereby accept Christ, still, the same Believer will then place his faith in his own good works, and ignore the Cross, thereby doing the very same thing that he's claiming the unredeemed cannot do.

The Believer has to learn that he must repent not only of the bad things he does, whatever they might be, but the good things as well. Now that comes as a shock doesn't it?

Abraham had to give up Ishmael. He did not at all desire to do that. Ishmael was the work of his own flesh, the scheming of his own mind, the result of his own efforts. He loved Ishmael, who was a type of the flesh. But Ishmael had to go. Ishmael and Isaac could not stay under the same roof, and neither can the flesh and the Spirit of God at the same time be dominant. One or the other will go.

Even though it cost Abraham something to give up Ishmael, as it costs us something to give up our own efforts and abilities, still, it had to be.

Ishmael had to go, and our depending upon the flesh has to go as well.

WHAT IS THE FLESH?

Paul used this term over and over again, actually, nearly a hundred times. Almost every time he was speaking of it in a negative sense.

In simple terms, the *"flesh"* is simply the individual's own personal ability, talents, efforts, good works, knowledge, intellectualism, etc. Within themselves, these things aren't wrong. Where the wrong comes in, is when our faith is placed in these efforts, whatever they might be, instead of in Christ and what He has done for us at the Cross. It is so easy to depend on these things and, as stated, especially considering that we load it up with all type of religious phraseology, making ourselves believe that it is Scriptural, when all the time it's flesh.

But as it was very difficult for Abraham to give up Ishmael, which was a type of the flesh, it is very difficult for us to give up our own efforts also. They are the product of our own scheming and abilities. So, we think highly of these efforts. But the truth is, the Lord can have none of it.

The Believer must never depend upon his own ability and strength, whatever it might be, but altogether upon Christ and what Christ did at the Cross. This is where the offense of the Cross comes in. It offends us to be told that our beautiful, religious phraseology and efforts are of no consequence, and actually that they are harmful. We blanch at that and, in fact, don't like to hear it.

That's the reason that Preachers who are extolling the flesh, in other words, telling you how that you can improve yourself by changing your habits, or doing 101 other similar things, are so popular. We like to hear that. We like to think we can get it done. The truth is, no matter how Saved and Spirit-filled we are, we can't do it! If it's not Christ and the Cross, and our Faith exclusively in that Finished Work, then it's the flesh. And let the Reader understand the following:

"So then they that are in the flesh cannot please God" (Rom. 8:8).

Gideon won a tremendous victory, but he did so only by following to the letter that which the Lord told him to do. It is the same presently.

We follow the Word of God as it regards God's Prescribed Order, and we gain the Victory. Otherwise, and no matter how good our other efforts may seem to be, we will lose!

(23) "AND THE MEN OF ISRAEL GATHERED THEMSELVES TOGETHER OUT OF NAPHTALI, AND OUT OF ASHER, AND OUT OF ALL MANASSEH, AND PURSUED AFTER THE MIDIANITES.

(24) "AND GIDEON SENT MESSENGERS THROUGHOUT ALL MOUNT EPHRAIM, SAYING, COME DOWN AGAINST THE MIDIANITES, AND TAKE BEFORE THEM THE WATERS UNTO BETH-BARAH AND JORDAN. THEN ALL THE MEN OF EPHRAIM GATHERED THEMSELVES TOGETHER, AND TOOK THE WATERS UNTO BETH-BARAH AND JORDAN.

(25) "AND THEY TOOK TWO PRINCES OF THE MIDIANITES, OREB AND ZEEB; AND THEY KILLED OREB UPON THE ROCK OREB, AND ZEEB THEY KILLED AT THE WINEPRESS OF ZEEB, AND

NOTES

PURSUED MIDIAN, AND BROUGHT THE HEADS OF OREB AND ZEEB TO GIDEON ON THE OTHER SIDE JORDAN."

The composition is:

1. Gideon intended to cut off the potential escape of the Midianites.

2. The capture of Oreb and Zeeb is celebrated in Psalms 83:11 and Isaiah 10:26.

3. We learn from all this just how important was this victory, which the Lord gave to Gideon. In fact, every single victory we win is important in the Eyes of God, and is recorded, as is here obvious. We should never forget that!

VICTORY

Now that God had given great victory, there was a time, place, and use for the many of Israel. As would be obvious, far more than the original 300.

Likewise, when the Lord opens the door to take the Gospel to hundreds of millions, there must be many who will step in the breach and help get the job done; however, Believers must make certain that what they're supporting is actually the true Gospel, and that their money is doing what they think it's doing.

The Lord now gives great victory to this multitude who He at first had rejected.

The Twenty-fifth Verse says, *"They took two princes of the Midianites."* They killed these princes and *"brought the heads of Oreb and Zeeb to Gideon."* Their names mean *"raven and wolf,"* symbolic of demon powers that had attempted to destroy Israel.

This is the posture in which God desires Israel to be. Instead of the raven and the wolf destroying Israel, Israel was to destroy the raven and the wolf. Every demon spirit must fall in the Name of Jesus. These demon powers respond to no other.

Whenever we go God's Way, which is the Way of the Cross, and do God's Bidding, even the lowliest Christian among us can come away with trophies of the *"raven"* and the *"wolf"* in his hands, victorious in the mighty Name of Jesus Christ. The way is simple:

The Believer, as we have repeatedly stated, must ever make Christ and the Cross the Object of his Faith. This is critical, and demanded by the Lord (Gal., Chpt. 5).

CHAPTER 8

(1) "AND THE MEN OF EPHRAIM SAID UNTO HIM, WHY HAVE YOU SERVED US THUS, THAT YOU CALLED US NOT, WHEN YOU WENT TO FIGHT WITH THE MIDIANITES? AND THEY DID CHIDE WITH HIM SHARPLY.

(2) "AND HE SAID UNTO THEM, WHAT HAVE I DONE NOW IN COMPARISON OF YOU? IS NOT THE GLEANING OF THE GRAPES OF EPHRAIM BETTER THAN THE VINTAGE OF ABIEZER?

(3) "GOD HAS DELIVERED INTO YOUR HANDS THE PRINCES OF MIDIAN, OREB AND ZEEB: AND WHAT WAS I ABLE TO DO IN COMPARISON OF YOU? THEN THEIR ANGER WAS ABATED TOWARD HIM, WHEN HE HAD SAID THAT.

(4) "AND GIDEON CAME TO JORDAN, AND PASSED OVER, HE, AND THE THREE HUNDRED MEN WHO WERE WITH HIM, FAINT, YET PURSUING THEM.

(5) "AND HE SAID UNTO THE MEN OF SUCCOTH, GIVE, I PRAY YOU, LOAVES OF BREAD UNTO THE PEOPLE WHO FOLLOW ME; FOR THEY BE FAINT, AND I AM PURSUING AFTER ZEBAH AND ZALMUNNA, KINGS OF MIDIAN.

(6) "AND THE PRINCES OF SUCCOTH SAID, ARE THE HANDS OF ZEBAH AND ZALMUNNA NOW IN YOUR HAND, THAT WE SHOULD GIVE BREAD UNTO YOUR ARMY?

(7) "AND GIDEON SAID, THEREFORE WHEN THE LORD HAS DELIVERED ZEBAH AND ZALMUNNA INTO MY HAND, THEN I WILL TEAR YOUR FLESH WITH THE THORNS OF THE WILDERNESS AND WITH BRIERS.

(8) "AND HE WENT UP THENCE TO PENUEL, AND SPOKE UNTO THEM LIKEWISE: AND THE MEN OF PENUEL ANSWERED HIM AS THE MEN OF SUCCOTH HAD ANSWERED HIM.

(9) "AND HE SPOKE ALSO UNTO THE MEN OF PENUEL, SAYING, WHEN I COME AGAIN IN PEACE, I WILL BREAK DOWN THIS TOWER."

The exegesis is:

1. Gideon had not consulted the Tribe of

Ephraim, nor asked their aid; now that the war had been so successful; the men of Ephraim were much displeased at not having been consulted.

2. Gideon seems to have known the answer of Solomon, even some 500 years before the birth of that great King. *"A soft answer turns away wrath"* (Prov. 15:1).

3. The men of Ephraim had captured the two mightiest princes of the Midianites.

4. For fear that Gideon should fail, and thereby that the Midianites would rise back up, the men of Succoth refused even food to his weary followers.

5. It is sad when petulance is shown because of a seeming slight in connection with the Lord's Work, as it was Ephraim, but it is so much sadder when sympathy is shown to the enemy, and help refused to the servants of God, who, though faint, are yet pursuing. The problem witnessed here is all too often the problem in the modern Church. Many Christians, instead of helping to win victories for the Lord, try to hinder those, it seems, who are winning victories.

6. It is not clear as to exactly what is meant by the statements rendered in Verse 7, concerning punishment; the lack of faith among the people of Succoth is what seems to have irritated Gideon the most, and rightly so!

7. From all of this, we see that Israel had become very fragmented, with each Tribe somewhat standing on its own, in other words, close to the place of being twelve distinct nations.

LACK OF UNITY

The Eighth Chapter records victory, inward strife, and idolatry. God has just given one of the greatest victories Israel has ever known; but now in the aftermath, whereas, the Spirit of the Lord had been followed totally at the outset, now the flesh will interrupt causing great difficulty. Sadly and regrettably, this is a perfect picture of the modern Church.

Every once in a while we follow the Holy Spirit totally. Great victories are always the result. Most of the time, however, the flesh intervenes causing terrible problems.

Verse 1 says, *"And they did chide with him sharply,"* speaking of the *"men of Ephraim"* chiding with Gideon. Through Gideon's obedience to God, the Ephraimites joined in victory and saw great results; however, instead of their being grateful for Gideon's leadership, and the Call of God on his life, which resulted in this great victory, instead, they *"did chide with him sharply."* The man of God will answer in humility and with wisdom.

The men of Ephraim were taught with tenderness, whereas, the men of Succoth were taught with thorns. Grace dealt with Ephraim because Ephraim responded with Grace. Succoth would not respond to Grace; therefore, it had to be dealt with by Righteousness. God help us to place ourselves in such a spiritual position that we, like Ephraim, will respond to Grace. Otherwise, God will demand Righteousness of us, of which we are bereft.

The Church has never quite understood this. It loves to portray its supposed righteousness, which is always self-righteousness. God will have no part of it, as He can have no part of it. He will only respond to the Righteousness of Christ within our lives, which always yields to Grace.

It would certainly seem that all of Israel would now be thrillingly happy, considering the great victory that Gideon had just won; however, it seems that that was not the case.

Regrettably, this spirit has come up through the sands of time, even unto this very hour. Most of the modern Church little cares or is little concerned about great victories won in the Name of the Lord. It only looks to itself. In fact, jealousy reigns much of the time, even as it seemed to do so during the time of Gideon.

FAITH

Gideon's great Faith would defeat the enemy, and, yet, others would enjoy the victory and the fruit. Gideon, as any true man of God, will find no fault with this. The man of Faith is always satisfied with having done the work committed to him. He wants all to be likewise blessed. Now we will see how God deals with the sin of self-righteousness.

SELF-RIGHTEOUSNESS

Verse 5 says, *"And he said unto the men of Succoth, Give, I pray you, loaves of bread*

unto the people who follow me." The people of Succoth would not give the bread; therefore, Gideon said, *"I will tear your flesh with the thorns of the wilderness and with briers."* The same God Who extends Grace will also respond with Judgment as it regards self-righteousness. In fact, God cannot abide self-righteousness in any form.

Regrettably, the Eighth Verse says, *"The men of Penuel answered him as the men of Succoth."* They too were met with the Judgment of God, and from Gideon. God looks very unkindly on that which will oppose His Work.

What is self-righteousness?

It is any type of supposed righteousness, which one accrues to oneself, as a result of the doing of religion. It is righteousness based on good works, good deeds, or the not doing of bad deeds, etc. In other words, it is all man-devised. God will have none of it and, in fact, is greatly opposed to any type of self-righteousness.

The only Righteousness that God will honor, is that which comes from His Son Jesus Christ, and due to the Cross, can be imputed to any person who trusts Christ and not at all in themselves. It is called, *"The Righteousness of God"* (Rom. 1:17; 3:5, 21-22). This Righteousness is received strictly by Faith (Rom. 9:30). This means that the undeserving Saint exercises Faith in Christ and what Christ did at the Cross. Then, even as stated, a perfect, pure, spotless Righteousness, the Righteousness of Christ, is imputed to such a person. That is the only way that Righteousness can be obtained. Jesus gave a perfect illustration of this.

RELATIVE RIGHTEOUSNESS

It is the parable of the Pharisee and the Publican.

They both went up to the Temple to pray. Jesus records the prayer of the Pharisee first of all.

The man said, *"God, I thank You, that I am not as other men are, extortioners, unjust, adulterers, or even as this Publican."*

This is *"relative righteousness"* meaning that such a person judges their supposed righteousness by comparing it to others. They do more good things than others do, or don't do some bad things that others do; consequently, their righteousness is judged strictly on the points system so-called.

The Pharisee then said, *"I fast twice in the week, I give tithes of all that I possess."* This is *"works righteousness,"* thinking that one is righteous simply because of certain good things he does, etc. The Lord will not accept relative righteousness or works righteousness. Regrettably, the modern Church seems to be filled with both.

Our Lord then addressed the praying of the Publican.

First of all, a Publican was looked at by fellow Jews as the proverbial scum of the Earth. They were, in the eyes of most Jews, guilty of high treason against Israel because they were tax collectors, having sold out to Rome.

But this Publican, *"Smote upon his breast, saying, God be merciful to me a sinner."* The Scripture also says that he *"would not lift up so much as his eyes unto Heaven."*

In other words, he knew he was a sinner and admitted such. He was asking for Mercy and Grace.

Our Lord said that *"This man* (the Publican) *went down to his house justified rather than the other."* Our Lord then quickly added, *"for everyone who exalts himself shall be abased; and he who humbles himself shall be exalted"* (Lk. 18:9-14).

The Lord certainly wasn't exalting the sinfulness of the Publican. He was simply saying that this man knew he was a sinner, wanted to get out of the sin, and was begging Mercy and Grace from the Lord. Such a prayer will always be answered.

At the same time, our Lord is saying that this Pharisee, despite all of these things he said of himself, was not justified in the Eyes of God and, thereby, unless he ultimately changed, died eternally lost.

(10) "NOW ZEBAH AND ZALMUNNA WERE IN KARKOR, AND THEIR HOSTS WITH THEM, ABOUT FIFTEEN THOUSAND MEN, ALL WHO WERE LEFT OF ALL THE HOSTS OF THE CHILDREN OF THE EAST: FOR THERE FELL AN HUNDRED AND TWENTY THOUSAND MEN WHO DREW SWORD.

(11) "AND GIDEON WENT UP BY THE WAY OF THEM WHO DWELT IN TENTS

ON THE EAST OF NOBAH AND JOGBEHAH, AND SMOTE THE HOST: FOR THE HOST WAS SECURE.

(12) "AND WHEN ZEBAH AND ZALMUNNA FLED, HE PURSUED AFTER THEM, AND TOOK THE TWO KINGS OF MIDIAN, ZEBAH AND ZALMUNNA, AND DISCOMFITED ALL THE HOST.

(13) "AND GIDEON THE SON OF JOASH RETURNED FROM BATTLE BEFORE THE SUN WAS UP,

(14) "AND CAUGHT A YOUNG MAN OF THE MEN OF SUCCOTH, AND ENQUIRED OF HIM: AND HE DESCRIBED UNTO HIM THE PRINCES OF SUCCOTH, AND THE ELDERS THEREOF, EVEN THREESCORE AND SEVENTEEN MEN.

(15) "AND HE CAME UNTO THE MEN OF SUCCOTH, AND SAID, BEHOLD ZEBAH AND ZALMUNNA, WITH WHOM YOU DID UPBRAID ME, SAYING, ARE THE HANDS OF ZEBAH AND ZALMUNNA NOW IN YOUR HAND, THAT WE SHOULD GIVE BREAD UNTO YOUR MEN WHO ARE WEARY?

(16) "AND HE TOOK THE ELDERS OF THE CITY, AND THORNS OF THE WILDERNESS AND BRIERS, AND WITH THEM HE TAUGHT THE MEN OF SUCCOTH.

(17) "AND HE BEAT DOWN THE TOWER OF PENUEL, AND KILLED THE MEN OF THE CITY.

(18) "THEN SAID HE UNTO ZEBAH AND ZALMUNNA. WHAT MANNER OF MEN WERE THEY WHOM YOU SLEW AT TABOR? AND THEY ANSWERED, AS YOU ARE, SO WERE THEY; EACH ONE RESEMBLED THE CHILDREN OF A KING.

(19) "AND HE SAID, THEY WERE MY BRETHREN, EVEN THE SONS OF MY MOTHER: AS THE LORD LIVES, IF YOU HAD SAVED THEM ALIVE, I WOULD NOT KILL YOU.

(20) "AND HE SAID UNTO JETHER HIS FIRSTBORN, UP, AND KILL THEM. BUT THE YOUTH DREW NOT HIS SWORD: FOR HE FEARED, BECAUSE HE WAS YET A YOUTH.

(21) "THEN ZEBAH AND ZALMUNNA SAID, RISE YOU, AND FALL UPON US: FOR AS THE MAN IS, SO IS HIS STRENGTH. AND GIDEON AROSE, AND SLEW ZEBAH

AND ZALMUNNA, AND TOOK AWAY THE ORNAMENTS THAT WERE ON THEIR CAMELS' NECKS."

The diagram is:

1. Gideon's attention was directed at the two kings, Zebah and Zalmunna, so some of the 15,000 may have escaped; however, to be sure, they would no more harm Israel.

2. Considering the conversation of Verse 18, it seems that these two heathen kings seemed not to have known that the men whom they killed were brothers of Gideon. As to exactly when his brothers had lost their lives, we aren't told.

3. The items of Verse 21, were crescent-shaped ornaments of gold and silver, which, as well as *"chains,"* were hung as ornamentation on their camels' necks, denoting their royalty.

HARSH JUDGMENT

As to why the leading Elders of the cities of Succoth and Penuel tried to oppose Gideon, we aren't told. It seems that not only did they oppose him verbally but, as well, they did everything they could do, at least within their power, to hinder him.

Gideon did nothing at the time, but after defeating the enemy, and doing so totally, he then comes back to the twin cities, and proverbially speaking, wipes them clean. In other words, it seems like he killed most, if not all, of the men of the two villages.

Should he have done that?

No!

One can well imagine his feelings considering their attitude toward him. He had risked his life and, as well, and above all, the Lord had given a great victory, of which they seemed to appreciate very little. As stated, these were fellow Israelites, and should have done all they could have done to help him. But sadly, there are many in the modern Church who conduct themselves in a very similar way. They have little help, if any, at all for the Lord's anointed. From Chapter Five of Judges, we know what the Holy Spirit thinks of such action and attitude.

(22) "THEN THE MEN OF ISRAEL SAID UNTO GIDEON, RULE YOU OVER US, BOTH YOU, AND YOUR SON, AND YOUR SON'S SON ALSO: FOR YOU HAVE DELIVERED

US FROM THE HAND OF MIDIAN.

(23) "AND GIDEON SAID UNTO THEM, I WILL NOT RULE OVER YOU, NEITHER SHALL MY SON RULE OVER YOU: THE LORD SHALL RULE OVER YOU.

(24) "AND GIDEON SAID UNTO THEM, I WOULD DESIRE A REQUEST OF YOU, THAT YOU WOULD GIVE ME EVERY MAN THE EARRINGS OF HIS PREY. (FOR THEY HAD GOLDEN EARRINGS, BECAUSE THEY WERE ISHMAELITES.)

(25) "AND THEY ANSWERED, WE WILL WILLINGLY GIVE THEM. AND THEY SPREAD A GARMENT, AND DID CAST THEREIN EVERY MAN THE EARRINGS OF HIS PREY.

(26) "AND THE WEIGHT OF THE GOLDEN EARRINGS THAT HE REQUESTED WAS A THOUSAND AND SEVEN HUNDRED SHEKELS OF GOLD; BESIDE ORNAMENTS, AND COLLARS, AND PURPLE RAIMENT THAT WAS ON THE KINGS OF MIDIAN, AND BESIDE THE CHAINS THAT WERE ABOUT THEIR CAMELS' NECKS.

(27) "AND GIDEON MADE AN EPHOD THEREOF, AND PUT IT IN HIS CITY, EVEN IN OPHRAH: AND ALL ISRAEL WENT THITHER A WHORING AFTER IT: WHICH THING BECAME A SNARE UNTO GIDEON, AND TO HIS HOUSE.

(28) "THUS WAS MIDIAN SUBDUED BEFORE THE CHILDREN OF ISRAEL, SO THAT THEY LIFTED UP THEIR HEADS NO MORE. AND THE COUNTRY WAS IN QUIETNESS FORTY YEARS IN THE DAYS OF GIDEON."

The pattern is:

1. In essence, the men of Israel wanted Gideon to be a king over them; however, the time predicted by Moses that a king would, in fact, rule over Israel was not yet come (Deut. 17:14-15).

2. The golden ornaments of Verse 26 were worth approximately $340,000 in 2004 currency.

3. The *"Ephod"* made by Gideon, became a thing of worship, which was very displeasing to the Lord. Why did Gideon do what he did, and why did Israel worship this thing?

4. What is more commendable and pleasing to the religious mind than to use the wealth of the enemy in making an Ephod?

Was not an Ephod a Bible garment? Was it not of Divine ordination? And Gideon put his foot in the snare; and the very man who had destroyed a gross form of idolatry in his home and his city set up a refined form of the same evil in his kingdom. Idolatry comes so easy!

5. In today's modern vernacular, anything as it pertains to God, which is not anchored squarely in Christ and the Cross, is looked at by the Lord as idolatry (Gal. 1:8-9).

IDOLATRY

Sadly, Satan is an angel of light and a minister of self-righteousness, who knows how to set a snare for the feet of God's truest servants. This will be a religious snare, and we speak of the Ephod, as almost all snares are. He would take the gold of the Ishmaelites, which had belonged to the Midianites, and *"make an Ephod thereof."* And then the Scripture says, *"and all Israel went thither a whoring after it."*

The Ephod was a beautiful garment worn by the High Priest in which the Urim and the Thummim were kept. Somehow in Gideon's thinking a golden Ephod representing the wisdom and direction of the Holy Spirit would be most appropriate. This thing would *"become a snare unto Gideon, and to his house,"* as all religiosity is.

Most of the *"whoring"* of the Church is after that which is religious. We make our denominations into golden Ephods, or our Church into a golden Ephod, or our doctrine into a golden Ephod, or our good works, etc., *"and all of these things become snares."* This thing became an idol, as so much in the Church today no longer constitutes true worship of God but is, in fact, an idol. God help us!

This is the reason that John the Beloved said, *"little children, keep yourselves from idols. Amen"* (I Jn. 5:21).

(29) "AND JERUB-BAAL THE SON OF JOASH WENT AND DWELT IN HIS OWN HOUSE.

(30) "AND GIDEON HAD THREESCORE AND TEN SONS OF HIS BODY BEGOTTEN: FOR HE HAD MANY WIVES.

(31) "AND HIS CONCUBINE WHO WAS IN SHECHEM, SHE ALSO BORE HIM A SON,

WHOSE NAME HE CALLED ABIMELECH.

(32) "AND GIDEON THE SON OF JOASH DIED IN A GOOD OLD AGE, AND WAS BURIED IN THE SEPULCHRE OF JOASH HIS FATHER, IN OPHRAH OF THE ABIEZRITES."

The overview is:

1. Gideon remains to us as one of the most remarkable characters of the Old Testament, not indeed without faults and blemishes, and not wholly unspoiled by prosperity, but still a great man, and an imminent servant of God.

2. Even though Gideon had 70 sons, one of his sons, Abimelech, would prove to be a great hindrance and an embarrassment to the Work of God.

3. Israel experienced forty years of quietness and rest in the *"days of Gideon,"* and all because of the great deliverance that the Lord performed through him.

(33) "AND IT CAME TO PASS, AS SOON AS GIDEON WAS DEAD, THAT THE CHILDREN OF ISRAEL TURNED AGAIN, AND WENT A WHORING AFTER BAALIM, AND MADE BAAL-BERITH THEIR GOD.

(34) "AND THE CHILDREN OF ISRAEL REMEMBERED NOT THE LORD THEIR GOD, WHO HAD DELIVERED THEM OUT OF THE HANDS OF ALL THEIR ENEMIES ON EVERY SIDE:

(35) "NEITHER SHOWED THEY KINDNESS TO THE HOUSE OF JERUB-BAAL, NAMELY, GIDEON, ACCORDING TO ALL THE GOODNESS WHICH HE HAD SHOWED UNTO ISRAEL."

The synopsis is:

1. Hervey says, *"Forgetfulness of God is often the parent of ingratitude to men. The heart of stone which is not touched by the love of Christ is also insensible to the kindness of man."*

2. *"As soon as Gideon was dead,"* the Scripture says, then Israel *"went a whoring after Baalim."*

The Church can rise no higher than its leadership.

3. Once the spiritual slide downward begins, it accelerates quickly!

APOSTASY

Several things are said here. They are:

A. Gideon died;

B. Israel went after Baalim;

C. The Children of Israel forgot the Lord; and,

D. When they turned on the Lord, they also turned on the house of Gideon.

As is so painfully obvious in this Book, bereft of proper leadership, and we speak of proper Spiritual Leadership, Israel founders. It is no different presently!

For the Church to thrive, there must be strong Spiritual Leadership, which necessitates an adherence, even a strict adherence to the Word of God. If the proper leadership is lacking, exactly as Israel did so long ago and the Church does presently, it goes *"a whoring after the world."*

As Israel forgot the Lord Who delivered them, likewise, the modern Church forgets the Lord Who Saved them.

In doing so, as Israel was grossly unkind to the house of Gideon, likewise, the apostate Church persecutes the True Church.

CHAPTER 9

(1) "AND ABIMELECH THE SON OF JERUB-BAAL WENT TO SHECHEM UNTO HIS MOTHER'S BRETHREN, AND COMMUNED WITH THEM, AND WITH ALL THE FAMILY OF THE HOUSE OF HIS MOTHER'S FATHER, SAYING,

(2) "SPEAK, I PRAY YOU, IN THE EARS OF ALL THE MEN OF SHECHEM, WHETHER IS BETTER FOR YOU, EITHER THAT ALL THE SONS OF JERUB-BAAL, WHICH ARE THREESCORE AND TEN PERSONS, REIGN OVER YOU, OR THAT ONE REIGN OVER YOU? REMEMBER ALSO THAT I AM YOUR BONE AND YOUR FLESH.

(3) "AND HIS MOTHER'S BRETHREN SPOKE OF HIM IN THE EARS OF ALL THE MEN OF SHECHEM ALL THESE WORDS: AND THEIR HEARTS INCLINED TO FOLLOW ABIMELECH; FOR THEY SAID, HE IS OUR BROTHER.

(4) "AND THEY GAVE HIM THREESCORE AND TEN PIECES OF SILVER OUT OF THE HOUSE OF BAAL-BERITH,

WHEREWITH ABIMELECH HIRED VAIN AND LIGHT PERSONS, WHICH FOLLOWED HIM.

(5) "AND HE WENT UNTO HIS FATHER'S HOUSE AT OPHRAH, AND KILLED HIS BRETHREN THE SONS OF JERUB-BAAL, BEING THREESCORE AND TEN PERSONS, UPON ONE STONE: NOTWITHSTANDING YET JOTHAM THE YOUNGEST SON OF JERUB-BAAL WAS LEFT; FOR HE HID HIMSELF.

(6) "AND ALL THE MEN OF SHECHEM GATHERED TOGETHER, AND ALL THE HOUSE OF MILLO, AND WENT, AND MADE ABIMELECH KING, BY THE PLAIN OF THE PILLAR THAT WAS IN SHECHEM."

The construction is:

1. Abimelech was a son of Gideon. It is amply illustrated in this Chapter that he who sows to the flesh shall of the flesh reap corruption.

2. Abimelech, born of the will of the flesh, became a channel and an instrument of evil to Israel. Israel would have fared much better, and the family of Gideon had he never been born!

3. When Gideon looked at this baby when he was born, little did he realize that he had given conception to a monster. A wrong action, which, at the time, seems harmless, bears bitter fruit in after-years. To become king of sorts, he would murder all of his brothers, some 69 total; consequently, I think the word *"monster"* is not too harsh.

ABIMELECH, THE SIXTH JUDGE, A USURPER

The Ninth Chapter is a story of rebellion, which even characterizes, at times, the Church of the Living God. Abimelech is the culprit. He was the son of Gideon and a concubine who lived at Shechem (Judg. 8:31). If Gideon had wholly followed the Bible, this monster would have never been born.

Abimelech aspired kingship after the death of Gideon and did rule three years after killing Gideon's 70 other sons, except Jotham, his brother.

Working through his mother's people in Shechem and appealing to the city Elders who naturally desired their city to become great, Abimelech sought to become king with

Shechem as his Capital. He was given money by the Elders which enabled him to hire assassins to destroy the other sons of Gideon, giving him no rival from that source. He was then made king, although not approved or selected by God.

A WORK OF THE FLESH

The Fourth Verse says, *"Wherewith Abimelech hired vain and light persons, which followed him,"* presents the terrible apostasy which followed Israel's great revival under Gideon. Gideon's calling was a Work of the Spirit. Abimelech's calling was a work of the flesh. One brought life, the other death. In Chapters 8 and 9 we have the picture of the Spiritual Church and the carnal Church.

Throughout this Chapter Gideon is spoken of by the name of Jerub-baal.

Why?

The name means, *"is an idol anything?"*

The nickname given Gideon portrays his war against these idol gods in Israel and, as well, the Holy Spirit desired that it be known, and known so by this nickname, that an idol is nothing. And yet this Chapter will proclaim what happened to Israel after she went *"a whoring after Baalim."*

In this Chapter, the people of God sink to the lowest depths. It is not a very pleasant picture of those who would bring the Messiah into the world; however, the Bible records not only the victories, but the failures of God's People as well!

Gideon was roused by the Call of God to seek his country's deliverance from a galling yoke, and to restore the worship of the true God in his native land. With self-devotion and unflinching enthusiasm, he gave himself to his task, and accomplished it at the risk of his life, without a thought of himself or any selfish ends.

To the contrary, Abimelech, seeking power for himself, pretending to have in view the people's interest, and, to secure their favor, restored an abominable idolatry. His kingdom, founded in bloodshed, gross bloodshed, abetted by falsehood, and fostered by a base and cruel policy, had no end or motive in view but self-aggrandizement.

(7) "AND WHEN THEY TOLD IT TO JOTHAM, HE WENT AND STOOD IN THE

TOP OF MOUNT GERIZIM, AND LIFTED UP HIS VOICE, AND CRIED, AND SAID UNTO THEM, HEARKEN UNTO ME, YOU MEN OF SHECHEM, THAT GOD MAY HEARKEN UNTO YOU.

(8) "THE TREES WENT FORTH ON A TIME TO ANOINT A KING OVER THEM; AND THEY SAID UNTO THE OLIVE TREE, REIGN YOU OVER US.

(9) "BUT THE OLIVE TREE SAID UNTO THEM, SHOULD I LEAVE MY FATNESS, WHEREWITH BY ME THEY HONOUR GOD AND MAN, AND GO TO BE PROMOTED OVER THE TREES?

(10) "AND THE TREES SAID TO THE FIG TREE, COME YOU, AND REIGN OVER US.

(11) "BUT THE FIG TREE SAID UNTO THEM, SHOULD I FORSAKE MY SWEETNESS, AND MY GOOD FRUIT, AND GO TO BE PROMOTED OVER THE TREES?

(12) "THEN SAID THE TREES UNTO THE VINE, COME YOU, AND REIGN OVER US.

(13) "AND THE VINE SAID UNTO THEM, SHOULD I LEAVE MY WINE, WHICH CHEERS GOD AND MAN, AND GO TO BE PROMOTED OVER THE TREES?

(14) "THEN SAID ALL THE TREES UNTO THE BRAMBLE, COME YOU, AND REIGN OVER US.

(15) "AND THE BRAMBLE SAID UNTO THE TREES, IF IN TRUTH YOU ANOINT ME KING OVER YOU, THEN COME AND PUT YOUR TRUST IN MY SHADOW: AND IF NOT, LET FIRE COME OUT OF THE BRAMBLE, AND DEVOUR THE CEDARS OF LEBANON.

(16) "NOW THEREFORE, IF YOU HAVE DONE TRULY AND SINCERELY, IN THAT YOU HAVE MADE ABIMELECH KING, AND IF YOU HAVE DEALT WELL WITH JERUB-BAAL AND HIS HOUSE, AND HAVE DONE UNTO HIM ACCORDING TO THE DESERVING OF HIS HANDS;

(17) "(FOR MY FATHER FOUGHT FOR YOU, AND ADVENTURED HIS LIFE FAR, AND DELIVERED YOU OUT OF THE HAND OF MIDIAN:

(18) "AND YOU ARE RISEN UP AGAINST MY FATHER'S HOUSE THIS DAY, AND HAVE SLAIN HIS SONS, THREESCORE

AND TEN PERSONS, UPON ONE STONE, AND HAVE MADE ABIMILECH, THE SON OF HIS MAIDSERVANT, KING OVER THE MEN OF SHECHEM, BECAUSE HE IS YOUR BROHTER;)

(19) "IF YOU THEN HAVE DEALT TRULY AND SINCERELY WITH JERUB-BAAL AND WITH HIS HOUSE THIS DAY, THEN REJOICE YOU IN ABIMELECH, AND LET HIM ALSO REJOICE IN YOU:

(20) "BUT IF NOT, LET FIRE COME OUT FROM ABIMELECH, AND DEVOUR THE MEN OF SHECHEM, AND FROM THE HOUSE OF MILLO, AND LET FIRE COME OUT FROM THE MEN OF SHECHEM, AND FROM THE HOUSE OF MILLO, AND DEVOUR ABIMELECH.

(21) "AND JOTHAM RAN AWAY, AND FLED, AND WENT TO BEER, AND DWELT THERE, FOR FEAR OF ABIMELECH HIS BROTHER."

The overview is:

1. As stated in Verse 5, Jotham was the youngest son of Gideon, and the only one left alive of the slaughter of his 69 brothers — all murdered by Abimelech.

2. Jotham's allegory was both a Parable and a Prophecy. It had an immediate fulfillment; for the men of Shechem elected the bramble to rule over them, and mutual destruction was the result.

3. But the allegory had a wider significance. In the Scriptures, Israel is figured as a fig tree, an olive tree, and a vine. These symbolize National Blessing, Covenant Blessing, and Spiritual Blessing. The bramble is a fore-picture of the coming Antichrist. In the future dark day of Israel's rebellion, she will turn aside from all Divine fullness, and put her trust in the rule of the Antichrist; and mutual destruction will be the result.

THE ALLEGORY OF JOTHAM

Concerning this allegory given by a man, even some 3,200 years ago, and at an extremely low spiritual tide, one would never dream that it refers to the happenings of the present time (2006), and more particularly, that which is soon to come. Only the Holy Spirit could divine such Knowledge. To be sure, Jotham had no idea whatsoever that what he was saying had any meaning other

NOTES

than his present time. But it definitely did!

As the world at this present time views the situation in the Middle East, and especially the great dilemma of Israel, most do not dream that it is all a fulfillment of Bible Prophecy.

MODERN ISRAEL AND HER DILEMMA

Israel is surrounded by enemies, enemies we might quickly add, which have vowed her destruction. She has Hamas on the south and Hezbollah on the north. It is virtually impossible for Israel to tell which constitutes religious fanatics, and which don't.

Whatever she does, something or nothing, the rockets continue to fall on her cities.

On top of all of that, almost all of the world blames Israel for the situation in the Middle East, not really caring that Israel is not at fault at all.

Most think that Israel's dilemma is because they will not give these wonderful Palestinians the land area in which they could form a state. The truth is, Israel has offered them every single thing for which they have asked, with the exception of East Jerusalem.

The continuing Truth is, the Palestinians have no interest in statehood at all. They want the entirety of the land area of Israel, and on top of that, they want every Jew dead. They consider the Land of Israel as Muslim land, and they have vowed to ultimately regain it, and will use any method at their disposal.

The Land of Israel comprises about one tenth of one percent of the land area of the Middle East, with all the balance occupied by Arabs, and Iran occupied by the Persians.

The Arabs have declared war on Israel five times, and have lost each conflict. Stop and think about the following for a moment:

Had Israel lost even one of these wars, there would be no Israel today. But even though Israel won these conflicts, and especially consider that each one was begun by the other side, the Palestinians have been allowed to remain, and have actually been helped by the Israelis.

The problem goes all the way back to Abraham. It began with Isaac and Ishmael. The Muslims falsely claim that Ishmael is the true son, and that the Promise of God is centered up in him. Of course, the Bible teaches the exact opposite. So, the problem is a spiritual problem. It is the religion of Islam pitted against Christianity and Judaism.

FACTS CONCERNING ISRAEL AND JERUSALEM

The following should be noted, even though it is little recognized by the world.

• Israel became a state in approximately 1312 B.C., two millennia before Islam even came into being.

• Arab refugees from Israel began calling themselves *"Palestinians"* in 1967, two decades after modern Israeli statehood. In fact, there are no such thing as Palestinians, the name being derived from the Philistines of Biblical times. The individuals now in Israel referring to themselves as such, actually are Jordanians, Egyptians, Syrians, etc.

• After Joshua conquered the land in approximately 1400 B.C., Jews ruled it for an approximate 1,000 years and maintained a continuous presence there for well over 3,000 years.

• For about 3,000 years, Jerusalem was the Jewish Capital. It was never the Capital of any Arab or Muslim entity. Even under Jordanian rule, Jerusalem was not made the Capital, and no Arab leader came to visit it.

• Jerusalem is mentioned over 700 times in the Bible, but not once is it mentioned in the Koran.

• King David founded Jerusalem; Mohammed never set foot in it.

• Jews pray facing Jerusalem, Muslims face Mecca. If they are between the two cities, Muslims pray facing Mecca with their backs to Jerusalem.

• In 1948, Arab leaders urged their people to leave, promising to cleanse the land of Jewish presence. Approximately sixty-eight percent of them fled without ever setting eyes on an Israeli soldier.

• Virtually the entire Jewish population of Muslim countries had to flee as the result of violence against them.

• Some 630,000 Arabs left Israel in 1948, while close to a million Jews were forced to leave the Muslim countries in which they then resided.

• Despite the vast territories occupied by the Arabs in the Middle East, all Arab refugees were and are deliberately prevented from going to these countries. In other words, the Jordanians will not allow any Palestinians to integrate from Israel to that country. It is the same with all other Arab lands. Why?

The refugees forced by the Muslim world to remain in Israel are used to gain the sympathy of the balance of the world. They actually have no interest in the welfare of the people, desiring only to cause Israel problems. As stated, they have vowed to take the entirety of the Land of Israel. Then it would be renamed Palestine.

• Fatah and Hamas constitutions still call for the destruction of Israel. Israel ceded most of the West Bank and all of Gaza to the Palestinian authority, and even provided it with arms. It seems that Uncle Sam is not the only one who is Uncle Sap.

• During the Jordanian occupation, Jewish holy sites were vandalized and were off limits to Jews. Under Israeli rule, all Muslim and Christian holy sites are accessible to all faiths.

THE FUTURE FOR ISRAEL

As stated, Jotham, when giving his allegory or parable concerning the trees, and especially when he said, *"Then said all the trees unto the bramble, Come you, and reign over us,"* dared realize that he was speaking of something which would happen thousands of years in the future.

Israel, as stated, is pressed severely as to what she should do. The truth is, almost anything she does comes out to be wrong. As well, virtually every nation in the world and, in fact, all except the United States are opposed to Israel. In fact, the entirety of the world minus the U.S. just wishes that Israel would go away. In fact, they wouldn't care if the Muslims crushed this tiny state tomorrow. These problems will continue, and even exacerbate, until a strong man appears on the horizon of the world, and who will be able to solve Israel's problems, at least for a short time. Whatever name the world will give him is yet to be determined. Israel will think he is their Messiah, and will announce such to the entirety of the world. In effect, they will be saying to the *"bramble, Come you, and reign over us."* He will be the Antichrist.

For a short period of time, the Antichrist will most definitely solve Israel's problems. So much so, in fact, that they will be able to build their Temple, and will even begin daily sacrifices (Dan. 9:27). They will then say *"peace and safety."* That's what the Apostle Paul was talking about when he said, *"For when they shall say, peace and safety; then sudden destruction comes upon them, as travail upon a woman with child; and they shall not escape"* (I Thess. 5:3).

What is he talking about?

THE RISE OF THE ANTICHRIST

This one who Israel will think is the Messiah, and who will laud all over the world, will suddenly show his true colors. He will launch a surprise attack against Israel, causing them to suffer their first defeat since becoming a Nation in 1948. That is the *"sudden destruction"* of which Paul speaks.

Israel will then enter into the most depressing period of the entirety of her history, surpassing even that of the Holocaust. It will be three and a half years of unmitigated hell, actually the last half of the Great Tribulation. Jesus said it would be worse than anything the world has ever known and, in fact, would never know such again. The truth is, Israel will then come close to total annihilation. In fact, she would be totally annihilated were it not for the greatest event that human history has ever known, and we speak of the Second Coming. Then the True Messiah, the Lord Jesus Christ, the One Whom they crucified, will come back in answer to their prayers, overthrow the Antichrist, and all of his armies, thereby rescuing Israel with the greatest victory that she has ever known. She will then accept Him as Messiah, Lord, and above all, as Saviour (Zech. 13:1).

(22) "WHEN ABIMELECH HAD REIGNED THREE YEARS OVER ISRAEL,

(23) "THEN GOD SENT AN EVIL SPIRIT BETWEEN ABIMELECH AND THE MEN OF SCHECHEM; AND THE MEN OF SHECHEM DEALT TREACHEROUSLY WITH ABIMELECH:

(24) "THAT THE CRUELTY DONE TO

THE THREESCORE AND TEN SONS OF JERUB-BAAL MIGHT COME, AND THEIR BLOOD BE LAID UPON ABIMELECH THEIR BROTHER, WHICH KILLED THEM; AND UPON THE MEN OF SHECHEM, WHICH AIDED HIM IN THE KILLING OF HIS BRETHREN.

(25) "AND THE MEN OF SHECHEM SET LIERS IN WAIT FOR HIM IN THE TOP OF THE MOUNTAINS, AND THEY ROBBED ALL WHO CAME ALONG THAT WAY BY THEM: AND IT WAS TOLD ABIMELECH.

(26) "AND GAAL THE SON OF EBED CAME WITH HIS BRETHREN, AND WENT OVER TO SHECHEM: AND THE MEN OF SHECHEM PUT THEIR CONFIDENCE IN HIM.

(27) "AND THEY WENT OUT INTO THE FIELDS, AND GATHERED THEIR VINEYARDS, AND TRODE THE GRAPES, AND MADE MERRY, AND WENT INTO THE HOUSE OF THEIR GOD, AND DID EAT AND DRINK, AND CURSED ABIMELECH.

(28) "AND GAAL THE SON OF EBED SAID, WHO IS ABIMELECH, AND WHO IS SHECHEM, THAT WE SHOULD SERVE HIM? IS NOT HE THE SON OF JERUB-BAAL? AND ZEBUL HIS OFFICER? SERVE THE MEN OF HAMOR THE FATHER OF SHECHEM: FOR WHY SHOULD WE SERVE HIM?

(29) "AND WOULD TO GOD THIS PEOPLE WERE UNDER MY HAND! THEN WOULD I REMOVE ABIMELECH. AND HE SAID TO ABIMELECH, INCREASE YOUR ARMY, AND COME OUT."

The overview is:

1. If men desire evil, as did Abimelech, God will see to it that they get evil.

2. As should be obvious from these Passages, the Lord sees everything that takes place. At some point, He will avenge the evil.

3. The Lord allowing an evil spirit to come into the situation, proclaims the fact, as should be obvious, that He is the Master of all things.

THE LORD AND THE EVIL SPIRIT

Verse 23 says, *"Then God sent an evil spirit between Abimelech and the men of Shechem."* The results were, *"And the men of Shechem dealt treacherously with Abimelech."*

The Believer should understand, that every single thing done to him or her, is either caused by the Lord or allowed by the Lord. Of course, the Lord never causes anyone to sin; however, He does allow such, that is, if the individual is so inclined to do so.

In all of this, we learn that the Lord controls Satan and all his minions of darkness, in every capacity. In other words, Satan can only do what the Lord allows him to do.

In this instance, the Lord used a demon spirit to bring about division between Abimelech and the men of Shechem.

Why did He do that?

He did it because of the cruelty that had been carried out by Abimelech on his 69 brothers. In other words, he murdered them.

What we sow, we will ultimately reap. We must never forget that!

Regarding evil spirits, such should never be a bother to the Child of God, and won't be a bother, that is, if the Believer will place his Faith exclusively in Christ and what Christ has done at the Cross. It was at the Cross that Satan and all his minions of darkness were totally and completely defeated (Col. 2:14-15).

Satan was defeated by Jesus removing the means by which Satan holds man in captivity and bondage. That means is *"sin."* It was done at Calvary's Cross. There Jesus atoned for all sin, past, present, and future, at least for all who will believe (Jn. 3:16).

Now, and we speak of all the time since the Cross, Satan can hold mankind in bondage, only by the ones thusly held, giving their consent. By that we mean the following:

Those who do not know the Lord and will not accept the Lord, thereby, continue to be ruled by demon spirits.

But regrettably, most Christians are also oppressed in one way or the other by demon spirits, simply because they do not know and understand God's Prescribed Order of Victory, which is the Cross, and our Faith in that Finished Work. Whether it is understood or not, when the Believer places his faith in something other than Christ and the Cross, he is giving his consent to be held in bondage. He may disagree with that statement, but that's exactly what is happening (Gal. 5:1).

Protection from Satan and all evil spirits is guaranteed upon the Believer placing his Faith exclusively in Christ and the Cross, which then gives the Holy Spirit latitude to work. To be sure, Satan wants no part of the Lord Jesus Christ or the Cross on which He died; likewise, he wants no part of the Holy Spirit. Protection is guaranteed upon proper Faith (Rom. 6:14; 8:1-2, 11).

(30) "AND WHEN ZEBUL THE RULER OF THE CITY HEARD THE WORDS OF GAAL THE SON OF EBED, HIS ANGER WAS KINDLED.

(31) "AND HE SENT MESSENGERS UNTO ABIMELECH PRIVILY, SAYING, BEHOLD, GAAL THE SON OF EBED AND HIS BRETHREN BE COME TO SHECHEM; AND, BEHOLD, THEY FORTIFY THE CITY AGAINST YOU.

(32) "NOW THEREFORE UP BY NIGHT, YOU AND THE PEOPLE WHO ARE WITH YOU, AND LIE IN WAIT IN THE FIELD:

(33) "AND IT SHALL BE, THAT IN THE MORNING, AS SOON AS THE SUN IS UP, YOU SHALL RISE EARLY, AND SET UPON THE CITY: AND, BEHOLD, WHEN HE AND THE PEOPLE WHO ARE WITH HIM COME OUT AGAINST YOU, THEN MAY YOU DO TO THEM AS YOU SHALL FIND OCCASION.

(34) "AND ABIMELECH ROSE UP, AND ALL THE PEOPLE WHO WERE WITH HIM, BY NIGHT, AND THEY LAID WAIT AGAINST SHECHEM IN FOUR COMPANIES.

(35) "AND GAAL THE SON OF EBED WENT OUT, AND STOOD IN THE ENTERING OF THE GATE OF THE CITY: AND ABIMELECH ROSE UP, AND THE PEOPLE THAT WERE WITH HIM, FROM LYING IN WAIT."

The diagram is:

1. Zebul, it appears, was governor of the city under Abimelech.

2. As is here obvious, God relates the lives of both the good and the bad.

3. Without God, treachery, subterfuge, deceit, are commonplace!

(36) "AND WHEN GAAL SAW THE PEOPLE, HE SAID TO ZEBUL, BEHOLD, THERE COME PEOPLE DOWN FROM THE TOP OF THE MOUNTAINS. AND

ZEBUL SAID UNTO HIM, YOU SEE THE SHADOW OF THE MOUNTAINS AS IF THEY WERE MEN.

(37) "AND GAAL SPOKE AGAIN AND SAID, SEE THERE COME PEOPLE DOWN BY THE MIDDLE OF THE LAND, AND ANOTHER COMPANY COME ALONG BY THE PLAIN OF MEONENIM.

(38) "THEN SAID ZEBUL UNTO HIM, WHERE IS NOW YOUR MOUTH, WHEREWITH YOU SAID, WHO IS ABIMELECH, THAT WE SHOULD SERVE HIM? IS NOT THIS THE PEOPLE THAT YOU HAVE DESPISED? GO OUT, I PRAY NOW, AND FIGHT WITH THEM.

(39) "AND GAAL WENT OUT BEFORE THE MEN OF SHECHEM, AND FOUGHT WITH ABIMELECH.

(40) "AND ABIMELECH CHASED HIM, AND HE FLED BEFORE HIM, AND MANY WERE OVERTHROWN AND WOUNDED, EVEN UNTO THE ENTERING OF THE GATE.

(41) "AND ABIMELECH DWELT AT ARUMAH: AND ZEBUL THRUST OUT GAAL AND HIS BRETHREN, THAT THEY SHOULD NOT DWELL IN SHECHEM."

The structure is:

1. The quick succession of events shows that the political situation of Israel at this time, is one of unstable equilibrium. The movement of affairs is rapid, as if the stage were being cleared for the real and important action that is to follow (Pulpit).[1]

2. So natural does the development of events appear, that there is danger of overlooking the overruling providence of God.

3. While Zebul served Abimelech faithfully, still, his devotion appears strangely misplaced.

(42) "AND IT CAME TO PASS ON THE MORROW, THAT THE PEOPLE WENT OUT INTO THE FIELD; AND THEY TOLD ABIMELECH.

(43) "AND HE TOOK THE PEOPLE, AND DIVIDED THEM INTO THREE COMPANIES, AND LAID WAIT IN THE FIELD, AND LOOKED, AND, BEHOLD, THE PEOPLE WERE COME FORTH OUT OF THE CITY; AND HE ROSE UP AGAINST THEM, AND SMOTE THEM.

(44) "AND ABIMELECH, AND THE

COMPANY THAT WAS WITH HIM, RUSHED FORWARD, AND STOOD IN THE ENTERING OF THE GATE OF THE CITY: AND THE TWO OTHER COMPANIES RAN UPON ALL THE PEOPLE WHO WERE IN THE FIELDS, AND KILLED THEM.

(45) "AND ABIMELECH FOUGHT AGAINST THE CITY ALL THAT DAY; AND HE TOOK THE CITY; AND KILLED THE PEOPLE THAT WERE THEREIN, AND BEAT DOWN THE CITY, AND SOWED IT WITH SALT.

(46) "AND WHEN ALL THE MEN OF THE TOWER OF SHECHEM HEARD THAT, THEY ENTERED INTO AN HOLD OF THE HOUSE OF THE GOD BERITH.

(47) "AND IT WAS TOLD ABIMELECH, THAT ALL THE MEN OF THE TOWER OF SHECHEM WERE GATHERED TOGETHER.

(48) "AND ABIMELECH GAT HIM UP TO MOUNT ZALMON, HE AND ALL THE PEOPLE THAT WERE WITH HIM; AND ABIMELECH TOOK AN AX IN HIS HAND, AND CUT DOWN A BOUGH FROM THE TREES, AND TOOK IT, AND LAID IT ON HIS SHOULDER, AND SAID UNTO THE PEOPLE WHO WERE WITH HIM, WHAT YOU HAVE SEEN ME DO, MAKE HASTE, AND DO AS I HAVE DONE.

(49) "AND ALL THE PEOPLE LIKEWISE CUT DOWN EVERY MAN HIS BOUGH, AND FOLLOWED ABIMELECH, AND PUT THEM TO THE HOLD, AND SET THE HOLD ON FIRE UPON THEM: SO THAT ALL THE MEN OF THE TOWER OF SHECHEM DIED ALSO, ABOUT A THOUSAND MEN AND WOMEN."

The overview is:

1. When we read these accounts of murder, rape, and outright destruction, we wonder, how could such be?

The answer is simple, these are individuals who are led by their own selfish ambition and pride, with no thought of God, even though His Name may be occasionally used.

2. Most of the world is presently in the same condition as the accounts being illustrated in these Passages. In fact, the only semblance of order in this world, is that which is brought about by force, or influenced by Christianity.

3. The judgment of Abimelech involves Zebul. There comes a time when we share the guilt of the master in continuing to serve him. An honorable departure should be sought in such a case. *"The Lord will provide."* Otherwise we could find ourselves involved in the same judgment.

(50) "THEN WENT ABIMELECH TO THEBEZ, AND ENCAMPED AGAINST THEBEZ, AND TOOK IT.

(51) "BUT THERE WAS A STRONG TOWER WITHIN THE CITY, AND THITHER FLED ALL THE MEN AND WOMEN, AND ALL THEY OF THE CITY, AND SHUT IT TO THEM, AND GAT THEM UP TO THE TOP OF THE TOWER.

(52) "AND ABIMELECH CAME UNTO THE TOWER, AND FOUGHT AGAINST IT, AND WENT HARD UNTO THE DOOR OF THE TOWER TO BURN IT WITH FIRE.

(53) "AND A CERTAIN WOMAN CAST A PIECE OF A MILLSTONE UPON ABIMELECH'S HEAD, AND ALL TO BREAK HIS SKULL.

(54) "THEN HE CALLED HASTILY UNTO THE YOUNG MAN HIS ARMOURBEARER, AND SAID UNTO HIM, DRAW YOUR SWORD, AND KILL ME, THAT MEN SAY NOT OF ME, A WOMEN KILLED HIM. AND HIS YOUNG MAN THRUST HIM THROUGH, AND HE DIED.

(55) "AND WHEN THE MEN OF ISRAEL SAW THAT ABIMELECH WAS DEAD, THEY DEPARTED EVERY MAN UNTO HIS PLACE.

(56) "THUS GOD RENDERED THE WICKEDNESS OF ABIMELECH, WHICH HE DID UNTO HIS FATHER, IN KILLING HIS SEVENTY BRETHREN:

(57) "AND ALL THE EVIL OF THE MEN OF SHECHEM DID GOD RENDER UPON THEIR HEADS: AND UPON THEM CAME THE CURSE OF JOTHAM THE SON OF JERUB-BAAL."

The construction is:

1. In all of this we see the low state to which Israel had fallen, and all because of sin.

2. There is no talisman in the name of Abimelech, the son of Shechem, now that he is dead. His body is left to the wolves and vultures. Only *"the memory of the just smells sweet, and blossoms in the dust."* The saintly

NOTES

departed rule us from their graves. For instance, the Name of the Crucified and Eternal, Infinite Power.

3. In the moment of his death, Abimelech seems not to care for his soul, but is rather anxious to save his reputation. He thinks it has been dishonored because it could be said that a woman killed him. How stupid for one to spend one's last moments concerned about the insignificant.

THE DEATH OF THE WICKED

Most men die as they have lived. Some few on their death beds, even as the dying thief on the Cross, cry to the Lord for Mercy and Grace. To be sure, such Mercy and Grace are never withheld. But mostly it isn't so!

Many years ago I spoke for a few moments to a man who was worth many millions of dollars, and who was dying. I asked him, *"are you sure that you are ready to meet God?"*

He thought for a moment, and then answered, *"I don't know!"*

I then stated, *"Well don't you think it's time to make it right?"* His answer was very revealing.

"I've lived too long in this manner, and I can't change now."

He died a few days later. Maybe he called on the Lord in his last moments, and I sincerely pray he did, but I sincerely doubt that it happened. In fact, his last words were, *"I am burning, I am burning."* And then he died!

That man was my uncle. I was born in his home on March 15, 1935. He gave the money to build the little church in which my entire family was Saved. God dealt with him over and over, and in varied and many ways, all, it seems to no avail.

Abimelech had a godly father, but that didn't save him. He saw the Hand of God in operation as few individuals have seen it in the great victory won by his father over the enemy. But it couldn't save him.

In his military strategy, he tried to copy his godly father in breaking up his force into several companies, but still, none of that meant that he was Saved. He died lost, his last thoughts concerning how he would be remembered.

How will you be remembered?

CHAPTER 10

(1) "AND AFTER ABIMELECH THERE AROSE TO DEFEND ISRAEL TOLA THE SON OF PUAH, THE SON OF DODO, A MAN OF ISSACHAR; AND HE DWELT IN SHAMIR IN MOUNT EPHRAIM.

(2) "AND HE JUDGED ISRAEL TWENTY AND THREE YEARS, AND DIED, AND WAS BURIED IN SHAMIR.

(3) "AND AFTER HIM AROSE JAIR, A GILEADITE, AND JUDGED ISRAEL TWENTY AND TWO YEARS.

(4) "AND HE HAD THIRTY SONS WHO RODE ON THIRTY ASS COLTS, AND THEY HAD THIRTY CITIES, WHICH ARE CALLED HAVOTH-JAIR UNTO THIS DAY, WHICH ARE IN THE LAND OF GILEAD.

(5) "AND JAIR DIED, AND WAS BURIED IN CAMON."

The diagram is:

1. The information given in these five Verses concerning the two Judges *"Tola"* and *"Jair,"* presents the sum total.

2. If one would count the number of years each Judge served, as well as the number of years of servitude to various heathen countries round about, one would come up with more than *"450 years, until Samuel,"* as stated by Paul (Acts 13:20); therefore, the answer lies in the fact that the tenure of these Judges at times overlapped.

3. It seems that the Judgeships of Tola and Jair, which were some 45 years, present a lull before the storm. In their days we read of no invasions of their foes; consequently, no Gideon comes forth to herald miraculous things. The only events chronicled are the peaceful ridings of Jair's sons upon their colts amidst their ancestral cities.

TOLA AND JAIR THE SEVENTH AND EIGHTH JUDGES OF ISRAEL

To speculate too heavily about both Tola and Jair would not be wise. But yet, there are some things we do know. The best men are not always best known. We know nothing of Tola and Jair in comparison with what we know of Abimelech. Yet, the very fact that little is said of them is a proof that quite possibly they were good and honest men. All too often, we are too ready to mistake notoriety for fame and both for signs of greatness. We must also remember, that they are not the greatest men who make the most noise in the world (Pulpit).[1]

Who the enemies were from whom Tola was raised up to save Israel we are not told.

Incidentally, the Hebrew name *"Jair"* is preserved in the New Testament under the Greek form of *"Jairus"* (Mk. 5:22).

(6) "AND THE CHILDREN OF ISRAEL DID EVIL AGAIN IN THE SIGHT OF THE LORD, AND SERVED BAALIM, AND ASHTAROTH, AND THE GODS OF SYRIA, AND THE GODS OF ZIDON, AND THE GODS OF MOAB, AND THE GODS OF THE CHILDREN OF AMMON, AND THE GODS OF THE PHILISTINES, AND FORSOOK THE LORD, AND SERVED NOT HIM.

(7) "AND THE ANGER OF THE LORD WAS HOT AGAINST ISRAEL, AND HE SOLD THEM INTO THE HANDS OF THE PHILISTINES, AND INTO THE HANDS OF THE CHILDREN OF AMMON.

(8) "AND THAT YEAR THEY VEXED AND OPPRESSED THE CHILDREN OF ISRAEL: EIGHTEEN YEARS, ALL THE CHILDREN OF ISRAEL WHO WERE ON THE OTHER SIDE JORDAN IN THE LAND OF THE AMORITES, WHICH IS IN GILEAD.

(9) "MOREOVER THE CHILDREN OF AMMON PASSED OVER JORDAN TO FIGHT ALSO AGAINST JUDAH, AND AGAINST BENJAMIN, AND AGAINST THE HOUSE OF EPHRAIM; SO THAT ISRAEL WAS SORE DISTRESSED."

The composition is:

1. The Scripture says, *"And the Children of Israel did evil again in the sight of the LORD."* An old sin is an easy sin!

2. We find here that Israel has sunk to an all-time low. This appears to be the lowest point of debasement that they touched at this period of their history.

3. Israel seemed to forget, or else they didn't know, that the Lord, Whom they were supposed to serve, could bring about any situation He so desired. It is still the same presently. Everything that happens to a Child of God is either caused or allowed by the Lord. This we must never forget.

4. The words of Verse 8 may be translated *"broke and crushed them."* In earlier days, when serving one false god, they were oppressed but on one side, but now, serving a multitude of idols, they are oppressed on both sides. This fact is as true for men and nations presently as it was then.

THE ANGER OF THE LORD

As we have repeatedly stated, without proper leadership Israel debases herself, and does so to a greater degree than ever it seems! She lapses once again into acute idolatry. As stated, an old sin is an easy sin.

Why would they leave the Lord and serve the gods of Syria, Zidon, Moab, etc.? In fact, these were the only people on Earth who had any knowledge at all of Jehovah, the True God. These idols were only figments of man's imagination. True, demon spirits aided and abetted evil men in the invention of such wicked things, but still, the idols were nothing.

Over and over again, the Prophets exclaimed the simple truth as to how something made by man could be greater than the man who made it?

Concerning modern times, while most of the world doesn't worship such idols, still, most of the world makes idols out of things such as money, sports, fame, power, prestige, entertainment, etc. In fact, the greatest idol of all at the present time is religion. It is my contention that men have to be delivered from religion exactly as they are delivered from alcohol or drugs, etc. In fact, the demon of religion is far more powerful than these other things mentioned.

I think that history proves the fact that if proper Spiritual Leadership is lacking, men in one form or the other, will go into idolatry. As it held true for Israel then, it holds true for the modern Church presently. Regrettably and sadly, there is presently precious little true Spiritual Leadership. As a result, the Church is heading pell-mell toward apostasy, if, in fact, it has not already arrived at that sordid destination.

The Scripture bluntly says, *"The children of Israel did evil again . . . and forsook the LORD, and served not Him."*

The results? The Scripture also says,

NOTES

"And the anger of the LORD was hot against Israel."

The results? *"And He sold them into the hands of the Philistines, and into the hands of the children of Ammon."*

The word *"sold"* in the Hebrew is *"makar,"* and means *"sold as a slave."* The idea is, if Israel was going to serve the gods of this heathen, then they must as well, belong to the heathen.

If one wants sin, God will give sin to that individual. In other words, He will allow them to go the limit. They will find that the price is far higher than they desire to pay, or even can pay.

THREE ASPECTS TO SIN

If one looks at sin closely, one will see all of these aspects of sin. It doesn't present a pretty picture. They are:

1. The Pleasure Of Sin: Sin has an allurement, an enticement to it, which promises great pleasure. In fact, there is a momentary pleasure to sin, which makes it so attractive. The Word of God says of Moses, and concerning this very thing, and I quote from THE EXPOSITOR'S STUDY BIBLE:

"By Faith Moses, when he was come to years (refers to him coming to the age of 40 [Ex. 2:11]), *refused to be called the son of Pharaoh's daughter* (in effect, he refused the position of Pharaoh of Egypt, for which he had been trained because he had been adopted by Pharaoh's daughter);

"Choosing rather to suffer affliction with the people of God (proclaims the choice Moses made; he traded the temporal for the Eternal) *than to enjoy the pleasures of sin for a season* (presents the choice which much be made, affliction or the pleasures of sin);

"Esteeming the reproach of Christ greater riches than the treasures in Egypt (he judged the reproach was greater than the throne of Egypt): *for he had respect unto the recompense of the reward.* (Moses habitually 'looked away' from the treasures in Egypt, and purposely fixed his eye on the Heavenly Reward.)

"By Faith he forsook Egypt (which, spiritually speaking, every Believer must do), *not fearing the wrath of the king* (Pharaoh tried to kill him at that time [Ex. 2:15]): *for he endured, as seeing Him Who is invisible.* (This

speaks of Christ, Whom Moses saw by Faith.)

"Through Faith he kept the Passover (means that he *'instituted the Passover'* according to the Word of the Lord), *and the sprinkling of Blood* (referred to the Blood of the Pascal Lamb on the lintels and doorposts of the houses [Ex. 12:22]), *lest He Who destroyed the firstborn should touch them.* (Every Israelite's house was safe that night because of the blood being applied to the doorposts, a Type of the Blood of Christ applied to our hearts, which stops the Judgment of God)" (Heb. 11:24-28).

The Twenty-fifth Verse mentions the *"pleasures of sin."* But it also states that these pleasures are *"for a season,"* meaning, only for a short time.

The *"pleasure"* soon leads to something else.

2. The Bondage Of Sin: Drinking is a lot of fun, some say. But the twenty million people in this nation who are alcoholics do not any more think it's fun. They want to quit but they can't. They are now in bondage, where sin always leads.

Some twenty million Americans who are hooked on gambling, started out as *"fun,"* but it no longer fits that category. Now they can't stop, even though they have gambled away everything that matters. They are in bondage.

Millions of people begin taking drugs as a lark. It's fun! It's a pleasure! But in a little bit they find that it's no longer fun, they are hooked!

Without fail, sin, in one way or the other, will always take the person into bondage. It enslaves people. Admittedly, some are enslaved much worse than others; irrespective, slavery in one form or the other is the result.

The kid starts out smoking, because it's *"cool"* to do so. In fact, it's enjoyable, it's a pleasure! But in a little bit, it ceases to be a pleasure, and becomes a living Hell. Let us say it again: all sin in one form or the other, leads to bondage.

There is only one cure for this bondage, only one, and that is the Lord Jesus Christ and what He did for us at the Cross. That's why Paul said, *"We preach Christ Crucified"* (I Cor. 1:23). There is no other answer for this dread malady. If the Church preaches any other solution, it is preaching a lie! If it

preaches any other so-called panacea, it is preaching a lie! If it fosters any other scheme or fad, it is fostering a lie! For men to be delivered from sin, the Cross alone is the answer. That's why Paul also said:

"For I determined not to know any thing among you (with purpose and design, Paul did not resort to the knowledge or philosophy of the world regarding the Preaching of the Gospel), *save Jesus Christ, and Him Crucified* (that and that alone is the Message which will save the sinner, set the captive free, and give the Believer perpetual Victory)" (I Cor. 2:2).

3. The Eternal Destiny Of Sin: The first aspect of sin is *"pleasure."* The second aspect of sin is *"bondage."* The third aspect of sin is *"Hell,"* and we're speaking of that eternal abode, which at this moment holds most all who have ever lived.

Hell is located in the heart of the Earth (Mat. 12:40). Every unsaved person immediately upon dying goes to Hell (Lk. 16:19-31). As well, the fire of Hell is literal (Lk. 16:23-24).

The Sixteenth Chapter of Luke also proclaims the fact that all souls there are conscious. They think! They feel! They remember! As well, Hell is eternal (Rev. 20:10).

THE CROSS OF CHRIST AND ETERNAL HELL

The only thing standing between man and eternal Hell is the Cross of the Lord Jesus Christ. There, our Lord paid the ransom, a ransom incidentally, which was owed by man to God, but which man could never pay. Jesus paid it all, and did so by the giving of Himself on the Cross as a Perfect Sacrifice, which satisfied the demands of a thrice-Holy God.

In order to be Saved and to miss Hell, men must accept Christ as their Saviour and as their Lord (Jn. 3:16). One can be Saved no other way. Jesus Himself said, *"I am the Way, the Truth, and the Life: no man comes unto the Father, but by Me"* (Jn. 14:6).

Men may not like the idea and actually the reality, that Jesus Christ, and Jesus Christ Alone is the way, but that happens to be the Truth. Men can serve Mohammed if they like, but it will bring no Salvation. They can serve Buddha or Confucius if they like, but it will bring no Salvation. Men can serve the Virgin Mary and the Pope if they like, but it will bring no Salvation! In fact, men can serve their own Church, whatever that Church might be, but it will bring no Salvation. Peter said it well:

"*Neither is there Salvation in any other* (proclaims unequivocally that Jesus Alone holds the key to Salvation and, in fact, is Salvation)*: for there is none other name under Heaven given among men whereby we must be Saved*" (Acts 4:12).

(10) "AND THE CHILDREN OF ISRAEL CRIED UNTO THE LORD, SAYING, WE HAVE SINNED AGAINST YOU, BOTH BECAUSE WE HAVE FORSAKEN OUR GOD, AND ALSO SERVED BAALIM.

(11) "AND THE LORD SAID UNTO THE CHILDREN OF ISRAEL, DID NOT I DELIVER YOU FROM THE EGYPTIANS, AND FROM THE AMORITES, FROM THE CHILDREN OF AMMON, AND FROM THE PHILISTINES?

(12) "THE ZIDONIANS ALSO, AND THE AMALEKITES, AND THE MAONITES, DID OPPRESS YOU; AND YOU CRIED TO ME, AND I DELIVERED YOU OUT OF THEIR HAND.

(13) "YET YOU HAVE FORSAKEN ME, AND SERVED OTHER GODS: WHEREFORE I WILL DELIVER YOU NO MORE.

(14) "GO AND CRY UNTO THE GODS WHICH YOU HAVE CHOSEN; LET THEM DELIVER YOU IN THE TIME OF YOUR TRIBULATION."

The synopsis is:

1. Williams says, "*But there was sufficient energy of life in Israel to bring out the cry of confession. To be conscious of misery is a sign of life. Because of the deceitfulness of the heart, and because of the deceitfulness of sin, bondage is accepted after a slight struggle, and then, after a time, the slave becomes unconscious of the slavery.*

2. "*The confession, 'we have sinned against You' showed true repentance, for it showed a sense of injury done to God, and not merely sorrow because of the miseries that lay upon themselves. Remorse within itself is not repentance — mental distress because of the painful results of sin is not repentance; but a sense of the grief and dishonor*

NOTES

occasioned to God, and sorrow because He has been sinned against, that is Repentance. David and Simon Magus illustrate true and false repentance. The one cried, 'I have sinned against the Lord.' His first thought was God and His Glory. The other said, 'pray for me that none of these things come upon me.' His first thought was himself and to secure exemption from punishment."[2]

3. These idols, these so-called gods were merely figments of men's imaginations. They didn't even exist! So why did Israel, who had the privilege of having relationship with Jehovah, the only True God, desire to submit themselves to such evil?

Why does the modern Church forsake the Bible, and follow strange doctrines devised by men?

4. The problem was, and is, the sin nature. This is the nature of man that bends itself toward sin, and all because of the Fall. While they had no excuse, still, before the Cross, they did not have the Holy Spirit abiding within their lives on a permanent basis; therefore, Israel was, for all practical purposes, denied much of the help the Holy Spirit now gives.

5. Even presently, if the Believer doesn't understand that all victory is received and maintained by our Faith in Christ and the Cross, the sin nature will once again begin to dominate such a person (Rom. 8:32; 6:12-14).

CRY TO GOD FOR HELP

The Lord sold Israel into slavery, in order that they might ultimately come to their spiritual senses, and cry to Him for help, which they did! This was the very purpose of the Judgment. God, at times, will sell us to the enemy, allowing us to be squeezed just enough so that we will also "*Cry unto the Lord.*"

The truth is, even though Israel cried to the Lord, Verses 10 through 14 record an insincere repentance. It was a halfhearted confession by Israel, which elicited no favorable response from God.

Israel did admit that they had sinned, and that their sin had been against God, which was, in fact, an excellent first step. But still, it seems, that they were not yet ready to come to the place that God demanded — a place of total contrition.

So, the Lord tells them, why not cry to these gods, which they have been serving, the gods of the Zidonians, of the Amalekites, of the Maonites, etc.?

He wants them to see, and on no uncertain terms, just exactly how stupid they have been in forsaking Him, and turning to these monstrosities!

INSANITY

All sin, and in whatever shape, is a form of insanity. Without the Lord, men do not think right, do not act right, do not conduct themselves right, hence, the reason for the problems of this world.

It was insane to turn from Jehovah to serve these idol gods! It was insane to think that these things could help them in even the slightest way! It was insane to leave the Lord Who had delivered them from all the powers of darkness, and had given them this land, a land flowing with milk and honey!

IS SIN A CHOICE?

Yes and no!

Many Christians have the erroneous idea that before they were Saved they had no choice but to commit sin. In other words, looking back, they realize that Satan would override their will; however, now that they are Saved, many have the idea, wrongly we might quickly add, that now their willpower is strong enough that they can easily say "*no*" to sin.

In fact, most Preachers claim that sin is a matter of choice, and if a person does sin, it's just because they want to sin, etc.

While sin is a matter of choice, it's not a choice in the manner in which most think.

The choice is, and we are addressing ourselves to Believers, do we trust Christ and what He has done for us at the Cross, or do we trust something else? That's where the choice is, and that alone!

The willpower of the Believer does not increase after he is Saved. In fact, Paul said the following, and I quote from THE EXPOSITOR'S STUDY BIBLE:

"*For I know that in me (that is, in my flesh,) dwells no good thing* (speaks of man's own ability, or rather the lack thereof in

comparison to the Holy Spirit, at least when it comes to spiritual things)*: for to will is present with me* (Paul is speaking here of his willpower; regrettably, most modern Christians are trying to live for God by means of willpower, thinking falsely that since they have come to Christ, they are now free to say '*no*' to sin; that is the wrong way to look at the situation; the Believer cannot live for God by the strength of willpower; while the will is definitely important, it alone is not enough; the Believer must exercise Faith in Christ and the Cross, and do so constantly; then he will have the ability and strength to say '*yes*' to Christ, which automatically says, '*no*' to the things of the world)*; but how to perform that which is good I find not* (outside of the Cross, it is impossible to find a way to do good)" (Rom. 7:18).

Clearly and plainly the Apostle hear tells us that willpower is not strong enough to overcome sin. The truth is this:

If the Believer doesn't have his Faith exclusively in Christ and the Cross, which then gives the Holy Spirit the latitude to help him, Satan can force that person against their will. Now I realize a lot of Christians don't like to hear that. Some even deny it, but Paul is here plainly stating that that is the case. Think about it for a moment!

SIN AND THE BELIEVER

As a Believer, someone who loves the Lord, do you want to sin?

Of course not!

In fact, no person who is truly a Believer desires to sin. When they do sin, they feel like a dog that's just been unfaithful to his master, and they can't wait to get before the Lord and rid themselves of the problem (I Jn. 1:9). If one is a true Christian, that's the way that one feels.

So why does such a Believer sin?

They don't want to sin, they don't desire to sin, they're trying not to sin, so why do they sin?

They sin, at least most of the time, despite having struggled against it, and fought against it with all of their strength, simply because Satan overrode their will, and forced them into a position in which they didn't want to be.

Now some might read that and think, if Satan has forced them against their will, then they are not responsible. That isn't true. They are most definitely responsible.

How are they responsible?

They are responsible simply because they have omitted or failed to follow God's Prescribed Order of Victory, which is Faith in Christ and what Christ has done at the Cross. That's how they are responsible and, in fact, that's their real sin. What they have done as it regards acts of sin, is merely the symptom of not having their faith placed in the correct object — the Cross of Christ.

Believers need to repent not only of the bad things they've done, but they need to also repent of the good things they have done.

What do we mean by that?

We need to repent of depending upon the good deeds we have accomplished, the faithfulness we have rendered to the Church, even one's dependence on his prayer life, as good as that might be in its own right. These are all good things, because they are good things, they deceive us.

We're not saying that these good things should be given up. In fact, if possible, they should be increased. But this I do say:

We must not depend on these things, must not place our faith in these things, must not think that they merit us anything with God. Our Faith must exclusively be in Christ and what He has done for us at the Cross. In fact, that's the only type of Faith that God will really honor. So, our Repentance should include a lot of things other than merely the bad things we have done, as I trust we have properly explained (Rom. 5:1-2).

(15) "AND THE CHILDREN OF ISRAEL SAID UNTO THE LORD, WE HAVE SINNED: DO THOU UNTO US WHATSOEVER SEEMS GOOD UNTO YOU; DELIVER US ONLY WE PRAY THEE, THIS DAY.

(16) "AND THEY PUT AWAY THE STRANGE GODS FROM AMONG THEM, AND SERVED THE LORD: AND HIS SOUL WAS GRIEVED FOR THE MISERY OF ISRAEL.

(17) "THEN THE CHILDREN OF AMMON WERE GATHERED TOGETHER, AND ENCAMPED IN GILEAD. AND THE CHILDREN OF ISRAEL ASSEMBLED THEMSELVES TOGETHER, AND ENCAMPED

IN MIZPEH.

(18) "AND THE PEOPLE AND PRINCES OF GILEAD SAID ONE TO ANOTHER, WHAT MAN IS HE WHO WILL BEGIN TO FIGHT AGAINST THE CHILDREN OF AMMON? HE SHALL BE HEAD OVER ALL THE INHABITANTS OF GILEAD."

The construction is:

1. The Soul of the Lord being *"grieved"* means that He literally could not bear their suffering any longer. He would answer their prayer and deliver them.

2. The Lord has never turned aside those who sincerely come to Him, no matter the past.

3. What we're seeing in Verses 15 through 18 constitutes genuine Repentance.

REPENTANCE

There is a fivefold part to Israel's Repentance. Never mind that it took place some 3,300 years ago. It is appropriate for us presently as well! That fivefold part is:

WE HAVE SINNED

The first principle of true Repentance is to admit one's sin. One must make confession or acknowledgment of his sins to be forgiven (I Jn. 1:9). In essence, the person must say the same thing about himself that God says. He must repent not only of the bad, as we have stated, but the good as well. Sadly, this is what hinders most Christians. Some of us have become very adept at repenting of the bad; however, we find it very difficult, if not impossible to repent of the Pharisaical good. True Repentance demands that we repent not only of our bad, but our good also.

As we've already stated, the *"good"* that we do is not wrong. That's not the idea. The idea is, that we depend on these good things, in essence, making them the object of our Faith, which God cannot tolerate. So we have to repent of that. It doesn't mean stop doing the good, it just means that we place our Faith where it ought to be, in Christ and the Cross.

LORD, DO WITH US WHAT YOU LIKE

Israel said to the Lord, *"Do Thou unto us whatsoever seems good unto You."*

This is wholehearted surrender to the Will

of God and obedience to Him. This type of Repentance makes no claim upon God. We acknowledge that we deserve terrible Judgment. By rights, we should be condemned to Hell. We parade no goodness before Him, seeking to justify ourselves.

DELIVER US

This is an earnest appeal for deliverance from enemies, and from sin, which is also necessary for full consecration. God cannot deliver us until we admit we cannot deliver ourselves.

Man's constant fault is that he thinks that he can set himself free. Remember, sin cannot deliver sin; sickness cannot heal sickness; bondage cannot deliver bondage; and, flesh cannot deliver flesh. There is only one Deliverer, and He is God.

The very word *"Deliverer,"* infers that the power of enslavement is so great, that the individual cannot deliver himself. Consequently, there has to be one who is stronger than the enemy. Man within himself, does not carry such strength.

In fact, there is only One Who is stronger, and that One is the Lord Jesus Christ. Our Lord addressed Himself to this when He spoke of the *"strongman's house."* That strongman is Satan. In order for this strongman's house to be spoiled along with his goods, there has to be One Who is stronger Who can do these things. As stated, that One is the Lord Jesus Christ (Mat. 12:29).

Satan was totally and completely defeated at Calvary's Cross, and that defeat consisted of all sin being atoned, which took away the legal right that Satan had to hold man captive. With all sin removed, Satan's legal right was also removed.

So, Jesus has delivered us, at least all who will believe, because He is stronger, much stronger than Satan. Paul said:

"Who gave Himself for our sins (the Cross), *that He might deliver us from this present evil world* (the Cross alone can set the captive free), *according to the Will of God and our Father* (the standard of the entire process of Redemption)" (Gal. 1:4).

PUT AWAY THE STRANGE GODS

This consisted of all idols and idol worship.

Repentance demands that we quit the sin business.

This attitude manifested true Repentance and sincerity. Sadly, Israel abounded in strange gods. These gods were Baal and Ashtaroth.

Regrettably, the strange gods did not pass away with Israel; they abound presently in the modern Church.

The *"power of positive thinking gospel,"* is a strange god. The *"possibility thinking gospel,"* is a strange god. The *"health and wealth gospel,"* is a strange god. The *"dominion teaching,"* is a strange god. The *"psychological way,"* is a strange god. The *"Purpose Driven Life scheme,"* is a strange god. The *"Government of Twelve,"* is a strange god. *"Denominationalism"* is a strange god.

In other words, any message that's not *"Jesus Christ and Him Crucified,"* presents itself as a *"strange god."*

SERVE THE LORD

One can make confession and a pretense of consecration with the mouth; he can pose as being truly penitent and desperate and carry out the acts of Verse 15 all without true Repentance.

The way to tell if true Repentance is put into practice, is when one begins to do the things that one should do as it regards living for God. Putting into practice what we say is worth more than all Burnt Offerings, sacrifices, and, of course, superficial promises.

To put away all gods and truly serve Jehovah is all that God has ever required of man. When anyone does this, he will be reconciled to God and have Him on his side in any problem.

Whenever Israel met God's Conditions, and these conditions are not difficult to meet, the Lord will always respond with Deliverance, Forgiveness, Mercy, Grace, and an exhibition of His Power, all on behalf of the penitent one.

The Lord loves to do wonderful and beautiful things for His Children. We only have to meet His Conditions. If we think He has somewhat been short with us, we should check ourselves. It can be assured, that the fault lies with us and not with Him.

CHAPTER 11

(1) "NOW JEPHTHAH THE GILEADITE WAS A MIGHTY MAN OF VALOUR, AND HE WAS THE SON OF AN HARLOT: AND GILEAD BEGAT JEPHTHAH.

(2) "AND GILEAD'S WIFE BORE HIM SONS; AND HIS WIFE'S SONS GREW UP, AND THEY THRUST OUT JEPHTHAH, AND SAID UNTO HIM, YOU SHALL NOT INHERIT IN OUR FATHER'S HOUSE; FOR YOU ARE THE SON OF A STRANGE WOMAN.

(3) "THEN JEPHTHAH FLED FROM HIS BRETHREN, AND DWELT IN THE LAND OF TOB: AND THERE WERE GATHERED VAIN MEN TO JEPHTHAH, AND WENT OUT WITH HIM."

The exposition is:

1. Perhaps because Jephthah was the son of a harlot, he was despised, rejected, and hated; however, God used him greatly, even as we shall see. In fact, he is one of the specimen names found in God's Faith Hall of Fame (Heb. 11:32).

2. If a person's heart is toward God, irrespective of the past, God can use such a person, and often does so in order to rebuke His People, and to confound man's wisdom and power.

3. The men of Verse 3 were individuals who were broken and bankrupt. They gravitated toward Jephthah, as, at a later time, similar individuals joined David in the cave of Adullam.

JEPHTHAH THE NINTH
JUDGE OF ISRAEL

The Holy Spirit delineates immediately two things about Jephthah. The Spirit says:

A. He was *"a mighty man of valour."*

B. *"He was the son of an harlot."*

While man has no control over the circumstances of his birth, he has all the control in the world over the circumstances of his life and death. Jephthah could not help the sin of his father, but it seems that his brothers (half brothers) took it out on him. Let us state this truth:

There is no such thing as an illegitimate child, only illegitimate parents!

They thrust him out of his inheritance, thereby denying him that which was rightly his. Instead of fighting them, *"Jephthah fled from his brethren, and dwelt in the land of Tob."*

All too often such happens in modern Christendom. It happens because so-called Believers do not know the Word of God or else they're not interested in the Word of God, and simply desire to use the situation at hand to further their own cause and desires, whatever that might be.

But as his brothers would ultimately see, the wrong they did him, would ultimately come back to haunt them, as it always does.

(4) "AND IT CAME TO PASS IN PROCESS OF TIME, THAT THE CHILDREN OF AMMON MADE WAR AGAINST ISRAEL.

(5) "AND IT WAS SO, THAT WHEN THE CHILDREN OF AMMON MADE WAR AGAINST ISRAEL, THE ELDERS OF GILEAD WENT TO FETCH JEPHTHAH OUT OF THE LAND OF TOB:

(6) "AND THEY SAID UNTO JEPHTHAH, COME, AND BE OUR CAPTAIN, THAT WE MAY FIGHT WITH THE CHILDREN OF AMMON.

(7) "AND JEPHTHAH SAID UNTO THE ELDERS OF GILEAD, DID NOT YOU HATE ME, AND EXPEL ME OUT OF MY FATHER'S HOUSE? AND WHY ARE YOU COME UNTO ME NOW WHEN YOU ARE IN DISTRESS?

(8) "AND THE ELDERS OF GILEAD SAID UNTO JEPHTHAH, THEREFORE WE TURN AGAIN TO YOU NOW, THAT YOU MAY GO WITH US, AND FIGHT AGAINST THE CHILDREN OF AMMON, AND BE OUR HEAD OVER ALL THE INHABITANTS OF GILEAD.

(9) "AND JEPHTHAH SAID UNTO THE ELDERS OF GILEAD, IF YOU BRING ME HOME AGAIN TO FIGHT AGAINST THE CHILDREN OF AMMON, AND THE LORD DELIVER THEM BEFORE ME, SHALL I BE YOUR HEAD?

(10) "AND THE ELDERS OF GILEAD SAID UNTO JEPHTHAH. THE LORD BE WITNESS BETWEEN US, IF WE DO NOT SO ACCORDING TO YOUR WORDS.

(11) "THEN JEPHTHAH WENT WITH THE ELDERS OF GILEAD, AND THE PEOPLE MADE HIM HEAD AND CAPTAIN

OVER THEM: AND JEPHTHAH UTTERED ALL HIS WORDS BEFORE THE LORD IN MIZPEH."

The pattern is:

1. Evidently, Jephthah had made a name for himself in some way, as it regards military expertise.

2. The Seventh Verse proclaims the fact that his expulsion was not the private act of his own brothers only turning him out of the house they lived in, but rather a tribal act at which the elders of Gilead had taken a part.

3. As is obvious in the Eleventh Verse, Jephthah was a man of Faith and, thereby, desired the Will of God in these matters.

JEPHTHAH THE CAPTAIN

The Bible is full of instances of men who have gained power and fame through the overcoming of difficulties. Time and God are on the side of them who, not withstanding temptation, are found faithful. And is there not One Who outshines all others in this? The Stone which the builders rejected is become the Headstone of the corner. His Life, His Ministry, and we speak of our Lord Jesus Christ, are our incentive and example (Phil. 2:5-11).

And at the same time, a social stigma, which Jephthah had the misfortune to experience is worse to bear up against than many of the greatest calamities which do not involve such. This man is forced to take up his abode in a far off border town, near to Ammon, the hereditary enemy of Israel. In this capacity, he must have made a name for himself in opposing Israel's enemies, with his exploits having reached the ears of the leaders of Israel.

Whatever his circumstances, we find that the worship of Jehovah is maintained, and the heart of this man, this chieftain, beats true to all the traditions of Israel. Now he would be called upon to serve his country. Despite what his brothers and the Elders of Israel seemed to have thought of him in the beginning, he has proven himself as a godly man, whatever their thoughts and actions. And now, the Lord will vindicate this man's Faith.

BEFORE THE LORD

The Eleventh Verse says, "And the people

made him head and captain over them: and Jephthah uttered all his words before the LORD in Mizpeh."

Pulpit says, "The expression 'before the Lord' is used in Ex. 34:34; Lev. 1:3; and Judg. 21:2, and elsewhere to signify the special presence of the Lord which was to be found in the Tabernacle or with the Ark, or where there was the Priest with an Ephod. And this must be the meaning of the expression here."[1]

Jephthah was installed at the national place of gathering and consultation for Gilead. It was all done under the auspices of the Presence of the Lord, thereby, the Will of God.

Whether, however, the Ark was brought there, or the Altar, or a Priest with an Ephod, or whether some substitute was devised, which the unsettled times might justify, it is impossible to say from want of information; however, whatever was done was evidently completely sanctioned by the Lord.

(12) "AND JEPHTHAH SENT MESSENGERS UNTO THE KING OF THE CHILDREN OF AMMON, SAYING, WHAT HAVE YOU TO DO WITH ME, THAT YOU ARE COME AGAINST ME TO FIGHT IN MY LAND?

(13) "AND THE KING OF THE CHILDREN OF AMMON ANSWERED UNTO THE MESSENGERS OF JEPHTHAH, BECAUSE ISRAEL TOOK AWAY MY LAND, WHEN THEY CAME UP OUT OF EGYPT, FROM ARNON EVEN UNTO JABBOK, AND UNTO JORDAN: NOW THEREFORE RESTORE THOSE LANDS AGAIN PEACEABLY.

(14) "AND JEPHTHAH SENT MESSENGERS AGAIN UNTO THE KING OF THE CHILDREN OF AMMON:

(15) "AND SAID UNTO HIM, THUS SAITH JEPHTHAH, ISRAEL TOOK NOT AWAY THE LAND OF MOAB, NOR THE LAND OF THE CHILDREN OF AMMON:

(16) "BUT WHEN ISRAEL CAME UP FROM EGYPT, AND WALKED THROUGH THE WILDERNESS UNTO THE RED SEA, AND CAME TO KADESH;

(17) "THEN ISRAEL SENT MESSENGERS UNTO THE KING OF EDOM, SAYING, LET ME, I PRAY YOU, PASS THROUGH YOUR LAND: BUT THE KING OF EDOM WOULD NOT HEARKEN

THERETO. AND IN LIKE MANNER THEY SENT UNTO THE KING OF MOAB: BUT HE WOULD NOT CONSENT: AND ISRAEL ABODE IN KADESH.

(18) "THEN THEY WENT ALONG THROUGH THE WILDERNESS, AND COMPASSED THE LAND OF EDOM, AND THE LAND OF MOAB, AND CAME BY THE EAST SIDE OF THE LAND OF MOAB, AND PITCHED ON THE OTHER SIDE OF ARNON, BUT CAME NOT WITHIN THE BORDER OF MOAB: FOR ARNON WAS THE BORDER OF MOAB.

(19) "AND ISRAEL SENT MESSENGERS UNTO SIHON KING OF THE AMORITES, THE KING OF HESHBON; AND ISRAEL SAID UNTO HIM, LET US PASS, WE PRAY YOU, THROUGH YOUR LAND INTO MY PLACE.

(20) "BUT SIHON TRUSTED NOT ISRAEL TO PASS THROUGH HIS COAST: BUT SIHON GATHERED ALL HIS PEOPLE TOGETHER, AND PITCHED IN JAHAZ, AND FOUGHT AGAINST ISRAEL.

(21) "AND THE LORD GOD OF ISRAEL DELIVERED SIHON AND ALL HIS PEOPLE INTO THE HAND OF ISRAEL, AND THEY SMOTE THEM: SO ISRAEL POSSESSED ALL THE LAND OF THE AMORITES, THE INHABITANTS OF THAT COUNTRY.

(22) "AND THEY POSSESSED ALL THE COASTS OF THE AMORITES, FROM ARNON EVEN UNTO JABBOK, AND FROM THE WILDERNESS EVEN UNTO JORDAN.

(23) "SO NOW THE LORD GOD OF ISRAEL HAS DISPOSSESSED THE AMORITES FROM BEFORE HIS PEOPLE ISRAEL, AND SHOULD YOU POSSESS IT?

(24) "WILL NOT YOU POSSESS THAT WHICH CHEMOSH YOUR GOD GIVES YOU TO POSSESS? SO WHOMSOEVER THE LORD OUR GOD SHALL DRIVE OUT FROM BEFORE US, THEM WILL WE POSSESS.

(25) "AND NOW ARE YOU ANY THING BETTER THAN BALAK THE SON OF ZIPPOR, KING OF MOAB? DID HE EVER STRIVE AGAINST ISRAEL, OR DID HE EVER FIGHT AGAINST THEM,

(26) "WHILE ISRAEL DWELT IN HESHBON AND HER TOWNS, AND IN AROER AND HER TOWNS, AND IN ALL THE CITIES THAT BE ALONG BY THE COASTS OF ARNON, THREE HUNDRED YEARS? WHY THEREFORE DID YOU NOT RECOVER THEM WITHIN THAT TIME?

(27) "WHEREFORE I HAVE NOT SINNED AGAINST YOU, BUT YOU DO ME WRONG TO WAR AGAINST ME: THE LORD THE JUDGE BE JUDGE THIS DAY BETWEEN THE CHILDREN OF ISRAEL AND THE CHILDREN OF AMMON.

(28) "HOWBEIT THE KING OF THE CHILDREN OF AMMON HEARKENED NOT UNTO THE WORDS OF JEPHTHAH WHICH HE SENT HIM."

The construction is:

1. The king of the children of Ammon demanded the surrender of a certain area of land as the only condition of peace.

2. That of which the king of Ammon speaks in Verse 13 took place over 300 years before.

3. In effect, Jephthah in Verse 24 is pitting the Lord God against the idols of the Ammonites.

4. Jephthah now advances another argument to prove the justice of his cause and the unreasonableness of the Ammonite claim. If the territory in question was Moabite property, how came it that Balak lay no claim to it? So, if Balak, those long years before, had laid no claim to this area, neither should the Ammonites.

EFFORTS OF SATAN

The Thirteenth Verse says that Ammon was demanding Israel's possession. Satan will always demand your possession. If he can stop you from occupying it, he will. If you occupy it, he will try to dislodge you. He will do so by denying the Bible if possible, and if not, by warring against you.

Jephthah's answer is, *"So whomsoever the LORD our God shall drive out from before us, them will we possess."*

In effect, Jephthah is putting the ball in their court. In other words he is saying to them, *"If your god is able to take the land, so be it, but if our God, Jehovah prevails, then the victory belongs to us."*

What Jephthah proposes presents itself as sacred history, with the seal of God upon it. He recounts the details of the conquest by Israel those many years before, so far as they are relevant. He then asked the question as to why for 300 years Israel's occupancy of the disputed territory had never been contested?

(29) "THEN THE SPIRIT OF THE LORD CAME UPON JEPHTHAH, AND HE PASSED OVER GILEAD, AND MANASSEH, AND PASSED OVER MIZPEH OF GILEAD, AND FROM MIZPEH OF GILEAD HE PASSED OVER UNTO THE CHILDREN OF AMMON.

(30) "AND JEPHTHAH VOWED A VOW UNTO THE LORD, AND SAID, IF YOU SHALL WITHOUT FAIL DELIVER THE CHILDREN OF AMMON INTO MY HANDS,

(31) "THEN IT SHALL BE, THAT WHATSOEVER COMES FORTH OF THE DOORS OF MY HOUSE TO MEET ME, WHEN I RETURN IN PEACE FROM THE CHILDREN OF AMMON, SHALL SURELY BE THE LORD'S, AND I WILL OFFER IT UP FOR A BURNT OFFERING."

The exposition is:

1. The Spirit of the Lord is what is guiding Jephthah, and he makes his move according to the Lord's Command.

2. Williams says, *"The word 'and' in the Thirty-first Verse in the Hebrew, is frequently translated 'or' in the Scriptures; so, it would then read, 'shall surely be the LORD's, or I will offer it up for a Burnt Offering.'"*[2]

3. Jephthah did not offer up his daughter as a Burnt Offering as some think, but rather consecrated her to perpetual virginity, thereby ending the family tree with her.

THE SPIRIT OF THE LORD

The Twenty-ninth Verse gives us the secret of Victory in the Church, *"Then the Spirit of the LORD came upon Jephthah."*

God's Spirit will only come upon a man of Faith; it will not come upon the flesh. Self-righteous pride could never accept this.

Jephthah is the son of a harlot, the result of a sinful act of his father and, thereby, cursed, or so they thought! So, all good Israelites must reject him; however, Faith overcomes sin, for only Faith in the Vicarious Atoning Work of the Lord Jesus Christ can overcome sin.

The *"Spirit of the LORD"* did not come on the leaders of Israel; it did not come upon the High Priest; it did not come upon the Levites; it came upon Jephthah.

THE WORK OF THE SPIRIT BEFORE THE CROSS

In the Twenty-ninth Verse when it speaks of the *"Spirit of the LORD coming upon Jephthah,"* this is the manner in which the Holy Spirit worked before the Cross.

Due to the blood of bulls and goats being unable to take away sins, meaning that animal blood, although necessary, still was woefully insufficient, the sin debt remained, and could not be atoned (Heb. 10:4).

So, the Holy Spirit during those times would come upon certain individuals called by the Lord, such as Jephthah, in order to help carry out the task assigned to them. When that task was completed, the Spirit of God would lift.

That's what Jesus was talking about when He said to His Disciples shortly before the Crucifixion, *"He* (the Holy Spirit) *dwells with you, and shall be in you"* (Jn. 14:17).

There is a vast difference in the Holy Spirit dwelling with someone, than being in someone. Since the Cross, every Believer becomes a Temple of the Holy Spirit, with the Holy Spirit dwelling within us permanently (I Cor. 3:16).

The difference in all of this is the *"Cross."*

At the Cross, the terrible sin debt which hung over man, and which man could not pay, was completely alleviated by Jesus offering up Himself in Sacrifice. This means that all sin was atoned, past, present, and future, at least for all who will believe (Jn. 3:16).

With all sin atoned, meaning that the sin debt was forever lifted, thereby paid, and paid in full, the Holy Spirit could now come into the heart and life of the Believer, which He does at conversion (Jn. 3:5-8).

Due to the Cross, we now have a much better Covenant, based on better Promises (Heb. 8:6).

(32) "SO JEPHTHAH PASSED OVER UNTO THE CHILDREN OF AMMON TO FIGHT AGAINST THEM; AND THE LORD DELIVERED THEM INTO HIS HANDS.

(33) "AND HE SMOTE THEM FROM AROER, EVEN TILL YOU COME TO MINNITH, EVEN TWENTY CITIES, AND UNTO THE PLAIN OF THE VINYARDS, WITH A VERY GREAT SLAUGHTER. THUS THE CHILDREN OF AMMON

WERE SUBDUED BEFORE THE CHILDREN OF ISRAEL."

The diagram is:

1. The Spirit of the Lord coming upon Jephthah, guaranteed his success. All the armies in the world could not have defeated him.

2. That which the Lord anoints, He is bound to honor.

3. Victory is intended for every Believer, and can be had by every Believer, providing Faith is properly placed in Christ and the Cross (Rom. 6:1-14; 8:1-2, 11; Gal. 6:14).

VICTORY

The Thirty-second Verse says, *"And the LORD delivered them into his hands."*

In the Fifteenth Verse of the Tenth Chapter, Israel had cried to God for the Lord to deliver them. God would hear that cry and answer that petition. Jephthah would be the instrument the Lord would use to deliver Israel.

Many people want deliverance but not God's Way. If it can come through their denomination or their Church with them setting the rules, then they will accept it. This means that most people, never receive deliverance simply because they want to dictate the terms, and God will have none of it.

All Deliverance comes exclusively from Christ through the Cross. In other words, Christ is the Source, while the Cross is the Means. Let it ever be understood, there is no other Source, and there are no other Means.

(34) "AND JEPHTHAH CAME TO MIZPEH UNTO HIS HOUSE, AND, BEHOLD, HIS DAUGHTER CAME OUT TO MEET HIM WITH TIMBRELS AND WITH DANCES: AND SHE WAS HIS ONLY CHILD; BESIDE HER HE HAD NEITHER SON NOR DAUGHTER.

(35) "AND IT CAME TO PASS, WHEN HE SAW HER, THAT HE RENT HIS CLOTHES, AND SAID, ALAS, MY DAUGHTER! YOU HAVE BROUGHT ME VERY LOW, AND YOU ARE ONE OF THEM THAT TROUBLE ME: FOR I HAVE OPENED MY MOUTH UNTO THE LORD, AND I CANNOT GO BACK.

(36) "AND SHE SAID UNTO HIM, MY FATHER, IF YOU HAVE OPENED YOUR

MOUTH UNTO THE LORD, DO TO ME ACCORDING TO THAT WHICH HAS PROCEEDED OUT OF YOUR MOUTH; FORASMUCH AS THE LORD HAS TAKEN VENGEANCE FOR YOU OF YOUR ENEMIES, EVEN OF THE CHILDREN OF AMMON.

(37) "AND SHE SAID UNTO HER FATHER, LET THIS THING BE DONE FOR ME: LET ME ALONE TWO MONTHS, THAT I MAY GO UP AND DOWN UPON THE MOUNTAINS, AND BEWAIL MY VIRGINITY, I AND MY FELLOWS.

(38) "AND HE SAID, GO. AND HE SENT HER AWAY FOR TWO MONTHS: AND SHE WENT WITH HER COMPANIONS, AND BEWAILED HER VIRGINITY UPON THE MOUNTAINS.

(39) "AND IT CAME TO PASS AT THEN END OF TWO MONTHS, THAT SHE RETURNED UNTO HER FATHER, WHO DID WITH HER ACCORDING TO HIS VOW WHICH HE HAD VOWED: AND SHE KNEW NO MAN. AND IT WAS A CUSTOM IN ISRAEL,

(40) "THAT THE DAUGHTERS OF ISRAEL WENT YEARLY TO LAMENT THE DAUGHTER OF JEPHTHAH THE GILEADITE FOUR DAYS IN A YEAR."

The structure is:

1. Jephthah did not put his daughter to death and offer up her body as a burnt sacrifice to Jehovah, for such sacrifices were sternly forbidden in the Law (Lev. 18:21; 20:2-5).

2. He rather dedicated his daughter to Jehovah by a perpetual virginity. This is conclusive from the statement in Verse 39 that after her father had performed his vow, *"she knew no man,"* that is, she never was married.

3. Considering that no children would be born into this family, this meant that the line of Jephthah would end with his death and her death; however, Jephthah is mentioned in Hebrews 11:32 as one of the great giants of Faith. And so he was!

JEPHTHAH'S VOW

That vow had been, *"If you shall without fail deliver the children of Ammon into my hands, then it shall be, that whatsoever comes forth of the doors of my house to meet me, when I return in peace from the children of Ammon, shall surely be the LORD's, and I will offer it up for a Burnt Offering."*

The word *"house"* in the Hebrew is *"payith"* and has several meanings, one of which is *"without,"* therefore, it could mean within the house, or it could mean without the house, which would refer to the entirety of the possessions of Jephthah. For instance, the term is used at times such as, *"the house of Obededom"* (II Sam. 6:10). In other words, it refers to far more than a mere domicile.

Jephthah would not have been talking about his domicile, referring to the four walls so to speak, because the only thing that could come out of such a dwelling would be a human being. So, he was speaking of the entirety of his possessions, which would have included flocks of lambs, etc.

Jephthah's daughter was the first one to come out of the house to meet him upon him returning from his great victory. Considering his vow, she would be consecrated to the Lord all of her life, meaning she would not marry, meaning that there would be no children born into this family, meaning as well that the family line would cease with Jephthah and his daughter.

The question begs to be asked, should Jephthah, noting the circumstances, have asked the Lord to forgive him for this rash vow and, thereby, not submit his daughter to perpetual loneliness?

Concerning the law of vows, the Scripture says, *"If a man vow a vow unto the LORD, or swear an oath to bind his soul with a bond; he shall not break his word, he shall do according to all that proceeds out of his mouth"* (Num. 30:2).

Concerning a father and his daughter, it also says, *"If a woman also vow a vow unto the LORD, and bind herself by a bond, being in her father's house in her youth;*

"And her father hear her vow, and her bond wherewith she has bound her soul, and her father shall hold his peace at her; then all her vows shall stand, and every bond wherewith she has bound her soul shall stand."

And then it says, *"But if her father disallow her in the day that he hears; not any of her vows, or of her bonds wherewith she has bound her soul, shall stand: and the LORD shall forgive her, because her father disallowed her"* (Num. 30:3-5).

The idea is concerning the father and his daughter, that if the father was so minded, he could disallow her vow, and the Lord would forgive her.

Williams says, *"There was release for a woman, but she could not effect it herself; only one who was related to her, and who loved her, could do so."*[3]

There is some small indication, I think, that Jephthah could have asked the Lord to forgive him for this rash vow, insomuch as it included his daughter with her having no say.

One might say, such was Israel. She vowed at Sinai to perform all that Jehovah commanded. Her Divine Bridegroom and husband permitted the vow; but she, having failed to keep it, came, therefore, under the sentence of death. To redeem her from this doom, her Husband, in Grace, took it upon Himself, and so delivered her from her vow. She could not deliver herself.

Perhaps the questions concerning Jephthah and his vow will never be answered this side of Heaven. But this one thing is certain, this man was true to God and in every respect, and nothing could be greater than that.

CHAPTER 12

(1) "AND THE MEN OF EPHRAIM GATHERED THEMSELVES TOGETHER, AND WENT NORTHWARD, AND SAID UNTO JEPHTHAH, WHEREFORE PASSED YOU OVER TO FIGHT AGAINST THE CHILDREN OF AMMON, AND DID NOT CALL US TO GO WITH YOU? WE WILL BURN YOUR HOUSE UPON YOU WITH FIRE.

(2) "AND JEPHTHAH SAID UNTO THEM, I AND MY PEOPLE WERE AT GREAT STRIFE WITH THE CHILDREN OF AMMON; AND WHEN I CALLED YOU, YOU DELIVERED ME NOT OUT OF THEIR HANDS.

(3) "AND WHEN I SAW THAT YOU DELIVERED ME NOT, I PUT MY LIFE IN MY HANDS, AND PASSED OVER AGAINST THE CHILDREN OF AMMON, AND THE LORD DELIVERED THEM INTO MY HAND: WHEREFORE THEN ARE YOU COME UP UNTO ME THIS DAY, TO FIGHT AGAINST ME?

(4) "THEN JEPHTHAH GATHERED TOGETHER ALL THE MEN OF GILEAD, AND FOUGHT WITH EPHRAIM: AND THE MEN OF GILEAD SMOTE EPHRAIM, BECAUSE THEY SAID, YOU GILEADITES ARE FUGITIVES OF EPHRAIM AMONG THE EPHRAIMITES, AND AMONG THE MANASSITES.

(5) "AND THE GILEADITES TOOK THE PASSAGES OF JORDAN BEFORE THE EPHRAIMITES: AND IT WAS SO, THAT WHEN THOSE EPHRAIMITES WHICH WERE ESCAPTED SAID, LET ME GO OVER; THAT THE MEN OF GILEAD SAID UNTO HIM, ARE YOU AN EPHRAIMITE? IF HE SAID, NO;

(6) "THEN SAID THEY UNTO HIM, SAY NOW SHIBOLETH: AND HE SAID SIBBOLETH: FOR HE COULD NOT FRAME TO PRONOUNCE IT RIGHT. THEN THEY TOOK HIM, AND KILLED HIM AT THE PASSAGES OF JORDAN: AND THERE FELL AT THAT TIME OF THE EPHRAIMITES FORTY AND TWO THOUSAND."

The diagram is:

1. Carnal men with carnal ideas as were the Ephraimites, tread where Angels fear to tread. In the first place, they had no right whatsoever to speak to Jephthah in this fashion; second, did they not realize that they were insulting the man who had just defeated the Ammonites, and, above all, that God was with him?

2. It seems that Jephthah asked the help of Ephraim when he was first made chief of the Gileadites, and they refused, partly because they thought the attempt desperate, and partly because it seems they were offended at his leadership.

3. The forty-two thousand of Verse 6 probably should have been translated *"forty plus two thousand, i.e., 2,040."*

INWARD STRIFE

The Twelfth Chapter is a sad picture of the Church in strife.

Verse 1 says, *"And the men of Ephraim gathered themselves together."* Regrettably, they gathered themselves together to destroy that which God had blessed. The flesh ever persecutes the Spirit.

Why didn't they gather themselves together

against Ammon when these heathen were threatening Israel? They were claiming that Jephthah did not give them an invitation to fight with him against Ammon. The Second Verse declares that he did, *"And when I called you, you delivered me not out of their hands."*

Perhaps they were, as many Christians, so preoccupied with their own doings that they paid little attention to the Call. And then again, and more than likely, at the first they didn't think that Jephthah had any chance of winning.

Now that a great victory has been won, they reasoned that had they been there, they could have helped gather the spoil, which, no doubt, was voluminous; however, they were not there, and so they were denied the spoil. They were angry about that if, in fact, that was the real problem. How many Believers presently are being called by God to help take this Gospel to the world; to help push back the darkness; to help bring in the harvest; but because of Spiritual Deafness they do not hear? Jesus said, *"If any man have ears to hear, let him hear."*

Ephraim had no ears to hear. Sadly, most of Christendom has no ears to hear. Now, they will want to destroy the man whom God has used to save them from Ammonite oppression. Once again we say, the flesh cannot abide the Spirit.

Now we have a civil war between brethren, for the Third Verse says, *"You come up unto me this day, to fight against me?"*

This is a sad picture of the modern Church. There are enemies galore to fight, but, instead, we fight each other.

The Sixth Verse says, *"And there fell at that time of the Ephraimites forty and two thousand."* As stated, it probably should have been translated 2,040.

How many casualties are there in the Church because of inner strife? How much of our energy do we spend in fighting among ourselves instead of against the enemy?

Perhaps some of the old animosity against Jephthah remained in the heart of Ephraim. I think it is evident that they were little pleased with God's choice, as the Church is seldom pleased with God's choice.

(7) "AND JEPHTHAH JUDGED ISRAEL SIX YEARS. THEN DIED JEPHTHAH THE

GILEADITE, AND WAS BURIED IN ONE OF THE CITIES OF GILEAD."

The overview is:

1. Jephthah and Abdon present a contrast. The one risked his life, won a great victory, and delivered Israel; and after a childless life was buried in an unknown grave. Such is the gratitude of man!

2. The other risked nothing that is recorded. He had forty sons and thirty grandsons, and his grave is described with great minuteness.

3. However, the Holy Spirit in Hebrews 11:32 places Jephthah's valorous name among the golden tablets of the Eternal Records and ignores Abdon. God never forgets those who trust and serve Him, however much they may be forgotten by man.

(8) "AND AFTER HIM IBZAN OF BETH-LEHEM JUDGED ISRAEL.

(9) "AND HE HAD THIRTY SONS, AND THIRTY DAUGHTERS, WHOM HE SENT ABROAD, AND TOOK IN THIRTY DAUGHTERS FROM ABROAD FOR HIS SONS. AND HE JUDGED ISRAEL SEVEN YEARS.

(10) "THEN DIED IBZAN, AND WAS BURIED AT BETH-LEHEM.

(11) "AND AFTER HIM ELON, A ZEBULONITE, JUDGED ISRAEL; AND HE JUDGED ISRAEL TEN YEARS.

(12) "AND ELON THE ZEBULONITE DIED, AND WAS BURIED IN AIJALON IN THE COUNTRY OF ZEBULUN.

(13) "AND AFTER HIM ABDON THE SON OF HILLEL, A PIRATHONITE, JUDGED ISRAEL.

(14) "AND HE HAD FORTY SONS AND THIRTY NEPHEWS, WHO RODE ON THREESCORE AND TEN ASS COLTS: AND HE JUDGED ISRAEL EIGHT YEARS.

(15) "AND ABDON THE SON OF HILLEL THE PIRATHONITE DIED, AND WAS BURIED IN PIRATHON IN THE LAND OF EPHRAIM, IN THE MOUNT OF THE AMALEKITES."

The structure is:

1. From no record of Ibzan's Judgeship being preserved, we may infer that no important events took place in his time.

2. There is nothing to record save how long these particular three Judges judged, when they died, and where they were buried.

NOTES

We infer, indeed, from the fact that there were Judges, the continual care of God for His People, and from the absence of invasion and servitude, that the people at that time, did not forsake God.

3. It would seem that Jephthah's battles, and the great victory won, were in some way, perhaps the greatest cause of all, the reason for the calm. It was a calm after the storm.

IBZAN, ELON, AND ABDON, THE TENTH, ELEVENTH AND TWELFTH JUDGES OF ISRAEL

From no record of Ibzan's Judgeship being preserved, except this domestic incident of Verse 9, we may infer, as in the case of Jair, that no important events took place in his time (Pulpit).[1]

Basically the same is said of Elon and Abdon.

As previously stated, no doubt, the great victory won by Jephthah was at least partly, if not totally, responsible for the present calmness of the times.

CHAPTER 13

(1) "AND THE CHILDREN OF ISRAEL DID EVIL AGAIN IN THE SIGHT OF THE LORD; AND THE LORD DELIVERED THEM INTO THE HAND OF THE PHILISTINES FORTY YEARS.

(2) "AND THERE WAS A CERTAIN MAN OF ZORAH, OF THE FAMILY OF THE DANITES, WHOSE NAME WAS MANOAH; AND HIS WIFE WAS BARREN, AND BORE NOT.

(3) "AND THE ANGEL OF THE LORD APPEARED UNTO THE WOMAN, AND SAID UNTO HER, BEHOLD NOW, YOU ARE BARREN, AND BEAREST NOT: BUT YOU SHALL CONCEIVE, AND BEAR A SON.

(4) "NOW THEREFORE BEWARE, I PRAY YOU, AND DRINK NOT WINE NOR STRONG DRINK, AND EAT NOT ANY UNCLEAN THING:

(5) "FOR, LO, YOU SHALL CONCEIVE, AND BEAR A SON; AND NO RAZOR SHALL COME ON HIS HEAD: FOR THE CHILD SHALL BE A NAZARITE UNTO GOD FROM

THE WOMB: AND HE SHALL BEGIN TO DELIVER ISRAEL OUT OF THE HAND OF THE PHILISTINES.

(6) "THEN THE WOMAN CAME AND TOLD HER HUSBAND, SAYING, A MAN OF GOD CAME UNTO ME, AND HIS COUNTE-NANCE WAS LIKE THE COUNTENANCE OF AN ANGEL OF GOD, VERY TERRIBLE: BUT I ASKED HIM NOT WHENCE HE WAS, NEITHER TOLD HE ME HIS NAME:

(7) "BUT HE SAID UNTO ME, BEHOLD, YOU SHALL CONCEIVE, AND BEAR A SON; AND NOW DRINK NO WINE NOR STRONG DRINK, NEITHER EAT ANY UNCLEAN THING: FOR THE CHILD SHALL BE A NAZARITE TO GOD FROM THE WOMB TO THE DAY OF HIS DEATH."

The construction is:

1. Over and over again, we see this ter-rible disposition of Israel. They go into deep sin; and to bring them to their senses, the Lord allows them to be taken over by the heathen.

2. After they suffer immeasurably for a pe-riod of time, they begin to call on the Name of the Lord, begging for help; and, always, the Lord would hear and answer, even as He will always hear and answer such a plea. But what a sad commentary on the plight of the human heart.

3. The Philistines now become promi-nent, and continued to be so up to the time of David, when they were finally subdued.

4. The Philistine represents a fact: Samson, whom we will study in the next four Chap-ters, represents a principle.

5. The fact is, there are enemies within the Christian's heart, for the Philistine was an inward, and not an outward foe. The prin-ciple is that this inward enemy can only be defeated by the Believer understanding that his victory comes exclusively through Christ and what Christ has done at the Cross, de-manding our ever constant Faith in Christ and the Cross. Then, and then only, can the Holy Spirit function and work within our lives, bringing about the desired consecra-tion (I Cor. 1:17-18, 21, 23; 2:2; Gal. 6:14).

6. The description given in Verse 2 con-cerning the parents of Samson presents that which is very similar to Abraham and Sarah (Gen. 17:19; 18:10, 14), to Hannah (I Sam.

NOTES

1:17), to Elisabeth (Lk. 1:13), and to the Blessed Virgin (Lk. 1:31). The Angel of Je-hovah, incidentally was the same Angel Who appeared to Gideon, actually, the Lord Jesus Christ in angelic form.

7. Until Samson would be born, his mother was to consecrate herself as a Nazarite.

8. Samson was to be a Nazarite from his mother's womb. That meant that he was not to drink any type of intoxicating drink, or even grape juice. He was not to cut his hair, nor was he to go near a dead body, even that of his nearest relation. If the last rule was inadvertently broken, the Nazarite had to undergo closely-detailed purification rites. If it is to be noticed, Samson would not ac-tually deliver Israel from the Philistines, but most definitely would begin the process.

EVIL

Verse 1 says, *"Did evil again."* This rep-etition presents a sorry note concerning Is-rael and yet, I wonder if it's not characteris-tic of the majority of the Church. There are two major pictures presented to us in the Book of Judges:

A. The Compassion, Grace, and Mercy of the Lord in forgiving Israel over and over again, as well as coming to her rescue.

B. The terrible weakness of God's chosen People, which too much characterizes the majority, as well of the Christian Church.

How many Christians is it said of them that they *"Did evil again"* and that over and over?

Verse 1 also says, *"And the LORD deliv-ered them into the hand of the Philistines forty years."* The Philistines now become prominent and continue to be so up to the time of David, when they are finally subdued.

The fact is, as stated, that there are en-emies within the Christian's heart, for as also stated, the Philistine was an inward and not an outward foe. The inward enemy can only be defeated by one subscribing fully to God's Prescribed Order of Victory; hence, the Lord called Samson to be a Nazarite.

GOD'S PRESCRIBED ORDER OF VICTORY

I would strongly encourage the reader to obtain for yourself our Study Guide, THE

CROSS OF CHRIST, GOD'S PRESCRIBED ORDER OF VICTORY. This is a subject we will allude to again and again in this Volume, and simply because it is the single most important thing as it regards the Child of God.

God's Prescribed Order of Victory is in brief, the Cross of our Lord Jesus Christ. As we've stated over and over, Christ is the Source, while the Cross is the Means.

God demands that we live a holy life, a consecrated life, a dedicated life, free from the bondages of this world, free from the snares of Satan. The Holy Spirit said through the Apostle Paul, *"I beseech you therefore, Brethren* (I beg of you please), *by the Mercies of God* (all is given to the Believer, not because of merit on the Believer's part, but strictly because of the *'Mercy of God'*), *that you present your bodies a Living Sacrifice* (the word *'Sacrifice'* speaks of the Sacrifice of Christ, and means that we cannot do this which the Holy Spirit demands unless our Faith is placed strictly in Christ and the Cross, which then gives the Holy Spirit latitude to carry out this great work within our lives), *holy* (that which the Holy Spirit Alone can do), *acceptable unto God* (actually means that a holy physical body, i.e., *'temple,'* is all that He will accept), *which is your reasonable service* (reasonable if we look to Christ and the Cross; otherwise impossible!)*"* (Rom. 12:1).

To defeat the Philistine, i.e., *"this inward foe,"* the Believer must understand that within himself, no matter how personally strong he might think he is, he simply cannot carry out this which the Lord demands. In order to be what we can be and, in fact, to be what we must be, the Holy Spirit Alone, as stated, can carry out this work within our lives. He doesn't demand much of us, but He does demand one thing, and that is that our Faith be exclusively in Christ and the Cross (Rom. 6:1-14; 8:1-2, 11). As well, it is demanded that our Faith be in Christ and the Cross on a continuous even a daily basis. Jesus said so (Lk. 9:23).

THE BARREN WOMAN

Verse 2 says, and concerning the wife of Samson's prospective father, *"and his wife was barren."* That which God will use to bring a deliverer will at the same time allow

Satan much latitude to hinder; consequently, he will make Manoah's wife barren, and the Lord will allow it. God allows Satan this type of latitude for two purposes:

A. To create in the heart and life of the party in question total trust and dependence on the Lord.

B. That the work be totally of the Spirit and none of the flesh.

It is the same presently.

As someone has well said, *"Desperation always precedes Revelation."* I think that has proved correct in the experience of life more often than not.

The things of God do not come easily, and neither do they come quickly. So often, even as we here observe, the Lord will allow Satan the means by which he causes great hindrance.

I suppose the question must be asked, as to how many through whom the Lord desires to bring forth a great thing, but they lose Faith and quit. I suspect that number is far larger than anyone realizes.

While circumstances possibly mean everything to we poor human beings, they mean nothing to God. He is able to do whatever needs to be done, irrespective as to what it might be.

In the midst of wayward Israel, God's People gone astray, we will find that a woman who has been barren now becomes pregnant, and from her a deliverer will come forth.

Bluntly, the modern Church is barren! It has lost its way! But yet somewhere, in some place, possibly by the one least expected, a Spiritual Pregnancy is about to take place. God is going to do a great thing! I believe that!

THE ANGEL OF THE LORD

Verse 3 says, *"And the Angel of the LORD appeared unto the woman."*

This was a pre-incarnate appearance of the Lord Jesus Christ. His Message would be simple, *"You shall conceive and bear a son."*

The desperate need of the modern Church is to hear the Voice of the Lord. There is nothing more powerful than, *"Thus saith the Lord."* Regrettably, the Church all too often hears the racket of what proposes to be God, but seldom is. Mostly it is the voice of false doctrine, error, apostasy, and heresy. But when the Lord appears, and He must appear for His Work to be done, great things begin to happen.

Let me ask the question again, *"Is it possible that somewhere in this nation, or somewhere else in this world, that one, or more, or even many, have just been made Spiritually Pregnant, which means, that despite all that Hell could try to do, the drought is over?"*

I can hear the voice of the great Prophet saying, *"Get thee up, eat and drink; for there is a sound of abundance of rain"* (I Ki. 18:41).

THE NAZARITE

Verses 4 and 5 proclaim that both mother and son would be Nazarites. The Fifth Verse says, *"For the child shall be a Nazarite unto God from the womb."* All Nazarites were to let their hair grow and to abstain from all fruit of the vine. These two Verses have a double meaning. They are:

A. The Fourth Verse is a picture of what God demanded of Israel in that they would ultimately bring the True Nazarite into the world, and we speak of the Lord Jesus Christ. This means that the entirety of the Nation of Israel, and for all time, at least until Christ would be born, was spiritually to be a Nazarite. Regrettably, they failed, but the Lord Jesus Christ, the True Nazarite did not fail. In fact, Jesus is the True Israel, the True Man, and the True Church.

B. The order of the Nazarite ordained by God demanded total consecration, and was, in effect, a sign of weakness, as long hair meant weakness. So, the Lord would take Samson, place the Nazarite vow upon him, denoting great weakness, and then put His Spirit upon Samson to make him the strongest man upon the face of the Earth. This is a picture of what Israel should have been, what the Church ought to be, and what we as Believers ought to be also, spiritually speaking.

THE NAZARITE VOW

The Nazarite vow was threefold:

• Do not touch a dead body; death is a portrayal of the Fall of man, and is a result of sin.

• No alcoholic beverage of any nature was to be consumed, not even grape juice, or even the grapes on the vine.

• Do not cut the hair; as an example, the

great Prophet Samuel was a Nazarite, as was John the Baptist.

THE NAZARITE SPIRIT

Inasmuch as Jesus has now come, and inasmuch as all sin has been addressed at the Cross of Calvary, all the physical restrictions of the ancient Nazarite vow have been lifted; however, the Nazarite spirit, which means separation from the world unto God, is to be a part and parcel of every Believer. But yet, the Believer should understand, that rules and regulations must never become a part of our Faith, that being entirely in Christ and what He has done for us at the Cross. Paul said:

"Let no man therefore judge you in meat, or in drink, or in respect of an holyday, or of the new moon, or of the Sabbath Days (the moment we add any rule or regulation to the Finished Work of Christ, we have just abrogated the Grace of God)*:*

"Which are a shadow of things to come (the law, with all of its observances, was only meant to point to the One Who was to come, namely Christ)*; but the Body* (Church) *is of Christ* (refers to 'substance and reality,' as opposed to shadow)*"* (Col. 2:16-17).

The Apostle then said:

"Wherefore if you be dead with Christ (actually says, 'in view of the fact that you died with Christ') *from the rudiments of the world* (the way of the world), *why, as though living in the world, are you subject to Ordinances* (refers to trusting something other than Christ and the Cross for Salvation and Victory),

"(Touch not; taste not; handle not [there is no Salvation or Victory in rules and regulations]*;*

"Which all are to perish with the using;) (This refers to the fact that they don't work because they are of human origin. Therefore, new ones are made that work no better than the old, which is the way of man.) *after the commandments and doctrines of men?* (This means it is not of God, and must be avoided at all costs)*"* (Col. 2:20-22).

TOTAL VICTORY IN CHRIST

The total Victory of the Child of God, and I speak of how all of this pertains to our life and living, is found completely in Christ and what He did for us at the Cross, and our Faith in that Finished Work (I Cor. 1:17-18, 23; 2:2; Gal., Chpt. 5).

The great sin of the modern Church, and perhaps it's always been the problem, is the Believer trying to establish his own righteousness, which is the very thing that caused the fall of Israel (Rom. 10:1-4). One trying to establish one's own righteousness by whatever means adopted, only seeks in establishing self-righteousness, which, of course, God can never accept.

THE RIGHTEOUSNESS OF GOD

The only way that true Righteousness, the Righteousness of God can be obtained by the Believer, is by the Believer exhibiting Faith in Christ, Who has made a Perfect, spotless Righteousness possible, and did so by going to the Cross. The Believer is to ever exhibit Faith in Christ, and what He did for us at the Cross, which guarantees this spotless Righteousness instantly being imputed to us. Whenever the Church attempts to bring about this Righteousness by any scheme, any method, any effort, any way, other than by simple Faith in Christ and the Cross, such then becomes self-righteousness. Paul said, *"I do not frustrate the Grace of God* (if we make anything other than the Cross of Christ the object of our Faith, we frustrate the Grace of God, which means we stop its action, and the Holy Spirit will no longer help us)*: for if Righteousness come by the Law* (any type of Law), *then Christ is dead in vain.* (If I can successfully live for the Lord by any means other than Faith in Christ and the Cross, then the Death of Christ was a waste)" (Gal. 2:21).

(8) "THEN MANOAH INTREATED THE LORD, AND SAID, O MY LORD, LET THE MAN OF GOD WHICH YOU DID SEND COME AGAIN UNTO US, AND TEACH US WHAT WE SHALL DO UNTO THE CHILD THAT SHALL BE BORN.

(9) "AND GOD HEARKENED TO THE VOICE OF MANOAH; AND THE ANGEL OF GOD CAME AGAIN UNTO THE WOMAN AS SHE SAT IN THE FIELD: BUT MANOAH HER HUSBAND WAS NOT WITH HER.

(10) "AND THE WOMAN MADE HASTE, AND RAN, AND SHOWED HER HUSBAND, AND SAID UNTO HIM, BEHOLD, THE MAN HAS APPEARED UNTO ME, WHO CAME UNTO ME THE OTHER DAY.

(11) "AND MANOAH AROSE, AND WENT AFTER HIS WIFE, AND CAME TO THE MAN, AND SAID UNTO HIM, ARE YOU THE MAN WHO SPOKE UNTO THE WOMAN? AND HE SAID, I AM.

(12) "AND MANAOAH SAID, NOW LET YOUR WORDS COME TO PASS. HOW SHALL WE ORDER THE CHILD, AND HOW SHALL WE DO UNTO HIM?

(13) "AND THE ANGEL OF THE LORD SAID UNTO MANOAH, OF ALL THAT I SAID UNTO THE WOMAN LET HER BEWARE.

(14) "SHE MAY NOT EAT OF ANY THING THAT COMES OF THE VINE, NEITHER LET HER DRINK WINE OR STRONG DRINK, NOR EAT ANY UNCLEAN THING: ALL THAT I COMMANDED HER LET HER OBSERVE.

(15) "AND MANOAH SAID UNTO THE ANGEL OF THE LORD, I PRAY YOU, LET US DETAIN YOU, UNTIL WE SHALL HAVE MADE READY A KID FOR YOU.

(16) "AND THE ANGEL OF THE LORD SAID UNTO MANOAH, THOUGH YOU DETAIN ME, I WILL NOT EAT OF YOUR BREAD: AND IF YOU WILL OFFER A BURNT OFFERING, YOU MUST OFFER IT UNTO THE LORD. FOR MANOAH KNEW NOT THAT HE WAS AN ANGEL OF THE LORD.

(17) "AND MANOAH SAID UNTO THE ANGEL OF THE LORD, WHAT IS YOUR NAME, THAT WHEN YOUR SAYINGS COME TO PASS WE MAY DO YOU HONOUR?

(18) "AND THE ANGEL OF THE LORD SAID UNTO HIM, WHY ASK YOU THUS AFTER MY NAME, SEEING IT IS SECRET?

(19) "SO MANOAH TOOK A KID WITH A MEAT OFFERING, AND OFFERED IT UPON A ROCK UNTO THE LORD: AND THE ANGEL DID WONDEROUSLY; AND MANOAH AND HIS WIFE LOOKED ON.

(20) "FOR IT CAME TO PASS, WHEN THE FLAME WENT UP TOWARD HEAVEN FROM OFF THE ALTAR, THAT THE ANGEL OF THE LORD ASCENDED IN THE FLAME OF THE ALTAR. AND MANOAH AND HIS WIFE LOOKED ON IT, AND FELL ON THEIR FACES TO THE GROUND.

NOTES

(21) "BUT THE ANGEL OF THE LORD DID NO MORE APPEAR TO MANOAH AND TO HIS WIFE. THEN MANOAH KNEW THAT HE WAS AN ANGEL OF THE LORD.

(22) "AND MANOAH SAID UNTO HIS WIFE, WE SHALL SURELY DIE, BECAUSE WE HAVE SEEN GOD.

(23) "BUT HIS WIFE SAID UNTO HIM, IF THE LORD WERE PLEASED TO KILL US, HE WOULD NOT HAVE RECEIVED A BURNT OFFERING AND A MEAT OFFERING AT OUR HANDS, NEITHER WOULD HE HAVE SHOWN US ALL THESE THINGS, NOR WOULD AS AT THIS TIME HAVE TOLD US SUCH THINGS AS THESE."

The construction is:

1. No matter how evil that Israel became, there were always a few who still looked to God, even as evidently did Manoah and his wife.

2. The faith of Manoah was very admirable, and his ignorance very deplorable. For if not rebuked, he would have given Divine honor to a person whom he believed to be a creature and not the Creator; however, this was, in fact, a preincarnate appearance of the Lord Jesus Christ.

3. In essence, when asked what was His Name, the Angel replied, *"Wonderful."* This, in the Hebrew Text is the same word as in Isaiah 9:6. His doing wondrously and ascending up to Heaven in the flame of fire proved Him to be entitled to this great Name.

Christ is a wonderful Saviour. He is Wonderful for what He is to sinners, and Wonderful because of what He does for Saints.

4. It seems that Manoah's wife had a deeper insight into the things of the Lord than did her husband. The Divine directions respecting the child having been given to the mother is a striking instance of the fact that the boy's future, as with all boys, largely depends upon a mother's proper training.

Her reasoning was right; the fact that the Angel accepted the Sacrifice was an evidence of Salvation and Life, and not of condemnation and death. The truth is, Jesus is All in All!

Sinners are Saved, not so much by their acceptance of Christ, but by God's acceptance of Christ on our behalf; but sinners must accept the Saviour in order to profit by the Divine acceptance of His Person and Work (Jn. 1:12).

WONDERFUL

The Eighth Verse says, *"Then Manoah entreated the LORD."* He said, *"Teach us what we shall do."*

This humble entreaty was rewarded by a favorable response from the Lord, even as He always does. Men today are entreating everyone and everything except the Lord. Oh, if we would only ask Him to *"teach us what we shall do."*

Verse 9 says, *"And God hearkened to the voice of Manoah,"* as God always will do upon such a humble request.

The Eighteenth Verse says, *"Why ask you thus after My Name, seeing it is 'secret'?"* The word, *"secret,"* in the Hebrew means *"wonderful,"* and should have been translated accordingly. It not only means that He (the Lord Jesus Christ) is wonderful, but that He does wondrously as is recorded in Verse 19.

Christ is wonderful in every respect. He was wonderful in His miraculous Conception, wonderful in His Birth, wonderful in His Life, wonderful in His Perfection, wonderful in His Healings and Miracles, wonderful in His carrying out the Redemption Plan by giving Himself as a Sacrifice on the Cross, wonderful in His atoning for all sin, wonderful in His Resurrection, wonderful in His Ascension, wonderful in His Exaltation, wonderful in His sending back the Holy Spirit, even as He promised. Truly, He is *"wonderful."*

As well, He is wonderful in His keeping Power, will be wonderful in the Rapture of the Church, will be wonderful in defeating the Antichrist in the Battle of Armageddon, will be wonderful in His Second Coming, will be wonderful in His restoring Israel to her rightful place, will be wonderful as the King of kings and Lord of lords for the entirety of the world during the Kingdom Age, in fact, will be wonderful forever and forever!

THE FLAME OF THE ALTAR

Not knowing what to do, Manoah actually invited the Lord to stay for a meal. He was corrected almost immediately.

The Lord told him to offer a *"Burnt Offering"* as well as a *"Meat Offering,"* with the latter being actually a Grain Offering, in reality a Thanksgiving Offering.

Manoah offered up the *"Burnt Offering"* on a rock, along with the *"Meat Offering,"* and when the flame of the offering went up toward Heaven from off the Altar, the Scripture says *"The Lord ascended in the flame of the Altar."*

Everything the Lord has ever done for the human race, has always been predicated on the Cross of Calvary, of which the old Levitical Offerings were Types. As we have said over and over, and will continue to say, *"Christ is the Source of all things that we receive from God, and the Cross is the Means by which all of these things are made possible to us."* Regrettably, the modern Church little understands this or even believes it. In fact, the modern Cross, could be constituted only as a new cross, which God will never accept.

THE OLD CROSS AND
THE NEW CROSS

The new cross is not a place of Sacrifice, but rather of self-will. It involves no sacrifice, because it does not see man for what man really is — a vile sinner.

The old Cross, the Cross of the Bible, is a place of Sacrifice, of the shedding of blood, of the giving of one's life, a place of death. This was absolutely necessary because of man's terrible condition. Born in sin, under the Judgment and Wrath of God, because God must always be unalterably opposed to sin, man's dilemma was acute, meaning that he had no solution. But God did have a solution.

God became Man, and while He did many things as a Man, the Man Christ Jesus, still, His overriding objective was always the Cross (I Pet. 1:18-20). It was there that the price was paid.

The old Levitical Law for all of its nuances and concepts, could not open the Veil which led into the Holy of Holies. The Cross alone could do that and, in fact, did do that.

But the new cross envisions man in an entirely different perspective than the manner in which the Bible describes man. I quote from THE EXPOSITOR'S STUDY BIBLE:

"What then? Are we better than they?" (Are Jews better than Gentiles?) *No, in no wise: for we have before proved both Jews and Gentiles, that they are all under sin* (points to the supposed claim of the Jews of superiority, which is refuted);

"As it is written (Ps. 14:1-3), *there is none righteous, no, not one* (addresses the complaint of the Jews and clinches the argument with the Scriptures, which the Jews could not deny):

"There is none who understands (proclaims total depravity), *there is none who seek after God* (man left on his own will not seek God and, in fact, cannot seek God; he is spiritually dead).

"They are all gone out of the Way (speaks of the lost condition of all men; the *'Way'* is God's Way), *they are together become unprofitable* (refers to the terrible loss in every capacity of wayward man); *there is none who does good, no, not one* (the Greek Text says, *'useless!'*).

"Their throat is an open sepulcher (the idea is of an open grave, with the rotting remains sending forth a putrid stench); *with their tongues they have used deceit* (speaks of guile, deception, hypocrisy, etc.); *the poison of asps is under their lips* (man cannot be trusted in anything he says):

"Whose mouth is full of cursing (wishing someone evil or hurt) *and bitterness* (bitter and reproachful language):

"Their feet are swift to shed blood (the world is filled with murder, killing, and violence):

"Destruction and misery are in their ways (all brought about by sin):

"And the way of peace have they not known (and cannot know until Christ returns):

"There is no fear of God before their eyes (there is no fear of God, because unbelieving man does not know God).

"Now we know that what things soever the Law says, it says to them who are under the Law (is meant first of all to inform the Jews that Verses 10 through 18 apply to them as well as the Gentiles): *that every mouth may be stopped* (the Gentiles were claiming ignorance, while the Jews were claiming exception from Judgment), *and all the world may become guilty before God* (states the case exactly as it is, meaning all need a Saviour)" (Rom. 3:9-19).

As I think is overly obvious, the Holy Spirit

here does not draw a very favorable picture of man. In fact, the way we learn as to how vile that man actually is, is by the price that was paid in order for man to be redeemed. That price was God giving His Only Son, and giving Him in Sacrifice, which price is beyond our comprehension, to say the least. Unfortunately, the modern Church doesn't seem to see it that way; therefore, it proposes a new cross, that of its own making, which translates into *"another Jesus, promoted by another spirit, which presents another gospel"* (II Cor. 11:4).

The Church, which proposes to be of Jesus Christ must come back to the Cross!

(24) "AND THE WOMAN BORE A SON, AND CALLED HIS NAME SAMSON: AND THE CHILD GREW, AND THE LORD BLESSED HIM.

(25) "AND THE SPIRIT OF THE LORD BEGAN TO MOVE HIM AT TIMES IN THE CAMP OF DAN BETWEEN ZORAH AND ESHTAOL."

The exegesis is:

1. Israel had at this time fallen so completely into the power of the enemy that only a Nazarite could be used by God to deliver them. But, as always, so in this case, man failed. Christ was the True Nazarite. The source of His Strength was a secret unknown to the world.

2. At that time, Israel was in a worse bondage than that of the Philistines, who didn't even know the Lord; and He, the Lord Jesus Christ, in the power of full consecration, walked among sinners separate from them — separate from evil — yet He was in the midst of them as their Light and their Salvation. So, as Samson, our Lord began to save His People from the Philistine in His First Advent and, as David, He will complete His Saving Work in His Second Advent.

3. All victory was and is won through the Cross!

SAMSON WAS THE THIRTEENTH JUDGE

In some ways, Verses 24 and 25 are a portrayal of the Church. As Samson's birth was miraculous, so the birth of the Church was miraculous as well.

The Church grew and the Lord blessed it.

As well, the *"Spirit of the LORD"* moved on the Church *"at times."*

Also, Samson's terrible spiritual declension portrays the Church exactly. And then, finally, Samson's victorious conclusion portrays the Church, and we speak of the True Church at the time of the Rapture as a *"Glorious Church."*

The name Samson is difficult to decipher as it regards its meaning. Probably the closest rendering would be *"to minister."* If this is correct, it would be a reference to his dedication to God as a Nazarite from his mother's womb, the only thing his mother knew about him when she gave him the name.

The phrase, *"And the Spirit of the LORD began to move him at times,"* presents an uncommon expression. It is almost as the Spirit of God could move upon Samson not at all as much as would be desired, but could only function in what might be described as *"fits"* and *"starts."*

And yet, when we think about the situation, it probably could be said that even under the New Covenant, which is a much better Covenant, still, the Holy Spirit has to work with us in approximately the same way. He has to prod us along, gradually, hopefully, bringing us to the place He so desires.

Among those used by God in the Bible, Samson is probably ridiculed the most. And yet we find that he is listed in God's Faith Hall of Fame (Heb. 11:32).

Not for a moment excusing Samson's glaring failures, but still, as we shall see, regarding the Mission for which God called and empowered him, he had, it seems almost no help at all from the balance of Israel. In fact, they seemed to oppose him. To be sure, such action is no excuse for failure, but before Judgment is rendered, we need to do our best to look at each situation as God looks at it. As we peruse the next three Chapters, hopefully we will learn some things, not only about Samson, but about ourselves as well!

CHAPTER 14

(1) "AND SAMSON WENT DOWN TO TIMNATH, AND SAW A WOMAN IN

TIMNATH OF THE DAUGHTERS OF THE PHILISTINES.

(2) "AND HE CAME UP, AND TOLD HIS FATHER AND HIS MOTHER, AND SAID, I HAVE SEEN A WOMAN IN TIMNATH OF THE DAUGHTERS OF THE PHILISTINES: NOW THEREFORE GET HER FOR ME TO WIFE.

(3) "THEN HIS FATHER AND HIS MOTHER SAID UNTO HIM, IS THERE NEVER A WOMAN AMONG THE DAUGHTERS OF YOUR BRETHREN, OR AMONG ALL MY PEOPLE, THAT YOU GO TO TAKE A WIFE OF THE UNCIRCUMCISED PHILISTINES? AND SAMSON SAID UNTO HIS FATHER, GET HER FOR ME: FOR SHE PLEASES ME WELL.

(4) "BUT HIS FATHER AND HIS MOTHER KNEW NOT THAT IT WAS OF THE LORD, THAT HE SOUGHT AN OCCASION AGAINST THE PHILISTINES: FOR AT THAT TIME THE PHILISTINES HAD DOMINION OVER ISRAEL."

The diagram is:

1. Williams said, *"Samson's history illustrates the tendency of the Christian to fall at any moment from the position of wholehearted separation unto God into all that in which the world finds its joy and strength. We find here that while God made use of Samson's marriage to a Philistine in order to punish that people, still, that did not excuse Samson's folly and disobedience.*

"The Law of God said that there was to be no marriage with the heathen; therefore, had he yielded himself unto God, and his members as instruments of Righteousness (Rom. 6:13), how much greater and more glorious would have been the victories granted to him!"[1]

2. The depths of Satan may be recognized in his action toward Israel in connection with the Philistines. The other nations *"mightily oppressed"* Israel, but it is not stated that the Philistines did so. They simply *"ruled"* Israel; and so insensible had Israel become to slavery that they accepted this yoke.

This is the sad history of many a Christian life. Bondage to some inward form of evil is submitted to, its rule accepted, and spiritual insensibility results.

3. We find here that Satan introduces a

new form of rule and bondage as distinct from the former violence and cruelty; and it seems that Samson's countrymen were satisfied with it. He, therefore, could not get them to join him in a general revolt, as was the case with former Judges; and, therefore, it was necessary that a private cause of quarrel should arise. Samson's proposed marriage furnished such an occasion, and God used it to that end.

A DIFFERENT KIND OF BONDAGE

Verse 1 says, *"And Samson went down to Timnath."* It would be there he would see a daughter of the Philistines. This would prove to be a problem.

The Philistines, as we have stated, were an inward foe. In other words, they were not the Ammonites, the Moabites, the Edomites, or the Midianites, all outside the borders of Israel, that is if we conclude the Jordan River to be the eastern boundary. In fact, the Jordan River was not meant by the Lord to serve as an eastern boundary, but came to serve in that capacity due to particular events, etc.

The Philistines occupied the western part of the Tribe of Judah, actually that which bordered the Mediterranean. It was a space approximately 75 miles long, and at its widest about 40 miles. Its five principle cities were Gaza, Ashkelon, Ashdod, Gath, and Ekron. At this time, the time of Samson, they had *"dominion over Israel."*

It seems, as we shall see, that their dominion was loosely held, with Israel succumbing without much if any opposition. This was not at all pleasing to the Lord, so He will raise up Samson in order to deliver Israel.

Presently, the modern Christian has the sin nature to deal with. Through the sin nature, and the Believer not understanding what it is or how to overcome it, Satan erects a stronghold within our lives, meant to destroy us, or at least seriously weaken our testimony. As we previously stated, every attack by the enemy is for one purpose, to either destroy our Faith altogether, or to seriously weaken our Faith. It all pertains to our Faith.

The Lord is not pleased at all with sin dominating us in any fashion. He plainly says in His Word, *"For sin* (the sin nature) *shall not have dominion over you: for you are not under the Law, but under Grace"* (Rom. 6:14).

The way this is done, is by the Believer evidencing Faith in Christ and the Cross, and doing so on a perpetual basis (Rom. 6:3-5). But far too many modern Believers are satisfied to live under the dominion of the sin nature, exactly as Israel was regarding dominion by the Philistines. But let it be understood, Satan is never satisfied with half measures. His aim is to steal, kill, and destroy. And unless He is rooted out altogether, ultimately that is exactly what he will do.

SAMSON AND THE WORLD

The Second Verse says, *"Now therefore get her for me to wife."* Samson, as a type of the Church, *"marries the world,"* which is far too prevalent today. For when we look at Samson, we see the Church. When we look at his failures, we look at the Church. When we look at the concluding victory, we also see the Church.

God will use Samson despite his marriage to the world, once again portraying two things:

1. God's Mercy and Grace to Samson.

2. God's eagerness to deliver Israel and His Anger at the Philistines.

The Fourth Verse says, *"But his father and his mother knew not that it was of the LORD."*

The above Passage does not mean that God approved of or even condoned Samson taking a wife of *"the uncircumcised Philistines."* But it does mean that Samson's failure did not abrogate God's Judgment upon the Philistines. God would use a wayward Church, so to speak, to *"seek occasion against the Philistines."* And the reason?

"The Philistines had dominion over Israel." God desired to break that dominion. He was only partially able to do so because of Israel's failure.

(5) "THEN WENT SAMSON DOWN, AND HIS FATHER AND HIS MOTHER, TO TIMNATH, AND CAME TO THE VINEYARDS OF TIMNATH: AND, BEHOLD, A YOUNG LION ROARED AGAINST HIM.

(6) "AND THE SPIRIT OF THE LORD CAME MIGHTILY UPON HIM, AND HE RENT HIM AS HE WOULD HAVE RENT A KID, AND HE HAD NOTHING IN HIS HAND: BUT HE TOLD NOT HIS FATHER OR HIS MOTHER WHAT HE HAD DONE.

(7) "AND HE WENT DOWN, AND TALKED WITH THE WOMAN; AND SHE PLEASED SAMSON WELL.

(8) "AND AFTER A TIME HE RETURNED TO TAKE HER, AND HE TURNED ASIDE TO SEE THE CARCASS OF THE LION: AND, BEHOLD, THERE WAS A SWARM OF BEES AND HONEY IN THE CARCASS OF THE LION.

(9) "AND HE TOOK THEREOF IN HIS HANDS, AND WENT ON EATING, AND CAME TO HIS FATHER AND MOTHER, AND HE GAVE THEM, AND THEY DID EAT: BUT HE TOLD THEM NOT THAT HE HAD TAKEN THE HONEY OUT OF THE CARCASS OF THE LION."

The diagram is:

1. In a sense, the vineyards typify the Fruit of the Spirit.

2. Satan, as a roaring lion, seeks to stop the Spiritual progress of the Child of God (I Pet. 5:8).

3. The Spirit of the Lord enables Samson to kill this lion with his bare hands.

4. The *"honey"* represents here the Blessings of the Lord, which come to us in respect to the defeat of Satan, which we accomplish by our Faith; however, it must be Faith in Christ and the Cross; so, if the Believer *"walks after the Spirit"* (Rom. 8:1-2), Satan will be defeated, and his attack turned into Blessing.

5. The Spirit of the Lord has now begun His glorious Work in the life of Samson, and did so by strengthening him to such an extent that he could kill a lion with his bare hands, which typified Christ overcoming the powers of darkness, and bringing about the sweet results of victory; victory, incidentally, which is ours, because we are in Him (Jn. 14:20).

THE SPIRIT OF THE LORD

The Fifth Verse says, *"Then went Samson down."* Of course, it is speaking in the geographical sense; however, spiritually speaking, one can look at it in one of two ways. They are:

First of all, he went down in a spiritual

sense, meaning Spiritual Declension. Considering that he was on his way to see the Philistine woman, it is easy to come to that conclusion; however, the word *"down"* could refer to humility on the part of Samson. Considering that the Spirit of God came upon him mightily at this time, the latter conclusion might be closer to the spiritual intent, however, I think one could say without fear of contradiction, that both forces are always at play, in some manner, as it regards the Child of God. That is sad but true.

THE PRINCIPLE OF GOOD AND EVIL

Self-righteous Christians would take umbrage at the Lord using Samson, in fact, in any capacity. Actually, they wish the story of Samson wasn't even in the Bible.

In all of this, we must understand that God doesn't run His Government on the principle of good and evil.

What do we mean by that?

The principle of good and evil refers to the fact that God looks at an individual, and if He sees that which is good, then He uses the person. If He sees evil, and in any capacity, the person cannot be used. As stated, God does not function in that capacity. If He did, He would not use anyone.

While God never condones evil, never overlooks evil, and is totally opposed to evil in every respect, still, God looks at two things:

1. The heart of the individual.

2. What He can make of that person, despite their present weaknesses.

Regrettably, all too often, the Church tries to operate on the principle of good and evil. As stated, it *"tries."* Not being able to see and know the heart of the individual, such an effort all too often chooses the very one that God rejects.

The Psalmist said, *"Lord, if you mark iniquities, who can stand."* God looks at the heart of an individual and deals thusly with that individual regardless of the strength or the weakness. On this basis, *"The Spirit of the LORD came mightily upon him."* Sadly, a self-righteous Church can never accept God's Ways. That's the reason Jesus would say, *"The thieves and the harlots go into the Kingdom of God before you,"* when speaking to the Pharisees.

Did the Lord condone theft and harlotry? As Paul said, *"God forbid."* The truth is, the thief and the harlot knew what they were. The Pharisees would not admit what they were and would not repent or accept the Lord Jesus as their personal Saviour.

THE WEAPONS OF OUR WARFARE ARE NOT CARNAL

Samson killed the lion, and *"he had nothing in his hand."* This speaks of the fact that the *"weapons of our warfare are not carnal, but mighty through God, to the pulling down of strong holds"* (II Cor. 10:4).

If we attempt to oppose Satan by means of our own ability and strength, the Lord labels such as *"the flesh."* Such will never bring forth victory. The old song is right:

"Nothing in my hands I bring,
"Simply to the Cross I cling."

HONEY IN THE ROCK

The Psalmist said, *"He should have fed them also with the finest of the wheat: and with honey out of the rock should I have satisfied you"* (Ps. 81:16).

Even though the honey in the carcass of the lion was not honey out of the rock, still, it was similar.

The lion meant harm for Samson; however, Samson killed the lion with his bare hands, and some time later finds honey in the carcass of the lion.

The Lord intends for this to be a lesson to us. That which Satan means for our destruction, can be turned by the Lord into a Blessing.

And yet, this Blessing can come, only if we function in God's manner. That manner is Faith exclusively in Christ and the Cross (Gal. 6:14; Col. 2:14-15).

(10) "SO HIS FATHER WENT DOWN UNTO THE WOMAN: AND SAMSON MADE THERE A FEAST; FOR SO USED THE YOUNG MEN TO DO.

(11) "AND IT CAME TO PASS, WHEN THEY SAW HIM, THAT THEY BROUGHT THIRTY COMPANIONS TO BE WITH HIM.

(12) "AND SAMSON SAID UNTO THEM, I WILL NOW PUT FORTH A RIDDLE UNTO YOU: IF YOU CAN CERTAINLY DECLARE

IT ME WITHIN THE SEVEN DAYS OF THE FEAST, AND FIND IT OUT, THEN I WILL GIVE YOU THIRTY SHEETS AND THIRTY CHANGE OF GARMENTS:

(13) "BUT IF YOU CANNOT DECLARE IT ME, THEN SHALL YOU GIVE ME THIRTY SHEETS AND THIRTY CHANGE OF GARMENTS. AND THEY SAID UNTO HIM, PUT FORTH YOUR RIDDLE, THAT WE MAY HEAR IT.

(14) "AND HE SAID UNTO THEM, OUT OF THE EATER CAME FORTH MEAT, AND OUT OF THE STRONG CAME FORTH SWEETNESS. AND THEY COULD NOT IN THREE DAYS EXPOUND THE RIDDLE."

The overview is:

1. The Eleventh Verse indicates that Samson's family was one of wealth and position.

2. Riddles and their interpretation were a favorite form of entertainment at that particular time.

3. As it regards the Fourteenth Verse, in effect, Samson was telling the Philistines that the Spirit of the Lord had already begun to come upon him, which began with the killing of the lion, which was a type of Satan and the Philistines; the resultant honey was the sweetness that would come forth from this great deliverance; however, the Philistines, of course, had no idea as to what he meant.

(15) "AND IT CAME TO PASS ON THE SEVENTH DAY, THAT THEY SAID UNTO SAMSON'S WIFE, ENTICE YOUR HUSBAND, THAT HE MAY DECLARE UNTO US THE RIDDLE, LEST WE BURN YOU AND YOUR FATHER'S HOUSE WITH FIRE: HAVE YOU CALLED US TO TAKE THAT WE HAVE? IS IT NOT SO?

(16) "AND SAMSON'S WIFE WEPT BEFORE HIM, AND SAID, YOU DO BUT HATE ME, AND LOVE ME NOT: YOU HAVE PUT FORTH A RIDDLE UNTO THE CHILDREN OF MY PEOPLE, AND HAVE NOT TOLD IT ME. AND HE SAID UNTO HER, BEHOLD, I HAVE NOT TOLD IT MY FATHER NOR MY MOTHER, AND SHALL I TELL IT YOU?

(17) "AND SHE WEPT BEFORE HIM THE SEVEN DAYS, WHILE THEIR FEAST LASTED: AND IT CAME TO PASS ON THE SEVENTH DAY, THAT HE TOLD HER, BECAUSE SHE LAY SORE UPON HIM: AND

NOTES

SHE TOLD THE RIDDLE TO THE CHILDREN OF HER PEOPLE.

(18) "AND THE MEN OF THE CITY SAID UNTO HIM ON THE SEVENTH DAY BEFORE THE SUN WENT DOWN, WHAT IS SWEETER THAN HONEY? AND WHAT IS STRONGER THAN A LION? AND HE SAID UNTO THEM, IF YOU HAD NOT PLOWED WITH MY HEIFER, YOU HAD NOT FOUND OUT MY RIDDLE."

The synopsis is:

1. Samson knew that his wife had told them the answer.

2. Believer's, as this example portrays, but which Samson did not heed, must be separate from the world.

3. While the Bible most definitely teaches separation, it does not teach isolation (Mat. 5:14; II Cor. 6:14-18).

(19) "AND THE SPIRIT OF THE LORD CAME UPON HIM, AND HE WENT DOWN TO ASHKELON, AND KILLED THIRTY MEN OF THEM, AND TOOK THEIR SPOIL, AND GAVE CHANGE OF GARMENTS UNTO THEM WHICH EXPOUNDED THE RIDDLE. AND HIS ANGER WAS KINDLED, AND HE WENT UP TO HIS FATHER'S HOUSE.

(20) "BUT SAMSON'S WIFE WAS GIVEN TO HIS COMPANION, WHOM HE HAD USED AS HIS FRIEND."

The composition is:

1. While the Philistines would find the answer to the riddle, they as of yet had no idea as to who actually Samson was, nor the damage he would do to them.

2. He was betrayed on all counts: by the Philistines, typifying the world; by his wife, typifying companionship with the world; and by his friend, typifying an unholy alliance.

3. When we leave the Word of God, as Samson here did, the end results are never good!

THE SPIRIT OF THE LORD

From Verses 10 through 20, which concludes the Chapter, we witness Samson's continued association with the world. As well, we see the Spirit of the Lord's continued association with Samson. No, it does not show God condoning sin. It does show God's Compassion, Mercy, and Love.

As we read the story of Samson, how many

of us look with pity upon God's champion, never seeming to realize that we are no different or perhaps even worse.

Samson lost many battles; he also won many, but in the final analysis, he won the war. Above all, he would be included in God's great *"Hall of Fame"* in Hebrews, Chapter 11. What a compliment despite his failures! But still, this must be said about every Christian — despite our failures!

CHAPTER 15

(1) "BUT IT CAME TO PASS WITHIN A WHILE AFTER, IN THE TIME OF WHEAT HARVEST, THAT SAMSON VISITED HIS WIFE WITH A KID; AND HE SAID, I WILL GO IN TO MY WIFE INTO THE CHAMBER. BUT HER FATHER WOULD NOT SUFFER HIM TO GO IN.

(2) "AND HER FATHER SAID, I VERILY THOUGHT THAT YOU HAD UTTERLY HATED HER; THEREFORE I GAVE HER TO YOUR COMPANION: IS NOT HER YOUNGER SISTER FAIRER THAN SHE? TAKE HER, I PRAY YOU, INSTEAD OF HER.

(3) "AND SAMSON SAID CONCERNING THEM, NOW SHALL I BE MORE BLAMELESS THAN THE PHILISTINES, THOUGH I DO THEM A DISPLEASURE.

(4) "AND SAMSON WENT AND CAUGHT THREE HUNDRED FOXES, AND TOOK FIREBRANDS, AND TURNED TAIL TO TAIL, AND PUT A FIRBRAND IN THE MIDST BETWEEN TWO TAILS.

(5) "AND WHEN HE HAD SET THE BRANDS ON FIRE, HE LET THEM GO INTO THE STANDING CORN OF THE PHILISTINES, AND BURNT UP BOTH THE SHOCKS, AND ALSO THE STANDING CORN, WITH THE VINEYARDS AND OLIVES."

The exposition is:

1. The Wheat Harvest was in either late May or early June, the time of the Feast of Pentecost, which it seems Israel no longer celebrated, at least at this time.

2. Life is usually marked by folly, when self-will is the spring of action. To the contrary, when God's Will governs the life, prudence and prosperity result. Accordingly,

NOTES

Samson foolishly returned to the woman who so basely betrayed him.

3. The word *"foxes"* should have been translated *"jackals."*

THE PATIENCE OF THE HOLY SPIRIT

These Passages portray the folly of Samson's direction. But yet we learn from these Passages, some things about God's Direction, His Will, and His Plan. It must be ever understood that God uses all things, whether they be good or evil, to further His Cause and His Work.

God was neither the author of, nor did he condone Samson's courtship with the Philistine; therefore, Samson failed; however, the Lord would use this connection with the Philistines to His advantage, while at the same time never condoning Samson's actions.

If Samson had conducted himself correctly, God would have found another way to have destroyed the Philistines, with Samson at the same time being greatly blessed. As it was, Samson would fail God regarding his association with the heathen, and even though he would suffer great loss, still, God would further His Own cause by using what was at hand to destroy the enemies of Israel.

Killing thirty men in anger, as evidenced in the previous Chapter, and then tying firebrands to the tails of animals, were hardly the way of the Holy Spirit. But yet, the Lord helped Samson anyway, even as He does with us time and time again.

It is so easy to read these accounts of God's Champion, and point out Samson's wrongdoing, or even make fun of him. But the truth is, would we have done any better, or even as well?

We have to answer that by looking at our own lives presently, and then attempt to ascertain our service for God. If we will be honest with ourselves, we probably won't like what we see.

(6) "THEN THE PHILISTINES SAID, WHO HAS DONE THIS? AND THEY ANSWERED, SAMSON, THE SON IN LAW OF THE TIMNITE, BECAUSE HE HAD TAKEN HIS WIFE, AND GIVEN HER TO HIS COMPANION. AND THE PHILISTINES CAME UP, AND BURNT HER AND HER FATHER WITH FIRE."

The pattern is:

1. The type of people that Samson is dealing with, should by now be obvious as to what they were. They had little regard for anything. They were heathen, without God!

2. Still, it seems they little realized as to who exactly this man was, and the damage he would shortly do them.

3. In all of this, we see the Lord attempting to bring about a positive conclusion, which was the defeat of the Philistines, even though Samson was not exactly the most pliable subject in His Hands.

(7) "AND SAMSON SAID UNTO THEM, THOUGH YOU HAVE DONE THIS, YET WILL I BE AVENGED OF YOU, AND AFTER THAT I WILL CEASE.

(8) "AND HE SMOTE THEM HIP AND THIGH WITH A GREAT SLAUGHTER: AND HE WENT DOWN AND DWELT IN THE TOP OF THE ROCK ETAM.

(9) "THEN THE PHILISTINES WENT UP, AND PITCHED IN JUDAH, AND SPREAD THEMSELVES IN LEHI.

(10) "AND THE MEN OF JUDAH SAID, WHY ARE YOU COME UP AGAINST US? AND THEY ANSWERED, TO BIND SAMSON ARE WE COME UP, TO DO TO HIM AS HE HAS DONE TO US."

The exposition is:

1. In effect, Samson says to the Philistines as it regards what they did to his wife and her father, *"If this is the way you treat me, be sure that I will not cease until I have had my full revenge."*

2. The Believer may wonder as to how the Lord could be in all of these things? However, it must be understood that Israel at this particular time, was at an extremely low state spiritually. In fact, I think it can be said that Samson, for all of his weaknesses, was the best of the lot.

3. In a sense, Samson was a Type of Christ, at least as it regards his victories. These victories represent the Lord overcoming every enemy, all on our behalf.

VICTORY

The Eighth Verse says, *"And he smote them hip and thigh with a great slaughter."* It says nothing here about the Holy Spirit coming upon him; however, it is obvious that

the Spirit did come or Samson could not have done what he did.

We aren't told here how many Philistines were killed, but the words *"great slaughter"* indicated that the number was sizeable.

As is overly obvious in these Passages, whatever Samson did, he had no help at all from the leaders of Israel. As we shall see, if anything, they were at best neutral toward him, and at worse, opposing him.

As a result of the *"great slaughter"* the Philistines *"went up, and pitched in Judah, and spread themselves in Lehi."* No doubt, this numbered many thousands of men. But as is obvious in the Tenth Verse, the men of Israel had no part in what Samson had done, and as we shall see, actually was in opposition.

What a terrible indictment as it regards Israel! They didn't want to be bothered, they were quite satisfied and now accustomed to their bondage, even as are many modern Christians. They were now, as the great Prophet Jeremiah would later proclaim, a *"homeborn slave"* (Jer. 2:14).

(11) "THEN THREE THOUSAND MEN OF JUDAH WENT TO THE TOP OF THE ROCK ETAM, AND SAID TO SAMSON, KNOW YOU NOT THAT THE PHILISTINES ARE RULERS OVER US? WHAT IS THIS THAT YOU HAVE DONE UNTO US? AND HE SAID UNTO THEM, AS THEY DID UNTO ME, SO HAVE I DONE UNTO THEM.

(12) "AND THEY SAID UNTO HIM, WE ARE COME DOWN TO BIND YOU, THAT WE MAY DELIVER YOU INTO THE HAND OF THE PHILISTINES. AND SAMSON SAID UNTO THEM, SWEAR UNTO ME, THAT YOU WILL NOT FALL UPON ME YOURSELVES.

(13) "AND THEY SPOKE UNTO HIM, SAYING, NO; BUT WE WILL BIND YOU FAST, AND DELIVER YOU INTO THEIR HAND: BUT SURELY WE WILL NOT KILL YOU. AND THEY BOUND HIM WITH TWO NEW CORDS, AND BROUGHT HIM UP FROM THE ROCK.

(14) "AND WHEN HE CAME UNTO LEHI, THE PHILISTINES SHOUTED AGAINST HIM: AND THE SPIRIT OF THE LORD CAME MIGHTILY UPON HIM, AND THE CORDS THAT WERE UPON HIS ARMS BECAME AS FLAX THAT WAS BURNT WITH FIRE, AND HIS BANDS LOOSED FROM

OFF HIS HANDS.

(15) "AND HE FOUND A NEW JAWBONE OF AN ASS, AND PUT FORTH HIS HAND, AND TOOK IT, AND KILLED A THOUSAND MEN THEREWITH.

(16) "AND SAMSON SAID, WITH THE JAWBONE OF AN ASS, HEAPS UPON HEAPS, WITH THE JAW OF AN ASS HAVE I SLAIN A THOUSAND MEN.

(17) "AND IT CAME TO PASS, WHEN HE HAD MADE AN END OF SPEAKING, THAT HE CAST AWAY THE JAWBONE OUT OF HIS HAND, AND CALLED THAT PLACE RAMATH-LEHI.

(18) "AND HE WAS SORE ATHIRST, AND CALLED ON THE LORD, AND SAID, YOU HAVE GIVEN THIS GREAT DELIVERANCE INTO THE HAND OF YOUR SERVANT: AND NOW SHALL I DIE FOR THIRST, AND FALL INTO THE HAND OF THE UNCIRCUMCISED?

(19) "BUT GOD CLAVE AN HOLLOW PLACE THAT WAS IN THE JAW, AND THERE CAME WATER THEREOUT; AND WHEN HE HAD DRUNK, HIS SPIRIT CAME AGAIN, AND HE REVIVED: WHEREFORE HE CALLED THE NAME THEREOF EN-HAKKORE, WHICH IS IN LEHI UNTO THIS DAY.

(20) "AND HE JUDGED ISRAEL IN THE DAYS OF THE PHILISTINES TWENTY YEARS."

The structure is:

1. The language of these cowardly men, as portrayed in Verse 11, portrays the fact as to how completely the Philistine yoke was fastened upon the necks of Judah. The opposition of the world is bitter to the Nazarite Christian, but the opposition of the Church is more bitter.

The Philistines ruled over Israel and Israel was content to have it so. They did not wish to have a Nazarite in their midst who would disturb their peace and excite the world against them. They were quite ready to hand Samson over to a cruel death in order to maintain their so-called peace.

This condition of Spiritual degradation marks, and has marked, the history of the Christian Church. Instead of hailing Samson as a deliverer, his fellow Israelites treated him as an enemy.

NOTES

Believers are very quick to talk about the foibles of Samson, but very seldom mention the leaders of Israel, who were in far worse spiritual condition.

2. Evidently, the leaders of Israel had agreed with the Philistines that if they could deliver Samson to them, the Philistines would not start the war; the truth is, they didn't care about Samson, neither did they care about the Will of the Lord; they sought only to appease the world, which is the attitude of most of the modern Church.

3. By far, this given to us in the Fifteenth Verse was Samson's mightiest achievement to date. As stated, Israel should have helped him and, in fact, had they done so, they would have been delivered from the Philistine yoke at that moment. But they were so far away from God that they were quite satisfied with that yoke. They reasoned that their situation was not nearly so bad as it had been under other conquerors. So, they would live with this problem, and they didn't want Samson rocking the boat.

4. How so like far too many modern Believers. They are quite satisfied to live under the dominion of Satan, providing it doesn't get too bad. So, when they hear the Message of the Cross, which is the only means of Deliverance, they by and large shrug it off, thinking that such is not necessary for them. They know of others who desperately need the Message of the Cross, but they never put themselves in the same category. At best, such Christians are of no use to the Kingdom of God, and at worse, they lose their souls.

5. "Ramath-lehi" means "the casting away of the jawbone," and refers to the fact that the jawbone had no special qualities at all, but rather that this was carried out by the Spirit of God; had he not thrown away this item, Israel would have probably worshipped the thing; such is the human heart.

6. We may note from the Eighteenth Verse that the more God gives, the more He encourages us to ask.

7. The word "En-hakkore" means "the well of him who called, or cried" (Ps. 34:6).

THE PHILISTINES ARE
RULERS OVER US

The Israelites said to Samson, "Knowest

thou not that the Philistines are rulers over us?" It seems they had long since accepted this place and position. How tragic!

God's chosen People not only allow the enemy to subdue them, but rather seem to somewhat enjoy it. They would tolerate no Nazarite seeking to free them from their enemies. Never mind that Samson had been appointed by God! Never mind that his birth was a miracle birth! Never mind that the Holy Spirit mightily came upon him! Israel at this time had no desire for God, no desire for His Miracles, no desire for His appointed Leadership, nor any desire to be free. How so characteristic of the present-day Church. Satan rules us, and we *"love to have it so."*

The Twelfth Verse says, *"And they said unto him, We are come down to bind you, that we may deliver you into the hand of the Philistines."* What a tragedy!

They were quite ready to hand Samson over to a cruel death in order to maintain their status quo. This condition of spiritual degradation marks the history of the Church. They want no part of Samson; they want no part of the Plan of God. So, *"three thousand men of Judah"* will seek to deliver him to the Philistines.

What was Samson's opposition to them? There was no opposition at all. Facing them with meekness, he said to them, *"swear unto me, that you will not fall upon me yourselves."*

What irony! Samson is pleading with his own people not to kill him.

What would have been the result, had the leaders of Israel stood with Samson against the Philistines? What victory they would have won!

Let the reader peruse this Chapter carefully. Sadly and regrettably, it is a portrayal of so very much of the Kingdom of God.

THE REVELATION OF THE CROSS

It was in 1997 when the Lord gave me the Revelation of the Cross. It was not something new, actually that which had already been given to the Apostle Paul and, no doubt, to many others down through the centuries as well; however, due to the fact that the Cross has been so little preached in the last 50 years, this great Message is, in fact, brand-new to

most modern Christians. This means that the Church is by and large rudderless. Considering that the Holy Spirit works entirely within the framework of the Finished Work of Christ, which means that He will little function outside of the Believer expressing Faith in Christ and the Cross, and doing so exclusively, it also means that the Church is little led by the Spirit of God, if at all!

Once this great Revelation was given to me, I thought in my spirit that surely once the Church heard this Message, they would be very eager to receive what the Lord had given. To my dismay, I found that was not the case! For a little bit it threw me. How could they neglect something, ignore something, or outright resist something, which is so obviously from the Lord?

But I found, exactly as Samson found, that most were little interested. A few were, and thank God for the few, but most were not.

Exactly as Israel of old, the modern Church has come to terms with Satan. While Israel was not too very much disturbed by the condition in which they now found themselves, to be sure, the Lord was; hence, Him raising up Samson.

But Samson did not suit the religious leaders of Israel! They didn't like his methods, and they didn't like his ways. But little did they realize, that in rejecting him, they were as well rejecting the Spirit of God, and they were also rejecting Deliverance.

THE JAWBONE OF A MULE

Now Samson is bound and delivered over by Israel to the Philistines. What a travesty! What an insult by the religious leaders of Israel to the Lord! What an ungodly deed they had now done!

Now the Philistines come against Samson, and *"shouted against him."* They were, no doubt, telling him as to exactly what they were now going to do to him. But then *"the Spirit of the LORD came mightily upon him."*

When this happened, he broke the cords binding him as if though they were thread.

Looking around *"he found a new jawbone of an ass, and put forth his hand, and took it."* That was his weapon! Of itself, it was no weapon at all. Of itself, what could be done with such? But with *"the Spirit of the*

LORD" upon Samson, it became the mightiest weapon of all. Samson, with that one piece of bone, *"killed a thousand men."*

As should be overly obvious, in the natural such was not even remotely possible. But with God all things are possible!

It must be noted that Samson did not use his God-given strength against his own people as wrong as they were; he used it against the enemies of the Lord.

It is sad, Israel at that time, would rather be ruled by the Philistines then to have Samson, called of God, to deliver them. And yet, *"God's victories are usually won with despised instruments."* But the feeblest instrument is destruction to the enemy if God be behind it.

THE REFRESHING WATER

The Nineteenth Verse says, *"But God clave an hollow place that was in the jaw, and there came water thereout."* The sentence would have probably been better translated, *"But God clave an hollow place by the jawbone, and there came water thereout."*

The well that refreshed the fainting Samson was not found in the jawbone but in Lehi, the hollow place. It was a depression in the ground and was so named.

Samson would name the place *"Enhakkore."* It meant *"the caller's fount."* It implies that he called on God for water, and God supplied the need. God is our supply; there is no other. May we depend upon Him for everything.

This water was supplied by the Lord, and in a sense could be referred to as *"Living Water."*

The Power of God supplied the Victory, and the refreshing from the Lord supplied the rest, which was sorely needed! (Isa. 28:12).

CHAPTER 16

(1) "THEN WENT SAMSON TO GAZA, AND SAW THERE AN HARLOT, AND WENT IN UNTO HER.

(2) "AND IT WAS TOLD THE GAZITES, SAYING, SAMSON IS COME HITHER. AND THEY COMPASSED HIM IN, AND LAID WAIT FOR HIM ALL NIGHT IN THE GATE

OF THE CITY, AND WERE QUIET ALL THE NIGHT, SAYING, IN THE MORNING, WHEN IT IS DAY, WE SHALL KILL HIM.

(3) "AND SAMSON LAY TILL MIDNIGHT, AND AROSE AT MIDNIGHT, AND TOOK THE DOORS OF THE GATE OF THE CITY, AND THE TWO POSTS, AND WENT AWAY WITH THEM, BAR AND ALL, AND PUT THEM UPON HIS SHOULDERS, AND CARRIED THEM UP TO THE TOP OF AN HILL THAT IS BEFORE HEBRON."

The diagram is:

1. The word *"then"* tells us that this incident occurred after the slaughter of the thousand Philistines, but it doesn't tell us how long after. Samson could rend lions and conquer Philistines, but he could not rend his lust nor conquer his appetites.

2. There is only one way that victory over these things can be accomplished, not five ways, or two ways, just one way.

The Believer must understand that Christ is the Source of all things which we need, and the Cross is the Means. This means that the Believer should anchor his Faith squarely in Christ and the Cross, ever making such the Object of his Faith. This occasions the Holy Spirit, Who works entirely within the perimeters of the Finished Work of Christ, greatly helping us. In fact, He will help us only on these terms (Rom. 6:3-14; 8:1-2, 11).

3. The gate and the posts of Verse 3 must have weighed well over a thousand pounds or more. Within himself, Samson could not even remotely have done such a thing. But with the help of the Holy Spirit, it could be done and, in fact, was done.

4. In a sense, but without the unholy union, this was a Type of Christ, Who descended to Earth, not to have guilty union with its fallen inhabitants, but to redeem them. And, at the dawning of the day, he burst the bars of the tomb, and ascended to the Heavenly Hebron, thereby securing Eternal Life for the degraded sons of men (Jn. 3:16).

THE FORBEARANCE OF
THE HOLY SPIRIT

We see three things in these three Verses.

1. We see Samson cohabiting with a harlot.

2. We see the Gazites planning to kill Samson.

3. We see Samson, by the Spirit of God, literally ripping the gate and its posts out of the city wall, and carrying them to the top of the hill, which he had to do by the Spirit of God, as would be overly obvious.

How do we reconcile all of this?

That God condoned Samson consorting with a harlot?

As Paul would say, *"God forbid!"* God cannot condone sin of any nature, and to be sure this was a vile sin. So, that being the case, how could the Holy Spirit help him to perform the mighty deed of valor, which was accomplished?

There are two reasons.

1. First of all, and as we have previously stated, God does not work from the premise of good and evil. He works from an entirely different premise, which might vary with individuals. If the Lord used only perfect people, none would ever be used, simply because there are no perfect people. As well, our definition of sin is somewhat different than that of the Lord. All sin to Him is abhorrent, but, as well, He looks at some sins as despicable, of which we have little concern.

2. Also, just because the Lord continues, at times, to bless, and despite the waywardness of the individual in question, doesn't mean that He will continue to do such forever. The truth is, while the Holy Spirit will show great forbearance, and thank God He does, still, there will come a time that the sin will have to go, or else the Holy Spirit will take drastic action, which He ultimately did with Samson.

(4) "AND IT CAME TO PASS AFTERWARD, THAT HE LOVED A WOMAN IN THE VALLEY OF SOREK, WHOSE NAME WAS DELILAH.

(5) "AND THE LORDS OF THE PHILISTINES CAME UP UNTO HER, AND SAID UNTO HER, ENTICE HIM, AND SEE WHEREIN HIS GREAT STRENGTH LIES, AND BY WHAT MEANS WE MAY PREVAIL AGAINST HIM, THAT WE MAY BIND HIM TO AFFLICT HIM: AND WE WILL GIVE YOU EVERY ONE OF US ELEVEN HUNDRED PIECES OF SILVER.

(6) "AND DELILAH SAID TO SAMSON,

NOTES

TELL ME, I PRAY YOU, WHEREIN YOUR GREAT STRENGTH LIES, AND WHEREWITH YOU MIGHT BE BOUND TO AFFLICT YOU.

(7) "AND SAMSON SAID UNTO HER, IF THEY BIND ME WITH SEVEN GREEN WITHS THAT WERE NEVER DRIED, THEN SHALL I BE WEAK, AND BE AS ANOTHER MAN.

(8) "THEN THE LORDS OF THE PHILISTINES BROUGHT UP TO HER SEVEN GREEN WITHS WHICH HAD NOT BEEN DRIED, AND SHE BOUND HIM WITH THEM.

(9) "NOW THERE WERE MEN LYING IN WAIT, ABIDING WITH HER IN THE CHAMBER. AND SHE SAID UNTO HIM, THE PHILISTINES BE UPON YOU, SAMSON. AND HE BROKE THE WITHS, AS A THREAD OF TOW IS BROKEN WHEN IT TOUCHES THE FIRE. SO HIS STRENGTH WAS NOT KNOWN."

The exegesis is:

1. A Believer, when governed by self-will, can fall deeper into folly and sin than even a man of the world. This explains Samson's incredible conduct with Delilah.

2. By now, the Philistines were extremely wary of Samson; in fact, they could not see any way to defeat him; but yet, they knew there must be some secret to his strength; in fact, there was.

3. While it was not wrong for Samson to be in the territory of the Philistines, it was most definitely wrong for him to be in their territory in the capacity in which he now finds himself. Jesus ministered to sinners, and thank God He did, but He never joined them in their sin as did Samson.

WHAT IS THE SECRET
OF YOUR STRENGTH?

The balance of this Chapter records Satan's ever-present efforts to rob the Child of God of his Spiritual Power. The enticements and allurements of the world are powerful seductions. The one desire of the enemy is to rob Samson of his Spiritual Power. Strangely enough the Church does not want it, and the world seeks to destroy it.

The Fourth Verse says, *"Whose name was Delilah."*

This was Satan's greatest effort to date. It is very easy to condemn Samson because he was at fault. But at the same time, there is a side of this that most Christians do not consider.

Whenever one is called greatly by God as Samson was, then Satan is also allowed great latitude to hinder that Call. If we think that Samson was little more than a wayward *"oaf"* who had little spirituality, then we miss the point altogether. The truth is, he was a man of God; he judged Israel twenty years; the Holy Spirit mightily used him; and, as well, and certainly not in the least, he was listed in God's great *"Hall of Faith"* in Hebrews, Chapter 11. Years ago one Preacher appropriately said these words:

A. When you hear something bad about a fellow Christian, remember that you are hearing gossip and thereby should treat it as such.

B. Even if you feel that you know the facts, still, you have little knowledge of the powerful Spiritual Warfare involved.

C. If you had been placed in the same position, would you have done any better or even as well?

If we would but remember this simple admonition, our judgment of other Christians would be much less severe.

Samson was wrong, and he sinned for which he would pay a terrible price. But, yet, in all of Israel there was no one who had the Faith of Samson. He alone would begin to deliver Israel. And once again before Judgment is passed, remember:

There were but 16 individuals listed in God's *"Hall of Faith"* (Heb., Chpt. 11); Samson was one of them. The Church may not have wanted him and had no desire for his presence, but God wanted him.

(10) "AND DELILAH SAID UNTO SAMSON, BEHOLD, YOU HAVE MOCKED ME, AND TOLD ME LIES: NOW TELL ME, I PRAY YOU, WHEREWITH YOU MIGHT BE BOUND.

(11) "AND HE SAID UNTO HER, IF THEY BIND ME FAST WITH NEW ROPES THAT WERE NEVER OCCUPIED, THEN SHALL I BE WEAK, AND BE AS ANOTHER MAN.

(12) "DELILAH THEREFORE TOOK

NEW ROPES, AND BOUND HIM THEREWITH, AND SAID UNTO HIM, THE PHILISTINES BE UPON YOU, SAMSON. AND THERE WERE LIERS IN WAIT ABIDING IN THE CHAMBER. AND HE BROKE THEM FROM OFF HIS ARMS LIKE A THREAD."

The pattern is:

1. All sin is a form of insanity. Could not Samson see what Delilah was and what she was trying to do?

2. One of the most instructive observations we can make with a view to our own guidance is that of the extreme danger of self-confidence.

3. Humility is the very essence of the Christian character, and the moment that presumption takes the place of humility the danger to the soul commences (Pulpit).[1]

PRESUMPTION

What was in Samson's mind, we have no real way of knowing. As stated, it should have been obvious as to what Delilah was doing. But yet he seemed to be oblivious to what was actually taking place.

The secret of his strength was a very holy thing, which should have been between him and God Alone. At best, it could be conveyed to other godly people, but to do as he is now doing, is to cast his pearls before swine. To be sure, those swine will ultimately turn on him.

Samson did not overrate his strength when he submitted to be bound by the men of Judah, nor when he put the gates of Gath upon his shoulders, and carried them to the hill over against Hebron. But the transition to presumption commences as soon as we forget that we have nothing which we have not received, and begin to use what we have for our own purposes, and not for God's Glory, and then reckon upon its continuance, whatever use we make of it. When a gift or power generates self-conceit, as if it originated with ourselves, presumption has begun; the use of it for our own glorification is the next step; security in its continuance, however much we abuse it, is the third stage of presumption (Pulpit).[2]

The Holy Spirit will suffer such only for so long, even as we shall see.

(13) "AND DELILAH SAID UNTO

SAMSON, HITHERTO YOU HAVE MOCKED ME, AND TOLD ME LIES: TELL ME WHEREWITH YOU MIGHT BE BOUND. AND HE SAID UNTO HER, IF YOU WEAVE THE SEVEN LOCKS OF MY HEAD WITH THE WEB.

(14) "AND SHE FASTENED IT WITH THE PIN, AND SAID UNTO HIM, THE PHILISTINES BE UPON YOU, SAMSON. AND HE AWAKED OUT OF HIS SLEEP, AND WENT AWAY WITH THE PIN OF THE BEAM, AND WITH THE WEB."

The exposition is:

1. For the first time, Samson mentions his hair, which is a symbol of his strength.

2. It is not possible to have close communion with the world without at last becoming a part of the world.

3. That which happened to Samson will happen to anyone. As God doesn't change, neither do the allurements of the world, nor its dangers.

THE SECRET OF HIS STRENGTH

At first Samson mentioned his hands and then his feet, but now he mentions his hair. If one is on Satan's territory, ultimately one will divulge that which Satan desires. There is no human being who can defeat Satan on his own ground.

The Holy Spirit always respected Samson's will, as the Holy Spirit also respects our wills. Many times the Holy Spirit came upon him so that his great feats might be performed; however, the Holy Spirit did not now come upon him to stop the spiritual slide to destruction. That was his choice. The Holy Spirit will treat us accordingly.

Samson placed himself purposely in the path of the Evil One, on the territory of the Evil One, in the embrace of the Evil One. What happened should have been expected.

When the Believer, no matter how greatly used of God otherwise, places himself in the path of sin, he will find himself sooner or later unable to stop its advances. As with Samson, the Lord will allow such a person to proceed, even though it is to one's own destruction. How so much this must grieve the heart of God.

As someone has well said, *"If you put coals of fire in your bosom, you are going to get burned."*

NOTES

Now he mentions his hair.
Why?

As stated, sin, and Samson had already been engaging in sin, is about to spring its deadly trap. He had no business whatsoever being with this woman. Why was he ever attracted only to Philistine women? What was wrong with the beautiful young ladies of Israel?

As we have previously stated in this Volume, sin has an allurement to it, an enticement, an attraction. Forbidden fruit holds its allurement, strictly because it is forbidden. That's why the Law, even the Law of God, never succeeded in making one holy. The very idea of *"Thou shalt not,"* automatically has its wayward pull. In fact, God designed it that way, in order that man may see how helpless he really is. But yet, the failure is not the fault of the Law, but rather the fault of the man.

(15) "AND SHE SAID UNTO HIM, HOW CAN YOU SAY, I LOVE YOU, WHEN YOUR HEART IS NOT WITH ME? YOU HAVE MOCKED ME THESE THREE TIMES, AND HAVE NOT TOLD ME WHEREIN YOUR GREAT STRENGTH LIES.

(16) "AND IT CAME TO PASS, WHEN SHE PRESSED HIM DAILY WITH HER WORDS, AND URGED HIM, SO THAT HIS SOUL WAS VEXED UNTO DEATH;

(17) "THAT HE TOLD HER ALL HIS HEART, AND SAID UNTO HER, THERE HAS NOT COME A RAZOR UPON MY HEAD; FOR I HAVE BEEN A NAZARITE UNTO GOD FROM MY MOTHER'S WOMB: IF I BE SHAVED, THEN MY STRENGTH WILL GO FROM ME, AND I SHALL BECOME WEAK, AND BE LIKE ANY OTHER MAN.

(18) "AND WHEN DELILAH SAW THAT HE HAD TOLD HER ALL HIS HEART, SHE SENT AND CALLED FOR THE LORDS OF THE PHILISTINES, SAYING, COME UP THIS ONCE, FOR HE HAS SHOWED ME ALL HIS HEART. THEN THE LORDS OF THE PHILISTINES CAME UP UNTO HER, AND BROUGHT MONEY IN THEIR HAND.

(19) "AND SHE MADE HIM SLEEP UPON HER KNEES; AND SHE CALLED FOR A MAN, AND SHE CAUSED HIM TO SHAVE OFF THE SEVEN LOCKS OF HIS HEAD; AND SHE BEGAN TO AFFLICT HIM,

AND HIS STRENGTH WENT FROM HIM."

The exegesis is:

1. Samson should never have been in this place; it is not possible, I think for any Believer to submit himself to such a situation but that the end result will be exactly as that of Samson.

2. Fellowship with the world is at least one of the greatest dangers, if not the greatest danger, to the Child of God (I Jn. 2:15-17).

3. As Verse 18 proclaims, once again we see that the love of money is the root of all evil.

THE SEVEN LOCKS OF HIS HEAD

The Nineteenth Verse records the terrible moment, *"And she caused him to shave off the seven locks of his head."* Even though there is no Scriptural assurance, still, the Lord could have told Samson to braid his hair in seven braids. Seven is God's Perfect Number. It denotes fulfillment, totality, completion, perfection, and universality. Now the seven locks are gone. The Scripture says, *"His strength went from him."*

Obviously, the question should be asked, *"Why did the Holy Spirit not leave him when the other acts of sin were committed, such as marrying a heathen woman or committing adultery with a harlot?"* These things were terrible sins, but, yet, the Holy Spirit remained with him.

The answer is found, as it only can be found, in the Mercy and Grace of God. We may lament the fact that God showed Samson Mercy and Grace during these nearly twenty years of repeated offenses; however, instead of criticism, we should thank God, because God deals with us also with Compassion, Love, Grace, and Understanding.

But yet, God is no respecter of persons. The time will come, if victory is not attained, that the Lord will bring chastisement upon such a person and, in fact, severe chastisement (Heb. 12:5-11).

(20) "AND SHE SAID, THE PHILISTINES BE UPON YOU, SAMSON. AND HE AWOKE OUT OF HIS SLEEP, AND SAID, I WILL GO OUT AS AT OTHER TIMES BEFORE, AND SHAKE MYSELF. AND HE WIST NOT THAT THE LORD WAS DEPARTED FROM HIM.

(21) "BUT THE PHILISTINES TOOK HIM,

NOTES

AND PUT OUT HIS EYES, AND BROUGHT HIM DOWN TO GAZA, AND BOUND HIM WITH FETTERS OF BRASS; AND HE DID GRIND IN THE PRISON HOUSE."

The overview is:

1. There is nothing worse that can be said of a person than that the Spirit of the Lord has departed from him.

2. The Philistines put out his eyes and degraded him to the abject position of grinding meal and making sport of him. Such is ever the moral result of association with the world — it obtains the mastery, the Christian loses his eyesight and liberty, and becomes a mere purveyor of entertainments to the Church — and that is basically the far lower level to which the modern Church has succumbed. It is no more than a social center, which provides good entertainment. God help us!

3. There is only one way, one means of victory over the world, the flesh, and the Devil — only one! That one way is, *"Jesus Christ and Him Crucified"* (I Cor. 1:23).

THE DEPARTURE OF THE LORD

Samson tells Delilah that the secret of his strength is his hair, and that if it be shaved off, he will be like any other man.

It was shaved off, but yet he conducts himself as if the Spirit of the Lord remains present.

Did he not know that his hair was gone?

Either he didn't know it, or else he somehow believed that God would remain with him, despite the fact of the secret being revealed.

The words, *"And he wist not that the LORD was departed from him,"* are worse than anything that could be heard or done. As stated, however, if Victory over sin is not ultimately attained, the Spirit of the Lord will ultimately depart.

It is the business of the Holy Spirit to get sin out of our lives. That is the greater part of His Mission. If we cooperate with Him, Victory will be ours; otherwise, not so!

Samson did not cooperate with the Holy Spirit very well. I wonder if we do much better, if at all!

THE MANNER IN WHICH VICTORY IS ATTAINED OVER SIN

Sin is so bad, so powerful, that it has killed

every human being who has ever been born, with the exception of Enoch and Elijah. Thank God, Jesus defeated death, with all of its clinging vines, at the Cross of Calvary. In fact, sin is so bad so horrible, so powerful, that sin could be defeated only at the Cross. Paul wrote:

"But this Man (this Priest, Christ Jesus), *after He had offered One Sacrifice for sins forever* (speaks of the Cross), *sat down on the Right Hand of God* (refers to the great contrast with the Priests under the Levitical system, who never sat down because their work was never completed; the Work of Christ was a *'Finished Work,'* and needed no repetition)*" (Heb. 10:12).

To partake of the great victory won by Christ, and all on our behalf, the Believer need only exhibit Faith in Christ and what He did for us at the Cross. That being done, and done perpetually, even on a daily basis (Lk. 9:23), the Holy Spirit, Who works exclusively within the perimeters of the legal work of Christ on the Cross, then will help us mightily (Rom. 8:1-2, 11). He only demands Faith of us, but yet that our Faith have as its correct Object the Cross of Christ. This is very, very important! (Gal., Chpt. 5; 6:14).

(22) "HOWBEIT THE HAIR OF HIS HEAD BEGAN TO GROW AGAIN AFTER HE WAS SHAVED.

(23) "THEN THE LORDS OF THE PHILISTINES GATHERED THEM TOGETHER FOR TO OFFER A GREAT SACRIFICE UNTO DAGON THEIR GOD, AND TO REJOICE: FOR THEY SAID, OUR GOD HAS DELIVERED SAMSON OUR ENEMY INTO OUR HAND.

(24) "AND WHEN THE PEOPLE SAW HIM, THEY PRAISED THEIR GOD: FOR THEY SAID, OUR GOD HAS DELIVERED INTO OUR HANDS OUR ENEMY, AND THE DESTROYER OF OUR COUNTRY, WHICH KILLED MANY OF US.

(25) "AND IT CAME TO PASS, WHEN THEIR HEARTS WERE MERRY, THAT THEY SAID, CALL FOR SAMSON, THAT HE MAY MAKE US SPORT. AND THEY CALLED FOR SAMSON OUT OF THE PRISON HOUSE; AND HE MADE THEM SPORT: AND THEY SET HIM BETWEEN THE PILLARS.

(26) "AND SAMSON SAID UNTO THE LAD WHO HELD HIM BY THE HAND, SUFFER ME THAT I MAY FEEL THE PILLARS WHEREUPON THE HOUSE STANDS, THAT I MAY LEAN UPON THEM.

(27) "NOW THE HOUSE WAS FULL OF MEN AND WOMEN; AND ALL THE LORDS OF THE PHILISTINES WERE THERE; AND THERE WERE UPON THE ROOF ABOUT THREE THOUSAND MEN AND WOMEN, WHO BEHELD WHILE SAMSON MADE SPORT.

(28) "AND SAMSON CALLED UNTO THE LORD, AND SAID, O LORD GOD, REMEMBER ME, I PRAY YOU, AND STRENGTHEN ME, I PRAY YOU, ONLY THIS ONCE, O GOD, THAT I MAY BE AT ONCE AVENGED OF THE PHILISTINES FOR MY TWO EYES.

(29) "AND SAMSON TOOK HOLD OF THE TWO MIDDLE PILLARS UPON WHICH THE HOUSE STOOD, AND ON WHICH IT WAS BORNE UP, OF THE ONE WITH HIS RIGHT HAND, AND OF THE OTHER WITH HIS LEFT.

(30) "AND SAMSON SAID, LET ME DIE WITH THE PHILISTINES. AND HE BOWED HIMSELF WITH ALL HIS MIGHT; AND THE HOUSE FELL UPON THE LORDS, AND UPON ALL THE PEOPLE WHO WERE THEREIN. SO THE DEAD WHICH HE KILLED AT HIS DEATH WERE MORE THAN THEY WHICH HE KILLED IN HIS LIFE.

(31) "THEN HIS BRETHREN AND ALL THE HOUSE OF HIS FATHER CAME DOWN, AND TOOK HIM, AND BROUGHT HIM UP, AND BURIED HIM BETWEEN ZORAH AND ESHTAOL IN THE BURYING-PLACE OF MANOAH HIS FATHER. AND HE JUDGED ISRAEL TWENTY YEARS."

The construction is:

1. The fallen Believer can come back; the hair, spiritually speaking, can begin to grow again.

2. The Philistines equated Samson's loss of strength as their god, Dagon, defeating Jehovah, the God of the Israelites. Dagon had the head, breast, and hands of a human, and the balance of the body shaped like a fish.

3. They didn't seem to realize that his hair had grown back, that is if they had any understanding at all of its meaning, which they probably didn't.

4. This pavilion was held up by two pillars, which Samson would use to destroy these Philistines.

5. The type of prayer prayed by Samson will always be heard by the Lord. The term *"Lord GOD"* refers to the *"God of Covenants,"* which, in itself, speaks volumes.

6. I wonder what these thousands of Philistines were thinking, when they saw him put his arms around these two pillars? The jesting and the mocking could probably be heard for quite a distance.

7. Samson did not commit suicide, but rather gave his life, in a sense as did Christ.

8. Had his brethren and all the house of his father come down when he was alive, instead of only when he was dead, the situation might have been different.

THE HAIR IS GROWING AGAIN

The Philistines, not understanding spiritual things, saw no threat at all in Samson's hair again beginning to grow. Let the reader understand, spiritually speaking, the hair can grow again. Many years before, Job the great Patriarch made this statement. He said, *"For there is hope of a tree, if it be cut down, that it will sprout again, and that the tender branch thereof will not cease"* (Job 14:7).

In this one Verse, we are told that even if a man does fall on hard times, if he will believe God, the fallen tree can sprout and grow again.

The Evil One loves to tell Believers that they have wrecked everything, and there is no more hope, and they might as well quit. He is a liar!

As long as a person can call on God, and do so sincerely, the Lord can make the tree grow again, can make the hair grow again. He has done it with untold millions, and he can do it for you.

Samson is crying out to his God begging for forgiveness, and asking the Lord, no doubt, to restore him. To be sure, the Holy Spirit will answer his prayer.

MAKE SPORT OF
THE MAN OF GOD

The Twenty-fifth Verse says, *"Call for Samson, that he may make us sport."* The Hebrew word for *"sport"* seems to imply that

Samson danced before the crowd, becoming the most humiliating of spectacles. Satan relishes this moment, not knowing that what looks like Samson's defeat is, in effect, Samson's victory. God will hear him as he prays. There can be no higher acclaim than that.

The Thirty-first Verse says, *"Then his brethren and all the house of his father came down, and took him, and brought him up, and buried him."*

Notice the word *"then."*

It is remarkable that they now come. Why did they not come previously? Why did they not help him fight against the powers of darkness? The casual, carnal reader of this portion of Judges may in skimming the surface see only the failure of Samson; however, the Holy Spirit, in fact, shows us the failure of Israel instead.

Concerning Samson, despite his problems, despite his many failures, despite his wrong direction, the Holy Spirit closes out the Book on him by saying, *"And of Samson . . . who through Faith subdued Kingdoms, wrought Righteousness, obtained Promises, stopped the mouths of lions"* (Heb. 11:32-33).

I don't think more could be said that would be greater than that.

May we do as well!

CHAPTER 17

(1) "AND THERE WAS A MAN OF MOUNT EPHRAIM, WHOSE NAME WAS MICAH.

(2) "AND HE SAID UNTO HIS MOTHER, THE ELEVEN HUNDRED SHEKELS OF SILVER THAT WERE TAKEN FROM YOU, ABOUT WHICH YOU CURSED, AND SPOKE OF ALSO IN MY EARS, BEHOLD, THE SILVER IS WITH ME; I TOOK IT. AND HIS MOTHER SAID, BLESSED BE YOU OF THE LORD, MY SON.

(3) "AND WHEN HE HAD RESTORED THE ELEVEN HUNDRED SHEKELS OF SILVER TO HIS MOTHER, HIS MOTHER SAID, I HAD WHOLLY DEDICATED THE SILVER UNTO THE LORD FROM MY HAND FOR MY SON, TO MAKE A GRAVEN IMAGE AND A MOLTEN IMAGE: NOW THEREFORE I

WILL RESTORE IT UNTO YOU.

(4) "YET HE RESTORED THE MONEY UNTO HIS MOTHER; AND HIS MOTHER TOOK TWO HUNDRED SHEKELS OF SILVER, AND GAVE THEM TO THE FOUNDER, WHO MADE THEREOF A GRAVEN IMAGE AND A MOLTEN IMAGE: AND THEY WERE IN THE HOUSE OF MICAH.

(5) "AND THE MAN MICAH HAD AN HOUSE OF GODS AND MADE AN EPHOD, AND TERAPHIM, AND CONSECRATED ONE OF HIS SONS, WHO BECAME HIS PRIEST.

(6) "IN THOSE DAYS THERE WAS NO KING IN ISRAEL, BUT EVERY MAN DID THAT WHICH WAS RIGHT IN HIS OWN EYES."

The composition is:

1. The balance of this Book no longer concerns itself with Judges raised up by the Lord, but rather the internal affairs of Israel. It is done, of course, for purpose, which is to show the inward moral condition of the Nation, which was despicable, to say the least. It is a sad picture of confusion, idolatry, sin, and violence; it all resulted from neglect of the Bible. Four times in this section of the Book it states, *Every man did that which was right in his own eyes."*

2. Evidently, Micah had stolen a certain amount of silver from his mother. As we shall see, it is connected with idolatry.

3. As we see here, the greater part of Israel, of which the Holy Spirit desires that this household serve as a type, equated the Lord and idols as one and the same.

4. Presently, any doctrine in the modern Church which is not based squarely on the Foundation of *"Christ and Him Crucified"* (I Cor. 1:23), pure and simple, is idolatry. Such false worship is *"another Jesus, brought about by another spirit, which gives us another gospel"* (II Cor. 11:4). If that, in fact, is correct, and it definitely is, due to the paucity of the preaching of the Cross (I Cor. 1:21), almost the entirety of the modern Church world is corrupted by idolatry (I Jn. 5:21).

5. Far too many modern Churches are actually founders of graven and molten images, but in a different form now than then; it is now in the form of Denominationalism, methodology, false doctrine, etc.

6. These images, together with the Ephod,

NOTES

Teraphim, and Priests, suggest that this domestic chapel was a corrupt imitation of the Tabernacle. All were contrary to the Word of God.

7. The Word commanded one place of worship only; it forbade images. And it permitted none to be Priests but the sons of Aaron. No description is given in the Bible of the "teraphim;" however, it is believed they were a particular object shaped in the form of an idol, which was consulted.

8. The difference between now and then is that the people are not so much presently doing that which is right in their own eyes, but rather in the eyes of someone else, who is rather a wolf in sheep's clothing (Mat. 7:14-20).

WRONG DIRECTION

Chapters 17 through 21 record the terrible spiritual declension of Israel through the 400 odd years of the Judges. In reading these Chapters, one can well see the terrible superstitious state of a nation, a country, or a people who are without God. God is talked about but not served. Basically, man makes up his own religion as he goes, completely ignoring the True Word of God.

At this time in Israel's history, they had the five Books of the Law written by Moses, as well as the Book of Joshua, and probably the Book of Job. Regrettably, Israel ignored these Books. Chaos, murder, and rebellion were the result.

Man's carnal ways always lead him to think he can reach God by his own efforts. He will try through money and false gods.

In the Third Verse Micah's mother says, *"I had wholly dedicated the silver unto the LORD from my hand for my son, to make a graven image."* She will call Him *"LORD,"* meaning *"Covenant God."* But she will understand very little of what she says.

How many Christians at this time are taking their money and using it for what purports to be the Work of God, but, in reality, will make nothing but a *"house of gods"*?

In the Fifth Verse the Holy Spirit, by using the word *"gods,"* emphatically states that none of this was the Work of the Lord but was from man's unregenerate heart. Sadly, most of the modern Church world is spending its money to make a *"house of gods."*

Then the Holy Spirit in Verse 6 emphatically states, *"but every man did that which was right in his own eyes,"* meaning that it was not right in God's Eyes.

When Believers leave the Word of God, even as the modern Church is now doing, the end result, in one form or the other, is that which we are given, as stated, in Chapters 17 through 21. Many centuries may separate the present from those days of long ago; however, the problem is the same.

Sin is the problem. It always has been, it is now, and it always will be, at least until the Lord changes things, which He will do in the coming Perfect Age (Rev., Chpts. 21-22).

The only solution to this problem, and I mean the only solution, is *"Jesus Christ and Him Crucified"* (I Cor. 1:23). Unfortunately, the modern Church is projecting everything to a gullible Christian public, instead of the right thing. The Cross of Christ, which is the only answer, is being preached not at all. Yes, there is an exception here and there, but as a whole, no! Let us say it again, and because it is so very, very important:

The answer for man's dilemma and, in fact, the only answer for man's dilemma is the Cross of Christ! But sadly and regrettably, the modern Church is projecting everything except that which is the right thing.

(7) "AND THERE WAS A YOUNG MAN OUT OF BETH-LEHEM-JUDAH OF THE FAMILY OF JUDAH, WHO WAS A LEVITE, AND HE SOJOURNED THERE.

(8) "AND THE MAN DEPARTED OUT OF THE CITY FROM BETH-LEHEM-JUDAH TO SOJOURN WHERE HE COULD FIND A PLACE: AND HE CAME TO MOUNT EPHRAIM TO THE HOUSE OF MICAH, AS HE JOURNEYED.

(9) "AND MICAH SAID UNTO HIM, FROM WHERE DO YOU COME? AND HE SAID UNTO HIM, I AM A LEVITE OF BETH-LEHEM-JUDAH, AND I GO TO SOJOURN WHERE I MAY FIND A PLACE.

(10) "AND MICAH SAID UNTO HIM, DWELL WITH ME, AND BE UNTO ME A FATHER AND A PRIEST, AND I WILL GIVE YOU TEN SHEKELS OF SILVER BY THE YEAR, AND A SUIT OF APPAREL,

NOTES

AND YOUR VICTUALS. SO THE LEVITE WENT IN.

(11) "AND THE LEVITE WAS CONTENT TO DWELL WITH THE MAN; AND THE YOUNG MAN WAS UNTO HIM AS ONE OF HIS SONS.

(12) "AND MICAH CONSECRATED THE LEVITE; AND THE YOUNG MAN BECAME HIS PRIEST, AND WAS IN THE HOUSE OF MICAH.

(13) "THEN SAID MICAH, NOW KNOW I THAT THE LORD WILL DO ME GOOD, SEEING I HAVE A LEVITE TO MY PRIEST."

The composition is:

1. The statement in Verse 7 doesn't mean that this Levite was from the Tribe of Judah, because a Levite couldn't be from the Tribe of Judah, but rather the Tribe of Levi. It means he had made his home in Bethlehem, which was in the realm of the Tribe of Judah.

2. If Phinehas, the High Priest and the Nation had obeyed the Scriptures, this Levite would not have had to travel about looking for a place to serve.

3. Micah called his chapel a *"House of God,"* which it actually is in the original Hebrew, but the Holy Spirit called it a house of idols (Vs. 5). The true House of God was neglected and is hard to find then as it is today; and too often when found, amusements rather than worship characterize it (21:21-23). It seems that Preachers are for sale now, just as they were then.

4. The statement of Verse 13 didn't exactly turn out that way. Micah was afterwards robbed of both his idols and his Priest. He had, like some people at the present time, a little knowledge of Scriptural Worship, but only sufficient to make him idolatrous and superstitious.

DEVIATION FROM THE WORD OF GOD

Pulpit says, *"The writer of the five last Chapters of the Book of Judges had a painful task to perform. Writing the history of his people, and they the people of God, he had to tell a tale of violence, plunder, bloodshed, brutality, civil war, and extermination, on the secular side, and of superstition, schism, and idolatry on the religious side of history."*[1] As stated, it did not present itself as a very pretty picture.

It all resulted from neglect of the Bible. Had they read and obeyed the five Books of Moses they would have been a holy and a happy people. But they were self-willed; and four times in this section of the Book it states, *"and every man did that which was right in his own eyes."*

The Tenth Verse says that Micah thinks that this meandering Levite can be his own personal *"father and Priest."* He would buy him a suit of clothes and three meals a day for sixty dollars.

How many preachers in the world of Christendom presently are for sale? Preachers sell out for various reasons: some for guaranteed sustenance as this Levite; some to deacon boards; some to their denominational hierarchy. Sadly, this Chapter characterizes the majority of modern preachers. Their services are for sale to the highest bidder.

The Thirteenth Verse says, *"Now I know that the LORD will do me good, seeing I have a Levite to my Priest."*

What a shame, God's true Tabernacle was ignored. His Word was ignored as well. When the Church deviates from the Word of God, superstition, foolishness, and absurdity become the rule.

It was not God's Will that a Priest function in any household. They were to function only at the Tabernacle. No house was to set up its own place of worship; that, as well, must be at the Tabernacle; however, the Word of God was completely ignored. Regrettably, Micah's *"positive confession"* will do him no good. The next Chapter will relate how that his gods are stolen, and his place of *"worship"* desecrated. It must be plainly understood that evil begets evil. A little leaven will ultimately corrupt and rot the whole lump.

CHAPTER 18

(1) "IN THOSE DAYS THERE WAS NO KING IN ISRAEL: AND IN THOSE DAYS THE TRIBE OF THE DANITES SOUGHT THEM AN INHERITANCE TO DWELL IN; FOR UNTO THAT DAY ALL THEIR

INHERITANCE HAD NOT FALLEN UNTO THEM AMONG THE TRIBES OF ISRAEL.

(2) "AND THE CHILDREN OF DAN SENT OF THEIR FAMILY FIVE MEN FROM THEIR COASTS, MEN OF VALOUR, FROM ZORAH, AND FROM ESHTAOL, TO SPY OUT THE LAND, AND TO SEARCH IT; AND THEY SAID UNTO THEM, GO, SEARCH THE LAND: WHO WHEN THEY CAME TO MOUNT EPHRAIM, TO THE HOUSE OF MICAH, THEY LODGED THERE.

(3) "WHEN THEY WERE BY THE HOUSE OF MICAH, THEY KNEW THE VOICE OF THE YOUNG MAN THE LEVITE: AND THEY TURNED IN THITHER, AND SAID UNTO HIM, WHO BROUGHT YOU HERE? AND WHAT ARE YOU DOING IN THIS PLACE? AND WHAT HAVE YOU HERE?

(4) "AND HE SAID UNTO THEM, THUS AND THUS DEALT MICAH WITH ME, AND HAS HIRED ME, AND I AM HIS PRIEST.

(5) "AND THEY SAID UNTO HIM, ASK COUNSEL, WE PRAY YOU, OF GOD, THAT WE MAY KNOW WHERE OUR WAY WHICH WE GO SHALL BE PROSPEROUS.

(6) "AND THE PRIEST SAID UNTO THEM, GO IN PEACE: BEFORE THE LORD IS YOUR WAY WHEREIN YOU GO.

(7) "THEN THE FIVE MEN DEPARTED, AND CAME TO LAISH, AND SAW THE PEOPLE WHO WERE THEREIN, HOW THEY DWELT CARELESS, AFTER THE MANNER OF THE ZIDONIANS, QUIET AND SECURE; AND THERE WAS NO MAGISTRATE IN THE LAND, THAT MIGHT PUT THEM TO SHAME IN ANY THING; AND THEY WERE FAR FROM THE ZIDONIANS, AND HAD NO BUSINESS WITH ANY MAN.

(8) "AND THEY CAME UNTO THEIR BRETHREN TO ZORAH AND ESHTAOL: AND THEIR BRETHREN SAID UNTO THEM, WHAT DO YOU SAY?

(9) "AND THEY SAID, ARISE, THAT WE MAY GO UP AGAINST THEM: FOR WE HAVE SEEN THE LAND, AND, BEHOLD, IT IS VERY GOOD: AND ARE YOU STILL? BE NOT SLOTHFUL TO GO, AND TO ENTER TO POSSESS THE LAND.

(10) "WHEN YOU GO, YOU SHALL COME UNTO A PEOPLE SECURE, AND TO A LARGE LAND: FOR GOD HAS GIVEN IT INTO YOUR HANDS; A PLACE WHERE

THERE IS NO WANT OF ANY THING THAT IS IN THE EARTH."

The exegesis is:

1. The time frame of this Chapter probably occurred when Othniel was the Judge in Israel. The portion assigned to the Tribe of Dan was in the area of the Philistines (Josh. 19:40); however, it seems they did not have enough Faith to overcome the Philistines; so, instead, and out of the Will of God, they undertook an expedition against a small and defenseless people in the extreme north of the land, built a city there, which they called *"Dan"* — thus, originating the expression *"from Dan even to Beersheba"* — and publicly established idolatry. This is probably the reason for the omission of their name in Revelation, Chapter 7.

2. The action of the Danites in asking this Levite to divine for them — no doubt, by means of the Teraphim or the Ephod — shows how far at this early date the Word of God was departed from. They ought to have been shocked and grieved at a Levite assuming priestly functions; and they should have been indignant at the existence of a house of idols in rivalry with the Tabernacle of Jehovah.

3. Even though they used the Name of *"God,"* there is no record that the Holy Spirit had allotted to the Tribe of Dan this territory up north. This was their own doings, and, accordingly, would not turn out well.

OUT OF THE WILL OF GOD

The First Verse says, *"The Tribe of the Danites sought them an inheritance to dwell in."*

It seems that either they had not occupied their rightful inheritance designed for them by the Holy Spirit, or that a portion of the Danites (some 600 men) went to the extreme northern part of Israel to establish a second area of occupation. They would build a city there, which they called *"Dan"* — thus originating the expression, *"from Dan even to Beersheba."*

Men are ever desirous, it seems, to leave that which God has appointed for them and to draw their own boundaries. They fail as fail they must. The only thing the Danites established in the northern part of Israel was a continued and greater idolatry.

The Fourth Verse says concerning their dealing with the priests at Micah's house, *"And has hired me, and I am his priest."* How many preachers in one way or the other are *"hired?"* Thus they become hirelings.

The Fifth Verse says, *"Ask counsel, we pray you, of God, that we may know whether our way which we go shall be prosperous."*

Most of the Christian world is asking counsel of that which purports to be of God, but, in reality, is not. They are asking counsel of the psychologists, psychiatrists, and therapists, worldly counselors who claim to be Biblical, at least some do, but are not; however, it is seldom that the modern Church actually seeks the counsel of God.

Men always love to have their self-made plans sanctioned by religion. It all seems so righteous, holy, and desirable. In fact, the world today is full of religion, but precious little of God. It is full of *"little gods,"* but experiences precious little of the God of Glory. How many people today are asking God to prosper their unscriptural way? It must be understood that God cannot bless anything that is unscriptural.

The Sixth Verse says that the hired priest would give them the blessing they so desired, *"Go in peace: before the LORD is your way wherein you go."*

The action of the Danites in asking this Levite to divine for them shows how far the Word of God had already departed from them. They should have been shocked and grieved at the Levite assuming priestly functions. As well, they should have been indignant of the insistence of a house of idols in place of the Tabernacle of Jehovah.

All of this is a perfect picture of man devising his own religious government, his own salvation so to speak, his own way, which he claims is of God. Let us say it again:

If it's not exactly according to the Word of God, then it can never be sanctioned by God. And if it is according to the Word of God, whatever it might be, it will have the Cross of Christ as its foundation.

THE PURPOSE DRIVEN LIFE SCHEME

Some time back, Frances handed me a book entitled *"The Purpose Driven Life,"* and asked me to read it, and tell her what I thought about it.

I read six or seven pages and then laid it down. A little bit later she came in, seeing the book on the coffee table, asked me, *"Did you read it?"* Of course, I could not have read it in that period of time.

I said to her, *"No, I only read a few pages."*

She then asked, *"You're not going to read the balance of it?"*

My answer was to the point, *"No, I don't have to read any more of it to know what it is."*

Reading the first few pages I knew that the man who wrote the book wasn't preaching or teaching the Cross; therefore, I knew that whatever it was that he was teaching, was not Biblical, was not of God, and consequently was not going to help anyone whatsoever. In fact, such foolishness, only hinders and hurts; it never helps.

It doesn't make any difference that hundreds of thousands of Churches have opted for *"The Purpose Driven Life"* scheme, or that thousands of preachers laud its doctrine, if it's not the Cross of Christ, then it's not the Gospel (I Cor. 1:17-18, 23; 2:2). Let us say it again:

THE ONLY ANSWER IS THE CROSS OF CHRIST

Man has a problem, a problem for which he has no solution. He has tried everything to address this need down through the ages. In the last 100 years humanistic psychology has been the big thruway, but without any success. Regrettably and unfortunately, the modern Church has opted for the ways of the world, and to be sure, those ways will afford no more solution for the Church than it does for the world.

As stated, there is only one answer, one solution to this dilemma, and that is the Cross of Jesus Christ.

To have that solution applied to one's heart and life, one must first of all make the Lord Jesus the Saviour of his soul, and the Lord of his life. In other words, he must be Born-Again (Jn. 3:3, 16).

Then he must anchor his Faith exclusively in Christ and the Cross, not allow it to be moved elsewhere, in effect, keeping it in the Cross all of his life. In effect, and according

NOTES

to the Words of our Saviour, it would be very good for each Believer to renew their Faith thusly even on a daily basis. Jesus said, and I quote from THE EXPOSITOR'S STUDY BIBLE:

"And He said to them all, If any man will come after Me (the criteria for Discipleship), *let him deny himself* (not asceticism as many think, but rather that one denies, one's own willpower, self-will, strength, and ability, depending totally on Christ), *and take up his cross* (the benefits of the Cross, looking exclusively to what Jesus did there to meet our every need) *daily* (this is so important, our looking to the Cross; that we must renew our Faith in what Christ has done for us, even on a daily basis, for Satan will ever try to move us away from the Cross as the Object of our Faith, which always spells disaster), *and follow Me* (Christ can be followed only by the Believer looking to the Cross, understanding what it accomplished, and by that means alone [Rom. 6:3-5, 11, 14; 8:1-2, 11; I Cor. 1:17-18, 21, 23; 2:2; Gal. 6:14; Eph. 2:13-18; Col. 2:14-15])" (Lk. 9:23).

And then our Lord said:

"And whosoever does not bear his cross (this doesn't speak of suffering as most think, but rather ever making the Cross of Christ the Object of our Faith; we are Saved and we are victorious not by suffering, although that sometimes will happen, or any other similar things, but rather by our Faith, but always with the Cross of Christ as the Object of that Faith), *and come after Me* (one can follow Christ only by Faith in what He has done for us at the Cross; He recognizes nothing else), *cannot be My Disciple* (the statement is emphatic! If it's not Faith in the Cross of Christ, then it's faith that God will not recognize, which means that such people are refused)" (Lk. 14:27).

These statements as given by Christ, as stated, are emphatic. In other words, and to use some street terminology, they leave nothing for wiggle room. It's the Cross of Christ or it's nothing! Let us say it again:

Man has a problem, and the only solution for that problem is the Cross of Christ.

(11) "AND THERE WENT FROM THENCE OF THE FAMILY OF THE DANITES, OUT OF ZORAH AND OUT OF ESHTAOL, SIX

HUNDRED MEN APPOINTED WITH WEAPONS OF WAR.

(12) "AND THEY WENT UP, AND PITCHED IN KIRJATH-JEARIM, IN JUDAH: WHEREFORE THEY CALLED THAT PLACE MAHANEH-DAN UNTO THIS DAY: BEHOLD, IT IS BEHIND KIRJATH-JEARIM.

(13) "AND THEY PASSED THENCE UNTO MOUNT EPHRAIM, AND CAME UNTO THE HOUSE OF MICAH.

(14) "THEN ANSWERED THE FIVE MEN WHO WENT TO SPY OUT THE COUNTRY OF LAISH, AND SAID UNTO THEIR BRETHREN, DO YOU KNOW THAT THERE IS IN THESE HOUSES AN EPHOD, AND TERAPHIM, AND A GRAVEN IMAGE, AND A MOLTEN IMAGE? NOW THEREFORE CONSIDER WHAT YOU HAVE TO DO.

(15) "AND THEY TURNED THITHERWARD, AND CAME TO THE HOUSE OF THE YOUNG MAN THE LEVITE, EVEN UNTO THE HOUSE OF MICAH, AND SALUTED HIM.

(16) "AND THE SIX HUNDRED MEN APPOINTED WITH THEIR WEAPONS OF WAR, WHICH WERE OF THE CHILDREN OF DAN, STOOD BY THE ENTERING OF THE GATE.

(17) "AND THE FIVE MEN WHO WENT TO SPY OUT THE LAND WENT UP, AND CAME IN THITHER, AND TOOK THE GRAVEN IMAGE, AND THE EPHOD, AND THE TERAPHIM, AND THE MOLTEN IMAGE: AND THE PRIEST STOOD IN THE ENTERING OF THE GATE WITH THE SIX HUNDRED MEN WHO WERE APPOINTED WITH WEAPONS OF WAR.

(18) "AND THESE WENT INTO MICAH'S HOUSE, AND FETCHED THE CARVED IMAGE, THE EPHOD, AND THE TERAPHIM, AND THE MOLTEN IMAGE. THEN SAID THE PRIEST UNTO THEM, WHAT ARE YOU DOING?

(19) "AND THEY SAID UNTO HIM, HOLD YOUR PEACE, LAY YOUR HAND UPON YOUR MOUTH, AND GO WITH US, AND BE TO US A FATHER AND A PRIEST: IS IT BETTER FOR YOU TO BE A PRIEST UNTO THE HOUSE OF ONE MAN, OR THAT YOU BE A PRIEST UNTO A TRIBE AND A FAMILY IN ISRAEL?

(20) "AND THE PRIEST'S HEART

NOTES

WAS GLAD, AND HE TOOK THE EPHOD, AND THE TERAPHIM, AND THE GRAVEN IMAGE, AND WENT IN THE MIDST OF THE PEOPLE.

(21) "SO THEY TURNED AND DEPARTED, AND PUT THE LITTLE ONES AND THE CATTLE AND THE CARRIAGE BEFORE THEM."

The exegesis is:

1. Ceremonial religion and violence, robbery, and plunder readily accord; and the richer the ceremonial the feebler and poorer becomes the moral consciousness.

2. Mankind has religious affections. Consequently, he must have objects on which to exercise these affections. Hence, the passion for images, pictures, crosses, and symbols in what is properly called *"worship."*

3. The priest of Verse 20 was for sale, and the Tribe of Dan paid more, so he went with them. How many modern preachers are doing the same thing?!

THE PRIEST AND
THE MONEY

It is obvious that this priest, the man of our illustration, has but one thing on his mind, and it isn't serving God, but rather, it's how much money that he's going to get! Regarding his ministry, such as it was, the highest bidder won his services.

I wonder how many modern preachers fall into the same category?

Christian Television, so-called, is a microcosm of the Church. First of all there are the outright shysters, selling their miracle water, or miracle oil, etc. I call them *"snake oil boys."* Due to the gullibility of so many, these particular preachers so-called, seem to do very well.

And then there are the preachers, while not peddling holy water, etc., still, promising riches if the people will only send so much money. I wonder why the snake oil boys don't take their own potion, and why the preachers with the get rich quick schemes, don't practice what they preach?

And then there are those who preach the *"feel good gospel."* Theirs is a morality message, which tickles the ears. Everyone wants higher morals, but the question is, how are these things obtained?

With these preachers, it's just a psychological gimmick, which, of course, doesn't work. Morals most definitely can be improved, but only by the Believer expressing Faith in Christ and what Christ did at the Cross. Then the Holy Spirit can develop His Fruit in one's heart and life (Gal. 5:22-24).

And then there is the ceremonial religion, which is obviously not Scriptural, but yet appeals to many.

And finally, there are the few, and precious few there are, who are truly preaching the Gospel of Jesus Christ. And to be sure, it is most difficult to find such Preachers. As someone has well said, they are as scarce as proverbial hens teeth.

(22) "AND WHEN THEY WERE A GOOD WAY FROM THE HOUSE OF MICAH, THE MEN WHO WERE IN THE HOUSES NEAR TO MICAH'S HOUSE WERE GATHERED TOGETHER, AND OVERTOOK THE CHILDREN OF DAN.

(23) "AND THEY CRIED UNTO THE CHILDREN OF DAN. AND THEY TURNED THEIR FACES, AND SAID UNTO MICAH, WHAT AILS YOU, THAT YOU COME WITH SUCH A COMPANY?

(24) "AND HE SAID, YOU HAVE TAKEN AWAY MY GODS WHICH I MADE, AND THE PRIEST, AND YOU ARE GONE AWAY: AND WHAT HAVE I MORE? AND WHAT IS THIS THAT YOU SAY UNTO ME, WHAT AILS YOU?

(25) "AND THE CHILDREN OF DAN SAID UNTO HIM, LET NOT YOUR VOICE BE HEARD AMONG US, LEST ANGRY FELLOWS RUN UPON YOU, AND YOU LOSE YOUR LIFE, WITH THE LIVES OF YOUR HOUSEHOLD.

(26) "AND THE CHILDREN OF DAN WENT THEIR WAY: AND WHEN MICAH SAW THAT THEY WERE TOO STRONG FOR HIM, HE TURNED AND WENT BACK UNTO HIS HOUSE."

The composition is:

1. A goodly number of men who were neighbors to Micah joined him to try to retrieve the stolen items from the children of Dan.

2. It is strange, Micah worships gods, which he made, and which can be taken by others, proving they are of no value; and,

NOTES

yet, almost all the modern world functions presently in the same manner. It worships gods that it has made, and the god of religion is the biggest god of all.

3. Micah's distress at the loss of his gods and priest portray religion. One can lose religion, but one cannot lose the Lord, at least in this fashion!

RELIGION

Religion is that which is conceived by man, given birth by man, and developed by man. It purports to reach God, or else to better one's self in some way. It is not of God. Anything that man has, man touches, man devises, or man conceives, is automatically polluted, meaning it's not of the Lord, and the Lord can have nothing to do with it.

That's the reason that anything other than the Cross is not of God, and simply because it is devised by man. Man may load it with Scriptures, may make his efforts very religious, but again we state, if it's not the Cross of Christ, then in some way, it is religion.

That's one of the reasons that man doesn't like the Cross. It is all of God and none of him. Men love to have a part in their own Salvation, a way which they have personally made, an effort which is of their sweat. This is why Cain was not happy at all with the Altar and the slain lamb. He recognized the need for sacrifice and, as well, the need for an Altar; however, he felt the produce of his own hands, was much more acceptable than that of a slain lamb. In fact, he was too nice to kill a lamb, but not too nice at all to murder his brother. Such characterizes modern day religion as nothing else!

(27) "AND THEY TOOK THE THINGS WHICH MICAH HAD MADE, AND THE PRIEST WHICH HE HAD, AND CAME UNTO LAISH, UNTO A PEOPLE WHO WERE AT QUIET AND SECURE: AND THEY SMOTE THEM WITH THE EDGE OF THE SWORD, AND BURNT THE CITY WITH FIRE.

(28) "AND THERE WAS NO DELIVERER, BECAUSE IT WAS FAR FROM ZIDON, AND THEY HAD NO BUSINESS WITH ANY MAN; AND IT WAS IN THE VALLEY THAT LIES BY BETH-REHOB. AND THEY BUILT A CITY, AND DWELT THEREIN.

(29) "AND THEY CALLED THE NAME OF THE CITY DAN, AFTER THE NAME OF DAN THEIR FATHER, WHO WAS BORN UNTO ISRAEL: HOWBEIT THE NAME OF THE CITY WAS LAISH AT THE FIRST."

The overview is:

1. The Holy Spirit using the name of *"Israel"* in Verse 29 emphasizes the depth of Dan's guilt in setting up idolatry.

2. The Twenty-seventh Verse says of the city called *"Laish,"* that *"they smote them with the edge of the sword, and burnt the city with fire"* — and they did it all in the Name of God.

More blood has been spilled regarding religion than for any other reason in the history of mankind. Where religion rules, violence results.

3. The Twenty-ninth Verse says, *"And they called the name of the city Dan."* Changing the name of the city from Laish to Dan did not in any fashion make it a city of God. The heathen they replaced, in fact, were closer to God than these Danites. The heathen did not know better; the Tribe of Dan did!

(30) "AND THE CHILDREN OF DAN SET UP THE GRAVEN IMAGE: AND JONATHAN, THE SON OF GERSHOM, THE SON OF MANASSEH, HE AND HIS SONS WERE PRIESTS TO THE TRIBE OF DAN UNTIL THE DAY OF THE CAPTIVITY OF THE LAND.

(31) "AND THEY SET THEM UP MICAH'S GRAVEN IMAGE, WHICH HE MADE, ALL THE TIME THAT THE HOUSE OF GOD WAS IN SHILOH."

The overview is:

1. Actually, Jonathan of Verse 30 was the grandson of Moses. His contemporary in the High Priesthood was Phinehas, the grandson of Aaron. Manasseh had no son called Gershom. Instead of the word *"Manasseh,"* the Hebrew word is *"Mosheh,"* Moses. It was altered to Manasseh, but all ancient authorities agree that it was a substitution for Moses in order to spare the reputation of the great Law-Giver and preserve the honor of his name and memory among Israel.

2. In I Chronicles 24:20 Jonathan is called *"Sheubael,"* which means *"he returned to God."* It is supposed to be the name of Jonathan after his Repentance, and it is used of him

afterward. As is here obvious, God has no grandchildren.

3. The Thirty-first Verse tells us of these idols being set up all over the land *"all the time that the House of God was in Shiloh."* Why was this so?

The answer is obvious. There was no Power of God at Shiloh. The priests were corrupt; therefore, the land was corrupt. The Tabernacle had been turned into little more than an idol itself; therefore, the rest of the land would be filled with idols as well.

4. As the Church goes, so goes the nation. If there is a declining, weak, vacillating Church (as we now have), the nation as well will be weak and vacillating.

The strength of America is the Church (the True Body of Christ). The strength of the Church is its devotion to the Word of God. Regrettably, there is precious little devotion at the present time, and as a result, precious little strength; therefore, so goes the nation.

CHAPTER 19

(1) "AND IT CAME TO PASS IN THOSE DAYS, WHEN THERE WAS NO KING IN ISRAEL, THAT THERE WAS A CERTAIN LEVITE SOJOURNING ON THE SIDE OF MOUNT EPHRAIM, WHO TOOK TO HIM A CONCUBINE OUT OF BETH-LEHEM-JUDAH.

(2) "AND HIS CONCUBINE PLAYED THE WHORE AGAINST HIM, AND WENT AWAY FROM HIM UNTO HER FATHER'S HOUSE TO BETH-LEHEM-JUDAH, AND WAS THERE FOUR WHOLE MONTHS.

(3) "AND HER HUSBAND AROSE, AND WENT AFTER HER, TO SPEAK FRIENDLY UNTO HER, AND TO BRING HER AGAIN, HAVING HIS SERVANT WITH HIM, AND A COUPLE OF ASSES: AND SHE BROUGHT HIM INTO HER FATHER'S HOUSE: AND WHEN THE FATHER OF THE DAMSEL SAW HIM, HE REJOICED TO MEET HIM.

(4) "AND HIS FATHER IN LAW, THE DAMSEL'S FATHER, RETAINED HIM; AND HE ABODE WITH HIM THREE DAYS: SO THEY DID EAT AND DRINK, AND

LODGED THERE.

(5) "AND IT CAME TO PASS ON THE FOURTH DAY, WHEN THEY AROSE EARLY IN THE MORNING, THAT HE ROSE UP TO DEPART: AND THE DAMSEL'S FATHER SAID UNTO HIS SON IN LAW, COMFORT YOUR HEART WITH A MORSEL OF BREAD, AND AFTERWARD GO YOUR WAY.

(6) "AND THEY SAT DOWN, AND DID EAT AND DRINK BOTH OF THEM TOGETHER: FOR THE DAMSEL'S FATHER HAD SAID UNTO THE MAN, BE CONTENT, I PRAY YOU, AND TARRY ALL NIGHT, AND LET YOUR HEART BE MERRY.

(7) "AND WHEN THE MAN ROSE UP TO DEPART, HIS FATHER IN LAW URGED HIM: THEREFORE HE LODGED THERE AGAIN.

(8) "AND HE AROSE EARLY IN THE MORNING ON THE FIFTH DAY TO DEPART: AND THE DAMSEL'S FATHER SAID, COMFORT YOUR HEART, I PRAY YOU. AND THEY TARRIED UNTIL AFTERNOON, AND THEY DID EAT BOTH OF THEM.

(9) "AND WHEN THE MAN ROSE UP TO DEPART, HE, AND HIS CONCUBINE, AND HIS SERVANT, HIS FATHER IN LAW, THE DAMSEL'S FATHER, SAID UNTO HIM, BEHOLD, NOW THE DAY DRAWS TOWARD EVENING, I PRAY YOU TARRY ALL NIGHT: BEHOLD, THE DAY GROWS TO AN END, LODGE HERE, THAT YOUR HEART MAY BE MERRY; AND TO MORROW GET YOU EARLY ON YOUR WAY, THAT YOU MAY GO HOME."

The overview is:

1. As exactly to the time frame this took place, we aren't told; however, it was definitely before the time of Saul.

2. The Lord said that Moses, because of the hardness of their hearts, suffered them to have more than one wife, but that in the beginning it was not so. The Levite, therefore, in having a secondary wife — they were called concubines — did not stand in a dishonorable relation to her.

3. This woman, in sinning against her husband, little dreamed of the dreadful doom that would result from her action. The Devil pays hard wages.

Concerning this, Williams says, "The terrible

NOTES

story pictures the misery, shame and ruin that comes upon the heart that, unfaithful to the True Husband, lives in guilty union with the world. The night in such a heart is dark indeed; and all the world gives is abuse and not honor."[1]

THE MORAL EVIL OF THE PEOPLE OF GOD

The closing Chapters of the Book of Judges picture the moral darkness that settles down upon a nation or a Church when the Bible is disregarded, and men follow the religious and social teachings of their own hearts, which is exactly what is happening presently in the modern Church.

The terrible message of this Levite was necessary to awaken the Nation, so deep was the impure sleep into which Israel had fallen.

In this Chapter we will see terrible depravity. Verse 1 says, "A certain Levite sojourning on the side of Mount Ephraim, who took to him a concubine."

Concubines were secondary wives and one might say, customary in those times; however, Jesus would say that Moses, because of the hardness of their hearts, suffered them to have more than one wife, but that in the beginning it was not so. The Levite, therefore, in having a secondary wife was allowed such action because of his hardened heart, but this was not the perfect Plan of God. Men usually try to push away from God's Direction as far as possible, and yet still claim they are Scriptural, even though by the narrowest of margins. Oh, how so much the heart of man would be blessed if he would strive constantly to get closer to God, instead of seeing how far away he can get and still be "in Grace."

The Second Verse says, "And his concubine played the whore against him." Sadly, this concubine was but a picture of the entirety of Israel that was "playing the whore" against God.

Verses 3 through 9 portray this "certain Levite" going to get his concubine to bring her home. If the people had been as zealous toward God as they were their "property" how much different the Nation might have been.

Pulpit says, "It is certainly not without a purpose that we have in Holy Scripture from *time to time exhibitions of sin in its most repulsive and revolting forms. The general rule which tells us that 'it is a shame even to speak of those things which are done of them in secret' is, as it were, violated on these occasions, because it is more important that the depravity of which human nature is capable at its worst should be revealed, than that the blush of shame should be prevented by its concealment. Sin, in some of its forms, is so disguised, and toned down, and softened, that the natural mind of man does not shrink from it with abhorrence or perceive its deadly nature, or its fatal consequences. But it is essential that sin should be known to be what it is, and especially that it should be made clear by what gradual descents a man may glide from one stage of wickedness to another, till, under favoring circumstances, he reaches a depth of vileness that at one time would have seemed impossible. As well, the process by which this descent is reached is not difficult to trace.*

"There is in every man a certain moral sense which restrains him from the commission of certain acts, whether of falsehood, dishonesty, cruelty, injustice, sensuality, or any other form of sin. And while that moral sense is maintained in its vigour, such acts may appear to him impossible for him to commit. But this moral sense is weakened, and more or less broken down by every action done in contradiction to its authority. At each successive stage of descent there is less shock to the weakened moral sense by the aspect of such or such sins that there was at the preceding stage. The sin, whatever it might be, appears less odious, and the resisting power is less strong."[2]

FALLEN MAN HAS A PROBLEM, AND THE ONLY ANSWER TO THAT PROBLEM IS THE CROSS OF CHRIST

I want the reader to slowly read that heading again, *"Fallen man has a problem, and the only answer to that problem is the Cross of Christ."* Now notice, I said, *"The only answer."* Paul wrote:

"But this Man (this Priest, Christ Jesus), *after He had offered One Sacrifice for sins forever* (speaks of the Cross), *sat down on the Right Hand of God* (refers to the great

contrast with the Priests under the Levitical system, who never sat down because their work was never completed; the Work of Christ was a *'Finished Work,'* and needed no repetition)*;*

"From henceforth expecting till His enemies be made His footstool. (These enemies are Satan and all the fallen Angels and demon spirits, plus all who follow Satan.)

"For by one Offering He has perfected forever them who are Sanctified. (Everything one needs is found in the Cross [Gal. 6:14])*"* (Heb. 10:12-14).

Please notice that the Scripture says *"One Sacrifice for sins forever."* This means that the work was totally completed, meaning that all sin, past, present, and future, is atoned, and is proven by the fact that Jesus is now *"sat down on the Right Hand of God."* This means that God has accepted His Sacrifice.

The word *"forever"* means that there will never be a need for another Sacrifice. That's the reason that Paul also referred to this Sacrifice as *"the Blood of the Everlasting Covenant"* (Heb. 13:20).

The word *"Everlasting"* means that this Covenant, made possible by the Cross, will never have to be replaced, never have to be amended, not in any form, and because it is perfect.

This is the answer, the only answer for man's dilemma. That's why we must preach the Cross.

PREACHING THE CROSS

Paul also said, *"For after that in the Wisdom of God the world by wisdom knew not God* (man's puny wisdom, even the best he has to offer, cannot come to know God in any manner), *it pleased God by the foolishness of preaching* (preaching the Cross) *to save them who believe.* (Paul is not dealing with the art of preaching here, but with what is preached.)

And then, *"But we preach Christ Crucified* (this is the Foundation of the Word of God and, thereby, of Salvation), *unto the Jews a stumblingblock* (the Cross was the stumblingblock), *and unto the Greeks foolishness* (both found it difficult to accept as God a dead Man hanging on a Cross, for such Christ was to them)*;*

"But unto them which are called (refers to those who accept the Call, for the entirety of mankind is invited [Jn. 3:16; Rev. 22:17]), *both Jews and Greeks* (actually stands for both *'Jews and Gentiles'*), *Christ the Power of God* (what He did at the Cross atoned for all sin, thereby, making it possible for the Holy Spirit to exhibit His Power within our lives), *and the Wisdom of God.* (This Wisdom devised a Plan of Salvation which pardoned guilty men and at the same time vindicated and glorified the Justice of God, which stands out as the wisest and most remarkable Plan of all time)*"* (I Cor. 1:21, 23-24).

Is the modern Church preaching the Cross?

I think the answer to that is obvious, no it isn't!

What does it actually mean to preach the Cross?

It means that the preacher must understand, exactly as the heading states, that man has a severe problem, a problem incidentally that is terminal, and the only answer for that problem, and I mean the only answer, is the Cross of Christ. There sin was fully, totally, and completely addressed, because that was the only place it could be addressed. In fact, Jesus came to this world to do a lot of things, but His main Objective was ever the Cross.

The preacher must understand that every single thing we receive from God, and in totality, comes to us strictly from Christ as the Source, and the Cross as the Means. In other words, the Cross is the Means by which all of these wonderful things are given to us. That's the reason that Paul said:

"For Christ sent me not to baptize (presents to us a Cardinal Truth), *but to preach the Gospel* (the manner in which one may be saved from sin): *not with wisdom of words* (intellectualism is not the Gospel), *lest the Cross of Christ should be made of none effect.* (This tells us in no uncertain terms that the Cross of Christ must always be the emphasis of the Message)*"* (I Cor. 1:17).

When the preacher fully understands that the Cross of Christ is not only an absolute necessity for Salvation, but, as well, for Sanctification, then he is fully preaching the Cross. That being the case, he will not try to promote humanistic psychology, *"The*

NOTES

Purpose Driven Life" foolishness, or any other so-called panacea, but only the Cross. In fact, once he understands the Cross as he should, and that refers to understanding it not only for Salvation but, as well, for Sanctification, he will begin to see false doctrine for what it is, whereas without a proper understanding of the Cross, there is no such illumination.

Properly preaching the Cross is not so much what one says, even though that is extremely important, but actually what one believes.

ALL SPIRITUAL MATURITY IS PREDICATED ON A PROPER UNDERSTANDING OF THE CROSS

If the Believer, preacher or otherwise, doesn't understand the Cross as it regards both Salvation and Sanctification, there will be precious little maturity in the Word of God. All maturity, and we mean all maturity, is bound up in one's proper understanding of the Cross. That's the reason that Paul also said:

"For I determined not to know any thing among you (with purpose and design, Paul did not resort to the knowledge or philosophy of the world regarding the Preaching of the Gospel), *save Jesus Christ, and Him Crucified* (that and that alone is the Message which will save the sinner, set the captive free, and give the Believer perpetual victory)*"* (I Cor. 2:2).

(10) "BUT THE MAN WOULD NOT TARRY THAT NIGHT, BUT HE ROSE UP AND DEPARTED, AND CAME OVER AGAINST JEBUS, WHICH IS JERUSALEM; AND THERE WERE WITH HIM TWO ASSES SADDLED, HIS CONCUBINE ALSO WAS WITH HIM.

(11) "AND WHEN THEY WERE BY JEBUS, THE DAY WAS FAR SPENT; AND THE SERVANT SAID UNTO HIS MASTER, COME I PRAY YOU, AND LET US TURN IN INTO THIS CITY OF THE JEBUSITES, AND LODGE IN IT.

(12) "AND HIS MASTER SAID UNTO HIM, WE WILL NOT TURN ASIDE HITHER INTO THE CITY OF A STRANGER, THAT IS NOT OF THE CHILDREN OF ISRAEL;

WE WILL PASS OVER TO GIBEAH.

(13) "AND HE SAID UNTO HIS SERVANT, COME, AND LET US DRAW NEAR TO ONE OF THESE PLACES TO LODGE ALL NIGHT, IN GIBEAH, OR IN RAMAH.

(14) "AND THEY PASSED ON AND WENT THEIR WAY; AND THE SUN WENT DOWN UPON THEM WHEN THEY WERE BY GIBEAH, WHICH BELONGS TO BENJAMIN.

(15) "AND THEY TURNED ASIDE THITHER, TO GO IN AND TO LODGE IN GIBEAH: AND WHEN HE WENT IN, HE SAT HIM DOWN IN A STREET OF THE CITY: FOR THERE WAS NO MAN WHO TOOK THEM INTO HIS HOUSE TO LODGING.

(16) "AND, BEHOLD, THERE CAME AN OLD MAN FROM HIS WORK OUT OF THE FIELD AT EVENING, WHICH WAS ALSO OF MOUNT EPHRAIM; AND HE SOJOURNED IN GIBEAH: BUT THE MEN OF THE PLACE WERE BENJAMITES.

(17) "AND WHEN HE HAD LIFTED UP HIS EYES, HE SAW A WAYFARING MAN IN THE STREET OF THE CITY: AND THE OLD MAN SAID, WHERE ARE YOU GOING? AND FROM WHERE HAVE YOU COME?

(18) "AND HE SAID UNTO HIM, WE ARE PASSING FROM BETH-LEHEM-JUDAH TOWARD THE SIDE OF MOUNT EPHRAIM; FROM THENCE AM I: AND I WENT TO BETH-LEHEM-JUDAH, BUT I AM NOW GOING TO THE HOUSE OF THE LORD; AND THERE IS NO MAN WHO RECEIVES ME TO HOUSE.

(19) "YET THERE IS BOTH STRAW AND PROVENDER FOR OUR ASSES; AND THERE IS BREAD AND WINE ALSO FOR ME, AND FOR YOUR HANDMAID, AND FOR THE YOUNG MAN WHICH IS WITH YOUR SERVANTS: THERE IS NO WANT OF ANY THING.

(20) "AND THE OLD MAN SAID, PEACE BE WITH YOU; HOWSOEVER LET ALL YOUR WANTS LIE UPON ME; ONLY LODGE NOT IN THE STREET.

(21) "SO HE BROUGHT HIM INTO HIS HOUSE, AND GAVE PROVENDER UNTO THE ASSES: AND THEY WASHED THEIR FEET, AND DID EAT AND DRINK."

The synopsis is:

1. Gibeah was in a sense, a suburb of Jerusalem.

NOTES

2. Pulpit says, *"The absence of the common rites of hospitality toward strangers was a sign of the degraded character of the men of Gibeah. In those days, there were very few inns; consequently, travelers stayed, normally, in people's homes (Lk. 11:5-13)."*[3]

3. The *"House of the LORD"* referred to in Verse 18, probably refers to the Tabernacle at Shiloh.

4. In other words, the statement of Verse 19 means that he would not be a burden on anyone, because he had his own food, etc.

BELIEVERS AND UNBELIEVERS

The Eleventh Verse says, *"Let us turn in into this city of the Jebusites, and lodge in it."*

At that time the Jebusites, who were supposed to have been exterminated by the Tribe of Judah, still occupied Jerusalem. So, from this we see another failure on Israel's part; however, the Twelfth Verse says, *"We will pass over to Gibeah."*

They would have been far better off to have stayed with the heathen Jebusites than the depraved Benjamites, for the Tribe of Benjamin occupied Gibeah.

There is nothing more cruel or ungodly than the people of the Lord who have lost their way, and Israel had lost her way.

The great name of Joshua and what God did in his particular time, and the traditions of the surviving Elders who followed in the way of Joshua, must have set before Israel a standard of righteousness, and impressed them with a sense of being the people of God. But they had not acted up to their high calling. Doubtless they had mingled with the heathen and learned their works. Their hearts had declined from God, from His Fear and Service. Idolatry had eaten as a canker into their moral principle. Its shameful licentiousness had enticed and overcome them. To be sure, the Spirit of God was vexed with them to say the least!

The problem was, the Light of God's Word was quenched in the darkness of gross materialism. The results were, an utter callousness of conscience. They began to sneer at virtue, and to scoff at the fear of God. When the fear of God was gone, the honor due to man and due to themselves would soon dissipate as well. Thus, it came to pass at the time of this history that the whole community was sunk to the level of the vilest heathenism. The truth is, the Believers were in far worse condition than the unbelievers.

THE SNAKE OIL PREACHERS

I'm afraid that *"materialism"* is running rampant in the modern Church as well. That being the case, the next step will be the utter vileness of which we see here, which stain is already beginning to appear in certain religious denominations ordaining homosexuals to preach, etc.

Materialism is a doctrine that claims *"that the only or the highest values or objectives lie in material well-being and in the furtherance of material progress. It is a preoccupation with or stress upon material rather than spiritual things."* Such presents the modern *"money gospel"* which has left a mark upon most of that which claims to be Gospel. While Scriptures, of course, are used in this phony gospel, to be sure, the Word of God is not the criteria, but is used only to pull in the gullible, which it is very successful in doing.

How many times do you turn on that which purports to be Christian Television, and the preacher is telling people how to get rich, how to amass more money, with every type of gimmick being used to further this effort. The truth is, the only people who get rich are the preachers. I refer to this as the *"snake oil gospel"* and its purveyors as *"snake oil preachers."*

The phrase *"snake oil"* goes back many years ago, with salesmen offering some type of colored water, or some such liquid, claiming that it would heal all type of diseases, and work magic incantations, etc.

In the realm of preachers, this comes under two types:

The first type is overt. They are hawking *"miracle water"* or *"miracle oil,"* or some such foolishness, which unfortunately, there always seems to be ready takers. In other words, you get their *"miracle water,"* or *"miracle oil,"* and you're going to be healed, but above all, your going to get rich, meaning all type of wonderful things are going to start to fall on you.

Then we have the covert type of *"snake oil preacher."* What do we mean by that?

They do not peddle *"miracle water,"* or some such like foolishness, they rather couch their terminology in much more sophisticated terms. They purport to show you from the Scriptures, how you can be rich beyond your wildest dreams. Then you are encouraged to get their books or tapes, which will graphically explain the process. And above all, if you give money to them, whomever they might be, this will insure your proposed blessing.

Irrespective, and no matter what face is worn, pure and simple, it is *"snake oil."* Let me be a little more blunt!

THE CROSS OF CHRIST

If the preacher is not preaching the Cross of the Lord Jesus Christ as the answer to the human dilemma, and the only answer to the human dilemma, then in some way, even whether he intends to or not, he is peddling snake oil. What he is proposing will not do the people any good. Let's look at Paul and see what he had to say about this.

He said, *"If you be circumcised, Christ shall profit you nothing"* (Gal. 5:2).

What the great Apostle is saying is that if the Galatians, or anyone else for that matter, places their faith in anything except Christ and Him Crucified, and that exclusively, all that Jesus did on the Cross, all the victory which He purchased for us, and at a dear price I might quickly add, *"shall profit you nothing."* He then said, *"Christ is become of no effect unto you"* (Gal. 5:4).

What did he mean by that?

He meant, that the entire Plan of Redemption, all that Christ came to this world to do, all, in fact, that He did do, will be of no benefit whatsoever to the individual who places his faith in anything except Christ and the Cross exclusively. For *"Christ to become of no effect unto us,"* places such a person in a very disconcerted position. Sadly and regrettably, that is, however, the position of most modern Christians. Christ is of no effect unto them.

He went on to say, *"whosoever of you are justified by the Law* (seek to be Justified by the Law); *you are fallen from Grace* (fallen from the position of Grace, which means the

Believer is trusting in something other than the Cross; it actually means, *'to apostatize'*)" (Gal. 5:4).

WHAT DOES IT MEAN TO FALL FROM GRACE?

First of all, plain and simple, it means for one to place their Faith in something other than Christ and the Cross.

The Grace of God is simply the Goodness of God extended to undeserving Believers. However, we must never forget that the Grace of God comes to us exclusively by the Means of the Cross. It is the Cross of Christ which makes the Grace of God possible.

All the Believer has to do in order to have a continued, uninterrupted supply of Grace, i.e., *"The Goodness of God,"* extended to him, is to keep his Faith anchored in the Cross, and as our Lord said, even on a daily basis (Lk. 9:23).

It is the Holy Spirit Who superintends the giving of the Grace of God to us (Rom. 8:1-2, 11; Gal. 5:5). He works exclusively within the parameters of the Finished Work of Christ (Rom. 8:2). In fact, He will not work outside of those parameters. Consequently, He demands that our Faith be exclusively in Christ and what Christ has done for us in His Finished Work. That's the reason that Paul also said, *"For the preaching* (Message) *of the Cross is to them who perish foolishness; but to we who are Saved it is the Power of God"* (I Cor. 1:18).

The *"power"* is registered in the Holy Spirit. He gives it to us on the premise of what Christ has done at the Cross, and our Faith in that Finished Work.

When a Believer fails to place his faith in Christ and the Cross and do so exclusively, or else he moves his faith from Christ and the Cross to something else, even as the Galatians were doing, that individual is *"fallen from Grace."* Sadly and regrettably, that means that virtually the entirety of the modern Church has *"fallen from Grace."* The end result, to say the least, will not be pleasant.

Untold millions of Believers will simply quit believing, will ultimately quit, and will lose their souls. Even the Believers who do not quit, and even though they are Saved, will live far beneath their Spiritual privileges,

and because of having their faith in the wrong thing.

Unfortunately, most Christians have been taught that *"falling from Grace,"* means that one has committed some grave sin, etc.

No it doesn't!

In fact, that's the very person who desperately needs the Grace of God, and will receive it, providing they dutifully repent, and once again place their faith in Christ and the Cross, and nothing else.

WHEN PETER DENIED THE LORD DID HE FALL FROM GRACE?

No!

Peter failed, and failed miserably, which brought him tremendous condemnation and sorrow, but he did not Fall. In other words, he never quit believing in Christ, despite his terrible situation in which he found himself that day.

However, Peter at one juncture of his life and Ministry, did begin to fall from Grace. It is recorded in the Second Chapter of Galatians. Concerning this incident, Paul said, *"I withstood him to the face* (means Paul openly opposed and reproved him, even though Peter was the eldest), *because he was to be blamed* (for abandoning the Cross and resorting to Law).

"For before that certain came from James (gives us all too well another example as to why Apostles, or anyone else for that matter, are not to be the final word, but rather the Word of God itself), *he* (Peter) *did eat with the Gentiles* (Peter knew the Gospel of Grace): *but when they were come* (those from James in Jerusalem), *he withdrew and separated himself, fearing them which were of the Circumcision.* (The problem was *'man fear.'* Some of the Jewish Christians were still trying to hold to the Law of Moses, which means they accepted Jesus as the Messiah, but gave no credence to the Cross whatsoever. This ultimately occasioned the necessity of Paul writing the Epistle to the Hebrews.)

"And the other Jews (in the Church at Antioch) *dissembled likewise with him* (with Peter); *insomuch that Barnabas also was carried away with their dissimulation* (hypocrisy)" (Gal. 2:11-13).

Every evidence is that Peter took Paul's

rebuke, and got his faith organized again. In other words, his falling from Grace was very short.

Now most would look at the situation where Peter denied the Lord as being far worse than this occasion here with Peter reverting back to Law; however, the latter stood to do the Church far more harm than the first episode. In fact, concerning Peter's gross failure of denial, Luke quoted our Lord as saying:

"*Simon, Simon, behold, Satan has desired to have you* (portrays to us a glimpse into the spirit world, which was very similar to the same request made by Satan concerning Job), *that he may sift you as wheat* (Satan tempts in order to bring out the bad, while God tests in order to bring out the good; the simple truth is, God, at times using Satan as His instrument in addressing character, causes men to seek God's Holiness rather than their own)*:

"*But I have prayed for you, that your faith fail not* (Satan's attack is always delivered against Faith, for if that fails all fails)*: and when you are converted, strengthen your brethren* (does not refer to being Saved again, but rather coming to the right path of trust and dependence on the Lord, instead of on self; that lesson learned, one is then able to strengthen the Brethren)*" (Lk. 22:31-32).

I think it is obvious that God answered the prayer of His Son as it regards Peter. Peter's Faith did not fail, meaning he did not quit as did Judas. Let us say it again:

Regrettably, most of the modern Church thinks that "*falling from Grace*" is committing some type of heinous sin. No, that's not falling from Grace. As stated, that person is in dire need of the Grace of God, which Grace God will extend, if the individual will only humble himself or herself.

Falling from Grace has to do with one's Faith being transferred from Christ and the Cross to something else. And it doesn't matter how religious the something else is, even how good it might be in its own right. Listen again to Paul:

"*For Christ sent me not to baptize* (presents to us a Cardinal Truth), *but to preach the Gospel* (the manner in which one may be Saved from sin)*: not with wisdom of words*

(intellectualism is not the Gospel), *lest the Cross of Christ should be made of none effect.* (This tells us in no uncertain terms that the Cross of Christ must always be the emphasis of the Message)*" (I Cor. 1:17).

The Holy Spirit here through Paul is telling us that the "*Cross of Christ*" is actually the "*Gospel.*" That being the case, we must not allow other things, as right as they may be in their own way, even as Water Baptism, to be emphasized. Our Faith must ever be in Christ as the Source and the Cross as the Means.

If our faith is placed in something else, even as the faith of the modern Church basically is, the end result will ultimately be the same as it was with Israel of old — vile sins of every description.

(22) "NOW AS THEY WERE MAKING THEIR HEARTS MERRY, BEHOLD, THE MEN OF THE CITY, CERTAIN SONS OF BELIAL, BESET THE HOUSE ROUND ABOUT, AND BEAT AT THE DOOR, AND SPOKE TO THE MASTER OF THE HOUSE, THE OLD MAN, SAYING, BRING FORTH THE MAN WHO CAME INTO YOUR HOUSE, THAT WE MAY KNOW HIM.

(23) "AND THE MAN, THE MASTER OF THE HOUSE, WENT OUT UNTO THEM, AND SAID UNTO THEM, NO, MY BRETHREN, NO, I PRAY YOU, DO NOT SO WICKEDLY; SEEING THAT THIS MAN IS COME INTO MY HOUSE, DO NOT THIS FOLLY.

(24) "BEHOLD, HERE IS MY DAUGHTER A MAIDEN, AND HIS CONCUBINE; THEM I WILL BRING OUT NOW, AND HUMBLE YOU THEM, AND DO WITH THEM WHAT SEEMS GOOD UNTO YOU: BUT UNTO THIS MAN DO NOT SO VILE A THING.

(25) "BUT THE MEN WOULD NOT HEARKEN TO HIM: SO THE MAN TOOK HIS CONCUBINE, AND BROUGHT HER FORTH UNTO THEM; AND THEY KNEW HER, AND ABUSED HER ALL THE NIGHT UNTIL THE MORNING: AND WHEN THE DAY BEGAN TO SPRING, THEY LET HER GO.

(26) "THEN CAME THE WOMAN IN THE DAWNING OF THE DAY, AND FELL DOWN AT THE DOOR OF THE MAN'S HOUSE WHERE HER LORD WAS, TILL IT WAS LIGHT.

(27) "AND HER LORD ROSE UP IN THE MORNING, AND OPENED THE DOORS

OF THE HOUSE, AND WENT OUT TO GO HIS WAY: AND, BEHOLD, THE WOMAN HIS CONCUBINE WAS FALLEN DOWN AT THE DOOR OF THE HOUSE, AND HER HANDS WERE UPON THE THRESHOLD.

(28) "AND HE SAID UNTO HER, UP, AND LET US BE GOING. BUT NONE ANSWERED. THEN THE MAN TOOK HER UP UPON AN ASS, AND THE MAN ROSE UP, AND GOT HIM UNTO HIS PLACE."

The overview is:

1. The men of Verse 22 were homosexuals; it would have been better for the Levite to have spent the night with the heathen Jebusites than with the professed children of God; for the latter had already become viler than the former, although Joshua was not long dead!

2. The singular resemblance of the whole narrative to that in Genesis, Chapter 19 suggests that the Israelites, by their contact with the accursed Canaanites, had reduced themselves to the level of Sodom and Gomorrah.

The illustration given in this Chapter proclaims the wisdom of the command to destroy utterly these workers of abomination. Some sins are worse than others, and the sin of homosexuality is one of the most vile.

It is the only sin that has occasioned the destruction of entire cities, and we speak of Sodom and Gomorrah, and done so instantly, and done so by God.

3. The United States, and especially this country, because of the great Gospel Light it has been given, will ultimately face the Judgment of God in its sanctioning of so-called homosexual marriages. The sin itself is bad enough; however, to legitimize it, which this nation is doing, will ultimately bring upon our heads the Wrath of God, and rightly so.

4. Lot's last night in Sodom gives a similar illustration of the loathsome depths to which men sink when they cease to retain God in their knowledge (Rom. 1:18-32).

5. As Verse 25 records what was done, this tells us how despicable was her husband, who allowed such a thing to happen.

The woman died from the abuse she had taken that night. God help us!

HOMOSEXUALITY

Some sins are worse than others, Jesus

said so!

The Scripture says, *"Jesus answered, You could have no power at all against Me, except it were given you from above* (tells us the degree of control exercised by God): *therefore he who delivered Me unto you has the greater sin* (we learn from this that some sins are worse than others, thereby we learn that the Jews were held by God as more culpable than the Romans)" (Jn. 19:11).

Jesus also said, *"Woe unto you, Scribes and Pharisees, hypocrites! for you devour widows' houses, and for a pretence make long prayer* (projects a false piety which deceives people, and the most helpless at that): *therefore you shall receive the greater damnation* (this tells us that religious wickedness is the greatest wickedness of all)" (Mat. 23:14).

Homosexuality is a sin! A grievous sin! I don't think it's the worse sin of all, that being as just stated, *"religious wickedness;"* nevertheless, homosexuality is abominable.

HOW SHOULD HOMOSEXUALS BE TREATED?

Homosexuals are human beings just like anyone else. They should be treated with the same dignity and respect. Jesus died for them the same as He died for all of humanity.

While the true Believer is extremely opposed to homosexuality, we should not be opposed to homosexuals. In other words, the homosexual should not be treated with disdain. It is the same for the gambler. While all Believers are opposed to gambling, we should not be opposed to the gambler. While we are opposed to drug addiction, we must not be opposed to the drug addict. While we are opposed to alcoholism, we should not be opposed to the alcoholic. Jesus loved the sinners, but hated the sin. That must be our motif as well (Jn. 3:16).

CAN A HOMOSEXUAL BE SAVED?

Most definitely! Anyone can be Saved if they will come to Christ. When Jesus died on the Cross of Calvary, He died for the whole of humanity. In fact, Calvary was for homosexuals, and for the alcoholic, and for gamblers, and for the drug addict. In fact, Jesus died for all of humanity, no matter how vile, how wicked, how ungodly the person may be.

In fact, Calvary left no sin unatoned, whether past, present, or future, at least for all who will believe (Jn. 3:16).

However, having said that, once the homosexual comes to Christ, homosexuality must be laid aside. Our Lord doesn't save in sin, but rather from sin.

That doesn't mean that he or she might not have a tug or a pull, even severely so, after conversion. In fact, that most probably will be the case; however, the very premise of the Gospel is to deliver us from sin. Paul said and concerning Christ, *"Who gave Himself for our sins* (the Cross), *that He might deliver us from this present evil world* (the Cross alone can set the captive free), *according to the Will of God and our Father* (the Standard of the entire process of Redemption)*"* (Gal. 1:4).

Once the homosexual comes to Christ, or anyone else for that matter, their faith must be placed exclusively in Christ and the Cross, and they must not allow it to be moved elsewhere. In fact, the entirety of the Sixth Chapter of Romans proclaims to us the manner in which the Believer is to overcome. Christ is the Source of our Salvation and our Victory, and the Cross is the Means by which it is given unto us. It only requires Faith on our part, and Faith exclusively in Christ and the Cross.

This being done, Faith placed exclusively in the Cross of Christ, the Holy Spirit, Who is God, and Who of necessity can do anything, will then use His Almighty Power, all on our behalf, enabling us to live the life we ought to live, which includes victory over the terrible sin of homosexuality.

If the Believer doesn't place his faith in Christ and the Cross, but rather something else, this greatly hinders the Holy Spirit from helping us, considering that the Holy Spirit works entirely within the parameters of the Finished Work of Christ, which means that such a Believer is going to continue to have real problems.

However, we must quickly add, that none of this means, and I am speaking of our Faith being correctly placed in Christ and the Cross, that Satan will cease all operations against us, and there will be never more a problem. In fact, Satan will not stop trying

NOTES

to hinder the Child of God. He will test one's metal so to speak! So, the Believer placing his Faith correctly in Christ and the Cross, and thinking that this will forego all temptation, is going to be in for a rude awakening.

It may even be possible, and more than likely will happen, that such a Believer will fail. The reason is, our Faith is never quite what we think it is, and is not as anchored in the Cross as we think it is. But remember this, and as one good Baptist Preacher said: *"We might fail, but the Cross never fails!*

ARE HOMOSEXUALS BORN THAT WAY?

No!

However, that needs an explanation.

Every human being, due to the Fall in the Garden of Eden, is born with a sin nature. In our nature, which is given over to sin, and because of original sin, there are proclivities in certain people toward certain types of sins, more than it is in others. In other words, some will have a proclivity toward alcohol, or gambling, or homosexuality, or jealousy, or envy, etc. While everyone has such proclivities, some types are more pronounced in some people than others.

This doesn't mean that one is born a kleptomaniac, or pathological liar, or a homosexual, etc. It does mean that they are born with tendencies a little more than usual toward those particular vices or bondages. With these proclivities, many gravitate toward the problem, giving vent to the situation and, thereby, become totally enslaved.

Science claims that it has located particular genes in the person, which has the tendency to push one, for instance, toward alcoholism, etc. They think if they can replace that perverted gene with a healthy gene, that the problem can be eliminated; however, the problem is really not in the gene, the problem is in what causes the gene to be like it is, whatever that might be. That problem is a Spiritual problem. That's the reason that a person has to be *"born again."* When Born-Again happens, in effect, the person is actually *"regened."* Paul says:

"Not by works of righteousness which we have done (presents the utter impossibility of man performing works of Righteousness

which will save him), *but according to His Mercy He saved us* (the initiative of Salvation springs entirely from the Lord, and is carried out by Means of the Cross), *by the washing of Regeneration* (in effect, the Born-Again Believer is regened, which is brought about by a cleansing process, with the Blood having cleansed from all sin, both its power and its guilt [I Jn. 1:7]), *and renewing of the Holy Spirit* (proclaims the Member of the Godhead Who actually carries out the work of Regeneration in the heart and life of the Believing sinner, which He does by exhibited Faith in Christ on the part of the individual)" (Titus 3:5).

When one is Born-Again, one is regenerated, which, in effect, is *"regened."* That is the only cure for the problem. No matter what science does, they will never be able to solve the problem, at least by the means of science. As stated, it is a Spiritual problem, all as a result of the Fall, and can be addressed properly only by the Believing sinner evidencing Faith in Christ, Who paid the price that we might be Saved.

Again we state, no, the homosexual was not born that way, and neither was the alcoholic, or the gambler, etc.

James, the Lord's brother tells us how the individual is pulled into the bondages of darkness. He said:

"Let no man say when he is tempted, I am tempted of God (we must not assume that enticement to sin comes from God; it never does!)*: for God cannot be tempted with evil, neither tempts He any man* (God's omnipotent Holy Will fully resists any direction towards sin)*:*

"But every man is tempted, when he is drawn away of his own lust, and enticed. (The temptation to sin appeals to a moral defect in us, even in the best, for none are perfect.)

"Then when lust has conceived (speaks of evil lusts), *it brings forth sin* (as stated, these temptations do not come from God, but from the appetites of man's sinful nature, which is a result of the Fall; the sin nature can be held at bay, and is meant to be held at bay by the Believer anchoring his Faith in the Cross of Christ, which will then give the Holy Spirit latitude to help)*: and sin, when it is finished, brings forth death.* (This refers to Spiritual

death, because sin separates man from God.)

"Do not err, my beloved Brethren (James is saying to Believers, *'don't be deceived; sin is the ruin of all that is good'*)*"* (James 1:13-16).

Incidentally, the *"gene"* is *"an element of the germ plasm that controls transmission of a hereditary character."*

The men of Gibeah who demanded that the visitor be given unto them were homosexuals. Angry because he wasn't given to them and the woman was, they killed her.

It should be quickly said, that homosexuality carries with it acute forms of violence. This doesn't mean that every homosexual is a murderer, or of the type listed here in the Word of God, but it does mean that some are, more than usual, and that this bondage drives some to that terrible place of murder and abomination.

BIBLICAL ACCOUNTS OF HOMOSEXUALITY

The first account given in the Bible of such is found in Genesis, Chapter 19. It speaks of the men of the city of Sodom demanding of Lot that he give up the visitors who were in his house. These men were homosexuals or Sodomites. Incidentally, the name *"Sodomite,"* which is another name for homosexuals, came from this incident. It was one of the reasons, that God destroyed both Sodom and Gomorrah.

The Lord specifically stated, *"You shall not lie with mankind, as with womankind: it is abomination"* (Lev. 18:22).

He also said, *"If a man also lie with mankind, as he lies with a woman, both of them have committed an abomination: they shall surely be put to death; their blood shall be upon them"* (Lev. 20:13).

The command for the death penalty for homosexuality was under the Law; it was not carried over under the New Covenant, even though the sin is still just as repugnant.

The Lord also said, *"There shall be no whore of the daughters of Israel, nor a sodomite of the sons of Israel.*

He then said, *"You shall not bring the hire of a whore, or the price of a dog, into the House of the LORD your God for any vow: for even both these are abomination unto the LORD your God"* (Deut. 23:17-18).

The word *"dog"* as used here in the Hebrew is *"kaleb,"* and means *"a male prostitute."* Moses is not speaking of the canine variety.

Concerning homosexuality, Paul said, *"For this cause God gave them up unto vile affections* (the Lord removed His restraints and, therefore, gave them unimpeded access to their desires)*: for even their women did change the natural use into that which is against nature* (in short, speaks of Lesbianism)*:

"And likewise also the men (homosexuality), *leaving the natural use of the woman* (speaks of the sex act which is performed between the man and his wife), *burned in their lust one toward another* (raging lust); *men with men working that which is unseemly* (specifies its direction, which is total perversion), *and receiving in themselves that recompence of their error which was meet* (refers to the penalty attached to wrongdoing).

"And even as they did not like to retain God in their knowledge (carries the idea of the human race putting God to the test for the purpose of approving or disapproving Him), *God gave them over to a reprobate mind* (Light rejected is Light withdrawn), *to do those things which are not convenient* (which are not fitting)*"* (Rom. 1:26-28). He then said, *"Who knowing the Judgment of God* (in essence, saying, 'do your worst, and it will not stop us'), *that they which commit such things are worthy of death* (Divine Judgment is implied), *not only do the same, but have pleasure in them who do them* (proclaims the result of the 'reprobate mind')*"* (Rom. 1:32).

Jude, the half brother of our Lord said, *"Even as Sodom and Gomorrah, and the cities about them in like manner* (the Greek Text introduces a comparison showing a likeness between the Angels of Verse 6 and the cities of Sodom and Gomorrah; but the likeness between them lies deeper than the fact that both were guilty of committing sin; it extends to the fact that both were guilty of the same identical sin), *giving themselves over to fornication, and going after strange flesh* (the Angels cohabited with women; the sin of Sodom and Gomorrah, and the cities around them, was homosexuality), *are set forth for and example, suffering the vengeance of eternal fire* (those who engage in the sin of homosexuality and refuse to repent will suffer the vengeance of the Lake of Fire)*"* (Jude, Vs. 7).

There is Salvation for the homosexual, as with anyone else; however, there is no Salvation for homosexuality!

(29) "AND WHEN HE WAS COME INTO HIS HOUSE, HE TOOK A KNIFE, AND LAID HOLD ON HIS CONCUBINE, AND DIVIDED HER, TOGETHER WITH HER BONES, INTO TWELVE PIECES, AND SENT HER INTO ALL THE COASTS OF ISRAEL.

(30) "AND IT WAS SO, THAT ALL WHO SAW IT SAID, THERE WAS NO SUCH DEED DONE NOR SEEN FROM THE DAY THAT THE CHILDREN OF ISRAEL CAME UP OUT OF THE LAND OF EGYPT UNTO THIS DAY: CONSIDER OF IT, TAKE ADVICE, AND SPEAK YOUR MINDS."

The exposition is:

1. The closing Chapters of the Book of Judges picture the moral darkness that settles down upon a nation, or a Church when the Bible is disregarded, and men follow the religious and social teachings of their own minds and hearts.

2. The general sense of the whole Nation was to call a national counsel to decide what to do. At least, and despite his cowardice, the Levite had succeeded in arousing the indignation of the Twelve Tribes to avenge this terrible wrong.

3. When men leave God and His Ways, we see here the result! Regrettably, America is heading in this same direction.

CHAPTER 20

(1) "THEN ALL THE CHILDREN OF ISRAEL WENT OUT, AND THE CONGREGATION WAS GATHERED TOGETHER AS ONE MAN, FROM DAN EVEN TO BEERSHEBA, WITH THE LAND OF GILEAD, UNTO THE LORD IN MIZPEH.

(2) "AND THE CHIEF OF ALL THE PEOPLE, EVEN OF ALL THE TRIBES OF ISRAEL, PRESENTED THEMSELVES IN THE ASSEMBLY OF THE PEOPLE OF GOD, FOUR HUNDRED THOUSAND FOOTMEN WHO DREW SWORD.

(3) "(NOW THE CHILDREN OF BENJAMIN HEARD THAT THE CHILDREN OF ISRAEL WERE GONE UP TO MIZPEH.) THEN SAID THE CHILDREN OF ISRAEL, TELL US, HOW WAS THIS WICKEDNESS?

(4) "AND THE LEVITE, THE HUSBAND OF THE WOMAN WHO WAS SLAIN, ANSWERED AND SAID, I CAME UNTO GIBEAH THAT BELONGS TO BENJAMIN, I AND MY CONCUBINE, TO LODGE.

(5) "AND THE MEN OF GIBEAH ROSE AGAINST ME, AND BESET THE HOUSE ROUND ABOUT UPON ME BY NIGHT, AND THOUGHT TO HAVE SLAIN ME: AND MY CONCUBINE HAVE THEY FORCED, THAT SHE IS DEAD.

(6) "AND I TOOK MY CONCUBINE, AND CUT HER IN PIECES, AND SENT HER THROUGHOUT ALL THE COUNTRY OF THE INHERITANCE OF ISRAEL: FOR THEY HAVE COMMITTED LEWDNESS AND FOLLY IN ISRAEL."

The structure is:

1. Mizpeh seemed to have been a national meeting place. As well, the phrase *"unto the LORD,"* could mean that the Tabernacle was brought here from Shiloh (Vs. 26).

2. How painful it must have been to the Spirit of God to have to record such vileness!

3. Williams says, *"The men of Israel were shocked at the fruits of the 'flesh' in the men of Gibeah but they were blind to the activities and power of that same principle of evil in themselves."*[1]

THE EVIL OF THE ENTIRETY OF THE NATION OF ISRAEL

If the Twentieth Chapter of Judges were studied carefully by all Christians, we would see ourselves as God sees us and would, consequently, be less judgmental in our attitude regarding others.

While it is certainly true that sin must be dealt with and put away, still, we must be very careful as to how this is done. In fact, concerning this present time, it can only be done in one way.

Paul said, *"Brethren, if a man be overtaken in a fault* (pertains to moral failure, and is brought about because one has ignorantly placed himself under Law; such a position guarantees failure), *you who are Spiritual*

(refers to those who understand God's Prescribed Order of Victory, which is the Cross), *restore such an one* (tell him he failed because of reverting to Law, and that Victory can be his by placing his Faith totally in the Cross, which then gives the Holy Spirit latitude to work, Who Alone can give the Victory) *in the spirit of meekness* (never with an overbearing, holier than thou attitude); *considering yourself, lest you also be tempted* (the implication is that if we do not handle such a case Scripturally we, thereby, open the door for Satan to attack us in the same manner as he did the failing brother).

"Bear ye one another's burdens (refers to sharing the heartache and shame of one who has spiritually failed), *and so fulfil the Law of Christ* (which is Love!).

"For if a man think himself to be something, when he is nothing (refers to a Believer who puts himself above the one who has failed in his own eyes), *he deceives himself.* (This presents one who has the conceited idea he is morally and Spiritually superior to what he actually is.)

"But let every man prove his own work (to put his Faith in the Cross to the test for the purpose of approving, which is done by seeing how well one obeys the Word of the Lord), *and then shall he have rejoicing in himself alone* (the spiritual man sees himself as he really is, totally dependent on Christ and the Cross), *and not in another.* (He will not then be rejoicing over the other man's failure.)

"For every man shall bear his own burden. (When each Believer sees his own failings, which we all have, he will have no inclination to compare himself with others, at least as it regards a superior position)" (Gal. 6:1-5).

Even though we have already explained it in the accompanying notes, and because of its great significance, let's diagram what Paul has just said.

SCRIPTURAL RESTORATION

• The *"fault"* here addressed in Verse 1 is not a minor infraction, but rather a severe moral failure.

• For one to be labeled *"spiritual"* by the Holy Spirit, one must understand God's

Prescribed Order of Victory, which is the Cross of Christ.

• The *"Restoration process"* pertains to explaining to the person that failure has resulted because their faith has been in something other than Christ and the Cross. The individual is encouraged, even strongly so, to bring his faith back to Christ and the Cross, because Victory is found only in the Cross. Then the Holy Spirit, Who works entirely within the framework of the Cross, can then function on our behalf (Rom. 8:1-22, 11).

• This is to never be done with an overbearing, holier than thou attitude, but rather *"in the spirit of meekness."*

• The individual being used by the Lord as it regards the Restoration process, should function with the understanding that if he conducts himself wrong toward the failing brother or sister, the Holy Spirit will see to it that such an individual faces the same type of temptation.

• *"Bearing one another's burdens"* refers to the fact that the failing individual should be treated with dignity and respect, and never in an unkind way. That and that alone will *"fulfil the Law of Christ"* which is *"Love."*

It seems that the man whose concubine had been murdered, raised attention, and did so quickly, when he cut her body into pieces, and sent pieces throughout all the country of Israel.

It is doubtful that the 400,000 soldiers of Verse 2 all came to Mizpeh, but rather that representatives, i.e., *"Chiefs,"* came to represent them.

(7) "BEHOLD, YOU ARE ALL CHILDREN OF ISRAEL; GIVE HERE YOUR ADVICE AND COUNSEL.

(8) "AND ALL THE PEOPLE AROSE AS ONE MAN, SAYING, WE WILL NOT ANY OF US GO TO HIS TENT, NEITHER WILL WE ANY OF US TURN INTO HIS HOUSE.

(9) "BUT NOW THIS SHALL BE THE THING WHICH WE WILL DO TO GIBEAH; WE WILL GO UP BY LOT AGAINST IT;

(10) "AND WE WILL TAKE TEN MEN OF AN HUNDRED THROUGHOUT ALL THE TRIBES OF ISRAEL, AND AN HUNDRED OF A THOUSAND, AND A THOUSAND OUT OF TEN THOUSAND, TO FETCH VICTUAL FOR THE PEOPLE, THAT THEY MAY DO,

WHEN THEY COME TO GIBEAH OF BENJAMIN, ACCORDING TO ALL THE FOLLY THAT THEY HAVE WROUGHT IN ISRAEL.

(11) "SO ALL THE MEN OF ISRAEL WERE GATHERED AGAINST THE CITY, KNIT TOGETHER AS ONE MAN.

(12) "AND THE TRIBES OF ISRAEL SENT MEN THROUGH ALL THE TRIBE OF BENJAMIN, SAYING, WHAT WICKEDNESS IS THIS THAT IS DONE AMONG YOU?

(13) "NOW THEREFORE, DELIVER US THE MEN, THE CHILDREN OF BELIAL, WHICH ARE IN GIBEAH, THAT WE MAY PUT THEM TO DEATH, AND PUT AWAY EVIL FROM ISRAEL. BUT THE CHILDREN OF BENJAMIN WOULD NOT HEARKEN TO THE VOICE OF THEIR BRETHREN THE CHILDREN OF ISRAEL."

The construction is:

1. While advice and counsel were sought as it regards what to do, there is no record, however, that they sought the Lord, at least at this time, which would prove to be disastrous.

2. They were filled with anger because of the conduct of these men against a Levite and his wife; but there is no record of their sense of the terribleness of this sin against God, and of the evil of the idolatry, which, at the time, existed in their midst. So it is presently.

A sin against God is lightly regarded, but a sin against society is mercilessly judged.

3. The word *"lot"* as used in Verse 9, could refer to the Urim and Thummim; however, if this, in fact, is the case, it doesn't mean they asked the Will of the Lord in the matter regarding whether to go or not, but rather who would go.

4. It is believed that the leaders of the other Tribes did not really approach Benjamin properly; irrespective, Benjamin's response was totally wrong, and they would suffer dearly, along with all of Israel.

THE RESULTS OF SEEKING THE COUNSEL OF MEN AND NOT OF GOD

At any rate, the request from Israel to the Tribe of Benjamin was just and right. They said in the Thirteenth Verse, *"Deliver us the men, the children of Belial, which are in Gibeah, that we may put them to death."* The consequences were that the entire Tribe of Benjamin would resist this demand.

The Believer should seek the Face of the Lord about anything and everything, be it little or large. We must desire His Mind, His Will, His Direction, in other words, solely what He wants and desires.

The problem is, when catastrophe befalls us, we then go to the Lord, but having ignored Him on about everything else, we little know how to approach Him when we really do need help. The truth is, the Believer needs the Help of the Lord, the Guidance of the Lord, the Direction of the Lord, in all things. Be they little or large, be they great or small, the Lord has a Perfect Will in any and every case. We should seek that Will, find that Will, and then follow that Will.

A PERSONAL EXPERIENCE

In the year 2000, the Lord laid it on my heart to establish a Radio Network all over the nation, and the Lord, as well, told me how this Network was to be programmed.

In 2004 (if I remember the year correctly), the Lord began to deal with me about a certain Station in Palm Springs, California. In fact, a Construction Permit for a Station had come open in this area about a year before, and we had tried to obtain it, but just simply did not have the money.

The Lord began to deal with me about the Station, and I reckoned in my mind, that since it had been about a year, surely someone else had purchased the Construction Permit.

At any rate, following the Lord, I had David Whitelaw to call the man who owned the Permit.

(A Construction Permit simply means that the F.C.C. in Washington has given permission for the owner of this permit to build a Station. In fact, there was no Station there, but there was a permit available to build one. These permits are almost impossible to come by. The owner had applied for this one nearly ten years earlier. That's how long it takes, if it's possible to get one at all.)

Upon contacting the owner, he exclaimed to us, that if we had called a few days earlier that the Station would have been available; however, he went on to say that the contracts had just been signed for the Station

to be sold to someone else.

As I went to prayer again that afternoon, the Lord strongly impressed me to tell the man that if the other contract fell down, that he should call us, which we did, and he promised to do so.

I knew it was the Lord Who encouraged me to call the brother, but I reasoned in my mind that there surely was no use, because these things are so valuable, so hard to come by, that I couldn't feature the people not going through with the deal.

In prayer that particular afternoon at my home after coming from the office, I began to importune the Lord for this Station. I felt strongly in my spirit that I should ask the Lord to perform a Miracle.

For the last few months I had found myself saying, as it concerned certain situations, *"Lord give it to us, if it be Your Will!"*

All of us, at least those who are sensible, surely want the Perfect Will of God and, in fact, desire nothing that's not His Will. However, I sensed in my spirit that the Lord was not pleased with me praying in this manner. And then He spoke to my heart. He said:

"Do not say again when praying about this thing, 'Lord, give it to me if it be Your Will.' You are hindering your Faith when you say that." He then went on to say:

"I know that you want My Will, and only My Will. Knowing that, if you ask for something and it's not My Will, I will step in and stop the situation; Otherwise, you are to claim that which you feel you should have, and claim it in no uncertain terms."

POSSESSIVE FAITH

I'll admit, that I was somewhat shaken by what the Lord told me. But I saw instantly that it was right. In fact, I had felt all along, especially the last few months, when I would use that term, *"Lord, give it to me if it is Your Will,"* that what I was saying was not exactly pleasing to the Lord.

Some may argue with this, claiming that it's always proper to say, *"Lord if it be Your Will."* To be sure it is, that is if we have a single doubt about the subject at hand or the direction to be taken. Anyone with any Spiritual and Scriptural sense, wants the Perfect Will of God. And as it regards my own person, I've been too far down this road to want otherwise. I want nothing but the Will of God, and in all things. I have no personal agenda of my own, I seek only what the Will of the Lord is.

However, I could see that what I was doing was hindering my Faith. In fact, it was placing me on confusing ground.

You see the Lord has given all Believers the distinct privilege of participating in His Work, and doing so grandly. In these matters, we have much latitude. In other words, if we fall down, the Work simply won't be done. The idea, which many Christians have, that whatever the Lord wants to do, He will do, is basely wrong. As stated, the Lord has given us great latitude and privilege in working with Him. The great ingredient here is Faith.

I did exactly as the Lord told me to do. I claimed that Station, even though as far as I knew, the Station had been sold to someone else.

The next morning the owner called, stating that the other people had fallen down, meaning they were unable to follow through with the contract. *"The Station is yours,"* he said! I immediately said, *"We want it."*

PRAYER FOR FINANCES

The next afternoon when I went to prayer, I was elated at what the Lord had done; however, the truth was, we had no money to buy the Station. We had signed a contract that we would pay a certain amount of money down, and then so much a month. I didn't have that money, and didn't know where in the world I could get it.

And then while in prayer, the Lord began to move on my heart, telling me exactly what to do as to how to raise these funds. We followed His Directions minutely, and the funds were raised.

Today our Palm Springs, California Station, KPSH-FM, 90.9 on the dial, airs this great Message of the Cross twenty-four hours a day, seven days a week, covering the entirety of the Coachella Valley, reaching approximately a half million people. As well, we have eighty other Stations on the air all across this United States.

Now why would the Lord deal with me as

He did as it regards this particular Station? Was this Station more important than the other Stations?

I can't answer that. All I can relate is that which the Lord did. I wish I could say that the Lord directed and directs us regarding every Station. I believe He definitely does give us direction, but I have experienced no such moving as I did with the Palm Springs Station as it regards our other Stations.

I personally feel that the Lord wanted to show me something about Faith, which He did.

If Israel had sought the Lord, and had done so minutely, seeking His Direction in all that they did, the outcome would have been totally different. As it was, the entirety of the Nation would suffer greatly.

(14) "BUT THE CHILDREN OF BENJAMIN GATHERED THEMSELVES TOGETHER OUT OF THE CITIES UNTO GIBEAH, TO GO OUT TO BATTLE AGAINST THE CHILDREN OF ISRAEL.

(15) "AND THE CHILDREN OF BENJAMIN WERE NUMBERED AT THAT TIME OUT OF THE CITIES TWENTY AND SIX THOUSAND MEN WHO DREW SWORD, BESIDE THE INHABITANTS OF GIBEAH, WHICH WERE NUMBERED SEVEN HUNDRED CHOSEN MEN.

(16) "AMONG ALL THIS PEOPLE THERE WERE SEVEN HUNDRED CHOSEN MEN LEFTHANDED; EVERY ONE COULD SLING STONES AT AN HAIR BREADTH, AND NOT MISS.

(17) "AND THE MEN OF ISRAEL, BESIDE BENJAMIN, WERE NUMBERED FOUR HUNDRED THOUSAND MEN WHO DREW SWORD: ALL THESE WERE MEN OF WAR."

The exegesis is:

1. Satan loves it when God's People are fighting each other.

2. According to Verse 15, there must have been about three or four thousand people in the city of Gibeah, especially considering that they had *"seven hundred chosen men of battle."*

3. This would be the beginning of a catastrophe!

(18) "AND THE CHILDREN OF ISRAEL AROSE, AND WENT UP TO THE HOUSE

OF GOD, AND ASKED COUNSEL OF GOD, AND SAID, WHICH OF US SHALL GO UP FIRST TO THE BATTLE AGAINST THE CHILDREN OF BENJAMIN? AND THE LORD SAID, JUDAH SHALL GO UP FIRST.

(19) "AND THE CHILDREN OF ISRAEL ROSE UP IN THE MORNING, AND ENCAMPED AGAINST GIBEAH.

(20) "AND THE MEN OF ISRAEL WENT OUT TO BATTLE AGAINST BENJAMIN; AND THE MEN OF ISRAEL PUT THEMSELVES IN ARRAY TO FIGHT AGAINST THEM AT GIBEAH.

(21) "AND THE CHILDREN OF BENJAMIN CAME FORTH OUT OF GIBEAH, AND DESTROYED DOWN TO THE GROUND OF THE ISRAELITES THAT DAY TWENTY AND TWO THOUSAND MEN."

The diagram is:

1. According to Verse 18, Israel did not ask the Lord as to whether they should go or not, but as to who were to go.

2. Why would the Lord tell Judah to go forth to the battle, and then they would lose this great number?

The truth is, had the Children of Israel acted at the beginning as they did later on, in Verse 26, they would not have suffered the two defeats of Verses 21 and 25.

Their planning without God was one of the fruits of that fallen nature which they shared in common with the men of Gibeah. It is true that after they had made their plans, they prayed, but only after the plans were made.

3. Williams says, concerning this, *"There is instruction in this for Believers for all times. Before the Tribes were fitted to judge evil in others they needed a sharp discipline to teach them to judge evil in themselves. So dead in their souls had the people become that they never thought of asking God how the matter was to be dealt with; nor were they conscious that they themselves were guilty of sins, which cried out for Divine Wrath.*

"It was necessary, therefore, that they should learn a deep moral lesson; for God cannot give victories to man's natural will."[2]

THE DEEP MORAL LESSON

At this time Israel should have asked the

Lord what they should do; however, they made their own plans, *"and went up to the House of God, and asked counsel of God, and said, which of us shall go up; first to the battle against the children of Benjamin?"*

They did not ask if they should go up or how they should proceed. They merely asked which Tribe should go first. In other words they made their plans and then asked God to bless them. If they had allowed the Lord to make their plans, possibly the lives of some 60,000 men could have been spared (Vs. 18). This Verse also says, *"And the LORD said, Judah shall go up first."*

The men of Israel were shocked at what happened in Gibeah, as they certainly should have been; however, they were blind to the activities and power of evil in themselves. This is the reason Jesus carefully warned us not to judge (Mat. 7:1-5). The Lord would use this occasion not only to punish Benjamin but to punish the balance of Israel as well. The reason was that Israel was not conscious that they themselves were guilty of sins, which cried out for Divine Wrath.

Judah, along with the balance of the Israelites, would lose the battle that day and see some 22,000 of their men killed. They will learn, and it has already begun, a most painful lesson! Let us say it again:

PUNISHMENT

Punishing fellow Believers is solely in the domain of the Lord. It is never proper for Believers to take it upon themselves, whomever they might be, to level punishment on others.

Why?

The Holy Spirit through James answered this question:

"There is one Law-Giver, Who is able to save and to destroy (presents God as the only One Who can fill this position)*: who are you who judges another?* (The Greek actually says, 'But you — who are you?' In other words, 'who do you think you are?')" (James 4:12).

No Believer is spiritually qualified to punish another Believer, that position being in the domain of God Alone!

Jesus suffered our punishment on the Cross; therefore, when we think to level punishment on someone else, we are doing two things, which are very repulsive in the Eyes of God.

1. We aren't worthy to punish anyone else, considering that we are a long ways from being perfect ourselves.

2. Jesus has already suffered the punishment on our behalf; therefore, to claim that a fellow Believer must be punished is, in essence, saying that what Jesus suffered at Calvary was not enough, and that we must add more punishment to what He suffered. I think it is obvious on the surface, as to how impertinent and presumptuous such a position is.

If a fellow Believer has, in fact, done something wrong, and refuses to repent, we very likely would have to withdraw fellowship from such a person. However, we must do so with a hope that he will come back; consequently, we must continue to pray for him.

In the first battle, Israel would lose 22,000 men. This should have been a wake-up call that something was wrong. The Lord had told them, in answer to their request that *"Judah shall go up first."* Now, Judah will suffer severely.

(22) "AND THE PEOPLE THE MEN OF ISRAEL ENCOURAGED THEMSELVES, AND SET THEIR BATTLE AGAIN IN ARRAY IN THE PLACE WHERE THEY PUT THEMSELVES IN ARRAY THE FIRST DAY.

(23) "(AND THE CHILDREN OF ISRAEL WENT UP AND WEPT BEFORE THE LORD UNTIL EVENING, AND ASKED COUNSEL OF THE LORD, SAYING, SHALL I GO UP AGAIN TO BATTLE AGAINST THE CHILDREN OF BENJAMIN MY BROTHER? AND THE LORD SAID, GO UP AGAINST HIM.)

(24) "AND THE CHILDREN OF ISRAEL CAME NEAR AGAINST THE CHILDREN OF BENJAMIN THE SECOND DAY.

(25) "AND BENJAMIN WENT FORTH AGAINST THEM OUT OF GIBEAH THE SECOND DAY, AND DESTROYED DOWN TO THE GROUND OF THE CHILDREN OF ISRAEL AGAIN EIGHTEEN THOUSAND MEN; ALL THESE DREW THE SWORD."

The overview is:

1. Verse 25 proclaims the fact that these men were strong men of war, and yet they were beaten; in fact, in the two battles they had lost some forty thousand men, which,

NOTES

as is obvious, is a catastrophe.

2. In the case of Israel, the first feeling of indignation at a great wrong, the shame at the pollution of the name of Israel, their common inheritance, and their grief at the dishonor done to the Name of God, were righteous and commendable feelings. However, they acted on those feelings, instead of getting the direct Will of God.

3. The truth is, this pure stream of their indignation became fouled by far baser passion.

THE ACKNOWLEDGMENT
OF THEIR OWN SIN

The Twenty-third Verse says, *"Israel went up and wept before the LORD until evening, and asked counsel of the LORD, saying, Shall I go up again to battle against the children of Benjamin my brother?"* Once again the Lord will say, *"Go up against him."*

Still, despite the terrible slaughter that Israel experienced, it seems they were yet lacking in the acknowledgement of their own sin. How hard it is for us to see ourselves. How quick we are to condemn others. Self-righteousness can always point out the flaws, faults, and foibles of everyone else; however, self-righteousness cannot see its own crime, its own sin, or its own folly. It, thereby, continues to point a finger of accusation at others.

Once again, and to be sure, the Tribe of Benjamin had sinned sorely. They should have been dealt with but only in God's Way. Israel did three things wrong:

1. They failed to acknowledge their own grievous culpability in sins that probably were equally as bad.

2. They took it upon themselves to be God's Instrument of chastisement even though they were not worthy and, indeed, could never be. God would not tolerate it.

3. They failed to ask God's Guidance and Direction regarding what He wanted. They set out to do what they wanted and, thereby, met with disaster.

So, God would use the occasion to humble not only the Tribe of Benjamin, but all of Israel as well.

The second battle would also end in disaster. The Twenty-fifth Verse says, *"And destroyed down to the ground of the Children of Israel again eighteen thousand men."*

Now there would be true Repentance before God.

(26) "THEN ALL THE CHILDREN OF ISRAEL, AND ALL THE PEOPLE, WENT UP, AND CAME UNTO THE HOUSE OF GOD, AND WEPT, AND SAT THERE BEFORE THE LORD, AND FASTED THAT DAY UNTIL EVENING, AND OFFERED BURNT OFFERINGS AND PEACE OFFERINGS BEFORE THE LORD.

(27) "AND THE CHILDREN OF ISRAEL ENQUIRED OF THE LORD, (FOR THE ARK OF THE COVENANT OF GOD WAS THERE IN THOSE DAYS,

(28) "AND PHINEHAS, THE SON OF ELEAZAR, THE SON OF AARON, STOOD BEFORE IT IN THOSE DAYS,) SAYING, SHALL I YET AGAIN GO OUT TO BATTLE AGAINST THE CHILDREN OF BENJAMIN MY BROTHER, OR SHALL I CEASE? AND THE LORD SAID, GO UP; FOR TOMORROW I WILL DELIVER THEM INTO YOUR HAND."

The overview is:

1. The offering up of *"Burnt Offerings"* and *"Peace Offerings"* proclaims the fact that Israel is now engaging in true Repentance, because their Faith is once again in the shed Blood of the Lamb.

2. The Nation at last draws near to God in Repentance and sorrow, confessing themselves to be sinners. As interpreted by the New Testament, they confessed their own guilt, they declared themselves worthy of the Wrath of God and they pleaded the Person and Work of Christ, the Lamb of God, for pardon and acceptance.

3. Their souls now humbled and taught, they were in a fit moral state to go up against Gibeah. It indeed deserved wrath, and will receive that wrath, but Israel merited wrath herself, and had, in a figure, to suffer it in and with Christ before drawing the sword against Benjamin.

4. God recognizes nothing with the exception of Christ and what He has done for us at the Cross. This means that man is recognized only so long as his Faith is in Christ, and more than all, what Christ has done for us at the Cross.

This shows that man understands as to who exactly he is, a sinner in need of a Saviour, and exactly as to Who Christ is, the

NOTES

only Redeemer.

5. Deliverance will come, even as stated in Verse 28; however, it will come only on the basis of the slain Lamb; we must never forget that, because it hasn't changed unto this moment and, will never change; that's why Paul referred to it as *"The Everlasting Covenant"* (Heb. 13:20).

TRUE REPENTANCE

The Twenty-sixth Verse says, *"And came unto the House of God, and wept, and sat there before the LORD, and fasted that day until evening, and offered Burnt Offerings and Peace Offerings before the LORD."*

Now they are recognizing their own sin as well as the sin of Benjamin. Now the Lord will deliver Benjamin into their hand. Repentance without it being based on the Foundation of the Cross of Calvary is no repentance at all. At least it's not repentance that God will recognize.

All sin is addressed at the Cross; therefore, all Repentance must be based on the Cross also.

God forgives us only on the basis of the Sacrifice of the Lamb of God, Who paid the price for our sins, and not only ours, but for the sins of the whole world, and for all time.

So, Israel had to go to the Cross, thereby, repenting of their own sins, before they could fully be used by the Lord.

(29) "AND ISRAEL SET LIERS IN WAIT ROUND ABOUT GIBEAH.

(30) "AND THE CHILDREN OF ISRAEL WENT UP AGAINST THE CHILDREN OF BENJAMIN ON THE THIRD DAY, AND PUT THEMSELVES IN ARRAY AGAINST GIBEAH, AS AT OTHER TIMES.

(31) "AND THE CHILDREN OF BENJAMIN WENT OUT AGAINST THE PEOPLE, AND WERE DRAWN AWAY FROM THE CITY; AND THEY BEGAN TO SMITE OF THE PEOPLE, AND KILL, AS AT OTHER TIMES, IN THE HIGHWAYS, OF WHICH ONE GOES UP TO THE HOUSE OF GOD, AND THE OTHER TO GIBEAH IN THE FIELD, ABOUT THIRTY MEN OF ISRAEL.

(32) "AND THE CHILDREN OF BENJAMIN SAID, THEY ARE SMITTEN DOWN BEFORE US, AS AT THE FIRST. BUT THE CHILDREN OF ISRAEL SAID, LET US

FLEE, AND DRAW THEM FROM THE CITY UNTO THE HIGHWAYS.

(33) "AND ALL THE MEN OF ISRAEL ROSE UP OUT OF THEIR PLACE, AND PUT THEMSELVES IN ARRAY AT BAAL-TAMAR: AND THE LIERS IN WAIT OF ISRAEL CAME FORTH OUT OF THEIR PLACES, EVEN OUT OF THE MEADOWS OF GIBEAH.

(34) "AND THERE CAME AGAINST GIBEAH TEN THOUSAND CHOSEN MEN OUT OF ALL ISRAEL, AND THE BATTLE WAS SORE: BUT THEY KNEW NOT THAT EVIL WAS NEAR THEM.

(35) "AND THE LORD SMOTE BENJAMIN BEFORE ISRAEL: AND THE CHILDREN OF ISRAEL DESTROYED OF THE BENJAMITES THAT DAY TWENTY AND FIVE THOUSAND AND AN HUNDRED MEN: ALL THESE DREW THE SWORD.

(36) "SO THE CHILDREN OF BENJAMIN SAW THAT THEY WERE SMITTEN: FOR THE MEN OF ISRAEL GAVE PLACE TO THE BENJAMITES, BECAUSE THEY TRUSTED UNTO THE LIERS IN WAIT WHICH THEY HAD SET BESIDE GIBEAH.

(37) "AND THE LIERS IN WAIT HASTED, AND RUSHED UPON GIBEAH; AND THE LIERS IN WAIT DREW THEMSELVES ALONG, AND SMOTE ALL THE CITY WITH THE EDGE OF THE SWORD.

(38) "NOW THERE WAS AN APPOINTED SIGN BETWEEN THE MEN OF ISRAEL AND THE LIERS IN WAIT, THAT THEY SHOULD MAKE A GREAT FLAME WITH SMOKE RISE UP OUT OF THE CITY.

(39) "AND WHEN THE MEN OF ISRAEL RETIRED IN THE BATTLE, BENJAMIN BEGAN TO SMITE AND KILL OF THE MEN OF ISRAEL ABOUT THIRTY PERSONS: FOR THEY SAID, SURELY THEY ARE SMITTEN DOWN BEFORE US, AS IN THE FIRST BATTLE.

(40) "BUT WHEN THE FLAME BEGAN TO ARISE UP OUT OF THE CITY WITH A PILLAR OF SMOKE, THE BENJAMITES LOOKED BEHIND THEM, AND, BEHOLD, THE FLAME OF THE CITY ASCENDED UP TO HEAVEN.

(41) "AND WHEN THE MEN OF ISRAEL TURNED AGAIN, THE MEN OF BENJAMIN WERE AMAZED: FOR THEY SAW THAT EVIL WAS COME UPON THEM.

(42) "THEREFORE THEY TURNED THEIR BACKS BEFORE THE MEN OF ISRAEL UNTO THE WAY OF THE WILDERNESS; BUT THE BATTLE OVERTOOK THEM; AND THEM WHICH CAME OUT OF THE CITIES THEY DESTROYED IN THE MIDST OF THEM.

(43) "THUS THEY ENCLOSED THE BENJAMITES ROUND ABOUT, AND CHASED THEM, AND TRODE THEM DOWN WITH EASE OVER AGAINST GIBEAH TOWARD THE SUNRISING.

(44) "AND THERE FELL OF BENJAMIN EIGHTEEN THOUSAND MEN; ALL THESE WERE MEN OF VALOUR.

(45) "AND THEY TURNED AND FLED TOWARD THE WILDERNESS UNTO THE ROCK OF RIMMON: AND THEY GLEANED OF THEM IN THE HIGHWAYS FIVE THOUSAND MEN; AND PURSUED HARD AFTER THEM UNTO GIDOM, AND KILLED TWO THOUSAND MEN OF THEM.

(46) "SO THAT ALL WHICH FELL THAT DAY OF BENJAMIN WERE TWENTY AND FIVE THOUSAND MEN WHO DREW THE SWORD; ALL THESE WERE MEN OF VALOUR.

(47) "BUT SIX HUNDRED MEN TURNED AND FLED TO THE WILDERNESS UNTO THE ROCK RIMMON, AND ABODE IN THE ROCK RIMMON FOUR MONTHS.

(48) "AND THE MEN OF ISRAEL TURNED AGAIN UPON THE CHILDREN OF BENJAMIN, AND SMOTE THEM WITH THE EDGE OF THE SWORD, AS WELL THE MEN OF EVERY CITY, AS THE BEAST, AND ALL WHO CAME TO HAND; ALSO THEY SET ON FIRE ALL THE CITIES THAT THEY CAME TO."

The synopsis is:

1. Counting both the men of Israel and those of Benjamin, the total loss was a little over 65,000; all because of sin in the realm of vice, which plagued Benjamin, and self-righteousness which plagued the men of Israel.

2. It is ironic that more were lost to self-righteousness than to vice. Think about the sorrow and heartache that this brought to untold thousands of families in Israel, husbands, fathers, brothers, and sons!

3. Sin will take one further than one

desires to go, and cost more than one can afford to pay.

SELF-RIGHTEOUSNESS

The Thirty-fifth Verse says, *"And the LORD smote Benjamin before Israel."* That day Benjamin would lose 25,100 men. But notice, the Passage says, *"The LORD smote."*

How much our self-righteous indignation flares up when we think of the foibles of others. How so quick we are to show how unrighteous the other person is and how righteous we are. And how so quick God will tolerate none of it.

Sin must be dealt with, but in God's Way. He will not tolerate self-righteous action. Self-righteousness cost Israel about 40,000 men. These were husbands, brothers, etc., loved ones, who would not go home to their families, ever again, simply because they were so quick to judge the hideous sins of others and too quick to hide their own; however, God sees all. Let us say it again, *"God sees all."*

CHAPTER 21

(1) "NOW THE MEN OF ISRAEL HAD SWORN IN MIZPEH, SAYING, THERE SHALL NOT ANY OF US GIVE HIS DAUGHTER UNTO BENJAMIN TO WIFE.

(2) "AND THE PEOPLE CAME TO THE HOUSE OF GOD, AND ABODE THERE TILL EVENING BEFORE GOD, AND LIFTED UP THEIR VOICES, AND WEPT SORE;

(3) "AND SAID, O LORD GOD OF ISRAEL, WHY IS THIS COME TO PASS IN ISRAEL, THAT THERE SHOULD BE TO DAY ONE TRIBE LACKING IN ISRAEL?

(4) "AND IT CAME TO PASS ON THE MORROW, THAT THE PEOPLE ROSE EARLY, AND BUILT THERE AN ALTAR, AND OFFERED BURNT OFFERINGS AND PEACE OFFERINGS.

(5) "AND THE CHILDREN OF ISRAEL SAID, WHO IS THERE AMONG ALL THE TRIBES OF ISRAEL WHO CAME NOT UP WITH THE CONGREGATION UNTO THE LORD? FOR THEY HAD MADE A GREAT OATH CONCERNING HIM WHO CAME NOT UP TO THE LORD TO MIZPEH, SAYING,

HE SHALL SURELY BE PUT TO DEATH.

(6) "AND THE CHILDREN OF ISRAEL REPENTED THEM FOR BENJAMIN THEIR BROTHER, AND SAID, THERE IS ONE TRIBE CUT OFF FROM ISRAEL THIS DAY."

The synopsis is:

1. When people are governed by excitement, and not by the Word of God, they bind themselves by oaths, which lead to difficulty, and even to bloodshed.

2. It is true that the Benjamites merited punishment, because their refusal to judge the evil at Gibeah showed that they thought little of it, or that they sympathized with it.

3. And again, had Israel followed the Word of the Lord from the beginning, and had they waited upon God for direction, how different would be the history of this Chapter.

GOVERNMENT ACCORDING TO THE WORD OF GOD

Israel at this stage was governed by error, excitement, and personal zeal, but not by the Word of God.

The men of Jabesh-Gilead certainly deserved punishment, and had Israel sought the Lord earnestly, seeking His Will regarding the matter, no doubt, this Chapter would have been very different; however, when man takes matters into his own hands, judging from a position of self-righteousness, the end result will always be disaster, even as it was in these particular happenings.

The Fourth Verse says, *"And built there an Altar, and offered Burnt Offerings and Peace Offerings."* The Scripture does not say if they were at Shiloh or not, or if they were, why they did not use the Brazen Altar that was already there. It could be that some of the enemies of Israel during one of the servitudes in the period of the Judges destroyed the Brazen Altar and even other parts of the Tabernacle. The following facts seems to apply:

• If the Altar that was built was elsewhere from Shiloh, this would not have been according to the Direction of God.

• Or if the Altar built was at Shiloh, it shows that Israel had been lax in obeying God regarding the daily Sacrifices.

• Despite the error, it seems that Israel at least was trying to find her way back to God — hence, the building of the Altar.

One may wonder as to why the Holy Spirit desired these very unsavory experiences to be placed in the Bible, especially considering that they were all committed by God's chosen People?

Of course, anything the Holy Spirit does, is always for purpose and reason, and considering that He is God, it is, as well, perfect.

I'm sure there were many reasons the Holy Spirit desired this account, as unsavory as it is; however, the main purpose, I think, is that men will see the level to which even God's chosen People will sink, morally speaking, when they do not abide by the Word of God. The Lord had a proper Government, which Israel should have embraced; however, if it is to be noticed, several times the statement is used, *"Every man did that which was right in his own eyes."*

This tells us that Israel was not following the Government of God, as laid down in the Pentateuch, but was rather devising their own government, doing whatever it was they thought best at the time, which almost all the time was wrong.

BIBLICAL GOVERNMENT

From the very beginning, God has always had Government, which, if followed, will bring about the desired positive results. Unfortunately, man has ever tried to change that Government. It is no less a problem now than it was then.

The Government of God is the Word of God. As Believers we are meant to abide by the Word, to subscribe to the Word, to ask for the Lord's Help, even on a daily basis, that we obey the Word. Our Churches are to be operated according to the Word of God, our business decisions should be operated according to the Word of God, in fact, the Word of God must be the criteria for all things.

Unfortunately, the constitution and by-laws of most religious Denominations, are larger than the Bible, sadly and regrettably, oftentimes, with little thought given to the Word of God.

Once again, it's *"every man doing that which is right in his own eyes."* Let it ever be understood, it's only God's Eyes that really matter, not those of men.

As an example, Church should bear the

NOTES

earmarks of the Book of Acts. The Holy Spirit laid down the guidelines, gave us direction, and told us in this Book, along with the Epistles as to how to apply Doctrine. Let us say it again:

If our local Church does not bear the earmarks of the Book of Acts, then whatever it is, it's not a Church that God recognizes as such. I suppose one could ask the following question:

If the Apostle Paul, or Simon Peter, etc., walked into one of our services, and could understand the language that we speak, would they feel at home, or would things seem strange to them?

It all goes back to Government. Is the Word of God governing our personal lives? Is the Word of God governing our Churches? Is the Word of God governing our homes? Is the Word of God governing our life and living?

(7) "HOW SHALL WE DO FOR WIVES FOR THEM WHO REMAIN, SEEING WE HAVE SWORN BY THE LORD THAT WE WILL NOT GIVE THEM OF OUR DAUGHTERS TO WIVES?

(8) "AND THEY SAID, WHAT ONE IS THERE OF THE TRIBES OF ISRAEL THAT CAME NOT UP TO MIZPEH TO THE LORD? AND, BEHOLD, THERE CAME NONE TO THE CAMP FROM JABESH-GILEAD TO THE ASSEMBLY.

(9) "FOR THE PEOPLE WERE NUMBERED, AND, BEHOLD THERE WERE NONE OF THE INHABITANTS OF JABESH-GILEAD THERE.

(10) "AND THE CONGREGATION SENT THITHER TWELVE THOUSAND MEN OF THE VALIANTEST, AND COMMANDED THEM, SAYING, GO AND SMITE THE INHABITANTS OF JABESH-GILEAD WITH THE EDGE OF THE SWORD, WITH THE WOMEN AND THE CHILDREN.

(11) "AND THIS IS THE THING THAT YOU SHALL DO, YOU SHALL UTTERLY DESTROY EVERY MALE, AND EVERY WOMAN WHO HAS LAIN BY MAN.

(12) "AND THEY FOUND AMONG THE INHABITANTS OF JABESH-GILEAD FOUR HUNDRED YOUNG VIRGINS, WHO HAD KNOWN NO MAN BY LYING WITH ANY MALE: AND THEY BROUGHT THEM UNTO THE CAMP TO SHILOH, WHICH IS IN THE

LAND OF CANAAN.

(13) "AND THE WHOLE CONGREGATION SENT SOME TO SPEAK TO THE CHILDREN OF BENJAMIN WHO WERE IN THE ROCK RIMMON, AND TO CALL PEACEABLY UNTO THEM.

(14) "AND BENJAMIN CAME AGAIN AT THAT TIME; AND THEY GAVE THEM WIVES WHICH THEY HAD SAVED ALIVE OF THE WOMEN OF JABESH-GILEAD: AND YET SO THEY SUFFICED THEM NOT.

(15) "AND THE PEOPLE REPENTED THEM FOR BENJAMIN, BECAUSE THAT THE LORD HAD MADE A BREACH IN THE TRIBES OF ISRAEL."

The overview is:

1. Evidently, all or at least most of the women of Benjamin had been killed, causing the death toll to rise to astronomical proportions. What a horror!

2. Again, several thousand people are killed. And the truth is, none of this was necessary. The Lord did not tell them to do this thing. If they made a rash vow, which they evidently did (Vs. 5), they should have asked the Lord to forgive them, which He most definitely would have done, and let the matter rest. However, the men of Israel were, no doubt, very angry, considering their losses, that the men of Jabesh-gilead did not participate. So they would kill them, and so they did!

3. Once again, we see here government without God. The results, as always, are disastrous!

THE TRAGEDY OF SELF-WILL!

It is a sobering thought to observe the flourishing Tribe of Benjamin, which is now reduced to a handful of men, possibly about 600, clinging for life to an inaccessible rock, but having to mourn the loss of wives and daughters, and sisters and children, all ruthlessly slaughtered with the edge of the sword, but yet, this is the picture that greets us.

Well over a hundred thousand people, counting the women and children, had lost their lives in this horror — all in a few days, and all because of a departure from the Word. There is no way that we can imagine the heartache, the sorrow, the pain, the suffering, all brought about because of a departure from

the Word of God.

It doesn't matter that these were God's chosen People! It doesn't matter that some of them had seen great Miracles of the past, all performed by the Lord! It doesn't matter, what their history had been! It only matters as to what they are now, and what they are now is the result of self-will.

All of these things are meant to be a warning for us. Paul said, *"Now all these things happened unto them for examples* (as a warning; we had best heed those warnings)*: and they are written for our admonition, upon whom the ends of the world are come* (should have been translated, *'to whom the fulfillment of the ages has arrived,'* i.e., *'the Church Age')"* (I Cor. 10:11).

Then the great Apostle added, *"Wherefore let him who thinks he stands* (is addressed to all Believers) *take heed lest he fall.* (This means to not merely fall from fellowship as some teach, but to fall from Eternal Salvation. This won't happen if the Cross is ever in view)" (I Cor. 10:12).

CONFUSION!

If it is to be noticed, the people built an Altar and offered *"Burnt Offerings and Peace Offerings,"* and then made the decision to go murder thousands of the inhabitants of Jebus-gilead. How can the two, the sacrifices and the murder be reconciled?

They can't!

None of this was the Work of the Lord and, thereby, none of it was the Will of the Lord. These individuals, despite their religiosity, were acting upon their own self-will; therefore, let us make the following statement:

All of this is a perfect picture of religion. Cain was too nice to offer up a lamb in sacrifice, but not too nice to cut the jugular vein of his brother, thereby murdering him (Gen., Chpt. 4).

Whatever religiosity it was in which these people engaged themselves, while the offering up of sacrifices was definitely right, the motive was wrong. They were seeking to please God in all the wrong ways.

Millions presently, and I suppose it has always been that way, engage themselves every week in extensive religiosity as it regards their Churches, but do so with the wrong motives, with the wrong direction, in fact, that which is not Biblical. Such is religion!

It was religion that murdered the Lord Jesus Christ. It is ironical; these people killed the Lord in the Name of the Lord! When we depart from the Word of God, the only other place to go is religion. And please remember, the accounts that we are reading in Chapters 17 through 21, all portray religion. In fact, religion is a murderous business!

(16) "THEN THE ELDERS OF THE CONGREGATION SAID, HOW SHALL WE DO FOR WIVES FOR THEM WHO REMAIN, SEEING THE WOMEN ARE DESTROYED OUT OF BENJAMIN?

(17) "AND THEY SAID, THERE MUST BE AN INHERITANCE FOR THEM WHO BE ESCAPED OF BENJAMIN, THAT A TRIBE BE NOT DESTROYED OUT OF ISRAEL.

(18) "HOWBEIT WE MAY NOT GIVE THEM WIVES OF OUR DAUGHTERS: FOR THE CHILDREN OF ISRAEL HAVE SWORN, SAYING, CURSED BE HE WHO GIVES A WIFE TO BENJAMIN.

(19) "THEN THEY SAID, BEHOLD, THERE IS A FEAST OF THE LORD IN SHILOH YEARLY IN A PLACE WHICH IS ON THE NORTH SIDE OF BETHEL, ON THE EAST SIDE OF THE HIGHWAY THAT GOES UP FROM BETH-EL TO SHECHEM, AND ON THE SOUTH OF LEBONAH.

(20) "THEREFORE THEY COMMANDED THE CHILDREN OF BENJAMIN, SAYING, GO AND LIE IN WAIT IN THE VINEYARDS;

(21) "AND SEE, AND, BEHOLD, IF THE DAUGHTERS OF SHILOH COME OUT TO DANCE IN DANCES, THEN COME YOU OUT OF THE VINEYARDS, AND CATCH YOU EVERY MAN HIS WIFE OF THE DAUGHTERS OF SHILOH, AND GO TO THE LAND OF BENJAMIN.

(22) "AND IT SHALL BE, WHEN THEIR FATHERS OR THEIR BRETHREN COME UNTO US TO COMPLAIN, THAT WE WILL SAY UNTO THEM, BE FAVOURABLE UNTO THEM FOR OUR SAKES: BECAUSE WE RESERVED NOT TO EACH MAN HIS WIFE IN THE WAR: FOR YOU DID NOT GIVE UNTO THEM AT THIS TIME, THAT YOU SHOULD BE GUILTY.

(23) "AND THE CHILDREN OF BENJAMIN DID SO, AND TOOK THEM WIVES,

NOTES

ACCORDING TO THEIR NUMBER, OF THEM WHO DANCED, WHOM THEY CAUGHT: AND THEY WENT AND RETURNED UNTO THEIR INHERITANCE, AND REPAIRED THE CITIES, AND DWELT IN THEM.

(24) "AND THE CHILDREN OF ISRAEL DEPARTED THENCE AT THAT TIME, EVERY MAN TO HIS TRIBE AND TO HIS FAMILY, AND THEY WENT OUT FROM THENCE EVERY MAN TO HIS INHERITANCE."

The synopsis is:

1. The word "inheritance" as used in Verse 17, should have been translated "succession," thereby reading, "there must be heirs to succeed, and therefore we must find wives for them."

2. Williams says, "It gives a sad picture of the condition of the nation at this time that, although the Benjamites lived within a short distance of Shiloh where the Tabernacle was pitched, yet so complete was their neglect of it that the minute directions of Verse 19 had to be given them to enable them to find it; and, further, the mention of only one yearly Feast — God having commanded three — was an added proof of departure from His Word."[1]

3. The "dances" of Verse 21 shows how heathen customs had invaded the House of God; for no such dancing was ordained in the Book of Leviticus; it is all a mournful illustration of that today which professes to be the House of God; all too often, amusement displaces worship.

4. The Passage of Verse 22 could be translated, "you need not fear the guilt of the broken oath, because you did not give your daughters, so as to violate the oath, but they were taken from you by force."

RIGHT AND WRONG

As is obvious in these Passages, Israel keeps committing one wrong after the other, all trying to assuage the mess in which they now find themselves.

Only one time did Israel go before the Lord earnestly seeking guidance and direction. That is found in 20:26-28. But then, instead of continuing to seek the Lord for leading and guidance, they once again lapsed into their old ways, trying to solve the problem themselves, whatever was the problem.

Why is it so hard, even for Believers presently, to earnestly seek the Lord for leading and guidance regarding all that we do? Why do we not do that at the beginning, instead of being forced into such action by great trouble?

If any and every Believer will look back at negative situations, which cause great problems and difficulties, they will find that every single time, they departed from the Word of God. In other words, had they obeyed the Word, the situation would not have happened.

Now this doesn't mean that a proper obedience of the Word of God will forego all problems and difficulties; unfortunately, trouble, at times, comes to the Child of God through no fault of his own. But many problems can be avoided, if we will only stay true to the Word.

(25) "IN THOSE DAYS THERE WAS NO KING IN ISRAEL: EVERY MAN DID THAT WHICH WAS RIGHT IN HIS OWN EYES."

The composition is:

1. As should be obvious, the lessons of this Book are painful, but yet necessary. These lessons teach us that our Faith must ever be registered in Christ and what He has done for us at the Cross. That being done, the Holy Spirit will have latitude within our lives. To be sure, prayer and the study of the Word will then become prominent within our experience (Rom. 6:1-14; 8:1-2, 11).

2. Let it ever be understood that no height of Christian experience, nor miraculous manifestations, as glorious as they might be, can keep the soul from falling. Our daily fellowship with God, meditation upon and obedience to His Holy Word, and the ever-present Power of the indwelling Holy Spirit, which can only come about, as stated, by Faith in Christ and the Cross, can preserve the Christian from spiritual declension (Gal. 6:14).

3. It is a solemn truth that experiences of the past, as wonderful as they may have then been, are useless to the heart that is out of fellowship with God. Israel's history abundantly illustrates this fact. God help us to learn from the myriad of illustrations given in this Book, as painful as they are!

4. We should ever remember, that which

seems to be right in our own eyes, may not be right in the Eyes of God. We can only determine what is right in the Eyes of God, by going to, and abiding by His Word.

Of everything we need, Jesus Christ is the Source, and as well, we must never forget, that the Cross is the Means.

CONCLUSION

It is August 10, 2006, as I conclude this commentary on Judges. May it be a Blessing to you.

BIBLIOGRAPHY

CHAPTER 1

[1] George Williams, *The Student's Commentary On The Holy Scriptures*, Grand Rapids, Kregel Publications, 1949, pg. 121.

CHAPTER 2

[1] George Williams, *The Student's Commentary On The Holy Scriptures*, Grand Rapids, Kregel Publications, 1949, pg. 121.
[2] H.D.M Spence, *The Pulpit Commentary: Vol. 3*, Grand Rapids, Eerdmans Publishing Company, 1978, pg. 25.

CHAPTER 4

[1] George Williams, *The Student's Commentary On The Holy Scriptures*, Grand Rapids, Kregel Publications, 1949, pg. 123.
[2] Ibid., pg. 123.

CHAPTER 6

[1] George Williams, *The Student's Commentary On The Holy Scriptures*, Grand Rapids, Kregel Publications, 1949, pg. 125.

CHAPTER 9

[1] H.D.M Spence, *The Pulpit Commentary: Vol. 3*, Grand Rapids, Eerdmans Publishing Company, 1978, pg. 109.

CHAPTER 10

[1] H.D.M Spence, *The Pulpit Commentary: Vol. 3*, Grand Rapids, Eerdmans Publishing Company, 1978, pg. 112.

[2] George Williams, *The Student's Commentary On The Holy Scriptures*, Grand Rapids, Kregel Publications, 1949, pg. 127.

CHAPTER 11

[1] H.D.M Spence, *The Pulpit Commentary: Vol. 3*, Grand Rapids, Eerdmans Publishing Company, 1978, pg. 120.
[2] George Williams, *The Student's Commentary On The Holy Scriptures*, Grand Rapids, Kregel Publications, 1949, pgs. 127-128.
[3] Ibid., pg. 93.

CHAPTER 12

[1] H.D.M Spence, *The Pulpit Commentary: Vol. 3*, Grand Rapids, Eerdmans Publishing Company, 1978, pg. 136.

CHAPTER 14

[1] George Williams, *The Student's Commentary On The Holy Scriptures*, Grand Rapids, Kregel Publications, 1949, pg. 129.

CHAPTER 16

[1] H.D.M Spence, *The Pulpit Commentary: Vol. 3*, Grand Rapids, Eerdmans Publishing Company, 1978, pg. 168.
[2] Ibid., pg. 169.

CHAPTER 17

[1] H.D.M Spence, *The Pulpit Commentary: Vol. 3*, Grand Rapids, Eerdmans Publishing Company, 1978, pg. 181.

CHAPTER 19

[1] George Williams, *The Student's Commentary On The Holy Scriptures*, Grand Rapids, Kregel Publications, 1949, pg. 132.
[2] H.D.M Spence, *The Pulpit Commentary: Vol. 3*, Grand Rapids, Eerdmans Publishing Company, 1978, pg. 194.
[3] Ibid., pg. 193.

CHAPTER 20

[1] George Williams, *The Student's Commentary On The Holy Scriptures*, Grand Rapids, Kregel Publications, 1949, pg. 133
[2] Ibid., pg. 133.

NOTES

CHAPTER 21

[1] George Williams, *The Student's Commentary On The Holy Scriptures*, Grand Rapids, Kregel Publications, 1949, pgs. 133-134.

REFERENCE BOOKS

Atlas Of The Bible — Rogerson
Strong's Exhaustive Concordance Of The Bible
The New Bible Dictionary — Tyndale
The Pulpit Commentary — H.D.M. Spence
The Student's Commentary On The Holy Scriptures — George Williams
Webster's New Collegiate Dictionary

NOTES

THE
BOOK OF RUTH

—■—

THE INTRODUCTION

As to exactly when the short Book of Ruth was written, is not known. It is almost certain that it was written after the time of the Judges, simply because the writer said in Verse 1 of the First Chapter, *"In the days when the Judges ruled."*

As well, the Book closes with the name of David, who was possibly the great-grandson of Ruth. So, the Book was written possibly during the time of David, or shortly thereafter.

That the Book closes with King David, speaks volumes. The personality of the man demands that Ruth the Moabitess was in his thoughts. Moreover, King David was free from the many narrownesses of spirit that belittle multitudes of other minds. He recognized the gracious relationship of the God of Israel to all the families of the Earth, especially considering that Ruth was a Gentile. Hence, he would not be ashamed of the Moabitish link in his genealogy. He would be proud of it, and all the more, it is likely, because of a peculiarly critical period of his own history. He had been on terms of intimacy and confidence with the king of Moab.

Pulpit says, *"At the time when he had to flee for his life from the presence of Saul, and take refuge in the cave of Adullam, it is said, in I Samuel 22:3-4 that he went to Mizpeh of Moab, 'and said unto the king of Moab, let my father and my mother, I pray you, come forth, and be with you, till I know what God will do for me. And he brought them before the king of Moab; and they dwelt with him all the while that David was in the hold.'*

"It would not be doing violence to suppose

that, in David's communication with the king of Moab, he made mention of the Moabitish link in his genealogy, and of the incidents connected with it. If Ruth, an ancestor of his own, had been hospitably received in Judah, would it be asking too much if the grandson of that ancestor might, with his wife, (David's Mother and Dad), be hospitably received for a season in Moab? And so, it stands to reason that the Book of Ruth was probably written during the time of David or, as stated, very soon thereafter."[1]

THE AUTHOR

As to who wrote this beautiful and yet short Book, is utterly unknown. Many attribute it to the great Prophet Samuel, and it is quite possible that Samuel did write the Book. Probably there is more evidence that he did pen this great work, and under the guidance of the Holy Spirit, more so than any other. But to say for certain, one cannot!

THE REASON FOR THE BOOK OF RUTH

The following is a beautiful statement given in the Pulpit Commentary. I quote: *"Many have supposed that the true reason of the Book is a matter of genealogy. The ground on which this opinion is maintained is the fact that there is a little bit of genealogy in the five Verses with which the Book concludes. This bit of genealogy connects Pharez the son of Judah with David the son of Jessie. The line passed through Boaz, the husband of Ruth. It is an important historical relationship, more especially to us Christians; for as Christ was 'the Son of*

David," He was the son of Boaz too, and consequently the Son of Ruth the Moabitess — a Gentile link.

"The fact is all the more significant and suggestive as, in ascending the genealogical ladder upward to Abraham, the father of the Messianic people, we discover that there were other Gentile links which connected the favored descendants of the Patriarch with the outlying 'families of the Earth,' and which likewise show, in consequence of the moral peculiarity attaching to them, how wondrous was the boon conferred upon men, when the Lord of Glory humbled Himself to become the 'kinsman' and the 'friend' of those whose name is 'sinners.'"[2]

It is August 8, 2006 as I begin the work on this short Book of Ruth. To have the honor and privilege of doing this, to me is a Blessing from the Lord unparalleled. I thank Him for the opportunity.

Continuing with what has just been stated, I do not look at this as work or labor, but rather as a privilege. What an honor it is to study the Word of God. What a Blessing it is to profit from its many benefits. As we have repeatedly stated, *The Bible is the only revealed truth in the world and, in fact, ever has been.*

If our efforts are a Blessing to you, even in a small degree, we give the Lord all the Praise and all the Glory. If in some way you enjoy our efforts, and feel that you have learned a little more about the Word of God due to these efforts, then we both will have been blessed.

CHAPTER 1

(1) "NOW IT CAME TO PASS IN THE DAYS WHEN THE JUDGES RULED, THAT THERE WAS A FAMINE IN THE LAND. AND A CERTAIN MAN OF BETH-LEHEM-JUDAH WENT TO SOJOURN IN THE COUNTRY OF MOAB, HE, AND HIS WIFE, AND HIS TWO SONS.

(2) "AND THE NAME OF THE MAN WAS ELIMELECH, AND THE NAME OF HIS WIFE NAOMI, AND THE NAME OF HIS TWO SONS MAHLON AND CHILION,

NOTES

EPHRATHITES OF BETH-LEHEM-JUDAH. AND THEY CAME INTO THE COUNTRY OF MOAB, AND CONTINUED THERE."

The exposition is:

1. In Old Testament times, famines were sent by the Lord upon Israel as a Judgment because of spiritual declension.

2. The name *"Bethlehem"* means *"house of bread."*

3. Going to a country outside of Israel to live was forbidden by the Lord; and yet, we will see how the Lord would take this wrong and turn it into right, but with great loss, as accompanies all failure.

4. Elimelech and Naomi would find that it would be better to be in a famine in that which belonged to the Lord, as did Israel, than to be in a place of prosperity, and it be filled with idolatry, as was Moab.

MOAB

In these two Verses so much is stated. Let's look first of all at the geographical location stated here — Beth-lehem-Judah. It is given to us in this manner because there was another Bethlehem in Israel, namely in the area of the Tribe of Zebulun (Josh. 19:15); therefore, the writer, whomever he might have been, specifies that the Bethlehem mentioned here, is in the portion of the Tribe of Judah.

Some time ago, on one of our trips to Israel, in which we were accompanied by our Television crew, we did a short piece on the fields of Bethlehem. Standing and looking at those rolling fields as they stretched out toward the little city of Bethlehem, I knew from Bible study, that this was simply one of the most important places on the face of the Earth.

It was the home of Boaz, the area of Ruth's gleaning, and of her marriage to Boaz. In these pastures was trained, in the household of Jessie, and among his stalwart sons, the youthful David, who became the hero and the darling, in fact, the King of Israel.

In New Testament history, between the pastures of Bethlehem and the stars of Heaven was sung the Angel's song of good will and peace. Here was born the Son of David, Who was the Son of God. So, in a sense, very few places on the Earth, if any, could even begin to rival the significance, and I speak of the spiritual significance, of this beautiful area. So, this is the setting of this Book of Ruth.

Even though the very name Bethlehem means *"house of bread,"* signifying that it is a very fertile area, at the commencing of our story, famine grips the land.

FAMINE

Famines, at times, were used by God as a portrayal of His Anger because of spiritual declension. This famine, no doubt, signified such, especially considering the last few Chapters of the Book of Judges.

It could also be said that America's problems regarding the weather, the oil situation, Iraq, terrorism, etc., can be laid at the doorstep of spiritual declension. As well, the cause of the spiritual declension in this nation, is the spiritual declension of the Church. Never, at least since the Reformation, has the Church around the world been in such terrible spiritual condition. Less people are being Saved today than ever. Fewer Believers are being baptized with the Holy Spirit presently than at any time in the last 100 years. And for this problem to be rectified, the Church must come back to the Cross of Christ. There is no other solution!

The Church, in whatever stripe, can institute whatever reforms it so desires; however, until it comes back to the Cross, which is the Foundation of the Word of God, the foundation of Biblical Christianity, there will be no Revival. Everything is tied up in the Cross.

I personally believe this is at least one reason that the Lord has spared our Television Ministry and, as well, has raised up SonLife Radio. We are using these instruments of communication to proclaim the Message of the Cross, and to do so with all the strength that we have. We believe that this is what the Lord has told us to do.

It is ironical, the very name *"Bethlehem"* means *"house of bread."* So here we have poverty in the plenty.

One could well say that the United States has been the repository for the greatest Move of God the world has even known. In fact, it is the secret and strength of all our Blessings. But yet, and because of spiritual declension, as we have stated, there is a famine of the Word of God in the land, as never before. As

it was with Israel of old, so it is with America and the world today.

THE HEATHEN COUNTRY OF MOAB

The Scripture says that Elimelech and Naomi and their two sons *"went to sojourn in the country of Moab."* They, no doubt, intended on staying but a short time. Their sojourn, however, would last for some ten years.

Better to be in a famine in that which God has ordained, than to go to the land of idols. They would find that their situation there would not improve.

I'm afraid the modern Church is doing the same thing, only in a little different way. It is embracing the idols of this world, and, thereby, forsaking the Word of God. The end result will be no different with the modern Church than it was with the family of Elimelech.

The word *"sojourn"* means *"to dwell as a foreigner."* It was a place he and his family did not belong.

Moab was the son of Lot by an incestuous union with his eldest daughter (Gen. 19:37). Both the descendants and the land were known as Moab, and the people also as Moabites. The country was located on the lower part of the eastern side of the Dead Sea. Their god was *"Chemosh,"* which included the sacrifices of little children as a burnt offering.

Josephus says that the time of these happenings was during the Judgeship of Eli, the High Priest. As well, the name *"Elimelech"* means, *"God is King."* *"Naomi"* means, *"God is sweet."*

THE WORD OF GOD

It is noteworthy, while the information is given as to Elimelech and Naomi going to Moab, and of the negative circumstances which transpired there, it is enough to say and reply that there is no hint in the Text itself that the step taken was blamable or blamed. As someone has said, and probably should be repeated, *"No man ought to be condemned, whether dead or alive, without proofs of guilt; and no certain proofs of guilt appear in this present case."*

So how can we reconcile Elimelech and Naomi leaving Bethlehem and going to a heathen country such as Moab, with the tremendous blessing that accrued from this, namely Ruth?

That's a good question!

To understand the why of all of this, we have to first of all understand that God uses all things to His Glory, whatever those things might be. As well, the Lord is able to take our wrong, put it in His Right and thereby make everything right.

Our immediate reaction to all of this is, if Elimelech and Naomi had not gone to Moab, Ruth could not have been Saved, and her name would have been missing in the genealogy of Christ; however, the Lord, Who knows all things, past, present, and future, knew that Elimelech and Naomi would do this thing; therefore, He accordingly worked out His Plan.

But what if they had not gone, the question may be asked?

That is an incorrect question, and for this reason.

Through foreknowledge, God knows everything. So He knew, as stated, they would do this thing; therefore, He would work His Plan regarding Ruth.

OMNISCIENCE

It is difficult for us to understand Omniscience, which refers to perfect knowledge of all things, past, present, and future. By our human comprehension we are limited. So, the idea of one knowing all things, past, present, and future and, thereby, forming plans according to that perfect knowledge, explains the situation. Such belongs to Deity and not mere mortals.

We as human beings can function only according to the very limited knowledge we have as it regards the past and the present — and limited it is. So, we have to think in those terms. But God is not limited. He knows all things, and functions accordingly. That's at least one of the reasons that we find only the facts given to us in this Book of Ruth concerning the happenings, but no blame attributed. While wrong things were done, as is obvious, that is not really the moral of the illustration. The moral pertains to the Salvation of Ruth, which is really the subject matter of the story.

But yet, we should not fail to learn the truths presented in this illustration as it regards wrong direction, etc., and allow it to be a lesson to us personally.

(3) "AND ELIMELECH NAOMI'S HUSBAND DIED; AND SHE WAS LEFT, AND HER TWO SONS.

(4) "AND THEY TOOK THEM WIVES OF THE WOMEN OF MOAB; THE NAME OF THE ONE WAS ORPAH, AND THE NAME OF THE OTHER RUTH: AND THEY DWELLED THERE ABOUT TEN YEARS.

(5) "AND MAHLON AND CHILION DIED ALSO BOTH OF THEM; AND THE WOMAN WAS LEFT OF HER TWO SONS AND HER HUSBAND."

The exposition is:

1. Verse 3 proclaims the fact that to be out of the Will of God always brings suffering.

2. It was not forbidden in the Law for a Hebrew to marry a Moabite woman, but a Moabite, because of being cursed by God, was forbidden to enter the congregation of the Lord (Deut. 23:3); however, Faith could overcome that, which it did with Ruth.

4. Two Books in the Bible are named after women — Ruth and Esther. In the one, a Gentile woman marries a Hebrew and, in the other, a Hebrew woman marries a Gentile. Both marriages predict, as foretold, that the Gentiles, as such, are to be brought into the Kingdom of God in connection with Israel (Gen. 12:3; 18:18; 22:18; 26:4; Ps. 72:17; Acts 3:25).

5. The Fourth Verse says that this family dwelled in Moab for about ten years. It's very easy, spiritually speaking, to go into wrong direction; however, very hard to leave that wrong direction in order to come back to the right way.

NAOMI, A TYPE OF ISRAEL

Naomi is a picture of Israel in the last days under the *"famine of the Antichrist,"* when they will flee to *"Moab,"* which will take place at the midpoint of the Great Tribulation. In the coming Great Tribulation Israel will lose much. In fact, that which is transpiring presently in Israel and Lebanon August, 2006, is but a precursor of what is soon to happen regarding the seven year Great Tribulation that's coming upon this world (Mat. 24:21).

The great Prophet Jeremiah spoke of this coming time as *"the time of Jacob's trouble."* However, he then said, *"but he shall be saved out of it"* (Jer. 30:7).

The Great Tribulation will conclude with the Battle of Armageddon portrayed to us in Ezekiel, Chapters 38 and 39. The Battle of Armageddon will conclude with the Second Coming of the Lord (Rev., Chpt. 19). Then, Israel will come to Christ, typified by Boaz in our story, who is a Type of Christ. Then Naomi (Israel) and her daughter-in-law Ruth, who is a Gentile and typifies the Church, will come into the riches of our heavenly Boaz, the Lord Jesus Christ, which will begin the thousand year Kingdom Age.

So, the story of Ruth is far more than meets the eye. That which happened approximately 100 years before the time of David carries not only the illustration of the Salvation of a soul, which is so very, very important, but, as well, has prophetic overtones that reaches out even to us presently.

GENTILES

The Fourth Verse brings into view the two Moabite girls, Orpah and Ruth, who had married the two sons of Elimelech and Naomi, Mahlon and Chilion.

Theological critics have here again raised the question, was it sinful for these Hebrew young men to take in marriage the daughters of Moab?

The Jewish Targums did not hesitate regarding their decision. They said, *"And they transgressed the edict of the Word of the Lord, and took to themselves alien wives of the daughters of Moab."* It is noteworthy, however, that in the Text itself, even to which we have already alluded, and throughout the entire Book, there is nothing of the nature of condemnation, not even the least hint of blame. In fact, it was not forbidden in the Law for a Hebrew to marry a Moabite woman. A Canaanite yes, a Moabite no (Deut. 7:3).

Some say that the name *"Ruth"* means *"beauty"* and others say it means *"friend."* Some have even proposed that Ruth was looked at as *"the Rose of Moab."* Orpah, regrettably will soon fade from view. Ruth by contrast will set an example of Righteousness that defies all description.

Although a Gentile she will be placed, and due to her marriage with Boaz, in the genealogy of the Lord Jesus Christ, and nothing could be greater than that (Mat. 1:5). As well, and, as stated, she was the great-grandmother of David, the great King of Israel.

IS RUTH A TYPE OF THE CHURCH?

I think so, but only in a limited way, and I speak of coming into the riches of Christ, which both Israel and the Church will do at the beginning of the Kingdom Age.

Williams has some thoughts on this, which I think are very important. He said, *"Naomi typifies Israel in the latter day — in exile from Canaan, a widow, impoverished, and having no heir. She returns to the Land of Promise bringing Ruth, that is, the Gentile with her. They and their property are redeemed by Boaz, i.e., Christ; the nearer kinsman, i.e., the Law being unable to do so, and unwilling, because it necessitated union with a Gentile, i.e., Ruth.*

"Israel having departed from God, and the Gentile being far off from God and outside of the Promises, the Law had no power to establish either of them in blessing.

"In this Book is recorded the operations of Grace in blessing those who merited no Grace; and of the prosecution of God's purposes despite the sin and disorder which marked that time; for God never fails to act even in the midst of evil; and having decreed that Ruth the Gentile should be an ancestress of the Messiah, He bent every circumstance to the accomplishment of that purpose."[1]

DEATH

Abruptly and bluntly we are told that Elimelech died, and then a little later Mahlon and Chilion died, leaving Naomi with her two daughters-in-law, Orpah and Ruth.

It has been said, *"Many men have had affliction, but none like Job; many women have had affliction, but none like Naomi."*

Why did the Lord allow this to happen?

To be sure, the deaths of these three men were definitely the work of the Lord. The reasons are given to us in this Book.

Were these three men, Elimelech, Mahlon, and Chilion men of faith? The Scripture is silent; however, the blunt way in which the occasion of their deaths is given, probably indicates, that they were not individuals of faith.

WHAT DO WE MEAN, MEN OF FAITH?

Unless a Believer is of Faith, meaning that he or she believes God, and does so without reservation, desiring that the Will of God be carried out in his or her life, such Will simply cannot be carried out. In other words, God Who works entirely on the premise of Faith as it lodges in the heart and life of the individual, can only function according to that Faith or the lack thereof. If I had to guess, and one can only guess, I would have to say that these three men were not individuals of faith, which would have greatly hindered the Lord from carrying out His Purposes and Will as it regards what actually did transpire.

Did they die lost?

Most likely not; however, I do believe that there are many Believers who simply are set aside, with some of them even prematurely losing their lives, simply because of not being a person of Faith. This doesn't mean that every Believer who dies prematurely falls into that category. But it does mean that some definitely do. Listen to Paul as he explains the Lord's Supper. He said:

"Wherefore whosoever shall eat this bread, and drink this cup of the Lord, unworthily (tells us emphatically that this can be done, and is done constantly, I'm afraid), *shall be guilty of the Body and Blood of the Lord* (in danger of Judgment, subject to Judgment).

"But let a man examine himself (examine his Faith as to what is its real object), *and so let him eat of that bread, and drink of that cup* (after careful examination).

"For he who eats and drinks unworthily, eats and drinks damnation to himself (does not necessarily mean the loss of one's soul, but rather temporal penalties, which can become much more serious), *not discerning the Lord's Body.* (Not properly discerning the Cross refers to a lack of understanding regarding the Cross. All of this tells us that every single thing we have from the Lord, comes to us exclusively by means of the Cross of

Christ. If we do not understand that, we are not properly *'discerning the Lord's Body.'*)

"For this cause (not properly discerning the Lord's Body) *many* (a considerable number) *are weak and sickly among you* (the cause of much sickness among Christians), *and many sleep.* (This means that many Christians die prematurely. They don't lose their souls, but they do cut their lives short. This shows us, I seriously think, how important properly understanding the Cross is)" (I Cor. 11:27-30).

(6) "THEN SHE AROSE WITH HER DAUGHTERS IN LAW, THAT SHE MIGHT RETURN FROM THE COUNTRY OF MOAB: FOR SHE HAD HEARD IN THE COUNTRY OF MOAB HOW THAT THE LORD HAD VISITED HIS PEOPLE IN GIVING THEM BREAD.

(7) "WHEREFORE SHE WENT FORTH OUT OF THE PLACE WHERE SHE WAS, AND HER TWO DAUGHTERS IN LAW WITH HER; AND THEY WENT ON THE WAY TO RETURN UNTO THE LAND OF JUDAH.

(8) "AND NAOMI SAID UNTO HER TWO DAUGHTERS IN LAW, GO, RETURN EACH TO HER MOTHER'S HOUSE: THE LORD DEAL KINDLY WITH YOU, AS YOU HAVE DEALT WITH THE DEAD, AND WITH ME.

(9) "THE LORD GRANT YOU THAT YOU MAY FIND REST, EACH OF YOU IN THE HOUSE OF HER HUSBAND. THEN SHE KISSED THEM; AND THEY LIFTED UP THEIR VOICE, AND WEPT.

(10) "AND THEY SAID UNTO HER, SURELY WE WILL RETURN WITH YOU UNTO YOUR PEOPLE.

(11) "AND NAOMI SAID, TURN AGAIN, MY DAUGHTERS: WHY WILL YOU GO WITH ME? ARE THERE YET ANY MORE SONS IN MY WOMB, THAT THEY MAY BE YOUR HUSBANDS?

(12) "TURN AGAIN, MY DAUGHTERS, GO YOUR WAY; FOR I AM TOO OLD TO HAVE AN HUSBAND. IF I SHOULD SAY, I HAVE HOPE, IF I SHOULD HAVE AN HUSBAND ALSO TONIGHT, AND SHOULD ALSO BEAR SONS;

(13) "WOULD YOU TARRY FOR THEM TILL THEY WERE GROWN? WOULD YOU STAY FOR THEM FROM HAVING HUSBANDS? NO, MY DAUGHTERS; FOR IT

GRIEVES ME MUCH FOR YOUR SAKES THAT THE HAND OF THE LORD IS GONE OUT AGAINST ME."

The pattern is:

1. Concerning Verse 6, the Jewish Targums say that an Angel spoke to her and gave this information; in other words, the famine was over; it evidently lasted a number of years.

2. It seems that Naomi, at least at this stage, had so little faith in the Promises of God, and such a poor experience as the result of her own disobedience, that she discouraged her daughters-in-law from returning with her. This she should not have done; however, the same faithlessness that caused her and her family to leave Israel plagues her still. But, as we shall see, when she does return to Israel, her faith will begin to come back. Moab was not the place of faith, as the world system is never the place of faith. Israel was the place of Faith, and so it is presently, spiritually speaking.

3. Regarding Verse 9, Naomi knew that there was no *"rest"* in the land of Moab, because it was a place of idolatry.

4. Naomi felt that she had suffered the tragic loss of her husband and two sons because of being out of the Will of God, by leaving Israel to come to Moab. There was, no doubt, some truth in that; however, we must always remember, God doesn't work from what might have been, but rather from *"what is."*

THERE IS BREAD IN BETHLEHEM

The Sixth Verse says, *"For she had heard in the country of Moab how that the LORD had visited His People in giving them bread."*

The Jewish Targums say that an Angel spoke to her and gave this information. At any rate, she knew the famine was over.

This which the Lord did at that particular time, in giving bread to His People, which ended the famine, I want the Lord to do in this particular time, and in a greater way than ever.

Yes, we have seen God do great things; however, He is always able to do greater. I want the news to go out all over the world, into every city, town, and village, which says, *"The Lord is giving His People bread in Baton Rouge."* I want it for the whole world, but of

course, I want it for the area of my domicile.

THE WORD OF THE LORD

If I remember correctly, it was early 1992. We were having two prayer meetings a day at that time, which we did for over ten years, and which I more or less personally continue. It was in the morning prayer meeting. There were only six or seven of us gathered, and we had met in the boardroom of the Ministry.

As I began to seek the Lord that morning, mostly asking for His Help as it regarded my own personal situation. But all of a sudden, the Spirit of the Lord covered me, and greatly so. The Lord spoke to my heart and, in essence, said:

"You are asking help for yourself, and that I will give; however, the entirety of the Church desperately needs help." He then quoted to me the words of Isaiah the Prophet, and applying them to the Church. He said:

"The whole head is sick, and the whole heart faint. From the sole of the foot even unto the head there is no soundness in it; but wounds, and bruises, and putrifying sores: they have not been closed, neither bound up, neither mollified with ointment."

As most Bible students know, that comes from Isaiah 1:5-6.

And then He said to me, *"I will begin a move at Family Worship Center in Baton Rouge, Louisiana, that will girdle the globe."*

It was short and to the point!

To be frank, a thousand questions filled my mind. What did the Lord mean by that? Why would the Lord use me at all?

As stated, this was in 1992, some five years before the Lord would give me the great Revelation of the Cross.

As to exactly what the Lord meant as it regards a move beginning here in Baton Rouge and girdling the globe, I cannot honestly say. I definitely do believe that it has an awful lot to do with the Message of the Cross. As to exactly how it will be carried out, and what will be carried out, only the future will tell; however, this one thing I know, what the Lord said He would do, He will do!

Naomi heard the great word, *"there is bread once again in Bethlehem."* Oh Lord help us, and in whatever capacity You desire to give such, that the news will go out all over the world *"there is bread once again in Baton Rouge, or wherever the Lord chooses to move."*

Famine is a terrible thing, and to be sure, this Nation and, in essence, the entirety of the world, is in a famine as it regards the Word of God. To hear that such a famine is over, it has concluded, it has ended, and there is plenty of bread available, is the greatest thing that anyone could ever hear. Spiritually speaking, it completely transcends anything that is physical, meaning that it is far greater.

ELIJAH THE PROPHET

My mind goes back to the time of Elijah. Israel was in a sad state, with drought and famine having plagued the land for over three years. Then there was the great contest between Elijah and all the prophets of Baal, which took place at Mount Carmel.

The Scripture tells us, *"And Elijah said unto all the people, Come near unto me. And all the people came near unto him. And he repaired the Altar of the LORD that was broken down.* (The 'Altar' was a type of the coming Cross, and what Jesus would do there. As is obvious, Israel no longer believed in the Altar of Jehovah and, above all, what it represented, namely the Cross. Elijah repaired the Altar, which had once been used, but had fallen into disrepair. The Church presently desperately needs to *'repair the Altar of the Lord that is broken down.'* In other words, it desperately needs to reestablish its faith in Christ and the Cross)*" (I Ki. 18:30).

The rest of the illustration proclaims the fact that the fire fell on the Altar and consumed the Burnt Sacrifice, which was a type of the Judgment of God which would fall on Christ when He hung on the Cross, with Him suffering death, and all on our behalf.

The Scripture then says, *"And Elijah said unto Ahab, Get thee up, eat and drink; for there is a sound of abundance of rain* (the people had been directed back to the Cross, of which the Altar was a type, and now the rain of the Spirit could fall; before the Holy Spirit can work, the Church must come back to the Cross; there is no other way!)*" (I Ki. 18:41).

As I have stated, I believe the Lord giving me the Revelation of the Cross, which

by no means is new, but is actually what was given to the Apostle Paul, but yet, that from which the Church has departed, is a portend of what is going to happen. As I have repeatedly stated, the Church must come back to the Cross before there can be *"bread in Bethlehem."*

During the time of Elijah, drought and famine had plagued the land. Everything was burnt to a crisp, which was a type of Israel's spiritual condition. But when Israel was directed back to the Cross, which they were with Elijah repairing the Altar, then the rain came, the rain of the Spirit, so to speak.

This is what I believe is happening, and is going to happen in the United States of America and, in fact, the entirety of the world.

There is bread in Bethlehem!

JEWISH LAW

The Eleventh Verse says, *"Are there yet any more sons in my womb, that they may be your husbands?"*

Jewish Law stated that if the husband died then the wife was to marry his brother, that is if he had a brother. If that was impossible, as it was in this case, she was to marry the next of kin who was not already married. This is the reason for Naomi's words, *"no more sons in my womb"* (Deut. 25:5-9).

Quite possibly these customs were strange to these two Moabite girls, but yet they were probably well acquainted with Jewish Law by now.

The reason for this had to do with all the families of Israel. Each family was important, very important! Through one certain family in Israel at this time, the Messiah would come. Actually, it would be in the Tribe of Judah (Gen. 49:10). And then in this Tribe, the Lord later told David, that the Messiah would come through his family (II Sam., Chpt. 7). And yet, every family was important, because the Lord would chose from various families in Israel, the certain individuals to stand in the Office of the Prophet, with some of these Prophets giving us the Word of God, as the Lord used them. So, every family was very special in Israel, hence, the reason for every effort being made to maintain each family name.

(14) "AND THEY LIFTED UP THEIR

VOICE, AND WEPT AGAIN: AND ORPAH KISSED HER MOTHER IN LAW; BUT RUTH CLAVE UNTO HER.

(15) "AND SHE SAID, BEHOLD, YOUR SISTER IN LAW IS GONE BACK UNTO HER PEOPLE, AND UNTO HER GODS: RETURN THOU AFTER YOUR SISTER IN LAW.

(16) "AND RUTH SAID, INTREAT ME NOT TO LEAVE YOU, OR TO RETURN FROM FOLLOWING AFTER YOU: FOR WHERE YOU GO, I WILL GO; AND WHERE YOU LODGE, I WILL LODGE: YOUR PEOPLE SHALL BE MY PEOPLE, AND YOUR GOD MY GOD:

(17) "WHERE YOU DIE, WILL I DIE, AND THERE WILL I BE BURIED: THE LORD DO SO TO ME, AND MORE ALSO, IF OUGHT BUT DEATH PART YOU AND ME.

(18) "WHEN SHE SAW THAT SHE WAS STEDFASTLY MINDED TO GO WITH HER, THEN SHE LEFT SPEAKING UNTO HER.

(19) "SO THEY TWO WENT UNTIL THEY CAME TO BETHLEHEM. AND IT CAME TO PASS, WHEN THEY WERE COME TO BETHLEHEM, THAT ALL THE CITY WAS MOVED ABOUT THEM, AND THEY SAID, IS THIS NAOMI?

(20) "AND SHE SAID UNTO THEM, CALL ME NOT NAOMI, CALL ME MARA: FOR THE ALMIGHTY HAS DEALT VERY BITTERLY WITH ME.

(21) "I WENT OUT FULL, AND THE LORD HAS BROUGHT ME HOME AGAIN EMPTY: WHY THEN CALL YOU ME NAOMI, SEEING THE LORD HAS TESTIFIED AGAINST ME, AND THE ALMIGHTY HAS AFFLICTED ME?

(22) "SO NAOMI RETURNED, AND RUTH THE MOABITESS, HER DAUGHTER IN LAW, WITH HER, WHICH RETURNED OUT OF THE COUNTRY OF MOAB: AND THEY CAME TO BETH-LEHEM IN THE BEGINNING OF BARLEY HARVEST."

The structure is:

1. Orpah left, and we never hear from her again; how sad!

2. From the statement in Verse 15, *"unto her gods,"* it is obvious that the great contending factor here was the gods of Moab versus the God of Israel. Orpah chose *"her gods,"* and missed the greatest thing could ever happen to any individual — Eternal Life.

In essence, Naomi asked Ruth if that is what she is going to do as well! Exactly as to what Naomi had in mind, we can only guess. It seems that she didn't want to promise them things that she could not fulfill. This seems to have been her intention. But yet, in all of this her Faith, it seems, was very, very low.

3. Verses 16 and 17 record what has to be, one of the greatest statements, one of the greatest affirmations of Salvation, found in the entirety of the Word of God. In essence, it is that which must characterize all who come to Christ. It is the statement of Faith given by Ruth.

In this consecration, there is no looking back. The die is cast. Ruth will forever turn her back on the world of idolatry and rebellion against God. She will forever throw in her lot with those who worship the Lord of Glory. Even when she dies, she does not want to be sent back to Moab, but rather buried in the land of Israel, which she was. She cut all ties with the past, even her family, and everything else. This is exactly the consecration that is demanded by God of all who come to Him. Anything less constitutes no Salvation at all.

4. The words *"they said"* in Verse 19, proclaim a wealth of information. They carry the idea that the poverty which envelopes Naomi was obvious to all. Beside that, her husband and two sons were absent, meaning they were dead. As well, and above all, she is accompanied by a Moabitess, which was a reproach within itself. Little did the people of Bethlehem realize that this Moabitess would be the ancestress of the Messiah.

5. In the thinking of Naomi, *"empty"* as given in Verse 21, described her situation; however, she was far more full than she could even begin to think; Ruth would prove to be the greatest blessing of all; unbelief sees *"empty,"* while Faith sees *"full."*

6. Verse 22 proclaims the Holy Spirit desiring us to know who Ruth is, that we might know what Ruth becomes; He is at the same time, telling us, as He changed Ruth's life, He can change our lives, as well.

7. The time in question here described was April, Passover time. In effect, the Holy Spirit is saying, *"when I see the Blood, I will*

pass over you." There is no sin the Blood cannot cover. There is no life the cleansing of the Blood cannot change. It will change Ruth, it can change us!

THE WRONG DIRECTION

Orpah is dealt with first of all. The evidence is that she considered the situation, and made her decision to reject the God of Israel, and to go back to *"her gods."* Those gods were *"Baal-Peor"* and *"Chemosh,"* both which demanded human sacrifice. The decision that Orpah made, and the direction she took, sadly and regrettably, is the direction taken by most all the world, and for all time.

Why is it that so few accept Christ?

Jesus said:

"Because straight is the gate, and narrow is the way, which leads unto life, and few there be that find it (every contrite heart earnestly desires to be among the *'few'*; the requirements are greater than most are willing to accept)*"* (Mat. 7:14).

So, why are there few who accept?

Jesus answered this as well. He said, *"When any one hears the Word of the Kingdom* (refers to the Word of God; it speaks of God's Way vs. Satan's way), *and understands it not* (does not refer to one who is incapable of understanding, but instead, to one who has no desire to understand), *then comes the wicked one* (Jesus compares Satan to a vulture), *and catches away that which was sown in his heart* (refers to Satan being allowed to do such a thing by the individual involved; the initiative does not lie with the Lord or with Satan, but with the person). *This is he which receives seed by the way side* (the word *'way side'* refers to the fact that the individual doesn't give it credence, i.e., *'unbelief'*).

"But he who receives the seed (Word of God) *into stony places* (refers to the second group), *the same is he who hears the Word, and anon* (immediately) *with joy receives it* (they make a good start, but then fall by the wayside);

"Yet has he not root in himself (refers to the *'stony places'*), *but endures for a while* (he hears the Word of God, believes it, and accepts Christ; it is all done with joy; but then something else happens): *for when tribulation or persecution arises because of*

the Word (which it definitely will), *by and by* (immediately) *he is offended* (the offense of the Cross [Gal. 5:11].)

"He also who received seed (the Word of God) *among the thorns is he who hears the Word* (he receives the Word; the soil is fertile and good with plenty depth); *and the care of this world* (ways of this world), *and the deceitfulness of riches* (deceitful, simply because the acquiring of such makes a person believe erroneous things), *choke the Word* (stops its growth), *and he becomes unfruitful* (such a one is ultimately lost [Jn. 15:2, 6].)

"But he who receives seed into the good ground (prepared ground — ground plowed up by the Spirit of conviction because of sin) *is he who hears the Word* (does so with eagerness), *and understands it* (he wanted to understand, and the Lord rewards such by giving more understanding); *which also bears fruit* (Christian growth), *and brings forth, some an hundredfold, some sixty, some thirty* (the idea is one hundredfold; the Holy Spirit strives to bring the thirty fold and the sixty fold up to a hundred fold [Jn. 15:1-8])*"* (Mat. 13:19-23).

The here and now is much more alluring to most than the there and then, with the latter speaking of eternity. Most, however, never think of eternity, only the present!

What could have been in the hearts of both of these women that one would say *"no"* to the Lord while the other would say *"yes?"* Both had the opportunity, but only one would accept. Her name is in history forever as the great-grandmother of David, and, ultimately of the Son of David, the Messiah.

THE GREAT ACCLAMATION

The consecration that Ruth makes is recorded in Verses 16 and 17, and is, in fact, the consecration that every person must make in coming to the Lord Jesus Christ. She said:

"For where you go, I will go; and where you lodge, I will lodge: your people shall be my people, and your God my God: Where you die, will I die, and there will I be buried: the LORD do so to me, and more also, if ought but death part you and me."

In this consecration there is no looking back. The die is cast. She will forever turn her back upon the world of idolatry. The same could be said for her family. In fact, the evidence is, she would never see them again.

She had learned about the God of Israel from Naomi. She had accepted the Christ as her Saviour, her Lord, and her Master. This means, as well, that she turned her back forever upon the gods of Moab. She had now found the peace that passes all understanding, the joy unspeakable and full of glory. Moab now holds nothing for her. Her eyes are cast upon God's Land, and God's People, of which she is now a part.

One should study this acclamation as given by Ruth very carefully.

• *"Where you go, I will go"*: By this statement she means that she is casting her lot with the People of God, and doing so forever. This meant, as well, that she would turn her back upon her own family, her Moabite friends, forever making the people of Israel now her kindred.

This phrase also means that whatever the hardship, whatever the difficulties, no matter what she is called upon to do, this she will do.

• *"Where you lodge, I will lodge"*: It doesn't matter where the lodging place will be, how spartan it is, or how palatial it is. In fact, the riches or lack thereof of the lodging present themselves as unimportant.

• *"Your people shall be my people, and your God my God"*: Jehovah is now her God, and will be her God forever! She has turned her back totally and completely on the idols of Moab. She is now with the People of God forever, and Jehovah is her God forever. Her own immediate family, although she loves them, are not considered here. She has a new family. In other words, she is cutting all ties with the past.

• *"Where you die, will I die, and there will I be buried"*: She has made her choice for life. There is no turning back. As stated, she will never see her family again, will never see Moab again, will never see again the places where she was born and raised. She has forever cast her lot with the People of God, and she tells Naomi, wherever it is that you will die, that is the place that I will die, for I am not leaving your side. From your lips I have found the Lord of Glory. You have pointed

to me the way. There is nothing else for me any other place. My past, my present, and my future is with you, and in reality, with your God and my Lord!

There could be no more beautiful affirmation and acclamation of this as given by Ruth. It forever rings down through the span of time that which it means as it regards a full consecration to the Lord. How so certain is the sound that comes from her lips! How so sure her consecration!

The Eighteenth Verse says, *"She was steadfastly minded."* Those who are, make it. Those who are not, don't!

THE PASSOVER

The journey from Moab to Bethlehem was only about 70 or 80 miles. Not much now, but a journey of some length then. It probably took them about a week to make the trip. The miles were insignificant, but the journey for both, Naomi and Ruth, was a journey of unprecedented proportions.

For Ruth, it was a journey from one life to another. A journey, in some measure, which would never end, meaning it has not ended even yet. And so it is as it regards any and every person who makes Jesus Christ their Saviour and their Lord. They have just embarked upon a journey that is eternal, and journey with such rewards that literally stagger the imagination.

It is Passover time, the time of the *"barley harvest."* In the time of the Judges, the Passover was little celebrated. So, how much that Ruth knew about this greatest Feast of all, celebrating the Deliverance of the Children of Israel from Egyptian bondage, we aren't told; nevertheless, the Holy Spirit wants us to know by inserting the statement, *"in the beginning of barley harvest,"* that it was Passover time.

Why is this so important?

It's important simply because Ruth would be the ancestress of the One Who would shed His immortal Glory, and take upon Himself the habiliments of human flesh, all for the purpose of going to the Cross, where He would there shed His Life's Blood, in order that the fallen sons of Adam's lost race might be Saved. *"When I see the Blood, I will pass over you."*

"Christ our Redeemer died on the Cross,
"Died for the sinner, paid all his due;
"Sprinkle your soul with the Blood of
    the Lamb,
"And I will pass, will pass over you."

"Chiefest of sinners, Jesus will save;
"All He has promised, that He will do;
"Washed in the fountain opened for sin,
"And I will pass, will pass over you."

"Judgment is coming, all will be there,
"Each one receiving justly his due;
"Hide in the saving sin-cleansing Blood,
"And I will pass, will pass over you."

"Oh great compassion! O boundless love!
"Oh lovingkindness, faithful and true!
"Find peace and shelter under the Blood,
"And I will pass, will pass over you."

THE ALMIGHTY

When Naomi and Ruth come into Bethlehem, Naomi is instantly recognized. Scores of people gather around them, asking the question *"Is this Naomi?"* She has been gone ten years, and now she returns home; however, she returns without her husband or two sons. Above that, she has a Moabitess girl with her, which, to say the least, was very unusual!

Naomi doesn't try to put a face on the situation, even as the questions fly at her thick and fast. Where is Elimelech? Where is Mahlon and Chilion? Who is this Moabite girl, beautiful, but yet a Moabite?

The Holy Spirit strongly desired that all would know who Ruth was. He referred to her as *"Ruth the Moabitess."*

Why?

The reasons, no doubt, are many! However, He wanted all to know, that Faith, which incidentally characterized Ruth, can rise above any dilemma. Despite the fact that she had been an idol worshipping Moabite, in fact, a people cursed by God, still, she would rise above all of that, actually, rise to such a height as to defy all description. Her Faith in God would take her there. Her consecration, portrays that.

Her Faith would take her to the land of Israel, to be a part of the People of God, and above all, to serve Jehovah, the only True

God. As well, she would be the great-grandmother of David, the mighty King of Israel, and above all of that, far above all of that, she would be the ancestress of the Son of David, the Lord Jesus Christ, the Saviour of mankind, the Baptizer with the Holy Spirit, the King of kings and Lord of lords, the First and the Last, the Alpha and the Omega.

Who is she, the Holy Spirit asks?!

Quickly the retort is given, *"She is a Moabitess, cursed by God, but yet rising above all of that, showing every human being who has ever lived, and no matter their circumstances, that through Faith in God, they can rise above these problems, and see great things, even as did Ruth!"*

AFFLICTION

Naomi said, *"The Almighty has afflicted me."*

What seems at times to be affliction, turns out to be a blessing, and this is exactly what happened.

While the Lord at times, does most definitely chastise us, and because He chastises those He loves, but everything He does, is always and without exception, for our good (Heb. 12:3-11).

It may not seem to be good when it's happening, such as the passing of Naomi's husband and two sons, which, as would be obvious, would be extremely hurtful, but at the same time, the Lord allowed this to happen, to which we have already alluded, for a reason. He could easily have stopped the deaths of this man and his two sons, thereby, avoiding the pain and suffering that Naomi had to go through. But the Lord knew of certain things, and knowing those certain things, as He always does, it would be best that He would take these three men.

He knew that Ruth would turn her back on the idol gods of Moab, and would accept Him as the Lord of her life. He also knew that she would be the great-grandmother of David, and ultimately the ancestress of the Messiah, although she would not ever know those things until she was taken home to Glory. But she knows now, and she is satisfied!

As well, Naomi knows now, and is satisfied. I don't think, if you were to ask her at the present, that she would say as she said so long ago, *"The Almighty has afflicted me."* I think she would rather say, *"The Almighty has blessed me, and has done so abundantly!"*

CHAPTER 2

(1) "AND NAOMI HAD A KINSMAN OF HER HUSBAND'S, A MIGHTY MAN OF WEALTH, OF THE FAMILY OF ELIMELECH; AND HIS NAME WAS BOAZ.

(2) "AND RUTH THE MOABITESS SAID UNTO NAOMI, LET ME NOW GO TO THE FIELD, AND GLEAN EARS OF CORN AFTER HIM IN WHOSE SIGHT I SHALL FIND GRACE. AND SHE SAID UNTO HER, GO, MY DAUGHTER.

(3) "AND SHE WENT, AND CAME, AND GLEANED IN THE FIELD AFTER THE REAPERS: AND HER HAP WAS TO LIGHT ON A PART OF THE FIELD BELONGING UNTO BOAZ, WHO WAS OF THE KINDRED OF ELIMELECH."

The exegesis is:

1. In a sense, Boaz is a Type of Christ; and Ruth, a Gentile, is a type of the Church. The terrible losses in the land of Moab portray the dispersion and, thereby, Judgment of Israel.

2. Boaz will prove to be the kinsman redeemer of Ruth. There is one Hebrew word for *"kinsman"* and *"redeemer,"* for he only had *"the right to redeem"* who was a kinsman. Hence, it was necessary that the Lord Jesus Christ should become Man in order to redeem man. Ruth's marriage into the wealthy home into which she was brought, pictured the satisfying joy and fullness of Blessing which union with Christ secures for the heart that trusts Him (Williams).[1]

3. Verse 2 portrays the fact that Naomi was poverty stricken. The welfare system of Israel in that day, which was given by God in the Law of Moses, stated that the poor, during the harvest, could go into the fields and glean the leavings. In this Law, the reapers were instructed to not glean the corners of the fields, and to leave a little something along the way (Lev. 19:9; 23:22; Deut. 24:19).

4. We find that Ruth, although a beautiful young lady, was not adverse to hard work;

those who are, are seldom, if ever, used by the Lord.

5. The Third Verse says, *"Her hap was to light on a part of the field belonging to Boaz."*

As far as Ruth was concerned, she just happened to come on the field of Boaz, not really knowing where she was; of course, the Holy Spirit was guiding her all the way. She did not know Boaz, but the Lord did. When the Lord plans for us, beautiful things result; when we plan for ourselves, there are no positive results!

THE MIGHTY MAN OF WEALTH

Boaz is a Type of Christ, with Ruth being a Gentile, a type of the Church. The terrible losses in the land of Moab portray the dispersion, and, thereby, Judgment of Israel, that is even yet to come. It will take place at the midpoint of the Great Tribulation, when the Antichrist who has brokered a peace treaty between Israel and the Muslims, etc., will then himself break that treaty. He will attack Israel, with her suffering her first military defeat since becoming a Nation in 1948. She will then flee to Petra, which is in modern Jordan, nearby the Dead Sea. It was Moab during the time of Ruth.

The Antichrist will have bigger fish to fry, so to speak, in his efforts to take over the entirety of the world, and will leave Israel for another day. She will then filter back into the land, and especially into the city of Jerusalem. About three and a half years later, the Antichrist will once again, fresh from the great victories in the north and in the east, come down upon the land of Israel, with every intent of destroying these people, and doing so once and for all.

In fact, he most definitely would do so, annihilating Israel from the face of the Earth, but will be interrupted by the most cataclysmic event the world has ever known, the Second Coming (Rev., Chpt. 19).

He will then face power such as he has never known before, and will be defeated by the Lord Jesus Christ in short order.

Then Israel will accept Christ as her Saviour and her Lord. She will then realize that the One she crucified, was in reality her Messiah after all! In fact, there is Scriptural evidence, that every Jew in the world at that time will accept Christ (Isa. 11:11). As Naomi was ultimately blessed, Israel will then be blessed beyond measure.

The events which are transpiring presently in the Middle East, even as I dictate these notes (August 10, 2006), are but a precursor of all of this which we have just mentioned. Modern Israel is in a crushing dilemma, not knowing what to do. She is trying to fight Hezbollah, and yet she really doesn't know, at least for the most part, who Hezbollah actually is. By that I refer to those who belong to this so-called party of god. Though they occupy southern Lebanon, still, they are so mixed and mingled with the regular population, that it is not really known as to exactly who is what or what is who. So, Israel fighting the Hezbollah is pretty much like fighting a phantom.

As well, Hezbollah is funded by Iran, and as well, supplied with weapons. Syria delivers these weapons to this shadow army.

On top of all of that, her very reason for existing is to fight Israel. Any peace treaty she signs, will only be for a short duration until she can work out something to her favor, and then she will attack again. To Hezbollah and, in fact, most Muslims, the only good Jew is a dead Jew. Also, they consider that the land of Israel belongs to the Muslims. They don't want a part of it for a small state, they want all of it, and will do anything to achieve their goal. In fact, they refer to Israel as *"Little Satan,"* and America as *"Big Satan!"*

So, how does one defeat such an army — a shadow army? If they are defeated, they will merely regroup, reform themselves, and start all over again. For every member of Hezbollah who is killed, several more are ready to step in and take their place.

Considering all of this, how can Israel stop the rockets from coming into her country, and her soldiers being kidnapped and killed, even in the times of so-called *"peace?"*

The truth is, she can't! That's why the Antichrist will choose this very thing to make his debut. He will broker a peace between the Muslims and Israel, and other nations, thereby solving this thorny problem, which will gain the admiration of the world, and actually cause Israel to think of him,

and really accept him, as the Messiah. They will find to their utter dismay, that it will be the biggest mistake that they have ever made in modern times (Dan. 9:27).

THE LEADING OF THE HOLY SPIRIT

The Second Verse says, *"Let me now go to the field, and glean ears of corn."*

The welfare system of Israel in that day, as stated, was given by God in the Law of Moses, stating that the poor during the harvest could go into the fields and glean the leavings. Considering that Naomi was desperately poor, Ruth volunteers to go into the fields in order that they might have food. This shows that Ruth, even though a very lovely young lady, did not feel that she was too good to stoop to the lowest social level in order that she and her mother-in-law might have food to eat.

God can use no other kind. What a lesson we can learn from this. The old adage says, *"God helps those who help themselves."* It is not bad advice. In this we learn two things about Ruth:

• Her willingness to work, even at the lowest task and

• Her humility.

Verse 3 says, *"And her hap was to light on a part of the field belonging unto Boaz."* The way the Holy Spirit had these words constructed tells us that He was guiding Ruth constantly. She may have thought that she chose a field by chance; however, it was no chance at all. The Lord will be involved in every aspect of our lives if we will only give Him an opportunity to do so.

God's Agency does not supersede man's, nor does man's supersede God's. Each of us should be able to say, *"My Father works hitherto, and so do I."*

That memorable day when Ruth set out, probably early in the morning, she little knew where she was going. She just knew they had to have food; there was no other way for it to be obtained. She little understood, at least at this time, the Leading and Guidance of the Holy Spirit, but to be sure, He was guiding every step of the way.

Possibly she passed several fields, and then finally she saw one that somehow attracted her. This was the Holy Spirit pushing her in that direction. It belonged to Boaz, one of the wealthiest men in Bethlehem. She knew none of this, only that she hoped to get a little grain so that some bread could be made that night.

She had made the great consecration to the Lord, and is this the way that He rewards her?

Many have been led to believe in these modern times, that if anything at all is done for the Lord, that He rewards such handsomely.

The truth is, He does, but most of the time in a different way than we think.

In His rewarding of Ruth, He would demand some things of her. Had she been lazy, thinking she was too good to do such backbreaking work, the Lord could not have blessed her; however, He knew what kind of woman she was.

So, as she sets out in order to try to find a little food for she and Naomi, the Holy Spirit has a grand and glorious Plan, and He is guiding her all the way.

Do we understand here what is happening?

Do we realize that the Lord desires to lead and guide us in exactly the same way? She had made the bold consecration, and she meant to stand by what she had said.

Does one think that she might have grown discouraged at her decision to throw in her lot totally and completely with Naomi, as it regards the God of Israel?

I don't think so!

There is no hint in the Text that she ever even remotely was sorry for the choice she had made. Whatever it was that she did, even to this backbreaking work of stooping to find a little grain, she did it; it seems, with relish, thankful to the Lord for the privilege of doing so.

THE PLACE OF OUR APPOINTMENT

The Lord has a plan for every single Believer. None are excluded, meaning that all are included.

The full realization of that Plan requires many steps, with the Lord Leading and Guiding in them all. One of the biggest mistakes that we make as a Believer, is to fail to appreciate where the Lord has presently placed us. We have our eyes on something that maybe is not His Will. The correct way is as

Ruth, we should thank God for where we are, wherever it might be, determine to do our best for Him, leaving the promotion to His Leading and Guidance.

This was the place that God had placed Ruth and Naomi. It did not seem to be a very prosperous place on the surface. In fact, the wolf was at the door, so to speak. But yet, the Lord was behind it all! As Naomi and Ruth were planning as to how they would find a little food to eat, the Holy Spirit was planning as well; however, His Plans were much, much larger than those of Naomi's and Ruth's.

If the modern Believer treats with disdain the place where they presently are, failing to thank the Lord for their present position, whatever it might be, this greatly hinders the Holy Spirit from doing very much with us.

If the Lord has placed us in a McDonald's Restaurant, we should determine to be the best hamburger flipper or the best clerk that the store has. The Lord demands no less of us.

However, if we whine about our present position, thinking we are too good to fill such a post, we are, in effect, insulting the Lord. Also, we are hindering anything that He might want to do for us, in elevating us, which He fully intends to do — that is if we will only function according to His Word and His Will.

Did Ruth think of herself too good to glean in the fields? Did she think of herself as too good to be thought of as on welfare? Did she complain to the Lord that He wasn't treating her right? Did she turn on Naomi as many do, always seeking to place the blame somewhere else? Did she blame God, and then stupidly tell Him that she forgave Him for her present lot, as much of modern Christendom now advocates? The answer is *"No!"*

Gleaning in the fields was all that she knew to do. So she did it with all the dignity that was hers, and the Lord rewarded her accordingly.

He will do the same for you!

(4) "AND, BEHOLD, BOAZ CAME FROM BETH-LEHEM, AND SAID UNTO THE REAPERS, THE LORD BE WITH YOU. AND THEY ANSWERED HIM, THE LORD BLESS YOU.

(5) "THEN SAID BOAZ UNTO HIS SERVANT WHO WAS SET OVER THE

REAPERS, WHOSE DAMSEL IS THIS?

(6) "AND THE SERVANT WHO WAS SET OVER THE REAPERS ANSWERED AND SAID, IT IS THE MOABITISH DAMSEL WHO CAME BACK WITH NAOMI OUT OF THE COUNTRY OF MOAB:

(7) "AND SHE SAID, I PRAY YOU, LET ME GLEAN AND GATHER AFTER THE REAPERS AMONG THE SHEAVES: SO SHE CAME, AND HAS CONTINUED EVEN FROM THE MORNING UNTIL NOW, THAT SHE TARRIED A LITTLE IN THE HOUSE.

(8) "THEN SAID BOAZ UNTO RUTH, HEAREST THOU NOT, MY DAUGHTER? GO NOT TO GLEAN IN ANOTHER FIELD, NEITHER GO FROM HENCE, BUT ABIDE HERE FAST BY MY MAIDENS:

(9) "LET YOUR EYES BE ON THE FIELD THAT THEY DO REAP, AND GO THOU AFTER THEM: HAVE I NOT CHARGED THE YOUNG MEN THAT THEY SHALL NOT TOUCH YOU? AND WHEN YOU ARE ATHIRST, GO UNTO THE VESSELS, AND DRINK OF THAT WHICH THE YOUNG MEN HAVE DRAWN.

(10) "THEN SHE FELL ON HER FACE, AND BOWED HERSELF TO THE GROUND, AND SAID UNTO HIM, WHY HAVE I FOUND GRACE IN YOUR EYES, THAT YOU SHOULD TAKE KNOWLEDGE OF ME, SEEING I AM A STRANGER?

(11) "AND BOAZ ANSWERED AND SAID UNTO HER, IT HAS FULLY BEEN SHOWED ME, ALL THAT YOU HAVE DONE TO YOUR MOTHER IN LAW SINCE THE DEATH OF YOUR HUSBAND: AND HOW YOU HAVE LEFT YOUR FATHER AND YOUR MOTHER, AND THE LAND OF YOUR NATIVITY, AND ARE COME UNTO A PEOPLE WHICH YOU KNEW NOT HERETOFORE.

(12) "THE LORD RECOMPENSE YOUR WORK, AND A FULL REWARD BE GIVEN YOU OF THE LORD GOD OF ISRAEL, UNDER WHOSE WINGS YOU ARE COME TO TRUST.

(13) "THEN SHE SAID, LET ME FIND FAVOUR IN YOUR SIGHT, MY LORD; FOR THAT YOU HAVE COMFORTED ME, AND FOR THAT YOU HAVE SPOKEN FRIENDLY UNTO YOUR HANDMAID, THOUGH I BE NOT LIKE UNTO ONE OF YOUR HANDMAIDENS.

NOTES

(14) "AND BOAZ SAID UNTO HER, AT MEALTIME COME THOU HITHER, AND EAT OF THE BREAD, AND DIP YOUR MORSEL IN THE VINEGAR. AND SHE SAT BESIDE THE REAPERS: AND HE REACHED HER PARCHED CORN, AND SHE DID EAT AND WAS SUFFICED, AND LEFT.

(15) "AND WHEN SHE WAS RISEN UP TO GLEAN, BOAZ COMMANDED HIS YOUNG MEN, SAYING, LET HER GLEAN EVEN AMONG THE SHEAVES, AND REPROACH HER NOT:

(16) "AND LET FALL ALSO SOME OF THE HANDFULS OF PURPOSE FOR HER, AND LEAVE THEM, THAT SHE MAY GLEAN THEM, AND REBUKE HER NOT.

(17) "SO SHE GLEANED IN THE FIELD UNTIL EVENING, AND BEAT OUT THAT SHE HAD GLEANED: AND IT WAS ABOUT AN EPHAH OF BARLEY.

(18) "AND SHE TOOK IT UP, AND WENT INTO THE CITY: AND HER MOTHER IN LAW SAW WHAT SHE HAD GLEANED: AND SHE BROUGHT FORTH, AND GAVE TO HER THAT SHE HAD RESERVED AFTER SHE WAS SUFFICED."

The diagram is:

1. Boaz was extremely wealthy. He was of the Tribe of Judah, and in the direct line of the Messiah.

2. The question of Verse 5, even though asked casually by Boaz, would be answered by the Holy Spirit. Ruth would be the great-grandmother of David, and, thereby, of the Son of David.

3. To those around her, Ruth was reduced to the level of gleaning, as she was poverty stricken; also, she was a Moabitess, with all its resultant connotations; however, Heaven would answer the question in a much different way.

4. Boaz had done far more than merely take notice of her. Her action towards him denotes humility, a trait, incidentally enjoyed by precious few.

5. Boaz makes it clear that he had already been informed of her consecration as a proselyte to the Hebrew Faith, and of her decision to leave her own people, her native land, and its gods, to live with a people who were strangers to her. He then pronounced a Blessing

from the God of Israel upon her. The Hebrew Targum adds to this answer of Boaz:

"It has been certainly told me by the word of the wise, that what the Lord has decreed (Deut. 23:3). *And it has surely said to me by prophecy, that Kings and Prophets shall proceed from you because of the good which you have done."*

6. Boaz, in his instructions to the reapers, directed them to give Ruth greater liberty than that commanded by the Law. The *"handfuls of purpose,"* in effect, state that handfuls of grain were to be dropped just for her. As stated, she was truly favored.

WHO IS THIS DAMSEL?

Boaz is mentioned nineteen times in the Book of Ruth. His greeting to the reapers was, *"The LORD be with you."* And they answered him, *"The LORD bless you."* This was the daily greeting of godly men and their servants in Israel.

This was the same as the owner of the field asking for the presence of God to be with the workers, and for divine protection and preservation as they labored. It was the same when the servants expressed a desire for the owner to be blessed of God that he might enjoy the increase of the field and have wisdom regarding how to use it for God's Glory.

If such mutual love and respect were shared alike by employer and employees in all lands at the present time, it would be as near the days of Heaven on Earth as possible.

Boaz comes to this particular field to check with the reapers to see how things are going. He notices the Moabitess, and asks, *"Whose damsel is this?"*

This question, even though asked casually by Boaz, would be answered by the Holy Spirit. Ruth would be the great-grandmother of David, and, thereby, of the Son of David. Of course, none of this was known at the time and, in fact, would not be known throughout the lifetimes of both Ruth and Boaz. But Faith would bring it to pass, and most certainly, they now both know, and know it very well, at the present time.

This young lady and this man who characterized this Book, and of whom we write, we will all one day meet, that is, if we make Heaven our Eternal Home.

These people, Boaz and Ruth are so very prominent in the Scriptures, simply because they are both in the lineage of the Messiah. Boaz by direct lineage, and Ruth by marriage, thereby uniting the Jew and the Gentile.

In order to redeem the fallen sons of Adam's lost race, God would have to become man, go to a Cross, which was ever His Destination. Angels couldn't do this thing, because they were of another Creation. God as God couldn't do this thing, because God, as stated, cannot die. So God would have to become man, the Man, Christ Jesus, in which many things would be done; however, the ever present goal, that which had been decided from before the foundation of the world, was the Cross. There His Life's Blood would be poured out. There, Mercy was great, and Grace was free. There, all sin would be atoned, past, present, and future, at least for all who will believe (Jn. 3:16). If man was to be Saved, snatched back from the very jaws of Hell, then this is the price that had to be paid, and only God could pay it. Ruth and Boaz figure so prominently in all of this, thereby, giving us insight into the lives of some of these who would be in this great lineage.

HUMILITY

When Boaz spoke to Ruth, the Scripture says, *"Then she fell on her face, and bowed herself to the ground."* This denotes her humility.

The great compliment of humility is enjoyed by so few of the majority of Christendom and yet, it is possibly the greatest Grace that God could ever bestow upon anyone. The only personal thing that Jesus ever said about Himself was, *"I am meek and lowly in heart."*

Ruth would say, *"I am a stranger."* She was, in fact, a stranger to the commonwealth of Israel, an alien to the Promises of God; however, great Grace would change her from a stranger to a joint heir (Rom. 8:17).

HANDFULS OF PURPOSE

The Eleventh Verse says, *"And Boaz answered and said unto her, It has fully been shown me."*

The news, evidently, had gotten around all over the little village of Bethlehem concerning this beautiful Moabitess. Everyone knew of her consecration, how she had converted to the God of Israel, thereby, forever forsaking the idols of Moab. They knew of her consecration, and they knew of her Faith. In fact, it seems that she was the talk of Bethlehem. When Boaz asked as to who she was, I greatly suspect, that he already suspicioned who she was.

He continued his answer to her by saying, *"The LORD recompense your work, and a full reward be given you of the LORD God of Israel, under Whose wings you are come to trust."*

What a beautiful way of proclaiming the Salvation of Ruth.

He then tells the reapers to *"let fall also some of the 'handfuls of purpose' for her."*

To be sure, our Heavenly Boaz will most definitely do the same for us, in leaving wherever He so desires, *"handfuls of purpose"* which will make our way easier. Every Believer should understand this, and every Believer should expect this. If we obey the Lord, as did Ruth, if we follow Him, as did Ruth, if we consecrate, as did Ruth, we can expect those *"handfuls of purpose,"* and expect them on a continuing basis. The old song says:

*"Hallelujah what a thought, Jesus full
   Salvation brought,
"Victory, yes victory!
"Let the powers of sin assail, Heaven's
   Grace shall never fail,
"Victory, yes Victory!"*

God is a Blessing God, as is illustrated here by the action of Boaz on behalf of Ruth. Why did he do this for her? Why did he show her this courtesy?

He did it for many reasons, quite possibly the greatest reason of all, whether he realized it at the moment or not, he was already falling in love with her.

Even though we were strangers, aliens from the commonwealth of Israel, and strangers to the Promise, still, despite our lowly Gentile position, poverty stricken, yet, He loved us. He came to where we were gleaning in the field, trying to get a little sustenance, and gave instructions that there should be

"handfuls of purpose" left on our behalf.

Oh, dear reader, do you not see that? Do you not feel that? Do you not sense that?

He loves you, and He wants to leave *"handfuls of purpose"* all on your behalf and He, as stated, will most definitely do so, if we will only believe Him.

Please note the following:

All of this was preceded by Ruth's humility. When he spoke to her, she fell to the ground in prostrated form, and asked him, *"Why have I found grace in your eyes, that you should take knowledge of me, seeing I am a stranger?"*

Yes, the correct question, and the correct answer was and is *"Grace."* No wonder John Newton wrote so long ago:

*"Amazing Grace how sweet the sound,
"That Saved a wretch like me.
"I once was lost, but now I'm found,
"I was blind, but now I see."*

WHAT IS GRACE?

Grace is simply the Goodness of God extended to undeserving Believers.

There is nothing we can do to earn the Goodness of God! There is nothing we can do to merit such. In fact, we deserve eternal punishment. But if we will exhibit Faith in Christ, humble ourselves before Him, even as Ruth did with Boaz, the Grace of God will be extended to us, and extended in an uninterrupted flow.

Actually, it is the Cross of Christ that makes Grace possible. Christ is the Source, and the Cross is the Means by which all of this is done.

Everything we receive from the Lord, and whatever it might be, is a gift from God. As stated, we didn't earn it, we did not merit it, as we could not earn or merit such. So it is a gift!

This *"Gift"* is received by us exhibiting Faith in Christ and what He did for us at the Cross, which then gives the Holy Spirit latitude to work within our lives, thereby making this Grace possible and, in fact, flowing to us like a veritable Niagara.

Due to the grace shown Ruth by Boaz in the leaving of *"handfuls of purpose,"* she was able to gather that day an ephah of barley.

This was a little bit over a half bushel, which was enough to make all the bread she and Naomi needed, plus some. However, as we shall see, this is just the beginning. It is an ephah of barley now, in just a little bit, she will own the entirety of the farm.

What a mighty God we serve!

(19) "AND HER MOTHER IN LAW SAID UNTO HER, WHERE HAVE YOU GLEANED TODAY? AND WHERE HAVE YOU WORKED? BLESSED BE HE WHO DID TAKE KNOWLEDGE OF YOU. AND SHE SHOWED HER MOTHER IN LAW WITH WHOM SHE HAD WORKED, AND SAID, THE MAN'S NAME WITH WHOM I WORKED TODAY IS BOAZ.

(20) "AND NAOMI SAID UNTO HER DAUGHTER IN LAW, BLESSED BE HE OF THE LORD, WHO HAS NOT LEFT OFF HIS KINDNESS TO THE LIVING AND TO THE DEAD. AND NAOMI SAID UNTO HER, THE MAN IS NEAR OF KIN UNTO US, ONE OF OUR NEXT KINSMEN.

(21) "AND RUTH THE MOABITESS SAID, HE SAID UNTO ME ALSO, YOU SHALL KEEP FAST BY MY YOUNG MEN, UNTIL THEY HAVE ENDED ALL MY HARVEST.

(22) "AND NAOMI SAID UNTO RUTH HER DAUGHTER IN LAW, IT IS GOOD, MY DAUGHTER, THAT YOU GO OUT WITH HIS MAIDENS, THAT THEY MEET YOU NOT IN ANY OTHER FIELD.

(23) "SO SHE KEPT FAST BY THE MAIDENS OF BOAZ TO GLEAN UNTO THE END OF BARLEY HARVEST AND OF WHEAT HARVEST; AND DWELT WITH HER MOTHER IN LAW."

The exposition is:

1. The way that Ruth answered the question of Naomi as asked in Verse 19, proclaims more than a mere identification. She sensed something more, but Naomi would have to fill in the blanks, which she instantly did.

2. Regarding Verse 20, Naomi was speaking of the Law of the *"kinsman redeemer."* It referred to buying back a relative's property and to marrying his widow.

When a Hebrew was forced to sell his inheritance because of poverty, the nearest relative was to redeem it for him (Lev. 25:25). If one acted as a *"kinsman redeemer"* for one who had died without a son, he was obliged

NOTES

to marry the widow. Should he refuse to take possession of the property, he was not under obligation to marry the widow. Boaz had no right to redeem the property until the nearest kinsman refused, which he did.

3. During the time of barley harvest, which was in April, three Feasts were to be kept: Passover, Unleavened Bread, and Firstfruits. During the time of the wheat harvest, which came in the latter part of May or early June, was to be the Feast of Pentecost. It was 50 days after Passover.

WHERE HAVE YOU GLEANED TODAY?

This first day of gleaning when Ruth comes home, and bringing the grain with her, she is asked by her mother-in-law, *"Where have you gleaned today?"*

What a simple question, and yet, it is freighted with a glimpse of the ages. Of course, Naomi had no idea at all as to the portend of her question, but it would have significance far beyond her thinking.

Where Ruth gleaned that day, was that which had been designed by the Holy Spirit. It had a meaning that reached into eternity, including David as the great king of Israel, which would come about in approximately 100 years, but above all of that, the coming of the Messiah, which is actually the answer to the question asked that day by Naomi.

When a person gives their heart to Christ, everything changes. Not only are they changed personally, but direction is changed, and above all, eternal destiny is changed. Then, there is no limit to the worth of such a life, all because it is now linked with the Lord.

Could this young Moabite girl ever even think of dreaming that she would be in the lineage of the Messiah? I think not! But yet, she was and all because of her Faith. I am persuaded that if every Believer, whomever that Believer might be, will make the consecration that Ruth made when she said, *"Where you go, I will go; and where you lodge, I will lodge: your people shall be my people, and your God my God: Where you die, will I die, and there will I be buried,"* the consequences, extremely positive consequences, will be enormous! The Lord is not so much interested in what we were, as to what He can make of us, if only we will yield to Him.

THE ANSWER IS
THE CROSS OF CHRIST

God's Way is *"Jesus Christ and Him Crucified"* (I Cor. 1:23). This means that Jesus Christ, the Son of the Living God, God manifest in the flesh, paid the price on Calvary's Cross, in order that man may be lifted out of his terrible dilemma. To be sure, the Cross of Christ is the answer and, in fact, is the only answer.

Once the Believer understands what Jesus did at the Cross and that it refers not only to our Salvation, but, as well, to our Sanctification, then the Believer begins to see himself as he really is and, above all, he sees Christ as He really is. What he sees about himself will not present itself as a pretty picture. What he sees about Christ will be nothing but Perfection. Understanding the Cross as it regards Sanctification, the Believer comes to understand that within himself he cannot do anything, or merit anything from God whatsoever, no matter what he does. In other words, it is not in works, not in performance, not in our doing, not in religion, etc. It is all in Christ and the Cross.

Understanding that within himself, and no matter how godly he might think he is, or actually might be, still, within himself he can merit nothing from the Lord. It is hard for man to come to that place to realize this and to believe it, and especially religious man. We like to think that our good works, our good deeds, our faithfulness, our obedience, or whatever label we would like to use, merits us something with God. It doesn't. The reason is simple.

As a result of the Fall, man is polluted. Everything he touches he destroys, he pollutes, he sullies, he wrecks. And it doesn't matter who he is. Our only hope is in Christ, and what He has done for us at the Cross (Rom. 5:1-2; 6:1-14; 8:1-2, 11; I Cor. 1:17-18, 21, 23; 2:2; Gal., Chpt. 5; 6:14; Eph. 2:13-18; Col. 2:14-15).

When we understand that Christ is the Source of all things, and the Cross is the Means by which all of these things are given unto us, which requires Faith on our part,

NOTES

and we speak of Faith exclusively in Christ and the Cross, this is God's Prescribed Order of Life and Living, His Prescribed Order of Victory.

THE MEANING OF THE NEW
COVENANT IS THE MEANING
OF THE CROSS

When the Holy Spirit through Paul desired to give us an object lesson as to what the meaning of the New Covenant is, he gave it to us in the form of the Lord's Supper, which portrays, and in no uncertain terms, the Cross of Christ. The *"broken bread"* is a Type of His Body, which was given in Sacrifice. The *"cup"* is a Type of His precious shed Blood, which was spilled in order to pour out His Life, thereby offering up Himself, which Sacrifice God accepted as payment in full (I Cor. 11:23-32).

Why is the Message of the Cross so hard to believe? Why is it so hard to accept? Listen again to Paul:

"For the preaching (Word) *of the Cross is to them who perish foolishness* (spiritual things cannot be discerned by unredeemed people, but that doesn't matter; the Cross must be preached just the same, even as we shall see); *but unto us who are Saved it is the Power of God."* (The Cross is the Power of God simply because it was there that the total sin debt was paid, giving the Holy Spirit, in Whom the Power resides, latitude to work mightily within our lives)" (I Cor. 1:18).

The Greek word translated *"preaching"* as used here, is *"logos,"* and means *"Word, or Message."* Why the King James people translated it preaching I have no idea. It should read *"For the Word, or the Message of the Cross is to them who perish foolishness. . . ."*

Unfortunately, the Message of the Cross is not only foolishness to those who are perishing, i.e., *"unredeemed,"* but, as well, it is foolishness to many in the modern Church also!

If one doesn't understand the Cross, then one doesn't understand the New Covenant. In fact, one doesn't understand the Word of God. This is why so much false doctrine abounds. The individuals do not understand the Cross, and those who listen to their error, as well do not understand the Cross, and thereby accept something that is false.

The Cross of Christ is actually the very foundation of the entirety of the Gospel. Through foreknowledge God knew that He would make the world, would create man, and that man would fall. The Godhead then determined, even before the foundation of the world, that man would be redeemed by God becoming flesh, and thereby going to a Cross in order to satisfy the claims of Heavenly Justice. And this is exactly what happened. Peter said so (I Pet. 1:18-20). So, every Doctrine as it regards the Word of God must be built exclusively on the Cross of Christ, and if not, in some way that doctrine will be spurious.

THE BARLEY HARVEST AND THE WHEAT HARVEST

The harvests were the most important time of the year in Israel. Events were reckoned from harvest times.

The three great yearly gatherings of Israel took place at the time of the three harvest seasons (Ex. 23:16; 34:21-22). They are as follows:

1. The Feasts of Passover, Firstfruits, and Unleavened Bread were held every April in connection with the barley harvest.

2. The Feast of Pentecost was held seven weeks later at the time of the wheat harvest. It was during June. These two harvests, barley and wheat, characterized the time frame of our story concerning Ruth.

3. The Feast of Tabernacles was held at the end of the year at the time of the fruit harvest. It was October. The Feast of Trumpets and the Great Day of Atonement preceded that of Tabernacles.

Pulpit says, *"Ruth's gleaning labors extended to the close of the wheat-harvest, during which time, no doubt, there would be frequent opportunities for a growing intimacy between the beautiful gleaner and the worthy proprietor. Often too, we may rest assured, would Boaz be a visitor in the humble home of Naomi."*[2]

How beautiful it is to observe the Leading and Guiding of the Holy Spirit. How so wondrously He works! How so perfectly He leads!

May the Lord give us guidance and strength to follow His Leading!

CHAPTER 3

(1) "THEN NAOMI HER MOTHER IN LAW SAID UNTO HER, MY DAUGHTER, SHALL I NOT SEEK REST FOR YOU, THAT IT MAY BE WELL WITH YOU?

(2) "AND NOW IS NOT BOAZ OUR KINDRED, WITH WHOSE MAIDENS YOU WERE? BEHOLD, HE WINNOWS BARLEY TONIGHT IN THE THRESHINGFLOOR.

(3) "WASH YOURSELF THEREFORE, AND ANOINT YOU, AND PUT YOUR RAIMENT UPON YOU, AND GET THEE DOWN TO THE FLOOR: BUT MAKE NOT YOURSELF KNOWN UNTO THE MAN, UNTIL HE SHALL HAVE DONE EATING AND DRINKING.

(4) "AND IT SHALL BE, WHEN HE LIES DOWN, THAT YOU SHALL MARK THE PLACE WHERE HE SHALL LIE, AND YOU SHALL GO IN, AND UNCOVER HIS FEET, AND LAY YOU DOWN; AND HE WILL TELL YOU WHAT YOU SHALL DO."

The diagram is:

1. In this instance, Naomi may be labeled as a Type of the Holy Spirit, Who seeks our good. His Business is to ever lead us to Christ.

2. The *"threshingfloor"* is a Type of what the Holy Spirit does in our life. On the threshingfloor the husks were separated from the grain. This is a Type of what the Holy Spirit does for us by separating us from the *"flesh,"* i.e., *"the frail strength of man"* (Mat. 3:11).

3. Verse 3 presents Types of several things. They are:

• *"Wash yourself therefore"*: This is a type of Redemption (I Cor. 6:11).

• *"Anoint you"*: This speaks of the Baptism with the Holy Spirit, hence, the anointing which follows the Salvation experience.

• *"Put your raiment upon you"*: This is the garment of praise; it is not only an inward change, but it is an outward change, as well; it is the change effected by the Power of the Holy Spirit working within our hearts and lives; it speaks of an inward change that produces itself outwardly (Isa. 61:3).

• *"Get you down to the floor"*: This speaks of humility; the literal meaning of the word *"humility"* is *"a river that runs low"* (I Pet. 5:5).

4. There was nothing unseemly concerning that Ruth did as outlined in Verse 4. It was a part of Hebrew Law.

She was making a move, as instructed her by Naomi, which would bring Boaz to a place of decision. It is the same as the believing sinner coming to the feet of Christ, after which he will inherit everything that belongs to Christ, exactly as did Ruth regarding Boaz.

THE WORK OF THE HOLY SPIRIT

This Chapter is rich in its application and glorious in its study. Verses 1 through 4 portray to us the entirety of the Plan of God for our lives. The Holy Spirit, down through Scripture, at times does this. In a simple statement a great Truth will be brought out, but which the individual in question, whomever that may have been, is not aware, even as Naomi.

REST

When Naomi said to Ruth, *"I seek rest for you, that it may be well with you,"* whatever her intentions and thoughts at the moment, a picture is here painted, actually of the great Salvation process.

The *"rest"* of which she speaks, is not understood at all, until the individual actually enjoys that which it produces, which can only come about when one makes Jesus Christ the Saviour of the soul, and the Lord of the life.

There is a perpetual war that goes on between God and unredeemed humanity. It is the enmity between God and man, and because of sin. To be sure, man does not feel that enmity, near as much as the Lord. The reason for that is simple, it is the Lord Who man sins against, actually Who has been offended, and offended greatly!

Immediately after the Fall, God said to Satan through the serpent, *"And I will put enmity* (animosity) *between you and the woman* (presents the Lord now actually speaking to Satan, who had used the serpent; in effect, the Lord is saying to Satan, *'You used the woman to bring down the human race, and I will use the woman as an instrument to bring the Redeemer into the world, Who will save the human race'*), *and between*

your seed (mankind which follows Satan) *and her Seed* (the Lord Jesus Christ)*; it* (Christ) *shall bruise your head* (the victory that Jesus won at the Cross [Col. 2:14-15])*, and you shall bruise His Heel* (the sufferings of the Cross)*"* (Gen. 3:15).

This enmity was removed at the Cross of Calvary, at least for all who accept Christ as Saviour. Paul said:

"Having abolished in His Flesh (speaking of His Death on the Cross, by which He Redeemed humanity, which also means He didn't die spiritually, as some claim) *the enmity* (the hatred between God and man, caused by sin)*, even the Law of Commandments contained in Ordinances* (pertains to the Law of Moses, and more particularly the Ten Commandments)*; for to make in Himself of twain* (of Jews and Gentiles) *one new man, so making peace* (which again was accomplished by the Cross)*;*

"And that He (Christ) *might reconcile both* (Jews and Gentiles) *unto God in one body* (the Church) *by the Cross* (it is by the Atonement only that men ever become reconciled to God)*, having slain the enmity thereby* (removed the barrier between God and sinful man)*"* (Eph. 2:15-16).

With the enmity removed, there is *"rest"* for the individual, which makes the Born-Again experience totally unlike anything else in the world.

Whatever Naomi meant by her statement concerning *"rest,"* the Holy Spirit, as usual, goes far beyond, and I mean far beyond, our thinking!

WASHED

Of course, Naomi in speaking to Ruth, was simply telling her to take a bath. She wanted her to look her best for Boaz. But once again, the Holy Spirit has far more in mind.

Paul said, *"Do you not know that the unrighteous shall not inherit the Kingdom of God?* (This shoots down the unscriptural Doctrine of Unconditional Eternal Security.) *Be not deceived* (presents the same words of our Lord, *'Let no man deceive you'* [Mk. 13:5])*: neither fornicators, nor idolaters, nor adulterers, nor effeminate, nor abusers of themselves with mankind* (the proof of true Christianity is the changed life),

"Nor thieves, nor covetous, nor drunkards, nor revilers, nor extortioners, shall inherit the Kingdom of God (refers to those who call themselves *'Believers,'* but yet continue to practice the sins mentioned, whom the Holy Spirit says are not Saved, irrespective of their claims).

"And such were some of you (before conversion)*: but you are washed* (refers to the Blood of Jesus cleansing from all sin), *but you are Sanctified* (one's position in Christ), *but you are Justified* (declared not guilty) *in the Name of the Lord Jesus* (refers to Christ and what He did at the Cross, in order that we might be Saved), *and by the Spirit of our God* (proclaims the Third Person of the Triune Godhead as the Mechanic in this great Work of Grace)*"* (I Cor. 6:9-11).

Because of sin, this world is polluted, and polluted in every manner, be it spiritually, domestically, economically, physically, in fact, in every way. So, the very first thing that happens to the believing sinner upon coming to Christ, is that he or she is *"washed."* As stated, that refers to being washed by the Blood of the Lamb.

All of this is a spiritual process, which is gained by Faith. There's nothing about it that is physical. But yet, the result of this *"washing"* carries over into every aspect of life and living.

The Blood of Jesus Christ is the only thing that can cleanse the soul. Nothing else can. As stated, it is all done by Faith, by the believing sinner expressing Faith and confidence in Christ and what He has done for us at the Cross.

The *"washing"* that the believing sinner receives upon coming to Christ, which, of course, is spiritual, is a one-time affair, and need never be repeated, and because it pertains to our Justification. And yet, there are scores of *"washings"* which must be repeated over and over again, as it regards to the Sanctification of the Believer.

We live in a polluted world, and the Believer has to function in this world. To illustrate this, Jesus used a *"foot washing"* to illustrate our walk before God, and the need for constant cleansing.

The Scripture says, *"He rose from supper* (He rose from the table when the preparation

had been completed), *laid aside His Garments* (physically, His outer robe; spiritually, He laid aside the expression of His Deity, while never losing the possession of His Deity)*; and took a towel* (refers to the action of the lowliest slave or servant in a household; it represents the servant spirit possessed by Christ), *and girded Himself* (wrapped Himself in the towel; spiritually speaking, it refers to His Human Body provided for Him by the Father [Heb. 10:5] in order to serve as a Sacrifice on the Cross for sin).

"After that He poured water into a basin (spiritually, it referred to the Holy Spirit, which would pour from Him like a River [Jn. 7:38-39]), *and began to wash the Disciples' feet* (presenting the servant principle which we are to follow, but even more particularly the cleansing guaranteed by the Holy Spirit concerning our daily walk, which comes about according to our Faith in Christ and what He did for us at the Cross), *and to wipe them with the towel wherewith He was girded* (refers to the Incarnation, which made possible His Death on Calvary, that atoned for all sin and made cleansing possible for the human race).

"Then comes He to Simon Peter (seems to indicate it was Peter to whom He first approached)*: and Peter said unto Him, Lord, do you wash my feet?* (*'The flesh'* cannot understand spiritual realities; it is too backward or too forward, too courageous or too cowardly; it is incapable of ever being right, and it is impossible to improve, consequently, it must *'die.'*)

"Jesus answered and said unto him, What I do you know not now; but you shall know hereafter (when Peter was filled with the Spirit, which he was on the Day of Pentecost).

"Peter said unto Him, You shall never wash my feet (the Greek Text actually says, *'Not while eternity lasts'*; Calvin said, *'With God, obedience is better than worship'*). *Jesus answered him, If I wash you not, you have no part with Me* (the statement as rendered by Christ speaks to the constant cleansing needed regarding our everyday walk before the Lord, which the washing of the feet [our walk], at least in part, represented).

*"Simon Peter said unto Him, Lord, not my feet only, but also my hands and my head

(Chrysostom said, *'In His deprecation He was vehement, and his yielding more vehement, but both came from his love'*).

"Jesus said to him, he who is washed needs not save to wash His feet (as stated, pertains to our daily walk before God, which means that the Believer doesn't have to get Saved over and over again; the *'head'* refers to our Salvation, meaning that we do not have to be repeatedly Saved, while the *'hands'* refer to our *'doing,'* signifying that this doesn't need to be washed because Christ has already done what needs to be done; all of this is in the spiritual sense), *but is clean every whit* (refers to Salvation, and pertains to the Precious Blood of Jesus that cleanses from all sin; the infinite Sacrifice needs no repetition)*" (Jn. 13:4-10).

HOW IS THIS CONSTANT WASHING FOR SANCTIFICATION CARRIED OUT?

It is carried out in a variety of ways.

First of all, the Scripture says, *"Christ also loved the Church, and gave Himself for it* (presents the great Sacrifice which characterizes the God kind of Love); *That He might sanctify and cleanse it* (speaks of the view to the final presentation of the Church in perfect Holiness at the coming Great Day) *with the washing of water by the Word* (actually means the *'Word'* washes and cleanses one exactly as water),

"That He might present it to Himself (it is Christ Himself Who is to present the Church, and He is to present it to Himself) *a glorious Church* (made possible by the Cross), *not having spot, or wrinkle, or any such thing* (which the Cross alone can do); *but that it should be Holy and without blemish.* (This is our position in Christ, made possible by the Cross)*" (Eph. 5:25-27).

So this tells us that the study of the Word of God actually acts as a washing and cleansing agent for the Believer, which is a continuous process, inasmuch as the Believer needs to study the Word constantly.

Second, one's constant Faith in Christ and what He has done for us at the Cross, provides a constant cleansing process. Paul said:

"But God forbid that I should glory (boast), *save in the Cross of our Lord Jesus Christ* (what the opponents of Paul sought to escape at the price of insincerity is the Apostle's only basis of exultation), *by Whom the world is crucified unto me, and I unto the world.* (The only way we can overcome the world, and I mean the only way, is by placing our Faith exclusively in the Cross of Christ and keeping it there)*" (Gal. 6:14).

We have before us the two great cleansing agents which every Believer constantly needs, hence, the many washings of Sanctification, which are the Word of God, and the Cross of Christ. In one sense, they are both the same!

ANOINTED

Naomi then told Ruth to anoint herself, which in a sense spoke of applying some type of perfume. Simply put, to make her smell good. But once again, the Holy Spirit has something far greater in mind.

After one comes to Christ, the next great step is the Baptism with the Holy Spirit, from which the anointing springs.

Jesus said, *"The Spirit of the Lord is upon Me* (we learn here of the absolute necessity of the Person and Work of the Holy Spirit within our lives), *because He has anointed Me . . .* (Jesus is the ultimate Anointed One; consequently, the Anointing of the Holy Spirit actually belongs to Christ, and the Anointing we have actually comes by His Authority [Jn. 16:14])*" (Lk. 4:18).

The Bible teaches that the Baptism with the Holy Spirit is a separate and distinct work subsequent to Salvation. In other words, one must first be Saved before one can be baptized with the Holy Spirit. Jesus said, *"Even the Spirit of Truth* (the Greek says, *'The Spirit of the Truth,'* which refers to the Word of God; actually, He does far more than merely superintend the attribute of Truth, as Christ *'is Truth'* [I Jn. 5:6]); *Whom the world cannot receive* (the Holy Spirit cannot come into the heart of the unbeliever until the person makes Christ his or her Saviour; then He comes in), *because it sees Him not, neither knows Him* (refers to the fact that only Born-Again Believers can understand the Holy Spirit and know Him)*" (Jn. 14:17).

There are five instances in the Book of Acts, which proclaim individuals being baptized with the Holy Spirit. Those five instances are found in Acts 2:1-4; 8:14-17; 9:17;

10:44-46; 19:1-7. In other words, one is not baptized with the Holy Spirit at the time of conversion, as many claim, although one is definitely born of the Spirit. There is a vast difference; however, in being *"born of the Spirit,"* than being *"baptized with the Spirit."* We are speaking here of being *"baptized with the Spirit."*

The Bible also teaches that every person who is baptized with the Spirit, speaks with other tongues. There is no exception.

Acts 2:1-4 proclaims these recipients speaking with other tongues.

In Acts, Chapter 8, the Scripture doesn't say that the Samaritans spoke with tongues, but Peter said to Simon the Sorcerer, *"You have neither part nor lot in this matter* (the word *'matter'* in the Greek, as it is used here, is *'logos,'* and means *'a word or speech'*; Peter is referring to these Believers speaking with other tongues)*"* (Acts 8:21).

In Acts, Chapter 9, as well, it doesn't say that Paul spoke with Tongues, but it doesn't say he didn't either. In fact, it gives little information, merely saying in the words of Ananais, *"The Lord, even Jesus, Who appeared unto you in the way as you came, has sent me, that you might receive your sight, and be filled with the Holy Spirit"* (Acts 9:17).

But yet, Paul himself said, *"I thank my God, I speak with Tongues more than you all"* (I Cor. 14:18). No, the Apostle is not here speaking of linguistic ability, the ability to speak several languages, but rather, of the physical evidence of the Baptism with the Holy Spirit, which is speaking with other Tongues.

In Acts, Chapter 10, Cornelius and his household were Saved and baptized with the Holy Spirit all in one act. Of course, they were Saved first, as they had to be, and then moments later, baptized with the Holy Spirit. The Scripture says, *"For they heard them speak with Tongues, and magnify God"* (Acts 10:46).

In the Nineteenth Chapter of Acts when the Ephesian Believers were baptized with the Holy Spirit, the Scripture says, *"And when Paul had laid his hands upon them, the Holy Spirit came on them; and they spoke with Tongues, and prophesied"* (Acts 19:6).

Without the Baptism with the Holy Spirit, the Believer, and especially the preacher, is not going to do very much for the Lord. If the Book of Acts is the criteria, and it most definitely is, then it's imperative that every Believer be baptized with the Holy Spirit.

It is true that every person at the moment of conversion receives the Holy Spirit. In fact, one cannot be Saved without the regeneration of the Holy Spirit, Who, in fact, initiates the Salvation process. But, as stated, there is a vast difference in being born of the Spirit, and baptized with the Spirit.

The Baptism with the Spirit, in essence, proclaims the total and complete surrender of the individual to the Lord, and in every respect. It doesn't make one perfect, and doesn't really give one victory over sin, that taking place by Faith being evidenced in Christ and the Cross and that exclusively. But it does give the Believer power to carry out the Work of the Lord (Acts 1:8). In fact, without the Baptism with the Holy Spirit there is very little spirituality involved. Preachers who do not believe in the Baptism with the Holy Spirit, perform most of their duties simply by means of the flesh, which really carry out nothing for the Lord (Rom. 8:8).

NEW RAIMENT

Once a believing sinner is washed in the Blood of the Lamb, then baptized with the Holy Spirit, his life then becomes a paean of praise to the Lord. The great Prophet Jeremiah said, *"Praise the LORD of Hosts: for the LORD is good; for His Mercy endures forever: and of them who shall bring the Sacrifice of Praise into the House of the LORD. For I will cause to return the captivity of the land, as at the first, saith the LORD"* (Jer. 33:11).

What does the phrase *"Sacrifice of Praise"* actually mean?

It means that our praises to the Lord must be based entirely upon the Sacrifice of Christ, what He did for us at Calvary's Cross. If it's not Praise based upon that Sacrifice, then it's praise that God cannot accept.

Sadly and regrettably, most of the so-called praise that's tendered in most modern Churches, is not based on the Cross at all, but rather constitutes *"will worship"* (Col. 2:23).

NOTES

The Second Chapter of Colossians speaks of the Cross and what Jesus did there and, in effect, states that serving God, or pretending to do so, and all types of worship that are based on anything other than the Cross, is constituted as *"will worship,"* which means that it is *"worship devised and prescribed by man."* In other words, and as stated, it is not based on the Cross of Christ.

Let all understand, everything that we believe as it pertains to the Word of God and to the Lord, must be based squarely upon the Cross of Christ, or else it is unacceptable to the Lord. Peter said:

"Forasmuch as you know that you were not Redeemed with corruptible things, as silver and gold (presents the fact that the most precious commodities [silver and gold] could not redeem fallen man), *from your vain conversation* (vain lifestyle) *received by tradition from your fathers* (speaks of original sin that is passed on from father to child at conception);

"But with the Precious Blood of Christ (presents the payment, which proclaims the poured out Life of Christ on behalf of sinners), *as of a Lamb without blemish and without spot* (speaks of the lambs offered as substitutes in the Old Jewish economy; the Death of Christ was not an execution or assassination, but rather a Sacrifice; the Offering of Himself presented a Perfect Sacrifice, for He was Perfect in every respect [Ex. 12:5]):

"Who verily was foreordained before the foundation of the world (refers to the fact that God, in His Omniscience, knew He would create man, man would Fall, and man would be Redeemed by Christ going to the Cross; this was all done before the Universe was created; this means the Cross of Christ is the Foundation Doctrine of all Doctrine, referring to the fact that all Doctrine must be built upon that Foundation, or else it is specious), *but was manifest in these last times for you* (refers to the invisible God Who, in the Person of the Son, was made visible to human eyesight by assuming a human body and human limitations)" (I Pet. 1:18-20).

HUMILITY

The phrase, *"And get you down to the floor,"* speaks of humility, which characterizes the

person who is truly washed, truly baptized with the Holy Spirit, and has put on the garment of praise. At least that's the goal of the Holy Spirit. Regrettably, it doesn't always work out that way, but that's the way it should be, and that's the way it can be, that is if the Believer will function according to the Word as the Believer should.

In all of His three and a half years of public Ministry, Jesus only said one thing about Himself on a personal basis. He said:

"Come unto Me (is meant by Jesus to reveal Himself as the Giver of Salvation), *all you who labor and are heavy laden* (trying to earn Salvation by works), *and I will give you rest* (this 'rest' can only be found by placing one's Faith in Christ and what He has done for us at the Cross [Gal. 5:1-6]).

"Take My yoke upon you (the 'yoke' of the 'Cross' [Lk. 9:23]), *and learn of Me* (learn of His Sacrifice [Rom. 6:3-5]); *for I am meek and lowly in heart* (the only thing that our Lord Personally said of Himself): *and you shall find rest unto your souls* (the soul can find rest only in the Cross).

"For My yoke is easy, and My burden is light (what He requires of us is very little, just to have Faith in Him, and His Sacrificial Atoning Work)" (Mat. 11:28-30).

In the words, *"For I am meek and lowly in heart,"* we find the humility of Christ, which is to be our example.

Humility is an ongoing process, which can only be attained, and continued, by one expressing one's Faith exclusively in Christ and the Cross, understanding that Christ is ever the Source, and the Cross is ever the Means. In fact, this is something that must be done on a *"daily"* basis (Lk. 9:23). If the Believer doesn't understand properly that everything he receives comes to him from Christ as the Source, and that the Cross is the Means by which all of this is done, even as we have said repeatedly, then the Believer will never know humility, nor anything else the Lord has for us. Regrettably, untold millions of people are Saved, but they've never grown in the Lord, never realized all the things for which Christ has paid such a price, and simply because their faith is in the wrong object. Their faith must ever be in Christ and the Cross.

WHAT IS HUMILITY?

Humility is a state of mind as it regards the individual who sees himself as he really is, and Christ as He really is. This will result in the Believer conducting himself in a humble manner.

And that which I've just stated, the Believer seeing himself as he really is, and Christ as He really is, cannot be done without the Believer having his faith properly in the Cross. Until the Believer understands the Cross, he will really never understand himself, nor will he understand Christ, at least as he should.

Please note the following very carefully:

No Believer in the world has any standing with God whatsoever, no matter who he is, no matter what he has done, no matter what he hasn't done, except by and through the Lord Jesus Christ, and more particularly what He did for us at the Cross. Without Christ and His Atoning Work, we have no standing whatsoever. And let it ever be understood, it is the Cross of Christ that has made everything possible. That's why Satan fights it as he does.

If the Believer will place his Faith exclusively in Christ and the Cross, he will begin to see many changes in his life, even though many of those changes will come at a slow pace, and one of those changes will be a humble and contrite spirit.

HE WILL TELL YOU WHAT
YOU SHALL DO!

Concerning this, Williams says, *"Ruth for a time was satisfied with the gifts that flowed from the hand of Boaz, but the sweeter and deeper joy of union with Boaz himself was suggested to her by Naomi.*

"This marks an important stage in Christian experience, and underlies St. John 1:29 as contrasted with St. John 1:36. At first the forgiveness that Christ gives, together with His other gifts, satisfies the heart; but, later, a deeper desire is awakened to be occupied with the Giver rather than with His gifts, and the soul hungers for the closest intimacy with Himself."[1]

As we have stated, Boaz is a Type of Christ, and Christ Alone can *"tell us what we should*

do." He does it through His Word, through the act of the Spirit moving upon the heart, and sometimes through another Believer, but the facts are, if we will look to Him, He most definitely will *"tell us what we ought to do."*

Once again, this type of intimacy, which presents a joy unspeakable and full of glory, is possible only by the Believer having his Faith properly placed in Christ and the Cross. It can come no other way!

In this beautiful story of Ruth, we see a steady progression of Faith, which will ultimately catapult her to a place and position unparalleled. This is not limited only to Ruth, but is available to every Believer who will truly follow the Lord as did Ruth. Even though this event took place approximately 3,100 years ago, still, the principle is the same.

(5) "AND SHE SAID UNTO HER, ALL THAT YOU SAY UNTO ME I WILL DO.

(6) "AND SHE WENT DOWN UNTO THE FLOOR, AND DID ACCORDING TO ALL THAT HER MOTHER IN LAW BADE HER.

(7) "AND WHEN BOAZ HAD EATEN AND DRUNK, AND HIS HEART WAS MERRY, HE WENT TO LIE DOWN AT THE END OF THE HEAP OF CORN: AND SHE CAME SOFTLY, AND UNCOVERED HIS FEET, AND LAID HER DOWN."

The exposition is:

1. Naomi, being a Type of the Holy Spirit, at least in this instance, gives instructions, and Ruth promptly obeys.

2. All of this had to do with the Law of the Kinsman Redeemer, which we will momentarily study to a greater depth, which incidentally, Ruth probably little understood, but nevertheless obeys.

3. We as well do not understand everything the Holy Spirit tells us to do, but which explanation will become clearer later on. It is our business to obey.

ALL THAT YOU SAY
UNTO ME I WILL DO

This is the answer that Ruth gives to Naomi, *"All that you say unto me I will do."*

As a Believer we should read these words several times, and do so very slowly. If every Believer would say such to the Holy Spirit, Who seeks to lead and guide us into all Truth, our lives would be far different than they presently are (Jn. 16:13).

As we observe Ruth and Naomi leading and guiding her, we see relationship with Boaz deepening almost by the day. This is what the Holy Spirit seeks to do within our hearts and lives. It is His Business to draw us ever closer to the Lord Jesus Christ. The Spirit doesn't glorify Himself, but rather Christ. He ever seeks to lift up Christ, to build up Christ, all in our eyes, that we may see the Lord Jesus for Who He really is. As we have repeatedly stated, this can only be done by the Believer ever making the Cross of Christ the Object of his Faith (Rom. 6:1-14; 8:1-2, 11; Gal. 6:14).

The Holy Spirit probably speaks to us as little as He does, simply because we have little heeded Him in the past. If we will ardently tell the Lord that we desire His Leading and Guidance, asking Him to forgive us of our spiritual blunders of the flesh, and that we seriously and sincerely want to be led by the Spirit, this is a prayer that God will answer. The key is in the words of Ruth, *"All that You say unto me I will do."*

(8) "AND IT CAME TO PASS AT MID-NIGHT, THAT THE MAN WAS AFRAID, AND TURNED HIMSELF: AND, BEHOLD, A WOMAN LAY AT HIS FEET.

(9) "AND HE SAID, WHO ARE YOU? AND SHE ANSWERED, I AM RUTH YOUR HANDMAID: SPREAD THEREFORE YOUR SKIRT OVER YOUR HANDMAID; FOR YOU ARE A NEAR KINSMAN.

(10) "AND HE SAID, BLESSED BE YOU OF THE LORD, MY DAUGHTER: FOR YOU HAVE SHOWED MORE KINDNESS IN THE LATTER END THAN AT THE BEGINNING, INASMUCH AS YOU FOLLOWED NOT YOUNG MEN, WHETHER POOR OR RICH.

(11) "AND NOW, MY DAUGHTER, FEAR NOT; I WILL DO TO YOU ALL THAT YOU REQUIRE: FOR ALL THE CITY OF MY PEOPLE DOES KNOW THAT YOU ARE A VIRTUOUS WOMAN.

(12) "AND NOW IT IS TRUE THAT I AM YOUR NEAR KINSMAN: HOWBEIT THERE IS A KINSMAN NEARER THAN I."

The diagram is:

1. Let the Reader understand that there was nothing unseemly or untoward going on here. This was a custom in those days,

NOTES

regarding a Kinsman Redeemer who had not stepped up to carry out the Law.

2. In effect, what Boaz was saying as it regards Verse 10 is, *"The kindness which you are showing to your husband now that he is gone is still greater than what you did show him while he lived,"* hence, the words, *"more kindness in the latter end than at the beginning."*

3. For months, the small town had observed Ruth, and the conclusion was one of virtue, as it regarded her.

4. The kinsman nearer to Ruth is the one referred to in 4:1 as *"Ho, such a one."* We might say that this individual represented the Law. In effect, he had first claim. However, he refused the right of redemption. He refused because the Law can never save. Only Boaz, our Heavenly Redeemer can save.

BOLDNESS

The Eighth Verse says, *"And, behold, a woman lay at his feet."*

The boldness of Faith and love is very precious to the Lord Jesus Christ. He commands *"boldness"* in drawing near to Him (Heb. 4:16). To be timid, therefore, is to be disobedient, and it grieves His Heart. Ruth's boldness in drawing near to Boaz made her all the more precious in his eyes. Listen to Paul:

"Let us therefore come boldly unto the Throne of Grace (presents the seat of Divine Power, and yet the Source of boundless Grace), *that we may obtain Mercy* (presents that which we want first), *and find Grace to help in time of need* (refers to the Goodness of God extended to all who come, and during any *'time of need'*; all made possible by the Cross)" (Heb. 4:16).

When Jesus died on the Cross, the moment He said, *"Father, it is finished, into Your Hands I commend My Spirit,"* at that moment, and because the price was now paid, the giant Veil which hung between the Holy Place and the Holy of Holies in the Temple, ripped from the top to the bottom, and was done so by the Hand of God. In effect, this was stating that the way was now open for sinful man even into the very Throne of God, all made possible by the Cross. As we have said previously:

Within ourselves, even the best of us,

whomever that might be, we have no standing with God whatsoever. The standing we do have, our ability to enter into the Throne of Grace, and to do so boldly, is predicated solely on Christ and what He has done for us at the Cross. And let us make another statement in that respect:

Christ without the Cross afforded no entrance, paid no price, gave man no standing with God. It is the Cross which makes everything possible. It was at the Cross where the price was paid, where the Sacrifice of our Saviour was presented, where His Life's Blood was poured out, all being accepted as payment in full by God the Father.

The *"boldness"* here projected by Paul in Hebrews 4:16 is not because of who we are, but rather Who He is. It's not because of anything great we've done, but despite what we are, through Christ we are able to walk boldly into the very Throne of God, where we will ever have Mercy granted to us, and *"find Grace to help in time of need."* But let us say it again:

It is all made possible exclusively by Christ and the Cross!

A NEAR KINSMAN

In the Old Testament which we are now studying, Redemption had several meanings.

According to the theocratic arrangement in Israel, the land belonged to God and the Israelite families only possessed the right to use the fruit of the land. If a family forfeited this use because its parcel of land had to be sold or because there was no heir, the parcel was returned to the initial family at the year of Jubilee, which came every 50 years (Lev. 25:8-17). Prior to this year the nearest kinsman had the right and the responsibility to redeem the property, i.e., to liquidate the debt so that the property might be restored to its original owner, that is if he was able to do so (Lev. 25:23-28).

Closely related to this custom was that of marriage. The brother-in-law or other near kinsman of someone who had died without leaving a male heir was obliged to marry the widow of the deceased in order to preserve the family name and property rights. In the marriage of Boaz and Ruth both of the above customs were involved. Land had been lost

because of the poverty of Elimelech and Naomi. As well, when the husband of Ruth died they had no children, i.e., no *"male heir."* Therefore, Naomi called the son born to Boaz and Ruth a redeemer because he delivered her from the reproach she had incurred because her family had no surviving male heir (Ruth 4:14). The birth of an heir now delivered her owner, as it were, from an alien dominion and restored it to her. In a sense, in Jewish thinking, Ruth was not fully a proselyte Jew, until this baby boy was born, although she was totally right with God from the moment she made her confession of Faith as recorded in 1:16-17.

Naomi referred to Boaz as *"one of our redeemers"* because his position in the family gave him the right to effect the restoration of the family property. She called the son born of Boaz and Ruth, as stated, *"a redeemer"* because he delivered both Naomi and Ruth from their reproach.

As it regards *"kinsman redemption"* pertaining to Ruth, two things, as also stated, had to be redeemed. The land had to be redeemed, which it was, and Ruth had to be redeemed, which she was, and done so by her marriage to Boaz.

The child that was born as a result of the union of Boaz and Ruth would be the heir of the property, just as if he had been Mahlon's son, even though Boaz should have other and older sons by another wife who had died. Of course, this was not the case with Boaz, as he had not been married before marrying Ruth.

Boaz was a *"near kinsman"* but he was not the nearest kinsman, even as we shall see.

BLESSED OF THE LORD

Boaz said to Ruth that night, *"blessed be you of the LORD, my daughter."*

There is great evidence in the Text that Boaz had fallen in love with Ruth, but was reluctant to venture his feelings, simply because of his age. He was evidently old enough to be her father.

When she made her move, instead of being in the least degree offended by the step she had taken, he was relieved, and felt full of gratification on the on hand, and of gratitude on the other.

He realized that by her coming and laying

at his feet that night, and please understand there was nothing untoward about this, that she was doing all she knew to do to carry out the Law of the Kinsman Redeemer. That's why he said to her, *"You have made your latter kindness better than the former,"* meaning that she is continuing to be faithful to her dead husband.

Her employment of the word *"kinsman,"* was evidence to Boaz that she was thinking of the respect which she owed to her husband's memory. Her concern in discharging that duty of *"piety"* struck the heart of Boaz.

His answer to her was straight and to the point, *"And now, my daughter, fear not; I will do to you all that you require."* However, there was one obstacle in the way, and that is *"a kinsman nearer than I."*

In other words, there was an individual who was a nearer kinsman to the family, and had the first right of redemption, that is if he so desired. That problem must be addressed first. We will find that it holds a deep spiritual meaning.

(13) "TARRY THIS NIGHT, AND IT SHALL BE IN THE MORNING, THAT IF HE WILL PERFORM UNTO YOU THE PART OF A KINSMAN, WELL; LET HIM DO THE KINSMAN'S PART: BUT IF HE WILL NOT DO THE PART OF A KINSMAN TO YOU, THEN WILL I DO THE PART OF A KINSMAN TO YOU, AS THE LORD LIVES: LIE DOWN UNTIL THE MORNING.

(14) "AND SHE LAY AT HIS FEET UNTIL THE MORNING: AND SHE ROSE UP BEFORE ONE COULD KNOW ANOTHER. AND HE SAID, LET IT NOT BE KNOWN THAT A WOMAN CAME INTO THE FLOOR.

(15) "ALSO HE SAID, BRING THE VEIL THAT YOU HAD UPON YOU, AND HOLD IT. AND WHEN SHE HELD IT, HE MEASURED SIX MEASURES OF BARLEY, AND LAID IT ON HER: AND SHE WENT INTO THE CITY.

(16) "AND WHEN SHE CAME TO HER MOTHER IN LAW, SHE SAID, WHO ARE YOU, MY DAUGHTER? AND SHE TOLD HER ALL THAT THE MAN HAD DONE TO HER.

(17) "AND SHE SAID, THESE SIX MEASURES OF BARLEY GAVE HE ME; FOR HE SAID TO ME, GO NOT EMPTY UNTO

NOTES

YOUR MOTHER IN LAW.

(18) "THEN SAID SHE, SIT STILL, MY DAUGHTER, UNTIL YOU KNOW HOW THE MATTER WILL FALL: FOR THE MAN WILL NOT BE IN REST, UNTIL HE HAVE FINISHED THE THING THIS DAY."

The exegesis is:

1. Ruth knew very little about the procedures of the Kinsman Redeemer, but Boaz knew them minutely.

2. Relating to Verse 14, Boaz, in other words, spoke to Ruth, telling her that she should not relate to anyone what happened that night. There was no impropriety in Ruth's action. It was the Law and custom of the time.

To draw a portion of a kinsman's mantle over one was the legal way of claiming protection and Redemption. Ruth effected this with great delicacy and skill. She chose a public place, such as the threshingfloor, where many persons were present, not to embarrass Boaz, but to give him liberty to act as he wished, she made her claim under the cover of darkness. Boaz, whose character commands admiration, immediately responded to her faith and love.

3. Concerning Verse 17, Christ, symbolized by Boaz, will give us all that we need, and even more, according to what the Holy Spirit, symbolized by Naomi, has told us to do. When we follow the leading of the Spirit, we will not return empty.

4. Verse 18 symbolizes the principle of Salvation by Faith; the Second Chapter of Galatians contrasts two principles for the obtaining of life and righteousness:

The first is *"works of Law,"* which pertained to religious ceremonies, personal moral efforts, and works of the flesh; it can never save;

The second is *"Salvation by Faith,"* which depends on no works, but totally upon Christ and what He has done for us at the Cross; the Holy Spirit teaches us that nothing can be had upon the first principle, but everything upon the second; so, Ruth would *"sit still,"* wholly trusting Boaz, and, as a result, obtain her heart's desire.

FAITH VERSUS WORKS

The word of Naomi, who is a Type of the Holy Spirit, to Ruth was, *"sit still, my daughter, until you know how the matter will fall.*" The words *"sit still"* pertain to Ruth allowing Boaz, who is a Type of Christ, to do the things which must be done, which he alone could do. This is the biggest problem for the Child of God, which is to *"sit still."*

There is something in us, I suppose a clinging vine from the Fall, that wants to try to earn our Salvation, try to merit that which God gives us, and whether we realize it or not, we are constantly placing before our Lord these things we have done, thinking they merit us something. They don't!

Everything we receive from the Lord, and I mean everything, comes to us strictly and totally by Faith, and not at all by works. Let's take the latter first.

As we've already stated, and will continue to say, when it comes to receiving things from the Lord, *"works"* simply will not suffice. This pertains to the flesh and our own efforts, that which God cannot abide and cannot accept. But yet, we are constantly dishing up works to the Lord, and think because we cover them with Scriptures, that somehow this makes it right. We may call it Faith, but it's not Faith, but something else altogether.

To pinpoint the issue, the *"Purpose Driven Life"* scheme is a case in point. So is the *"Government of Twelve."* So is the *"Confession Message."* So is *"Denominationalism!"*

Untold millions of Christians are mired down in these *"works,"* plus scores of directions and schemes we have not mentioned, but which will do them no good, but rather will do harm. But yet, this is where the problem actually is.

I am persuaded, that if the Believer doesn't understand the Cross, doesn't place his faith exclusively in Christ and the Cross, that he simply cannot understand Faith, cannot understand the Promises of God, and simply cannot receive from God.

If it is the kind of Faith that God honors, it is Faith that is placed exclusively in Christ and the Cross. It simply means that the Believer understands, that there is nothing he can do to merit the great and beautiful things which the Lord desires to give to us. We receive it as a gift, which means that we exhibit Faith in Christ and exclusively in

NOTES

Christ, and what He has done for us at the Cross. When this is done, and continues to be done, we will find the Lord giving us great and beautiful things, in a constant uninterrupted flow of Grace.

UNBELIEF

One of the greatest problems in the Church is the problem of *"unbelief!"* Most Christians, while all the time claiming they believe in the Cross of Christ, actually do not. How can they believe in the Cross, and at the same time, place their faith in something else? The problem is unbelief!

Many, if not most, Christians, which includes most preachers, despite what they say, simply do not believe that what Jesus did at the Cross answers man's dilemma. How do I know that?

I know that for the following reason. If preachers believe what Jesus did at the Cross was the answer for foundering humanity, they wouldn't place their faith in humanistic psychology. One cannot have both!

Or, if it's not humanistic psychology, it's something else in which they're placing their faith, such as their own pet schemes, or whatever it might be. But one would be surprised to know how that most all false doctrine is shot through with humanistic psychology. In fact, many, if not most, preachers are preaching psychology on Sunday mornings, and not even really knowing that they're doing so. Our society has been so shot through with this foolishness, and above all, the Church has accepted it in totality, so much so, in fact, that our very thinking has become warped by this false direction.

Believers, and especially preachers, need to get back to thinking the Bible way. They need to think constantly as it regards Christ and the Cross, because that's where the victory was won.

If even the weakest Christian will place his or her Faith exclusively in Christ and the Cross, believe it with their whole heart, little by little, they will find themselves growing in Grace and the Knowledge of the Lord. They will find to their amazement, that Spiritual Strength will begin to flood their hearts and lives. In fact, their understanding of the Word of God will change, and their maturity will start to develop. In fact, everything hinges on the Cross, and what Jesus there did.

Do you believe that? (I Cor. 1:17-18, 21, 23; 2:2; Gal., Chpt. 5; 6:14; Col. 2:14-15).

CHAPTER 4

(1) "THEN WENT BOAZ UP TO THE GATE, AND SAT HIM DOWN THERE: AND, BEHOLD, THE KINSMAN OF WHOM BOAZ SPOKE CAME BY; UNTO WHOM HE SAID, HO, SUCH A ONE! TURN ASIDE, SIT DOWN HERE. AND HE TURNED ASIDE, AND SAT DOWN.

(2) "AND HE TOOK TEN MEN OF THE ELDERS OF THE CITY, AND SAID, SIT YE DOWN HERE. AND THEY SAT DOWN.

(3) "AND HE SAID UNTO THE KINSMAN, NAOMI, WHO IS COME AGAIN OUT OF THE COUNTRY OF MOAB, SELLS A PARCEL OF LAND, WHICH WAS OUR BROTHER ELIMELECH'S:

(4) "AND I THOUGHT TO ADVERTISE YOU, SAYING, BUY IT BEFORE THE INHABITANTS, AND BEFORE THE ELDERS OF MY PEOPLE. IF YOU WILL REDEEM IT, REDEEM IT: BUT IF YOU WILL NOT REDEEM IT, THEN TELL ME, THAT I MAY KNOW: FOR THERE IS NONE TO REDEEM IT BESIDE YOU; AND I AM AFTER YOU. AND HE SAID, I WILL REDEEM IT.

(5) "THEN SAID BOAZ, WHAT DAY YOU BUY THE FIELD OF THE HAND OF NAOMI, YOU MUST BUY IT ALSO OF RUTH THE MOABITESS, THE WIFE OF THE DEAD, TO RAISE UP THE NAME OF THE DEAD UPON HIS INHERITANCE.

(6) "AND THE KINSMAN SAID, I CANNOT REDEEM IT FOR MYSELF, LEST I MAR MY OWN INHERITANCE: YOU REDEEM MY RIGHT TO YOURSELF; FOR I CANNOT REDEEM IT.

(7) "NOW THIS WAS THE MANNER IN FORMER TIME IN ISRAEL CONCERNING REDEEMING AND CONCERNING CHANGING, FOR TO CONFIRM ALL THINGS; A MAN PLUCKED OFF HIS SHOE, AND GAVE IT TO HIS NEIGHBOUR: AND THIS WAS A TESTIMONY IN ISRAEL.

(8) "THEREFORE THE KINSMAN SAID UNTO BOAZ, BUY IT FOR YOU. SO HE DREW OFF HIS SHOE.

(9) "AND BOAZ SAID UNTO THE ELDERS, AND UNTO ALL THE PEOPLE, YOU ARE WITNESSES THIS DAY, THAT I HAVE BOUGHT ALL THAT WAS ELIMELECH'S, AND ALL THAT WAS CHILION'S AND MAHLON'S, OF THE HAND OF NAOMI.

(10) "MOREOVER RUTH THE MOABITESS, THE WIFE OF MAHLON, HAVE I PURCHASED TO BE MY WIFE, TO RAISE UP THE NAME OF THE DEAD UPON HIS INHERITANCE, THAT THE NAME OF THE DEAD BE NOT CUT OFF FROM AMONG HIS BRETHREN, AND FROM THE GATE OF HIS PLACE: YOU ARE WITNESSES THIS DAY."

The diagram is:

1. In Old Testament times, business was conducted at the gate of the city.

2. The kinsman referred to as *"Ho, such a one,"* was nearer kin to Naomi, whoever he was, than was Boaz.

3. The explanation to the man as given by Boaz, meant that he must marry Ruth, as well as redeem the land. If a child was born to such a union, that child would inherit the land when the parents died, even though the father may even have other children who were older. In this manner, the inheritance would not be lost, which was the intention.

4. Boaz had to purchase Ruth, at least to effect the transaction, from a kinsman who had a prior claim, but who declared that he could not redeem her.

The Law has a prior claim on sinners, but it cannot redeem them. Christ, the Divine Kinsman, became Man in order to redeem. It cost Boaz nothing to redeem Ruth, beyond the setting aside of himself and his own interests, but it cost Christ everything to redeem sinners.

5. In regard to all of this, Ruth, a *"wild olive tree,"* was grafted into, and became a partaker of, *"the root and fatness of the olive tree,"* i.e., Israel; but she could not boast that this was due to any commanding personal claim; all she could say was, *"Why have I found grace in your eyes, seeing I am a Gentile?"* (2:10).

6. When land was sold, the one previously owning the land would give his shoe to the one who had bought it, signifying that he freely gave up his right to walk upon the soil in favor of the person who had acquired the possession.

7. By all the names mentioned in Verse 9, even though there was only one estate, there was a succession in the proprietorship.

THE KINSMAN REDEEMER

Boaz had determined this day to settle the matter. He probably knew that the nearer kinsman frequented the business section of the city, which was at the gate, every day; therefore, Boaz goes to the gate of the city, *"and sat there."*

There was no way as he went that day to complete this transaction, one way or the other, that he could have had any idea at all as to how important it actually was.

We look back now on the situation, knowing the full story and what it all meant, realizing that Ruth would be the great-grandmother of David, and above all, far above all, the ancestress of the Messiah.

The Lord has a Plan for every Believer, a Plan that reaches into eternity, but which we now only know in part. This makes it even more important that we conduct ourselves for the Lord with the same degree of responsibility as did Boaz, Naomi, and Ruth. I think far too many modern Believers have their minds on the here and now, and not at all on the there and then.

Much attention is given in the Word of God as to how we conduct ourselves, how we treat what God has given us, how we should act with responsibility.

Jesus spelled it out graphically so in the *"parable of the talents."*

The one who *"was afraid, and went and hid his talent in the earth,"* in effect, actually lost everything. Instead of adding to his talent, he did nothing; consequently, the Lord took away the one talent that he had, and gave it to the one who had ten talents (Mat. 25:14-30).

Once the matter was settled, we see that Boaz left no stone unturned, in order that this business be conducted, exactly as the Lord would have had it conducted.

THE LAW

The Second Verse, *"And lo, the kinsman of whom Boaz had spoken was passing; and he said, Ho, such a one! Turn hither and sit here, and he turned and sat down."*

There is evidence in the original Hebrew Text that Boaz called his kinsman by his name, but the writer does not tell us what that name is. I think the reason is according to the following:

"Ho, such a one," represents the Law. It had a nearer claim on humanity than did Christ, even as *"Ho, such a one,"* had a nearer claim on Naomi and her possessions, than did Boaz.

As witnesses, Boaz selected ten men who could hear this conversation and attest to the decisions here made.

REDEMPTION

The Fourth Verse proclaims Boaz saying to *"Ho, such a one, if you will redeem it."*

The answer was quick in coming back, *"I cannot redeem it for myself."*

In fact, the Law could never redeem. It was not actually created by God to redeem. It, in fact, was ordained by God that sin would appear to be sin, in other words, to define what sin was and is, and to show the horror of sin. There was no, nor is there any, redeeming virtue in the Law.

In fact, in the latter part of the Fourth Verse, *"Ho, such a one,"* actually says, *"I will redeem it."* But after Boaz explained to him what he had to do, which was not only to purchase the land, but, as well, to marry Ruth, he could not do such, and because he was already married.

When it is properly understood what has to be done in order for mankind to be redeemed, then it is also properly understood that the Law can never function in this capacity. As Paul said, *"If Righteousness come by the Law, then Christ is dead in vain"* (Gal. 2:21).

The trouble is, man has ever felt that his own works, merit, and personal efforts could redeem himself. It fails as fail it must! But yet Christian man keeps on trying.

WHAT IS LAW?

Instead of trying to enumerate all the things

that constitute Law, suffice to say that if it's not Christ and the Cross exclusively, then whatever it might be, it is Law. While it's not the Law of Moses, still, it's law that we have devised ourselves, or else some Church has devised, or some Preacher has devised, etc.

I had a young Minister to write me some time back, someone incidentally who had a particular problem. He had left the Ministry for a particular period of time, and was now ensconced in a large Church in a major American city.

His *"rehabilitation program"* consisted of the following:

• He was to meet three times a week with his psychological counselor;

• He was to read two Chapters a day in the Bible;

• He was to not fail to be in every Service at the Church; and,

• He was not to go any more than 30 miles outside the city.

As stated, this was his rehabilitation program. When he wrote me, he was ecstatic with joy, exclaiming as to how this was going to make him a new man.

I wrote him back, in essence, saying, *"My dear Brother, I know you mean well, and I know the people who are working with you mean well; however, these things you have named will in no way deliver you from your problem."*

If I remember correctly, he answered me almost immediately, and in a nice way told me that he was very confident that this was going to do the job.

I wonder why we do not use at least as much common sense with the Gospel as we do with other things?

In the first place, what in the world good is it going to do him not going over 30 miles outside of the city? As well, I can vouch say that the psychological counseling will do no good whatsoever, and will probably do harm. While everybody should be faithful to Church, still, that will have no effect upon him either, nor any of the other things that could be mentioned.

Sin is a powerful factor. There is only one way that it could be addressed, and that one way was the Cross of Christ. There Jesus atoned for all sin, past, present, and future,

at least for all who will believe (Jn. 3:16). When one puts one's Faith exclusively in the Sacrifice of Christ, the Holy Spirit Who is God, and Who, consequently can do anything, will begin to work on behalf of such an individual (Rom. 8:2).

A person has to be delivered from sin, that's exactly what Jesus did at the Cross. So, why is it that preachers, and especially those who claim to be spirit-filled, refuse to believe what I've just said about the Cross?

Among other things, once again, it is the problem of man feeling that his own personal efforts, can meet the need. They can't! Incidentally, the young man in question, despite his *"Rehabilitation Program,"* fell into sin again!

ONE'S STANDING WITH GOD

Man has no standing with God, outside of Jesus Christ and Him Crucified. Let me say that again:

Find me the Godliest man on the face of the Earth, and I must proclaim and do so loudly, that outside of Jesus Christ and the Cross, such a man has no standing with God whatsoever. God never accepts us because of our works, etc., but only on the merit of Christ and what He has done for us at the Cross. It only requires Faith on our part, and I am referring to Faith in Christ and His Atoning Work. When one thinks of that for a moment, then one begins to see himself as he really is.

Millions think they have a standing with the Lord based on the Church to which they belong, or the Denomination to which they belong, or according to how much money they've given, or the good works that they have carried out and are carrying out, etc. It is very hard for man, and especially religious man, to look at his works and say *"out!"* To look at the good things he has done and is doing, and say *"out!"* But the Truth is, we simply cannot redeem ourselves. And whenever we claim to believe in the Cross, and then ignore the Cross, thereby placing our emphasis on something else, whether we realize it or not, we've just resorted to Law, a position which God can never honor.

TRANSFER OF THE PROPERTY

In Old Testament times, whenever a

property transaction was handled, the one who owned the property and had sold it to another individual, pulled off his shoe and gave it to the person who had purchased the land. In essence, he was saying that he did not have the right anymore to walk upon this property and call it his own. Now, with his shoe being given to the purchaser, the man could walk on it and know that it was his. It was attested to by witnesses, hence, the ten men of Verse 2.

And this is what Boaz did. He purchased the land, in order that it be kept in the original family name. The man who was nearer kin, even though he had not owned the land, and received no money in this transaction, still, pulled off his shoe and gave it to Boaz, signifying that he had renounced his purchasing rights in favor of Boaz.

(11) "AND ALL THE PEOPLE WHO WERE IN THE GATE, AND THE ELDERS, SAID, WE ARE WITNESSES. THE LORD MAKE THE WOMAN WHO IS COME INTO YOUR HOUSE LIKE RACHEL AND LIKE LEAH, WHICH TWO DID BUILD THE HOUSE OF ISRAEL: AND DO YOU WORTHILY IN EPHRATAH, AND BE FAMOUS IN BETHLEHEM:

(12) "AND LET YOUR HOUSE BE LIKE THE HOUSE OF PHAREZ, WHOM TAMAR BORE UNTO JUDAH, OF THE SEED WHICH THE LORD SHALL GIVE YOU OF THIS YOUNG WOMAN.

(13) "SO BOAZ TOOK RUTH, AND SHE WAS HIS WIFE: AND WHEN HE WENT IN UNTO HER, THE LORD GAVE HER CONCEPTION, AND SHE BORE A SON.

(14) "AND THE WOMEN SAID UNTO NAOMI, BLESSED BE THE LORD, WHICH HAS NOT LEFT YOU THIS DAY WITHOUT A KINSMAN, THAT HIS NAME MAY BE FAMOUS IN ISRAEL.

(15) "AND HE SHALL BE UNTO YOU A RESTORER OF YOUR LIFE, AND A NOURISHER OF YOUR OLD AGE: FOR YOUR DAUGHTER IN LAW, WHICH LOVES YOU, WHICH IS BETTER TO YOU THAN SEVEN SONS, HAS BORN HIM.

(16) "AND NAOMI TOOK THE CHILD, AND LAID IT IN HER BOSOM, AND BECAME NURSE UNTO IT.

(17) "AND THE WOMEN HER

NOTES

NEIGHBOURS GAVE IT A NAME, SAYING, THERE IS A SON BORN TO NAOMI; AND THEY CALLED HIS NAME OBED: HE IS THE FATHER OF JESSE, THE FATHER OF DAVID."

The exposition is:

1. The latter phrase of Verse 11, *"and be famous in Bethlehem,"* is more a Prophecy than a statement; Bethlehem will ever be famous; the reason is that the Son of David, the great descendant of Ruth, would be born in Bethlehem some 1,200 years later; how beautifully and wondrously this Prophecy has come to pass.

2. To be sure, this *"House"* of Verse 12 was blessed far more than the house of Pharez could ever be blessed and, in fact, every other house, for it would be the House of the Lord Jesus Christ.

3. When Ruth looked at her newborn baby, I wonder what the thoughts were in her mind. Little did she realize the consequences of it all, and neither do we!

4. It is Ruth's little son who is the kinsman referred to, the nearest kinsman, still nearer than Boaz. To be sure, the child, who would be the grandparent of David and, ultimately, the Son of David, is linked to fame in a greater way than even these women could think.

5. Verse 17 means that the baby was born to Naomi through Boaz and Ruth who were fulfilling the Law by raising up seed for her dead husband and keeping his name alive; their seed was reckoned, or counted, to carry on his place in Israel (Deut. 25:5-10); this *"Son,"* who would be born of Israel (Naomi), will one day rule the world; His Name ultimately would be *"The Lord Jesus Christ,"* the Son of David, the Son of Abraham (Mat. 1:1).

THE PROPHECY

Everything that is linked to Christ, and in any positive way, is of significance far beyond our comprehension; consequently, whoever made the statement in Verse 11, whatever they meant to say, and whatever they meant it to be, was actually a Prophecy, and of gargantuan proportions.

The statement, *"The LORD make the woman who is come into your house like Rachel and like Leah,"* refers to Ruth. To be sure that request has not only come true, but true in a greater way than ever. In fact, what the Lord did through Ruth, was to bring forth the True Israel, even as He was the True Church and the True Man. Of course, we speak of the Lord Jesus Christ.

Regrettably, the *"House of Israel"* was almost destroyed, because this *"House"* rejected the One Who was brought forth by this union. But still, this *"House"* will be restored, rebuilt, but not until it accepts the One in question. Again, we speak of the Lord Jesus Christ. Their reception and acceptance of Him will be at the Second Coming.

To be sure, the statement, *"And be famous in Bethlehem,"* has been fulfilled far beyond the comprehension of anyone. David would be born in Bethlehem, who would be the crowning king of Israel, but above all, the King of kings would be born in Bethlehem, the Lord Jesus Christ.

Every year hundreds of thousands of Christians visit this little town, which is a suburb of Jerusalem, and all because of the Lord Jesus Christ Who was born there.

What Bethlehem will be in the coming Kingdom Age we aren't told; however, understanding that it is the Holy Spirit who framed the word *"famous in Bethlehem,"* we must ascertain that this *"fame"* will last forever.

Why the Holy Spirit through the speaker of this Prophecy mentions *"Pharez,"* we aren't exactly told. It could be because Pharez' descendants, the Pharezites of the Tribe of Judah, were particularly numerous and hence, the good wishes of Boaz's fellow-townsmen (Num. 26:20-21).

In fact, Judah became the most powerful Tribe, with the Southern Kingdom, after the split, being referred to as *"Judah."*

THE RESTORER AND THE NOURISHER

After the child is born, whose name would be called *"Obed,"* who would be the father of Jesse, who would be the father of David, another great Prophecy is given. Once again, we are not told who the speaker was, but yet we know the inspiration is from the Holy Spirit.

Even though the speaker was referring to the child that was born to Boaz and Ruth, still, the Holy Spirit is referring to far more

than that. He is referring to the Lord Jesus Christ, Who would be the Restorer and the Nourisher. This Christ is to all who will accept Him as Saviour and Lord, irrespective as to whom they might be, whether Jew or Gentile.

THE RESTORER

Through the Fall, Satan has stolen, or destroyed so much of what God intended for man to be. Man has tried every conceivable way to restore this which has been lost, but has been unsuccessful, because man, as man, has no answer to his dilemma. There is One, however, Who can restore all that has been lost, and that is the Lord Jesus Christ. Jesus Christ is God. When He came to this world, He did so in the form of Man (Isa. 7:14).

In order for man to be restored, the broken Law of God would have to be addressed and satisfied. This means the terrible sin debt would have to be paid, a debt, which man could not pay. From before the foundation of the world (I Pet. 1:18-20), it had been decreed that this debt would be paid by God becoming Man, and going to the Cross, where the price would be paid, and paid by the Son of Man giving His Life as a ransom for many. This He did. In other words, His Destination was ever the Cross, and because it is through the Cross alone, that the restoration process can be affected. Let's say it in another way:

Man has no standing with God whatsoever, or in any capacity, at least that is positive, except through Jesus Christ and what He did for us at the Cross. With Faith placed in Christ, even though it is little understood by the believing sinner, the individual is Born-Again; however, once the person is Born-Again, then the Holy Spirit, through the Word of God (Rom. 6:1-14), makes it crystal clear, that our Faith must be anchored solely in Christ and the Cross. through this means, and this means alone, and we continue to speak of the Cross of Christ, is the restoration process effected (Rom. 8:1-2, 11; I Cor. 1:17-18, 21, 23; 2:2; Gal., Chpt. 5; 6:14; Eph. 2:13-18; Col. 2:14-15).

Unfortunately, much of the modern Church seeks to engage the restoration process, or to carry it forward, by any and every means other than the Cross. The effort is a labor in futility. It cannot be done that way. It is the Cross and the Cross alone, which paid the price, and made it possible for man to be restored (Jn. 3:3, 16).

WHAT DO WE MEAN BY THE CROSS?

Paul used the word *"Cross,"* as a metaphor, so to speak, to explain the entire Redemption process. That's why he said, *"For the Preaching of the Cross is to them who perish foolishness, but unto we who are Saved it is the Power of God"* (I Cor. 1:18).

He wasn't speaking of a wooden beam. If, in fact, the actual cross on which Jesus died could be found, it would be of no more significance than any other piece of wood. As well, it was not death per se that effects this great Redemption Plan, for death is an enemy; however, what that death afforded, is definitely the means by which the restoration process is engaged. So, it's the benefits of the Cross of which Paul spoke, and which we speak. What Jesus did there, and it was completed at the Cross, makes it possible for a man to be Born-Again, to be baptized with the Holy Spirit, to have Eternal Life, to have his name written in the Lamb's Book of Life, in fact, to be the recipient of all Blessings. It is the Cross of Christ which is the means of all of this. But again let us state:

We are speaking of the benefits of what Jesus did there, and the benefits only. That's the reason that Paul referred to the Cross as *"The Everlasting Covenant"* (Heb. 13:20). This means that this Redemption Plan is perfect, and in every respect. It means that it will never have to be complemented. It means it will never have to be deleted. Perfection cannot be improved upon, and what Jesus did at the Cross is perfection.

WHAT PART DOES THE
RESURRECTION HAVE TO
PLAY IN ALL OF THIS?

To answer the question before we look at the details, I might quickly add that the manner in which Paul used the term *"The Cross,"* referred to every aspect of the Redemption process, which included the suffering before the Cross, which pertains to

the beating, the nails, the crown of thorns, etc., the Cross itself, the Resurrection, the Ascension, and even the Exaltation of Christ (Heb. 1:3).

Now for the details:

The Resurrection, one might say, was of immense significance, far beyond our comprehension to say the least, in that it ratified all that had been done at the Cross; however, it must be understood, that the entire Redemption process was completed in totality at the Cross. So this means, that the Resurrection was not in doubt.

If Jesus had failed to atone for even one sin, then He could not have been raised from the dead. The Bible states, *"The wages of sin is death"* (Rom. 6:23). So, the fact that He was raised from the dead, guarantees that every sin was atoned.

There was no question about His Resurrection. Some Preachers claim that demons tried to stop Him from being raised from the dead, and He almost didn't make it, etc. You won't find anything like that in the Bible. Read carefully what our Lord said and did:

"From that time forth began Jesus to show unto His Disciples, how that He must go unto Jerusalem, and suffer many things of the Elders and Chief Priests and Scribes, and be killed, and be raised again the third day" (Mat. 16:21).

If it is to be noticed, He plainly says that *"He . . . would be raised again the third day."* In other words, it was a foregone conclusion. And, as stated, it was a foregone conclusion, because the total price of Redemption would be paid at Calvary's Cross.

The moment that Jesus died the Scripture says, *"And, behold, the Veil of the Temple* (that which hid the Holy of Holies; Josephus said it was sixty feet high from the ceiling to the floor, four inches thick, and was so strong, that four yoke of oxen could not pull it apart) *was rent in twain from the top to the bottom* (meaning that God Alone could have done such a thing; it also signified, that the price was paid completely on the Cross; signified by the rent Veil; regrettably, some say, the Cross — didn't finish the task with other things required; this Verse says differently)*" (Mat. 27:51).

The Blood of Jesus Christ shed at Calvary's

Cross, which referred to His Life being poured out (Eph. 2:13), paid the priced demanded by God, and paid it fully. This means that it was totally, fully, absolutely, completely paid at the Cross. Once again Paul says so:

"And that He (Christ) might reconcile both (Jews and Gentiles) unto God in one body (the Church) by the Cross (it is by the Atonement only that men ever become reconciled to God), having slain the enmity thereby (removed the barrier between God and sinful man)" (Eph. 2:16).

If it is to be noticed, Paul plainly says that all of this was done "by the Cross."

The reason we're going into this detail, is because some Preachers claim that the Atonement is not in the Cross but rather in the Resurrection. Others state that it is in the Exaltation of Christ. Paul said it was in the Cross (I Cor. 1:17-18, 21, 23; 2:2; Gal. 6:14; Col. 2:14-15). While, of course, the Resurrection was of immense significance, as were the Ascension and the Exaltation, still, these things were the result of the Cross. In other words, if the Cross had failed in any respect, there would have been no Resurrection, no Ascension, and no Exaltation.

For instance, in the entirety of the Book of Hebrews, which, in effect, is the story of the Cross, typified by the Levitical Offerings, the Resurrection is mentioned only one time, and then in connection with the Cross, even as it should have been (Heb. 13:20). Don't you think if the Redemption Plan was centered up in the Resurrection, that Paul would have mentioned it at least more than once in the great Book of Hebrews? I think so!

The facts are, the Word of God must be the criteria for all things. And the way to properly understand the Word of God, is to correlate all Verses which pertain to a given subject. If we pick and choose, then we'll come up with wrong answers.

For instance, if one properly studies the Word of God, they will have to come to the conclusion that the Apostle Paul "preached the Cross." Of course he mentioned the Resurrection, and gave great details about that great Truth in I Corinthians, Chapter 15, and elsewhere, as he did other particulars of the Gospel; however, the emphasis was always the Cross of Christ. One will have to

come to that conclusion, if one properly interprets the Word of God.

It is the Cross! The Cross! The Cross!

THE NOURISHER

The word "Restorer" in a sense has to do with the Salvation process, and more than all the initial experience of being Born-Again (Jn. 3:3).

The word "Nourisher," as it refers to Christ, has to do with the Believer being sustained, thereby, growing in Grace, and the Knowledge of the Lord (II Pet. 3:18).

Most Believers at least have some knowledge as it regards the initial Salvation process of being Born-Again. They link the Cross with that, either totally, or at least in some vague way. Unfortunately, the Word of Faith people do not link the Salvation process to the Cross at all, actually referring to the Cross as "past miseries," and "the greatest defeat in human history." They actually say that if one preaches the Cross that one is preaching death. They advocate, of course, that the Preacher major on the Resurrection and the Exaltation of Christ. Pure and simple, this is "another gospel" (Gal. 1:6-7).

But getting back to the subject of the majority of Christianity, when it comes to living for God, that is on a daily basis, most Believers have no knowledge whatsoever as to the part the Cross plays in this all-important process. In fact, to make the statement that the Cross of Christ plays a part in this, presents itself as a gross understatement. In fact, the Cross of Christ must, and without fail, be the emphasis, and in every respect. This means, to be nourished by Christ, and to be so on a daily basis, our Faith must be locked into Christ and the Cross, and that exclusively, and that constantly. Jesus said that if we were to come after Him, that we must deny ourselves, and take up the Cross daily, and follow Him (Lk. 9:23).

Actually, He also said, if we don't do this, that we "cannot be His Disciple" (Lk. 14:27).

Therefore, the way, and the only way that the Believer can be properly "nourished," and done so on a continuing basis, is that we understand that Christ is the Source of all things from God, and that the Cross is the means by which we receive these things.

Herein lies the controversy!

How many Preachers are preaching the Cross?

Not many!

In fact, Preachers are preaching about everything but the Cross. Some of the things they are preaching are good things, but some are being used out of context. Paul addressed this by saying:

"For Christ sent me not to baptize, but to preach the Gospel: not with wisdom of words, lest the Cross of Christ should be made of none effect" (I Cor. 1:17).

Paul wasn't demeaning Water Baptism, which is a proper Scriptural Ordinance. He was saying that the emphasis must not be on Water Baptism, as important as it is, nor must it be on the Lord's Supper, or Church Membership, or Manifestations, etc. While some of these things may be of great significance, still, the emphasis must always be on the Cross of Christ.

You can turn on your Television set, and watch preachers, and most of them are emphasizing everything other than the Cross; therefore, let it be clearly understood:

Whatever it is they are preaching, though it may be good in its own respect, and though in some way it may be Scriptural, even as was and is Water Baptism, still, if these things are preached as the *"nourisher,"* and regrettably, that's exactly the way they are being preached, then no positive results will accrue. It doesn't matter how glibly these things are stated, how cultured they may be stated, or even with what authority they may be stated, if it's not the Cross of Christ, whatever it is, it's not the Gospel, but rather, *"another gospel"* (Gal. 1:6-7; II Cor. 11:4).

All the *"nourishment"* we need comes from Christ, and in every respect, and in every capacity. But the Means by which He gives us these things, is the Cross, always the Cross! This means that it is the Cross of Christ which has made all of this possible.

Do you believe that?

You had best think about that question very carefully, because on your proper answer hangs *"the more Abundant Life"* promised by Christ, or the lack thereof!

(18) "NOW THESE ARE THE GENERATIONS OF PHAREZ: PHAREZ

NOTES

BEGAT HEZRON,

(19) "AND HEZRON BEGAT RAM, AND RAM BEGAT AMMINADAB,

(20) "AND AMMINADAB BEGAT NAHSHON, AND NAHSHON BEGAT SALMON,

(21) "AND SALMON BEGAT BOAZ, AND BOAZ BEGAT OBED,

(22) "AND OBED BEGAT JESSE, AND JESSE BEGAT DAVID."

The exegesis is:

1. Most of the time the genealogies given in the Bible, exactly as here, are not complete, and neither are they meant to be complete. They are merely meant to link certain individuals with others, although several times, at times, removed.

2. We know that Jesse was the father of David; however, we don't know for certain if Obed was the immediate father of Jesse, or several times removed. In the Hebrew there is no word for grandfather, or great-grandfather, etc. They are all looked at as the *"father."*

3. We know that Rahab married Salmon (Mat. 1:5); we also know that Salmon was not the immediate father of Boaz, simply because Rahab and Salmon lived several hundreds of years before Boaz; however, we do know that Salmon was the father of Boaz several times removed. So, when these genealogies are observed, they must be observed with the idea in mind, that the genealogy is not complete, and neither are they meant to be complete. As already stated, they are merely meant to link certain individuals with others, although at times, several times removed.

4. All of this is very important, because it is an integral part of the genealogy of King David's great descendant, his *"Lord,"* and ours. In other words, it pertains to the Incarnation of Christ, God becoming Man, in order to redeem humanity by dying on a Cross. Nothing is more important that that!

CONCLUSION

It is August 16, 2006, as I finish the Commentary on this small Book of Ruth. But what a study! What a privilege to have had the opportunity to look at least somewhat in depth, at each one of these Verses. What a Blessing it has been.

I would pray that in your study of this

Commentary on Ruth, that you would be blessed as much as we have been in endeavoring to bring this material to you. Thank you for being a part of this effort.

BIBLIOGRAPHY

INTRODUCTION

[1] H.D.M Spence, *The Pulpit Commentary: Vol. 4*, Grand Rapids, Eerdmans Publishing Company, 1978, pg. *x*.
[2] Ibid., pg. *vi*.

CHAPTER 1

[1] George Williams, *The Students Commentary On The Holy Scriptures*, Grand Rapids, Kregel Publications, 1949, pg. 135.

CHAPTER 2

[1] George Williams, *The Students Commentary On The Holy Scriptures*, Grand Rapids, Kregel Publications, 1949, pg. 136.
[2] H.D.M Spence, *The Pulpit Commentary: Vol. 4*, Grand Rapids, Eerdmans Publishing Company, 1978, pg. 43.

CHAPTER 3

[1] George Williams, *The Students Commentary On The Holy Scriptures*, Grand Rapids, Kregel Publications, 1949, pg. 136.

REFERENCE BOOKS

Strong's Exhaustive Concordance Of The Bible
The Interlinear Greek — English New Testament — George Ricker Berry
The New Bible Dictionary — Tyndale
The Pulpit Commentary — H.D.M. Spence
The Student's Commentary On The Holy Scriptures — George Williams
The Zondervan Pictorial Encyclopedia Of The Bible
Vine's Expository Dictionary Of New Testament Words
Webster's New Collegiate Dictionary
Young's Literal Translation Of The Holy Bible

NOTES

NOTES

NOTES

NOTES

NOTES

INDEX

The index is listed according to subjects. The treatment may include a complete dissertation or no more than a paragraph. But hopefully it will provide some help.

As well, even though extended treatment of a subject may not be carried in this Commentary, one of the other Commentaries may well include the desired material.

For all information concerning the *Jimmy Swaggart Bible Commentary,* please request a Gift Catalog.

You may inquire by using Books of the Bible.

- Genesis (639 pages) (11-201)
- Exodus (639 pages) (11-202)
- Leviticus (435 pages) (11-203)
- Numbers
  Deuteronomy (493 pages) (11-204)
- Joshua
  Judges
  Ruth (329 pages) (11-205)
- I Samuel
  II Samuel (528 pages) (11-206)
- I Kings
  II Kings (560 pages) (11-207)
- I Chronicles
  II Chronicles (528 pages) (11-226)
- Ezra
  Nehemiah
  Esther (288 pages) (11-208)
- Job (320 pages) (11-225)
- Psalms (688 pages) (11-216)
- Proverbs (320 pages) (11-227)
- Ecclesiastes
  Song Of Solomon (11-228)
- Isaiah (688 pages) (11-220)
- Jeremiah
  Lamentations (688 pages) (11-070)
- Ezekiel (508 pages) (11-223)
- Daniel (403 pages) (11-224)
- Hosea
  Joel
  Amos
  (will be ready Fall 2012) (11-229)

- Matthew (625 pages) (11-073)
- Mark (606 pages) (11-074)
- Luke (626 pages) (11-075)
- John (532 pages) (11-076)
- Acts (697 pages) (11-077)
- Romans (536 pages) (11-078)
- I Corinthians (632 pages) (11-079)
- II Corinthians (589 pages) (11-080)
- Galatians (478 pages) (11-081)
- Ephesians (550 pages) (11-082)
- Philippians (476 pages) (11-083)
- Colossians (374 pages) (11-084)
- I Thessalonians
  II Thessalonians (498 pages) (11-085)
- I Timothy
  II Timothy
  Titus
  Philemon (687 pages) (11-086)
- Hebrews (831 pages) (11-087)
- James
  I Peter
  II Peter (730 pages) (11-088)
- I John
  II John
  III John
  Jude (377 pages) (11-089)
- Revelation (602 pages) (11-090)

For telephone orders you may call 1-800-288-8350 with bankcard information. All Baton Rouge residents please use (225) 768-7000. For mail orders send to:

Jimmy Swaggart Ministries
P.O. Box 262550
Baton Rouge, LA 70826-2550

Visit our website: www.jsm.org